Fundamentals of Remote Sensing

Fundamentals of Remote Sensing

S.C. Bhatia
B.E. (Chemical), MBA

Published by
ATLANTIC
PUBLISHERS & DISTRIBUTORS (P) LTD
7/22, Ansari Road, Darya Ganj, New Delhi-110002
Phones : +91-11-40775252, 40775214, 23273880, 23275880
Fax : +91-11-23285873
Web : www.atlanticbooks.com
E-mail : orders@atlanticbooks.com

Branch Office: Chennai
Phones : +91-44-48531784, 28291383
E-mail : chennai@atlanticbooks.com

Printed & bound in India by Atlantic Print Services

Preface

Remote sensing has been defined as the detection, recognition or evolution of objects by means of distant sensing or recording devices. In recent decades, remote sensing technology has emerged to support data collection and analysis methods of potential interest. It holds importance for forest management also. Historically, digital remote sensing developed quickly from technology of aerial photo-interpretation science. Remote Sensing and Geographical Information Systems (GIS) deal with mapping technology, concepts of maps and all relevant terminology, which are necessary for the beginners to develop their skills in this new and upcoming technology.

This Reference book/Textbook provides basic principles and techniques of remote sensing, microwave remote sensing, remote sensing platforms and sensors and data analysis techniques. Further, the book also covers GIS data quality issues, GIS data analyses and modelling, attributes of data management, GIS data input and editing, integration and linkage of remote sensing and GIS.

Chapter 1 is devoted to fundamental considerations. Various definitions, units of measure and milestones in the history of remote sensing have been discussed in detail. Remotely sensed images are formed by many inter-related processes and an isolated focus on any single component will produce a fragmented understanding. Keeping this in mind, chapter 2 deals with remote sensing processes. Chapter 3 focuses on electromagnetic radiation. Various electromagnetic radiations, their properties and application/interaction with the atmosphere have been discussed in detail. Although the status of photography is challenged by continuing innovations in digital imaging technology, photography remains the most practical, inexpensive and widely used means of remote sensing. Further, the basic optical principles used for photography are also employed in optical systems of non-photographic sensors and we often use photographic film to record images generated by non-photographic sensors. Therefore, knowledge of photography forms a central core for understanding the field of remote sensing. Considering this, chapter 4 concentrates on photographic sensors. Chapter 5 deals with digital data and image processing. Various methods of digital data and image processing along with equipments used are briefly discussed. Chapter 6 is devoted to image interpretation. Various elements of image interpretation, data characteristics, image interpretation strategies are highlighted in this chapter.

Today, many corporations and national governments operate satellite remote sensing systems, specifically designed for observation of Earth's surface to collect information about crops, forests, water bodies, land use, cities and minerals. Such capabilities are well suited to creating and maintaining a worldwide cartographic infrastructure and to monitoring changes in the many broad-scale environmental issues that the world faces today. Considering this, chapter 7 focuses on land observation satellites. Chapter 8 describes the Active Microwave and Lidar (Light detection and ranging sensors), two sensor systems that would seem to differ greatly because they use energy in widely separated regions of the spectrum—the microwave and visible light spectra, respectively and record contrasting properties of Earth's surface.

In order to interpret thermal infrared (IR) images, one must understand the basic physical processes that control the interactions between thermal energy and matter, as well as thermal properties of matter that determine the rate and intensity of the interactions. Chapter 9 concentrates on thermal radiation and infrared images. Various thermal detectors, thermal scanners and thermal properties of objects are briefly discussed. Chapter 10 deals with image resolution. The chapter highlights the significance of image resolution as a concept that extends across many aspects of remote sensing such as target and system variables, operating conditions, measurement of resolution and interaction with landscape. In the context of digital analysis of remotely sensed data, pre-processing refers to those operations that are preliminary to the main analysis; considering this, chapter 11 focuses on pre-processing. Chapter 12 concentrates on image classification. Various informational and spectral classes along with their advantages and disadvantages are discussed briefly. Chapter 13 deals with field data which consists of observations collected at or near ground level in support of remote sensing analysis. Various kinds of field data along with locational information are discussed in detail. Chapter 14 focuses on accuracy assessment, various methods of measurement of map accuracy and sources of error classification are briefly discussed. Chapter 15 concentrates on hyperspectral remote sensing which is based upon examination of many narrowly spectral channels to examine images of Earth's surface. Chapter 16 focuses on the concept of the Geographic Information Systems (GIS); although implemented in many different forms it is ideally one that permits full utilisation of the goals of remote sensing.

Remote sensing can be useful for monitoring areas planted to specific crops, for detecting plant diseases and insect infestations and for contributing to accurate crop production forecasts. Chapter 17 focuses on plant sciences. Remote sensing has been valuable source of information over the course of the past few decades in mapping and monitoring forest activities. Considering this, chapter 18 deals with remote sensing for sustainable forest management. A major issue facing those with forest management questions is not simply the collection of data, but rather the interpretation of information extracted from those data. Converting remote sensing data into information is not a simple task. Remote sensing measurements have a physical or statistical relationship to the forest conditions of interest which may be uneconomical, impractical or impossible to measure directly over large areas. Chapter 19 focuses on earth sciences. This chapter addresses applications of remote sensing in earth sciences, which include geology, geomorphology and soil science. Chapter 20 concentrates on hydrospheric sciences. Most traditional means of monitoring the Earth's water depend largely upon measurements made at specific points or collections of samples from discrete locations. However, remote sensing can provide a valuable perspective concerning broad scale, dynamic patterns that can be difficult to examine in detail using point measurement only.

Study of land use and land cover reveals the overall pattern of mankind's occupation of the Earth's surface and the geographic organisation of its activities. Chapter 21 focuses on land use and land cover. Chapter 22 concentrates on global remote sensing. This chapter highlights the various instruments and programmes to gather data that will provide the geographical coverage and consistency required to compile global data sets to examine fundamental questions.

If susceptibility to natural hazards can be identified in the early stages of an integrated development planning study, measures can be introduced to reduce the social and economic impacts of potential disasters. Chapter 23 is devoted to natural hazards. All natural hazards are amenable in some degree to study by remote sensing because nearly all geologic, hydraulic and atmospheric phenomena that create hazardous situations are recurring events or processes that leave evidence of their previous occurrence. This evidence can be recorded, analysed and integrated into planning process. Most remote sensing studies concerned with natural hazards have been about an area's vulnerability to a disaster, the monitoring of events which could precipitate a disaster and influence the magnitude, extent and duration of disaster.

Glossary and Index have been provided at the end for quick reference. Diagrams, figures and tables supplement the text. All the topics have been covered in a cogent and lucid style to help the reader grasp the information quickly and easily.

The present book on *Fundamentals of Remote Sensing* is essential reading for all students and teachers of geology, earthquake engineering, life sciences, biotechnologies, bioinformatics, environment science and research scholars in remote sensing and allied fields. The book has been prepared with meticulous care, aiming at making the book error-free. Constructive suggestions are always welcome from readers of this book.

S.C. Bhatia

Contents at a Glance

Contents

1

Fundamental Considerations

INTRODUCTION

Pictures concisely convey information about positions, sizes and inter-relationships between objects. By their nature, they portray information about things that we can recognise as objects. These objects in turn can convey deep levels of meaning. Because human beings possess a high level of proficiency in deriving information from such images, we experience little difficulty in interpreting even those scenes that are visually complex. We are so competent in such tasks that it is only when we attempt to replicate these capabilities using computer programmes, for instance, that we realise how powerful our abilities are to derive this kind of intricate information. Each picture therefore can truthfully be said to distill the meaning of at least a thousand words.

This text is devoted to the analysis of a special class of pictures that employ an overhead perspective (e.g., maps, aerial photographs and similar images), including many that are based upon radiation not visible to the human eye. These images have special properties that offer unique advantages for the study of the earth's surface—we can see patterns instead of isolated points and relationships between features that otherwise seem independent. They are especially powerful because they permit us to monitor changes over time; to measure sizes, areas, depths and heights; and in general, to acquire information that is very difficult to acquire by other means. However, our ability to extract this kind of information is not innate—we must work hard to develop the knowledge and skills that allow us to use images.

Specialised knowledge is important because remotely sensed images have qualities that differ from those we encounter in everyday experience:

1. Image presentation.
2. Unfamiliar scales and resolutions.
3. Overhead views from aircraft or satellites.
4. Use of several regions of the electromagnetic spectrum.

This text explores these and other elements of remote sensing and some of its many practical applications. Our purpose in this Chapter is to briefly outline its content, origins and scope as a foundation for more specific chapters that follow.

Remote sensing is broadly defined as collecting and interpreting information about a target without being in physical contact with the object. Aircraft and satellites are the common platforms for remote sensing observations. The term remote sensing is commonly restricted to methods that employ electromagnetic energy (such as light, heat and radio waves) as the means of detecting and measuring target characteristics. This definition of remote sensing excludes electrical, magnetic and gravity surveys that measure force fields rather than electromagnetic radiation. Magnetic and radioactivity surveys are frequently made from aircraft but are considered airborne geophysical surveys rather than remote sensing.

DEFINITIONS

The field of remote sensing has been defined many times (Table 1.1). Examination of common elements in these varied definitions permits identification of the topic's most important themes. From a cursory look at these definitions, it is easy to identify a central concept: the gathering of information at a distance. This excessively broad definition, however, must be refined if it is to guide us in studying a body of knowledge that can be approached in a single course of study.

Table 1.1. Remote sensing: some definitions.

Remote sensing has been variously defined but basically it is the art or science of telling something about an object without touching it
Remote sensing is the acquisition of physical data of an object without touch or contact
Imagery is acquired with a sensor other than (or in addition to) a conventional camera through which a scene is recorded, such as by electronic scanning, using radiations outside the normal visual range of the film and camera—microwave, radar, thermal, infrared, ultraviolet, as well as multispectral, special techniques are applied to process and interpret remote sensing imagery for the purpose of producing conventional maps, thematic maps, resources surveys, etc., in the fields of agriculture, archaeology, forestry, geography, geology and others
Remote sensing is the observation of a target by a device separated from it by some distance
The term 'remote sensing' in its broadest sense merely means 'reconnaissance at a distance'
Remote sensing, though not precisely defined, includes all methods of obtaining pictures or other forms of electromagnetic records of the Earth's surface from a distance and the treatment and processing the picture data. Remote sensing then in the widest sense is concerned with detecting and recording electromagnetic radiation from the target areas in the field of view of the sensor instrument. This radiation may have originated directly from separate components of the target area; it may be solar energy reflected from them; or it may be reflections of energy transmitted to the target area from the sensor itself
'Remote sensing' is the term currently used by a number of scientists for the study of remote objects (earth, lunar and planetary surfaces and atmospheres, stellar and galactic phenomena, etc.), from great distances. Broadly defined remote sensing denotes the joint effects of employing modern sensors, data-processing equipment, information theory and processing methodology, communications theory and devices, space and airborne vehicles and large-systems theory and practice for the purposes of carrying out aerial or space surveys of the earth's surface
Remote sensing is the science of deriving information about an object from measurements made at a distance from the object, i.e., without actually coming in contact with it. The quantity most frequently measured in present-day remote sensing systems is the electromagnetic energy emanating from objects of interest and although there are other possibilities (e.g., seismic waves, sonic waves and gravitational force), our attention is focused upon systems which measure electromagnetic energy

The kind of remote sensing to be discussed here is devoted to observation of the earth's land and water surfaces by means of reflected or emitted electromagnetic energy. This more focused definition excludes applications that could be reasonably included in broader definitions, such as sensing the earth's magnetic field or atmosphere or the temperature of the human body. Also, we will focus upon instruments that present information in an image format, so we must largely exclude instruments (e.g., certain lasers) that collect data at a distance, but do not portray the results in image format. Such excluded applications can of course, be considered 'remote sensing' in its broad meaning, but they are omitted here as a matter of convenience. For our purposes, the definition can be based on modification of concepts given in Table 1.1.

Thus '*Remote sensing is the practice of deriving information about the earth's land and water surfaces using images acquired from an overhead perspective, using electromagnetic radiation in one or more regions of the electromagnetic spectrum, reflected or emitted from the earth's surface*'.

MILESTONES IN THE HISTORY OF REMOTE SENSING

The scope of the field of remote sensing can be elaborated by examining its history to trace the development of some of its central concepts. A few key events can be offered to trace the evolution of the field (Table 1.2).

Table 1.2. Milestones in the history of remote sensing.

1800	Discovery of infrared by Sir William Herschel
1839	Beginning of practice of photography
1847	Infrared spectrum shown by A. H. L. Fizeau and J. B. L. Foucault to share properties with visible light
1850–1860	Photography from balloons
1873	Theory of electromagnetic energy developed by James Clerk Maxwell
1909	Photography from airplanes
1914–1918	World War I: aerial reconnaissance
1920–1930	Developmental and initial applications of aerial photography and photogrammetry
1929–1939	Economic depression generates environmental crises that lead to governmental applications of aerial photography
1930–1940	Development of radars in Germany, United States and United Kingdom
1939–1945	World war II: applications of nonvisible portions of electromagnetic spectrum; training of persons in acquisition and interpretation of airphotos
1950–1960	Military research and development
1956	Colwell's research on plant disease detection with infrared photography
1960–1970	First use of term 'remote sensing'
	TIROS weather satellite
	Skylab remote sensing observations from space
1972	Launch of Landsat I
1970–1980	Rapid advances in digital image processing
1980–1990	Landsat 4: new generation of Landsat sensors
1986	SPOT French Earth observation satellite
1980s	Development of hyperspectral sensors
1990s	Global remote sensing systems

Because the practice of remote sensing focuses upon the examination of images of the earth's surface, its origins lie in the beginnings of the practice of photography. The first attempts to form images by photography date from the early 1800s, when a number of scientists, now largely forgotten, conducted experiments with photosensitive chemicals. In 1839 Louis Daguerre (1789–1851) publicly reported results of his experiments with photographic chemicals; this date forms a convenient, although arbitrary, milestone for the birth of photography. The use of photography to record an aerial view of the earth's surface, from a captive balloon, dates from 1858. In succeeding years numerous improvements were made in photographic technology and in methods of acquiring photographs of the earth from balloons and kites. These aerial images of the earth are among the first to fit the definition of remote sensing given previously, but most must be regarded as curiosities rather than the basis for a systematic field of study.

The next milestone is the use of powered aircraft as platforms for aerial photography. In 1909 Wilbur Wright piloted the plane that acquired motion pictures of the Italian landscape near Centocelli; these are said to be the first aerial photographs taken from an airplane. The manoeuverability of the airplane provided the capability for the control of speed, altitude and direction required for systematic use of the airborne camera. World War I (1914–1918) marked the beginning of the acquisition of aerial photography on a routine basis. During the conflict, equipment was designed specifically for aerial photography and many people were trained in the processes of acquiring, processing and interpreting aerial photos. Although the aerial photography of this era was primitive by later standards, many of these individuals became pioneers in the application of aerial photography in civilian endeavours.

Numerous improvements followed from these beginnings. Camera designs were improved and tailored specifically for use in aircraft. The science of photogrammetry—the practice of making accurate measurements from photographs—was applied to aerial photography, with the development of instruments specifically designed for analysis of aerial photos. Although the fundamentals of photogrammetry had been defined much earlier, the field developed toward its modern form in the 1920s, with the application of accurate photogrammetric instruments. From these origins, another landmark was established: the more or less routine application of aerial photography in government programmes, initially for topographic mapping, but later for soil survey, geological mapping, forest surveys and agricultural statistics.

During this period, the well-illustrated volume by Lee, 'The Face of the Earth as seen from the Air', surveyed the range of possible applications of aerial photography in a variety of disciplines from the perspective of those early days. Although the applications that Lee envisioned were achieved at a slow pace, the expression of governmental interest assured continuity in the scientific development of the acquisition and analysis of aerial photography, increased the number of photographs available and trained many people in uses of aerial photography. Nonetheless, the acceptance of the use of aerial photography in most governmental and scientific activities developed slowly because of resistance among traditionalists, imperfections in equipment and technique and genuine uncertainties regarding the proper role of aerial photography in scientific inquiry and practical applications.

The worldwide economic depression of 1929–1939 was not only an economic and financial crisis, but for many nations also an environmental crisis. National concerns about social and economic impacts of rural economic development, widespread soil erosion, reliability of water supplies and similar issues lead to some of the first governmental applications of aerial surveys to record and monitor rural economic development. In the United States, the U.S. Department of Agriculture and the Tennessee Valley Authority led efforts to apply aerial photography to guide environmental planning and economic development. Such efforts formed an important contribution to the institutionalisation of the use of aerial photography in government and in creating a body of practical experience in applications of aerial photography.

These developments led to the eve of World War II (1939–1945), which forms the next milestone in our history. During the war years, use of the electromagnetic spectrum was extended from almost exclusive emphasis upon the visible spectrum to other regions, most notably the infrared and microwave regions (far beyond the range of human vision). Knowledge of these regions of the spectrum had been developed in both basic and applied sciences during the preceding 150 years (Table 1.2). However, during the war years, application and further development of this knowledge accelerated, as did dissemination of the means to apply it. Although research scientists had long understood the potential of the nonvisible spectrum, the equipment, materials and experience necessary to apply it to practical problems were not at hand. Wartime research and operational experience provided both the theoretical and the practical knowledge required for everyday use of the nonvisible spectrum in remote sensing.

Furthermore, wartime training and experience of the large numbers of pilots, camera operators and photointerpreters provided a large pool of experienced personnel who where able to transfer their skills and experience into civilian occupations after the war. Many of these people assumed leadership positions in the efforts of business, scientific and governmental programmes to apply aerial photography and remote sensing to a broad range of problems.

The postwar era saw the continuation of trends set in motion by wartime research. On the one hand, established capabilities found their way into civilian applications. On the other hand, the beginnings of the cold war between the Western democracies and the Soviet Union created the environment for further development of reconnaissance techniques, which were often closely guarded as defense secretes. As newer, more sophisticated instruments were developed, the superseded technologies were released for wider, nondefense, applications in the civilian economy.

Among the most significant developments in the civilian sphere was the work of Robert Colwell, who applied colour infrared film (popularly known as 'camouflage detection film,' developed for use in World War II) to problems of identifying small-grain cereal crops and their diseases and other problems in the plant sciences. Although many of the basic principles of his research had been established earlier, his systematic investigation of their practical dimensions forms a clear milestone in the development of the field of remote sensing. Even at this early date, Colwell delineated the outlines of modern remote sensing and anticipated many of the opportunities and difficulties of this field of inquiry.

The 1960s saw a series of important developments occur in rapid sequence. The first meteorological satellite (TIROS-1) was launched in April 1960. This satellite was designed for climatological and meteorological observations, but provided the basis for later development of land observation satellites. During this period, some of the remote sensing instruments originally developed for military reconnaissance and classified as defence secrets, were released for civilian use as more advanced designs became available for military application. These instruments extended the reach of aerial observation outside the visible spectrum into the infrared and microwave regions. It was in this context that the term 'remote sensing' was first used. Evelyn Pruit, a scientist working for the US Navy's Office of Naval Research, coined this term when she recognised that the term 'aerial photography' no longer accurately described the many forms of imagery collected using radiation outside the visible region of the spectrum. Early in the 1960s the US National Aeronautics and Space Administration (NASA) established a research programme in remote sensing—a programme that, during the next decade, was to support remote sensing research at institutions throughout the United States. During this same period, a committee of the US National Academy of Sciences (NAS) studied opportunities for application of remote sensing in the field of agriculture and forestry. In 1970, the NAS reported the results of their work in a document that outlined many of the opportunities offered by this emerging field of inquiry.

In 1972, the launch of Landsat 1, the first of many earth-orbiting satellites designed for observation of the earth's land areas, formed another milestone. Landsat provided, for the first time, systematic repetitive observation of the earth's land areas. Each Landsat image depicted large areas of the earth's surface in several regions of the electromagnetic spectrum, yet provided modest levels of detail sufficient for practical applications in many fields. Landsat's full significance may not yet be fully appreciated, yet it is possible to recognise three of its most important contributions. First, the routine availability of multispectral data for large regions of the earth's surface greatly expanded the number of people who acquired experience and interest in analysis of multispectral data. Multispectral data had been acquired previously, but were largely confined to specialised research laboratories. Landsat's data greatly expanded the population of scientists with interests in multispectral analysis.

Landsat's second contribution was to create an incentive for the rapid and broad expansion of uses of digital analyses for remote sensing. Before Landsat, image analyses were usually completed visually by examining prints and transparencies of aerial images. Analyses of digital images by computer were possible mainly in specialised research institutions; personal computers and the variety of image analysis programmes that we now regard as commonplace, did not exist. Although Landsat data were initially used primarily as prints or transparencies, they were also provided in digital form. The routine availability of digital data in a standard format created the context that permitted the growth in popularity of digital analysis and set the stage for the development of image analysis software that is now commonplace. A third contribution of the Landsat programme was its role as a model for development of other land observation satellites designed and operated by diverse organisations throughout the world. In the 1980s, scientists at the Jet Propulsion Laboratory (Pasadena, California) began, with NASA support, to develop instruments that could create images of the earth at unprecedented levels of spectral detail. Whereas previous multispectral sensors collected data in a few rather broadly defined spectral regions, these new instruments could collect 200 or more very precisely defined spectral regions. These instruments created the field of hyperspectral remote sensing, which is still developing as a field of inquiry. Hyperspectral remote sensing will advance remote sensing's analytical powers to new levels and will form the basis for a more thorough understanding of how the best develop future remote sensing capabilities.

By the 1990s, satellite systems had been designed specifically to collect remotely sensed data representing the entire earth. Although Landsat had offered such a capability in principle, in practice, effective global remote sensing requires sensors and processing techniques specifically designed to acquire broad-scale coverage. Such capabilities had existed on an adhoc basis since the 1980s, primarily developed from the synoptic scope of meteorological satellites. By December 1999, NASA had launched Terra-1, the first satellite of a system specifically designed to acquire global coverage to monitor changes in the nature and extent of earth's ecosystems. These data serve as a milestone marking the initiation of an era of broad-scale remote sensing of the earth.

Aerial photography is the original form of remote sensing and remains the most widely used method. Aerial photography analyses have played major roles in the discovery of many oil and mineral deposits around the world. These successes, using the visible portion of the electromagnetic spectrum, suggested that it might be possible to obtain comparable results by using other wavelength regions. In the 1960s, technological developments enabled the acquisition of images at other wavelengths, including thermal infrared (IR) and microwave. The development and deployment of manned and unmanned earth satellites began in the 1960s and provided and orbital vantage point for acquiring images of the earth. Descriptions of all these methods and interpretations of the images form the subject of this book.

UNITS OF MEASURE

This text employs the International System of units (SI), a modernised metric system adopted in 1960 that uses the following standard units and abbreviations:

meter	m
second	sec
kilogram	kg
gram	g
radian	rad

(Contd...)

milliradian	mrad
hertz	Hz
watt	W

(The SI abbreviation for second is actually s, but this text uses sec to avoid confusion with other abbreviations)

Distance is expressed in the multiples and fractions of meters shown in Table 1.3. Where appropriate for clarity, English units for distance will be used, with metric equivalents shown in parentheses.

Table 1.3. Metric nomenclature for distance.

Unit	*Symbol*	*Equivalent*	*Comment*
Kilometer	km	$1000 \text{ m} = 10^3 \text{ m}$	
Meter	m	$1.0 \text{ m} = 10^0 \text{ m}$	Basic unit
Centimeter	cm	$0.01 \text{ m} = 10^{-2} \text{ m}$	
Millimeter	mm	$0.001 \text{ m} = 10^{-3} \text{ m}$	
Micrometer	μm	$0.000001 \text{ m} = 10^{-6} \text{ m}$	Formerly called micron (μ)
Nanometer	nm	10^{-9} m	

Frequency (v) is the number of wave crests passing a given point in a specified period of time. Frequency was formerly expressed as 'cycles per second', but today we use hertz, the unit for a frequency of one cycle per second. The terms for designating frequencies are shown in Table 1.4.

Temperature is given in degrees Celsius (°C) or in degrees Kelvin (°K), which is also known as the absolute temperature scale. A temperature of –273°C is equivalent to 0°K. (The formal SI system omits the degree symbol for Kelvin temperatures, but the letter K alone may be confused with other constants that employ this letter; therefore '°K' is used in this text.) A few temperatures commonly given in degrees Fahrenheit (°F) will remain in that scale where conversion to degrees Celsius would be inconvenient.

In fractional statements, units in the denominator are identified by a negative superscript. For example, the property called thermal inertia (P) for a particular rock type is expressed as

$$P = 0.53 \text{ cal} \cdot \text{cm}^{-2} \cdot \text{sec}^{-1/2} \cdot {}^{\circ}\text{C}^{-1}$$

This expression means that for the particular rock type, thermal inertia (P) equals 0.53 calories per square centimetre per second to the square root per degree Celsius.

Table 1.4. Terms used to designate frequencies.

Unit	*Symbol*	*Frequency, cycles · sec*
Hertz	Hz	1
Kilohertz	kHz	10^3
Megahertz	MHz	10^6
Gigahertz	GHz	10^9

ELECTROMAGNETIC ENERGY

Electromagnetic energy refers to all energy that moves with the velocity of light in a harmonic wave pattern. A harmonic pattern consists of waves that occur at equal intervals in time. The wave concept explains how electromagnetic energy propagates (moves), but this energy can only be detected as it interacts with matter. In this interaction, electromagnetic energy behaves as though it consists of many individual bodies called photons that have such particlelike properties as energy and momentum. When light bends (refracts) as it propagates through media of different optical densities, it is behaving like waves. When a light meter measures the intensity of light, however, the interaction of photons with light-sensitive photodetector produces an electric signal that varies in strength proportional to the number of photons. The characteristics of electromagnetic energy that are significant for remote sensing are discussed below:

Properties of Electromagnetic Waves

Electromagnetic waves can be described in terms of their velocity, wavelength and frequency. All electromagnetic waves travel at the same speed (c). This velocity is commonly referred to as the speed of light, which is one form of electromagnetic energy. For electromagnetic waves moving through a vacuum, $c = 2{,}99{,}793 \text{ km} \cdot \text{sec}^{-1}$ or for practical purposes, $c = 3 \times 10^8 \text{ m} \cdot \text{sec}^{-1}$.

The wavelength (λ) of electromagnetic waves is the distance from any point on one cycle or wave to same position on the next cycle or wave. The micrometer (μm) is a convenient unit for designating wavelength of both visible and IR radiation. Optical scientists commonly employ nanometers (nm) for measurements of visible light to avoid using decimal numbers.

Unlike velocity and wavelength, which change as electromagnetic energy is propagated through media of different densities, frequency remains constant and is therefore a more fundamental property. Electronic engineers use frequency nomenclature for designating radio and radar energy regions. This book will use wavelength rather than frequency to simplify comparisons between all portions of the electromagnetic spectrum. Velocity (c), wavelength (λ) and frequency (ν) are related by:

$$c = \lambda\nu \quad \text{... (1.1)}$$

Interaction Mechanisms

Electromagnetic energy that encounters matter, whether solid, liquid or gas, is called incident radiation. Interactions with matter can change the following properties of the incident radiation: intensity, direction, wavelength, polarisation and phase. The science of remote sensing detects and records these changes. Scientists then interpret the resulting images and data to identify the characteristics of the matter that produced those changes. During interactions between electromagnetic radiation and matter, mass and energy are conserved according to basic physical principles. Figure 1.1 illustrates the five common results of those interactions. The incident radiation may be:

1. Transmitted, that is, passed through the substance. Transmission through media of different densities, such as from air into water, causes a change in the velocity of electromagnetic radiation. The ratio of the two velocities is called the index of refraction (n) and is expressed as:

$$n = \frac{c_a}{c_s} \quad \text{... (1.2)}$$

   where c_a is the velocity in a vacuum and c_s is the velocity in the substance.
2. Absorbed, giving up its energy largely to heating the matter.
3. Emitted by the substance, usually at longer wavelengths, as a function of its structure and temperature.
4. Scattered, that is, deflected in all directions. Surfaces with dimensions of relief or roughness, comparable to the wavelength of the incident energy produce scattering. Light waves are scattered

by molecules and particles in the atmosphere that have sizes similar to the dimensions of wavelengths of light.

5. Reflected, that is, returned from the surface of a material with the angle of reflection equal and opposite to the angle of incidence. Reflection is caused by surfaces that are smooth relative to the wavelength of incident energy. Polarisation or direction of vibration of the reflected waves may differ from that of the incident wave.

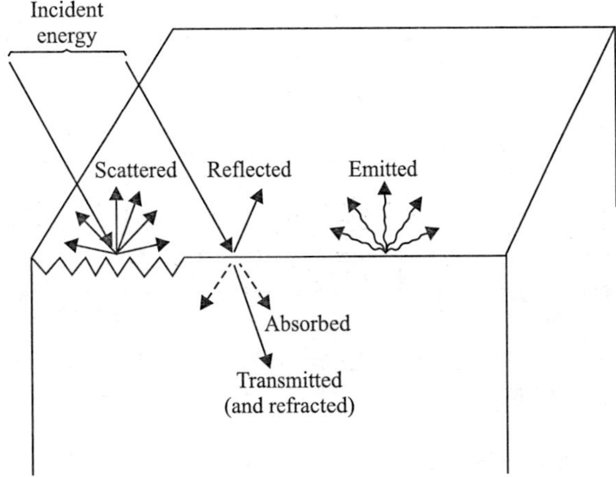

Fig. 1.1. Interaction mechanisms between electromagnetic energy and matter.

Emission, scattering and reflection are called surface phenomena because these interactions are determined primarily by properties of the surface, such as colour and roughness. Transmission and absorption are called volume phenomena because these interactions are determined by the internal characteristics of matter, such as density and conductivity. The particular combination of surface and volume interactions with any particular material depend both on the wavelength of the electromagnetic radiation and the specific properties of that material. These interactions between matter and energy are recorded on remote sensing images, from which one may interpret the characteristics of matter.

ELECTROMAGNETIC SPECTRUM

The electromagnetic spectrum is the continuum of energy that ranges from meters to nanometers in wavelength, travels at the speed of light and propagates through a vacuum such as outer space. All matter radiates a range of electromagnetic energy, with the peak intensity shifting toward progressively shorter wavelengths with increasing temperature of the matter.

Wavelength Regions

Figure 1.2 shows the electromagnetic spectrum, which is divided on the basis of wavelength into regions that are described in Table 1.5. The electromagnetic spectrum ranges from the very short wavelengths of the gamma-ray region (measured in fractions of nanometers) to the long wavelengths of the radio region (measured in meters). The horizontal scale in Fig. 1.2 is logarithmic in order to portray the shorter wavelengths. Notice that the visible region (0.4 to 0.7 μm wavelengths) occupies only a small portion of the spectrum. Energy reflected from the earth during daytime may be recorded as a function of wavelength. The maximum amount of energy is reflected at 0.5 μm wavelength, which corresponds to the green band of the visible region and is called the reflected energy peak (Fig. 1.2). The earth also radiates energy both day and night, with the maximum energy radiating at 9.7 μm wavelength. This radiant energy peak occurs in the thermal band of the IR region (Fig. 1.2).

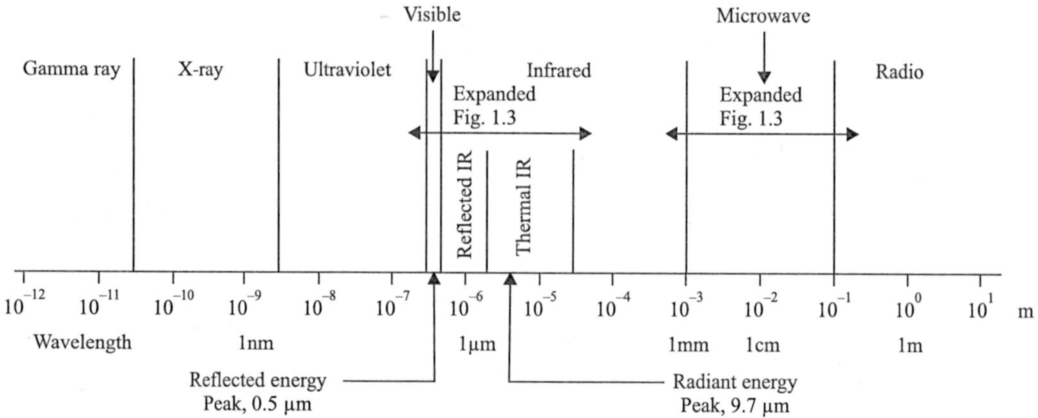

Fig. 1.2. Electromagnetic spectrum. Expanded versions of the visible, infrared regions and microwave regions and microwave regions are shown in Fig. 1.3.

Table 1.5. Electromagnetic spectral regions.

Region	*Wavelength*	*Remarks*
Gamma ray	<0.03 nm	Incoming radiation is completely absorbed by the upper atmosphere and is not available for remote sensing
X-ray	0.03–3.0 nm	Completely absorbed by atmosphere. Not employed in remote sensing
Ultraviolet	0.03–0.4 μm	Incoming wavelengths less than 0.3 μm are completely absorbed by ozone in the upper atmosphere
Photographic UV band	0.3–0.4 μm	Transmitted through atmosphere. Detectable with film and photodetectors, but atmospheric scattering is severe
Visible	0.4–0.7 μm	Imaged with film and photodetectors. Includes reflected energy peak of earth at 0.5 μm
Infrared	0.7–100 μm	Interaction with matter varies with wavelength. Atmospheric transmission windows are separated by absorption bands
Reflected IR band properties	0.7–3.0 μm	Reflected solar radiation that contains no information about thermal of materials. The band from 0.7 to 0.9 μm is detectable with film and is called the photographic IR band
Thermal IR band vidicon	3–5 μm, 8–14 μm	Principal atmospheric windows in the thermal region. Images at these wavelengths are acquired by optical-mechanical scanners and special systems but not by film
Microwave acquired	0.1–30 cm	Longer wavelengths can penetrate clouds, fog and rain. Images may be in the active or passive mode
Radar	0.1–30 cm	Active form of microwave remote sensing. Radar images are acquired at various wavelength bands
Radio	>30 cm	Longest wavelength portion of electromagnetic spectrum. Some classified radars with very long wavelength operate in this region

The earth's atmosphere absorbs energy in the gamma-ray, X-ray and most of the ultraviolet (UV) region; therefore, these regions are not used for remote sensing. Remote sensing records energy in the microwave, infrared and visible regions, as well as the long-wavelength portion of the UV region. Details of these regions are shown in Fig. 1.3. The horizontal axes again show wavelength on a logarithmic scale; the vertical axes show per cent atmospheric transmission of electromagnetic energy. Wavelength regions with high transmission are called atmospheric windows and are used to acquire remote sensing images.

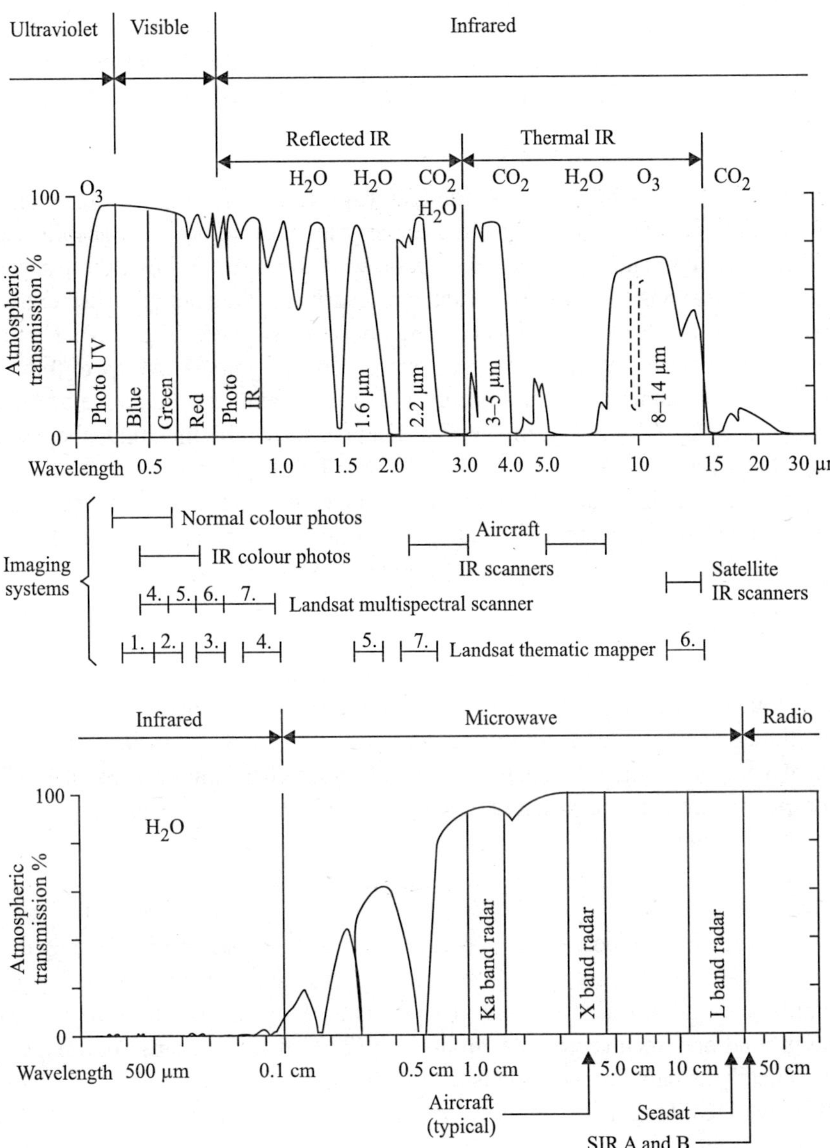

Fig. 1.3. Expanded diagrams of the visible and infrared regions (upper) and the microwave region (lower) showing atmospheric windows. Wavelength bands of commonly used remote sensing systems are indicated. Gases responsible for atmospheric absorption are shown.

The major remote sensing regions (visible, infrared and microwave) are further subdivided into bands, such as the blue, green and red bands of the visible region. The upper curve of Fig. 1.3 spans the UV through thermal IR regions. Bars below the curve show wavelength bands recorded by major imaging systems such as photography and scanners. For the Landsat systems the numbers identify specific bands recorded by these systems. Characteristics of the remote sensing regions are summarised in Table 1.5.

Passive remote sensing systems record the energy that naturally radiates or reflects from an object. An active system supplies its own source of energy, directing it at the object in order to measure the returned energy. Flash photography is an example of active remote sensing, in contrast to available-light photography, which is passive. The other common form of active remote sensing is radar (Table 1.3), which provides its own source of electromagnetic energy at microwave wavelengths.

Atmospheric Effects

Our eyes inform us that the atmosphere is essentially transparent to light and we tend to assume that this condition exists for all electromagnetic energy. In fact, the gases of the atmosphere absorb electromagnetic energy at specific wavelength intervals called absorption bands. Figure 1.3 shows these absorption bands, together with the gases responsible for the atmospheric absorption. Wavelengths shorter than 0.3 μm are completely absorbed by the ozone (O_3) layer in the upper atmosphere (Fig. 1.3). This absorption is essential to allow life on earth, because prolonged exposure to the intense energy of these wavelengths destroys living tissue. For example, sunburn occurs more readily at high mountain elevations than at sea level. Sunburn is caused by UV energy, much of which is absorbed by the atmosphere at sea level. At higher elevations however, there is less atmosphere to absorb the UV energy.

Clouds consist of aerosol-sized particles of liquid water that absorb and scatter electromagnetic radiation at wavelengths less than about 0.3 cm. Only radiation of microwave and longer wavelengths is capable of penetrating clouds without being scattered, reflected or absorbed.

IMAGE CHARACTERISTICS

In general usage, an image is any pictorial representation, irrespective of the wavelength or imaging device used to produce it. A photograph is an image that records wavelengths of 0.3 to 0.9 μm that have interacted with light-sensitive chemicals in photographic film. Images can be described in terms of certain fundamental properties regardless of the wavelength at which the image is recorded. These common fundamental properties are scale, brightness, contrast and resolution. Tone and texture of images are functions of the fundamental properties.

Scale

Scale is the ratio of the distance between two points on an image to the corresponding distance on the ground. A common scale on US Geological Survey topographic maps is 1:24000, which means that one unit on the map equals 24000 units on the ground. Thus 1 cm on the map represents 24000 cm (240 m) on the ground or 1 inch represents 24000 inch (2000 ft.). The maps and images of this book show scales graphically as bars. Image scale is determined by:

1. The effective focal length of the remote sensing device.
2. The altitude from which the image is acquired.
3. The magnification factor employed in reproducing the image.

The deployment of imaging systems on satellites has changed the concepts of image scale.

In this book, scales of images are designated as follows:

Small scale (greater than 1:5,00,000)	1 cm = 5 km or more (1 inch = 8 miles or more)
Intermediate scale (1:50000 to 1:5,00,000)	1 cm = 0.5 to 5 km (1 inch = 0.8 to 8 miles)
Large scale (less than 1:50000)	1 cm = 0.5 km or less (1 inch = 0.8 miles or less)

These designations differ from the traditional scale concepts of aerial photography. Twenty years ago, 1:62500 was the minimum scale of commercially available photographs and was considered small-scale. Today sensing systems on high-altitude aircraft and satellites can acquire photographs and images of excellent quality at much smaller scales. Optimum image scale is determined by how the images are to be interpreted. With the advent of satellite images, many investigators have been surprised at the amount and types of information that can be interpreted from very small scale images.

Brightness and Tone

Remote sensing systems detect the intensity of electromagnetic radiation that an object reflects, emits or scatters at particular wavelength bands. Variations in intensity of electromagnetic radiation from the terrain are commonly displayed as variations in brightness on images. On positive images, such as those in this book, the brightness of objects is directly proportional to the intensity of electromagnetic radiation that is detected from that object.

Brightness is the magnitude of the response produced in the eye by light; it is a subjective sensation that can be determined only approximately. Luminance is a quantitative measure of the intensity of light from a source and is measured with a device called a photometer or light meter. People who interpret images rarely, if ever, make quantitative measurements of brightness variations on an image. Variations in brightness may be calibrated with a gray scale such as the one in Fig. 1.4. Each distinguishable shade from black to white is a separate tone. In practice, most interpreters do not use an actual gray scale the way one would use a centimeter scale; they characterise areas on an image as light, intermediate or dark in tone, using their own mental concept of a gray scale.

Fig. 1.4. Gray scale.

On aerial photographs the tone of an object is primarily determined by the ability of the object to reflect incident sunlight, although atmospheric effects and the spectral sensitivity of the film are also factors. On images acquired in other wavelength regions, tone is determined by other physical properties of objects. On a thermal IR image, the tone of an object is proportional to the heat radiating from the object. On a radar image the tone of an object is determined by the intensity at which the transmitted beam of radar energy is scattered back to the receiving antenna.

Contrast Ratio

Contrast ratio (CR) is the ratio between the brightest and darkest parts of the image and is defined as:

$$CR = \frac{B_{max}}{B_{min}} \quad \text{... (1.3)}$$

where B_{max} is the maximum brightness of the scene and B_{min} is the minimum brightness. Figure 1.5 shows images of high, medium and low contrast together with profiles of brightness variations across each image. On a brightness scale of 0 to 10, the images in Fig. 1.5 have the following contrast ratios:

A. High contrast $CR = \frac{9}{2} = 4.5$

B. Medium contrast $CR = \frac{5}{2} = 2.5$

C. Low contrast $CR = \frac{3}{2} = 1.5$

Note that when $B_{min} = 0$, CR is infinity; when $B_{min} = B_{max}$, CR is unity. This discussion was summarised from Slater's extensive review, in which he describes other terms for contrast. In addition to describing an entire scene, contrast ratio is also used to describe the ratio between the brightness of an object on an image and the brightness of the adjacent background. Contrast ratio is a vital factor in determining the ability to resolve and detect objects.

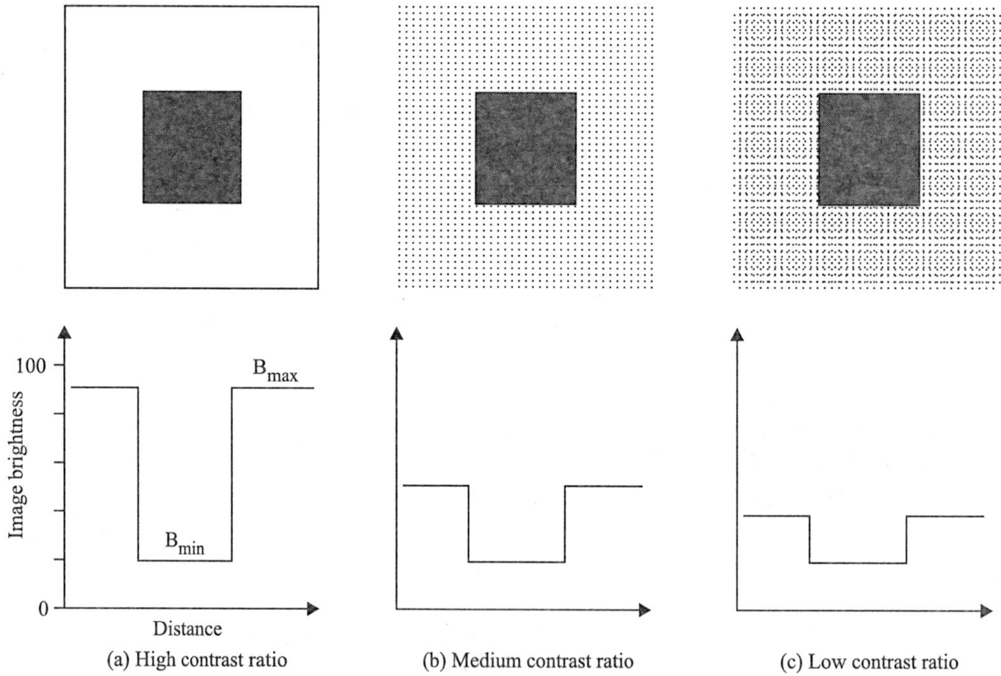

Fig. 1.5. Images of different contrast ratios with corresponding brightness profiles.

Images with a low contrast ratio are commonly referred to as 'washed out,' with monotonous, nearly uniform tones of gray.

Low contrast may result from the following causes:

1. The objects and background of the scene may have a nearly uniformly electromagnetic response at the particular wavelength band that the remote sensing system records. In other words, the scene has an inherently low contrast ratio.
2. Scattering of electromagnetic energy by the atmosphere can reduce the contrast of a scene. This effect is most pronounced in the shorter wavelength portions of the photographic remote sensing band.
3. The remote sensing system may lack sufficient sensitivity to detect and record the contrast of the terrain. Incorrect recording techniques can also result in low-contrast images even though the scene has a high contrast ratio when recorded by other means.

A low contrast ratio, regardless of the cause, can be improved by digital methods.

Spatial Resolution and Resolving Power

This text defines spatial resolution as the ability to distinguish between two closely spaced objects on an image. More specifically, it is the minimum distance between two objects at which the images of the objects appear distinct and separate. Objects spaced together more closely than the resolution limit will appear as a single object on the image.

Resolving power and spatial resolution are two closely related concepts. The term resolving power applies to an imaging system or a component of the system, whereas spatial resolution applies to the image produced by the system. For example, the lens and film of the camera system each have a characteristic resolving power that, together with other factors, determines the resolution of the photographs.

Spatial resolution of a photographic system is customarily determined by photographing a standard resolution target, such as the one shown in Fig. 1.6a, under specified conditions of illumination and magnification. The resolution targets or bar charts, consist of alternating black and white bars of equal width that are called line-pairs. Spacing of resolution targets is expressed in line-pairs per centimeter. For the target with 5 line-pairs $\cdot$ cm^{-1}, each black bar is 0.1 cm wide and separated by a white bar of the same width. The photograph is viewed under magnification and the observer determines the most closely spaced set of line-pairs for which the bars and spaces are discernable. Spatial resolution of the photographic system is stated as the number of line-pairs per millimeter of the resolved target. Human judgment and visual characteristics are critical components in this analysis, which therefore is not completely objective and reproducible. Spatial resolution is different for objects of different shape, size, arrangement and contrast ratio. An alternate method of describing resolution is the modulation transfer function (MTF), which employs a bar chart with progressively closer spacing of the bars. Angular resolving power is defined as the angle subtended by imaginary lines passing from the imaging system and two targets spaced at the minimum resolvable distance. Angular resolving power is commonly measured in radians. As shown in Fig. 1.7, a radian (rad) is the angle subtended by an arc BC of a circle having a length equal to the radius AB of the circle. Because the circumference of a circle has a length equal to 2π times the radius, there are 2π or 6.28, rad in a circle. A radian corresponds to 57.3° or 3438 minute and a milliradian (mrad) is 10^{-3} rad. In the radian system of angular measurement,

$$\text{Angle} = \frac{L}{r}\,\text{rad} \qquad \text{... (1.4)}$$

where L is the length of the subtended arc and r is the radius of the circle. A convenient relationship is that at a distance r of 1000 units, 1 mrad subtends an arc L of 1 unit. Figure 1.8 illustrates the angular resolving power of a remote sensing system (the eye) that can resolve the center bar chart of Fig. 1.6 at a distance of 5 m. This chart has 5 line-pairs $\cdot$ cm^{-1} and the bars are separated by 1 mm. For these targets with a high contrast ratio, the angular resolving power is 0.2 mrad.

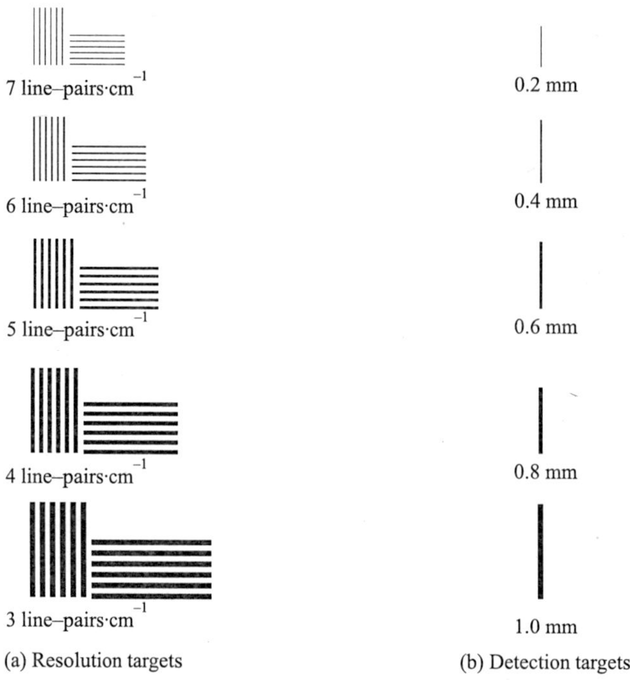

Fig. 1.6. Resolution and detection targets with high contrast ratio. View this chart from a distance of 5 m (16.5 ft.). For (a), determine the most closely spaced set of bars you can resolve. For (b), determine the narrowest bar you can detect.

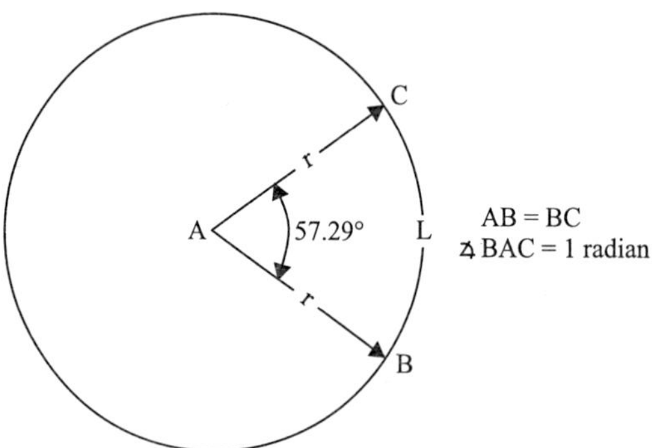

Fig. 1.7. Radian system of angular measurement.

Resolving power and spatial resolution will be discussed for each remote sensing system, one you should remember the following points:

1. Theoretical resolving power of a system is rarely achieved in actual operation.
2. Resolution alone does not adequately determine whether an image is suitable for a particular application.

3. Resolution is the minimum separation between two objects for which the images appear distinct and separate; it is not the size of the smallest object that can be seen. By knowing the resolution and scale of an image, however, one can estimate the size of smallest detectable object.

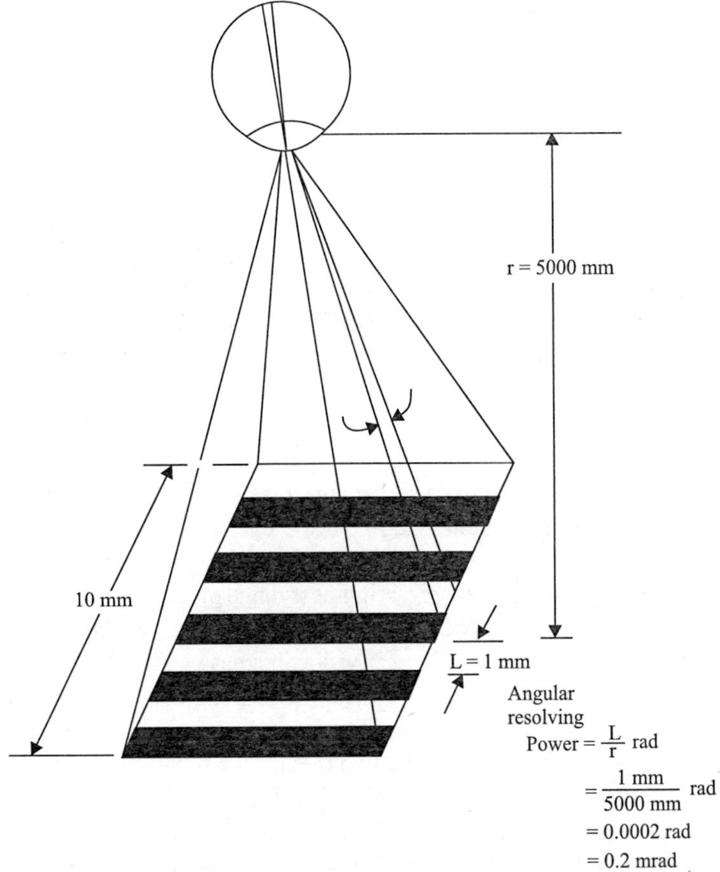

Fig. 1.8. Angular resolving power (in milliradians) for a remote sensing system that can resolve 5 line-pairs · cm^{-1} at a distance of 5 m.

Other Characteristics of Images

Detectability is the ability of an imaging system to record the presence or absence of an object, although the identity of the object may be unknown. An object may be detected even though it is smaller than the theoretical resolving power of the imaging system.

Recognisability is the ability to identify an object on an image. Objects may be detected and resolved and yet not be recognisable. For example, roads on an image appear as narrow lines that could also be railroads or canals. Unlike resolution, there are no quantitative measures for recognisability and detectability. It is important for the interpreter to understand the significance and correct use of these terms. A signature is the expression of an object on an image that enables the object to be recognised. Characteristics of an object that control its interaction with electromagnetic energy determine its signature. For example, the spectral signature of an object is its brightness measured at a specific wavelength of energy.

Texture is the frequency of change and arrangement of tones on an image. Fine, medium and coarse are some terms used to describe texture.

An interpretation key is a characteristics or combination of characteristics that enables an object to be identified on an image. Typical keys are size, shape, tone and colour. The associations of different characteristics are valuable keys. On images of cities, one may recognise single-family residential areas by the association of a dense street network, lawns and small buildings. The associations of certain landforms and vegetation species are keys for identifying different types of rocks.

VISION

Of our five senses, two detect electromagnetic radiation. Some of the nerve endings in our skin detect thermal IR radiation as heat but do not form images. Vision is the most important sense and accounts for most of the information input to our brain. Vision is not only an important remote sensing system in its own right, but it is also the means by which we interpret the images produced by other remote sensing systems. The following section analyses the human eye as a remote sensing system.

Structure of the Eye

For such a complex structure, the human eye in cross section, shown on Fig. 1.9, appears deceptively simple. Light enters through the clear cornea, which is separated from the lens by fluid called the aqueous humor. The iris is the pigmented part of the eye that controls the variable aperture called the pupil. It is commonly thought that variations in pupil size allow the eye to function over a wide range of light intensities. However, the pupil varies in area over a ratio of only 16:1 (maximum area 16 times the minimum area), whereas the eye functions over a brightness range of about 1,00,000:1. The pupil contracts to limit the light rays to the central and optically best part of the lens, except when the full opening is needed in dim light. The pupil also contracts for near vision, increasing the depth of field for near objects.

A common misconception is that the lens refracts (bends) the incoming rays of light to form the image. The amount that light bends when passing through two adjacent media is determined by the difference in the refractive indices (n) of the two media; the greater the difference, the greater the bending. For the eye the maximum difference is between air ($n = 1.0$) and the cornea ($n = 1.3$) and this interface is where the maximum light refraction occurs. Although the lens is relatively unimportant for forming the image, it is important in accommodating or focusing, for near and far vision. In cameras this accommodation is done by changing the position of the lens relative to the film. In the human eye, the shape rather than the position of the lens is changed by muscles that vary the tension on the lens. For near vision the muscles release tension, allowing the lens to become thicker in the center and assume a more convex cross section. With age the cells of the lens harden and the lens becomes too rigid to accommodate for different distances; as a result, bifocal glasses may become necessary to provide for near and far vision.

An inverted image is focused on the retina, a thin sheet of interconnected nerve cells that includes the light receptor cells, called rods and cones, that convert light into electrical impulses. Rods and cones receive their names from their longitudinal shapes when viewed microscopically. The cones function in daylight conditions to give colour or photopic, vision. The rods function under low illumination and only give vision in tones of gray, called scotopic, vision. Rods and cones are not uniformly distributed throughout the retinal surface. The maximum concentration and organisation of receptor cells is in the fovea (Fig. 1.9), a small region at the center of the retina that provides maximum visual acuity. You can demonstrate the existence and importance of the fovea by concentrating on a single letter on this page. The rest of the page and even the nearby words and letters appear indistinct because they are outside the field of view of the fovea. The eye is in continual motion to bring the fovea to bear on all parts of the page or scene. Close to the fovea is the blind spot, where the optic nerve joins the eye and there are no receptor cells. The electrical impulses from the receptor cells are transmitted to the brain, which interprets them as the visual perception.

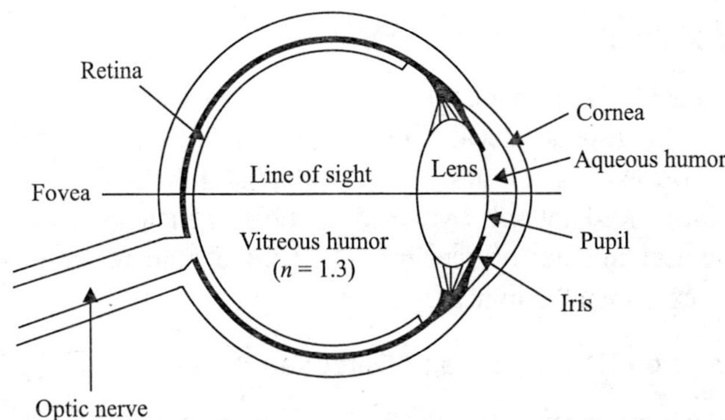

Fig. 1.9. Structure of the human eye.

Resolving Power of the Eye

The diameter of the largest receptor cells in the fovea determines the resolving power of the eye. Multiplying this maximum diameter (3 μm) by the refractive index of the vitreous humor (n = 1.3) determines an effective diameter (4 μm) for the receptor cells. The image distance or distance from the retina to the lens, is about 20 mm or 20000 μm. The effective width of the receptors is 4/20000 or 1/5000, of the image distance. Image distance is proportional to object distance, which is the distance from the eye to the object. An object forms an image that fills the width of a receptor if the object width is 1/5000 the object distance.

Therefore adjacent objects must be separated by 1/5000 the object distance for their images to fall on alternate receptors and be resolved by the eye.

One can demonstrate the resolving power of the eye by viewing the resolution targets of Fig. 1.6a at a distance of 5 m (16.5 ft.) and determining the most closely spaced set of line-pairs that can be resolved. Also determine the narrowest of the bars on Fig. 1.6b that you can detect. Make these determinations now, before reading further, because the following text may influence your perception of the targets.

For the high-contrast resolution targets of Fig. 1.6a at a distance of 5 m, the normal eye should be able to resolve the middle set that has 5 line-pairs · cm^{-1}. The black and white bars are 1 mm wide. The instantaneous field of view (IFOV) of any detector is the solid angle through which a detector is sensitive to radiation. Equation 1.4 is used to calculate the IFOV of the eye, where the radius (r) is 5000 mm and the length of the subtended arc (L) is 1 mm:

Figure 1.8 shows the relationships of the resolution targets to the IFOV of the eye. The 0.2-mrad IFOV of the eye means that a distance of 1000 units, the eye can resolve high-contrast targets that are spaced no closer than 0.2 units.

$$\mathrm{IFOV} = \frac{\mathrm{L}}{\mathrm{r}}\ \mathrm{rad}$$

$$= \frac{1\text{ mm}}{5000\text{ mm}}\text{ rad}$$
$$= 0.2 \times 10^{-3}\text{ rad}$$
$$= 0.2\text{ mrad}$$

Detection Capability of the Eye

When the detection targets of Fig. 1.6b are viewed from a distance of 5 m, most readers can detect the narrowest bar, which is 0.2 mm wide. Recall, however, that at this distance the minimum separation at which bar targets can be resolved is 1.0 mm. This test illustrates the difference between resolution and detection. Detection is influenced not only by the size of objects but also by their shape and orientation. For example, if dots are used in place of lines in Fig. 1.6b, the diameter of the smallest detectable dot would be considerably larger than 0.2 mm.

Effect of Contrast Ratio on Resolution and Detection

The resolution and detection targets in Fig. 1.10 have the same spacing as those in Fig. 1.6, but the contrast ratio has been reduced by the addition of a gray background. To evaluate the effect of the lower contrast ratio, view Fig. 1.10 from a distance of 5 m and determine which targets can be resolved and detected. Using this figure, most readers only resolve 3 line-pairs $\cdot$ cm^{-1} and the smallest detectable target is the line 0.6 mm wide. These dimensions are larger than the 5 line-pairs $\cdot$ cm^{-1} and the 0.2-mm line of the high-contrast target and demonstrate the effect of a lower contrast ratio on resolution and detection.

REMOTE SENSING SYSTEMS

The eye is a familiar example of a remote sensing system. The inorganic remote sensing systems described in this text belong to two major categories: framing systems and scanning systems.

Framing Systems

Framing systems instantaneously acquire an image of an area or frame, on the terrain. Cameras and vidicons are common examples of such systems (Fig. 1.11). The human eye can also be considered a framing system. A camera employs a lens to form an image of the scene at the focal plane, which is the plane at which the image is sharply defined. A shutter opens at selected intervals to allow light to enter the camera, where the image is recorded on photographic film. A vidicon is a type of television camera that records the image on a photosensitive electronically charged surface. An electron beam then sweeps the surface to detect the pattern of charge differences that constitutes the image. The electron beam produces a signal that may be transmitted and recorded on magnetic tape for eventual display on film.

Successive frames of camera of vidicon images may be acquired with forward overlap, as shown in Fig. 1.11. The overlapping portion may be viewed with a stereoscope to produce a three-dimensional view. Film is sensitive only to portions of the UV, visible and reflected IR regions (0.3 to 0.9 μm). The sensitivity range of special vidicons extends into the thermal band of the IR region. A framing system can instantaneously image a large area because the system has a dense array of detectors located at the focal plane. The eye has a network of rods and cones. The emulsion of camera film contains tiny grains of silver halide. A vidicon surface is coated with sensitive phosphors.

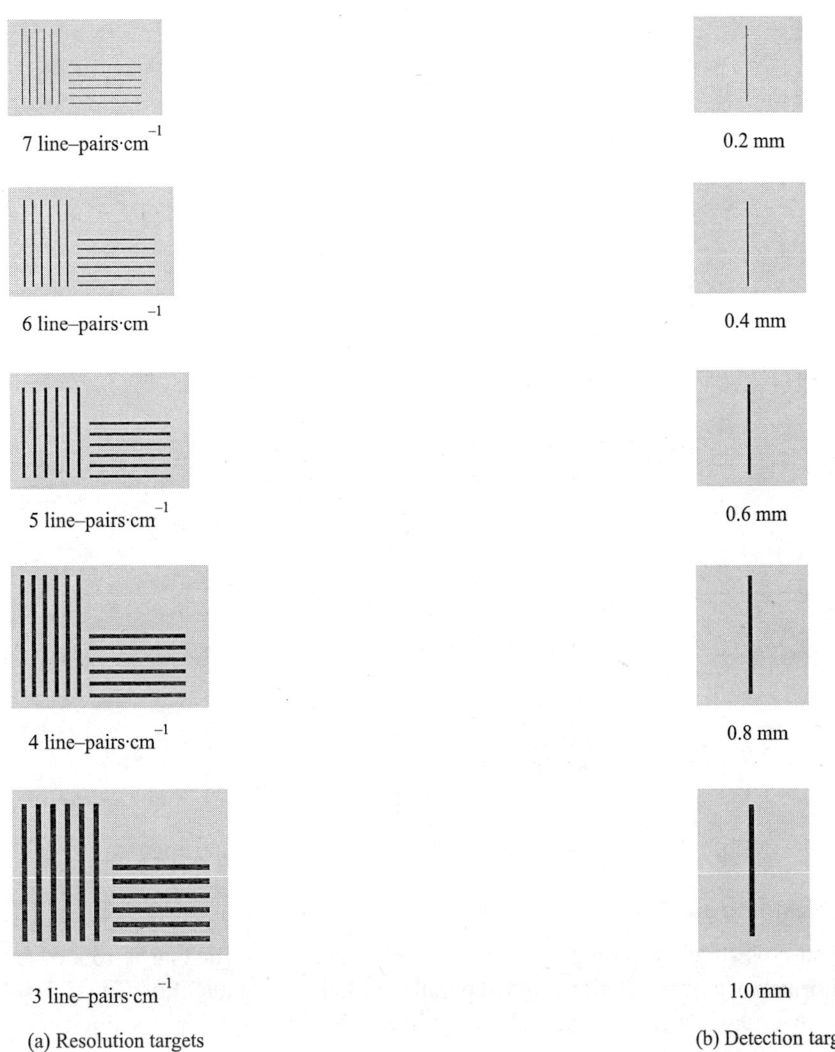

Fig. 1.10. Resolution and detection targets with low contrast ratio. View this chart from a distance of 5 m (16.5 ft.). For (a), determine the most closely spaced set of bars you can resolve. For (b) determine the narrowest bar you can detect. Compare these values with those determined from Fig. 1.6.

Scanning Systems

A scanning system employs a single detector with a narrow field of view which sweeps across the terrain to produce an image. When photons of electromagnetic energy radiated or reflected from the terrain encounter the detector, an electrical signal is produced that varies in proportion to the number of photons. The electrical signal is amplified, recorded on magnetic tape and played back later to produce an image. All scanning systems sweep the detector's field of view across the terrain in a series of parallel scan lines. There are four common scanning modes: cross-track scanning, circular scanning, along-track scanning and side scanning, which are diagrammed in Fig. 1.12.

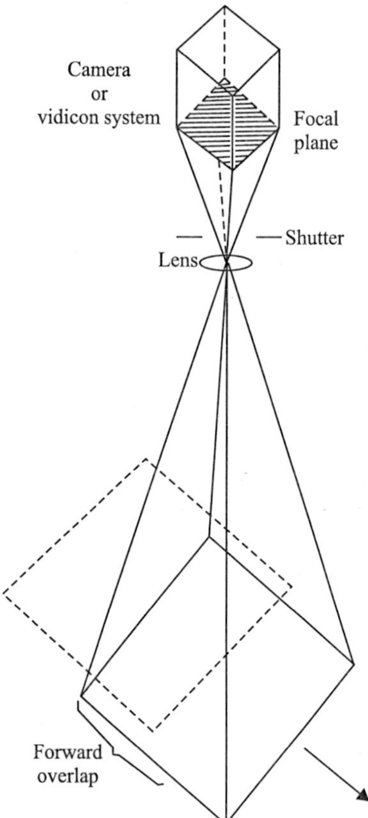

Fig. 1.11. Framing system for acquiring remote sensing images.

Cross-track scanning system

The widely used cross-track scanning systems employ a faceted mirror that is rotated by an electric motor, with a horizontal axis of rotation aligned parallel with the flight direction (Fig. 1.12a). The mirror sweeps across the terrain in a pattern of parallel scan lines oriented normal (perpendicularly) to the flight direction. Energy radiated or reflected from the ground is focused onto the detector by secondary mirrors (not shown).

The angular resolving power of a detector, measured in milliradians, determines the IFOV of the detector. As shown in Fig. 1.12a, the IFOV subtends an area on the terrain called a ground resolution cell. Dimensions of a ground resolution cell are determined by the detector's IFOV and the altitude of the scanning system. A detector with an IFOV of 1 mrad at an altitude of 10 km has a ground resolution cell of 10 by 10 m.

The angular field of view (Fig. 1.12a) is that portion of the mirror sweep, measured in degrees, that is recorded as a scan line. The angular field of view and the altitude of the system determine the ground swath, which is the width of the terrain strip represented by the image. Ground swath is calculated as:

$$\text{Ground swath} = \tan\left(\frac{\text{angular field of view}}{2}\right) \times \text{altitude} \qquad \text{... (1.5)}$$

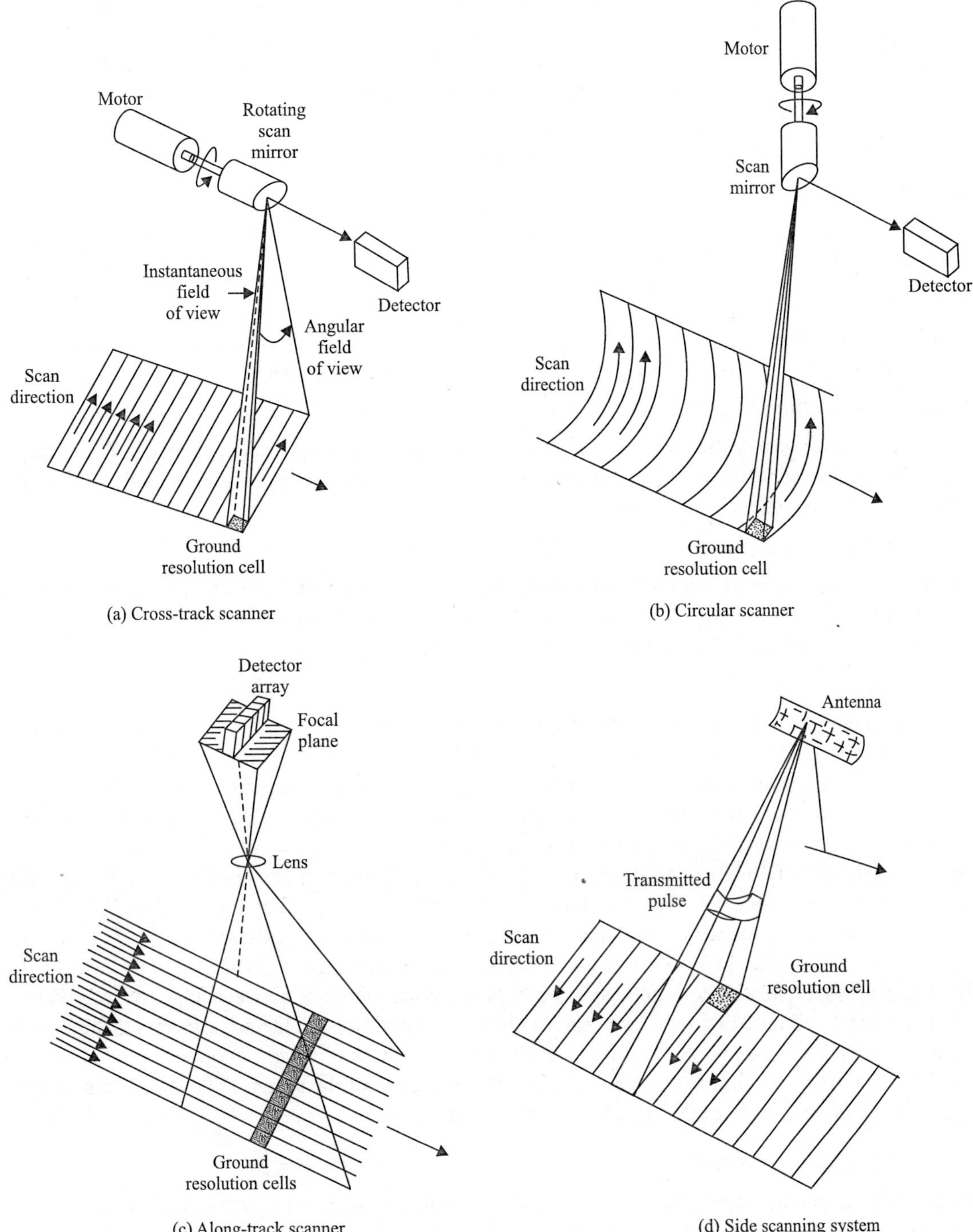

Fig. 1.12. Scanning systems for acquiring remote sensing images.

The distance between the scanner and terrain is greater at the margins of the ground swath than at its center. As a result, ground resolution cells are larger toward the margins than at the center, which results in a geometric distortion characteristic of cross-track scanner images. At the high altitude of satellites, a narrow angular field of view is sufficient to cover a broad swath of terrain. For this reason, the rotating mirror is replaced by a flat mirror that oscillates back and forth through an angle of approximately 15°.

The strength of the signal generated by a detector is a function of the following factors:

Energy flux

The amount of energy reflected or radiated from terrain is the energy flux. For visible detectors, this flux is lower on a dark day than on a sunny day.

Altitude

For a given ground resolution cell, the amount of energy reaching the detector is inversely proportional to the square of the distance. At greater altitude the signal strength is weaker.

Spectral bandwidth of the detector

The signal is stronger for detectors that respond to a broader-wavelength range of energy. For example, a detector that is sensitive to the entire visible range will receive more energy than a detector that is sensitive to a narrow band, such as visible red.

Instantaneous field of view

Both the physical size of the sensitive element of the detector and the effective focal length of the scanner optics determine the IFOV. A small IFOV is required for high spatial resolution but also restricts the signal strength (amount of energy received by the detector).

Dwell time

The time required for the detector IFOV to sweep across a ground resolution cell is the dwell time. A longer dwell time allows more energy to impinge on the detector, which creates a stronger signal.

For a cross-track scanner, the dwell time is determined by the detector IFOV and by the velocity at which the scan mirror sweeps the IFOV and across the terrain. As shown in Fig 1.13a, a typical airborne scanner with a detector IFOV of 1 mrad, a 90° angular field of view, operating at 2×10^{-2} sec per scan line, at an altitude of 10 km, has a dwell time of 1×10^{-5} sec per ground resolution cell. It is instructive to compare the dwell time with the ground speed of the aircraft. At a typical ground speed of 720 km $\cdot$ hr.$^{-1}$ or 200 m $\cdot$ sec^{-1}, the aircraft crosses the 10 m dimension of a ground resolution in 5×10^{-2} sec. The cross-track scanner time of 1×10^{-5} is 5×10^{3} times faster than the ground velocity of the aircraft. The high scanner speed relative to ground speed is required to prevent gaps between adjacent scan lines.

The short dwell time of cross-track scanners imposes constraints on the other factors that determine signal strength. For example, the IFOV and spectral bandwidth must be large enough to produce a signal of sufficient strength to overcome the inherent electronic noise of the system. The signal-to-noise ratio must be sufficiently high for the signal to be recognisable.

Circular scanning system

In a circular scanning system, the scan motor and mirror are mounted with a vertical axis of rotation that sweeps a circular path on the terrain (Fig. 1.12b). Only the forward portion of the sweep is recorded to produce images. An advantage of this system is that the distance between scanner and terrain is constant and all the ground resolution cells have the same dimensions. The major disadvantage is that most image processing and display systems are designed for linear scan data; therefore the circular scan data must be extensively reformatted prior to processing. Circular scanners have short dwell times comparable to those of cross-track scanners.

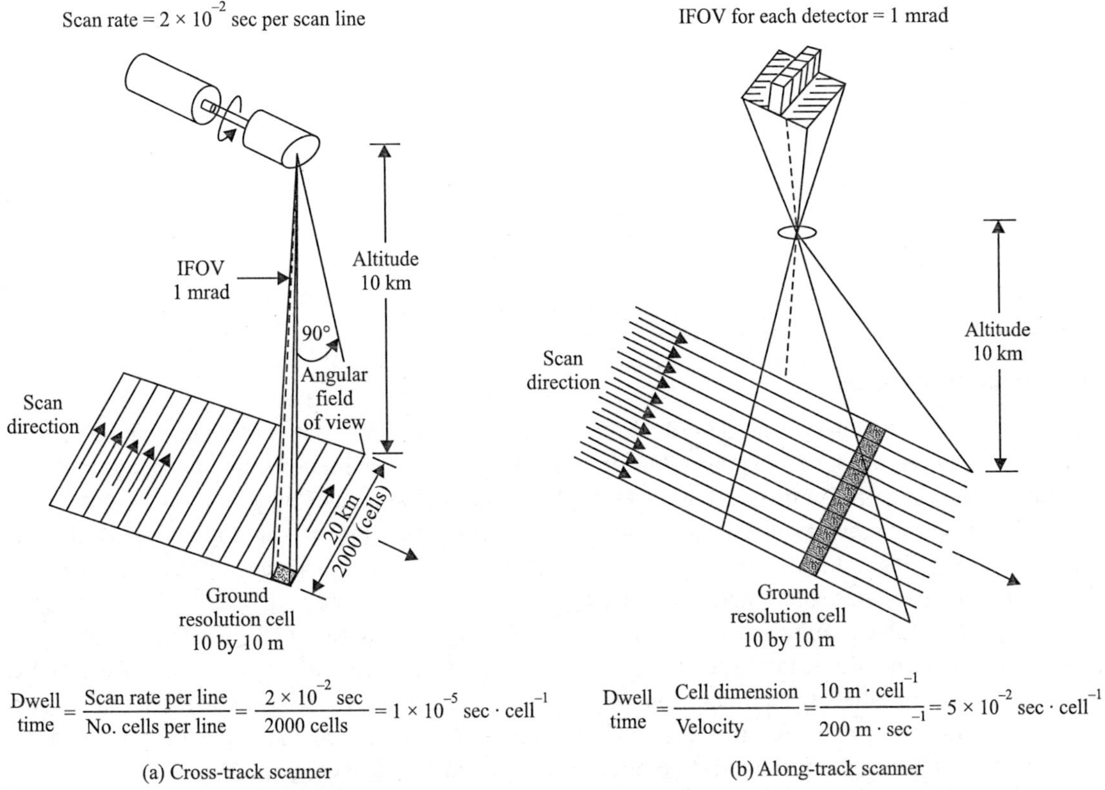

Fig. 1.13. Dwell time calculated for cross-track and along-track scanners.

Circular scanners are used for reconnaissance purposes in helicopters and low-flying aircraft. The axis of rotation is tilted to point forward and acquire images of the terrain well in advance of the aircraft position. The images are displayed in real time on a screen in the cockpit to guide the pilot.

Along-track scanning system

For scanner systems to achieve finer spatial and spectral resolution, the dwell time for each ground resolution cell must be increased. One method is to eliminate the scanning mirror and provide an individual detector for each ground resolution cell across the ground swath (Fig. 1.12c). The detectors are placed in a linear array in the focal plane of the image formed by a lens system. The long axis of the linear array is oriented normal to the flight path and the IFOV of each detector sweeps a ground resolution cell along the terrain parallel with the flight track direction (Fig. 1.12c). Along-track scanning refers to this movement of the ground resolution cells. These systems are also called pushbroom scanners because the detectors are analogous to the bristles of a broom pushed along the floor.

For along-track scanners, the dwell time of a ground resolution cell is determined by the ground velocity, as Fig. 1.13b illustrates. For a jet aircraft flying at 720 km $\cdot$ hr.$^{-1}$ or 200 m $\cdot$ sec^{-1}, the along-track dwell time for a 10-m cell is 5×10^{-2} sec, which is 5×10^3 times greater than the dwell time for a comparable cross-track scanner. The increased dwell time allows two improvements: (i) detectors can have smaller IFOVs, which provide finer spatial resolution; and (ii) detectors can have a narrower spectral bandwidth, which provides higher spectral resolution. The airborne imaging spectrometer is an along-track scanner with a spectral bandwidth of 0.01 μm. Typical cross-track scanners have bandwidths of 0.10 μm, which is a spectral resolution coarser by one order of magnitude.

Side scanning system

The three types of scanners just described are passive systems, since they detect and record energy naturally reflected or radiated from the terrain. Active systems, which provide their own energy sources, operate primarily in the side-scanning mode. The example in Fig. 1.12d is a radar system that transmits pulses of microwave energy to one side of the flight path (range direction) and records the energy scattered from the terrain back to the antenna. Another system is side-scanning sonar, which transmits pulses of sonic energy in the ocean to map bathymetric features.

Multispectral Systems

The framing and scanning systems described above record a single image that represents a single spectral band. For many remote sensing applications, it is essential to record a scene with multispectral images, multiple images acquired at different spectral bands. Multispectral images may be acquired by several means. Multiple cameras or vidicons may be mounted together and aligned to photograph the same area. The shutters are linked together and triggered simultaneously. Filters that transmit selected bands of energy are used to acquire black and white photographs. A typical cluster of four multispectral cameras records three visible bands (blue at 0.4–0.5 μm, green at 0.5–0.6 μm and red at 0.6–0.7 μm) and one reflected IR band (0.7–0.8 μm). Some multispectral cameras employ a single camera body and focal-plane shutter with four lenses and filters that produce four photographs of the same area on a single piece of film. Any three of the multispectral black and white positive films may be registered and projected in the additive primary colours (blue, green and red) to produce a colour composite photograph.

Framing systems for multispectral imaging have two major disadvantages:

1. Each image is acquired with a separate lens system and it may be difficult to register the multiple images.
2. The spectral range of camera systems is restricted to the visible region and part of the reflected IR region.

Today virtually all multispectral image data are acquired by scanner systems. Cross-track scanners employ a spectrometer to disperse the incoming energy into a spectrum (Fig. 1.14a). Detectors are positioned to record specific wavelength bands of energy (denoted λ_1, λ_2, λ_3 and λ_4 in the figure). The Landsat thematic mapper is a cross-track multispectral scanner that records seven bands of data: three visible bands, three reflected IR bands and one thermal IR band. A typical aircraft cross-track scanner, records 11 bands of data. As described earlier, the short dwell time of cross-track systems requires that the detector bandwidth be fairly broad, on the order of 0.05 to 0.10 μm.

Along-track multispectral scanners employ multiple arrays of linear detectors with each array recording a separate band of energy (Fig. 1.14b). Because of the extended dwell time, the detector bandwidth may be narrow and still produce an adequate signal. The SPOT satellite system uses a multispectral along-track scanner. More advanced along-track systems employ a spectrometer to disperse the incoming energy onto the detector arrays.

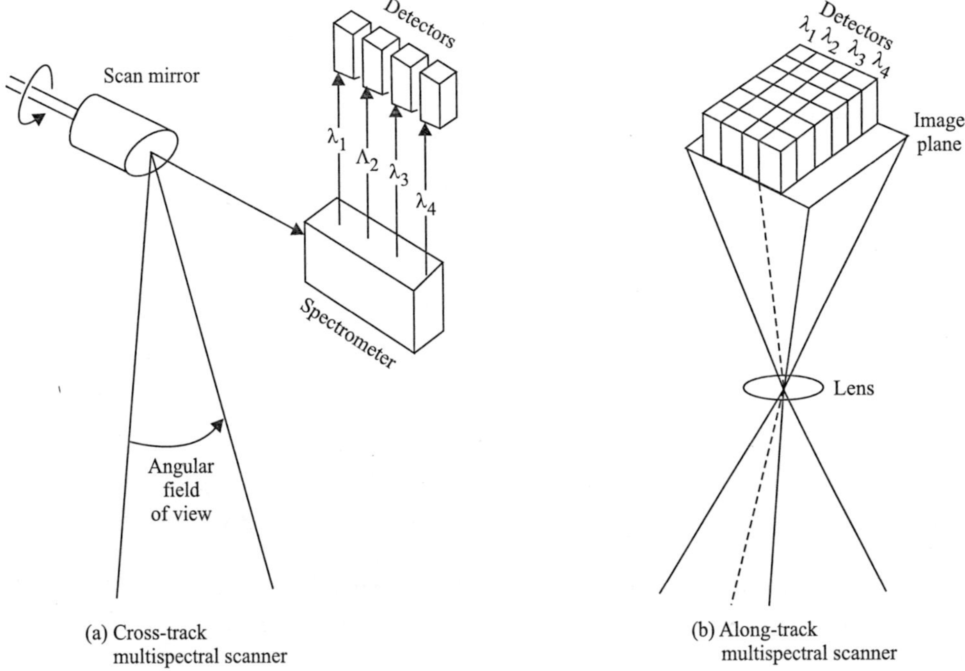

Fig. 1.14. Multispectral scanner systems.

SOURCES OF REMOTE SENSING INFORMATION

Several scientific journals devoted to remote sensing are published on a regular schedule by the technical societies listed in Appendix I. Membership in these societies is open to users of remote sensing data. There are also several journals published in languages other than English. In addition to these journals, many articles on remote sensing are published in journals devoted to other disciplines such as geology, geography and oceanography. Several of the societies listed in Appendix–I conduct remote sensing conferences on a regular basis.

In addition to the technical societies, there are a number of academic and research organisations (listed in Appendix II) that conduct conferences and workshops on various aspects of remote sensing. These organisations can provide information on forthcoming activities.

2

Remote Sensing Process

INTRODUCTION

Because remotely sensed images are formed by many interrelated processes, an isolated focus on any single component will produce a fragmented understanding. Therefore, our initial view of the field can benefit from a broad perspective that identifies the kinds of knowledge required for the practice of remote sensing (Fig. 2.1). Consider first the physical objects, consisting of buildings, vegetation, soil, water and the like. These are the objects that applications scientists wish to examine. Knowledge of the physical objects resides within specific disciplines, such as geology, forestry, soil science, geography and urban planning.

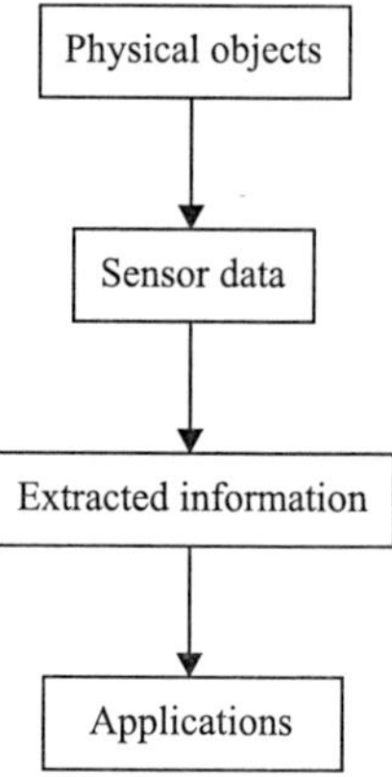

Fig. 2.1. Schematic overview of knowledge used in remote sensing.

Sensor data are formed as an instrument (e.g., a camera or radar) views the physical objects by recording electromagnetic radiation emitted or reflected from the landscape. Although the image domain can consist of pictorial images such as those familiar to us all, often images are most useful in their digital forms, which present information as numerical arrays that can be displayed and analysed by computers. For many of us, sensor data often seem to be abstract and foreign because of their unfamiliar overhead perspective, unusual resolutions and use of spectral regions outside the visible spectrum. As a result, effective use of sensor data requires analysis and interpretation to convert data to information that can be used to address practical problems, such as siting landfills or searching for mineral deposits.

These interpretations create extracted information, which consists of transformations of sensor data designed to reveal specific kinds of information (Fig. 2.1). Actually, a more realistic view (Fig. 2.2) illustrates that the same sensor data can be examined from alternative perspective to yield different interpretations. Therefore, a single image can be interpreted to provide information about soils, land use or hydrology, for example, depending on the specific image and the purpose of the analysis.

Finally, we proceed to the applications, in which the analysed remote sensing data can be combined with other data to address a specific practical problem, such as land-use planning, mineral exploration or water-quality mapping. When digital remote sensing data are combined with other geospatial data, applications are implemented in the context of geographic information systems (GISs). For example, remote sensing data may provide accurate land-use information that can be combined with soils, geologic, transportation and other information to guide the siting of a new landfill.

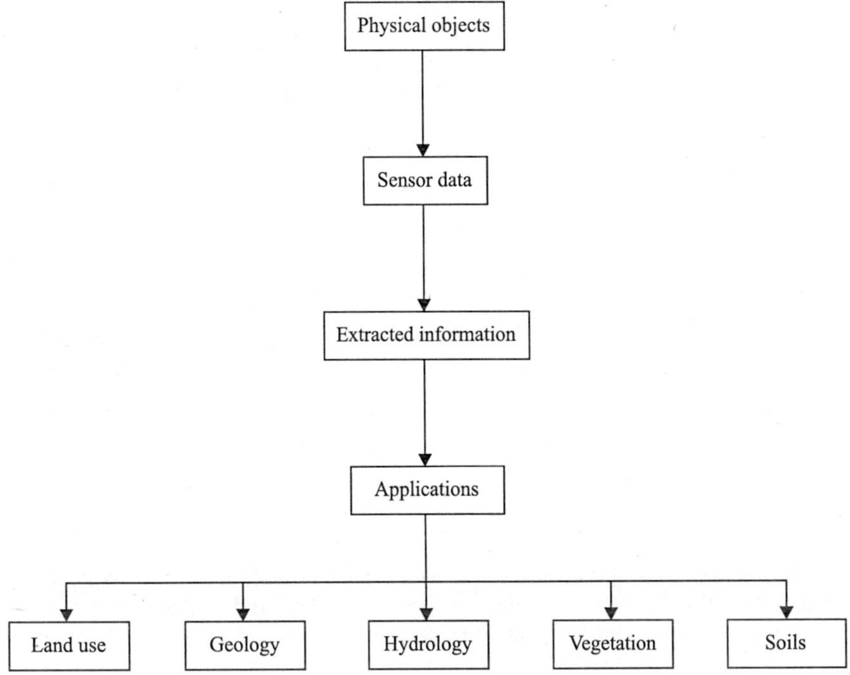

Fig. 2.2. Expanded view of the process outline in Fig. 2.1.

A SPECIFIC EXAMPLE

Let's consider how a remotely sensed image is acquired by tracing the path of energy used to make an image. A cursory examination of an aerial image of a deciduous forest (Fig. 2.3) can introduce some dimensions of the field of remote sensing (All of the concepts mentioned here will be discussed in detail in subsequent chapters).

Physical Features

Energy that reaches the earth from the sun is composed of many kinds of radiation, including that in the visible region of the spectrum (blue, green and red light), as well as other radiation (such as the infrared) outside the range of human vision. The solar beam must pass through the earth's atmosphere to reach the forest canopy; some of this energy is absorbed and scattered before it reaches the forest. Much scattering is selective by wavelength—for example, the atmosphere scatters blue light much more than it scatters green or red light. Of the remaining energy, some will reach the leaves of the tree canopy; of energy reaching the leaves, the infrared radiation (wavelengths just longer than those of visible radiation) will be reflected. The green region of the spectrum will be reflected by a different portion of the leaf, while blue and red radiation will be absorbed for use in photosynthesis. Energy that reaches the camera lens must again pass through the atmosphere, where it is again subject to attenuation.

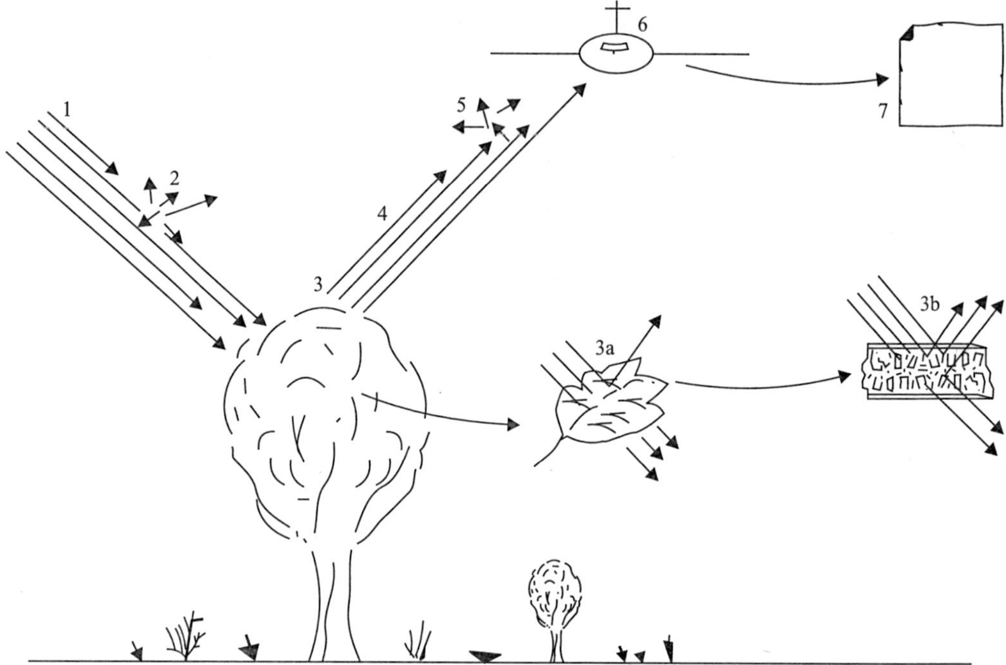

Fig. 2.3. Idealised overview of acquisition of a remotely sensed image. This diagram depicts a schematic view of some of the elements that must be considered in the acquisition and interpretation of a remote sensing image, as a means of illustrating the kinds of knowledge that constitute the field of remote sensing. In this examples, the image is derived from reflected solar radiation. Incoming solar radiation (1) is in part scattered or attenuated by the earth's atmosphere (2). The remaining energy reaches the earth's surface to interact with the features present on the landscape—in this example, a living tree (3). Much of the reflection of energy from the tree canopy is controlled by interactions with individual leaves (3a), which selectively absorb, transmit and reflect energy depending upon its wavelength (3b), as discussed in the text and in later chapters. The reflected energy (4) is again subject to atmospheric attenuation (5) before it is recorded by an airborne or satellite sensor (6). The results of a multitude of such interactions are recorded as a photograph-like image (7) or as an array of quantitative values. The image is then available for interpretation and analysis to derive information concerning the landscape, based upon the interpreter's examination of the image and knowledge of items 1 through 7.

Sensor Data

Thus, energy recorded by the camera lens is much different than the sunlight that entered the atmosphere. Some of the blue light was scattered by the atmosphere and reaches the camera without being reflected from the earth's surface. Blue, red, green and infrared have been reflected from the canopy, but reach the camera in proportions that differ from the proportions that were intercepted by the canopy. The film portrays these different kinds of radiation in different colours, which may not match those of the radiation they represent. This image represents a portion of the earth's surface, but its meaning is hidden from casual observation.

Extracted Information

Data within the image can be translated into information only through the process of image interpretation or image analysis. An image analyst, an individual skilled in the examination of images, studies the image to identify, for example, timber types and forest areas damaged by disease and insect activity. For some, much of this knowledge is based on everyday experience rather than formally structured learning. We do not need to 'learn' that deciduous trees lose their leaves in the winter or that wheat tends to be planted in fields of regular size and shape. This store of implicit knowledge is important because it forms such a large portion of what we know about a scene and because we often are unaware of its role in image analysis. More formal, explicit, knowledge of the landscape is especially significant in two contexts. First, we have no means of acquiring an implicit understanding of how radiation behaves outside the visible spectrum. So, knowledge that living vegetation is highly reflective in the near infrared portion of the spectrum must be acquired in a formalised learning situation. Second, our implicit knowledge has its geographic limits; when we travel outside the range of our experience, it is no longer valid in our assessment of the landscape. For example, there are large regions of the earth where crops are not customarily planted in regular fields and where trees do not all shed their leaves during the same season. Therefore, analysts often must consciously acquire information necessary to analyse image collected in areas outside the range of their direct experience.

Applications

Applications of remotely sensed data to practical problems usually require links to other kinds of information, including, for example, topography, political boundaries and pedologic, geologic or hydrologic data. In recent years, such links have increasingly been made within the framework of GISs. GISs are devoted to the analysis of geospatial data and especially to analysis of the inter-relationships between different kinds of data, matched to each other within a specific geographic region. Although there is no sharp line between remote sensing and GISs, it is only partially incorrect to state that remote sensing is primarily a means of collecting data and that GISs are primarily a means of storing and analysing data. At local levels of government, remote sensing imagery records large-scale representations of topography and drainage and the basic infrastructure of highways, buildings and utilities. At county and regional levels of detail, remotely sensed data provide a basis for outlining broad-scale patterns of development; to co-ordinate the relationships between transportation, residential, industrial and recreational land uses; to site landfills; and to plan future development. State governments require information from remotely sensed data for broad-scale inventories of natural resources; to monitor environmental issues, including land reclamation and water quality; and to plan economic development.

At broader levels of examination, national governments apply the methods of remote sensing and image analysis for environmental monitoring (both domestically and internationally), for management of lands, crop forecasting, disaster relief and to support activities to further national security and international relations. Remote sensing is also used to support activities of international scope, including analysis of broad-scale environmental issues, international development, disaster relief, aid for refugees and investigation of environmental issues of global scope.

These activities are conducted or supported by industrial and commercial enterprises that design and manufacture equipment, instruments and materials. Others operate systems to collect and distribute data to customers. And still others provide services to plan for effective acquisition of remotely sensed data and to analyse and interpret data to provide information for customers. Finally, some industrial and commercial organisations conduct basic research to develop and refine instruments and analysis.

Within subject-area disciplines, remote sensing imagery is almost always combined with other kinds of data. Geologists and geophysicists use remotely sensed images to study lithologies, structures, surface processes and geologic hazards. Hydrologists examine images that show land cover patterns, soil moisture status, drainage systems, sediment content of lake and rivers, ocean currents and other characteristics of water bodies. Geographers and planners examine imagery to study settlement patterns, inventory land resources and track changes in human uses of the landscape. Foresters use remote sensing and GISs to map timber stands, estimate timber volume, monitor insect infestations, fight forest fires and plan harvesting of timer. Agricultural scientists can examine the growth, maturing and harvesting of crops and monitor the progress of diseases, infestations and droughts to forecast their impact on crop yields. Soil scientists use remotely sensed imagery to plot boundaries of soil units and to examine relationships between soil patterns and those of land use and vegetation. In brief, remotely sensed imagery has found applications in virtually all fields that require the analysis of distributions of natural or human resources on the earth's surface.

KEY CONCEPTS OF REMOTE SENSING

Scientists usually attempt to avoid the pitfalls of relying upon improvised approaches for conducting research. Improvised or adhoc, methods may repeat previously discovered methodological errors, lead to trivial results, promote inefficiency or simply create inaccuracies. Instead, scientists prefer to base their methods upon systems of facts and methods found to yield consistent accurate results.

The practice of remote sensing is young enough that the basic facts and methods are not yet known completely. Scientists are still investigating to define many of the fundamental methods and concepts central to remote sensing. Nonetheless, it is useful to base our study of remote sensing upon a set of principles that seem to convey the essential dimensions of the practice of remote sensing. The principles outlined below are tentatively proposed as concepts that address ideas central to the practice of remote sensing, regardless of specific disciplinary applications.

Spectral Differentiation

Remote sensing depends upon observed spectral differences in the energy reflected or emitted from features of interest. Expressed in everyday terms, one might say that we look for differences in the 'colours' of objects. (This analogy may be useful even though remote sensing is often conducted outside the visible spectrum, where 'colours', in the usual meaning of the word, do not exist.) This principle is the basis of multispectral remote sensing, the science of observing features at varied wavelengths in an effort to derive information about these features and their distributions. The term 'spectral signature' has been used to refer to the spectral response of a feature, as observed over a range of wavelengths. For the beginning student, this term can be misleading because it implies a distinctiveness and a consistency that seldom can be observed in nature. For example, consider the notion of a spectral signature for 'corn'. A cornfield has one spectral response when it is planted, another as the plants emerge, another as the plants mature and yet another after harvest. Selection of a single time and place to designate a single spectral signature of 'corn' is futile. Yet the term conveys a more general concept that is useful, because at specific times and places the spectral response of cornfields may form the basis for reliable separation of corn from wheat, for example, even though neither crop forms universally applicable spectral signatures.

Radiometric Differentiation

Examination of any image acquired by remote sensing ultimately depends upon detection of differences in the brightness of objects and the features. The scene itself must have sufficient contrast (at a specific spectral region) in brightnesses and the remote sensing instrument must be capable of recording this contrast, before information can be derived from the image. As a result, the sensitivity of the instrument and the existing contrast in the scene between objects and their backgrounds, are always issues of significance in remote sensing investigation.

Spatial Differentiation

Every sensor is limited in respect to the size of the smallest area that can be separately recorded as an entity on an image. This minimum area determines the spatial detail—the fineness of the patterns—on the image. For some remote sensing systems, these smallest areal units—picture elements ('pixels')—are in fact discrete, distinct units, identifiable on the image. In other instances, the spatial detail (determined by the quality of a camera lens or the film that has been used) is less obvious, but is nonetheless present. Our ability to record spatial detail is influenced primarily by the choice of sensor and the altitude at which it is used to record images of the earth. Note also that some landscapes vary greatly in their spatial complexity—some may be represented clearly at coarse levels of detail, whereas others are so complex that the finest level of detail is required to record their essential characteristics.

Geometric Transformation

Every remotely sensed image represents a landscape in a specific geometric relationship determined by the design of the remote sensing instrument, specific operating conditions, terrain relief and other factors. The ideal remote sensing instrument would be able to create an image with accurate, consistent geometric relationships between points on the ground and their corresponding representations on the image. Such an image could form the basis for accurate measurements of areas and distances. In reality, of course, each image includes positional errors caused by the perspective of the sensor optics, the motion of scanning optics, terrain relief and earth curvature. Each source of error can vary in significance in specific instances, but the result is that geometric errors are inherent, not accidental, characteristics of remotely sensed images. In some instances we may be able to remove or reduce locational error, but it must always be taken into account before images are used as the basis for measurements of areas and distances.

Interchangeability of Pictorial and Digital Formats

Most remote sensing systems generate photograph-like images of the earth's surface. Any such image can be represented in digital form by systematically sub-dividing the image into tiny areas of equal size and shape, then representing the brightnesses of these areas by discrete values. Conversely, many remote sensing systems generate, as their first generation output, digital arrays that represent brightnesses of areas of the earth's surface in digital form. Digital images can be displayed as pictorial images by displaying each digital value as a brightness level scaled to the magnitude of the value.

The two forms for remote sensing data—pictorial and digital—represent different methods of display and representation, but there is no real difference in the information conveyed by the two forms. Any image can be portrayed in either form (sometimes with a loss of detail in converting from one form to another) according to the purposes of our investigation.

Remote Sensing Instrumentation Acts as a System

The image analyst must always be conscious of the fact that the many components of the remote sensing process act as a system and therefore cannot be isolated from one another. For example, upgrading the quality of a camera lens makes little sense unless we also use a film of sufficient quality to record the improvements produced by the superior lens, thus allowing the analyst to have the ability to derive improved information from the image.

Components of the system must be appropriate for the task at hand. This means that the interpreter must not only know intimately the remote sensing system, but also the subject of the interpretation, to include the amount of detail required, appropriate time of year to acquire the data, best spectral regions to use and so on. Like the physical components of the system, the interpreter's knowledge and experience also interact to form a whole.

Role of the Atmosphere

All energy reaching the remote sensing instrument must pass through a portion of the earth's atmosphere. For satellite remote sensing in the visible and near infrared, energy received by the sensor must pass through a considerable depth of the earth's atmosphere. In doing so, the sun's energy is altered in intensity and wavelength by particles and gases in the earth's atmosphere. These changes appear on the image in ways that degrade image quality or influence the accuracy of interpretations.

CAREER PREPARATION AND PROFESSIONAL DEVELOPMENT

For the student, a course of study in remote sensing offers opportunities to enter a field of knowledge that can contribute to several dimensions of a university education and subsequent personal and professional development. Students enrolled in introductory remote sensing courses often view the topic as an important part of their occupational and professional preparation. It is certainly true that skills in remote sensing are valuable in the initial search for employment. But is equally important to acknowledge that this topic should form part of a comprehensive programme of study that includes work in GIS and in-depth study of a specific discipline. A well-thought-out programme appropriate for a student's specific interests and strengths should combine studies in several interrelated topics, such as:

1. Geology, hydrology, geomorphology, soils.
2. Urban planning, transportation, urban geography.
3. Forestry, ecology, soils.

Such programmes are based on a foundation of supporting courses, including statistics, computer science and the physical sciences.

Students should avoid studies that provide only narrowly based, technique-oriented content. Such highly focused studies, perhaps with specific equipment or software, may provide immediate skills for entry-level positions, but they leave the student unprepared to participate in the broader assignments required for effective performance and professional advancement. Employers report that they seek employees who:

1. Have a good background in at least one traditional discipline.
2. Are reliable and able to follow instructions without detailed supervision.
3. Can write and speak effectively.
4. Work effectively in teams with others in other disciplines.
5. Are familiar with common business practices.

Possibly the most important but least visible contributions are to the development of conceptual thinking concerning the role of basic theory and method, integration of knowledge from several disciplines and proficiency in identifying practical problems in a spatial context. Although skills and knowledge of remote sensing are very important, it is usually a mistake to focus exclusively upon methodology and technique. At least two pitfalls are obvious. First, emphasis upon fact and technique without consideration of basic principles and theory provides a narrow, empirical foundation in a field that is characterised by diversity and rapid change. A student equipped with a narrow background is ill-prepared to compete with those trained in other disciplines or to adjust to unexpected developments in science and technology. Thus any educational experience is best perceived not as a catalog of facts to be memorised, but as an experience in how to learn to equip oneself for independent learning later, outside the classroom. This task requires a familiarity with basic references, fundamental principles and the content of related disciplines, as well as the core of facts that form the substance of a field of knowledge.

Second, many employers have little interest in hiring employees with shallow preparation in either their major discipline or in remote sensing. *Lillesand* reports that a panel of managers from diverse industries concerned with remote sensing recommended that prospective employees develop 'an ability and desire to interact at a conceptual level with other specialists'. *Campbell* quotes other supervisors who are also concerned that students receive a broad preparation in remote sensing and in their primary field of study:

1. It is essential that the interpreter have a good general education in an area of expertise. For example, you can make a geologist into a good photo geologist, but you cannot make an image interpreter into a geologist.
2. Often people lack any real philosophical understanding of why they are doing remote sensing and lack the broad overview of the inter-relationships of all earth science and earth-oriented disciplines (geography, geology, biology, hydrology, meteorology, etc.). This often creates delays in our work as people continue to work in small segments of the (real) world and don't see the inter-connections with another's research.

These same individuals have recommended that those students who are interested in remote sensing should complete courses in computer science, physics, geology, geography, biology, engineering, mathematics, hydrology, business, statistics and a wide variety of other disciplines. No student could possibly take all recommended courses during a normal programme of study, but it is clear that a haphazard selection of university courses or one that focused exclusively upon remote sensing courses, would not form a substantive background in remote sensing. In addition, many organisations have been forceful in stating that they desire employees who can write well and several have expressed an interest in persons with expertise in remote sensing who have knowledge of a foreign language. The key point is that educational preparation in remote sensing should be closely co-ordinated with study in traditional academic disciplines and should be supported by a programme of courses carefully selected from offerings in related disciplines.

Students should consider joining a professional society devoted to the field of remote sensing. In the United States and Canada, the American Society for Photogrammetry and Remote Sensing (ASPRS) is the principal professional organisation in this field. ASPRS offers students discounts on membership dues, publications and meeting registration and conducts job fairs at its annual meetings. ASPRS is organised on a regional basis, so local chapters conduct their own activities, which are open to student participation. Other professional organisations often have interest groups devoted applications of remote sensing within specific disciplines, often with similar benefits for student members.

Students should also investigate local libraries to become familiar with professional journals in the field. The field's principal journals include:

1. Photogrammetric engineering and remote sensing.
2. Remote sensing of environment.
3. International journal of remote sensing.
4. IEEE transactions on geoscience and remote sensing.
5. Computers and geosciences.

Although beginning students may not yet be prepared to read research articles in detail, those who make the effort to familiarise themselves with these journals will have prepared the way to take advantage of their content later. In particular, students may find Photogrammetric engineering and remote sensing useful because of its listing of job opportunities, scheduled meetings and new products.

The world of practical remote sensing has changed dramatically in recent decades. Especially since the early 1990s, commercial and industrial application of remote sensing have expanded dramatically to penetrate well beyond the specialised applications of an earlier era, to extend, for example, into marketing, real estate and agricultural enterprises. Aspects of remote sensing that formerly seemed to require a highly specialised knowledge became available to a much broader spectrum of users as data became less expensive and more widely available and as manufacturers designed software for use by the non-specialist.

These developments are leading to formation of a society in which remote sensing, GISs global positioning systems and related technological systems will become commonly used tools within the workplace, perhaps analogous in accessibility to spreadsheets, word processing or cell phones. In such a setting, citizens, especially the non-specialist, must be prepared to use spatial data effectively and appropriately and to understand its strengths and limitations. Because of the need to produce a wide variety of ready-to-use products tailored for specific populations of users, the remote sensing community will continue to require specialists, especially those who can link a solid knowledge of remote sensing with subject-area knowledge (e.g., hydrology, planning, forestry, etc.). People who will work in this field will require skills and perspective that differ greatly from those of previous graduates of only a few years earlier.

3

Electromagnetic Radiation

INTRODUCTION

With the exception of objects at absolute zero, all objects emit electromagnetic radiation. Objects also reflect radiation that has been emitted by other objects. By recording emitted or reflected radiation and applying a knowledge of its behaviour as it passes through the earth's atmosphere and interacts with objects, remote sensing analysts develop a knowledge of the character of features such as vegetation, structure, soils, rock or water bodies on the earth's surface.

Interpretation of remote sensing imagery depends on a sound understanding of electromagnetic radiation and its interaction with surfaces and the atmosphere. The discussion of electromagnetic radiation in this chapter builds a foundation to permit development in subsequent chapters of the many other important topics within the field of remote sensing.

The most familiar form of electromagnetic radiation is visible light, which forms only a small (but very important) portion of the full electromagnetic spectrum. The large segments of this spectrum that lie outside the range of human vision require our special attention because they may behave in ways that are quite foreign to our everyday experience with visible radiation.

ELECTROMAGNETIC SPECTRUM

Electromagnetic energy is generated by several mechanisms, including changes in the energy levels of electrons, acceleration of electrical charges, decay of radioactive substances and the thermal motion of atoms and molecules. Nuclear reactions within the sun produce a full spectrum of electromagnetic radiation, which is transmitted through space without experiencing major changes. As this radiation approaches the earth, it passes through the atmosphere before reaching the earth's surface. Some is reflected upward from the earth's surface; it is this radiation that forms the basis for photographs and similar images. Other solar radiation is absorbed at the surface of the earth and is then re-radiated as thermal energy. This thermal energy can also be used to form remotely sensed images, although they differ greatly from the aerial photographs formed from reflected energy. Finally, man-made radiation, such as that generated by imaging radars, is also used for remote sensing.

Electromagnetic radiation consists of an electrical field (E) that varies in magnitude in a direction perpendicular to the direction of propagation (Fig. 3.1). In addition, a magnetic field (H) oriented at right angles to the electrical field is propagated in phase with the electrical field.

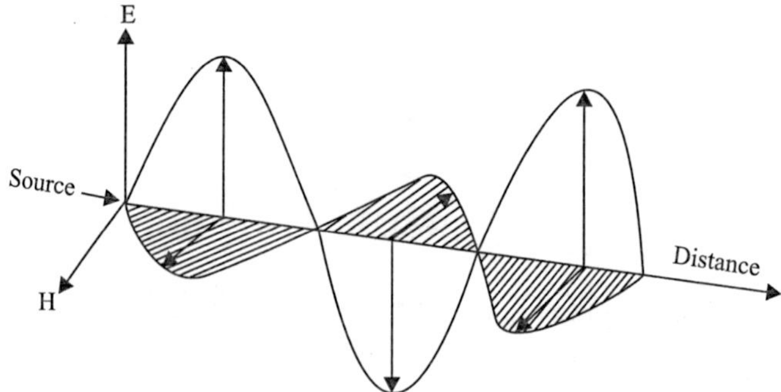

Fig. 3.1. Electric (E) and magnetic (H) components of electromagnetic radiation. The electric and magnetic components are oriented at right angles to one another and vary along an axis perpendicular to the axis of propagation.

Properties of Electromagnetic Energy

Electromagnetic energy displays three properties (Fig. 3.2):

1. Wavelength is the distance from one wave crest to the next. Wavelength can be measured in everyday units of length, although very short wavelengths have such small distances between wave crests that extremely short (and therefore less familiar) measurement units are required (Table 3.1).
2. Frequency is measured as the number of crests passing a fixed point in a given period of time. Frequency is often measured in Hertz, units each equivalent to one cycle per second (Table 3.2) and multiples of the Hertz.
3. Amplitude is equivalent to the height of each peak (Fig. 3.2). Amplitude is often measured as energy levels (formally known as spectral irradiance), expressed as watts per square meter per micrometer (i.e., as energy level per wavelength interval).

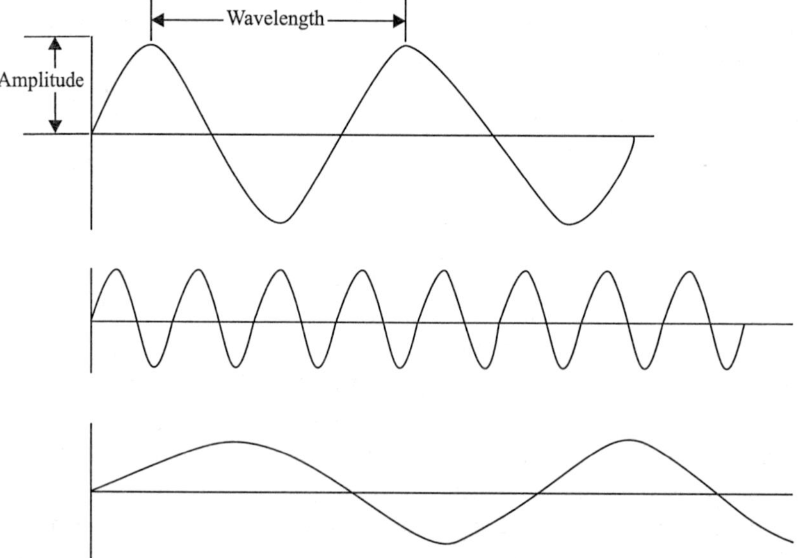

Fig. 3.2. Amplitude, frequency and wavelength. The center diagram represents high frequency, short wavelength; the bottom diagram shows low frequency, long wavelength.

Table 3.1. Units of length used in remote sensing.

Unit	*Distance*	
Kilometer (km)	1000 m	
Meter (m)	1.0 m	
Centimeter (cm)	0.01 m	$= 10^{-2}$ m
Millimeter (mm)	0.001 m	$= 10^{-3}$ m
Micrometer (μm)[a]	0.000001 m	$= 10^{-6}$ m
Nanometer (nm)		10^{-9} m
Ångstrom unit (Å)		10^{-10} m

[a]Formerly called the 'micron' (μ); the term 'micrometer' is now used by agreement of the General Conference of Weights and Measures.

Table 3.2. Frequencies used in remote sensing.

Unit	*Frequency (cycles per second)*
Hertz (Hz)	1
Kilohertz (kHz)	10^3 (=1000)
Megahertz (MHz)	10^6 (=1,000,000)
Gigahertz (GHz)	10^9 (=1,000,000,000)

The speed of electromagnetic energy (c) is constant at 299,893 kilometers (km) per second. Frequency (v) and wavelength (λ) are related:

$$c = \lambda v \qquad \text{... (3.1)}$$

Therefore, characteristics of electromagnetic energy can be specified using either frequency or wavelength. Varied disciplines and varied applications, follow different conventions for describing electromagnetic radiation, using either wavelength (measured in Angstrom units [Å], microns, micrometers, nanometers, millimeters, etc., as appropriate) or frequency (using Hertz, kilohertz, megahertz, etc., as appropriate). Although there is no authoritative standard, a common practice in the field of remote sensing is to define regions of the spectrum on the basis of wavelength, often using micrometers (each equal to one one-millionth of a meter, symbolised as μm), millimeters (mm) and meters (m) as units of length. Departures from this practice are common; for example, electrical engineers who work with microwave radiation traditionally use frequency to designate sub-divisions of the spectrum. This text will usually employ wavelength designations. The student should, however, be prepared to encounter different usages in scientific journals and in references.

MAJOR DIVISIONS OF THE ELECTROMAGNETIC SPECTRUM

Major divisions of the electromagnetic spectrum (Table 3.3) are, in essence, arbitrarily defined. In a full spectrum of solar energy there are no sharp breaks at the divisions indicated graphically in Fig. 3.3. Sub-divisions are established for convenience and by traditions within different disciplines, so do not be surprised to find different definitions in other sources or in references pertaining to other disciplines.

Two important categories are not shown in Table 3.3. The optical spectrum, from 0.30 to 15 μm, defines those wavelengths that can be reflected and refracted with lenses and mirrors. The reflective spectrum extends from about 0.38 to 3.0 μm; it defines that portion of the solar spectrum used directly for remote sensing.

Table 3.3. Principal divisions of the electromagnetic spectrum.

Division	*Limits*
Gamma rays	<0.03 nm
X-rays	0.03–300 nm
Ultraviolet radiation	0.30–0.38 μm
Visible light	0.38–0.72 μm
Infrared radiation	
Near infrared	0.72–1.30 μm
Mid-infrared	1.30–3.00 μm
Far infrared	7.0–1000 μm (1 mm)
Microwave radiation	1 mm–30 cm
Radio	≥ 30 cm

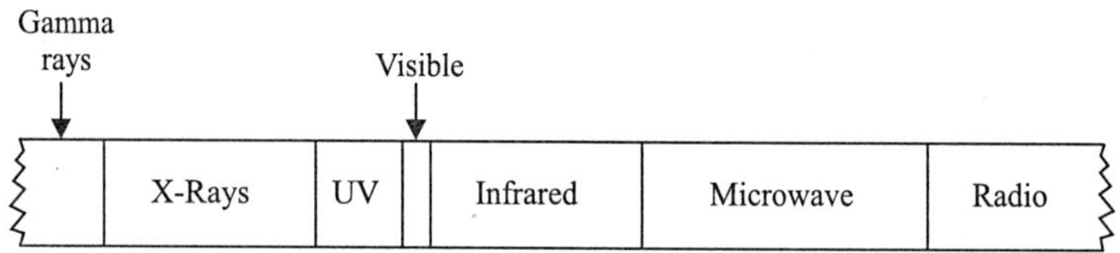

Fig. 3.3. Major divisions of the electromagnetic spectrum. This diagram gives only a schematic representation—sizes of divisions are not shown in correct proportions (see Table 3.3).

Ultraviolet Spectrum

For practical purposes, radiation of significance for remote sensing can be said to begin with the ultraviolet region, a zone of short-wavelength radiation that lies between the X-ray region and the limit of human vision. Often the ultraviolet region is sub-divided into the near ultraviolet (sometimes known as UV-A; 0.32 to 0.40 μm), the far ultraviolet (UV-B; 0.32 to 0.28 μm) and the extreme ultraviolet (UV-C; below 0.28 μm). Literally, 'ultraviolet' means 'beyond the violet', designating it as the region just outside the violet region, the shortest wavelengths visible to humans. Near ultraviolet radiation is known for its ability to induce fluorescence, emission of visible radiation, in some materials; it has significance for a specialised form of remote sensing. However, ultraviolet radiation is easily scattered by the earth's atmosphere, so it is not generally used for remote sensing of earth materials.

Visible Spectrum

Although the visible spectrum constitutes a very small portion of the spectrum, it has obvious significance in remote sensing. Limits of the visible spectrum are defined by the sensitivity of the human visual system. Optical properties of visible radiation were first investigated by Isaac Newton, who during 1665 and 1666 conducted experiments that revealed that visible light can be divided (using prisms or in our time, diffraction gratings) into three segments. Today we know these segments as the additive primaries, defined approximately from 0.4 to 0.5 μm (blue), 0.5 to 0.6 μm (green) and 0.6 to 0.7 μm (red) (Fig. 3.4). Primary colours are defined such that no single primary can be formed from a mixture of the other two and that all other colours can be formed by mixing the three primaries in appropriate proportions. Equal proportions of the three additive primaries combine to form white light.

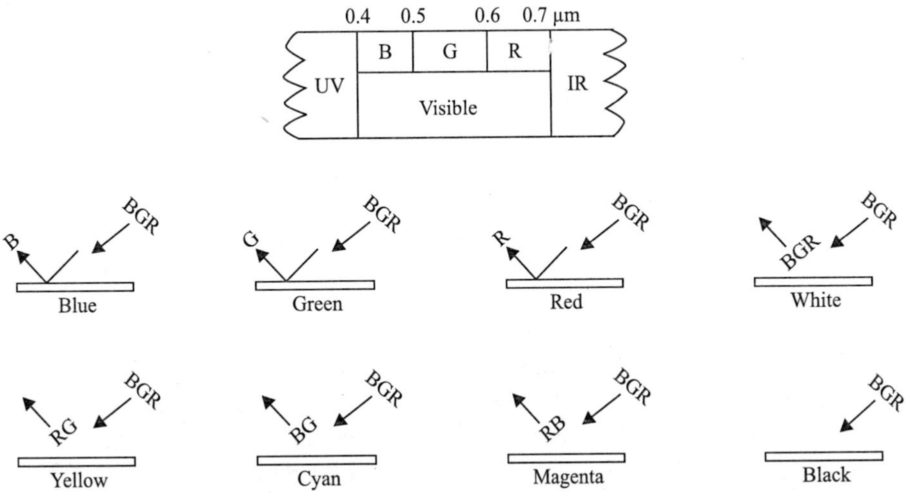

Fig. 3.4. Colours (B-Blue; G-Green; R-Red).

The colour of an object is defined by the colour of the light that it reflects (Fig. 3.4). Thus a 'blue' object is 'blue' because it reflects blue light. Intermediate colours are formed when an object reflects two or more of the additive primaries, which combine to create the sensation of 'yellow' (red and green), 'purple' (red and blue) or other colours. The additive primaries are significant whenever we consider the colours of light, as, for example, in the exposure of photographic films.

In contrast, representations of colours in films, paintings and similar images are formed by combinations of the three subtractive primaries that define the colours of pigments and dyes. Each of the three subtractive primaries absorbs a third of the visible spectrum (Fig. 3.4). Yellow absorbs blue light (and reflects red and green); cyan (a greenish-blue) absorbs red light (and reflects blue and green); and magenta (a bluish red) absorbs green light (and reflects red and blue light). A mixture of equal proportions of pigments of the three subtractive primaries yields black (complete absorption of the visible spectrum). The additive primaries are of interest in matters concerning radiant energy, whereas the subtractive primaries specify colours of the pigments and dyes used in reproducing colours on films, photographic prints and other images.

Infrared Spectrum

Wavelengths longer than the red portion of the visible spectrum are designated as the infrared region, discovered in 1800 by the British astronomer William Herschel (1738–1822). This segment of the spectrum is very large relative to the visible region, as it extends from 0.72 to 15 μm—making it more than 40 times as wide as the visible light spectrum. Because of its broad range, it encompasses radiation with varied properties. Two important categories can be recognised here. The first consists of near infrared and mid-infrared radiation—defined as those regions of the infrared spectrum closest to the visible. Radiation in the near infrared region behaves, with respect to optical systems, in a manner analogous to radiation in the visible spectrum. Therefore, remote sensing in the near infrared region can use films, filters and cameras with designs similar to those intended for use with visible light.

The second category of infrared radiation consists of the far infrared region, consisting of wavelengths well beyond the visible, extending into regions that border the microwave region (Table 3.3). This radiation is fundamentally different from that in the visible and the near infrared regions. Whereas near infrared radiation is essentially solar radiation reflected from the earth's surface, far infrared radiation is emitted by the earth. In everyday language, the far infrared consists of 'heat' or 'thermal energy'. Sometimes this portion of the spectrum is referred to as the emitted infrared.

Microwave Energy

The longest wavelengths commonly used in remote sensing are those from about 1 mm to 1 m in wavelength. The shortest wavelengths in this range have much in common with the thermal energy of the far infrared. The longer wavelengths merge into the radio wavelengths used for commercial broadcasts.

RADIATION LAWS

The propagation of electromagnetic energy follows certain physical laws. In the interests of conciseness, some of these laws are outlined in abbreviated form because our interest here is the basic relationships they express rather than the formal derivations that are available to the student in more comprehensive sources.

Isaac Newton was among the first to recognise the dual nature of light (and by extension, all forms of electromagnetic radiation), which simultaneously displays behaviours associated with both discrete and continuous phenomena. Newton maintained that light is a stream of minuscule particles ('corpuscles') that travel in straight lines. This notion is consistent with the modern theories of Max Planck and Albert Einstein. Planck discovered that electromagnetic energy is absorbed and emitted in discrete units called quanta or photons. The size of each unit is directly proportional to the frequency of the energy's radiation. Planck defined a constant (h) to relate frequency (v) to radiant energy (Q):

$$Q = hv \qquad \text{... (3.2)}$$

His model explains the photoelectric effect, the generation of electric currents by the exposure of certain substances to light, as the effect of the impact of these discrete units of energy (quanta) upon surfaces of certain metals, causing the emission of electrons. Newton knew of other phenomena, such as the refraction of light by prisms, that are best explained by assuming the electromagnetic energy travels in a wave-like manner. James Clerk Maxwell was the first to formally define the wave model of electromagnetic radiation. His mathematical definitions of the behaviour of electromagnetic energy are based upon the assumption from classical (mechanical) physics that light and other forms of electromagnetic energy propagate as a series of waves. The wave model best explains some aspects of the observed behaviour of electromagnetic energy (e.g., refraction by lenses and prisms and diffraction), whereas quantum theory provides explanations of other phenomena (notably, the photoelectric effect).

The rate at which photons (quanta) strike a surface is the radiant flux (ϕ_e), measured in watts (W); this measure specifies energy delivered to a surface in a unit of time. We also need to specify a unit of area; the irradiance (E_e) is defined as radiant flux per unit area (usually measured as watts per square meter). Irradiance measures radiation that strikes a surface, whereas the term radiant exitance (M_e) defines the rate at which radiation is emitted from a unit area (also measured in watts per square meter).

All objects with temperatures above absolute zero have temperature and emit energy. The amount of energy and the wavelengths at which it is emitted depend upon the temperature of the object. As the temperature of an object increases, the total amount of energy emitted also increases and the wavelength of maximum (peak) emission becomes shorter. These relationships can be expressed formally using the concept of the blackbody. A blackbody is a hypothetical source of energy that behaves in an idealised manner. It absorbs all incident radiation; none is reflected. A blackbody emits energy with perfect efficiency; its effectiveness as a radiator of energy varies only as temperature varies.

The blackbody is a hypothetical entity because in nature all objects reflect at least a small proportion of the radiation that strikes them and thus do not act as perfect re-radiators of absorbed energy. Although truly perfect blackbodies cannot exist, their behaviour can be approximated using laboratory instruments. Such instruments have formed the basis for the scientific research that has defined relationships between the temperatures of objects and the radiation they emit. Kirchhoff's law states that the ratio of emitted radiation to absorbed radiation flux is the same for all blackbodies at the same temperature. This law forms the basis for the definition of emissivity (ε), the ratio between the emittance of a given object (M) and that of blackbody at the same temperature (M_b):

$$\varepsilon = M/M_b \qquad \text{... (3.3)}$$

The emissivity of a true blackbody is 1 and that of a perfect reflector (a whitebody) would be 0. Blackbodies and whitebodies are hypothetical concepts, approximated in the laboratory under contrived conditions. In nature, all objects have emissivities that fall between these extremes (graybodies). For these objects, emissivity is a useful measure of their effectiveness as radiators of electromagnetic energy. Those objects that tend to absorb high proportions of incident radiation and then to re-radiate this energy will have high emissivities. Those that are less effective as absorbers and radiators of energy have low emissivities (i.e., they return much more of the energy that reaches them).

The Stefan-Boltzmann law defines the relationship between the total emitted radiation (W) (often expressed in watts $\cdot$ cm^{-2}) and temperature (T) (absolute temperature, K):

$$W = \sigma T^4 \qquad \text{... (3.4)}$$

Total radiation emitted from a blackbody is proportional to the fourth power of its absolute temperature. The constant (σ) is the Stefan-Boltzmann constant (5.6697×10^{-8}) (watts $\cdot m^{-2} \cdot K^{-4}$), which defines unit time and unit area. In essence, the Stefan-Boltzmann law states that hot blackbodies emit more energy per unit area than do cool blackbodies.

Wien's displacement law specifies the relationship between the wavelength of radiation emitted and the temperature of a blackbody:

$$\lambda = 2897.8/T \qquad \text{... (3.5)}$$

where λ is the wavelength at which radiance is at a maximum and T is the absolute temperature (K). As blackbodies become hotter, the wavelength of maximum emittance shifts to shorter wavelengths (Fig. 3.5).

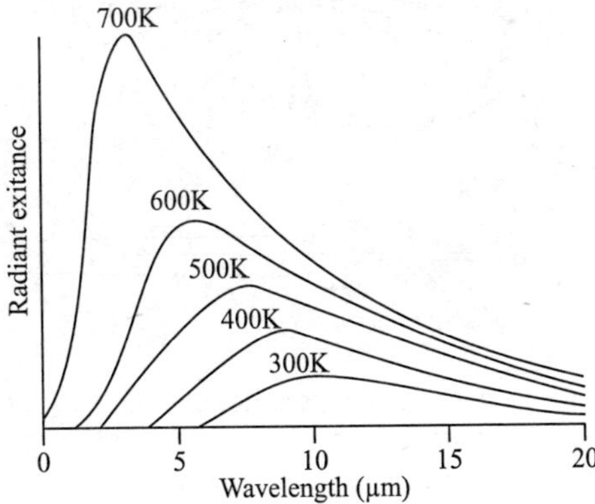

Fig. 3.5. Wien's displacement law. For Blackbodies at high temperatures, maximum radiation emission occurs at short wavelengths. Blackbodies at low temperatures emit maximum radiation at longer wavelengths.

All three of these radiation laws are important for understanding electromagnetic radiation. They have special significance later in discussions of detection of radiation in the far infrared spectrum.

INTERACTIONS WITH THE ATMOSPHERE

All radiation used for remote sensing must pass through the earth's atmosphere. If the sensor is carried by a low-flying aircraft, effects of the atmosphere upon image quality may be negligible. In contrast, energy that reaches sensors carried by earth satellites must pass through the entire depth of the earth's atmosphere. Under these conditions, atmospheric effects may have substantial impact upon the quality of images and data that the sensors generate. Therefore, the practice of remote sensing requires knowledge of interactions of electromagnetic energy with the atmosphere.

In cities we often are acutely aware of the visual effects of dust, smoke, haze and other atmospheric impurities due to their high concentrations. We easily appreciate their effects upon brightnesses and colours we see. But even in clear air, visual effects of the atmosphere are numerous, although so commonplace that we may not recognise their significance. In both settings, as solar energy passes through the earth's atmosphere, it is subject to modification by several physical processes, including (i) scattering; (ii) absorption; and (iii) refraction.

Scattering

Scattering in the redirection of electromagnetic energy by particles suspended in the atmosphere or by large molecules of atmospheric gases (Fig. 3.6).

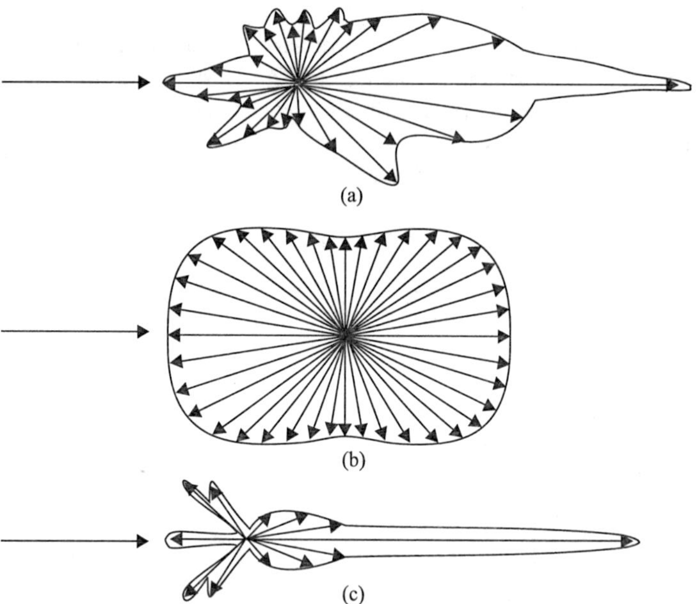

Fig. 3.6. Scattering behaviours of three classes of atmospheric particles. (a) Atmospheric dust and smoke form rather large irregular particles that create a strong forward-scattering peak, with a smaller degree of backscattering. (b) Atmospheric molecules are more nearly symmetric in shape, creating a pattern characterised by preferential forward and backscattering, but without the pronounced peaks observed in the first example. (c) Large water droplets create a pronounced forward-scattering peak, with smaller backscattering peaks.

The amount of scattering that occurs depends upon the sizes of these particles, their abundance, the wavelength of the radiation and the depth of the atmosphere through which the energy is travelling. The effect of scattering is to redirect radiation, so that a portion of the incoming solar beam is directed back toward space, as well as toward the earth's surface.

A common form of scattering was discovered by the British scientist Lord J. W. S. Rayleigh who demonstrated that a perfectly clean atmosphere, consisting only of atmospheric gases, causes scattering of light in a manner such that the amount of scattering increases greatly as wavelength becomes shorter. Rayleigh scattering occurs when atmospheric particles have diameters that are very small relative to the wavelength of the radiation. Typically, such particles could be very small specks of dust or some of the larger molecules of atmospheric gases, such as nitrogen (N_2) and oxygen (O_2). These particles have diameters that are much smaller than the wavelength of visible and near infrared radiation (on the order of diameters less than λ).

Because Rayleigh scattering can occur in the absence of atmospheric impurities, it is sometimes referred to as clear atmosphere scattering. It is the dominant scattering process high in the atmosphere, up to altitudes of 9 to 10 km, the upper limit for atmospheric scattering. Rayleigh scattering is wavelength-dependent, meaning that the amount of scattering changes greatly as one examines different regions of the spectrum (Fig. 3.7). Blue light is scattered about four times as much as is red light and ultraviolet light is scattered almost 16 times as much as is red light. Rayleigh's law states that this form of scattering is in proportion to the inverse of the fourth power of the wavelength.

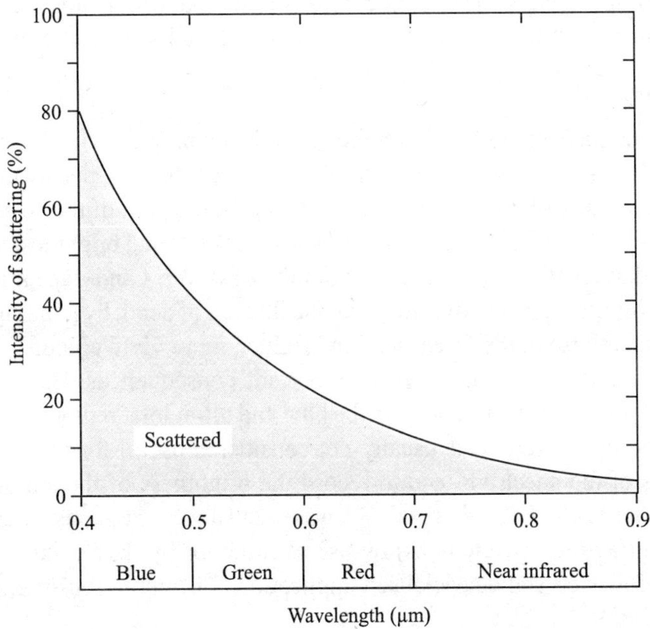

Fig. 3.7. Rayleigh scattering. Scattering is much higher at shorter wavelengths.

Rayleigh scattering is the cause both for the blue colour of the sky and for the brilliant red and orange colours often seen at sunset. At mid-day, when the sun is high in the sky, the atmospheric path of the solar beam is relatively short and direct, so an observer at the earth's surface sees mainly the blue light preferentially redirected by Rayleigh scatter. At sunset, observers on the earth's surface see only those wavelengths that pass through the longer atmospheric path caused by the low solar elevation; because only the longer wavelengths penetrate this distance without attenuation by scattering, we see only the reddish component of the solar beam. Variations of concentrations of fine atmospheric dust or of tiny water droplets in the atmosphere may contribute to variations in atmospheric clarity and therefore to variations in colours of sunsets.

Although Rayliegh scattering forms an important component of our understanding of atmospheric effects upon transmission of radiation in and near the visible spectrum, it applies only to a rather specific class of atmospheric interactions. German physicist Gustav Mie published an analysis that describes atmospheric scattering involving a broader range of atmospheric particles. Mie scattering is caused by large atmospheric particles, including dust, pollen, smoke and water droplets. Such particles may seem to be very small by the standards of everyday experience, but they are many times larger than those responsible for Rayleigh scattering. Those particles that cause Mie scattering have diameters that are roughly equivalent to the wavelength of the scattered radiation. Mie scattering can influence a broad range of wavelengths in and near the visible spectrum; Mie's analysis accounts for variations in the size, shape and composition of such particles. Mie scattering is wavelength-dependent, but not in the simple manner of Rayleigh scattering; it tends to be greatest in the lower atmosphere (0 to 5 km), where larger particles are abundant.

Non-selective scattering is caused by particles that are much larger than the wavelength of the scattered radiation. For radiation in and near the visible spectrum, such particles might be larger water droplets or large particles of airborne dust. 'Non-selective' means that scattering is not wavelength-dependent, so we observe it as a whitish or grayish haze—all visible wavelengths are scattered equally.

Effects of scattering

Scattering causes the atmosphere to have a brightness of its own. In the visible portion of the spectrum, shadows are not jet-black (as they would be in the absence of scattering), but are merely dark; we can see objects in shadows because of light redirected by particles in the path of the solar beam. The effects of scattering are also easily observed in vistas of landscapes—colours and brightnesses of objects are altered as they are positioned at locations more distant from the observer. Landscape artists take advantage of this effect, called atmospheric perspective, to create the illusion of depth by painting more distant features in sub-dued colours and those in the foreground in brighter, more vivid colours.

For remote sensing, scattering has several important consequences. Because of the wavelength dependency of Rayleigh scattering, radiation in the blue and ultraviolet regions of the spectrum (which is most strongly affected by scattering) is usually not considered useful for remote sensing. Images that record these portions of the spectrum tend to record the brightness of the atmosphere rather than the brightness of the scene itself. For this reason, remote sensing instruments often exclude short-wave radiation (blue and ultraviolet wavelengths) by use of filters or by decreasing sensitivities of films to these wavelengths (However, some specialised applications of remote sensing, not discussed here, do use ultraviolet radiation).

Scattering also directs energy from outside the sensor's field of view toward the sensor's aperture, thereby decreasing the spatial detail recorded by the sensor. Furthermore, scattering tends to make dark objects appear brighter than they would otherwise be and bright objects appear darker, thereby decreasing the contrast recorded by a sensor. Because 'good' images preserve the range of brightnesses present in a scene, scattering degrades the quality of an image.

Some of these effects are illustrated in Fig. 3.8. Observed radiance at the sensor, I, is the sum of I_S, radiance reflected from the earth's surface, conveying information about surface reflectance; I_O, radiation scattered from the solar beam directly to the sensor without reaching the earth's surface and I_D, diffuse radiation, directed first to the ground, then to the atmosphere, before reaching the sensor. Effects of these components are additive within a given spectral band:

$$I = I_S + I_O + I_D \qquad \text{... (3.6)}$$

I_S varies with differing surface materials, topographic slopes and orientation and angles of illumination and observation. I_O is often assumed to be more or less constant over large areas, although most satellite images represent areas large enough to encompass atmospheric differences sufficient to create variations in I_O. Diffuse radiation, I_D, is expected to be small relative to other factors, but varies from one land surface type to another, so in practice would be difficult to estimate. We should note the special case presented by shadows, in which $I_S = 0$, because the surface receives no direct solar radiation. However, shadows have their own brightness, derived from I_D and their own spectral patterns, derived from the influence of local land cover upon diffuse radiation. Remote sensing is devoted to the examination of I_S at different wavelengths to derive information about the earth's surface. Figure 3.9 illustrates how I_D, I_S and I_O vary with wavelength for surfaces of differing brightness.

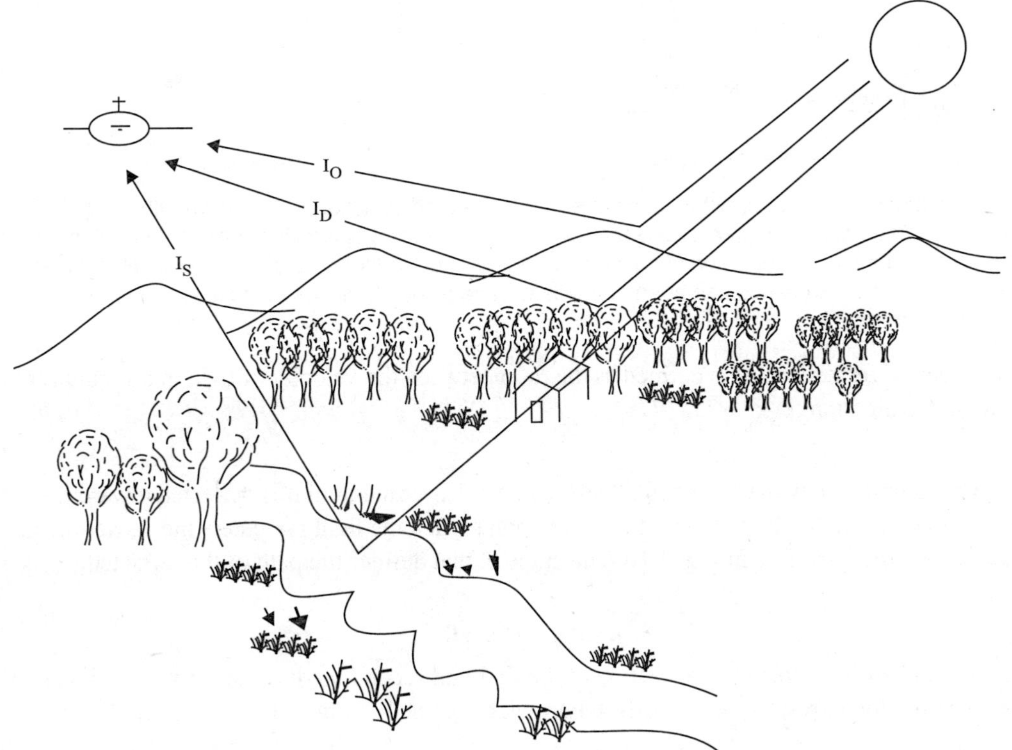

Fig. 3.8. Principal components of observed brightness. I_S represents radiation reflected from the ground surface, I_O is energy scattered by the atmosphere directly to the sensor and I_D represents diffuse light, directed to the ground, then to the atmosphere, before reaching the sensor. This diagram describes behaviour of radiation in and near the visible region of the spectrum.

Refraction

Refraction is the bending of light rays at the contact area between two media that transmit light. Familiar examples of refraction are the lenses of cameras or magnifying glasses, which bend light rays to project or enlarge images and the apparent displacement of objects submerged in clear water. Refraction also occurs in the atmosphere as light passes through atmospheric layers of varied clarity, humidity and temperature. These variations influence the density of atmospheric layers, which in turn causes a bending of light rays as they pass from one layer to another. Everyday examples are the shimmering appearances on hot summer days of objects viewed in the distance as light passes through hot air near the surface of heated highways, runways and parking lots.

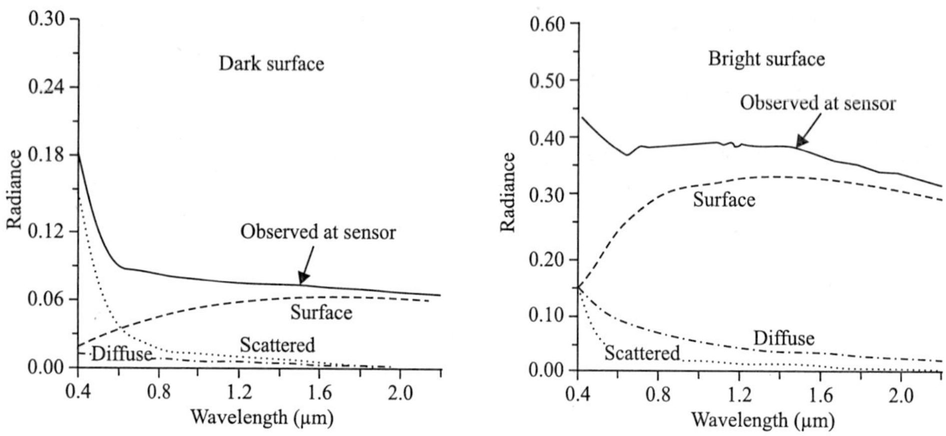

Fig. 3.9. Changes in reflected, diffuse, scattered and observed radiation over wavelength for dark (left) and bright (right) surfaces. This diagram shows the magnitude of the components illustrated in Fig. 3.8. Atmospheric effects constitute a larger proportion of observed brightness for dark objects than for bright objects, especially at short wavelengths. Radiance has been normalised; note also differences in the scaling of the vertical axes for the two diagrams.

The index of refraction (n) is defined as the ratio between the velocity of light in a vacuum (c) to its velocity in the medium (c_n):

$$n = c/c_n \qquad \text{... (3.7)}$$

Assuming uniform media, as the light passes into a denser medium it is deflected toward the surface normal, a line perpendicular to the surface at the point when the light ray enters the denser medium, as represented by the solid line in Fig. 3.10. The angle θ′ that defines the path of the refracted ray is given by Snell's law:

$$n \sin\theta = n' \sin\theta' \qquad \text{... (3.8)}$$

where n and n′ are the indices of refraction of the first and second media, respectively and θ and θ′ are angles measured with respect to the surface normal, as defined in Fig. 3.10.

Absorption

Absorption of radiation occurs when the atmosphere prevents or strongly attenuates, transmission of radiation or its energy through the atmosphere. (Energy acquired by the atmosphere is subsequently re-radiated at longer wavelengths.) Three gases are responsible for most absorption of solar radiation.

Ozone (O_3) is formed by the interaction of high-energy ultraviolet radiation with oxygen molecules (O_2) high in the atmosphere (maximum concentrations of ozone are found at altitudes of about 20 to 30 km in the stratosphere). Although naturally occurring concentrations of ozone are quite low (perhaps 0.07 parts per million at ground level, 0.1 to 0.2 parts per million in the stratosphere), ozone plays an important role in the earth's energy balance. Absorption of the high-energy, short-wavelength, portions of the ultraviolet spectrum (mainly λ less than 0.24 μm) prevents transmission of this radiation to the lower atmosphere.

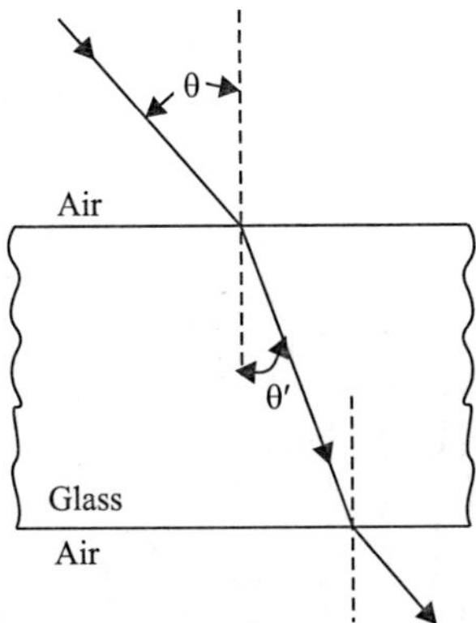

Fig. 3.10. Refraction. The path of a ray of light as it passes from one medium (air) to another (glass) and then again as it passes back to the first.

Carbon dioxide (CO_2) also occurs in low concentrations (about 0.03 per cent by volume of a dry atmosphere), mainly in the lower atmosphere. Aside from local variations caused by volcanic eruptions and mankind distribution of CO_2 in the lower atmosphere is probably relatively uniform (although human activities that burn fossil fuels have apparently contributed to increases during the past 100 years or so). Carbon dioxide is important in remote sensing because it is effective in absorbing radiation in the mid and far infrared regions of the spectrum. Its strongest absorption occurs in the region from about 13 to 17.5 μm, in the mid infrared.

Finally, water vapour (H_2O) is commonly present in the lower atmosphere (below about 100 km) in amounts that vary from 0 to about 3 per cent by volume. (Note the distinction between water vapour, discussed here and droplets of liquid water, mentioned previously). From everyday experience we know that the abundance of water vapour varies greatly from time to time and from place to place. Consequently, the role of atmospheric water vapour, unlike those of ozone and carbon dioxide, varies greatly with time and location. It may be almost insignificant in a desert setting or in a dry air mass, but may be highly significant in humid climates and in moist air masses. Furthermore, water vapour is several times more effective in absorbing radiation than are all other atmospheric gases combined. Two of the most important regions of absorption are in several bands between 5.5 and 7.0 μm and above 27.0 μm: absorption in these regions can exceed 80 per cent if the atmosphere contains appreciable amounts of water vapour.

Atmospheric Windows

Thus the earth's atmosphere is by no means completely transparent to electromagnetic radiation because these gases together form important barriers to transmission of electromagnetic radiation through the atmosphere. It selectively transmits energy of certain wavelengths; those wavelengths that are relatively easily transmitted through the atmosphere are referred to as atmospheric windows (Fig. 3.11). Positions, extents and effectiveness of atmospheric windows are determined by the absorption spectra of atmospheric gases. Atmospheric windows are of obvious significance for remote sensing—they define those wavelengths that can be used forming images. Energy at other wavelengths, not within the windows, is severely attenuated by the atmosphere and therefore cannot be effective for remote sensing. In the far infrared region, the two most important windows extend from 3.5 to 4.1 μm and from 10.5 to 12.5 μm. The latter is especially important because it corresponds approximately to wavelengths of peak emission from the earth's surface. A few of the most important atmospheric windows are tabulated in Table 3.4.

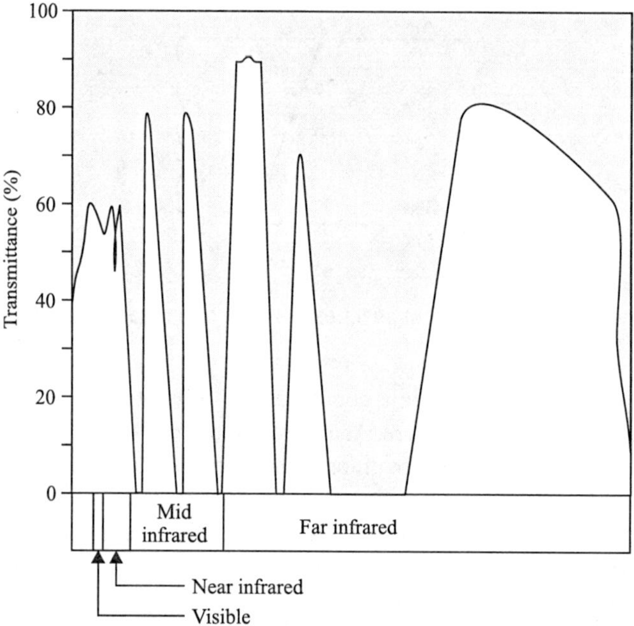

Fig. 3.11. Atmospheric windows. This is a schematic representation that can depict only a few of the most important windows. The shaded area represents absorption of electromagnetic radiation.

Table 3.4. Major atmospheric windows.

Ultraviolet and visible	0.30–0.75 μm
	0.77–0.91 μm
Near infrared	1.55–1.75 μm
	2.05–2.4 μm
Thermal infrared	8.0–9.2 μm
	10.2–12.4 μm
Microwave	7.5–11.5 μm
	20.0 + mm

Overview of Energy Interactions in the Atmosphere

Remote sensing is conducted in the context of all the atmospheric processes discussed thus far, so it is useful to summarise some of the most important points by outlining a perspective that integrates much of the preceding material. Figure 3.12 is an idealised diagram of interactions of shortwave solar radiation with the atmosphere; values are based upon typical or average, values derived from many places and many seasons, so they are by no means representative of values that might be observed at a particular time and place. This diagram represents only the behaviour of 'shortwave' radiation (defined loosely here to include radiation with wavelengths less than 4.0 μm). It is true that the sun emits a broad spectrum of radiation, but the maximum intensity is emitted at approximately 0.5 μm within this region and little solar radiation at longer wavelengths reaches the ground surface.

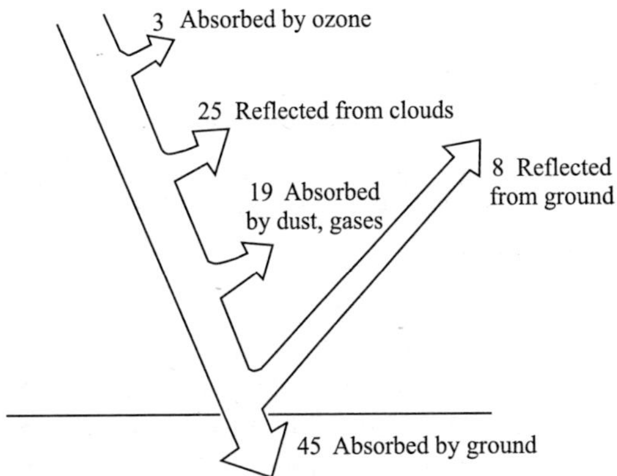

Fig. 3.12. Incoming solar radiation. This diagram represents radiation at relatively short wavelengths in and near the visible region. Values represent approximate magnitudes for the earth as a whole—conditions at any specific place and time would differ from those given here.

Of 100 units of shortwave radiation that reach the outer edge of the earth's atmosphere, about 3 units are absorbed in the stratosphere as ultraviolet radiation interacts with O_2 to form O_3. Of the remaining 97 units, about 25 are reflected from clouds and about 19 are absorbed by dust and gases in the lower atmosphere. About 8 units are reflected from the ground surface (this value varies greatly with different surface materials) and about 45 units ('about 50 per cent') are ultimately absorbed at the earth's surface. For remote sensing in the visible spectrum, it is the portion reflected from the earth's surface that is of primary interest, although knowledge of the quantity scattered is also important.

The 45 units that are absorbed are then re-radiated by the earth's surface. From Wien's displacement law (Equation 3.5), we know that the earth, being much cooler than the sun, must emit radiation at much longer wavelengths than does the sun. The sun, at 6000 K, has its maximum intensity at 0.5 μm (in the green portion of the visible spectrum); the earth, at 300 K, emits with maximum intensity near 10 μm, in the far infrared spectrum.

Terrestrial radiation, with wavelengths longer than 10 μm, is represented in Fig. 3.13. There is little, if any, overlap between the wavelengths of solar radiation, depicted in Fig. 3.12 and the terrestrial radiation, shown in Fig. 3.13. This diagram depicts the transfer of 143 units of long-wave radiation (as defined above) from the ground surface to the atmosphere, in three separate categories.

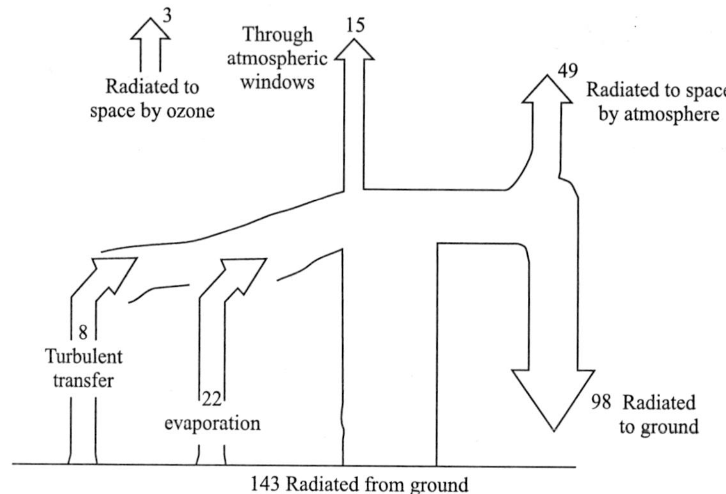

Fig. 3.13. Outgoing terrestrial radiation. This diagram represents radiation at relatively long wavelengths—what we think of as sensible heat or thermal radiation. Because the earth's atmosphere absorbs much of the radiation emitted by the earth, only those wavelengths that can pass through the atmospheric windows can be used for remote sensing.

About 8 units are transferred from the ground surface to the atmosphere by 'turbulent transfer' (heating of the lower atmosphere by the ground surface, which causes upward movement of air, then movement of cooler air to replace the original air). About 22 units are lost to the atmosphere by evaporation of moisture in the soil, water bodies and vegetation (this energy is transferred as the latent heat of evaporation). Finally, about 113 units are radiated directly to the atmosphere.

Because atmospheric gases are very effective in absorbing this long-wave (far infrared) radiation, much of the energy that the earth radiates is retained (temporarily) by the atmosphere. About 15 units pass directly through the atmosphere to space; this is energy emitted at wavelengths that correspond to atmospheric windows (chiefly 8 to 13 μm). Energy absorbed by the atmosphere is ultimately re-radiated to space (49 units) and back to the earth (98 units). For meteorology, it is these re-radiated units that are of interest because they are the source of energy for heating of the earth's atmosphere. For remote sensing, it is the 15 units that pass through the atmospheric windows that are of significance, as it is this radiation that conveys information concerning the radiometric properties of features on the earth's surface.

INTERACTIONS WITH SURFACES

As electromagnetic energy reaches the earth's surface, it must be reflected, absorbed or transmitted. The proportions accounted for by each process depend upon the nature of the surface, the wavelength of the energy and the angle of illumination.

Reflection

Reflection occurs when a ray of light is redirected as it strikes a non-transparent surface. The nature of the reflection depends upon sizes of surface irregularities (roughness or smoothness) in relation to the wavelength of the radiation considered. If the surface is smooth relative to wavelength, specular reflection occurs (Fig. 3.14a). Specular reflection redirects all or almost all, of the incident radiation in a single direction. For such surfaces, the angle of incidence is equal to the angle of reflection (i.e., in Equation 3.8, the two media are identical, so n = n′ and therefore θ = θ′). For visible radiation, specular reflection can occur with surfaces such as a mirror, smooth metal or a calm water body.

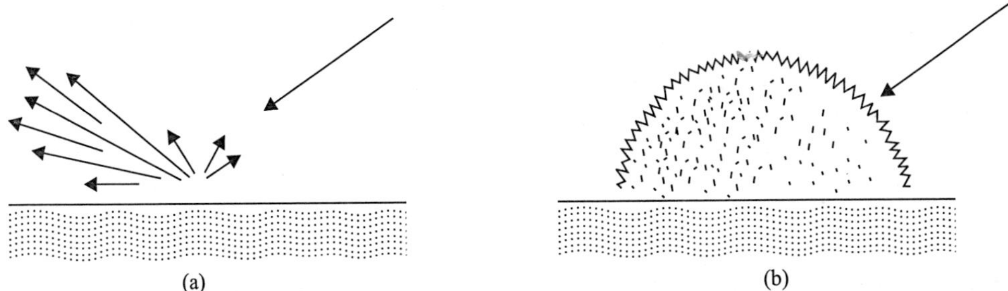

Fig. 3.14. Specular (a) and diffuse; (b) reflection. Specular reflection occurs when a smooth surface tends to direct incident radiation in a single direction. Diffuse reflection occurs when a rough surface tends to scatter energy more or less equally in all directions.

If a surface is rough relative to wavelength, it acts as a diffuse or isotropic, reflector. Energy is scattered more or less equally in all directions. For visible radiation, many natural surfaces might behave as diffuse reflectors, including, for example, uniform grassy surfaces. A perfectly diffuse reflector (known as a Lambertian surface) would have equal brightnesses when observed from any angle (Fig. 3.14b).

The idealised concept of a perfectly diffuse reflecting surface is derived from the work of Johann H. Lambert, who conducted many experiments designed to describe the behaviour of light. One of Lambert's laws of illumination states that the perceived brightness (radiance) of a perfectly diffuse surface does not change with the angle of view. This is Lambert's cosine law, which states that the observed brightness (I′) of such a surface is proportional to the cosine of the incidence angle (θ), where I is the brightness of the incident radiation as observed at zero incidence:

$$I' = I/\cos\theta \qquad \text{... (3.9)}$$

This relationship is often combined with the equally important inverse square law, which states that observed brightness decreases according to the square of the distance from the observer to the source:

$$I' = \frac{I}{D^2}(\cos\theta) \qquad \text{... (3.10)}$$

(Both the cosine law and the inverse square law are depicted in Fig. 3.15).

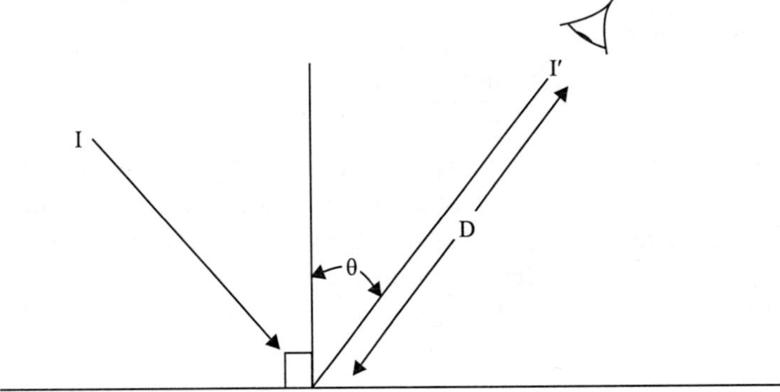

Fig. 3.15. Inverse square law and Lambert's cosine law.

Bidirectional Reflectance Distribution Function

Because of its simplicity and directness, the concept of a Lambertian surface is frequently used as an approximation of the optical behaviour of objects observed in remote sensing. However, the Lambertian model does not hold precisely for many, if not most, natural surfaces. Actual surfaces exhibit complex patterns of reflection determined by details of surface geometry (e.g., the sizes, shapes and orientations of plant leaves). Some surfaces may approximate Lambertian behaviour at some incidence angles, but exhibit clearly non-Lambertian properties at other angles.

Reflection characteristics of a surface are described by the bidirectional reflectance distribution function (BRDF). The BRDF is a mathematical description of the optical behaviour of a surface with respect to angles of illumination and observation, given that it has been illuminated with a parallel beam of light at a specified azimuth and elevation. (The function is 'bidirectional' in the sense that it accounts both for the angle of illumination and the angle of observation.) The BRDF for a Lambertian surface has the shape depicted in Fig. 3.14b, with even brightnesses as the surface is observed from any angle. Actual surfaces have more complex behaviour. Description of BRDFs for actual, rather than idealised, surfaces permits assessment of the degrees of which they approach the ideals of specular and diffuse surfaces (Fig. 3.16).

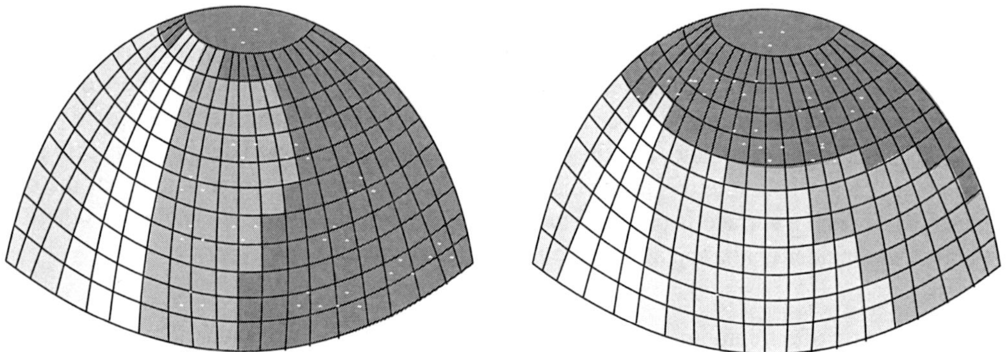

Fig. 3.16. BRDFs for two surfaces. The varied shading represents differing intensities of observed radiation.

Transmission

Transmission of radiation occurs when radiation passes through a substance without significant attenuation (Fig. 3.17). From a given thickness or depth, of a substance, the ability of a medium to transmit energy is measured as the transmittance (t):

$$t = \frac{\text{Transmitted radiation}}{\text{Incident radiation}} \quad \text{... (3.11)}$$

In the field of remote sensing, the transmittance of films and filters is often important. With respect to naturally occurring materials we often think only of water bodies as capable of transmitting significant amounts of radiation. However, the transmittance of many materials varies greatly with wavelengths, so our direct observations in the visible spectrum do not transfer to other parts of the spectrum. For example, plant leaves are generally opaque to visible radiation but transmit significant amounts of radiation in the infrared.

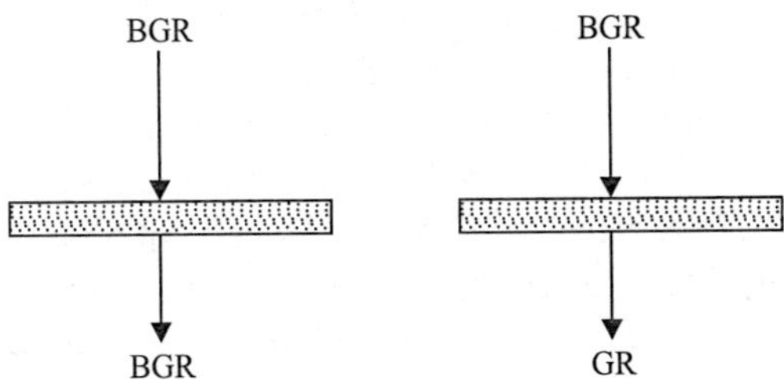

Fig. 3.17. Transmission. Incident radiation passes through an object without significant attenuation (left) or may be selectively transmitted (right). The object on the right would act as a yellow ('minus blue') filter, as it would transmit all visible radiation except for blue light.

Fluorescence

Fluorescence occurs when an object illuminated with radiation of one wavelength emits radiation at a different wavelength. The most familiar examples are some sulphide minerals, which emit visible radiation when illuminated with ultraviolet radiation. Other objects also fluoresce, although observation of fluorescence requires very accurate and detailed measurements, not now routinely available for most applications. Figure 3.18 illustrates the fluorescence of healthy and senescent leaves, using one axis to describe the spectral distribution of the illumination and the other to show the spectra of the emitted energy. These contrasting surfaces illustrate the effectiveness of fluorescence in revealing differences between healthy and stressed leaves.

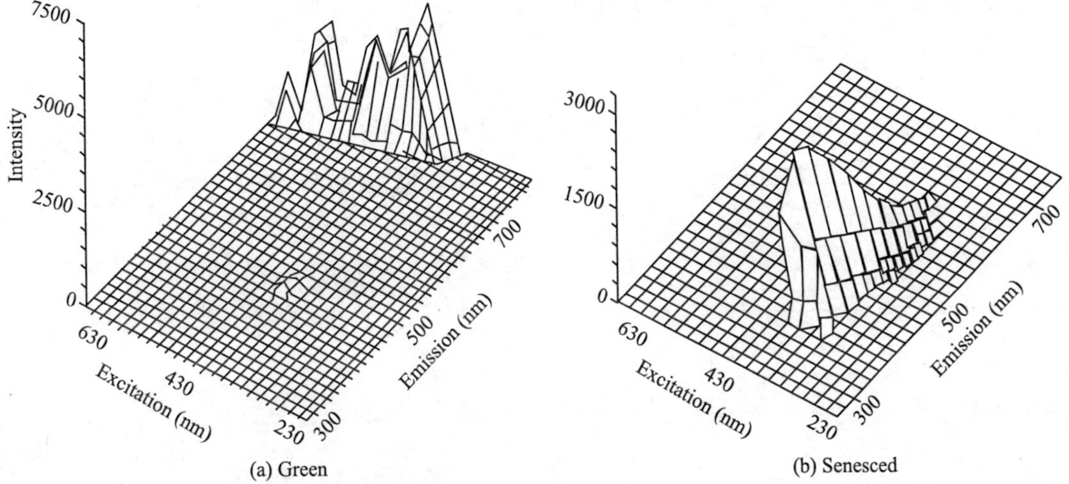

Fig. 3.18. Fluorescence. Exitation and emission are shown along the two horizontal axes (with wavelengths given in nanometers). The vertical axes show strength of fluorescence, with the two examples illustrating the contrast in fluorescence between healthy (a) and senescent (b) leaves.

Spectral Properties of Objects

Remote sensing consists of the study of radiation emitted and reflected from features at the earth's surface. In the instance of emitted (far infrared) radiation, the object itself is the immediate source of radiation. For reflected radiation, the source may be the sun, the atmosphere (by means of scattering of solar radiation) or man-made radiation (chiefly imaging radars).

A fundamental premise in remote sensing is that we can learn about objects and features on the earth's surface by studying the radiation reflected and/or emitted by these features. Using cameras and other remote sensing instruments, we can observe the brightnesses of objects over a range of wavelengths, so that there are numerous points of comparison between brightnesses of separate objects. A set of such observations or measurements constitute a spectral response pattern, sometimes called the spectral signature of an object (Fig. 3.19).

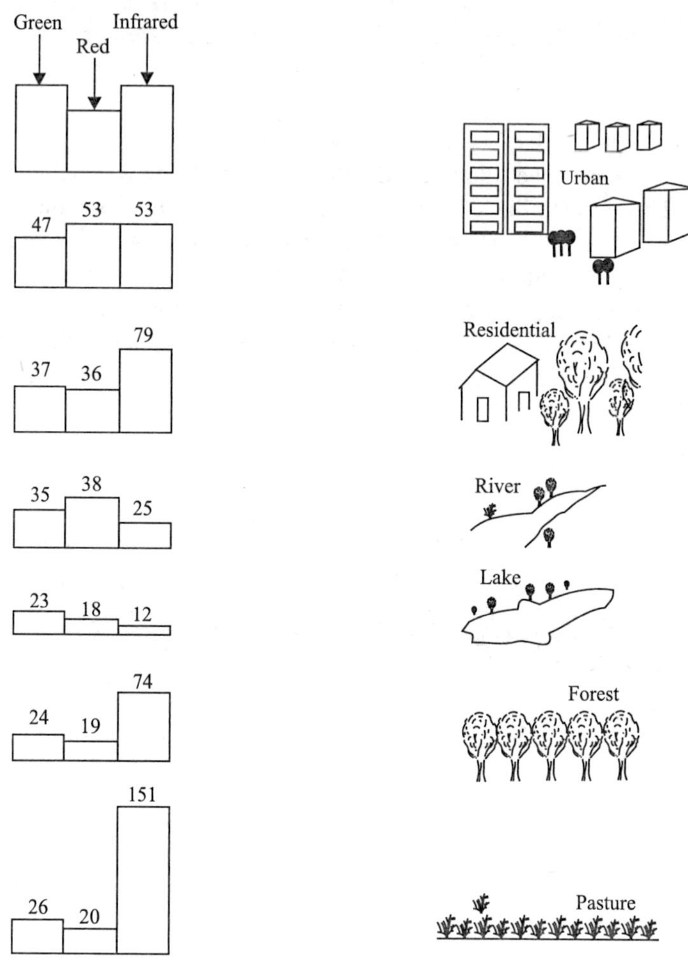

Fig. 3.19. Spectral signatures.

In the ideal, detailed knowledge of a spectral response pattern might permit identification of features of interest, such as separate kinds of crops, forests or minerals. This idea has been expressed as follows:

'Everything in nature has its own unique distribution of reflected, emitted and absorbed radiation. These spectral characteristics can—if ingeniously exploited—be used to distinguish one thing from another or to obtain information about shape, size and other physical and chemical properties'.

This statement expresses the fundamental concepts of the spectral signature, the notion that features display unique spectral responses that would permit clear identification, from spectral information alone, of individual crops, soils and so on, from remotely sensed images. In practice, it is now recognised that spectra of features change both over time (e.g., as a cornfield grows during a season) and over distance (e.g., as proportions of specific tree species in a forest change from place to place).

Nonetheless, the study of the spectral properties of objects forms an important part of remote sensing. Some research has been focused upon examination of spectral properties of different classes of features. Thus, although it may be difficult to define unique signatures for specific kinds of vegetation, we can recognise distinctive spectral patterns for vegetated and non-vegetated areas and for certain classes of vegetation and we can sometimes detect the existence of diseased or stressed vegetation. In other instances, we may be able to define spectral patterns that are useful within restricted geographic and temporal limits as a means of studying the distributions of certain plant and soil characteristics.

SUMMARY: THREE MODELS FOR REMOTE SENSING

Remote sensing typically takes one of three basic forms depending on the wavelengths of energy detected and on the purposes of the study. In the simplest form one records the reflection of solar radiation from the earth's surface (Fig. 3.20). This is the kind of remote sensing most nearly similar to everyday experience. For example, film in a camera records radiation from the sun after it is reflected from the objects of interest, regardless of whether one uses a simple hand-held camera to photograph a family scene or a complex aerial camera to photograph a large area of the earth's surface. This form of remote sensing mainly uses energy in the visible and near infrared portions of the spectrum. Key variables include atmospheric clarity, spectral properties of objects angle and intensity of the solar beam.

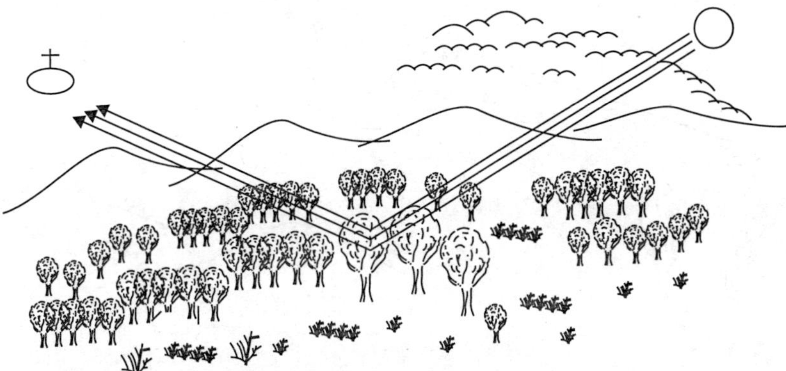

Fig. 3.20. Remote sensing using reflected solar radiation. The sensor detects solar radiation that has been reflected from features at the earth's surface. (See Fig. 3.12.)

A second strategy for remote sensing is to record radiation emitted from (rather than reflected from) the earth's surface. Because emitted energy is strongest in the far infrared spectrum, this kind of remote sensing requires special instruments designed to record these wavelengths. (There is no direct analogue to everyday experience for this kind of remote sensing.) Emitted energy from the earth's surface is mainly derived from short-wave energy from the sun that has been absorbed, then re-radiated at longer wavelengths (Fig. 3.21). Emitted radiation from the earth's surface reveals information concerning thermal properties of materials and man-made structures. Other sources of emitted radiation include geothermal energy, heat from steam pipes, power plants, buildings and forest fires. This example also represents 'passive' remote sensing, because it employs instruments designed to sense energy emitted by the earth, not energy generated by a sensor.

Fig. 3.21. Remote sensing using emitted terrestrial radiation. The sensor records solar radiation that has been absorbed by the earth, then re-emitted as thermal infrared radiation (Figs. 3.12 and 3.13.).

Finally, a third class of remote sensing instruments generate their own energy, then record the reflection of that energy from the earth's surface (Fig. 3.22). These are 'active' sensors—'active' in the sense that they provide their own energy, so they are independent of solar and terrestrial radiation. As an everyday analogy, a camera with a flash attachment can be considered to be an active sensor.

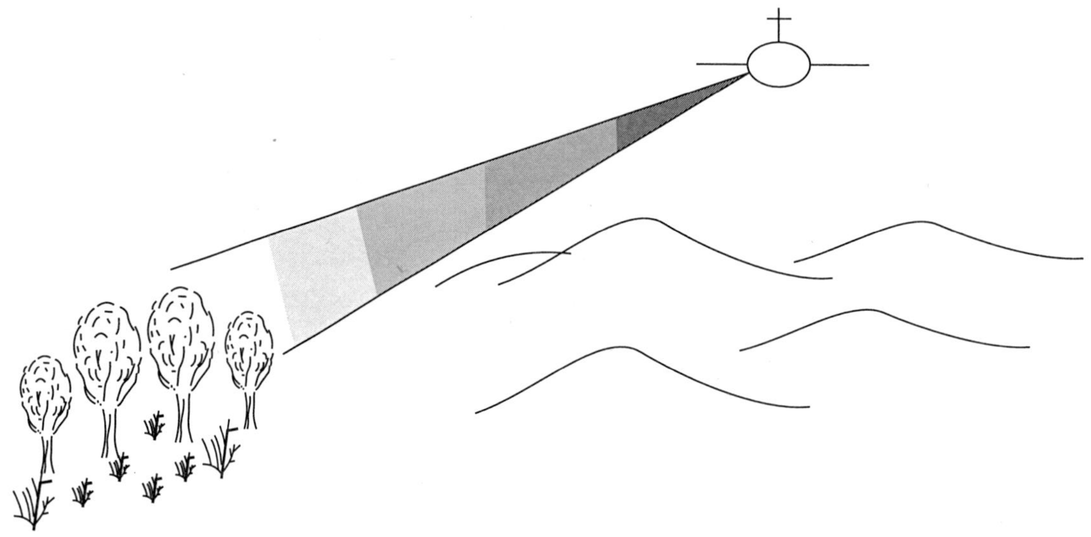

Fig. 3.22. Active remote sensing. The sensor illuminates the terrain with its own energy, then records the reflected energy as it has been altered by the earth's surface.

In practice, active sensors are best represented by imaging radars and lidars, which transmit energy toward the earth's surface from an aircraft or satellite, then receive the reflected energy to form an image. Because they sense energy provided directly by the sensor itself, such instruments have the capability to operate at night and during cloudy weather.

4

Photographic Sensors

INTRODUCTION

The word photography means 'to write with light'—a literal description of what the newly invented camera could do. Today our meaning is often expanded to include radiation just outside the visible spectrum, in the ultraviolet and near infrared regions.

Although the status of photography is challenged by continuing innovations in digital imaging technology, photography remains the most practical, inexpensive and widely used means of remote sensing. Further, the basic optical principals used for photography are also employed in optical systems of non-photographic sensors and we often use photographic film to record images generated by non-photographic sensors. Therefore, knowledge of photography forms a central core for understanding the field of remote sensing.

The formation of images by refraction of light is a surprisingly old practice. In antiquity, Greek and Arab scholars knew that images could be formed as light passed through a pinhole opening in a dark enclosure. Refraction of light at the tiny opening bends light rays to form an inverted image in a manner analogous to the effect of a simple lens. In medieval Europe, a device known as the camera obscura ('dark chamber') employed this principle to project an image onto a screen as an aid for artists, who could then trace the outline of the image as the foundation of more elaborate drawings or paintings. During the Renaissance, the addition of a simple convex lens improved the camera obscura, although there was still no convenient means of recording the image formed on the screen. Later, with the development of photographic emulsions (described below) as a means of making a detailed record of the image, the camera obscura began its evolution toward the everyday cameras that we know today, which in turn are models for the more complex cameras used for aerial survey.

Despite the current availability of more sophisticated imaging systems, aerial photography still remains the most accessible and versatile form of remote sensing imagery. Routine use of aerial photography has incalculable value throughout the world as a major source of information concerning the landscape and as the primary means of producing modern topographic maps. Its economic contributions to surveying of the earth and effective planning are considerable and it is clear that aerial photography will remain as a primary source of remote sensing imagery for many years to come.

AERIAL CAMERA

In their most basic elements, aerial cameras are similar to the simple handheld cameras we all have used. Both share the four main components of all cameras: (i) a lens to focus light on the film; (ii) a light-sensitive film to record the image; (iii) a shutter that controls entry of light into the camera; and (iv) the camera body, a light-tight enclosure that holds the film, lens and shutter in their correct positions.

In addition, aerial cameras include three other elements not usually encountered in our personal experiences with photography: the film magazine, the drive mechanism and the lens cone (Fig. 4.1).

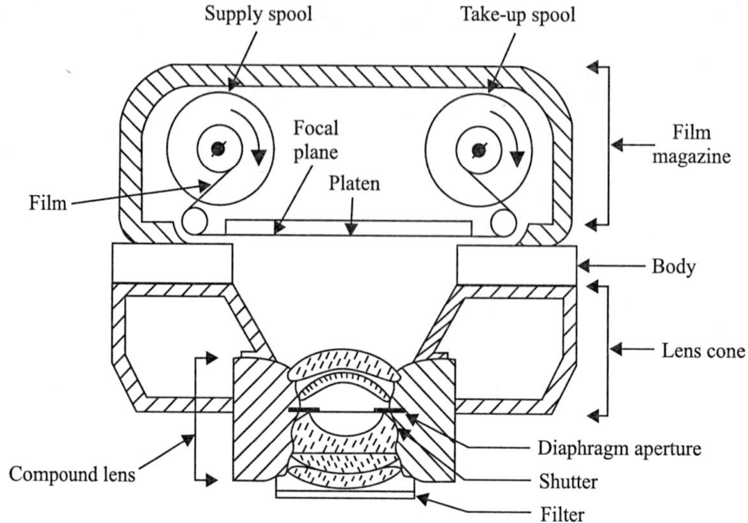

Fig. 4.1. Schematic diagram of an aerial camera, cross-sectional view.

Lens

The lens gathers reflected light and focuses it on the film. In its simplest form, a lens is a glass disk carefully ground into a shape with non-parallel curved surfaces (Fig. 4.2). The change in optical densities as light rays pass from the atmosphere to the lens and back to the atmosphere causes refraction of light rays; the sizes, shapes, arrangements and compositions of lenses are carefully designed to control this bending of light rays to maintain colour balance and to minimise optical distortions.

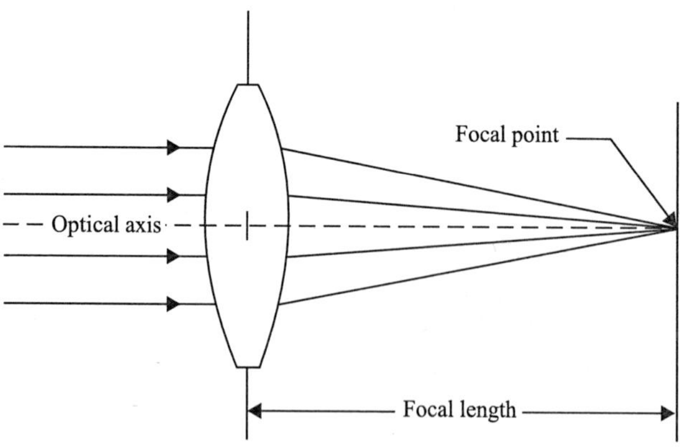

Fig. 4.2. Simple lens.

Optical characteristics of lenses are determined largely by the refractive index of the glass and the degree of curvature present in the lens surface. The quality of a lens is determined by the quality of its glass, the precision with which that glass is shaped and the accuracy with which it is positioned within a camera. Imperfections in lens shape contribute to spherical aberration, a source of error that distorts images and causes loss of image clarity. For modern aerial photography, spherical aberration is usually not a severe problem because most modern aerial cameras use lenses of very high quality.

Figure 4.2 shows the simplest of all lenses: a simple positive lens. Such a lens is formed from a glass disk with equal curvature on both sides; light rays are refracted at both edges to form an image. Most aerial cameras use compound lenses, formed from many separate lenses of varied sizes, shapes and properties. These many components are designed to correct for the errors that may be present in any single component, so the whole unit is much more accurate than any single element. For present purposes, consideration of a simple lens will be sufficient to define the most important features of lenses, even though a simple lens differs from those actually used in modern aerial cameras.

The optical axis joins the centers of curvature of the two sides of the lens. Although refraction occurs throughout a lens, a plane passing through the center of the lens, known as the image principal plane, is considered to be the center of refraction within the lens (Fig. 4.3). The image principal plane intersects the optical axis at the nodal point.

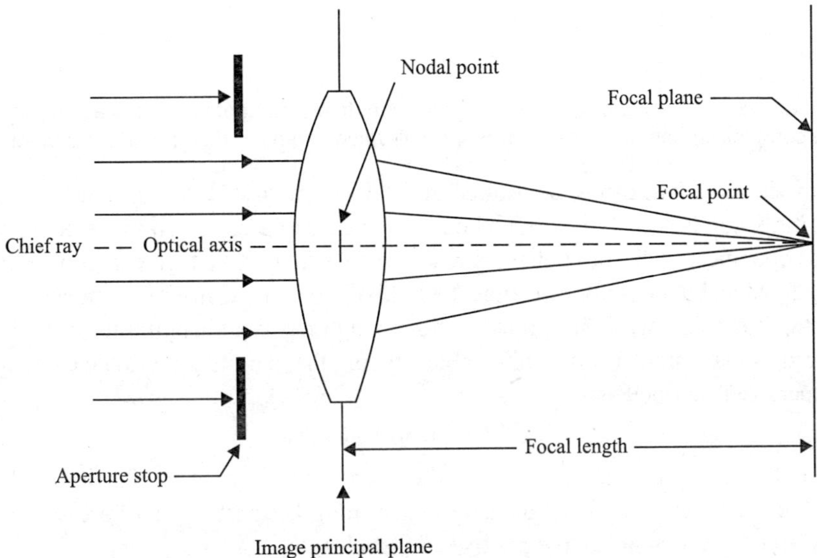

Fig. 4.3. Cross-sectional view of an image formed by a simple lens.

Parallel light rays reflected from an object at a great distance (at an 'infinite' distance) pass through the lens and are brought to focus at the principal focal point, the point at which the lens forms an image of the distant object. The chief ray passes through the nodal point without changing direction; all other rays are bent by the lens. A plane passing through the focal point parallel to the image principal plane is known as the focal plane. For handheld cameras, the distance from the lens to the object is important because the image is brought into focus at distances that increase as the object is positioned closer to the lens. For such cameras, it is important to use lenses that can be adjusted to bring each object to a correct focus as the distance from the camera to the object changes. For aerial cameras, the scene to be photographed is always at such large distances that the focus can be fixed at infinity, with no need to change the focus of the lens. For a simple positive lens, the focal length is defined as the distance from the center of the lens to the focal point, usually measured in inches or millimeters. (For a compound lens, the definition is more complex.) For a given lens, the focal length is not identical for all wavelengths. Blue light is brought to a focal point at a shorter distance than are red or infrared wavelengths (Fig. 4.4). This effect is the source of chromatic aberration. Unless corrected by lens design, chromatic aberration would cause the individual colours of an image to be out of focus in the photograph. Chromatic aberration is corrected in high-quality aerial cameras to assure that the radiation used to form the image is brought to a common focal point.

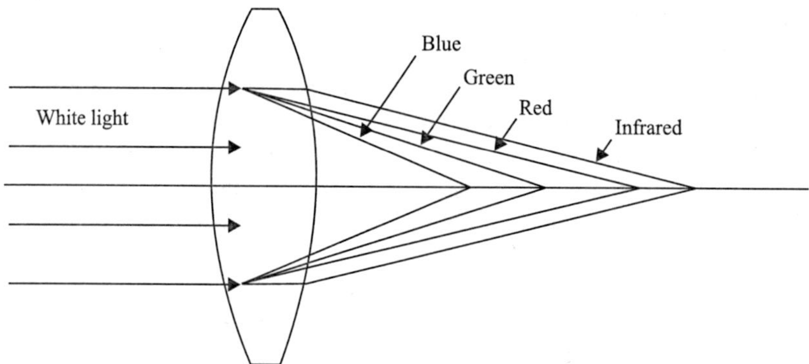

Fig. 4.4. Chromatic aberration. Energy of differing wavelengths is brought to a focus at varying distances from the lens. More complex lenses are corrected to bring all wavelengths to a common focal point.

The field of view of a lens can be controlled by field stop, a mask positioned just in front of the focal plane. An aperture stop is usually positioned near the center of a compound lens; it consists of a mask with a circular opening of adjustable diameter (Fig. 4.5). An aperture stop can control the intensity of light at the focal plane, but does not influence the field of view of the size of the image. Manipulation of the aperture stop controls only the brightness of the image without changing its size. Usually aperture size is measured as the diameter of the adjustable opening that admits light to the camera.

Relative aperture is defined as:

$$f = \text{Focal length/aperture size} \quad \text{... (4.1)}$$

where focal length and aperture are measured in the same units of length and f is the number, the relative aperture. A large f number means that the aperture opening is small relative to focal length; a small f number means that the opening is large relative to focal length.

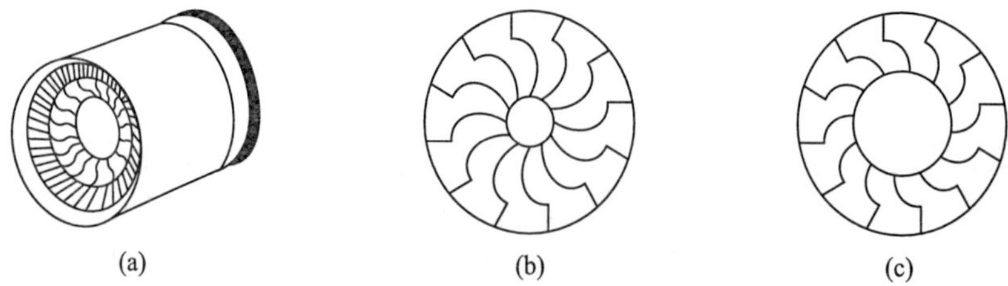

Fig. 4.5. Diaphragm aperture stop (a) Perspective view; (b) Narrow aperture; and (c) Wide aperture.

Why use f numbers rather than direct measurements of aperture? One reason is that standardisation of aperture with respect to focal length permits specification of aperture sizes using a value that is independent of camera size. Specification of an aperture as '23 mm' has no practical meaning unless we also know the size (focal length) of the camera. Specification of an aperture as 'f 4' has meaning for cameras of all sizes; we know that it is one-fourth of the focal length for any size camera.

The standard sequence of apertures is: f1, f1.4, f2, f2.8, f4, f5.6, f8, f11, f16, f22, f32, f64. This sequence is designed to change the amount of light by a factor of two as the f-stop is changed by one position. For example, a change from f2 to f2.8 halves the amount of light entering the camera; a change from f11 to f8 doubles the amount of light. A given lens, of course, is capable of using only a portion of the range of apertures mentioned above. Lenses for aerial cameras typically have rather wide fields of view. As a result, light reaching the focal plane from the edges of the field of view is typically dimmer than light reflected from object positioned near the center of the field of view. This effect creates a dark rim around the center of the aerial photograph—an effect known as vignetting. It is possible to employ an anti-vignetting filter, darker at the center and clearer at the periphery, which can be partially effective in evening brightnesses across the photography.

Shutter

The shutter controls the length of time that the film is exposed to light. The simplest shutters are often metal blades positioned between elements of the lens, forming 'intralens,' or between-the -lens,' shutters. An alternative form of shutter is the focal plane shutter, consisting of a metal or fabric curtain positioned just in front of the film, near the focal plane. The curtain is constructed with a number of slits; the choice of shutter speed by the operator selects the opening that produces the desired exposure. Although some aerial cameras use focal plane shutters, the-lens shutter is preferred for most aerial cameras. Between-the-lens shutter subjects the entire negative to illumination simultaneously and presents a clearly defined perspective that permits use of the image negative as the basis for precise measurements.

Film Magazine

The Film magazine (Fig. 4.1) is a light-tight container that holds the supply of film. The magazine usually includes a supply spool, holding perhaps several hundred feet of unexposed aerial film and a take-up spool to accept exposed film.

Lens Cone

The lens cone (Fig. 4.1) supports the lens and filters and holds them in their correct positions in relation to the film. The lens cone is usually detachable, to permit use of different lenses with the same camera body. The camera manufacturer carefully aligns the lens with the other components of the camera to assure geometric accuracy of photographs. Common focal lengths for typical aerial cameras are 150 mm (about 6 inch), 300 mm (about 12 inch) and 450 mm (about 18 inch).

Drive Mechanism

The drive mechanism advances the film after each exposure, using electric motors activated in co-ordination with the shutter and the motion of the plane. At the time of exposure, it is important that the film lie flat in the camera's focal plane. This function is performed by the platen, which for simple handheld cameras is a small, spring-mounted, metal plate positioned to hold the film flat at the instant of exposure. Because of the difficulty of holding large sheets of film flat, aerial cameras use special platens. A vacuum platen consists of a flat plate positioned at the focal plane; a vacuum pump draws air through small holes in the plate to hold the film flat and stationary during exposure. The vacuum sucks the film flat against the platen to prevent bending of the film or formation of bubbles of air as the film is positioned in the focal plane. The vacuum is released after exposure to allow the film to advance for the next exposure, then is applied again as the next frame is ready for exposure.

High-quality aerial cameras usually include a capability known as image motion compensation (or forward motion compensation), achieved by a mechanism that moves the film platen (or other components of the camera's optical system) during exposure at a speed and in a direction that compensates for the apparent motion of the image in the focal plane. As outlined in further section, high-resolution aerial films will have slower film speeds (i.e., will be less sensitive to light), so they will require slower shutter speeds, thus subjecting the image to blur when the aircraft is operated at relatively low altitudes. Image motion compensation permits the photographer to use a slower speed film than otherwise would be practical and therefore to acquire higher spatial resolution images at lower altitudes (where image motion is fastest) or at lower light levels than would otherwise be feasible.

KINDS OF AERIAL CAMERAS

Most civilian aerial photography has been acquired using metric cameras (sometimes called cartographic cameras) (Fig. 4.1). These are aerial cameras designed to provide high-quality images with a minimum of optical and geometric error. Metric cameras used for professional work have been calibrated at special laboratories operated by the manufacturer or by governmental agencies. During calibration, each camera is used to photograph a target image having features positioned with great accuracy. Then precise measurements are made of focal length, flatness of the focal plane and other variables. Such precise knowledge of the internal geometry of a camera permits photogrammetrists to make accurate measurements from photographs.

Other kinds of aerial cameras are less frequently used for routine photography, but may have uses for special applications. Reconnaissance cameras have been designed chiefly for military use. For such applications, geometric accuracy may be less important than the ability to take photographs at high air speed, at low altitude or under unfavourable light conditions. As a result, photographs from reconnaissance cameras do not have the geometric accuracy expected from those taken by metric cameras.

Strip cameras acquire images by moving film past a fixed slit that serves as a form of shutter (Fig. 4.6). The speed of film movement as it passes the slit is co-ordinated with the speed and altitude of the aircraft to provide proper exposure. The image is a long continuous strip of imagery without the individual frames formed by conventional cameras. Strip cameras are capable of acquiring high-quality images from planes flying at high speed and low altitudes—optical conditions that are so extreme that conventional cameras often cannot provide the fast shutter speeds necessary to acquire sharp images.

Panoramic cameras (Fig. 4.6) are designed to record a very wide field of view. Usually, a lens with a narrow field of view scans across a wide strip of land, so an image is formed by the side-to-side motion of the lens as the aircraft moves forward. Photographs from panoramic cameras show a long narrow strip of terrain that extends perpendicular to the flight track from horizon to horizon. Because of the forward motion of the aircraft during the side-to-side scan of the lens, panoramic photographs have serious geometric distortions that require correction before they can be used as the basis for measurements. Panoramic aerial photographs are useful because of the large areas they represent, but only the central portions are suitable for detailed interpretation because of the large variations in scale and detail present near the outside edges of the images.

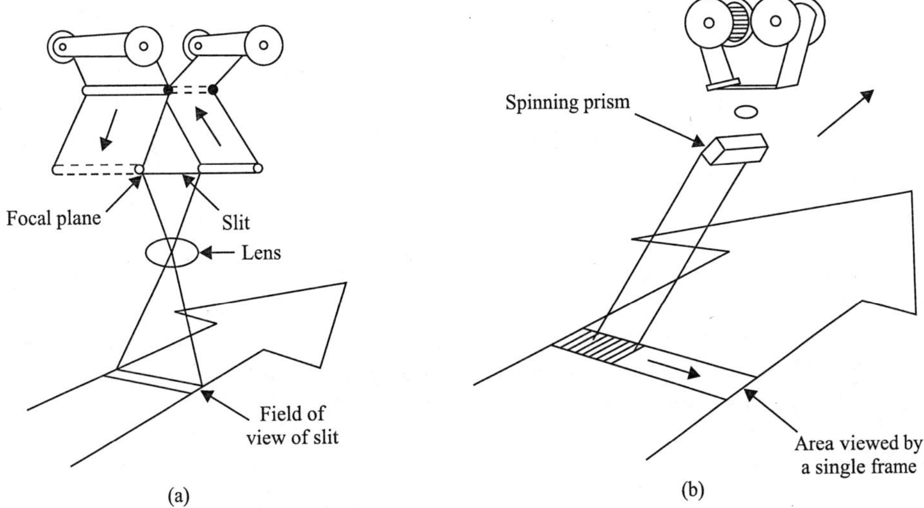

Fig. 4.6. (a) Strip camera and; and (b) panoramic camera.

BLACK-AND-WHITE AERIAL FILMS

Today the field of remote sensing encompasses a wide variety of sensors, both photographic and non-photographic. Yet we have only one practical medium for recording images on paper or film: the photographic emulsion. Therefore, even if we do not use a camera to record an image, we must still use photographic film to prepare film or paper copies of that image. Knowledge of the qualities and limitations of photographic film, therefore, is central to understanding the field of remote sensing.

In the late 1700s and early 1800s a number of amateur scientists experimented with light-sensitive (photosensitive) chemicals. For example, silver nitrate ($AgNO_3$), familiar to high school chemistry students, darkens when exposed to sunlight; therefore, a glass or metal plate coated with silver nitrate formed the basis for recording a crude image. Those areas on the plate where the light is brightest became dark; those where the light is dim remained light in tone.

Joseph Nicephone Niepce, a French chemist, is one of the many who experimented with such chemicals. He is often assigned credit for devising the first negative image. Niepce worked with Louis Daguerre, a French scientist and artist, to design a silver-coated metal plate treated with iodine vapour. Their invention was the first practical means of recording projected images.

Daguerrotypes, an early name for photographic images made using Daguerre's method, were used for many years, with many modifications. Many features of early photography differ greatly from modern equipment and practice and were clearly impractical for routine aerial photography. In the 1800s equipment was large, heavy and cumbersome. Exposure times were long, cameras required bright light and images were recorded on metal or glass plates, which were heavy, fragile and awkward. Nonetheless, many aerial photographs were taken in the early days of photography, mainly by using balloons or large kites as a means of elevating the camera. Of course, such photographs were primarily curiosities rather than scientific tools because of the difficulty of controlling the orientation of the camera. Furthermore, each photographer tended to have tailor-made equipment; photographers often prepared their own chemicals and used individually formulated emulsions. The lack of standardisation of equipment, materials and practice meant that even the fundamentals of photographic practice were as much an art as a science.

The more compact photographic equipment required for modern aerial photography was made possible by developments started by George Eastman, who invented roll film and improved and standardised methods of photographic processing. His invention of the Kodak camera and formation of the Eastman Kodak Company popularised the practice of photography by mass production of standardised photographic products. Widening the scope of photography greatly increased the number of people knowledgeable about photography, standardised photographic practice and decreased the cost of photographic materials. In brief, his work created the environment in which modern aerial survey could develop and grow into its present form.

Initially, photographic films were sensitive primarily to portions of the visible spectrum and could portray only those brightnesses in a single broad region of the spectrum. In contrast, modern photographic films can be designed to be sensitive to non-visible portions of the spectrum and can represent reflectances in much more specific spectral regions. Therefore, the photographer has a choice of films that can extend his or her reach beyond the visible spectrum.

Major Components

Aerial films have essentially the same structure as photographic films used in handheld cameras. The film base or support, is usually a thin (40 to 100 μm), flexible, transparent material that holds a light-sensitive coating. In the early days of photography, the support was often formed from metal or glass plates, but today such materials are inconvenient for everyday use. Modern films have bases of polyester film. These materials are useful because they can be fabricated into thin, lightweight, flexible strips that are strong enough to withstand the forceful motions of winding and unwinding as film is moved within the camera.

The base must be able to resist changes in size, caused by variation in temperature and humidity. Photogrammetrists measure distances on images so precisely that even small differences in image size due to shrinking or expanding of the base can introduce significant errors. Therefore, glass plates are still used for images that are to be used with some photogrammetric instruments because they are insensitive to variations in temperature and humidity.

The base is coated with a light-sensitive coating, the photographic emulsion (Fig. 4.7). Photosensitive coatings used in the early stages of photography were formed from silver nitrate (metallic silver dissolved in nitric acid). When a surface coated with silver nitrate is exposed to light, the silver nitrate darkens as the action of light changes it to metallic silver. The darkening effect increases as the light becomes more intense or as the length of exposure is increased. This effect provided a crude means of recording the image of a scene, but a number of practical problems (including the long exposures required to darken the coating) provided incentives to develop improved photosensitive coatings.

Modern emulsions consist of extremely small crystals of silver halide typically, silver bromide [95 per cent] and silver iodide [5 per cent] suspended in a gelatine matrix (possibly 5 μm thick). These crystals form the light-sensitive portion of modern films, just as silver nitrate was the light-sensitive agent in the early days of photography. Although the gelatine that holds the grains is ostensibly a mundane substance, it possesses several important characteristics. Silver halide crystals are insoluble and have other physical characteristics that prevent them from adhering directly to the base. Gelatine holds the crystals in suspension, permitting the manufacturer to spread them evenly on the base. Furthermore, gelatine is transparent, porous (to allow photographic chemicals to contact the crystals) and absorbs halogen gases released when light strikes the emulsion.

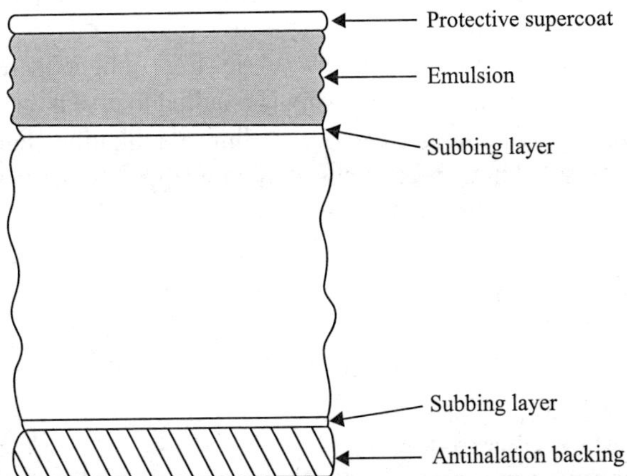

Fig. 4.7. Schematic cross-sectional view of black-and-white photographic film.

Physical characteristics of the silver halide crystals assume some importance. They are extremely small, irregular in shape, with many sharp edges–shapes that favour interception of photons that pass into the emulsion. The finer the size of the grains, the finer the detail that can be recorded. Coarser grains can record less detail, but produce a film with greater sensitivity to light. Thus the spatial resolution of a film is inversely related to its speed; as we increase the size of crystals to improve the film's sensitivity to light, the finest level of detail that the emulsion can record becomes coarser. Alternatively, if we design a film with very fine grains to record fine detail, the emulsion exhibits decreased sensitivity–we must have brighter light or use longer exposures.

Recent research by the Eastman Kodak Company has produced film emulsions with grains that are flat in shape. These new grains have essentially the same volume as those in older emulsions, but their surface area is greatly increased. The flat grains, oriented parallel to the film surface, expose large surface areas to the light, thereby increasing the speed of the film without decreasing the resolution of the film. At present that type of film has been developed and marketed for popular photography (colour prints only) rather than for aerial survey.

The film emulsion is coated with a thin layer of clear gelatine–the protective supercoat–designed to shield the emulsion from scratches during handling. Despite the presence of the supercoat, the emulsion is still vulnerable to damage from dust and from moisture and oil from handling with bare hands. As a result, analysts and interpreters should always wear cotton gloves when handling film or should protect film with transparent plastic sleeves.

Below the emulsion is a subbing layer, designed to ensure that the emulsion adheres to the base. On the reverse side of the base is an antihalation backing. This backing absorbs light that passes through the emulsion and the base, to prevent reflection back to the emulsion. In the absence of such a backing, the images of bright objects will be surrounded by halos caused by these reflections. The backing also acts as an anticurl agent, to counteract the curling effect of the emulsion that coats the upper side of the film.

When the shutter opens, it allows light to enter and strike the emulsion. The silver halide crystals are so small that even a small area of the film contains many thousands of crystals. When light strikes a crystal, it changes a very small portion of the crystal (perhaps only a single molecule) to metallic silver. The more intense the light striking a portion of the film, the greater the number of crystals affected. Thus the pattern of crystals influenced by light forms a record of patterns of light reflected from the scene. If it were possible to examine the exposed film without again subjecting it to the effects of light, it would appear no different than before exposure because of the extremely subtle effect of light upon the emulsion. At this point the image is recorded only as a latent image; processing is required to reveal this image.

Development is the process of bathing the exposed film in a alkaline chemical, the developer, that reduces the silver halide grains that have been exposed to light (Fig. 4.8). Crystals in the latent image that were altered minimally are now completely changed to metallic silver in a process that in effect amplifies the pattern recorded by the latent image. In the latent image only a tiny portion of each grain has been altered by the effect of light; after development, each grain exposed to light is changed entirely to metallic silver. The developer acts most rapidly on those grains that have been exposed to light, so those areas that were exposed to the most intense light have the greatest density of metallic silver in the final image.

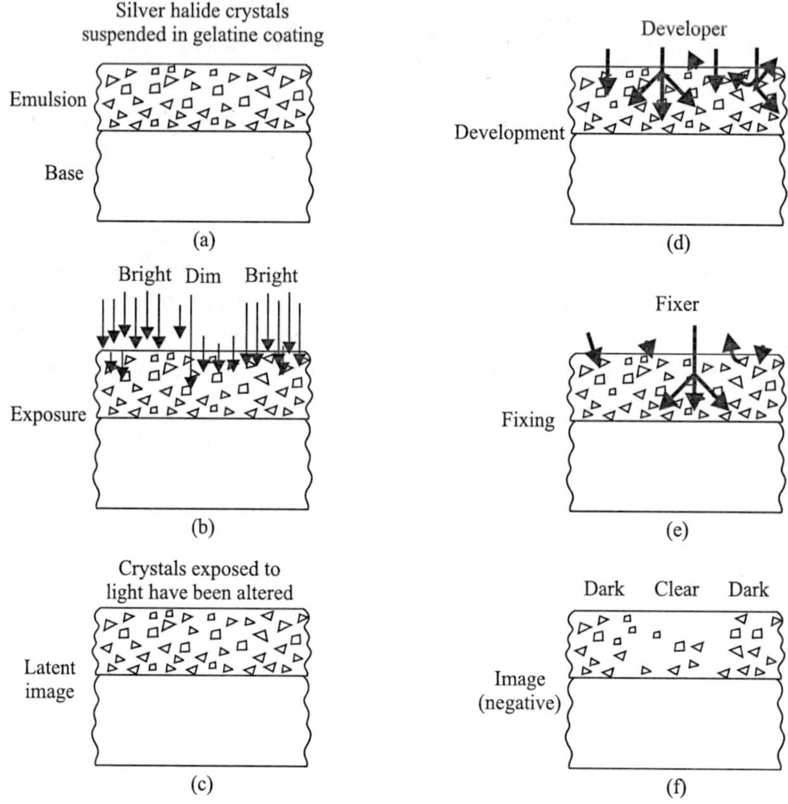

Fig. 4.8. Schematic representation of processing of black-and-white photographic film. (a) Basic structure of the film as seen in cross section; photosensitive chemicals are suspended in a gelatine coating on the film base; (b) During exposure, light strikes the emulsion at varied intensities, depending upon the brightness levels in the scene; (c) Light creates a chemical reaction in the photosensitive chemicals that changes only a few molecules of each grain, creating the latent image; (d) During development, the emulsion is bathed in an alkaline chemical that changes to metallic silver all grains modified in step; (e) Not shown here is the addition of an acidic chemical, the stop bath, that stops the action of the developer; (f) During fixing, unexposed grains are removed from the emulsion, leaving only those that had been exposed to light in (b); and (g) The final image is a negative; those areas exposed to the most intense light in (b) are darkest; those exposed to dim light are clear.

Application of an acidic stop bath allows exact control of the time the film is in contact with the developer by counteracting the chemical effect of the alkaline developer. Next a fixer is applied to dissolve, then remove, unexposed silver halide grains. If the fixer were not used, these unexposed grains would darken when the film was next exposed to daylight.

After development and fixing, the resulting image is a negative representation of the scene, because those areas that were brightest in the scene are represented by the greatest concentrations of metallic silver, which appears dark on the processed image. Thus, in the negative, brightnesses are reversed from their original values in the scene.

Film speed is a measure of the sensitivity of an emulsion to light. A fast film requires relatively low intensity of light for proper exposure; a slow film requires more light, meaning that the aperture must be opened wider or that a longer exposure time must be used. As mentioned previously, film speed is directly related to grain size and is inversely related to the ability of the film to record fine detail. Amateur photographers are familiar with the Deutsches Institut fur Normung (DIN) and American Standards Association (ASA) ratings for assessing the speeds of films for handheld cameras. The analogous scales for aerial films include the aerial film speed (AFS) and the aerial exposure index (AEI).

Contrast indicates the range of gray tones recorded by a film. High contrast means that the film records the scene largely in blacks and whites, with few intermediate gray tones. Low contrast indicates a representation largely in grays, with few really dark or really bright tones. Often the interpreter needs information about the intermediate brightnesses in a film, so for aerial photography low-contrast representation may be desirable. Fine-grained emulsions tend to have low contrast, so slower films tend to have higher spatial resolution and lower contrast than do the coarser-grained fast films. Emulsions on photographic papers typically have higher contrast than emulsions films, so interpreters often prefer to use film transparencies if they are available.

Spectral sensitivity records the spectral region to which a film is sensitive (Fig. 4.9). The spectral sensitivity curve for Kodak Tri-X Aerographic film 2403 shows typical features of black-and-white films (Fig. 4.9a). It is sensitive throughout the visible spectrum, but is also sensitive to ultraviolet radiation. Because of the scattering of these shorter (ultraviolet and blue) wavelengths, filters are often used with black-and-white aerial films to screen out blue light (Fig. 4.10).

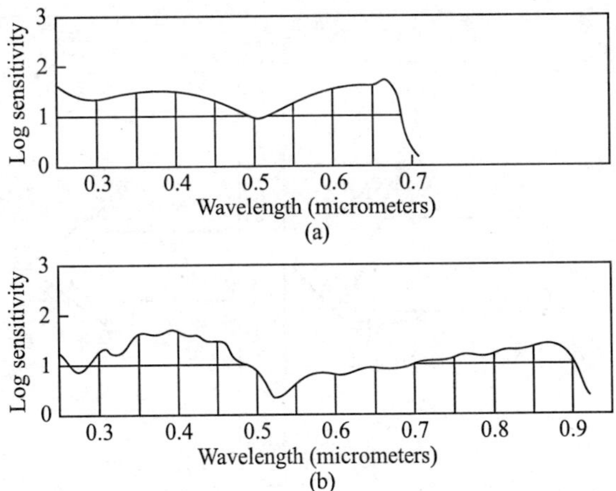

Fig. 4.9. Spectral sensitivities of two photographic films: (a) Black-and-white panchromatic film (Kodak Tri-X Aerographic film 2403); and (b) Black-and-white infrared film (Kodak Infrared Aerographic film 2424).

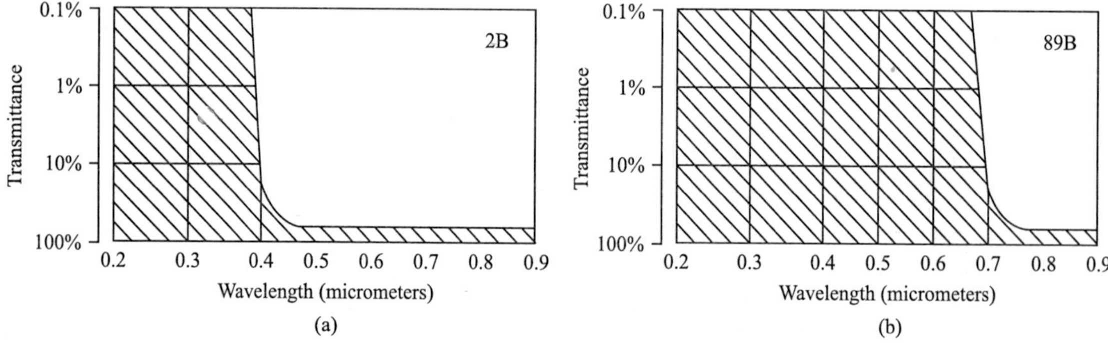

Fig. 4.10. Transmission curves for two filters: (a) Pale yellow filter (Kodak filter 2B) to prevent ultraviolet light from reaching the film; it is frequently used with panchromatic film; and (b) Kodak 89B filter used to exclude visible light, used with black-and-white infrared film (Shaded portions of the diagrams signify that the filter is blocking transmission of radiation at specified wavelengths).

This film presents a black-and-white representation of a scene (Fig. 4.10a) that is essentially in accord with our view of the scene as we see it directly with our own eyes. This is because the Tri-X film is an example of a panchromatic film, an emulsion that is sensitive to radiation throughout the visible spectrum, much the same as the human visual system is sensitive throughout the visible spectrum. The term orthochromatic designates films with preferred sensitively in the blue and green, usually with peak sensitivety in the green

Figure 4.9 also shows the spectral sensitivity curve for Kodak infrared Aerographic Film 2424, a black-and-white infrared film. Note that its sensitivity extends well beyond the visible into the infrared portion of the spectrum. Usually it is desirable to exclude visible radiation, so this film is often used with a deep red filter that blocks visible radiation, but allows infrared radiation to pass (Fig. 4.10). An image recorded by black-and-white infrared film (Fig. 4.11) is quite different from its representation in the visible spectrum. For example, living vegetation is many times brighter in the near infrared portion of the spectrum that it is in the visible portion, so vegetated areas appear bright white on the black-and-white infrared image.

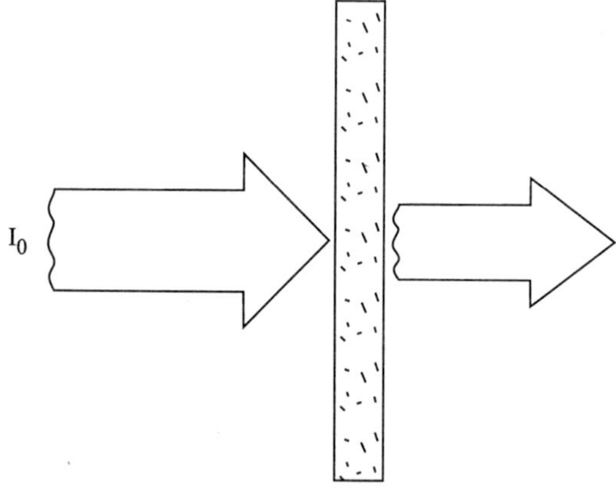

Fig. 4.11. Measurement of opacity.

Characteristic Curve

If we examine a negative after development and fixing, we find a pattern of dark and light related to the patterns of metallic silver formed in the processed film. Where the original scene was bright, the negative now has large amounts of silver, which create the dark areas. Where the original scene was dark, the film is clear, due to the absence of metallic silver.

We can see intermediate shades of brightness because the crystals in the emulsion are much smaller that the human eye can resolve. The areas that we perceive as shades of gray are actually variations in the abundance of the tiny grains of silver in the processed film. Thus each crystal is either present (black) or absent (clear), with shades of gray formed by variations in the abundance of crystals, which occur in proportion to the brightness of the original scene.

If we shine a light of intensity I_0 through a very small area of the negative (perhaps a fraction of a mm in diameter), the brightness of the light measured on the other side (I) is a measure of darkness of that region of the film (Fig. 4.11). I, of course, is less than I_0. The ratio is defined as the opacity.

$$I_0/I \qquad \text{... (4.2)}$$

The darkness of the film is of interest because it is related to the brightness of the original scene. By convention, the darkness of the film is expressed as density, defined as the $\log_{10}$ of opacity (Table 4.1).

Table 4.1. Transmission, opacity and density.

Percentage of light transmitted	*Opacity*	*Density (log_{10} opacity)*	*Example*
100	100/100 = 1	0	Clear
80	100/80 = 1.25	0.09	
50	100/50 = 2	0.3	
20	100/20 = 5	0.7	
10	100/10 = 10	1.0	
5	100/5 = 20	1.3	
1	100/1 = 100	2.	Dark sunglasses
0.1	100/0.1 = 1000	3.	
0.01	100/0.01 = 10000	4.	Very dark
0.0	100/0.0 = ∞	–	Opaque

The effect of light upon the emulsion of a film is determined by the product of intensity (i) ('brightness,' equivalent to irradiance) and time (t). For a given density, the product i × t has a constant value D, the exposure:

$$E = i \times t \qquad \text{... (4.3)}$$

In everyday photography we use this relationship whenever we compensate for use of a fast shutter speed by opening the aperture to allow more light to enter. The characteristic curve expresses the relationship between brightness in the scene and density on the film (Fig. 4.12). Or, more formally, it is a plot of the relationship between the density of a negative and the $\log_{10}$ of exposure. A specific emulsion will be characterised by a set of characteristic curves that differ in slope as development times vary. For present purposes, it is sufficient to consider only a single curve as an example.

The S-shape is typical of the characteristic curve. The lower part (the toe) is curved; the central part forms a straight line (the straight-line segment) and the upper portion (the shoulder) is curved. For scientific purposes, the straight-line segment is of interest; for a range of exposures, there is a consistent relationship between exposure and density. If exposure is increased by a certain amount, then the relationship depicted by the characteristic curve permits prediction of the corresponding increase in image density. The predictability of this relationship permits scientists to define consistent relationship between the darkness in a photograph and the brightness in the original scene. Given suitable controls, an image scientist can use measurements from the photography to learn about brightnesses in the scene. Note that the lowest point of the curve does not reach the bottom of the graph; this difference is the fog level–a very small amount of density caused by the development process itself, unrelated to exposure. At the other extreme, the shoulder of the characteristic curve, the curved shape indicates that further increases in exposure will not produce a corresponding increase in density. This effect is referred to as saturation–the exposure is so extreme that the density will no longer have a predictable association with exposure.

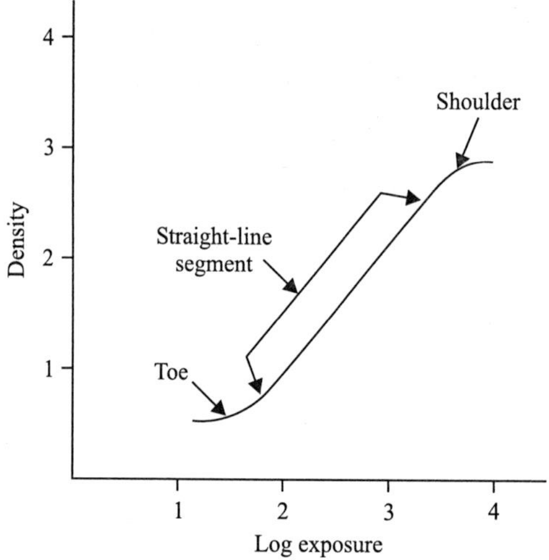

Fig. 4.12. Characteristic curve of a photographic emulsion.

Examine Fig. 4.13; here two characteristic curves illustrate how differences in the slope of the straight-line segment translate a given brightness range (BR) into different density ranges (DR) in the final processed images. If the slope of the straight-line segment is steep, then a small range in exposure translates into a big range in density. Such an image has high contrast, meaning that the image displays a large range in brightness. If the slope is shallow (Fig. 4.13b), a given range in scene brightness is translated into a smaller range in image brightness–a low contrast image.

Note that the toe and the shoulder of the curve do not depict consistent relationships between exposure and density. This means that for very high and very low exposures, the film will not produce the predictable densities that it will for exposures in the straight-line segment. That is, the film is no longer a scientific tool for portraying scene brightness because we cannot measure a density and then relate the density to the brightness of the original scene. Often, professional photographers will use the toe or the shoulder to create artistic effects in photographs, but scientists always avoid use of image measurements that may be based on very high or very low image densities–they have an unknown relationship to brightnesses in the scene they portray.

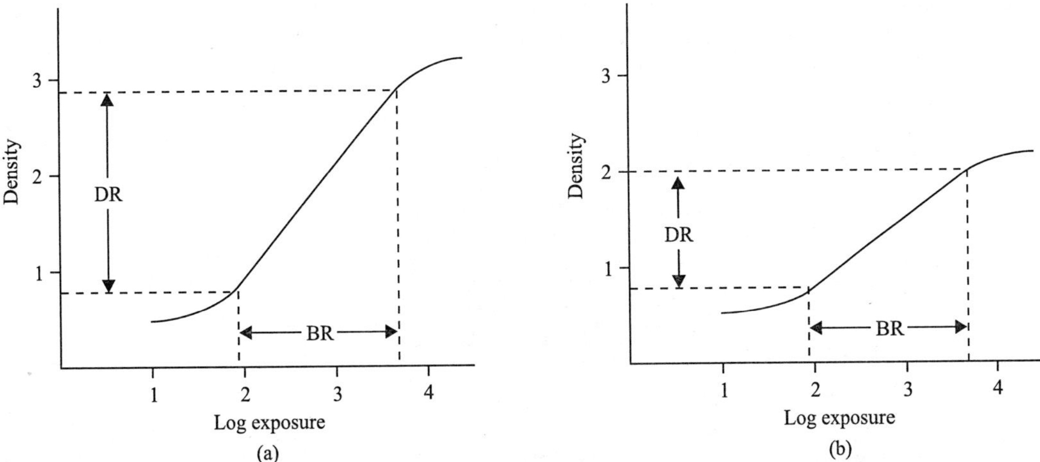

Fig. 4.13. Examples of characteristic curves.

Because photographic films are used to record images acquired by non-photographic sensors, knowledge of the characteristic curve is especially important in the field of remote sensing. Such sensors often record a large range of brightnesses—a range so large that it may exceed the capability of the film to record it. If so, the photographic record of the image will inevitably be inaccurate as a record of scene brightness. The very dark areas, the very bright areas or perhaps both will be represented in non-linear portions of the characteristic curve and the image will show only a small portion of the brightnesses present in the scene. It is partially for this reason that digital image data, which can represent very large ranges of brightnesses, often offer advantages in comparison with photographic images for some kinds of analyses.

COLOUR REVERSAL FILMS

Many of the colour films used in remote sensing are reversal films, similar to those used in handheld cameras for colour slides. Their basic elements are similar to those of black-and-white photographic film, except that they are coated with three separate emulsions, each sensitive to one of the three additive primaries (Fig. 4.14). The protective supercoat, the backing and the subbing layer are present and between the several emulsions are spacer layers of gelatine to prevent mixing of adjacent emulsions. The layer between the uppermost blue-sensitive emulsion and the middle (green-sensitive) emulsion is treated to act as a yellow filter to prevent blue light from passing through the upper layers to expose the lower emulsions. This filter is necessary because of the difficulty of manufacturing emulsions sensitive to red and green light without also sensitising them to blue light.

Upon exposure, blue light exposes the blue layer, passes through the blue layer, but is prevented from exposing the other two layers by the yellow filter (Fig. 4.15). Green light passes through the blue layer and exposes the green-sensitive emulsion. Red light passes through the upper emulsion to expose only the lower, red-sensitive layer. After processing, all areas not exposed to blue light on the blue-sensitive emulsion are represented by a yellow dye, while those areas exposed to blue are left clear. Areas exposed by green light on the green-sensitive emulsion are left clear; other areas are shown in magenta dye. Areas on the red-sensitive layer not exposed to red light are represented by cyan dye; images of red objects are clear on this emulsion. Thus each emulsion is sensitive to one of the additive primaries; after processing, each emulsion contains one of the subtractive primaries. The strategy of dying all areas not exposed in each separate emulsion differs fundamentally from the process used for the black-and-white films described earlier. Here there is no negative image; the dyes in the film processed combine to form a positive image in which brightness in the image corresponds (approximately) to brightness in the original scene.

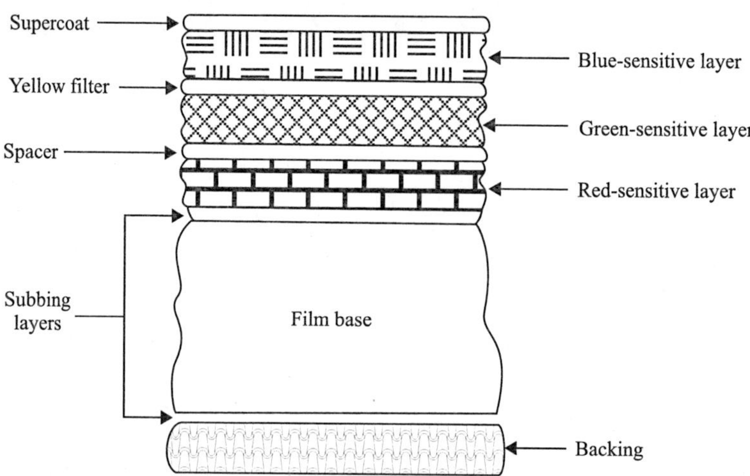

Fig. 4.14. Idealised cross-sectional diagram of colour reversal film.
(*Note*: Due to use of single colour, red, green and blue are depicted in different patterns for differentiation).

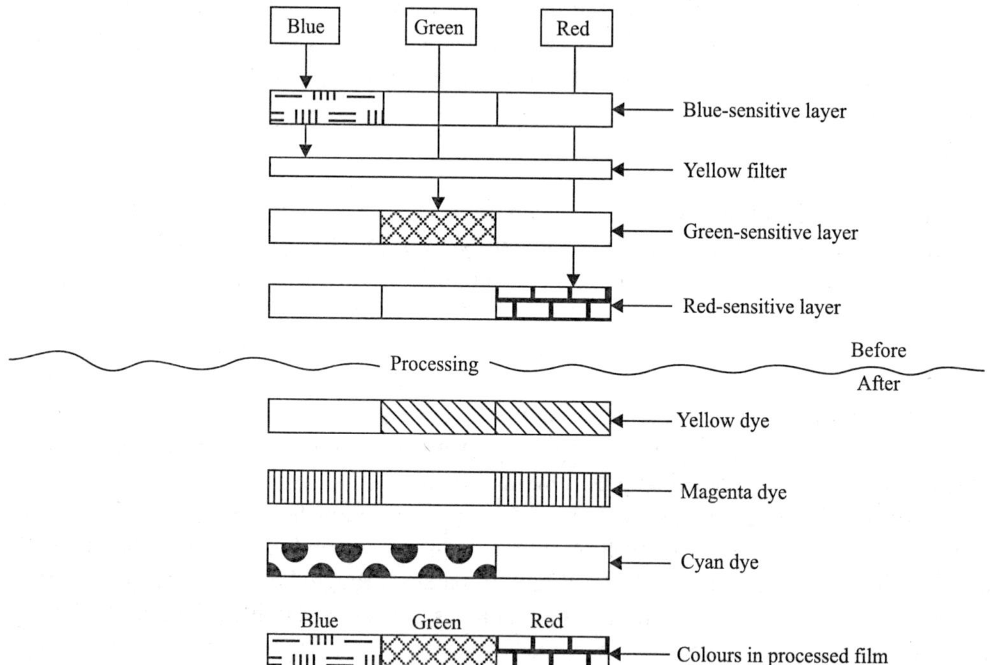

Fig. 4.15. Representation of colour reversal film.
(*Note*: Due to use of single colour, red, green and blue are depicted in different patterns for differentiation).

When the processed film is viewed as a transparency against a light source, the magenta and cyan dyes present in those areas exposed to blue light combine to form a blue colour. Likewise yellow and cyan combine to represent green and yellow and magenta combine to form red (Fig. 4.15). This process is the same as that used for production of the 35-mm colour or slides that are familiar to many readers, so it should be easy to visualise the result of this process, even though the explanation shown in Fig. 4.15 may seem rather abstract.

COLOUR INFRARED FILMS

Colour infrared (CIR) films are based upon the same principles as colour reversal films except for differences in the sensitivity of the emulsions and conventions in representation of colours. This film is used with a yellow filter to prevent blue light from entering the camera. The blue-sensitive layer is replaced by an emulsion sensitive to a portion of the near infrared region (Fig. 4.16). After developing, representation of colours in the scene is shifted one position in the spectrum, so that green in the scene appears as blue on the image, red appears as green and objects reflecting strongly in the near infrared are depicted on red. The comparison with normal colour films can be represented schematically as follows:

Object in the scene reflects:	Blue	Green	Red	Infrared
Colour reversal film represents the object as:	Blue	Green	Red	–
Colour infrared film represents the object as:	–	Blue	Green	Red

Most objects, of course, reflect in several portions of the spectrum, so the CIR image shows a variety of colour derived from the varied reflectances in the scene. CIR film is designed in a manner analogous to, but not identical to, that of colour reversal film (Fig. 4.17). A yellow filter over the camera lens excludes all blue light. Green light exposes the green-sensitive layer red light exposes the red-sensitive layer and IR radiation exposes the IR-sensitive layer. After processing, areas not exposed to the green light are coloured in yellow dye. Areas not exposed to red light are coloured magenta. And areas not exposed to IR radiation are represented as cyan. In the final transparency, cyan and magenta combine to represent green areas as blue, cyan and yellow combine to represent red areas as green and yellow and magenta combine to form the red colour that represents objects that reflect strongly in the near infrared.

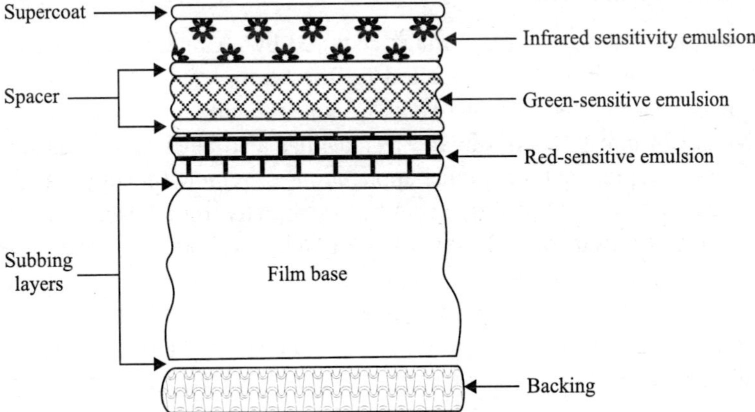

Fig. 4.16. Idealised cross-sectional diagram of colour infrared film.
(*Note*: Due to use of single colour, red, green and blue are depicted in different patterns for differentiation).

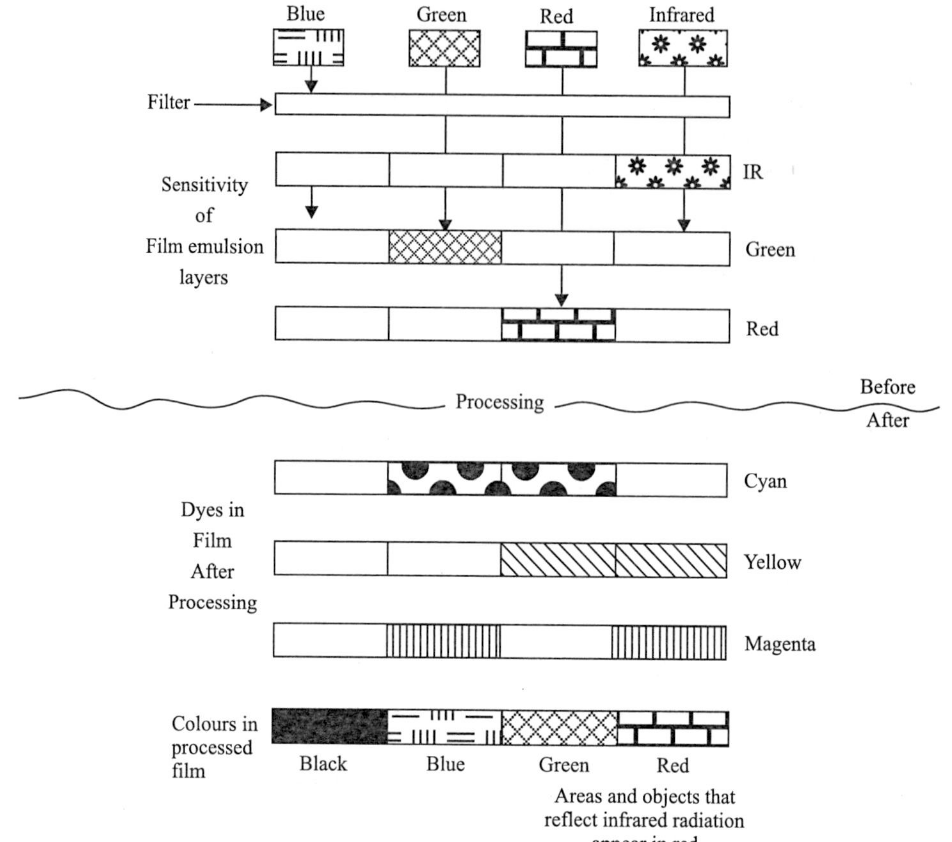

Fig. 4.17. Representation of colour infrared film.
(*Note*: Due to use of single colour, red, green and blue are depicted in different patterns for differentiation).

FILM FORMAT AND ANNOTATION

The term format designates the size of the image acquired by a camera. Mapping cameras generally produce a square image, with a size controlled by the width of the film. Common formats are 23 cm × 23 cm (approximately 9 inch × 9 inch) and 5.7 cm × 5.7 cm (approximately 2.5 inch × 2.5 inch). Film 35 mm in width (24 mm × 36 mm image format) has also been used for specialised purposes, although generally it is not practical for routine applications of remote sensing. The 23-cm format is a standard for most cartographic cameras; paper prints made directly from the negative (contact prints) are among the most frequently used form of aerial photography. Although enlargements of the original negative can be made to any size desired, the 23-cm format is convenient for storage and handling and because the prints are made directly from the negative without enlargement, the image retains maximum detail and sharpness. In some instances, paper prints are not made and the film is examined simply as a strip of film–a positive transparency–wound on large spools and viewed against an illuminated background. Because emulsion of transparencies typically represent a greater range of image tones than do paper prints, positive transparencies are often preferred for detailed interpretations and especially for colour and colour infrared films.

Most aerial photographs carry some form of annotation, markings that identify the photographs and provide details concerning their acquisition. Typically, aerial photographs are annotated in the forward edge of the photograph. Annotation consists of a series of letters and numerals that can vary in meaning from one aerial survey firm to the next, but usually they include the date of the photography, a series of letters and number that identify each project and the film roll number. Usually the last three digits specify the frame number, which shows the sequence in which photographs were taken. Other annotations, such as image scale, may also be included. In some instances the information may be recorded directly by the camera itself as the image is acquired; in other instances it may be added later as the film is processed and prepared for dissemination. The most sophisticated cameras may record on each frame information such as date, project identifier, focal length, time, image of a bubble level to indicate degree of tilt and locational co-ordinates provided by onboard global positioning systems.

GEOMETRY OF THE VERTICAL AERIAL PHOTOGRAPH

Aerial photographs can be classified according to the orientation of the camera in relation to the ground at the time of exposure (Fig. 4.18). Oblique aerial photographs have been acquired by cameras oriented toward the side of the aircraft. High oblique photographs (Fig. 4.18a) show the horizon; low oblique photographs (Fig. 4.18b) are taken with the camera aimed more directly toward the ground surface and do not show the horizon. Oblique photographs have the advantage of showing very large areas in a single image. Often those features in the foreground are easily recognised, as the view in an oblique photograph may resemble that from a tall building or mountain top. However, oblique photographs are not widely used, primarily because the drastic changes in scale that occur from foreground to back ground prevent convenient measurement of distances, areas and elevations.

Vertical photographs are acquired by a camera aimed directly at the ground surface from above (Fig. 4.18c). Although objects and features are often difficult to recognise from their representations on vertical photographs, the map-like view of the earth and the predictable geometric properties of vertical photographs provide practical advantages. It should be noted that few, if any, aerial photographs are truly vertical; most have some small degree of tilt due to aircraft motion and other factors. The term vertical photograph is commonly used to designate aerial photographs that are within a few degrees of a corresponding (hypothetical) truly vertical photograph.

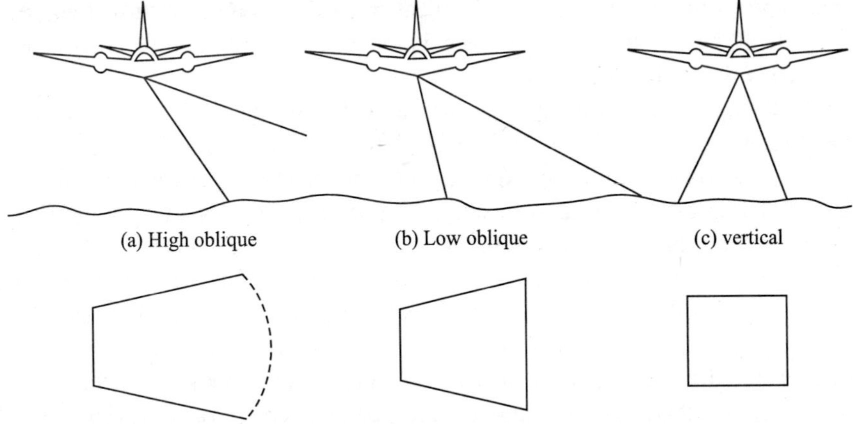

Fig. 4.18. Oblique and vertical aerial photographs.

Because the geometric properties of vertical and nearly vertical aerial photographs are well understood and can be applied to many practical problems, they form the basis for making accurate measurement using aerial photographs. The science of making accurate measurements from aerial photographs (or from any photograph) is known as photogrammetry. The following paragraphs outline some of the most basic elements of introductory photogrammetry. Aerial cameras are manufactured to include adjustable index marks attached rigidly to the camera so that the positions of the index marks are recorded on the photograph during exposure. These fiducial marks (usually four or eight in number) appear as silhouettes at the edges and/or corners of the photograph (Fig. 4.19). Lines that connect opposite pairs of fiducial marks intersect to identify the principal point, the optical center of the image. The ground nadir is defined as the point on the ground vertically beneath the center of the camera lens at the time the photography was taken (Fig 4.20). The photographic nadir is defined by the intersection with the photograph of the vertical line that intersects the ground nadir and the center of the lens (i.e., the image of the ground nadir).

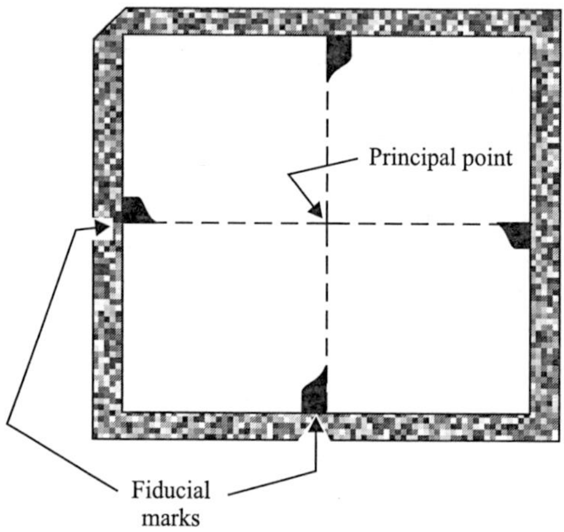

Fig. 4.19. Fiducial marks and principal point.

The isocenter can be defined informally as the focus of tilt. Imagine a truly vertical photograph that was taken at the same instant as the real, almost-vertical, image. The almost-vertical image would intersect with the (hypothetical) perfect image along a line that would form a 'hinge', the isocenter is a point on this hinge. On a truly vertical photograph, the isocenter, the principal point and the photographic nadir coincide. The most important positional or geometric, errors in the vertical aerial photograph can be summarised as follows.

1. Optical distortions are errors caused by an inferior camera lens, camera malfunction or similar problems. These distortions are probably of minor significance in most modern photography flown by professional aerial survey firms.
2. Tilt is caused by displacement of the focal plane from a truly horizontal position by aircraft motion (Fig. 4.20). The focus of tilt, the isocenter, is located at or near the principal point. Image areas on the upper side of the tilt are displaced further away from the ground than is the isocenter; these areas are therefore depicted at scales smaller than the nominal scale. Image areas on the lower side of the tilt are displaced down; these areas are depicted at scales larger than the nominal scale. Therefore, because all photographs have some degree of tilt, measurements confined to

one portion of the image run the risk of including systematic error caused by tilt (i.e., measurements may be consistently too large or too small). To avoid this effect, it is a good practice to select distances used for scale measurements as lines that pass close to the principal point; then errors caused by the upward tilt compensate for errors caused by the downward tilt. The resulting value for image scale is not, of course, precisely accurate for either portion of the image, but it will not include the large errors that can arise in areas located further from the principal point.

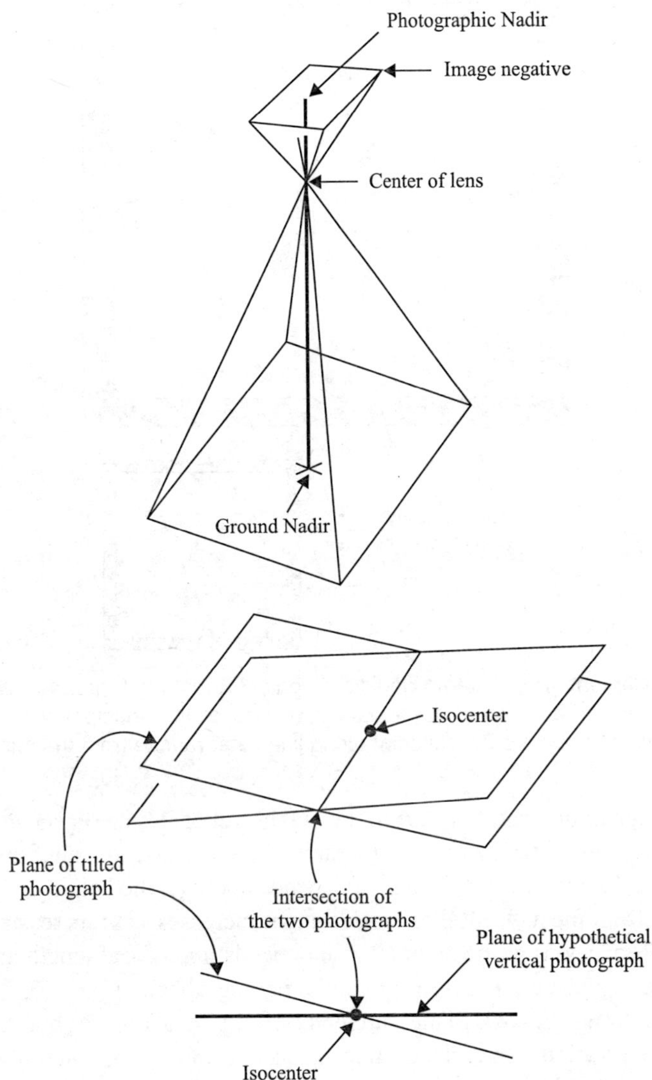

Fig. 4.20. Schematic representation of terms to describe geometry of vertical aerial photographs.

Because of routine use of high-quality cameras and careful inspection of photography to monitor photo quality, today the most important source of positional error in vertical aerial photography is probably relief displacement (Fig. 4.21). Objects positioned directly beneath the center of the camera lens will be photographed so that only the top of the object is visible (e.g., object A in Fig. 4.21). All other objects are positioned such that both their tops and their sides are visible from the position of the lens. That is, these objects appear to lean outward from the central perspective of the camera lens (e.g., see objects A in Fig. 4.21). Correct planimetric positioning of these features would represent only the top view, yet the photograph shows both the top and sides of the object. For tall features, it is intuitively clear that the base and the top cannot both be in their correct planimetric positions.

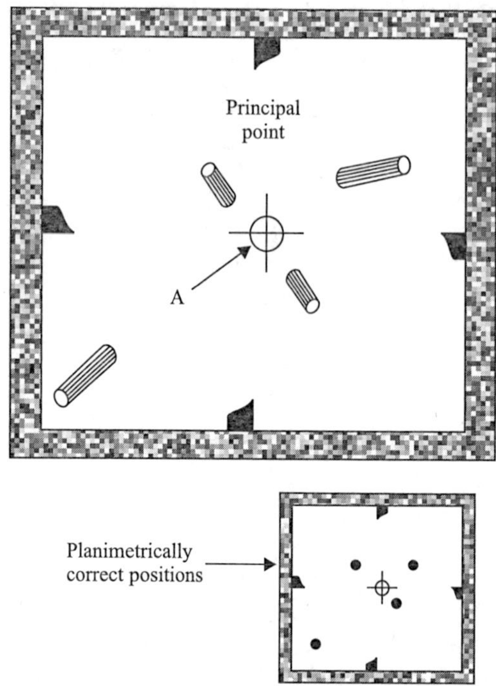

Fig. 4.21. Relief displacement. The diagram depicts a vertical aerial photograph of a level terrain with five towers of equal height located at different positions with respect to the principal point. Images of the tops of towers are displaced away from the principal point along lines that radiate from the nadir, as discussed in the text.

This difference in apparent location is due to the height (relief) of the object and forms an important source of positional error in vertical aerial photographs. The direction of relief displacement is always radial from the nadir; the amount of displacement depends upon: (i) the height of the object; and (ii) the distance of the object from the nadir. Relief displacement increases with increasing heights of features and with increasing distances from the nadir (It also depends upon focal length and flight altitude, but these may be regarded as constant for a few sequential photographs).

Relief displacement forms the basis of measurements of heights of objects, but its greatest significance is its role as a source of positional error. Uneven terrain can create significant relief displacement, so all measurements made directly from uncorrected aerial photographs are suspect.

COVERAGE BY MULTIPLE PHOTOGRAPHS

Pilots normally acquire vertical aerial photographs by flying a series of parallel flight lines that together build up complete coverage of a specific region. Each flight line consists of individual frames, usually numbered in sequence (Fig. 4.22). Often the camera operator can view the area to be photographed through a viewfinder attached to the camera or through a telescope-like instrument that observes the ground area below the plane. With the aid of these devices, the operator can manually trigger the shutter as aircraft motion brings predesignated landmarks into the field of view or can set controls to automatically acquire photographs at intervals tailored to provide the desired coverage.

Individual frames form ordered strips, as shown in (Fig. 4.22a). If the plane's course is deflected by a cross-wind, the positions of ground areas shown by successive photographs form the pattern shown in (Fig. 4.22b), known as drift. Crab (Fig. 4.22c) is caused by correction of the flight path to compensate for drift without a change in the orientation of the camera.

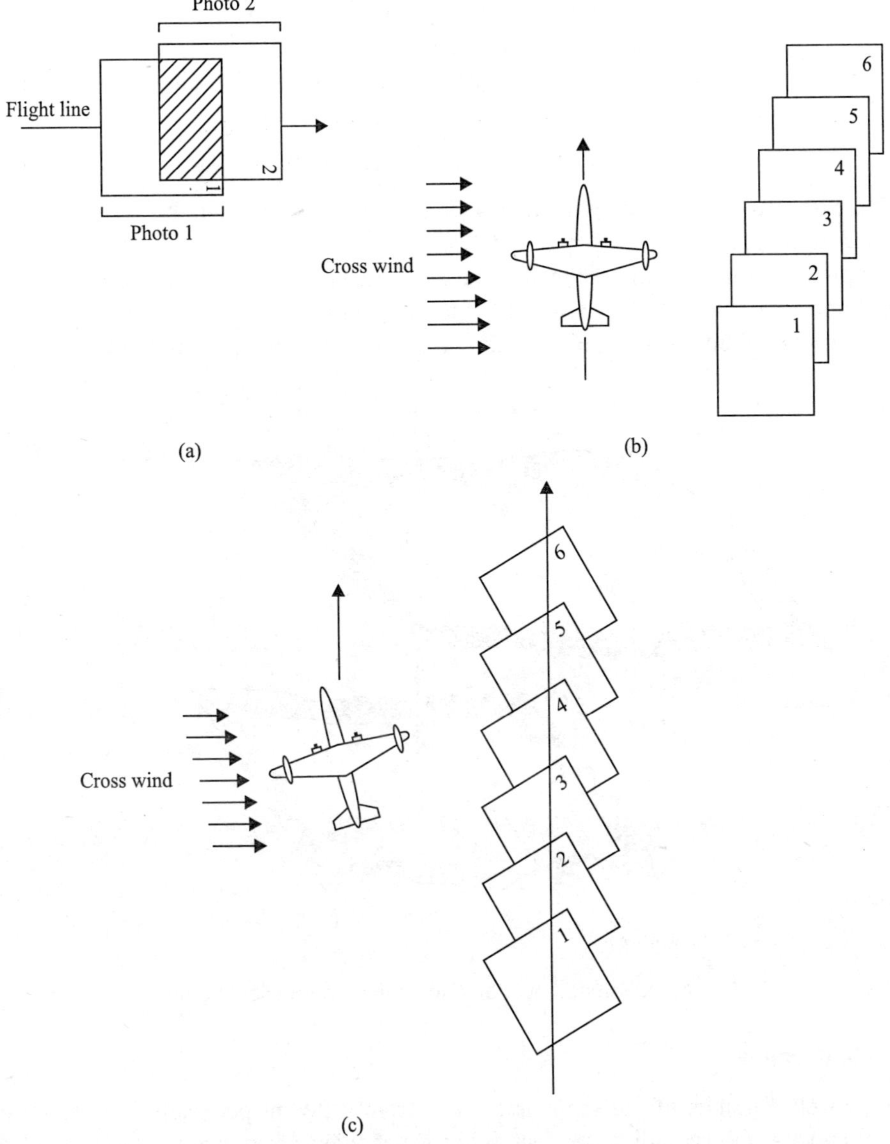

Fig. 4.22. Aerial photographic coverage: (a) forward overlap; (b) drift and; and (c) crab.

Usually flight plans call for a certain amount of forward overlap (Fig. 4.23), duplicate coverage by successive frames in a flight line, usually by about 50 to 60 per cent of each frame. If forward overlap is 50 per cent or more, then the image of the principal point of one photograph is visible on the next photograph in the flight line. These are known as conjugate principal points (Fig. 4.23). When it is necessary to photograph large areas, coverage is built up by means of several parallel strips of photography; each strip is called a flight line. Sidelap between adjacent flight lines may vary from about 5 to 15 per cent, in an effort to prevent gaps in coverage of adjacent flight lines.

However, as pilots and other crew members collect complete photographic coverage of a region, there may still be gaps (known as holidays) in coverage due to equipment malfunction, navigation errors, cloud cover or other problems. Sometimes photography flown later to cover holidays differs noticeably from adjacent images with respect to sun angle, vegetative cover and other qualities. For planning flight lines, the number of photographs required for each line can be estimated using the relationship:

$$\text{Number of photos} = \frac{\text{Length of flight line}}{(\text{gd of photo}) \times (1 - \text{overlap})} \qquad \text{... (4.4)}$$

where gd is the ground distance represented on a single frame, measured in the same units as the length of the planned flight line.

For example, if a flight line is planned to be 33 miles in length, each photograph is planned to represent 3.4 miles on a side and forward overlap is to be 0.60,

then $33/[3.4 \times (1 - 0.60)] = 33/(1.36) = 24.26$ or about 25 photographs are required.

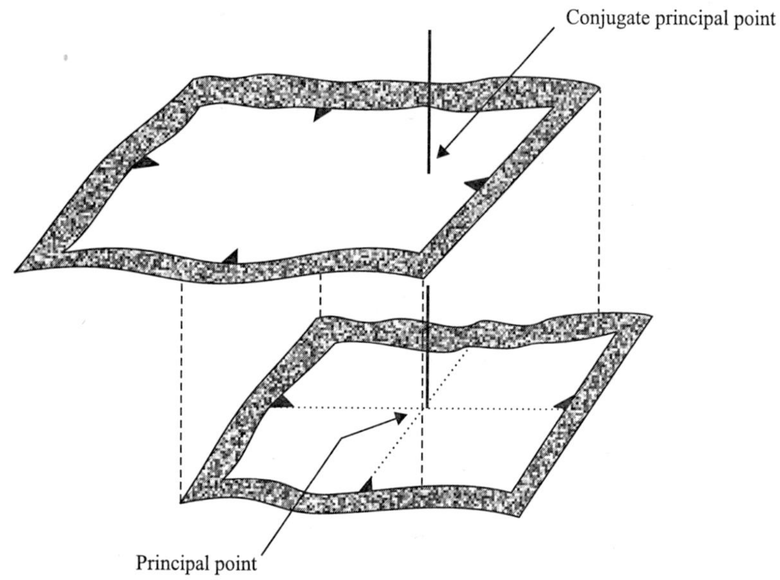

Fig. 4.23. Forward overlap and conjugate principal points.

Stereoscopic Parallax

If we have two photographs of the same area taken from different perspectives (i.e., from different camera positions), we observe a displacement of images of objects from one image to the other. You can observe this effect now by simple observation of nearby objects. Look up from this book at the objects near you. Close one eye, then open it and close the other. As you do this you observe a change in the appearance of objects from one eye to the next. Nearby objects are slightly different in appearance because one eye tends to see, for example, only the front of an object, whereas the other, because of its position (about 2.5 inch) from the other, sees the front and some of the side of the same object. This difference in appearances of objects due to change in perspective is known as stereoscopic parallax. The amount of parallax decreases as objects increase in distance from the observer. If you repeat the experiment looking out the window at a landscape you can confirm this effect by noting that distant objects display little or no observable parallax.

Stereoscopic parallax can therefore be used as a basis for measuring distance or height. Overlapping aerial photographs record parallax due to the shift in positions of the camera as aircraft motion carries the camera forward between successive exposures. If forward overlap is 50 per cent or more, then the entire ground area shown on a given frame can be viewed in stereo using three adjacent frames (a stereo triplet). Forward overlap of 50 to 60 per cent is common. This amount of overlap doubles the number of photographs required, but assures that the entire area can be viewed in stereo because each point on the ground will appear on two successive photographs in a flight line. Displacement due to stereo parallax is always parallel to the flight line. Tops of tall objects, nearer to the camera, show more displacement than do shorter objects, which are more distant from the camera. Measurement of parallax therefore provides a means of estimating heights of objects. Manual measurement of parallax can be accomplished as follows. Tape photographs of a stereo pair to a work table so the axis of the flight line is oriented from right to left (Fig. 4.24). For demonstration purposes, distances can be measured with an engineer's scale.

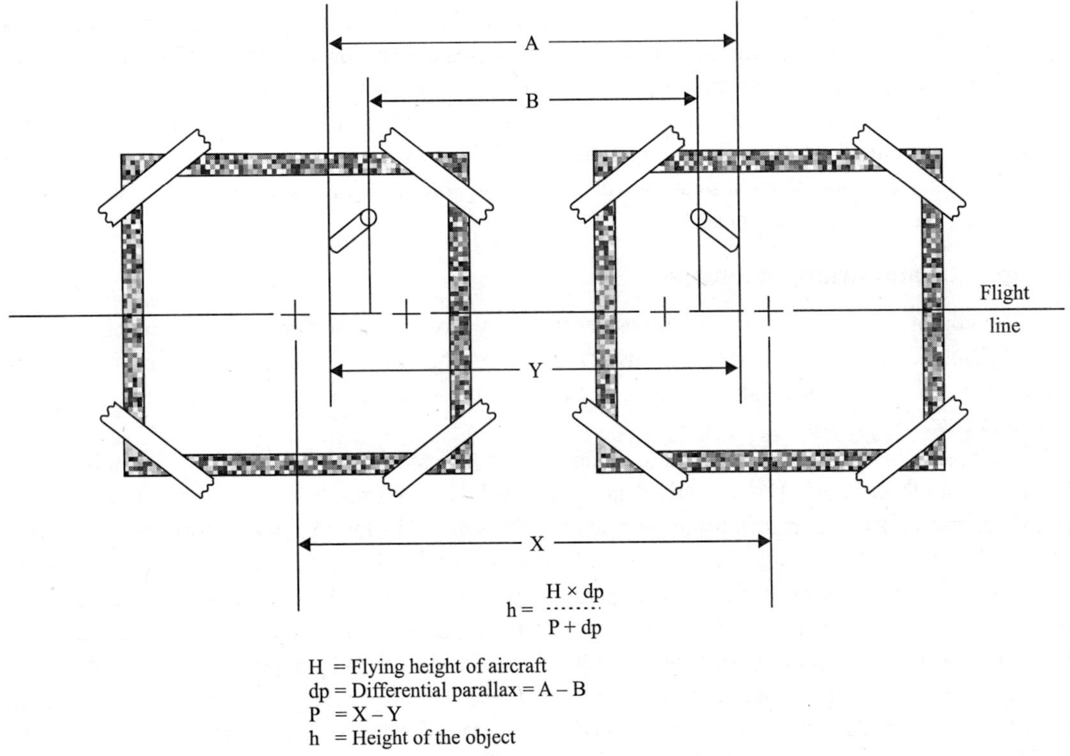

$$h = \frac{H \times dp}{P + dp}$$

H = Flying height of aircraft
dp = Differential parallax = A – B
P = X – Y
h = Height of the object

Fig. 4.24. Measurement of stereoscopic parallax.

1. Measure the distance between two principal points (X).
2. Measure the distance between separate images of the base of the object as represented on the two images (Y). Subtract this distance from that found in (1) to get P.
3. Measure top-to-top distances (B) and base-to-base (A) distances, then subtract to find dp.

In practice, parallax measurements can be made more conveniently using a parallax wedge or parallax bar devices that permit accurate measurement of small amounts of parallax.

Mosaics

A series of vertical aerial photographs that show adjacent regions on the ground can be joined together to form a mosaic. Aerial mosaics belong to one of two classes. Uncontrolled mosaics are formed by placing the photographs together in a manner that provides continuous coverage of an area, without concern for preservation of consistent scale and positional relationships. The most rudimentary form of uncontrolled mosaic is formed simply by placing the photographs in their correct sequence, but with only rough alignment at their edges. Then another photograph is taken of these individual photographs, forming a single image that gives an overview of the landscape within a given region. An uncontrolled mosaic of this kind is often used as an aerial index—a key to the locations and coverages of the individual photographs. An aerial index provides a means of identifying those particular photographs that might be needed for a specific purpose and does give a small-scale overview of a particular region. Uncontrolled mosaics cannot be used for measurements of distance or area because no effort has been made to ensure that images are positioned in their correct relative positions. Other kinds of uncontrolled mosaics can be made using only the center sections of individual photographs, with efforts to improve matching of detail at edges of images. Such mosaics are more attractive, but still lack the geometric accuracy necessary to provide a basis for accurate measurement. Controlled mosaics are formed from individual photographs assemble in manner that preserves correct positional relationships between the features they represent. Often the most accurate region of each photograph, that near the principal point, is cut out and used for the mosaic. Locational control must, of course, be provided by ground survey or by information from accurate maps. Controlled mosaics can be very expensive, but may have sufficient accuracy to serve as a map substitute in some instances.

Orthophotos and Orthophotomaps

Aerial photographs are not planimetric maps because they have geometric errors, most notably the effects of relief displacement, in the representations of the features they show. That is, objects are not represented in their correct relative positions and as a result the images cannot be used as the basis for accurate measurements.

Stereoscopic photographs can be used to generate a corrected form of an aerial photograph known as an ortho-photo that shows photographic detail without the errors caused by tilt and relief displacement. An instrument known as an ortho-photoscope can, for a given instant, project a corrected version of a very small portion of an image. An ortho-photoscope is an optical–mechanical instrument that, instead of exposing an entire image from a central perspective (i.e., through a single lens), exposes each small section individually in a manner that corrects for the elevation of that small section. The result is an image that has ortho-graphic properties rather than those of the central perspective of the original aerial photograph. The ortho-photoscope is capable of scanning an entire image piece by piece to generate a corrected version of that image. The projection orientation is adjusted to correct for tilt and the instrument continuously varies the projection distance to correct for relief displacement. Thus, as the instrument scans an image the operator views the ground surface in stereo and the new image is formed as a geometrically correct version of the original image. The result is a photo image that shows the same detail as the original aerial photograph but without the geometric errors introduced by tilt and relief displacement. Ortho-photomaps therefore can be used for most purposes as maps, because they show correct planimetric position and preserve consistent scale throughout the image. Ortho-photographs form the basis for ortho-photomaps, which are ortho-photographs presented in map format, with annotations, scale and geographic co-ordinates.

Ortho-photomaps are valuable because they show the fine detail of an aerial photograph without the geometric errors that are normally present and they can be compiled much more quickly and cheaply than the usual topographic maps. Therefore, they can be very useful as map substitutes in instances where topographic maps are not available; or as map supplements when maps are available, but the analyst requires the finer detail and more recent information, provided by an image.

Digital Ortho-photo Quadrangles

Digital ortho-photo quadrangles (DOQs) are ortho-photos prepared in a digital format, designed to correspond to the 7.5-minute quadrangles of the U.S. Geological Survey (USGS). DOQs are presented either as black-and-white or as colour images that have been processed to attain the geometric properties of a planimetric map.

DOQs are prepared from National Aerial Photography Programme (NAPP) photography (high-altitude photography, at 1:40000, supplemented by other aerial photography as needed. The rectification process is based upon the use of DEMs to represent variations in terrain elevation. The final product is presented to correspond to the matching USGS 7.5-minute quadrangle, with a supplementary border of imagery representing 50 to 300 m beyond the limits of the quadrangle, to facilitate matching and mosaicking with adjacent sheets. DOQs provide image detail equivalent to 2 m or so for DOQs presented in the quadrangle format and finer detail for quarter-quad DOQs.

PHOTOGRAMMETRY

Photogrammetry is the science of making accurate measurements from photographs. Photogrammetry applies the principles of optics and knowledge of the interior geometry of the camera and its orientation to reconstruct dimensions and positions of objects represented within photographs. Therefore, its practice requires detailed knowledge of specific cameras and the circumstances under which they were used and accurate measurements of features within photographs. Photographs used for photogrammetry have traditionally been prepared on glass plates or other dimensionally stable materials (i.e., materials that do not change in size as temperature and humidity change).

Photogrammetry can be applied to any photograph, provided the necessary information is at hand. However, by far the most frequent application of photogrammetry is the analysis of stereo aerial photography to derive estimates of topographic elevation for topographic mapping. With the aid of accurate locational information describing key features within a scene (ground control), photogrammetrists estimate topographic relief by estimating stereo parallax for any array of points within a region. Although stereo parallax can be measured manually, it is far more practical to employ specialised instruments designed for stereoscopic analysis.

Such instruments, known as analytical stereoplotters, reconstruct the orientations of photographs at the time they were taken. Operators then can view the image in stereo; by maintaining constant parallax visually, they can trace lines of uniform elevation. The quality of information derived from such instruments depends upon the quality of the photography, the accuracy of the data and the operator's skill in setting up the stereo model and tracing lines of uniform parallax. As the design of instruments improved, it eventually became possible to automatically match corresponding points on stereo pairs and thereby identify lines of uniform parallax with limited assistance from the operator.

DIGITAL PHOTOGRAPHY

Photographs can be electronically scanned to record the patterns of blacks, grays and whites as digital values, each representing the brightness of a specific point within the image. Although these values can be displayed in the form of a conventional photograph, the digital format offers advantages of compact storage and the power of numerical representation. Further, it is possible to manufacture cameras that replace the film in the focal plane with an array of light-sensitive detectors that directly record images in digital form, thereby bypassing the scanning step. Because this imaging system collects navigational and positional data that can be used with elevation data of the region imaged, it can produce imagery of high positional accuracy.

SOFTCOPY PHOTOGRAMMETRY

With further advances in instrumentation, it became possible to extend automation of the photogrammetric process so as to conduct the analysis completely within the digital domain. Satellite images or aerial photographs can be acquired digitally (or conventional photographs can be scanned to create digital products). With the use of global positioning systems to acquire accurate positional information and the use of data recorded from the aircraft's navigational system to record the orientations of photographs, it then became feasible to reconstruct the geometry of the image using those data gathered as the image was acquired. This process forms the basis for softcopy photogrammetry, so named because it does not require the physical (hardcopy) form of the photograph necessary for traditional photogrammetry. Instead the digital (softcopy) version of the image is used as input for a series of mathematical models that reconstruct the orientation of each image to create planimetrically correct representations. This process requires specialised computer software installed in workstations, which analyse digital data specifically acquired for the purpose of photogrammetric analysis. Softcopy photogrammetry offers advantages of speed and accuracy and also creates output data that are easily integrated into other production and analytical systems, including GIS.

SOURCES OF AERIAL PHOTOGRAPHY

Aerial photography can be acquired by (i) the user; or (ii) purchased from organisations that serve as repositories for imagery flown by others (archival imagery). In the first instance, aerial photography is produced upon request by firms that specialise in taking high-quality aerial photography. Such firms are listed in the business sections of most metropolitan phone directories. Customers may be individuals, governmental agencies or other businesses that use aerial photography. Such photography is, of course, customised to meet the specific needs of customers with respect to date, scale, film and coverage. As a result, costs may be prohibitive for many non-commercial uses.

Thus, for financial reasons, many users of aerial photography turn to archival photography as a means of acquiring the images they need. Although such photographs may not exactly meet users' requirements with respect to scale or date, low costs and ease of access may compensate for any shortcomings. For some tasks that require reconstruction of conditions at earlier dates (such as the

Environmental Protection Agency's search for abandoned toxic waste dumps), the archival images may form the only source of information.

It is feasible to take 'do-it-yourself' aerial photography. Many small cameras are suitable for aerial photography. Often the costs of local air charter services for an hour or so of flight time are relatively low. Small-format cameras, such as the usual 35-mm cameras, can be used for aerial photography if the photographer avoids the effects of aircraft vibration (Do not rest the camera against the aircraft). If the altitude is low and the atmosphere is clear, ordinary films can produce satisfactory results. Be sure to use a high-wing aircraft to ensure that the photographer will have a clear view of the landscape. If the camera can accommodate filters, it is possible to use other films (such as infrared or colour infrared) similar to those described above. Some experimentation may be necessary for the first-time user to obtain proper exposures, but most people can learn rather quickly to take satisfactory photographs. Usually the best lighting is when the camera is aimed away from the sun. Photographs acquired in this manner may be useful for illustrative purposes, although for scientific or professional work, the large-format, high-quality work of the fully equipped air survey firm is probably necessary.

Earth Science Information Center

The Earth Science Information Center (ESIC) is operated by the USGS as a central source for information pertaining to maps and aerial photographs: ESIC has a special interest in information pertaining to federal programmes and agencies, but also collects data pertaining to maps and photographs held by state and local governments. The ESIC headquarters is located at Reston, Virginia, but ESIC also maintains seven other offices throughout the United States; 31 other federal agencies have affiliated offices. ESIC can provide information to the public concerning the availability of maps and remotely sensed images. The following sections describe two programmes administered by ESIC that can provide access to archival aerial photography.

Aerial photography summary record system

The Aerial Photography Summary Record System (APSRS) is maintained by USGS as a computer-based information system for recording detailed information pertaining to aerial photography held by numerous federal, state and private organisations. Prior to the establishment of centralised records in 1975, citizens desiring comprehensive information on coverage by aerial photographs were required to query holdings by numerous agencies, which each followed different conventions in reporting coverage. After 1975, users could obtain information on the integrated holdings of numerous agencies, reported in a standard format.

Those who request information from APSRS receive information sorted by date; describing image scale, cloud cover and camera focal length; and identifying the organisation holding the photography. Coverage is indexed by USGS 7.5-minute quadrangles, which are listed by the latitude and longitude of the southeastern corner of each quadrangle. Users first identify the quadrangle that covers their area of interest and then use the latitude and longitude to search for coverage of the region. For each photographic mission, APSRS provides a listing giving the date of coverage, amount of cloud coverage, scale, film type and format, focal length and other qualities. Also listed is the agency that holds the photography; these listing are keyed to a directory that lists addresses so that the user can order copies of the photographs. Listings also include the Federal Information Processing Standards (FIPS) code for each area, which permits cross-reference to political and census units.

National aerial photography programme

The National Aerial Photography Programme (NAPP) acquires aerial photography for the coterminous United State, according to a systematic plan that ensures uniform standards. NAPP was initiated in 1987 by the USGS as a replacement for the National High Altitude Aerial Photography Programme (NHAP), begun in 1980 to consolidate the many federal programmes that use aerial photography. The USGS manages the NAPP, but it is funded by the federal agencies that are the primary users of its photography. Program oversight is provided by a committee of representatives from the USGS, the Bureau of Land Management, the National Agricultural Statistics Service, the National Resources Conservation Service (NRCS; previously known as the Soil Conservation Service), the Farm Service Agency (previously known as the Agricultural Stabilisation and Conservation Service), the US Forest Service and the Tennessee Valley Authority.

Under NHAP, photography was acquired under a plan to obtain complete coverage of the coterminous 48 states, then to update coverage as necessary to keep pace with requirements for current photography. Current plans call for updates at intervals of 5 years, although the actual schedules are determined in co-ordination with budgetary constraints. NHAP flight lines were oriented north–south, centered on each of four quadrants systematically positioned within USGS 7.5-minute quadrangles, with full stereoscopic coverage at 60 per cent forward overlap and sidelap of at least 27 per cent. Two camera systems were used to acquire simultaneous coverage: black-and-white coverage was acquired at scales of about 1:80000 using cameras with focal lengths of 6 inch. Colour infrared coverage was acquired at 1:58000 using a focal length of 8.25 inch. Dates of NHAP photography varied according to geographic region. Flight were timed to provide optimum atmospheric conditions for photography and to meet specifications for sun angle, snow cover and shadowing, with preference for autumn and winter seasons to provide images that show the landscape without the cover of deciduous vegetation. Specifications for NAPP photographs differ from those of NHAP. NAPP photographs are acquired at 20000-ft., altitude using a 6-inch, focal length lens. Flight lines are centered on quarter quads (1:24000-scale USGS quadrangles). NAPP photographs are planned for 1:40000, black-and-white or colour infrared film, depending on specific requirement for each area.

Photographs are available to all who may have an interest in their use. Their detail and quality permit use for land-cover surveys; assessment of agricultural, mineral and forest resources; as well as examination of patterns of soil erosion and water quality.

Thus aerial photography is a simple, reliable and inexpensive means of acquiring remotely sensed images. It has been used to make images from very low altitudes and from earth-orbiting satellites, so it can be said to be one of the most flexible strategies for remote sensing. Aerial photography is useful mainly in the visible and near infrared portions of the spectrum, but its principles are important throughout the field of remote sensing. For example, lenses are used in many non-photographic sensors and photographic films are used to record images acquired by a variety of instruments.

Aerial photographs form the primary source of information for compilation of many maps, especially large-scale topographic maps. Vertical aerial photographs are valuable as map substitutes or as map supplements. Geometric errors in the representation of location prevent direct use of aerial photographs as the basis for measurement of distance or area. But, as these errors are known and are well understood, it is possible for photogrammetrists to use photographs as the basis for reconstruction of correct positional relationships and the derivation of accurate measurements. Aerial photographs record complex detail of the varied patterns that constitute any landscape. Each image interpreter must develop the skills and knowledge necessary to resolve these patterns by disciplined examination of aerial images.

5

Digital Data and Image Processing

INTRODUCTION

So far, we have focused on examination of remotely sensed images as photographs or photograph-like images. Such images can also be represented in digital form, so that the pattern of image brightness (often in several spectral channels) forms an array of numbers recorded in digital form.

When an image is represented as numbers, brightness can be added, subtracted, multiplied, divided and in general subjected to statistical manipulation that is not possible if an image is presented only as a photograph. Thus, the digital format greatly increases our ability to display, examine and analyse remotely sensed data.

Although digital analysis of remotely sensed data dates from the early days of remote sensing, the launch of the first Landsat earth observation satellite in 1972 began an era of increasing interest in machine processing. Previously, digital remote sensing data could be analysed only at specialised remote sensing laboratories. The expensive equipment and highly trained personnel necessary to conduct routine machine analysis of data were not widely available, in part because of limited availability of digital remote sensing data and a lack of appreciation of their qualities.

After Landsat 1 began to generate a stream of digital data, analysts realised that the usual visual examination of Landsat images would not permit full exploitation of the information they conveyed. In time, routine availability of digital data increased interest among businesses and institutions, computers and peripheral equipment became less expensive, more personnel acquired the necessary training and experience, software became more widely available and managers developed knowledge of the capabilities of digital analysis for remote sensing applications. Today digital analysis has a significance that far exceeds that of purely visual interpretation of remotely sensed data.

Many types of remote sensing images are routinely recorded in digital form and then processed by computers to produce images for interpreters to study. The simplest form of digital image processing employs a microprocessor that converts the digital data tape into a film image with minimal corrections and calibrations. At the other extreme, large mainframe computers are employed for sophisticated interactive manipulation of the data to produce images in which specific information has been extracted and highlighted.

ELECTRONIC IMAGERY

Digital data can be created by a family of instruments that can systematically scan portions of the earth's surface, recording photons reflected or emitted from individual patches of ground, known as pixels ('picture elements'). A digital image is composed of many thousands of pixels, usually each too small to be individually resolved by the human eye. Each pixel represents the brightness of a small region on the earth's surface, recorded digitally as a numeric value, usually with separate values for each of several regions of the electromagnetic spectrum (Fig. 5.1).

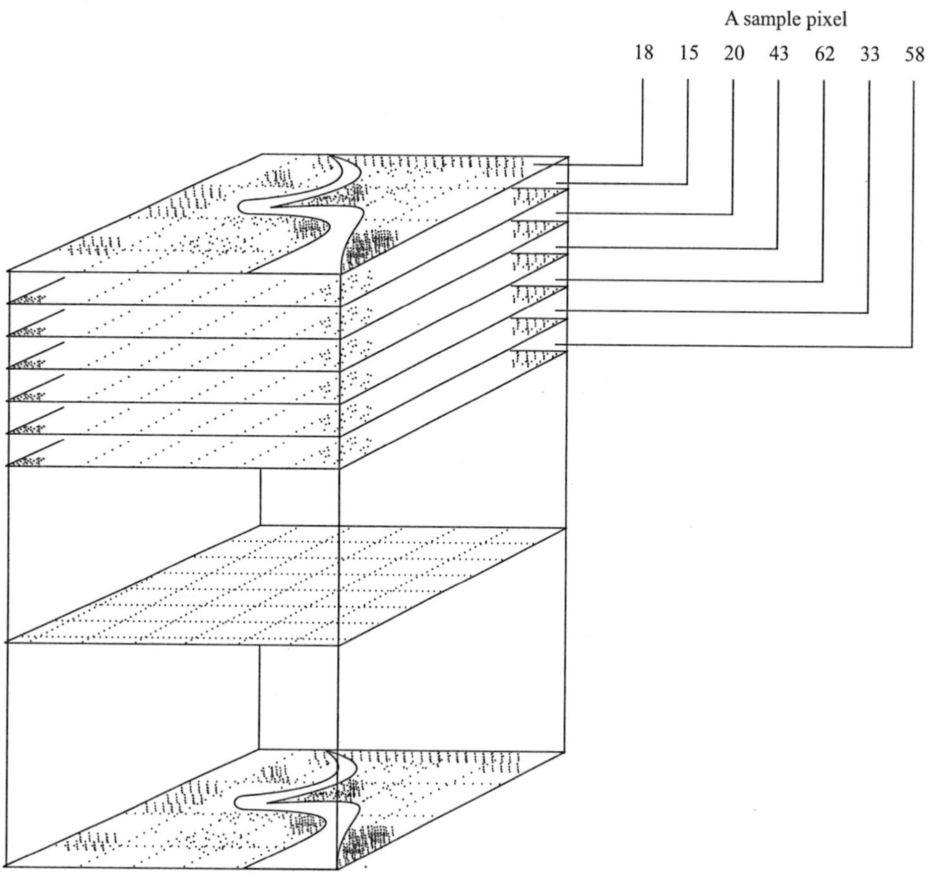

Fig. 5.1. Multispectral pixels.

Digital images can be generated by two kinds of instruments. Optical-mechanical scanners physically move mirrors or lenses to systematically aim the field of view over the earth's surface (Fig. 5.2). As the instrument scans the earth's surface, it generates an electrical current that varies in intensity as the land surface varies in brightness. Sensors sensitive in several regions of the spectrum use filters of separate energy into several spectral regions, each represented by separate electrical current. Each electrical signal must be sub-divided into distinct units to create the discrete values necessary for digital analysis. This conversion from the continuously varying analog signal to the discrete digital values is accomplished by sampling the current at a uniform interval (analog-to-digital or A-to-D, conversion) (Fig. 5.3). Because all signal values within this interval are represented as a single average, all variation within this interval is lost. Thus, the choice of sampling interval forms one dimension to the resolution of the sensor.

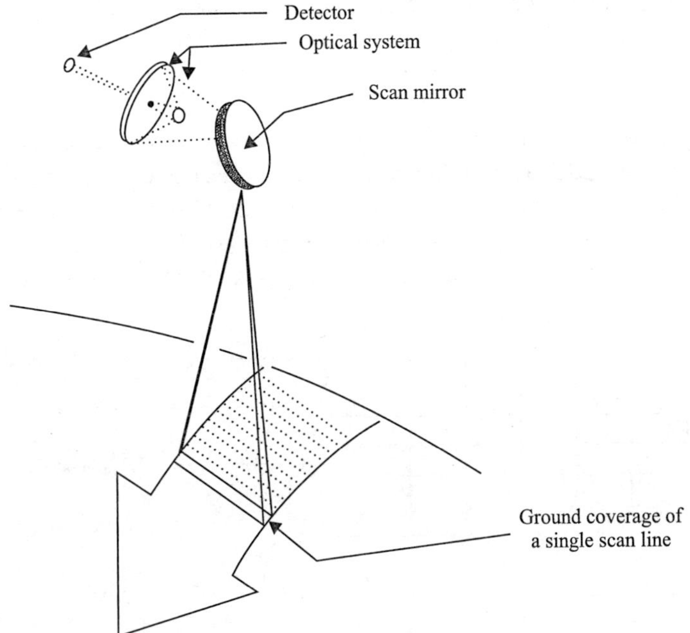

Fig. 5.2. Optical-mechanical scanner.

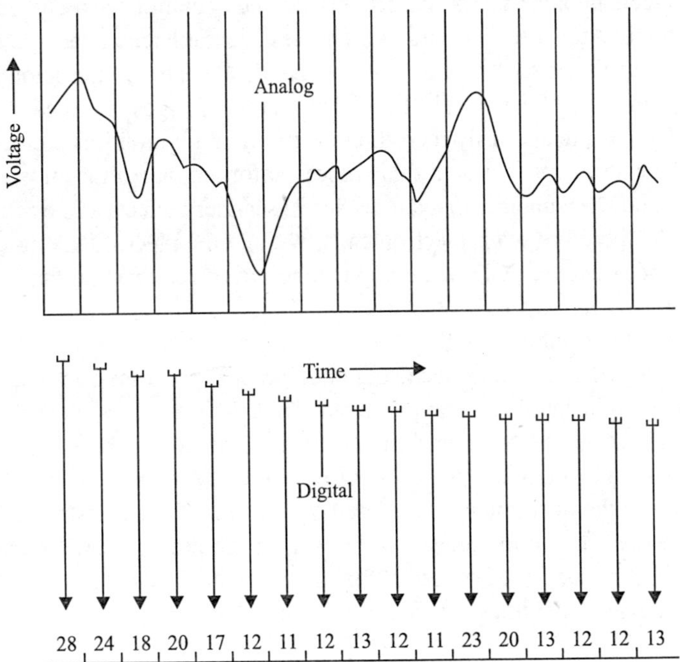

Fig. 5.3. Analog-to-digital conversion.

A second basic design for sensors uses charge-coupled devices (CCDs) (Fig. 5.4). A CCD is formed from light-sensitive material embedded in a silicon chip. The potential well receives photons from the scene, usually through an optical system designed to collect, filter and focus radiation. The sensitive components of CCDs can be manufactured to be very small, perhaps as small as 1 μm in diameter and sensitive to visible and near infrared radiation. These elements can be connected using microcircuitry to form arrays; detectors arranged in a single line form a linear array, detectors arranged in several rows and columns form two-dimensional arrays. Individual detectors are so small that a linear array smaller than 2 cm in length might have as many as 1000 separate detectors. Two-dimensional arrays of 800 × 800 have been used and larger arrays can be formed by mosaicking several smaller arrays together.

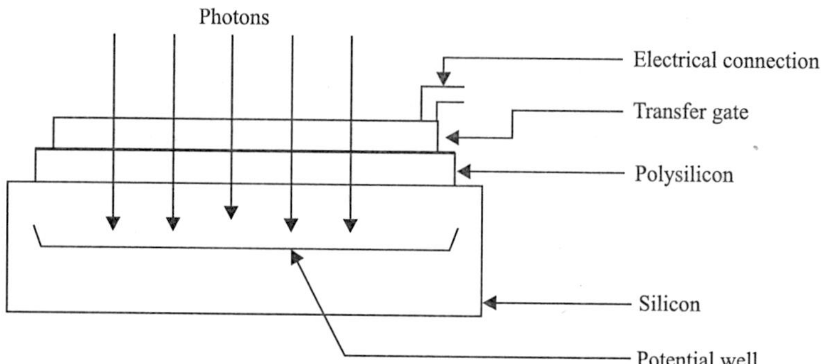

Fig. 5.4. Charge-coupled device (CCD).

Each detector collects photons that strike its surface and accumulates a charge proportional to the intensity of the radiation. At a specified interval, charges accumulated at each detector pass through a transfer gate, which controls the flow of information from the detectors. Microcircuits connect detectors within an array to form shift registers. Shift registers permit charges received at each detector to be passed to adjacent elements, temporarily recording the information until it is convenient to transfer it to another portion of the instrument. Through this process, information read from the shift register is read sequentially, much in the same manner that a mechanical scanner collects a line of data through its side-to-side motion. A CCD therefore scans electronically, without the mechanical motion necessary for the optical scanners described above. CCDs are compact; moreover, relative to other sensors, they are more efficient in detecting photons, so CCDs are especially effective when intensities are dim. Further, they tend to respond linearly to brightness, so they produce images that have more consistent relationships to scene brightness than is possible to produce using photographic processes.

An alternative imaging technology, complementary metal-oxide semi-conductors (CMOS), is used in camcorders and related consumer products. Recent improvements in CMOS-based instruments provide fine detail at a low cost and with a low power requirement. CCDs expose all pixels at the same instant, then read these values as the next image is acquired. In contrast, CMOS instruments expose a line at a time, then expose the next line in the image while data for the previous line is transferred. Therefore, pixels within a CMOS image are not exposed at the same instant. This quality, plus the advantage of the low noise that characterises CCD imagery, favours use of CCDs for digital remote sensing instruments.

Optical sensors often use prisms and filters to separate light into separate spectral regions. Electronic sensors usually use diffraction gratings, considered more efficient because of their effectiveness, small size and light weight. Diffraction gratings are closely spaced transmitting slits cut into a flat surface (a transmission grating) or grooves cut into a polished surface (reflection grating). Effective transmission gratings must be very accurately and consistently spaced and must have very sharp edges. Light from a scene is passed though a colluminating lens, designed to produce a beam of parallel rays of light that is oriented to strike the diffraction grating at an angle (Fig. 5.5).

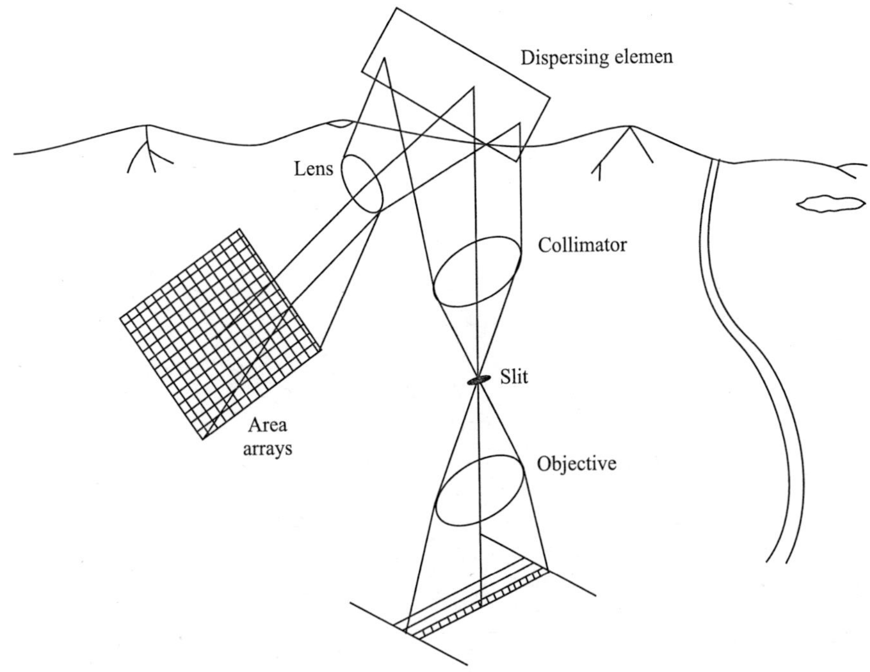

Fig. 5.5. Diffraction grating and colluminating lens.

Light striking a diffraction grating experiences both destructive and constructive interference as wavefronts interact with the grating. Destructive interference causes some wavelengths to be suppressed, whereas constructive interference causes others to be reinforced. Because the grating is oriented at an angle with respect to the beam of light, different wavelengths are diffracted at different angles and the radiation can be separated spectrally. This light can then illuminate detectors to achieve the desired spectral sensitivity.

CCDs can be positioned in the focal plane of a sensor such that they view a thin rectangular strip oriented at right angles to the flight path (Fig. 5.6). The forward motion of the aircraft or satellite moves the field of view forward along the flight path, building up coverage. By analogy, this means of generating an image is known as pushbroom scanning. (In contrast, mechanical scanning can be visualised by analogy to a whisk broom, which creates an image using the side-to-side motion of the scanner).

The instantaneous field of view (IFOV) refers to the area viewed by the instrument if it were possible to suspend the motion of the aircraft and the scanning of the sensor for an instant (Fig. 5.7). The IFOV therefore defines the smallest area viewed by the sensor and establishes a lower limit for the level of spatial detail that can be represented in a digital image. Although data in the final image can be aggregated so that an image pixel represents a ground area larger than the IFOV, it is not possible for pixels to carry information about ground areas smaller than the IFOV.

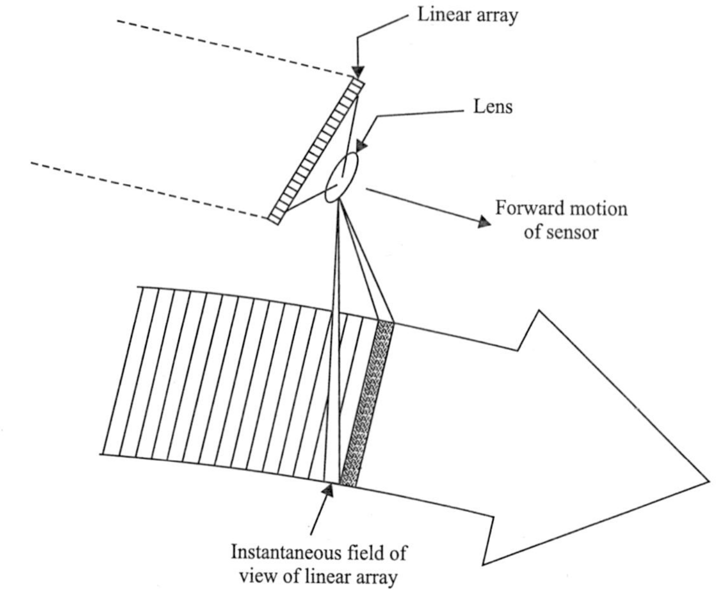

Fig. 5.6. CCD used in pushbroom scanning.

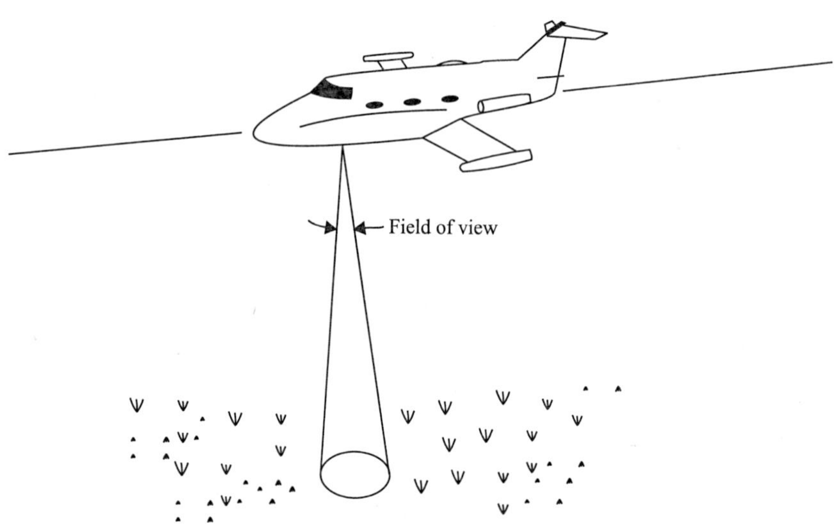

Fig. 5.7. Instantaneous field of view (IFOV).

Electronic sensors must be operated within the limits of their design capabilities. Altitudes and speeds of aircraft and satellites must be designed to match the sensitivities of the sensors such that detectors view a given ground area long enough to accumulate enough photons to generate strong signals (this interval is known as dwell time). At the lower end of an instrument's sensitivity is the dark current signal (Fig. 5.8). At low levels of brightness, a CCD can record a small level of brightness even when there is none in the scene. At an instrument's upper threshold, bright targets saturate the sensor's response—

the instrument fails to record further increases in target brightness. Between these limits, sensors are designed to generate signals that have predictable relationships with scene brightness; these relationships are established by careful calibration of each individual sensor. These characteristics of electronic sensors are analogous to the characteristic curve previously described for photographic films. In other words, they define the upper and lower limits of the system's sensitivity to brightness and the range of brightnesses over which a system can generate measurements with consistent relationships to scene brightnesses.

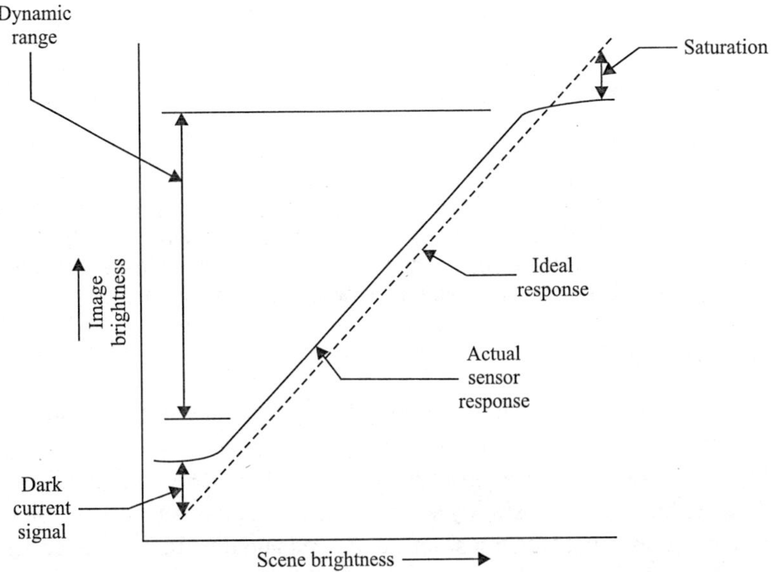

Fig. 5.8. Dark current, saturation and dynamic range.

The range of brightnesses that can be accurately recorded is known as the sensor's dynamic range. Most electronic sensors have rather large dynamic ranges compared to those of photographic films, computer displays or the human visual system. Therefore, photographic representations of electronic imagery tend to lose information at the upper and/or lower ranges of brightness. Because visual interpretation forms such an important dimension of our understanding of images, the way that photographic films, image displays (discussed below) and image-enhancement methods handle this problem forms an important dimension of the field of image analysis.

Each sensor creates responses unrelated to target brightness—that is, noise, created in part by accumulated electronic errors from various components of the sensor. (In this context 'noise' refers specifically to noise generated by the sensor, although the noise that the analyst receives originates not only in the sensor but also in the atmosphere, the interpretation process, etc.). For effective use, instruments must be designed such that their noise levels are small relative to the signal (brightness of the target). This is measured as the signal-to-noise ratio (S/N or SNR) (Fig. 5.9). Analysis desire signals to be large relative to noise, so the SNR should be large not only for bright targets, when the signal is large, but over the entire dynamic range of the instrument, especially at the lower levels of sensitivity, when the signal is small relative to noise. Engineers who design sensors must balance the radiometric sensitivity of the instrument with pixel size, dynamic range, operational altitude and other factors to maintain acceptable SNRs.

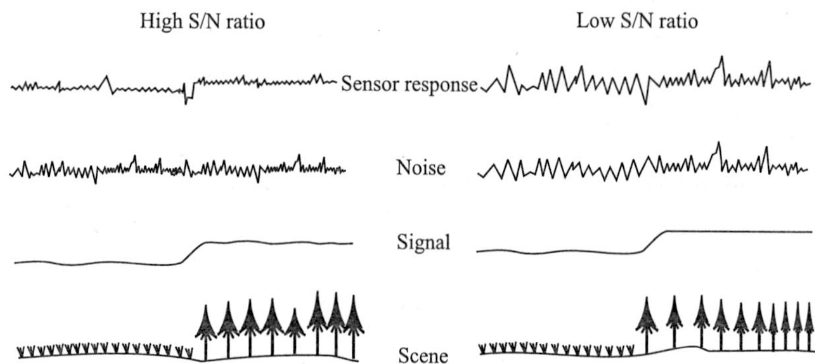

Fig. 5.9. Signal-to-noise ratio (S/N). At the bottom, a hypothetical scene is composed of two cover types. The signal records this region, with only a small difference in brightness between the two classes. Atmospheric effects, sensor error and other factors contribute to noise, which is added to the signal. The sensor then records a combination of signal and noise. When noise is small relative to the signal (left: high S/N ratio), the sensor conveys the difference between the two regions. When the signal is small relative to noise (right, low S/N ratio) the sensor cannot portray the difference in brightness between the two regions.

SPECTRAL SENSITIVITY

Because the various filters and diffraction gratings that instruments use to define the spectral limits (i.e., the 'colours' that they record) do not define discrete limits, spectral sensitivity varies across a specific defined interval. For example, an instrument designed to record radiation in the green region of the spectrum will not exhibit equal sensitivity across the green region, but will exhibit greater sensitivity near the center of the region than at the transitions to the red and blue regions on either side (Fig. 5.10). Defining the spectral sensitivity to be the extreme limits of the energy received would not be satisfactory because it is clear that the energy received at the extremes is so low that the effective sensitivity of the instrument is defined by a much narrower wavelength interval.

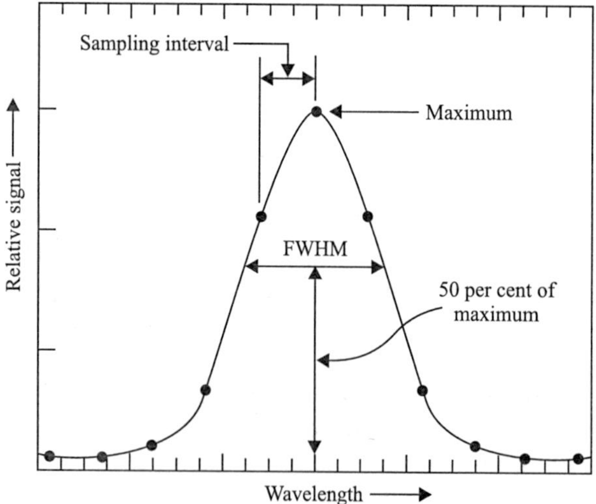

Fig. 5.10. Full width, half maximum.

As a result, the spectral sensitivity of an instrument is often specified using the definition of full width, half maximum (FWHM)—the spectral interval measured at the level at which the instrument's response reaches one-half of its maximum value (Fig. 5.10). Thus FWHM forms a definition of spectral resolution, the narrowest spectral interval that can be resolved by an instrument. (Even though the instrument is sensitive to radiation at the extreme limits, beyond the limits of FWHM, the response is so weak and unreliable at these limits that FWHM forms a measure of functional sensitivity). Figure 5.10 also illustrates the spectral sampling interval (known also as spectral bandwidth), which specifies the spectral interval used to record brightness in relation to wavelength.

DIGITAL DATA

Output from electronic sensors reaches the analyst as a set of numeric values. Each digital value is recorded as a series of binary values known as bits. Each bit records an exponent of a power of 2, with the value of the exponent determined by the position of the bit in the sequence. As an example, consider a system designed to record 7 bits for each digital value. This means that seven binary places are available to record the brightness sensed for each band of the sensor. The seven values record, in sequence, successive powers of 2. A '1' signifies that a specific power of 2 (determined by its position within the sequence) is to be evoked; a '0' indicates a value of zero for that position. Thus, the 7-bit binary number '1111111' signifies $2^6 + 2^5 + 2^4 + 2^3 + 2^2 + 2^1 + 2^0 = 64 + 32 + 16 + 8 + 4 + 2 + 1 = 127$. And '1001011' records $2^6 + 0^5 + 0^4 + 0^3 + 0^2 + 2^1 + 2^0 = 64 + 0 + 0 + 8 + 0 + 2 + 1 = 75$. Figure 5.11 shows different examples. Eight bits constitute a byte, intended to store a single character. Larger amounts of memory can be indicated in terms of kilobytes (KB) 1024 (2^{10}) bytes, megabytes (MB) 1,048,576 (2^{20}) bytes and gigabytes (GB), 1,073,741,824 (2^{30}) bytes (Table 5.1).

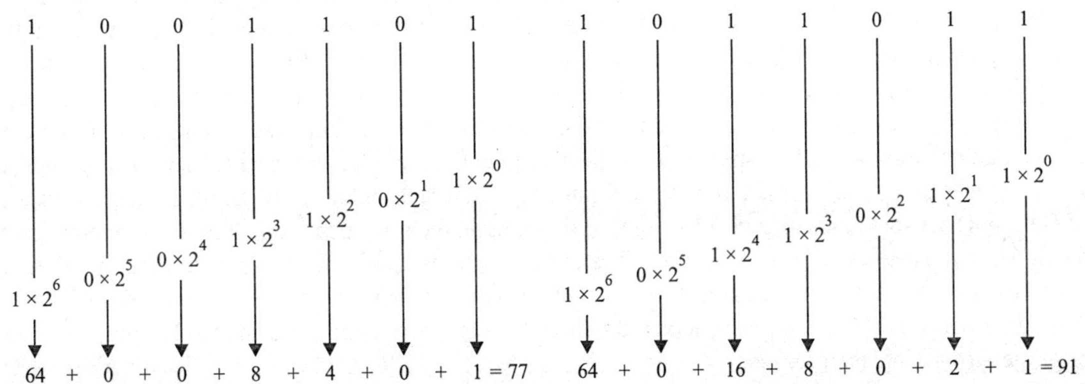

Fig. 5.11. Digital representation of values in 7 bits.

Table 5.1. Terminology for computer storage.

Bit	A binary digit (0 or 1)	
Byte	8 bits, 1 character	
Kilobyte (K or KB)	1024 bytes	(2^{10} bytes)
Megabyte (MB)	1,048,576 bytes	(2^{20} bytes)
Gigabyte (GB)	1,073,741,824 bytes	(2^{30} bytes)
Terabyte (TB)	1,099,511,627,776 bytes	(2^{40} bytes)

In this manner, discrete digital values for each pixel are recorded in a form suitable for storage on tapes or disks and for analysis by digital computer. These values, as read from tape or disk, are popularly known as 'digital numbers' (DNs), 'brightness values' (BVs) or 'digital counts', in part as a means of signifying that these values do not record true radiances from the scene.

The number of brightness values within a digital image is determined by the number of bits available. The 7-bit example given above permits a maximum range of 128 possible values (0–127) for each pixel. A decrease to 6 bits would decrease the range of brightness values to 64 (0–63); an increase to 8 bits would extend to range to 256 (0–255). Thus, the number of bits determines the radiometric resolution of a digital image. The number of bits available is determined by the design of the system, especially the sensitivity of the sensor (adding too many extra bits would simply record system noise rather than provide additional information about scene brightness) and its capabilities for recording and transmitting data (each added bit increases transmission requirements). If we assume that transmission and storage resources are fixed, then increasing the number of bits for each pixel means that we will have fewer pixels per image and the pixel sizes must be larger. Thus, design of remote sensing systems requires trade-offs between image coverage and radiometric, spectral and spatial resolutions.

Radiances

The brightness of radiation reflected from the earth's surface is measured as brightness (watts) per wavelength interval (micrometer) per angular unit (steradian); thus the measured brightness is defined with respect to wavelength (i.e., 'colour'), spatial area (angle) and intensity (brightness). Radiances record actual brightnesses, measured in physical units, given as real values (to include decimal fractions).

Use of digital numbers (DNs) facilitates the design of instruments and data communications and the visual display of image data. For visual comparison of different scenes or analyses that examine relative brightnesses, use of DNs is satisfactory. However, because a DN from one scene does not represent the same brightness as the same DN from another scene, DNs are not comparable from scene to scene if an analysis must examine actual scene brightnesses for purposes that require use of original physical units.

For such purposes, it is necessary to convert the DNs to the original radiances. This process requires knowledge of calibration data specific to each instrument. To ensure that a given sensor provides an accurate measure of brightness, it must be calibrated against targets of known brightness. The sensitivities of electronic sensors tends to drift over time, so to maintain their accuracy it is necessary to re-calibrate them. Although those sensors used in aircraft can be re-calibrated periodically, those used in satellites are not available after launch for the same kind of re-calibration. Typically, such sensors are designed so that they can observe calibration targets onboard the satellite or they are calibrated using landscapes of uniform brightness (e.g., in desert regions).

DATA FORMATS

Digital image analysis is usually conducted using 'raster' data structures in which each image is treated as an array of values (Fig. 5.12). Additional spectral channels form additional arrays that register to one another. Each pixel is treated as a separate unit, which can always be located within the image by its row and column coordinates. In most remote sensing analysis, coordinates originate in the upper left hand corner of an image and are referred to as rows and columns or as lines and pixels, to measure position down and to the right, respectively. Raster data structures offer advantages for manipulation of pixel values by image-processing systems, as it is easy to find and locate pixels and their values. The disadvantages are usually apparent only when we need to represent not the individual pixels, but areas of pixels as discrete patches or regions. Then the alternative structure, vector format, becomes more attractive. Vector format uses polygonal patches and their boundaries as the fundamental units for analysis and manipulation. The vector format is not appropriate for digital analysis of remotely sensed data, although sometimes we may wish to display the results of our analysis using a vector format. Almost always equipment and software for digital processing of remotely sensed data must be tailored for raster format.

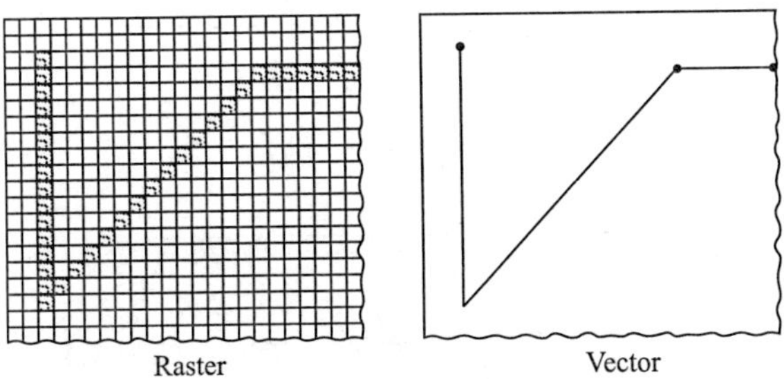

Fig. 5.12. Raster and vector formats.

Digital remote sensing data are typically organised according to one of three alternative strategies for storing image data. Consider an image consisting of four spectral channels, which together can be visualised as four superimposed images, with corresponding pixels in one band registering exactly to those in other bands.

One of the earliest formats for digital data was band interleaved by pixel (BIP). Data are organised in sequence values for line 1, pixels 1, band 1; then for line 1, pixel 1, band 2; then for line 1, pixel 1, band 3; and finally for line 1, pixel 1, band 4. Next are the four bands for line 1, pixel 2 and so on (Fig. 5.13). Thus, values for all four bands are written before values for the next pixel are represented. Any given pixel, once located within the data, is found with values for all four bands written in sequence one directly after the other. This arrangement may be advantageous in some situations, but for most applications it is awkward to sort through the entire sequence of data (which typically are very large in number) in order to sort the four bands into their respective images.

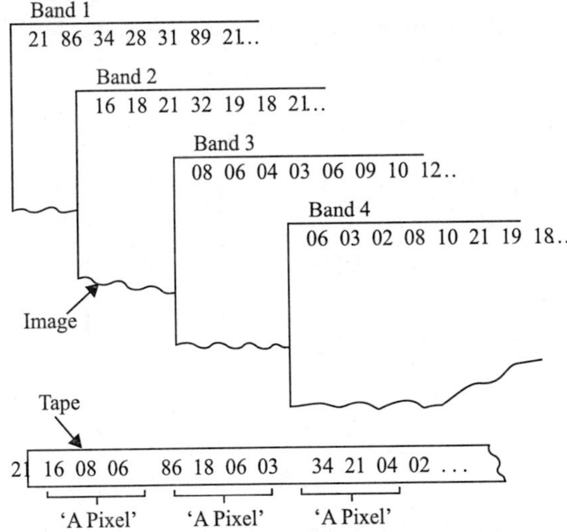

Fig. 5.13. Band interleaved by pixel (BIP) format.

The band interleaved by line (BIL) format treats each line of data as a separate unit (Fig. 5.14). In sequence the analyst finds line 1 for band 1, line 1 for band 2, line 1 for band 3, line 1 for band 4, line 2 for band 1, line 2 for band 2 and so on. Each line is represented in all four bands before the next line is encountered.

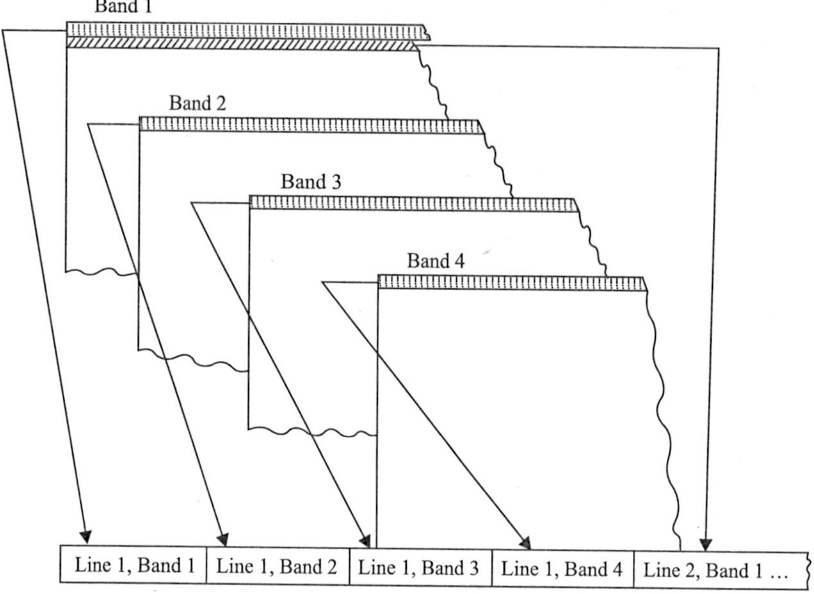

Fig. 5.14. Band interleaved by line (BIL) format.

A third convention for recording remotely sensed data is the band sequential (BSQ) format (Fig. 5.15). All data for band 1 are written in sequence, followed by all data for band 2 and so on. Each band is treated as a separate unit. For many applications, this format is the most practical, as it presents data in the format that most closely resembles the data structure used for the display and analysis. However, if areas smaller than the entire scene are to be examined, the analyst must read all four images before the sub-area can be identified and extracted.

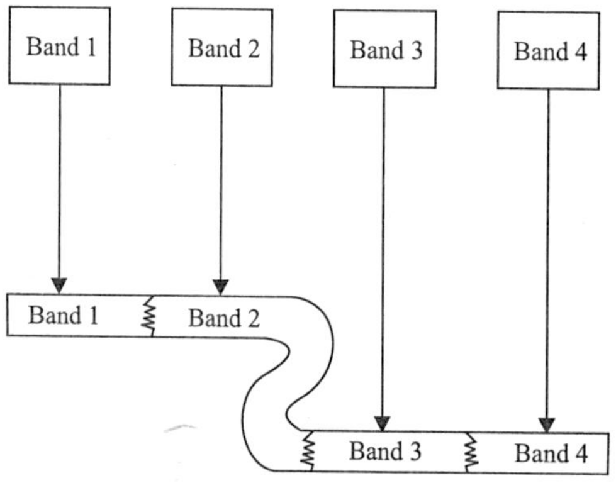

Fig. 5.15. Band sequential (BSQ) format.

Actual data formats used to distribute digital remote sensing data are usually variations on these basic alternatives. Exact details of data formats are specific to particular organisations and to particular forms of data, so whenever an analyst acquires data, he or she must make sure to acquire detailed information regarding the data format. Although organisations attempt to standardise formats for specific kinds of data, it is also true that data formats change as new mass storage media come into widespread use and as user communities employ new kinds of hardware or software.

The 'best' data format depends upon immediate context and often upon the specific software and equipment available. If all bands for an entire image must be used, then the BSQ and BIL formats are useful because they are convenient for reconstructing the entire scene in all four bands. If the analyst knows beforehand the exact position on the image of the sub-area that is to be studied, then the BIP format is useful because values for all bands are found together and it is not necessary to read through the entire data set to find a specific region. In general, however, the analyst must be prepared to read the data in the format in which they are received and to convert them into the format most convenient for use at a specific laboratory.

Data compression reduces the amount of digital data required to store or transmit information by exploiting the redundancies within a data set. If data arrays contain values that are repeated in sequence, then compression algorithms can exploit the repetition to reduce the size of arrays, while retaining the ability to restore the array to its original form. When the complete array is needed for analysis, then the original version can be restored by decompression. Because remotely sensed images require large amounts of storage and usually are characterised by modest levels of redundancies, data compression is an important tool for effective storage and transmission of digital remote sensing data. Compression and decompression are accomplished, for example, by executing computer programs that receive compressed data as input and produce a decompressed version as output.

The compression ratio compares the size of the original image to the size of the compressed image. A ratio of 2:1 indicates that the compressed image is one-half the size of the original. Lossless compression techniques restore compressed data to their exact original form; lossy techniques degrade the reconstructed image, although in some applications the visual impact of a lossy technique may be imperceptible. For digital satellite data, lossless compression techniques can achieve ratios from 1.04:1 to 1.9 to 1. For digitised cartographic data, ratios of 24:1 using lossy techniques have been reported to exhibit good quality. It is beyond the scope of this discussion to describe the numerous techniques and algorithms for image compression. Probably the most well-known compression standard is the JPEG (Joint Photographic Experts Group) format, a lossy technique that applies the discrete cosine transform (DCT) as a compression-decompression algorithm. Although the JPEG algorithm has been widely accepted as a useful technique for compression of continuous-tone photographs, it is not likely to be ideal for remote sensing and GIS data in general.

Generally stated, lossy compression techniques should not be applied to data intended for analysis or as archival copies. Lossy compression may be appropriate for images to present visual records of results of analytical process, provided they do not form input to other analyses.

IMAGE STRUCTURE

One can think of any image as consisting of tiny, equal areas or picture elements, arranged in regular rows and columns. The position of any picture element or pixel, is determined on an xy coordinate system; in the case of Landsat images, the origin is at the upper left corner of the image. Each pixel also has a numerical value, called a digital number (DN), that records the intensity of electromagnetic energy measured for the ground resolution cell represented by that pixel. Digital numbers range from zero to some higher number on a gray scale. The image may be described in strictly numerical terms on a three-coordinate system with x and y locating each pixel and *z* giving the DN, which is displayed as a gray-scale intensity value. Images may be originally recorded in this digital format, as in the case of Landsat. An image recorded initially on photographic film may be converted into digital format by a process known as digitisation.

IMAGE-PROCESSING OVERVIEW

Image-processing methods may be grouped into three functional categories; these are defined below together with lists of typical processing routines.

Image Restoration

Restoration processes are designed to recognise and compensate for errors, noise and geometric distortion introduced into the data during the scanning, transmission and recording processes. The objective is to make the image resemble the original scene. Image restoration is relatively simple because the pixels from each band are processed separately.

Image restoration compensates for data errors, noise, and geometric distortions introduced during the scanning, recording and playback operations.

1. Restoring periodic line dropouts.
2. Restoring periodic line striping.
3. Filtering of random noise.
4. Correcting for atmospheric scattering.
5. Correcting geometric distortions.

Image Enhancement

Enhancement is the modification of an image to alter its impact on the viewer. Generally enhancement distorts the original digital values; therefore enhancement is not done until the restoration processes are completed.

Image enhancement alters the visual impact that the image has on the interpreter in a fashion that improves the information content.

1. Contrast enhancement.
2. Intensity, hue and saturation transformations.
3. Density slicing.
4. Edge enhancement.
5. Making digital mosaics.
6. Producing synthetic stereo images.

Information Extraction

Image restoration and enhancement processes utilise computers to provide corrected and improved images for study by human interpreters. The computer makes no decisions in these procedures. However, processes that identify and extract information do utilise the computer's decision-making capability to identify and extract specific pieces of information. A human operator must instruct the computer and must evaluate the significance of the extracted information.

Information extraction utilises the decision-making capability of the computer to recognise and classify pixels on the basic of their digital signatures.

1. Producing principal-component images.
2. Producing ratio images.
3. Multispectral classification.
4. Producing change-detection images.

Once data are in hand, in either numeric or image form, the analyst is prepared to conduct an interpretation using some combination of manual or digital procedures. Figure 5.16 suggests an idealised sequence for a typical digital analysis, which is proposed as a schematic learning device for the student rather than as a detailed guide for actual analysis. Each step is briefly outlined below.

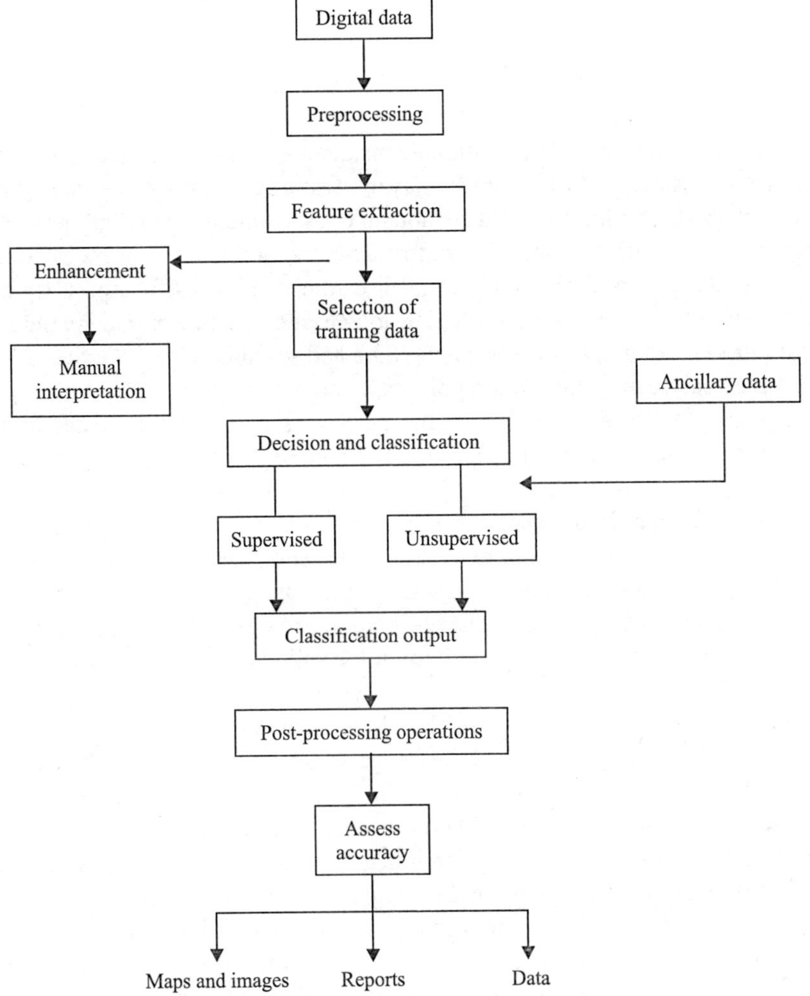

Fig. 5.16. Idealised sequence for digital analysis.

Pre-processing consists of those operations that prepare data for subsequent analysis, usually by attempts to correct or compensate for systematic errors. Three classes of pre-processing operations can be defined. The first are those that simply display or summarise, the data as a means of inspecting its characteristics and quality. These operations present histograms, scattergrams or statistical summaries that permit the operator to assess image quality and thereby determine subsequent pre-processing steps (if any) that may be necessary.

A second group of pre-processing operations are those that compensate for radiometric errors. These errors are caused by defects in sensor operation, atmospheric absorption and scattering, variations in scan angle, variations in illumination of the scene and system noise.

A third class of pre-processing operations corrects positional errors in relationships between image representations of ground features and their actual geographic relationships as they occur on the earth's surface. Geometric corrections are necessary because of systematic variations in the orientation of the vehicle that carries the sensor. Some are intrinsic to the sensor, caused, for example, by variations in the motion of the instrument; others, referred to as extrinsic errors, are the result of variations in the orientation of the platform or errors in recording platform position. Many of these errors are systematic and can be removed from the data before they reach the user. Other geometric transformations are not related to errors. Changing of scales and projection conversions, for example, are operations that simply alter sizes or locational reference systems without consideration of the presence of errors.

After pre-processing is complete, the analyst may use feature extraction to reduce the dimensionality of the data. In this context, a 'feature' should be thought of as 'useful information' in the data rather than as physical feature on the earth's surface. Thus, feature extraction is the process of isolating the most useful components of the data for further study while discarding the less useful aspects (errors, noise, etc.). (This term is misleading, but its use is established by long usage.) Feature extraction reduces the number of variables that must be examined, thereby saving time and resources.

At this point the analyst may choose to apply techniques to improve the visual appearance of the image by applying image enhancement to prepare the image for subsequent manual interpretation. Because image enhancement often drastically alters the original numeric data, image enhancement is normally used only for visual (manual) interpretation and is not used if further numeric analysis is desired.

There are several alternative approaches to decision and classification. In this step, data that have been subjected to pre-processing and feature extraction are subjected to quantitative analysis to assign individual pixels to specific classes. That is, individual pixels are grouped together image. These groups may correspond to regions on the ground that have common geologic or biologic properties and therefore may be useful to the analyst as a means of deriving information concerning subjects such as land use, water quality, geology and plant vigour. Figure 5.16 indicates the choice between the two alternative approaches to image classification. Supervised classification uses information derived from a few areas of known identity to classify the remainder of the image, consisting of those pixels of unknown identity. The analyst must carefully locate both on the ground and on the image areas that represent the classes of interest to be represented on the final product. These areas must be carefully selected as accurate samples of the broader categories they are to represent and their location must be carefully recorded to assist in delineation of these corresponding regions on the image. Once these 'training areas' or 'training fields', have been accurately located on the image, the classification procedure uses characteristics of these areas to assign pixels of unknown identity to each of the categories specified by the operator.

Unsupervised classification, the alternative to supervised classification, is the search for 'natural' groupings of pixels based upon their brightnesses is several spectral channels. The analyst then attempts to assign these 'natural' classes to the user-defined categories (e.g., 'forest' or 'water') that are of value to the scientists and planners who will use the results.

After classification is complete, it is necessary to assess its accuracy by comparing the categories on the classified images with areas of known identity on the ground. If such comparisons can be conducted for each category, the analyst can develop information that permits assessment of the categories that are most accurately classified and can document the quality of the results.

The final results of the analysis consist of maps (or images), data and a report. The maps and images provide the user with knowledge of the spatial distributions of the categories of interest and their patterns on the landscape. Data are provided by tabulations of classes and their areas. Finally, the report provides a clear account of the images examined, the procedures that were used and the results of the accuracy assessment. These three components of the results provide the user with full information concerning the source data, method of analysis, the outcome and its reliability.

EQUIPMENT FOR DIGITAL ANALYSIS

Digital analysis requires specialised equipment tailored for the storage, display and analysis of the large amounts of data that are necessary to record remotely sensed images. Remote sensing analysis has specific needs for input, storage, analysis and display of data that are often not fully met by standard equipment and programmes.

Computers

Although there was a time when some computers were specifically designed to analyse and display remotely sensed data, these computers were too expensive and inflexible for widespread use. Therefore, although remote sensing analysis may sometimes require extra memory, disk storage or peripheral devices, today the vast majority of remote sensing analysis uses general purpose computers and specialised remote sensing software.

The heart of any digital computer is its central processing unit (CPU), which consists of three components (Fig. 5.17). The control unit manages the flow of data and instructions to and from the CPU and to and from input and output devices. Once CPUs were massive networks of vacuum tubes, wires and switches that filled several rooms. Today the electrical pathways for a CPU are tiny circuits printed on silicon chips perhaps half the size of a credit card. Successive generations of chips have become increasingly more powerful and efficient, so the once arcane designations assigned by manufacturers to chips have become common shorthand for designating the power of a computer.

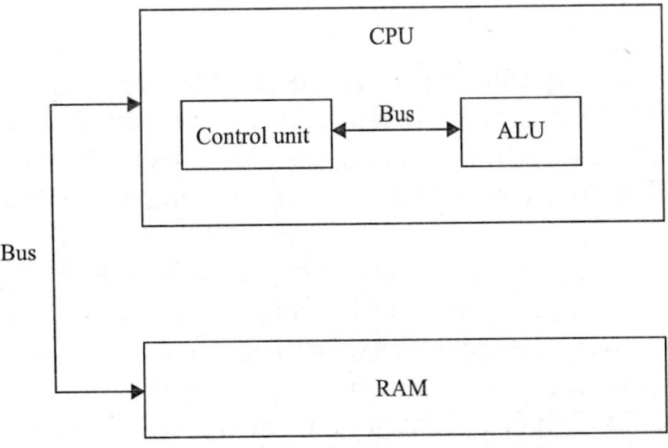

Fig. 5.17. Schematic representation of the CPU.

Within the CPU, the arithmetic/logic unit (ALU) manipulates input data to produce new (output) values that form results of a particular operation. Any computer program, when resolved into its simplest components, consists of a sequence of fundamental operations such as addition, multiplication and comparisons of values. These operations are often performed by specially designed silicon chips that form the ALU. Whereas most chips simply store bits that record data without altering the values, those in the ALU are designed to perform arithmetic or logical operations, so that the data they return to the CPU are altered from the data that they receive. The ALU receives data from the control unit, performs the required operations, then returns the results to the control unit. Although each operation of the ALU is itself very simple, a computer's power is achieved by its ability to perform millions of such simple operations quickly, with accuracy and with precision.

The third component of the CPU is its primary storage—the CPU's internal memory. Primary storage is known as random access memory (RAM), meaning that the CPU has direct access to each location in primary memory without sequential searching through preceding addresses and without mechanical movement (as are required with other forms of memory). Every value is stored in binary form, as described previously. The capabilities of main memory are a function of the number of bits used to record each value in memory, which is a function of the design of the chips that form the computer's main memory. Computers used for image processing now use 32 bit processors, meaning that each value stored in main memory is recorded with the precision of 32 bits, as explained previously. Because the CPU must load a program and data into primary storage, the amount of primary storage determines many of the capabilities of the computer. Small primary storage means that the computer can run rather short programs on small data sets; large primary storage means that the computer can run linger programs on larger data sets. For image-processing work, 256 megabytes (MB) of memory is common, with 512 MB available for more advanced systems.

The CPU, RAM and ALU are connected by data buses, electrical pathways that transfer data from one portion of the computer to another. A bus consists of wires, connectors and controllers; a bus must provide one wire for each bit required to specify the address of a location in memory, plus additional pathways to distinguish among the alternative data transfer options possible. For PCs, the design of the bus, often known as the expansion bus, determines the extent to which a computer's memory, speed and peripheral support can be expanded by adding or upgrading components. The capacity of the bus to transmit data determines the speed at which it can operate; current computers transmit data at 850 MHz or more, with speeds of 1.5 GHz representing an upper limit.

Mass Storage

Because remotely sensed data typically require very large storage capacities, image-processing systems use substantial amounts of disk storage. Disks can be manufactured from either rigid or flexible materials that are coated with a magnetised substance that is sensitised to record the bits that represent each digital value. The computer's disk drive rapidly spins the disk, allowing the computer to read data from both sides.

Rigid (hard) disks provide rapid access to the very large amounts of storage (perhaps 50–100 gigabytes [GB]) required for image processing. The flexible (floppy) disks have far smaller storage capacities (1.44 MB) and provide slower access to the data; they are used primarily for smaller computers, where the demands for storage and access are not as critical. Also available are a variety of removable disk drives that can store 100–250 MB (e.g., Iomega® Zip® drives) to 2 GB (e.g., Iomega® JAZ® drives) of data in a compact, transportable form.

Older computer systems used computer tapes, strips of coated plastic film that have been sensitised to record digital data when the write heads of tape drives encode them with magnetic marks that record bits and bytes, to record data. The computer tapes were manufactured in a range of sizes and capacities, some as small as the audio cassettes familiar to most readers. The amount of data recorded on a tape is determined in part by the density of data written to the tape; usually data are written at either 1600 bits per inch (BPI) or 6250 BPI (even older tapes may have been written at 800 BPI). Computers could read from and write to magnetic tape by means of tape drives, which could rapidly wind and unwind spools of tape. Sensitised read and write heads could sense the magnetic record of bits. Magnetic tapes once formed the primary means of providing archive (back-up) copies for use in the event a primary copy was accidentally destroyed.

Because tape drives were difficult to maintain, because tapes required special storage and handling precautions and because experience revealed that tape and their magnetic coatings deteriorated over time, tapes have been almost completely replaced by other mass storage media.

CD-ROM (compact disk, read-only memory) storage is the oldest and most reliable form of optical storage. Each CD-ROM consists of an internal disk coated with a very thin metal (usually aluminium) surface, then encased in a plastic shell. Data are recorded as microscopic indentations on the silver surface of the internal disc. CD-ROMs must be read using special drives, available as peripheral units or a standard equipment on personal computers. The CD-ROM drive reads the disk by directing a laser beam at the surface of the disk; by examining the way in which the laser is reflected from the disc, it can read the pattern of indentations formed when the disc was created. The CD-ROM forms a durable, reliable and stable storage medium, although some users find the inability to re-write data a disadvantage—conventional CD-ROM drives cannot alter the indentations of the internal disk, so there is no way to write new data to a disk.

Because each disk can hold 680 MB, it forms a compact, durable means of storing remote sensing data. Once encoded, CD-ROMs cannot be erased or re-written, so they are suitable primarily, in the context of remote sensing, as a means of transmitting raw image data that will be read many times.

Efforts to create more flexible mass storage have resulted in the CD-R and the CD-RW formats. CD-R (compact disc-recordable) are CDs that can be written by a user one time, but not altered once written. In contrast, a CD-RW (compact disc re-writable) drive can re-write the same disk several times. Disks written using CD-R and CD-RW devices can be read by CD-ROM drives. CD-RW and CD-R media are inexpensive—their principal disadvantage is that the ability to re-write data is limited. CD-R disks are not re-writable and until recently CD-RW discs had to be reformatted to recover the space take by deleted files; CD-RW rewriteability is imperfect because successive re-writes reduce the CD-RW disk's capacity. In recent years CD-ROM disks and CD-ROM drives have become so inexpensive that they can be used as a routine means of distributing image data.

Digital video disc (DVD) is another form of optical disc storage technology, analogous to CD technology, but faster and providing larger capacities. DVD is best known for its applications to cinema-like video data, but its large capacity and compact size offer obvious advantages for storage of other digital data, including digital remote sensing imagery. (It is important to note that although the discs used for video and computer applications may be physically identical, the application formats for DVDs used for video storage will differ from those used for data storage). Capacities of DVDs depend upon the format employed. A singled-sided DVD might hold 4.7 billion bytes. (Although the convention in the world of computer science is to specify capacity in multiples of 1024 (2^{10}) bytes, the commercial world of DVDs measures capacity in multiples of 1000 bytes, following usual conventions of SI units. Therefore, it is important to carefully evaluate the true capacity of DVD before relying on it to store a specific set of data, because for large capacities, the difference in the two conventions can be significant. At present, DVDs are not widely used to store remotely sensed data, although we can expect such applications to increase.

Image Display

For remote sensing computing, the image display is especially important because the analyst must be able to examine images and to inspect results of analyses, which often are themselves images. At the simplest level an image display can be thought of as a high-quality television screen, although those tailored specifically for image processing have image-display processors, which are special computers designed to very rapidly receive digital data from the main computer, then display them as brightnesses on the screen. The capabilities of an image display are determined by several factors. First is the size of the image it can display, usually specified by the number of rows and columns it can show at any one time. A large display might show 1600 rows and 1280 columns. A smaller display with respectable capabilities could show a 1024 × 768 image; others of much more limited capabilities could shown only smaller sizes, perhaps 800 × 600.

Second, a display has a given radiometric resolution, that is, for each pixel, it has a capability to show a range of brightnesses. One-bit resolution would give the capability to represent either black or white—certainly not enough detail to be useful for most purposes. In practice, 6 bits (64 brightness levels) are minimally necessary for gray-scale images to appear 'natural', and high-quality displays typically display 8 bits (256 brightness levels) or more.

A third factor controls the rendition of colour in the displayed image. The method of depicting colour is closely related to the design of the image display and the display processor. Image-display data are held in the frame buffer, a large segment of computer memory dedicated to handling data for display. The frame buffer provides one or more bits to record the brightness of each pixel to be shown on the screen (the 'bit plane'); thus the displayed image is generated, bit by bit, in the frame buffer. The more bits that have been designed in the frame buffer for each pixels, the greater the range of brightnesses that can be shown for that pixels, as explained above. For actual display on the screen, the digital value for each pixel is converted into an electrical signal that controls the brightness of the pixel on the screen. This requires a digital-to-analog (D-to-A) converter that translates discrete digital values into continuous electrical signals (the opposite function or the A-to-D converter mentioned previously).

Display of colour images requires a more complex process. For the simplest and cheapest colour displays (sometimes known as 'pseudocolour' displays), the image is stored in a single memory plane (Fig. 5.18). The colour for each pixel is determined by matching it to set of colours (a 'palette') stored in a segment of memory known as a look-up table. Values in the look-up table control the intensities of three A-to-D converters (one for each primary) that create colours on the display screen. The number of colours in the palette is determined by the number of bits in the look-up table. The values in the look-up table controls the brightness on the screen in the manner illustrated by Table 5.2. In this simple example, the intensity of each additive primary is controlled by only 1 bit, so only eight colours can be displayed at a given time. Each primary is either 'on' (1) or 'off' (0), resulting in the eight combinations shown in Table 5.2. If the look-up table has more bits, the primaries can be represented more subtly (rather than simply as 'on' or 'off'), so, for example, 4 bits give intensities from 0 to 15, 5 bits intensities from 0 to 31 and 7 bits intensities from 0 to 127. With more subtle variations of the brightnesses of the intensities, the colours on the screen assume a wider range of variations, more nearly approaching those we observe in nature. For example, with 7 bits the display could show red = 127, green = 0 and blue = 0 to produce a pure red on the screen. But it could also show a more subtle shade of colour by setting red = 127, green = 37 and blue = 65, a choice that would not be possible with the simpler system.

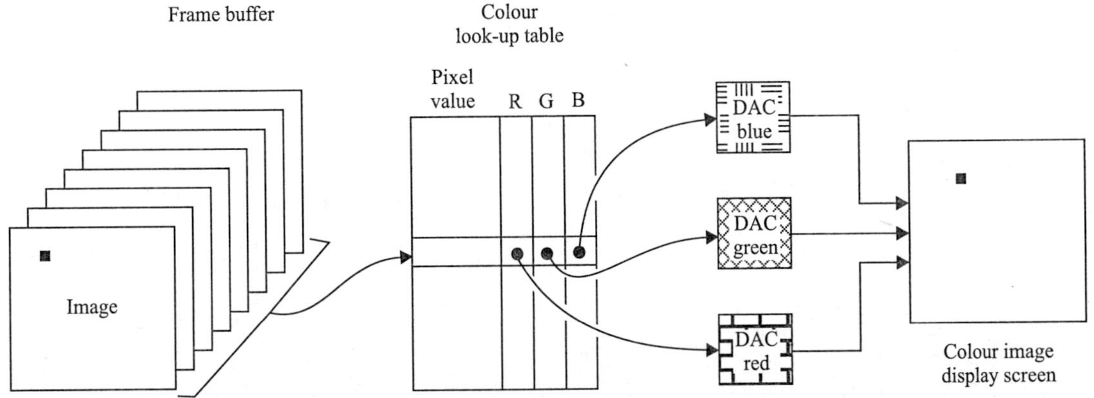

Fig. 5.18. Schematic diagram of a pseudocolour display.

Thus, the look-up table translates pixel values into intensities that can be displayed on the screen. Note that the look-up table may not have sufficient precision to accurately represent the varied detail within the data. (Certainly the example in Table 5.2 would not provide very much detail). The look-up table limits the number of colours that can be shown at a given time, but the analyst can re-configure (or 're-load') the look-up table to select another set of colours. The limitation of pseudocolour technology is both the restriction in the range of colours that can be shown at a given time and the time and inconvenience entailed in reloading and displaying colours.

Table 5.2. Example of look-up table for 3-bit frame buffer.

	Values from bit plane		
Colour on screen	*Red*	*Green*	*Blue*
Black	0	0	0
Red	1	0	0
Green	0	1	0
Blue	0	0	1
Yellow	1	1	0
Cyan	0	1	1
Magenta	1	0	1
White	1	1	1

The alternative form of representing colours is known as 'true', 'full' or 'analog' colour display (Fig. 5.19). A separate memory plane is required for each primary colour, each with its own look-up table and D-to-A converter. Because the three primary colours each reside in independent memory planes, manipulation of colours is much faster and easier than with pseudocolour systems. In addition, each primary colour has its own look-up table, which permits a much wider range of intensities for each primary and therefore a wider range of combinations on the screen, which in practice approximate the range of colours that might be observed in nature—hence the term 'true colour'. True-colour display shows much more realistic and attractive images than do pseudocolour displays, but are also more expensive.

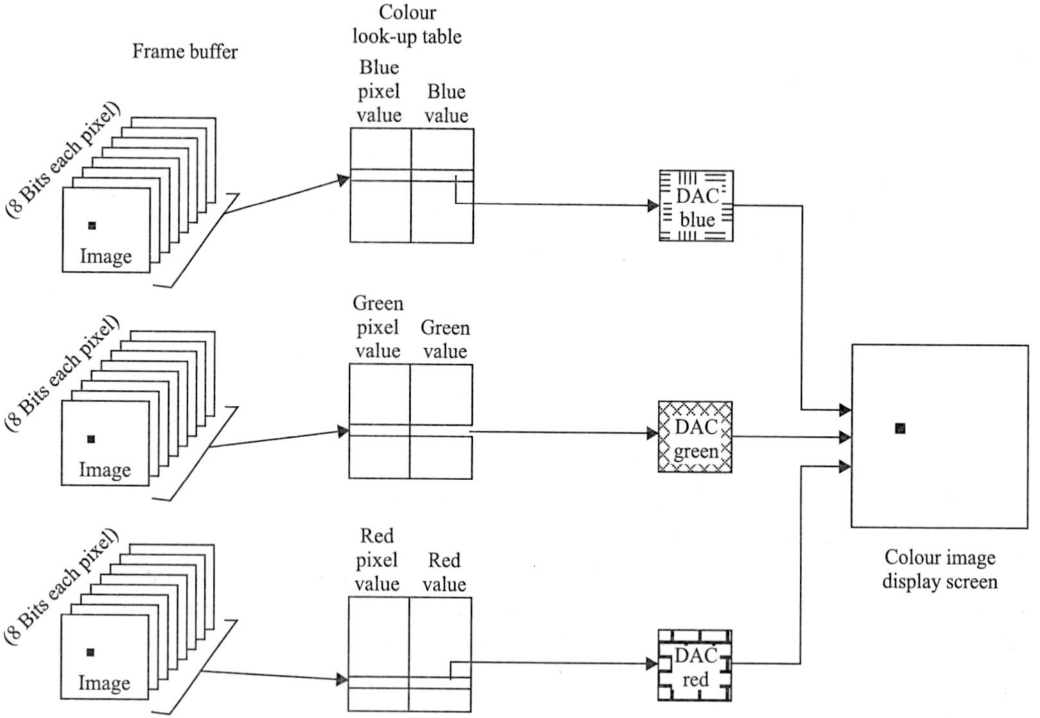

Fig. 5.19. Schematic diagram of a true-colour display.

Table 5.3 lists characteristics of current graphics standards. Image display is important because remote sensing instruments typically record a much wider range of values than can be accurately displayed by film products or by any single representation on an image display device. As a result, displays that provide the analyst with the means to conveniently change image scale, colour assignments, viewing area and the like provide a capability to explore visually the varied dimensions of an image. Such capabilities are not available with film images, where considerable effort is required to study varied representations of a digital image.

Table 5.3. Graphic standards for computer displays.

Name and designation	*Colours*	*Screen size*
Colour graphics adapter (CGA)	4	320 × 200
Extended graphics adapter (EGA)	16	640 × 350
Video graphics array (VGA)	16	640 × 450
Super VGA (S-VGA)	256	800 × 600
Extended graphics array (XGA)[a]	256	1024 × 768

[a] Today many PC displays employ screen sizes of 1280 × 1024. Available, but not now widely used are screen sizes of 1600 × 1280.

Film Recorders and Colour Printers

Film recorders are instruments designed to write image information directly to photographic paper or film. Usually the film is mounted on a cylindrical drum; during operation, the drum spins rapidly. A beam of light is varied in intensity in proportion to image brightness. As the drum spins, the light slowly moves the length of the image, exposing the entire image line by line. If a colour image is to be made, usually it is necessary to make three separate exposures, one for each primary colour. Many colour inkjet and colour laser printers and plotters (even some that are relatively inexpensive) now can provide paper copies of images of good quality that are satisfactory for many uses in the practice of remote sensing.

IMAGE-PROCESSING SOFTWARE

Digital remote sensing data can be interpreted by computer programs that manipulate the data recorded in pixels to yield information about specific subjects, as described in subsequent chapters. This kind of analysis is known as image processing, a term that encompasses a very wide range of techniques. Image processing requires a system of specialised computer programs tailored to the manipulation of digital image data. Although such programs vary greatly in purpose and in detail, it is possible to identify the major components likely to be found in most image-processing systems.

A separate specific portion of the system is designed to read image data, usually from CD-ROM or other storage media and to re-organise the data into the form to be used by the program. For example, many image-processing programs manipulate the data in BSQ format. Thus, the first step may be to read BIL or BIP data and then re-format the data into the BSQ format required for the analytical component of the system. Another portion of the system may permit the analyst to sub-divide the image into sub-images; to merge, superimpose or mosaic separate image and in general to prepare the data for analysis. The heart of the system consists of a suite of programs that analyse, classify and manipulate data to produce output image and statistics and data that may accompany them. Finally, a section of the image-processing system must prepare data for display and output, either to the display processor or to the line printer. In addition, the program requires 'housekeeping' sub-programs that monitor movement and labelling of files from one portion of the program to another, generate error messages and provide online documentation and assistance to the analysts.

Widely used image-processing systems run on PCs, Macintoshes or workstations. More elaborate systems can be supported by peripheral equipment, to including extra mass storage, digitisers, scanners, colour printers, disk drives and related equipment. Almost all such systems are directed by menus and graphic user interfaces that permit the analyst to select options from a list of options on the screen.

For students, some of these systems offer respectable capabilities for illustrating the basic capabilities for image processing. A partial list would include:

MultiSpec: *http://dynamo.ecn.purdue.edu/~biehl/MultiSpec*

TNTlite: *http://www.microimages.com*

INTERNET

Digital data once were available only through physical transfer of disks or tapes, usually an inconvenient, awkward process. Now the availability of the Internet has facilitated not only the acquisition of digital data, but also the equally troublesome task of searching indexes and archives to identify the appropriate coverage. The Internet is a network of computers connected by the world's telecommunications infrastructure of fiber-optic cables, phone lines, microwave relays and satellite links. This hardware infrastructure is supported by software that employs common conventions for the electronic transmission of data. Thus, the Internet consists of servers, computers that run programs designed to share their data with other computers by permitting remote access and clients, computers that run programs designed to access servers.

A large part of the power of the Internet derives from the simultaneous use of some computers as both clients and servers by the establishment of temporary links between computers at distant locations holding related data. Internet users, therefore, can access vast amounts of data residing at varied locations as if the data were immediately at hand. Further, because different users can define their own pathways through the network, it can be tailored with the specific requirements of varied users. Because servers are maintained by a vast and growing number of individuals, businesses, universities and other institutions, the amount and kinds of information available provides an unprecedented resource for students and researchers in the field of remote sensing.

To use these networks users require access to a computer, either an IBM-compatible PC or a Macintosh, equipped with communications software and a modern or ethernet card and access to communications such as a phone line or fiber-optic cable. Finally, Internet users require accounts or user identification, such as those issued by university computing centers or commercial networks, known as Internet service providers (ISPs).

The only real way for students to learn about the Internet is to actually use it. For university students, this is often relatively easy. Further, Internet resources are often changed frequently, so beginners should verify that they use current information.

6

Image Interpretation

INTRODUCTION

Earlier chapters in remote sensing as focused primarily on images of the earth's surface—map-like representations of the earth's surface based on the reflection of electromagnetic energy from vegetation, soil, water, rocks and man-made structures. From such images we learn much that cannot be derived from other sources. Yet such information is not presented to us directly: the information we seek is encoded in the varied tones and textures we see on each image.

To translate images into information, we must apply a specialised knowledge—knowledge that forms the field of image interpretation, which we can apply to derive useful information from the raw uninterpreted images we receive from remote sensing systems.

PROFICIENCY IN IMAGE INTERPRETATION

Proficiency in image interpretation is formed from three separate kinds of knowledge, of which only one—the final one listed here—falls within the scope of this text.

Subject

Knowledge of the subject of our interpretation—the kind of information that motivates us to examine the image—is the heart of the interpretation. Accurate interpretation requires familiarity with the subject of the interpretation. For example, interpretation of geologic information requires education and experience in the field of geology. Yet narrow specialisations are a handicap because each image records a complex mixture of many kinds of information, requiring application of broad knowledge that crosses traditional boundaries between disciplines. For example, accurate interpretation of geological information may require knowledge of botany and the plant sciences as a means of understanding how vegetation patterns on an image reflect geologic patterns that may not be directly visible. As a result, image interpreters should be equipped with a broad range of knowledge pertaining to the subjects at hand and their interrelationships.

Geographic Regions

Knowledge of the specific geographic region depicted on an image can be equally significant. Every locality has unique characteristics that influence the patterns recorded on an image. Often the interpreter may have direct experience within the area depicted on the image that can be applied to the interpretation.

In unfamiliar regions the interpreter may find it necessary to make a field reconnaissance or to use maps and books that describe analogous regions with similar climate, topography or land use.

Remote Sensing System

Finally, knowledge of the remote sensing system is obviously essential. The interpreter must understand how each image is formed and how each sensor portrays landscape features. Different instruments use separate portions of the electromagnetic spectrum, operate at different resolutions and use different methods of recording images. The image interpreter must know how each of these variables influences the image to be interpreted and how to evaluate their effects on his or her ability to derive useful information from the imagery. This chapter outlines how the image interpreter derives useful information from the complex patterns of tone and texture on each image.

CONTEXT FOR IMAGE INTERPRETATION

Human beings are well prepared to examine images, as our visual system and experience equip us to discern subtle distinctions in brightness and darkness, to distinguish between various image textures, to perceive depth and to recognise complex shapes and features. Even in early childhood we apply such skills routinely in everyday experience so that few of us encounter difficulties as we examine, for example, family snapshots or photographs in newspapers. Yet image analyses requires a conscious, explicit effort not only to learn about the subject matter, geographic setting and imaging systems (as mentioned above) in unfamiliar contexts, but also to develop our innate abilities for image analysis.

Three issues distinguish interpretation of remotely sensed imagery from interpretation conducted in everyday experience. First, remotely sensed images usually portray an overhead view—and unfamiliar perspective. Training, study and experience are required to develop the ability to recognise objects and features from this perspective. Second, many remote sensing images use radiation outside the visible portion of the spectrum—in fact, use of such radiation is an important advantage that we exploit as often as possible. Even the most familiar features may appear quite different in non-visible portions of the spectrum than they do in the familiar world of visible radiation. Finally, remote sensing images often portray the earth's surface at unfamiliar scales and resolutions. Commonplace objects and features may assume strange shapes and appearances as scale and resolution change from those to which we are accustomed.

This chapter outlines the art of image interpretation as applied to aerial photography. One cannot expect to become proficient in image analysis simply by reading about image interpretation. Experience forms the only sure preparation for skillful interpretation. Yet this chapter can highlight some of the issues that form the foundations for proficiency in image analysis.

In order to discuss this subject at an early point in the text, we must confine the discussion to interpretation of aerial photography, the only form of remote sensing imagery discussed thus far. But the principles, procedures and equipment described here are equally applicable to other kinds of imagery acquired by the sensors described in later chapters.

IMAGE INTERPRETATION TASKS

The image interpreter must routinely conduct several kinds of tasks, many of the which may be completed together in an integrated process. Nonetheless, for purposes of clarification, it is important to distinguish between these separate functions (Fig. 6.1).

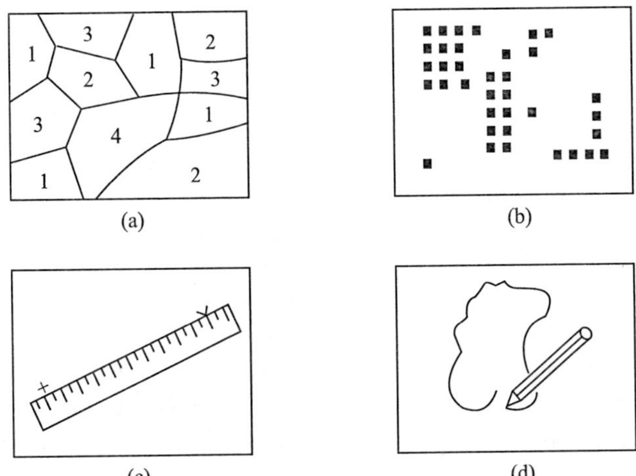

Fig. 6.1. Image interpretation skills. (a) Classification; (b) enumeration; (c) mensuration; and (d) delineation.

Classification

Classification is the assignment of objects, features or areas to classes based on their appearance on the imagery. Often a distinction is made between three levels of confidence and precision. Detection is the determination of the presence or absence of a feature. Recognition implies a higher level of knowledge about a feature or object, such that the object can be assigned an identity in a general class or category. Finally, identification means that the identity of an object or feature can be specified with enough confidence and detail to place it in a very specific class. Often an interpreter may qualify his or her confidence in an interpretation by specifying the identification as 'possible' or 'probable'.

Enumeration

Enumeration is the task of listing or counting discrete items visible on an image. For example, housing units can be classified as 'detached single-family home', 'multifamily complex', 'mobile home' and 'multistory residential' and then reported as numbers present within a defined area. Clearly, the ability to conduct such an enumeration depends upon an ability to accurately identify and classify items as discussed above.

Measurement/Mensuration

Measurement or mensuration, is an important function in many image interpretation problems. Two kinds of measurement are important. First is the measurement of distance and height and by extension, of volumes and areas as well. The practice of making such measurements forms the subject of photogrammetry, which applies knowledge of image geometry to the derivation of accurate distances. Although strictly speaking photogrammetry applies only to measurements from photographs, by extension it has analogs for the derivation of measurements from other kinds of remotely sensed images.

A second form of measurement is quantitative assessment of image brightness. The science of photometry is devoted to measurement of the intensity of light and include estimation of scene brightness by examination of image tone, using special instruments known as denstitometers, described below. If the measured radiation extends outside the visible spectrum, the term radiometry applies. Both photometry and radiometry apply similar instruments and principles, so they are closely related.

Delineation

Finally, the interpreter must often delineate or outline, regions as they are observed on remotely sensed images. The interpreter must be able to separate distinct areal units that are characterised by specific tones and textures and to identify edges or boundaries between separate areas. Typical examples include delineation of separate classes of forest or of land use—both occur only as areal entities (rather than as discrete objects). Typical problems include: (i) selection of appropriate levels of generalisation (e.g., when boundaries are intricate or when many tiny but distinct parcels are present); and (ii) placement of boundaries when there is a gradation (rather than a sharp edge) between two units.

The image analyst may simultaneously apply several of these skills in examining an image. Recognition, delineation and mensuration may all be required as the interpreter examines an image. Yet specific interpretation problems may emphasise specialised skills. Military photo interpretation often depends upon accurate recognition and enumeration of specific items of equipment, whereas land-use inventory emphasises delineation, although other skills are obviously important. Image analysts therefore need to develop proficiency in all of these skills.

ELEMENTS OF IMAGE INTERPRETATION

By tradition, image interpreters are said to employ some combination of the eight elements of image interpretation, which describe characteristics of objects and features as they appear on remotely sensed images. Image interpreters quite clearly use these characteristics together in very complex, but poorly understood, processes as they examine images. Nonetheless, it is convenient to list them separately as a way of emphasising their significance.

Image Tone

Image tone denotes the lightness or darkness of a region within an image. For black-and-white images, tone may be characterised as 'light', 'medium gray', 'dark gray', 'dark' and so on, as the image assumes varied shades of white, gray or black. For colour or CIR imagery, image tone refers simply to 'colour', described informally perhaps in such terms as 'dark green', 'light blue' or 'pale pink'. Image tone refers ultimately to the brightness of an area of ground as portrayed by the film in a given spectral region (or in three spectral regions, for colour or CIR film).

Image tone can also be influenced by the intensity and angle of illumination and by the processing of the film. Within a single aerial photograph, vignetting may create noticeable differences in image tone due solely to the position of an area within a frame of photography: the image becomes darker near the edges. Thus the interpreter must employ caution in relying solely on image tone for an interpretation, as it can be influenced by factors other than the absolute brightness of the earth's surface. Analysts should also remember that very dark or very bright regions on an image may be exposed in the non-linear portion of the characteristic curve, so they may not be represented in their correct relative brightnesses. Also, non-photographic sensors may record such a wide range of brightness values that they cannot all be accurately represented on photographic film—in such instances digital analyses may be more accurate.

Experiments have shown that interpreters tend to be consistent in interpretation of tones on black-and-white imagery, but less so in interpretation of colour imagery. Interpreter's assessment of image tone is much less sensitive to subtle differences in tone than are measurements by instruments (as might be expected). For the range of tones used in the experiments, human interpreter's assessment of tone expressed a linear relationship with corresponding measurements made by instruments. Cihlar and Protz's results imply that a human interpreter can provide reliable estimates of relative differences in tone, although he or she may not be capable of accurate description of absolute brightness.

Image Texture

Image texture refers to the apparent roughness or smoothness of an image region. Usually texture is caused by the pattern of highlighted and shadowed areas created when an irregular surface is illuminated from an oblique angle. Contrasting examples include the rough textures of a mature forest and the smooth textures of a mature wheat field. The human interpreter is very good at distinguishing subtle differences in image texture, so it is a valuable aid to interpretation—certainly equal in importance to image tone in many circumstances.

Image texture depends not only upon the surface itself, but also upon the angle of illumination, so it can vary as lighting varies. Also, good rendition of texture depends upon favourable image contrast, so images of poor or marginal quality may lack the distinct textural differences so valuable to the interpreter.

Shadow

Shadow is an especially important clue in the interpretation of objects. A building or vehicle, illuminated at an angle, casts a shadow that may reveal characteristics of its size or shape that would not be obvious from the overhead view alone. Because military photointerpreters often are primarily interested in identification of individual items of equipment, they have developed methods to use shadows to distinguish subtle differences that might not otherwise be visible. By extension, we can emphasise this role of shadow in interpretation of any man-made landscape in which identification of separate kinds of structures or objects is significant.

Shadow is of great significance also in interpretation of natural phenomena, even though its role may not be as obvious. For example, Fig. 6.2a depicts an open field in which scattered shrubs and bushes are separated by areas of open land. Without shadows, the individual plants might be too small and so nearly similar in tone to their background to be visible. Yet their shadows are large enough and dark enough, to create the streaked pattern on the imagery typical of this kind of land. A second example is shown in Fig. 6.2b. At the edge between mature forest and open land, the forest often casts a shadow that, at small scale, appears as a dark strip that enhances between the two zones as seen on the imagery.

Pattern

Pattern refers the arrangement of individual objects into distinctive recurring forms that facilitate the recognition on aerial imagery. Pattern on an image usually follows from a functional relationship between the individual features that compose the pattern. Thus the buildings in an industrial plant may have a distinctive pattern due to their organisation to permit economical flow of materials through the plant from receiving raw material to shipping of the finished product. The distinctive spacing of trees in an orchard arises from careful planting of trees at intervals that prevent competition between individual trees and permits convenient movement of equipment through the orchard.

Association

Association specifies the occurrence of certain objects or features, usually without the strict spatial arrangement implied by pattern. In the context of military photointerpretation, association of specific items has great significance, as, for example, when the identification of a specific class of equipment implies that other, more important, items are likely to be found nearby.

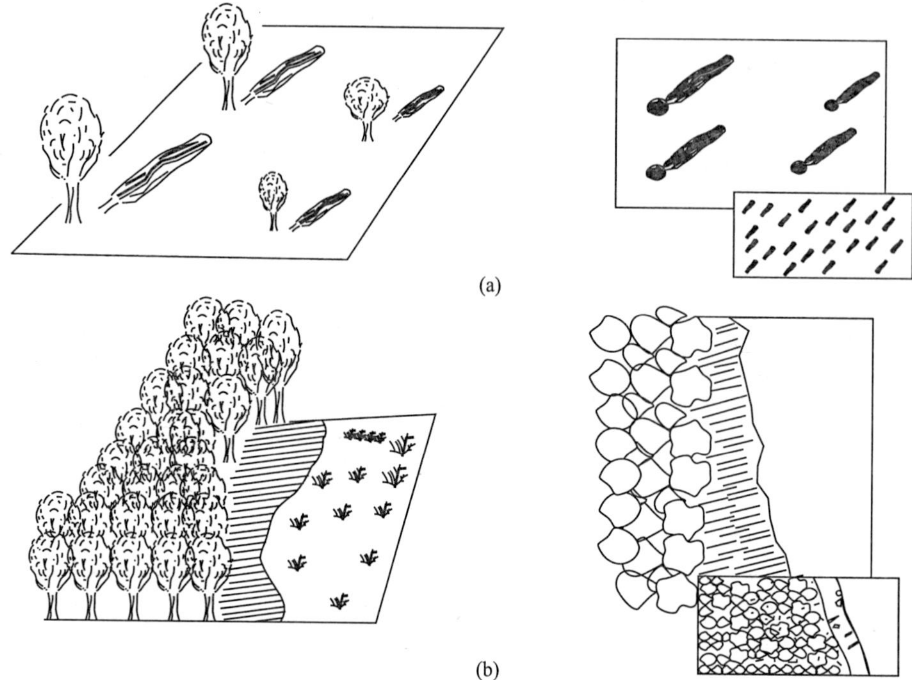

Fig. 6.2. Significance of shadow: (a) Characteristic pattern caused by shadows of shrubs cast on open field; and (b) Shadow at the edge of a forest enhances the boundary between two different land types.

Shape

Shapes of features are obvious clues to their identities. For example, individual structures and vehicles have characteristic shapes, which, if visible in sufficient detail, provide the basis for identification. Features in nature often have such distinctive shapes that shape alone might be sufficient to provide clear identification. For example, ponds, lakes and rivers occur in specific shapes unlike others found in nature. Often specific agricultural crops tend to be planted in fields that have characteristic shapes (perhaps related to the constraints of equipment used or the kind of irrigation that the farmer employs).

Size

Size is important in two ways. First, the relative size of an object or feature in relation to other objects on the image provides the interpreter with an intuitive notion of its scale and resolution, even though no measurements or calculations may have been made. This intuition is achieved via recognition of familiar objects (dwellings, highways, rivers, etc.), then extrapolation to relate the sizes of these known features to estimate the sizes and identities of those objects that might not be easily identified. This is probably the most direct and important function of size.

Second, absolute measurements can be equally valuable as interpretation aids. Measurements of the size of an object can confirm its identification based upon other factors, especially if its dimensions are so distinctive that they form definitive criteria for specific items or classes of items. Furthermore, absolute measurements permit derivation of quantitative information, including lengths, volumes or (sometimes) even rates of movement (e.g., of vehicles or ocean waves as they are shown in successive photographs).

Site

Site refers to topographic position. For example, sewage treatment facilities are positioned at low topographic sites near streams or rivers to collect waste flowing through the system from higher locations. Orchards may be positioned at characteristic topographic sites—often on hillsides (to avoid cold air drainage to low-lying areas) or near large water bodies (to exploit cooler spring temperatures near large lakes to prevent early blossoming).

DATA CHARACTERISTICS

A basic understanding of the characteristics of remote sensing data is necessary to consider the relevance of the multispectral or hyperspectral view of the forest. Such understanding is required to judge when the remote sensing perspective from above is the most appropriate view to select in a given problem context. In earlier chapters, some sense of the various data characteristics was provided, but now it is appropriate to become more specific. The comments are restricted to the two main portions of the electromagnetic spectrum (Fig. 6.3) currently used in remote sensing forestry applications: (i) optical/infrared; and (ii) active microwave. Of these two, optical/infrared imagery are presently the most common and this will likely to continue in the future.

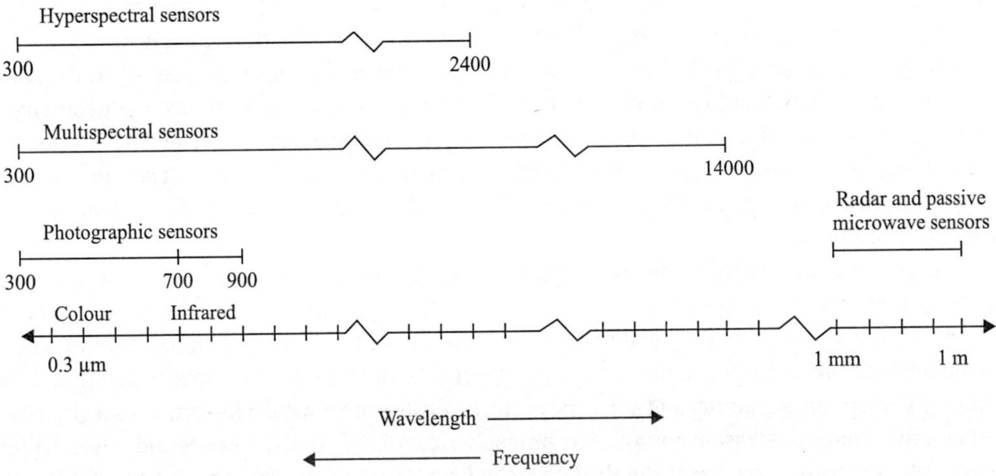

Fig. 6.3. Electromagnetic spectrum with regions of interest in forestry remote sensing. Although many sensors operate in different regions of the spectrum and provide data useful in forestry applications, the main regions of interest are the optical/infrared and microwave portions of the spectrum.

Other remote sensing image data acquired using other sensors or in different regions of the electromagnetic spectrum have specific characteristics that must be considered prior to their use in forestry applications. For example, lidar data are not yet operational in any region of the world yet their potential is enormous—the promise of accurate and reliable tree and canopy height information. Imagery acquired in the thermal, UV and passive microwave regions are typically used in specialised applications rather than as a general-purpose information source in forestry. In some applications, these other types of data are absolutely necessary—for example, thermal imagery can be used in reconstruction of surface temperature patterns which in some forests can be related to vegetation water stress and biodiversity. In other applications it is useful to be aware of the characteristics of these imagery as substitutes or ancillary information for the main optical and microwave imagery.

Optical Image Formation Process

In an ideal world, a remote sensing image would be formed directly from the reflectance provided by a target and received by a perfectly designed sensor. The only limiting factor would be the wavelength sensitivity of the sensor. Of course, reality means that remote sensing imagery is acquired in a process that is much more complex. Major complications arise from the quality of the sensor and the recording medium and in the process of acquiring the actual spectral measurement. An image, formed by observations of differing amounts of energy from reflecting surfaces, is affected by the original characteristics of these reflecting surfaces (such as leaves, bark, soil) and a whole host of other factors, such as the atmosphere and the adjacent surfaces involved in the image formation process.

The most important aspect of the image formation process is to understand how it is possible to create imagery in which it is not clear what element of the process—the spectral characteristics of the target, the illumination geometry or the atmosphere—has caused the particular appearance of the image. Ideally, the process should be completely and singularly invertible; that is, based on the appearance of the image it should be possible to reconstruct the cause of the appearance and as noted, in the ideal world the sole cause of image appearance would be the influence of the target. Unfortunately, the appearance of targets in imagery is affected by the fact that remote sensing measurements are typically acquired at specific angles in incidence (e.g., the solar and sensor positions). Surfaces reflect incoming energy in a pattern referred to as the bidirectional reflectance distribution function (BRDF): this effect is best considered as the difference in reflectance visible as the position of the viewer changes with respect to the source of light. Forests, in particular, are strongly directional in their reflectance; it is not just the geometry of the sensor and the source of illumination that are important, but the target as well. The BRDF effect is seen across the image as the target position changes within the filed of view of the sensor. Therefore, knowledge of the position of the sensor, the target and the originating energy source may be critical in using the collected measurements.

For example, radiometric processing of imagery can range from little or no consideration of atmospheric effects to a fully functional radiative transfer model of the atmosphere which considers atmospheric constituents, angular effects and optical paths. Much progress has been made in the development of an automatic and user-friendly procedure to correct specific sensor data—particularly Landsat TM—for atmospheric absorption, scattering and adjacency effects. On the other hand, Hall provides a good example of an alternative image processing approach to atmospheric radiative transfer codes and sensor calibration when reliable atmospheric optical depth data or calibration coefficients are not available—which, unfortunately, is often the case. It is this level of image processing that is of interest to those using remote sensing imagery, since it relies on approximations and simplifications of the more complex tools which are sometimes not readily available to all users of remote sensing data.

The factors affecting remote sensing spectral response include (in general order of importance):

1. The spectral properties (reflectance, absorption, transmittance) of the target.
2. The illumination geometry, including topographic effects.
3. The atmosphere.
4. The radiometric properties of the sensor (e.g., signal-to-noise ratio).
5. The geometrical properties of the target (e.g., leaf inclination).

The spectral response curve of green leaf vegetation and idealised biochemical compound reflectance curves are presented in Fig. 6.4. These curves illustrate the portions of the spectrum in which absorption and reflectance dominate for different compounds. For a green leaf, there is typically a small green peak reflectance (at approximately 550 nm) and a small red well of absorption by chlorophylls (at approximately

650 nm). The rapid rise in reflectance in the near-infrared (before 1000 nm) is known as the red-edge and there are several water absorption bands at longer wavelengths. These curves are idealised representations of the measurements; here, the concern is with gaining an appreciation of the sum effect that these factors and the different forest components such as bark, leaves and soil can have on the expression of these spectral measurements contained in remote sensing imagery. Understanding this basic pattern of reflectance and absorption can help with the interpretation of remote sensing imagery in forestry applications.

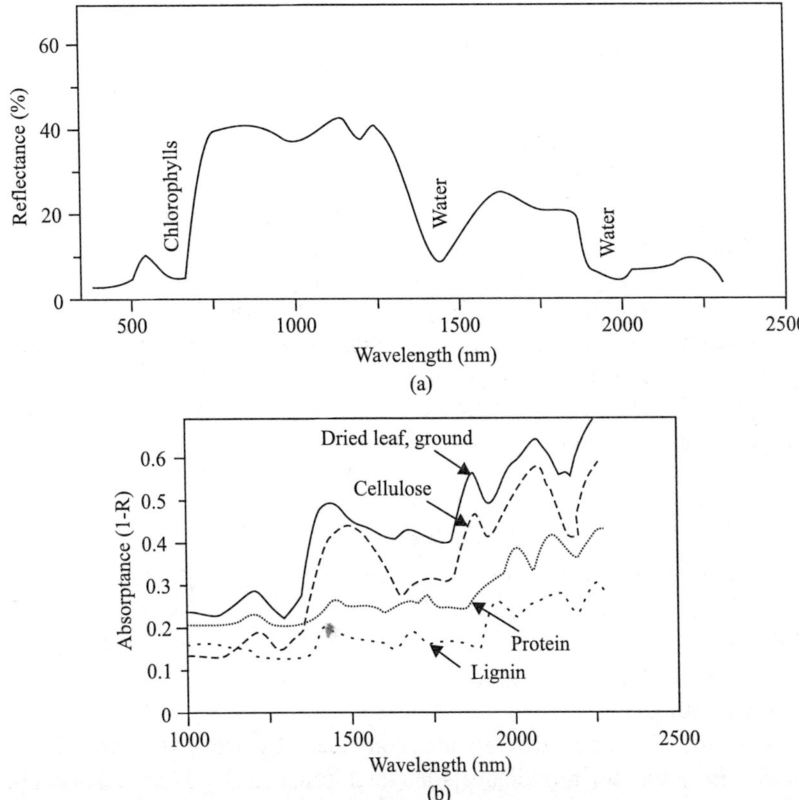

Fig. 6.4. Spectral response curves of vegetation illustrating the portions of the spectrum in which absorption and reflectance dominate. In (a) the total hemispherical spectral reflectance of conifer needles (whole, fresh and stacked five deep before data acquisition) is shown. Note the small green peak reflectance (at approximately 550 nm), the absorption by chlorophylls in the red region of the spectrum, the rapid rise in reflectance in the near-infrared (before 1000 nm) and the water absorption bands at longer wavelengths. In (b) a comparison is shown of the absorptance of oven-dried, ground deciduous leaves measured in a laboratory spectrophotometer compared to the absorptance characteristics of three biochemical compounds (lignin, protein, cellulose). The same features are visible in these curves, which differ primarily in the amount of absorption and reflectance. The original curves have been shifted up and down slightly to improve clarity.

At-Sensor Radiance and Reflectance

Remotely sensed data are typically presented to the user in the form of digital numbers (DN). These digital counts are consistent internally within the image and between different bands (or wavelengths) and therefore can be used in many image analysis tasks without further processing. However, to facilitate comparison between the same or different sensors at different times and the comparison between satellite, airborne and field-based sensors, conversion to physical units (standardised) is required. At-sensor radiance factors may be calculated from the digital numbers with the use of appropriate sensor calibration coefficients. These are published for civilian satellites following in-flight procedures using absolute calibration tests over terrestrial targets such as White Sands, New Mexico (the Landsat platforms) and La Crau, France (the SPOT satellite platforms). The coefficients are stored in the image data header files and are updated regularly by the various satellite operations groups. The at-sensor radiance equation may take the following form:

$$L_s = a_0 + a_1 \text{ DN} \qquad \text{... (6.1)}$$

where: L_s is the at-sensor radiance (W m^{-2} μm^{-1} sr^{-1}),

DN is the raw digital number and

a_0 to a_1 are the absolute calibration coefficients for the particular satellite or airborne sensor system under consideration.

A common approach to computing at-sensor radiances has been to use a normalisation equation with the maximum and minimum DN recorded in the scene. Then, a_0 to a_1 would be equivalent to a simple gain and offset, based on a scaled measure of the range of DN in the image plus a spectral reference. Spectral calibration targets are designed and deployed more easily during airborne remote sensing missions than during satellite overpasses. Similarly, radiometric calibration can be accomplished more easily in sensors that are returned periodically to the laboratory.

The measurement that is most useful in physical applications in forestry is reflectance, which is a property of the target alone. At-sensor reflectances can be calculated:

$$\rho = \frac{\pi d^2 L_s}{E_0 \cos \theta_z} \qquad \text{... (6.2)}$$

where: ρ is the apparent reflectance,

d is the normalised Earth/Sun distance,

L_s is the at-sensor radiance (W m^{-2} μm^{-1} sr^{-1}),

E_0 is the irradiance (W m^{-2} μm^{-1}) and

θ_z is the solar zenith angle.

For an airborne sensor, E_0 is estimated or recorded coincidentally with image acquisition by an incident light sensor measuring incoming solar irradiance; for a satellite sensor, E_0 is the exoatmosphere irradiance. The apparent reflectance does not consider atmospheric, topographic and view angle effects.

SAR Image Formation Process

The principles of microwave interaction with forests have been summarised by Henderson and Lewis. SAR sensors are active remote sensing devices; energy at known wavelengths is both generated and recorded by the instrument. The recorded energy is generally referred to as backscatter. Relationships between microwave backscattering coefficients and forest conditions have been reported as a function of the scattering properties of forests experimentally and empirically. Here the interest is in gaining an appreciation of the principal mechanisms involved in radar beam interactions with a forested landscape (Fig. 6.5); this will include volume scattering (from leaves and branches), direct scattering (from the ground and the stem/ground double-bounce) and other radiative transfers within the scene.

The wavelengths used in microwave sensing are typically long enough that they pass unimpeded through most atmospheric constituents and of course, since the source of illumination is provided, these sensors can operate independent of the Earth's rotation.

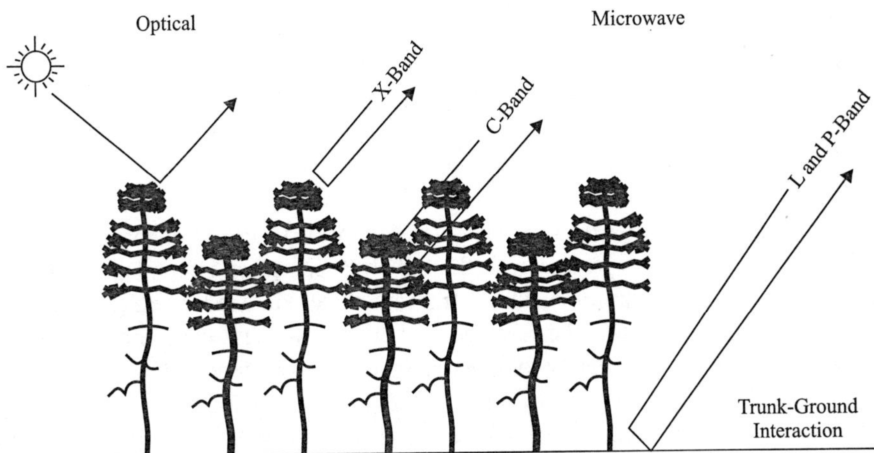

Fig. 6.5. SAR image interactions with forests. Different wavelengths of microwave energy have different penetrating ability in forest canopies; X-Band data (short wavelengths) are dominated by tree leaf interactions in much the same way that optical wavelength data are influenced by closed canopies. C-Band data (slightly longer wavelengths) are dominated by twig and small branch interactions; L and P-Band data (much longer wavelengths) are dominated by the trunk-ground interactions. Many other effects, including those caused by topography and incidence angles, can dominate or influence the SAR image data of forests.

SAR Backscatter

The most common mode of operation for active microwaves is the synthetic aperture radar (SAR) in which the forward motion of the platform is used to artificially generate a long antenna for reception of the microwave beam. This long antenna effectively increases the spatial detail of the subsequent image products. Microwave energy has wavelength range of approximately a centimeter to several meters; radar system wavelengths are designated with letters on the basis of the military code. In all of these systems, the radar equation is used to estimate the strength of the returning signal following emittance of a pulse:

$$P_s = \frac{P_t G_t}{4\pi R^2} \qquad \text{... (6.3)}$$

where: P_s is the power density of the scatterer,
P_t is the power at the transmitter,
G_t is the antenna gain and
R is the distance from the antenna.

The power reflected by the scatterer in the direction of the receiving antenna (S) is equal to P_s times the radar cross-section, which will differ by cover type, wavelength, polarisation and surface geometry.

Typically, image analysts are presented with a two-dimensional array of pixel intensities recorded as 8-bit or 16-bit digital counts, which are proportional to the backscattered amplitude (square-root of power), plus a range-dependent noise level. SAR image data contain shadowing (layover) effects and specular and Lambertian surfaces; in areas of significance relief topography can dominate satellite SAR image data to the point where they may be useless in forestry applications. In one study, Foody found that the topographic effect could reach 50 per cent of airborne SAR tonal variations of a vegetated study site. Simple empirical corrections for this effect have been reported with mixed results.

IMAGE INTERPRETATION STRATEGIES

An image interpretation strategy can be defined as a disciplined procedure that enables the interpreter to relate geographic patterns on the ground to their appearance on the image. Five categories of image interpretation strategies are defined below.

Field Observations

Field observations are required when the image and its relationship to ground conditions are so imperfectly understood that the interpreter is forced to go to the field himself or herself to make an identification. In effect, the analyst is unable to interpret the image from his or her knowledge and experience at hand and must gather observations to ascertain the relationship between the landscape and its appearance on the image. Field observations are, of course, a routine dimension to any interpretation as a check on accuracy or a means of familiarisation with a specific region. Here their use as an interpretation strategy refers to the fact that when they are required of the interpretation, their use reflects a rudimentary understanding of the manner in which a landscape is depicted on a specific image.

Direct Recognition

Direct recognition is the application of an interpreter's experience, skill and judgment to associate the image patterns with informational classes. The process is essentially a qualitative, subjective analysis of the image using the elements of image interpretation as visual and logical clues. In everyday experience direct recognition is applied in an intuitive manner; for image analysis, it must be disciplined process, involving a very careful systematic examination of the image.

Interpretation by Inference

Interpretation by inference is the use of a visible distribution to map one that is not itself visible on the image. The visible distribution acts as a surrogate or proxy (i.e., a substitute), for the mapped distribution. For example, soils are defined by vertical profiles that cannot be directly observed by remotely sensed imagery. But soil distributions are sometimes very closely related to patterns of landforms and vegetation that are recorded on the image. Thus they can form surrogates for the soil pattern; the interpreter infers the invisible soil distribution from other patterns that are visible. Application of this strategy requires a complete knowledge of the link between the proxy and the mapped distribution; attempts to apply imperfectly defined proxies produce inaccurate interpretations.

Probabilistic Interpretation

Probabilistic interpretations are efforts to narrow the range of possible interpretations by formally integrating non-image information into the classification process, often by means of quantitative classification algorithms. For example, knowledge of the crop calendar can restrict the likely choices when identifying crops of a specific region. If it is known that winter wheat is harvested in June, one's choice of possible crops for interpretation of an image from the month of August can be restricted to eliminate wheat as a likely choice and thereby avoid a potential classification error. Often such knowledge can be expressed as a statement of probability. Possibly certain classes might favour specific topographic sites, but occur over a range of sites, so a decision rule might express this knowledge as a 0.90 probability of finding the class on a well-drained site, but only a 0.05 probability of finding it on a poorly drained site. Several such statements systematically incorporated into the decision-making process can improve classification accuracy.

Deterministic Interpretation

A fifth strategy for image interpretation is deterministic interpretation, the most rigorous and precise approach to image interpretation. Deterministic interpretations are based on quantitatively expressed relationships that tie image characteristics to ground conditions. In contrast with the other methods, most information is derived from the image itself. Photogrammetric analysis of stereo pairs for terrain information is a good example. Suppose a scene is imaged from two separate positions along a flight path. The photogrammetrist can measure the apparent displacement. Based upon his or her knowledge of the geometry of the photographic system, he or she can reconstruct a topographic model of the landscape. The result is therefore the derivation of precise information about the landscape using only the image itself and a knowledge of its geometric relationship with the landscape. Relative to the other methods, very little non-image information is required.

Image interpreters, of course, may apply a mixture of several strategies in a given situation. For example, interpretation of soil patterns may require direct recognition to identify specific classes of vegetation, then application of interpretation by proxy to relate the vegetation pattern to the underlying soil pattern.

COLLATERAL INFORMATION

Collateral or ancillary, information refers to non-image information used to assist in the interpretation of an image. Actually, all image interpretations use collateral information in the form of the implicit, often intuitive, knowledge that every interpreter brings to an interpretation in the form of everyday experience and formal training. In its narrower meaning, it refers instead to the explicit, conscious efforts to employ maps, statistics and similar material to aid in analysis of an image. In the context of image interpretation, use of collateral information is permissible and certainly desirable, provided two conditions are satisfied. First, the use of such information is to be explicitly acknowledged in the written report; and second, the information must not be focused upon a single portion of the image or map to the extent that it produces uneven detail or accuracy in the final map. For example, it would be inappropriate for an interpreter to focus upon acquiring detailed knowledge of tobacco farming in an area of mixed agriculture if he or she then produced highly detailed, accurate delineations of the tobacco fields, but mapped other fields at lesser detail or accuracy.

Collateral information can consist of information from books, maps, statistical tables, field observations or other sources. Written material may pertain to the specific geographic area under examination or if such material is unavailable, it may be appropriate to search for information pertaining the analogous areas—similar geographic regions (possibly quite distant from the area of interest) characterised by comparable ecology, soils, landforms, climate or vegetation.

IMAGERY INTERPRETABILITY RATING SCALES

Remote sensing imagery can vary greatly in quality due both to environmental and to technical conditions influencing acquisition of the data. The National Imagery Interpretability Rating Scale (NIIRS) has been developed for single channel and panchromatic imagery and the Multispectral Imagery Interpretability Rating Scale (MS IIRS) has been developed for multispectral imagery. Such scales are based on evaluations using a large number of experienced interpreters to independently evaluate images of varied natural and man-made features, as recorded by images of varying characteristics. They provide a guide for evaluation if a specific form of imagery is likely to be satisfactory for specific purposes.

IMAGE INTERPRETATION KEYS

Image interpretation keys are valuable aids for summarising complex information portrayed as images. They have been widely used for image interpretation. Such keys serve either or both of two purposes: (i) they are a means of training inexperienced personnel in the interpretation of complex or unfamiliar topics; and (ii) they are a reference aid for experienced interpreters to organise information and examples pertaining to specific topics.

An image interpretation key is simply reference material designed to permit rapid and accurate identification of objects or features represented on aerial images. A key usually consists of two parts: (i) a collection of annotated or captioned images or stereograms; and (ii) a graphic or word description, possibly including sketches or diagrams. These materials are organised in a systematic manner that permits retrieval of desired images by, for example, date, season, region or subject.

Keys of various forms have been used for many years in the biological sciences, especially botany and zoology. These disciplines rely upon complex taxonomic systems that are so extensive that even experts cannot master the entire body of knowledge. The key therefore is a means of organising the essential characteristics of a topic in an orderly manner. It must be noted that scientific keys of all forms require a basic familiarity with the subject matter. A key is not a substitute for experience and knowledge, but a means of systematically ordering information so that an informed user can learn it quickly.

Keys were first routinely applied to aerial images during World War II, when it was necessary to train large numbers of inexperienced photointerpreters in the identification of equipment of foreign manufacture and in the analysis of regions far removed from the experience of most interpreters. The interpretation key formed an effective of organising and presenting the expert knowledge of a few individuals. After the war ended, interpretation keys were applied to many other subjects, including agriculture, forestry, soils and landforms. Their use has been extended from aerial photography to other forms of remotely sensed imagery. Today interpretation keys are still used for instruction and training, but they may have somewhat wider use as reference aids. Also, it is true that construction of a key tends to sharpen one's interpretation skills and encourages the interpreter to think more clearly about the interpretation process.

Keys designed solely for use by experts are referred to as technical keys. Non-technical keys are those designed for use by those with a lower level of expertise. Often it is more useful to classify keys by their formats and organisations. Essay keys consist of extensive written descriptions, usually with annotated images as illustrations. A file key is essentially a personal image file with notes; its completeness reflects the interests and knowledge of the compiler. Its content and organisation suit the needs of the compiler, so it may not be organised in a manner suitable for use by others.

INTERPRETIVE OVERLAYS

Often in resource-oriented interpretations it is necessary to search for complex associations of several related factors that together define the distribution or pattern of interest. For example, often soil patterns may be revealed by distinctive relationships between separate patterns of vegetation, slope and drainage. The interpretive-overlays approach to image interpretation is a way of deriving information from complex interrelationships between separate distributions recorded on remotely sensed images. The correspondence between several separate patterns may reveal other patterns not directly visible on the image (Fig. 6.6).

The method is applied by means of a series of individual overlays for each image to be examined. The first overlay might show the major classes of vegetation, perhaps consisting of dense forest, open forest, grassland and wetlands. A second overlay maps slope classes, including perhaps level, gently sloping and steep slopes. Another shows the drainage pattern and still others might show land use and geology.

Thus, for each image, the interpreter may have as many as five or six overlays, each depicting a separate pattern. By superimposing these overlays, the interpreter can derive information presented by the coincidence of several patterns. From his or her knowledge of the local terrain, the interpreter may know that certain soil conditions can be expected where the steep slopes and the dense forest are found together and that others are expected where the dense forest matches to the gentle slopes. From the information presented by several patterns, the interpreter can resolve information not conveyed by any single pattern.

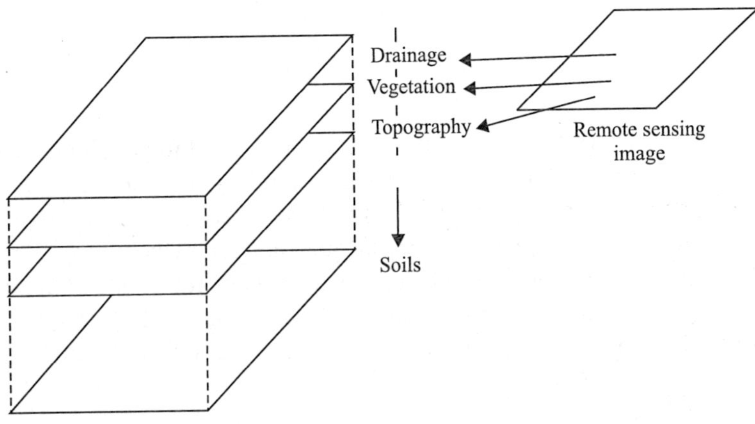

Fig. 6.6. Interpretive overlays.

PHOTOMORPHIC REGIONS

Another approach to interpretation of complex patterns is the search for photomorphic regions, regions of uniform appearance on the image. The interpreter does not attempt to resolve the individual components within the landscape (as he or she does when using interpretive overlays), but instead looks for their combined influence on image pattern. For this reason, application of photomorphic regions may be most valid for small-scale imagery where the coarse resolution tends to average together the separate components of the landscape. 'Photomorphic regions', then, are simply 'image regions' of relatively uniform tone and texture.

In the first step, the interpreter delineates regions of uniform image appearance, using tone, texture, shadow and the other elements of image interpretation as a means of separating regions. In some instances, interpreters have used densitometers to quantitatively measure image tone and variation in image tone as an aid to more subjective interpretation techniques.

In the second step, the interpreter matches photomorphic regions to useful classes of interest to the interpreter. For example, the interpreter must determine if specific photomorphic regions match to vegetation classes. This step obviously requires field observations or collateral information, because regions cannot be identified by image information alone. As the interpretation is refined, the analyst may combine some photomorphic regions or sub-divide others.

Delineation of photomorphic regions is a powerful interpretation tool, but one that must be applied with caution. Photomorphic regions do not always correspond neatly to the categories of interest to the interpreter. The appearance of one region may be dominated by factors related to geology and topography, whereas that of another region on the same image may be controlled by the vegetation pattern. And the image appearance of a third region may be the result of the interaction of several other factors.

IMAGE INTERPRETATION EQUIPMENT

Image interpretation can often be conducted with relatively simple, inexpensive equipment, although some tasks may require expensive items. Typically, an image interpretation laboratory is equipped for storage and handling of images both as paper prints and as film transparencies. Paper prints are most frequently 9 inch × 9 inch contact prints, often stored in sequence in a standard file cabinet. Larger prints and indices must be stored flat in a map cabinet.

Transparencies are available as individual 9 inch × 9 inch frames, but often they are stored as long rolls of film wound on spools and sealed in canisters to protect them from dust and moisture.

Light Tables

A light table is simply a translucent surface illuminated from behind to permit convenient viewing of film transparencies. In its simplest form, the light table is simply a box-like frame with a frosted glass surface. The viewing area in its largest form can be desk-size or can be as small as a briefcase. If role film is to be used, light tables must be equipped with special brackets to hold the film spools and rollers at the edges to permit the film to move freely without damage. More elaborate models have dimmer switches to control the intensity of the lighting, high-quality lamps to control the spectral properties of the illumination and sometimes power drives to wind and unwind long spools of film.

Measurement of Length

Ordinary household rulers are not satisfactory for photointerpretation. Analysts should use an engineer's scale or a ruler with accurate graduations. Both SI units (to at least 1 mm) and English units (to at least $\frac{1}{20}$ inch) are desirable. It is convenient for both measurement and calculation if English units are sub-divided into decimal divisions.

Measurement of Area

Areas on maps or remote sensing imagery can be measured using any of several techniques. At one time, the dot grid was the standard technique for measuring areas. An array of equally spaced dots, printed on a transparent overlay was superimposed over the area to be measured. The analyst could count the number of dots within a delineated area and then apply a formula that related the density of dots on the grid, the number of dots counted and the scale of the image to estimate the area in question. If applied properly, the dot grid was simple, inexpensive and reasonably accurate under most circumstances. However, this method is time-consuming and impractical for complex maps. The polar planimeter is a compact instrument with a moveable arm that can be used to trace the outline of an area; a dial at the base of the arm records the area outlined by the perimeter, usually as the map area (e.g., in square centimeters or square inches), which can then be converted to ground area. Planimeters are simple and reliable. However, accuracy requires the averaging of results from several repetitions, so this method is cumbersome when complex maps must be analysed. Today most analysts measure areas using some form of electronic digitiser, which records an electronic version of the outline traced by the analyst. From this electronic record, a microprocessor can compute areas and apply corrections for image scale. A special, less expensive, version of the electronic digitiser is the electronic planimeter (Fig. 6.7). The analyst can trace outlines with a moveable arm. Coordinates, areas and distance can be read from the display or transferred to a computer if desired. The keyboard permits the analyst to enter commands to the microprocessor and to enter identifying codes as areas are digitised.

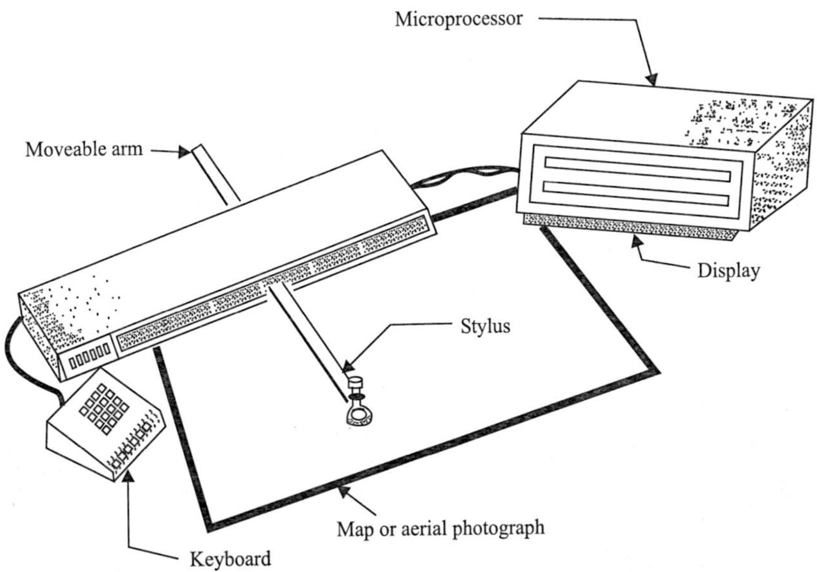

Fig. 6.7. Electronic planimeter. As the operator traces an outline using the moveable arm, the microprocesser records and displays coordinates, distances and areas, as required. The keyboard permits the operator to identify specific lines and regions within identifying codes.

Stereoscopes

Stereoscopes are devices that facilitate stereoscopic viewing of aerial photographs. The simplest and most common is the pocket stereoscope. Its compact size and inexpensive cost make it one of the most widely used remote sensing instruments. Typically, the pocket stereoscope (Fig. 6.8) consists of a body holding two low-power lenses attached to a set of collapsible legs that can be folded so the entire instrument is only a bit larger than a deck of playing cards. The body is usually formed from two separate pieces, each holding one of the two lenses that can be adjusted to control the spacing between the two lenses to accommodate the individual user.

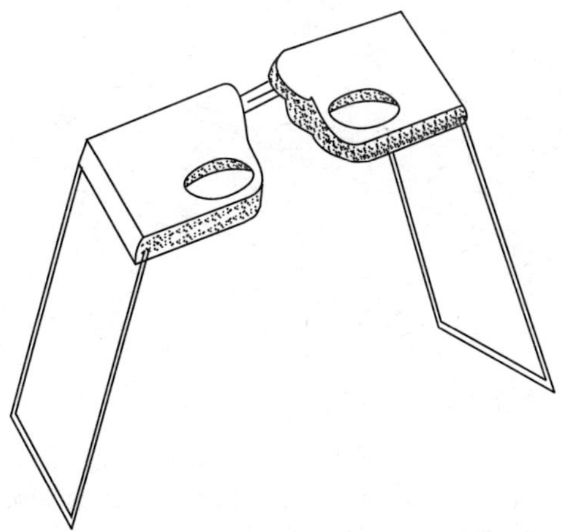

Fig. 6.8. Pocket stereoscope.

Other kinds of stereoscopes include the mirror stereoscope (Fig. 6.9), which permits stereoscopic viewing of large areas, usually at low magnification and the binocular stereoscope (Fig. 6.10), designed primarily for viewing transparencies on light tables. Often the binocular stereoscope has adjustable magnification that enables enlargement of portions of the image up to 20 or 40 times.

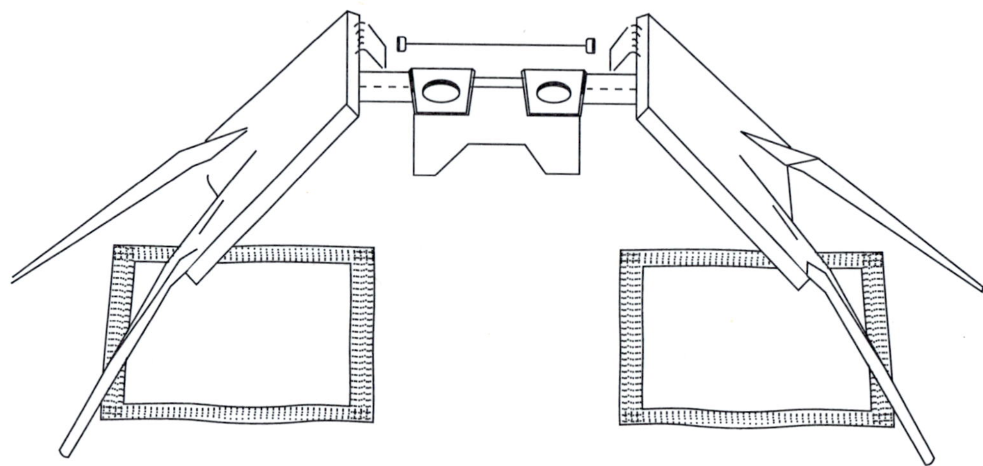

Fig. 6.9. Mirror stereoscope.

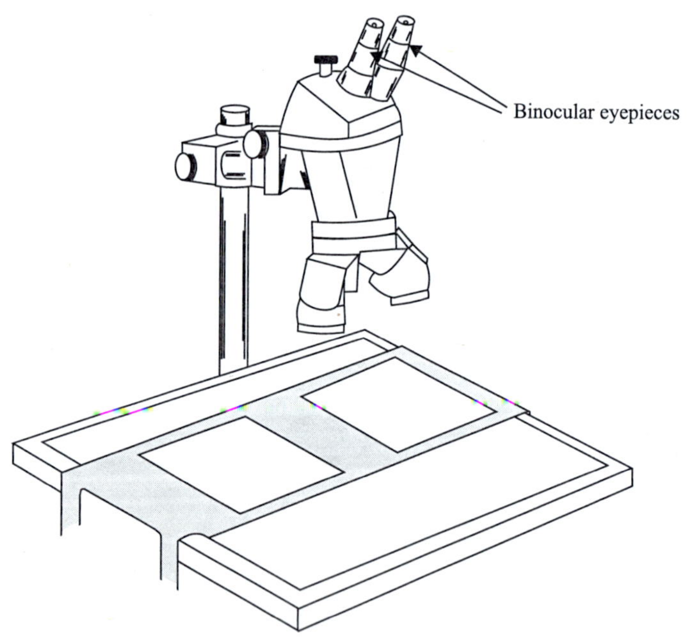

Fig. 6.10. Binocular stereoscope.

The stereoscope is only one of several devices designed to present separate images to each eye to create the stereo effect. Its way of doing this is known as the optical separation technique. Left and right images are presented side by side and an optical device is used to separate the analyst's view of the left and right images. The analyst views the image using special glasses with a red lens for the left eye and blue for the left eye. The coloured lenses cause the image intended for the other eye to blend into the background; the image intended for its own eye will appear as black. The anaglyph has been widely used for novelties, less often as an analytical device. A disadvantage is that it does not permit the analyst to view colour images.

The use of polarised lenses for stereovision is based on the projection of images for each eye through separate polarising filters (e.g., horizontal for the left eye, vertical for the right eye). The combined image must be viewed through special glasses that use orthogonal polarisations for the left and right lenses. This technique is one of the most effective means of stereoviewing for instructional and analytical applications. A proprietary variation of this technique (Crystal Eyes) displays left and right eye views of a digital image in sequential refresh scans on a monitor, then uses synchronised polarised shutter glasses to channel the correct image to the correct eye. This technique forms the basis for stereographic images in many virtual reality display environment. There are many other techniques that are effective to varying degrees for stereovision (including random dot stereograms, Magic Eye images and others)—most are less effective for scientific and analytical applications than stereoscopes and polarised lenses.

Magnification

Image analysts almost always wish to examine images using magnification, although the exact form depends upon individual preference and the nature of the task at hand. A simple, hand held reading glass is satisfactory in many circumstances. Tube magnifiers (Fig. 6.11) are low-power lenses (2× to about 8×) mounted in a transparent tube-like stand. The base may include a reticule calibrated in units as small as 0.001 ft. or 0.1 mm, to permit accurate measurement of small-scale images of objects. Sometimes it is necessary to use the much more expensive binocular microscopes for examination of film transparencies; such instruments may have magnification adjustable to as much as 40 ×, which will approach or exceed the limits of resolution for most images.

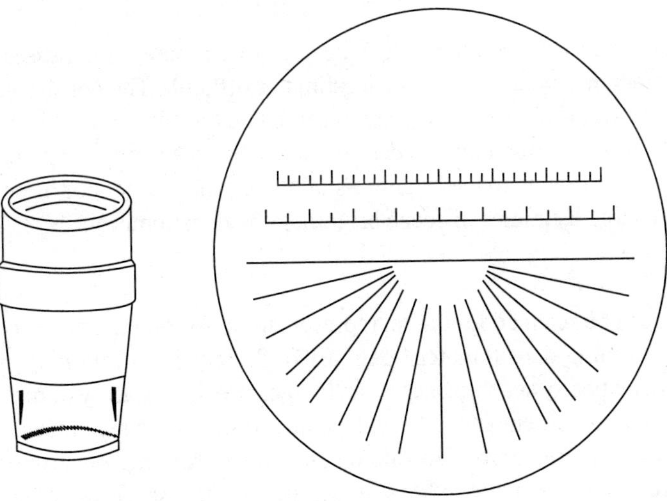

Fig. 6.11. Tube magnifier and reticule.

Densitometry

Densitometry is the science of making accurate measurements of film density. In the context of remote sensing, the objective is often to reconstruct estimates of brightness in the original scene or sometimes merely to estimate relative brightnesses on the film. A densitometer (Fig. 6.12) is an instrument that measures image density by directing a light of known brightness through a small portion of the image, then measuring its brightness as altered by the film. Typically, the light beam might pass through an opening perhaps 1 mm in diameter; use of smaller openings (measured sometimes in micrometers) is known as microdensitometry. Such instruments find densities for selected regions within an image; an interpreter might use a densitometer to make quantitative measurements of image tone. For colour or CIR images, filters are used to make three measurements, one for each of the three additive primaries.

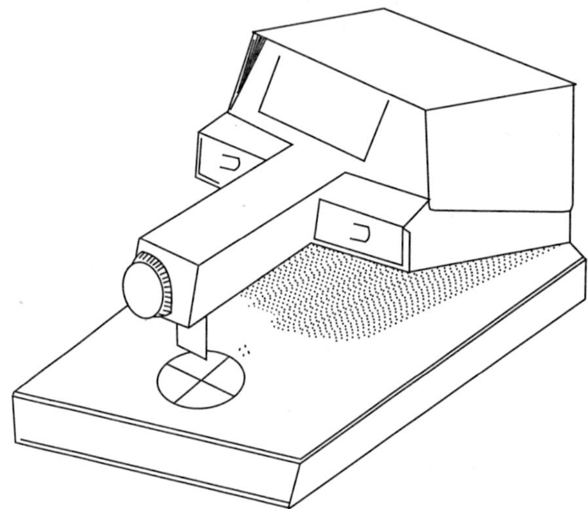

Fig. 6.12. Densitometer.

In principal, densitometric measurements can be used to estimate brightnesses in the original scene. However, several factors intervene to make such estimates difficult. The densitometer must be carefully calibrated; areas of known brightness must be represented on the film and subjected to same processing as the image to be examined. Measurements of densities that fall in the non-linear portion of the characteristic curve cannot, of course, be related to the brightness of the original scene. For these reasons and others, it is difficult to make reliable estimates of scene brightness by densitometry.

Image Scanning

Paper or film images can be scanned for digital representation. Among the most accurate instruments for image scanning are scanning densitometers (Fig. 6.13), designed to accurately and precisely measure image density by systematically scanning across an image, creating an array of digital values to represent the image pattern. Such instruments have been designed to very precisely measure position and image density, possibly using resolutions of a few micrometers or so. Although instruments designed for such precise tolerances are expensive, many other less precise, but still serviceable, scanners can sometimes be used for tasks that do not require high accuracy. Desktop scanners, although designed for office use, can be used to scan maps and images for visual analysis.

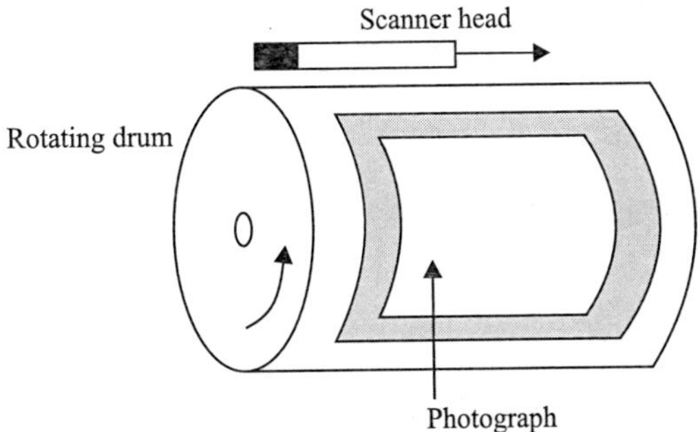

Fig. 6.13. Scanning densitometer.

Height Finder

The height finder (Fig. 6.14) is an instrument designed for use with a stereoscope; it permits estimation of topographic elevation or of the heights of features from stereo aerial photographs. The height finder is a bar that attaches at the base of the stereoscope; the bar holds two plastic tabs, one under each lens of the stereoscope. Both tabs are marked with a small black dot, but one tab is fixed in position, whereas the other can be moved from side to side along a scale that measures its movement left to right parallel to the bar.

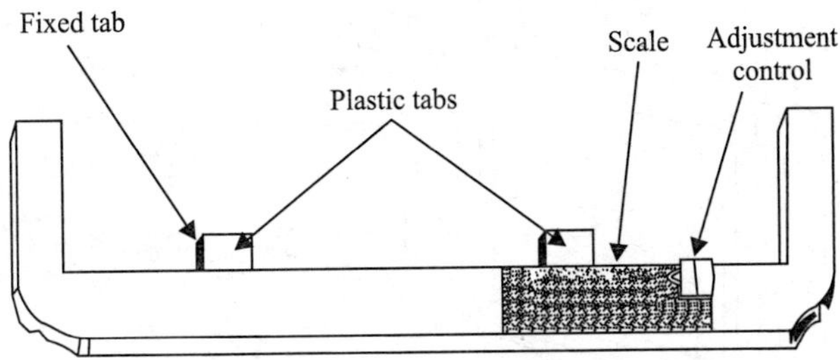

Fig. 6.14. Height finder.

The operator aligns the photographs for stereoscopic viewing after marking their principal points, their conjugate principal points and the flight line. The stereoscope is positioned for stereoscopic viewing as normal. Then the interpreter views the scene stereoscopically, positioning the moveable dot over the feature of interest. Adjustment of the moveable dot causes it to appear to float above the terrain surface; when it is positioned so it appears to rest on the terrain surface, a reading of the scale gives the parallax measurement for that point. A parallax factor is found by using a set of tables. Readings for several points, when combined with simple calculations, permit determination of elevation differences between the individual points (e.g., in feet or meters). If the photographs show a point of known elevation, then these points can be assigned elevations with reference to a datum (e.g., mean sea level); otherwise they provide only relative heights.

Data Transfer

Analysts often need to transfer information from one map or image to another to assure accurate placement of features, to update superseded information or to bring several kinds of information into a common format. Traditionally, these operations have been accomplished by optical projection of maps or images onto a working surface where they could be traced onto an overlay that registers the another image.

Manipulation of the optical system permitted the operator to change scale and to selectively enlarge or reduce portions of the image to correct for tilt and other geometric errors. As digital analysis has become more important, such devices are designed to digitise imagery and match them to other data, with computational adjustments for positional errors.

Digital Photointerpretation

Increasing use of digital photography and softcopy photogrammetry has blurred a previously distinct separation between manual and digital photointerpretation. Analyses that previously were conducted by visual examination of photographic prints or transparencies can now be completed by examination of digital images viewed on computer screens. Photogrammetric software permits projection of image detail in its correct planimetric location, without the positional or scale errors that might be present in the original imagery. In digital format the analyst can manipulate image contrast to improve interpretability of image detail.

Digital photogrammetric workstations (Fig. 6.15), often based on the usual PC or UNIX operating systems, can accept scanned film imagery, airborne digital imagery or digital satellite data. The full range of photogrammetric processes can be implemented digitally, including triangulation, compilation of digital terrain models (DTMs), feature digitisation, construction of orthophotos, mosaics and flythroughs. Analysts can digitise features onscreen ('heads-up' digitisation), using the computer mouse, to record and label features in digital format.

Fig. 6.15. Digital photogrammetric workstation. Operator is shown using polarising stereovision glasses.

PREPARATION FOR MANUAL INTERPRETATION

In general, the interpreter should be able to work at a large, well-lighted desk or work table with convenient access to electrical power. Often it is useful to be able to control lighting with blackout shades or dimmer switches. Basic equipment and materials, in addition to that described above, include a supply of translucent drafting film, an engineer's scale, protractors, triangles, dividers and the like. Maps, reference books and other supporting materials should be available as required.

If the interpretation is made from paper prints, special attention must be devoted to prevent folding, tearing or rough use that will cause the prints to become worn. Usually it is best to mark an overlay registered to the print rather than the print itself. The drafting tape used to attach drafting film must be selected specifically for its weak adhesive quality, which will not tear the emulsion; the stronger adhesive used on many of the popular brands of paper tape will damage paper prints.

If transparencies are used, special care must be give to their handling and storage. The surface of the transparency must be protected by a transparent plastic sleeve or handled only with clean cotton gloves. Moisture and oils naturally present on unprotected skin may damage the emulsion and dust and dirt will scratch the surface. Even if such damage is invisible to the unaided eye, it will later emerge as a major problem when high-power magnification is used.

For most interpretations, images should be oriented so that the shadows fall toward the analyst. Otherwise most individuals will see an apparent reversal in the relative elevations of terrain features: ridges will seem to be valleys and valleys will appear as ridgelines.

USE OF THE POCKET STEREOSCOPE

The pocket stereoscope is one of the most frequently used interpretation aids. As a result, every student should be proficient in its use. Although many students will require the assistance of the instructor as they learn to use the stereoscope, the following paragraphs may provide some assistance for beginners.

First, stereo photographs must be aligned so that the flight line passes left to right (as shown in Fig. 6.16). Check the photo numbers to be sure that the photographs have been selected from adjacent positions on the flight line. Usually (but not always) the numbers and annotations on photos are placed on the leading edge of the image: the edge of the image nearest the front of the aircraft at the time the image was taken. Therefore, these numbers should usually be oriented in sequence from left to right, as shown in Fig. 6.16. If the overlap between adjacent photos does not correspond to the natural positions of objects on the ground, then the photographs are incorrectly oriented.

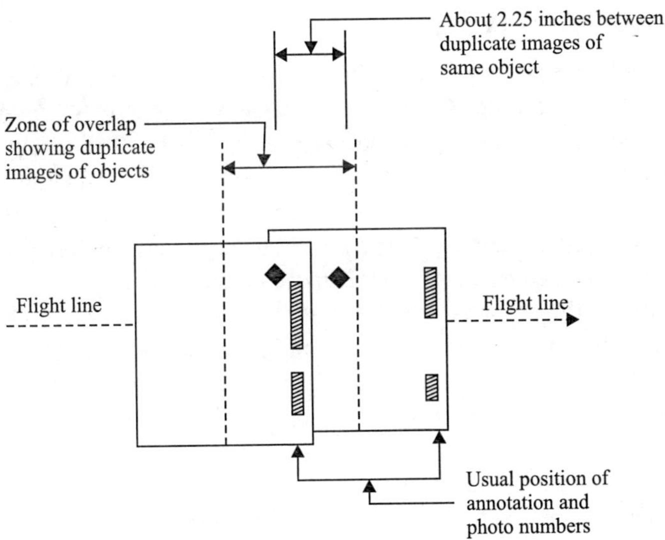

Fig. 6.16. Positioning aerial photographs for stereoscopic viewing.

Next, the interpreter should identify a distinctive feature on the image within the zone of stereoscopic overlap. The photos should then be positioned so that the duplicate images of this feature (one on each image) are approximately 64 mm (2.5 inch) apart. This distance represents the distance between the two pupils of a person of average size (referred to as the interpupillary distance), but for many it may be a bit too large or too small, so the spacing of photographs may require adjustment as the interpreter follows the procedure outlined here.

The pocket stereoscope should be opened so that its legs are locked in place to position the lens at their correct height above the photographs. The two segments of the body of the stereoscope should be adjusted so that the centers of the eyepieces are about 64 mm (2.5 inch) apart (or a slightly larger or smaller distance, as mentioned above). Then the stereoscope should be positioned so that the centers of the lenses are positioned above the duplicate images of the distinctive feature selected previously. Looking through the two lenses, the analyst sees two images of this feature; if the images are properly positioned, the two images will appear to 'float' or 'drift'.

The analyst can, with some efforts, control the apparent positions of the two images so that they fuse into a single image; as this occurs, the two images should merge into a single image that is then visible in three dimensions. Usually aerial photos show exaggerated heights, due to the large separation (relative to distance to the ground) between successive photographs as they were taken along the flight line. Although exaggerated heights can prevent convenient stereo viewing in regions of high relief, it can be useful in interpretations of subtle terrain features that might not otherwise be noticeable. The student who has successfully used the stereoscope to examine a section of the photo should then practice moving the stereoscope over the image to view the entire regions within the zone of overlap. As long as the axis of the stereoscope is oriented parallel to the flight line, it is possible to retain stereo vision while moving the stereoscope. If the stereoscope is twisted with respect to the flight line, the interpreter loses stereo vision. By lifting the edge of one of the photographs, it is possible to view the image regions near the edges of the photos.

IMAGE SCALE CALCULATIONS

Scale is a property of all images. As a result, anyone who works with aerial images and maps must be skilled in computation of image scale. Knowledge of image scale is essential for making measurements from images and for understanding the geometric errors present in all remotely sensed images. Work with image scale is not difficult, although it is easy to make simple mistakes that can result in serious errors.

Scale is simply an expression of the relationship between the image distance between two points and the actual distance between the two corresponding points on the ground. This relationship can be expressed in several ways. The word statement sets a unit distance on the map or photograph equal to the correct corresponding distance on the ground—for example, 'One inch equals one mile' or just as correctly, 'One centimeter equals five kilometers'. The first unit in the statement in the expression specifies the map distance, the second, the corresponding ground distance. A second method of specifying scale is the bar scale, which simply labels a line with sub-divisions that show ground distances.

The third method, the representative fractions (RF), is more widely used and often forms the preferred method of reporting image scale. The representative fraction is the ratio between image distance and ground distance. It usually takes the form '1:50000' or '1/50000', with the numerator set equal to 1 and the denominator equal to the corresponding ground distance. The representative fraction has meaning in any unit of length as long as both the numerator and the denominator are expressed in the same units.

Thus, '1:50000' can mean '1 inch on the image equals 50000 inch on the ground' or '1 cm on the image equals 50000 cm on the ground'.

A frequent source of confusion is converting the denominator into the larger units that we find more convenient to use for measuring large ground distance. With metric units, the conversion is usually simple; in the example given above, it is easy to see that 50000 cm is equal to 0.50 km and that 1 cm on the map represents 0.5 km on the ground. With English units, the same process is not quite so easy. It is necessary to convert inches to miles to derive '1 inch equals 0.79 miles' from 1:50000. For this reason, it is useful to know that 1 miles equals 63360 inch. Thus, 50000 inch is equal to 50000/63360 = 0.79 miles.

A typical scale problem requires estimation of the scale of an individual photograph. One method is to use the focal length and altitude method (Fig. 6.17):

$$RF = \frac{\text{Focal length}}{\text{Altitude}} \quad \text{... (6.4)}$$

Both values must be expressed in the same units. Thus, if a camera with a 6 inch focal length is flown at 10000 ft., the scale is 0.5/10000 = 1:20000. (Altitude always specifies the flying height above the terrain, not above sea level.) Because a given flying altitude is seldom the exact altitude at the time the photography was taken and because of the several sources that contribute to scale variations within a given photographs, we must always regard the results of such calculations as an approximation of the scale of any specific portion of the image. Often such values are referred to as the 'normal' scale of an image, meaning that it is recognised that the stated scale is an approximation and that image scale will vary within any given photograph.

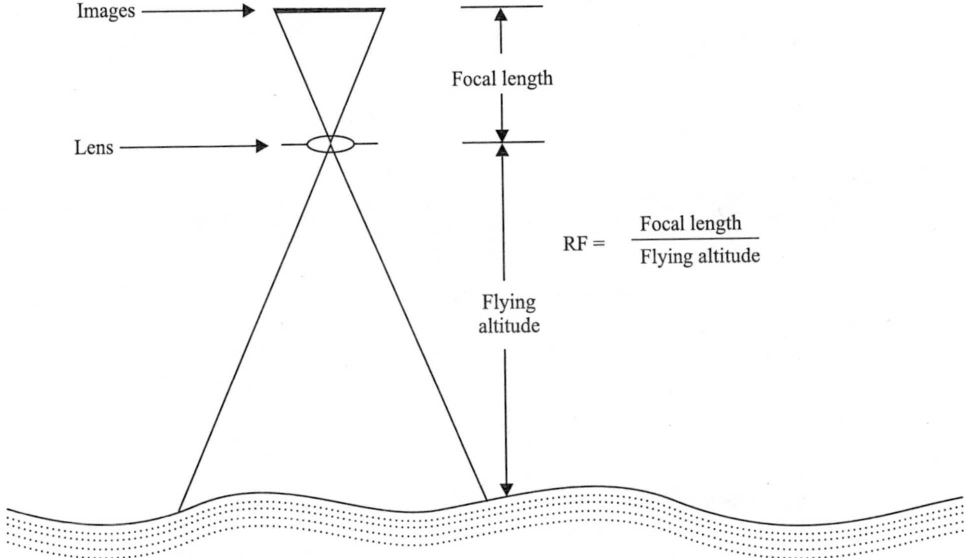

Fig. 6.17. Estimating image scale by focal length and altitude.

A second method is the use of a known ground distance. We identify two points on the aerial photograph that are also represented on a map. For example in Fig. 6.18, the image distance between points A and B is measured to be approximately 2.2 inch (5.6 cm).

From the map, the same distance is determined to correspond to a ground distance of 1,15,000 inch (about 1.82 miles). Thus the scale is found to be:

$$RF = \frac{\text{Image distance}}{\text{Ground distance}} = \frac{2.2 \text{ inch}}{1.82 \text{ miles}} = \frac{2.2 \text{ inch}}{1{,}15{,}000 \text{ inch}} \quad \text{... (6.5)}$$

$$= \frac{1}{52273}$$

In instances when accurate maps of the area represented on the photograph may not be available, the interpreter may not know focal length and altitude. Then an approximation of image scale can be made if it is possible to identify an object or feature of known dimensions. Such features might include a football field or baseball diamond; measurement of a distance from these features as they are shown on the image provides the 'image distance' value needed to use the relationship given above. The 'ground distance' is derived from our knowledge of the length of a football field or the distance between bases on a baseball diamond. Some photointerpretation manuals provide tables of standard dimensions of features commonly observed on aerial images, to include sizes of athletic fields (soccer, field hockey, etc.), lengths of railroad boxcars, distances between telephone poles and so on, as a means of using the known ground distance method.

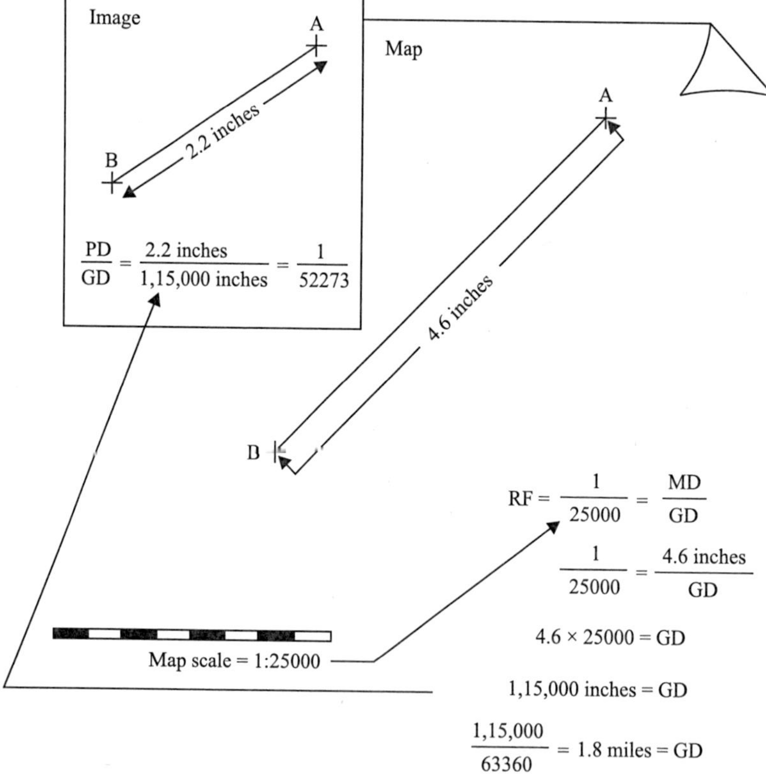

Fig. 6.18. Measurement of image scale using a map to derive ground distance.

A second kind of scale problem is the use of a known scale to measure a distance on the photograph. Such a distance might separate two objects on the photograph but not be represented on the map or the size of a feature has changed since the map was compiled. For example, we know that image scale is 1:15000. A pond not shown on the map is measured on the image as 0.12 inch in width. Therefore, we can estimate the actual width of the pond to be:

$$\frac{1}{15000} = \frac{\text{Image distance}}{\text{Ground distance}} \qquad \text{... (6.6)}$$

$$\frac{0.12 \text{ inch}}{\text{Unknown GD}} = \frac{\text{Image distance}}{\text{Ground distance}}$$

$$\text{GD} = 0.12 \times 15000 \text{ inch}$$

$$\text{GD} = 1800 \text{ inch or } 150 \text{ ft.}$$

This example can illustrate two other points. First, because image scale varies throughout the image, we cannot be absolutely confident that our distance for the width of the pond is accurate; it is simply an estimate, unless we have high confidence in our measurements and in the image scale at this portion of the photo. Second, measurement of short image distances are likely to have errors due simply to our inability to make accurate measurements of very short distances (e.g., the 0.12 inch distance measured above). As distances become shorter, our errors constitute a greater proportion of the estimated length. Thus an error of 0.005 inch is 0.08 per cent of a distance of 6 inch, but 4 per cent of our distance of 0.12 inch mentioned above. Thus the interpreter should exercise a healthy skepticism regarding measurements made from images unless he or she has taken great care to ensure maximum accuracy and consistency.

REPORTING RESULTS OF AN INTERPRETATION

An image interpreter possesses a specialised knowledge and experience that is not usually understood by those who use the information derived from remotely sensed images. These individuals may not appreciate the value and the reliability of the information nor may they realise that the same information may have certain errors and limitations. Thus the interpreter must be skilled not only in analysis of images, but also in the reporting of the results of the interpretation in a form that can be clearly understood by those who are not specialists in remote sensing.

Although the character of a report will vary greatly depending upon its topic, purpose and intended audience, it is possible to suggest a few general features that might be important in most circumstances. The repot itself might include six separate sections that outline: (i) objectives; (ii) equipment and materials; (iii) regional setting; (iv) procedure; (v) results; and (vi) conclusions.

Objectives

The objectives of the interpretation should be specified clearly so that no reader will misunderstand the scope or detail of the project. Examples are given in Table 6.1. Note that example A in Table 6.1 requires that the results be plotted on an accurate map for measurement of areas, whereas example B presents no such requirement, although it certainly is possible to mark census division boundaries on photographs. Officials who are to use the results may not realise the implications of these requirements, but the image analyst must anticipate problems that arise from these objectives (i.e., the requirements to register data to the map and to the census units, respectively) and devise suitable procedures to ensure that the objectives can be met.

Table 6.1. Objectives for image interpretation.

A. *For a land-use interpretation*:

To classify the land-use area of Montgomery County using five categories: forest, urban land, agricultural land, open water and barren land. Aerial photographs at 1:20000 dated April 1984 are to be used, with field surveys as necessary. Results are to be reported as a map at 1:50000 and as a table reporting areas in each category.

B. *For an inventory of housing units*:

To inventory housing units in Washington County, as of January 1985, then to report results by census sub-divisions. To identify each structure on each image either as a dwelling unit or as a non-dwelling unit. All structures must be assigned to categories that can be defined solely on the basis of their appearance on the image. Classification of dwelling units must be defined, then tested in early phases of the study, using field observations as necessary

Equipment and Materials and Regional Setting

Equipment and materials can be reported in a simple list as shown in Table 6.2. The regional setting should briefly outline the geographic setting of the area considered in the interpretation, both for the benefit of the person who will use the information and as a means of preparing the interpreter for the conditions that will be encountered within the image. This section could include brief descriptions of local climate, topography, agriculture, soils, industry, population and other factors that might pertain to interpretation of images of the region (Table 6.3).

Table 6.2. Equipment and materials.

Light tables

9 inch × 9 inch black-and-white aerial photographs (positive transparencies at 1:24000

Black-and-white paper enlargements at 1:8000

Descriptions of census division boundaries

Mylar drafting film

Magnifiers

Pens, pencils, drafting type, paper, etc.

Stereoscopes

IBM personal computer with dBASE III

Table 6.3. Example of a regional setting section of a report.

Landscape and climate

Topography is characterised by a series of parallel valleys and ridges. Valleys, oriented northeast-southwest, are underlain by limestones and shales and are separated by steep ridges underlain by sandstones and shales. Topography in valleys is rolling, with local relief of 3 to 30 m (10 to 100 ft.)

In valleys, soils are generally deep and well drained, with moderate to gentle slopes

Climate here is characterised by an average annual rainfall of about 1016 mm (40 inch), an average annual temperature of about 13°C (55°F) and about 200 frost-free days each year. Maximum precipitation is received during the summer months although late summer moisture deficits are common

Economic and social characteristics

Population in this region is largely rural; about 75 per cent of the land is farms, with only 2–3 per cent urban land

In addition to agriculture, important industries include light manufacturing, recreation and tourism, manufacture of forest products

Procedures

The procedures give a step-by-step description of the interpretation process in detail (Table 6.4). This section serves three purposes. First, it assures that the analyst has thought through the interpretation process in a way that is likely to anticipate problems before they arise. Second, a written description of procedures is especially important if several people are working together on the same project—to assure that results are consistent, all must follow the same procedure. Although written procedures are not in themselves sufficient to maintain high standards of uniformity, they are a necessary part of the process. Finally, the written procedures form a record of how the interpretation was conducted, so it is possible to answer questions that arise after the interpretation is complete, even though the individuals who actually conducted the interpretation may have moved to different job assignments in the interval since the project was completed.

Table 6.4. Example of a procedures section of a report.

(This example corresponds to Objective B, Table 6.1)

1. Plot census boundaries on photographs or on an overlay that registers to the photographs
2. Each structure is interpreted separately and assigned a unique identifying number within its census division
3. Interpretations usually will be made from the positive transparency, using the light table and the tube magnifier. Stereoscopes will be used to interpret paper prints in regions where detailed interpretation of multistory buildings is required. In urbanised areas, large-scale images are to be used to supplement the smaller scale photos
4. As interpretations are made, the classifications are recorded on an overlay that registers to the enlarged photograph. On this overlay the interpreter outlines each structure and marks it with the identifying number and a symbol that matches to one of the previously defined categories
5. When interpretation of a photograph is complete, data are recorded on the computer. Each record will specify structure number, category, census identifier, photo identification and the interpreter. The computer file permits recording of changes in interpretation, but all earlier interpretations are to be preserved
6. Overlays to the large-scale photographs form the authoritative graphic record of the interpretation and are marked to record the latest change, if changes in classification are necessary
7. For field use, the large-scale overlays are to be duplicated, then carried to the field and marked as necessary to record changes. Changes are to be recorded later on the computer (preserving all earlier interpretations). Field sheets are to be marked with a date and worker's initials and are to be retained for the duration of the project

Interpreters to work in teams. One examines the image using magnification, the other records the results on the overlay. Periodically tasks are rotated. Each team participates in recording information on the computer and in field verification work

The database system permits retrieval of information by census unit, by dwelling unit type, by photo or by interpreter. It also enables tabulation of data by census units at different levels and retrieval of data for each photo or each interpreter, if necessary to correct errors late in the process

Results

Results are reported in a brief narrative section that is supported by tables, maps and diagrams as appropriate. Frequently the interpretation will result in an inventory or enumeration of specific items or categories that can be reported in a detailed tabulation (Table 6.5). These tabulations should, of course, match the requirements of those who will use the information—for example, in Part B of Table 6.1, the categories should correspond to those of interest to the users and the values should be reported in appropriate units and with suitable detail to satisfy the intended use. The narrative can discuss points that may not be obvious from the table alone—to address topics such as relative accuracies or precision of values for the individual categories, for example.

Table 6.5. Example of a results section of a report.

A. For inventory of land use and land cover:	
Category	*Area (ha)*
Forested land	261
Coniferous	113
Deciduous	85
Mixed	63
Urban land	446
Residential	217
Commercial	93
Industrial	105
Transportation	31
Agricultural land	1139
Pasture	318
Cropland, irrigated	97
Cropland, non-irrigated	453
Orchards	85
Market gardens	101

B. For count of housing units:	
Category	*Number*
Single-family dwellings	251
Multiunit dwellings	23
Hotels and motels	12
Mobile home units	86

INTERPRETATION OF DIGITAL IMAGERY

Image interpretation was once practiced entirely within the realm of photographic prints and transparencies, using equipment and techniques outlined in the preceding sections. As digital analyses have increased in significance, so has the importance of interpretations on imagery as represented on computer displays. Although such interpretations are based on the same principles outlined above for traditional imagery, digital data have their own characteristics that require special treatment in the context of visual interpretation.

Image Enhancement

Image enhancement is the process of improving the visual appearance of digital images. Image enhancement has increasing significance in remote sensing because of the growing importance of digital analyses. Although some aspects of digital analysis may seem to reduce or replace traditional image interpretation, many of these procedures require analysts to examine images on computer displays, doing tasks that require many of the skills outlined in earlier sections of this chapter.

Most image-enhancement techniques are designed to improve the visual appearance of an image, often as evaluated by narrowly defined criteria. Therefore, it is important to remember that enhancement is often an arbitrary exercise—what is successful for one purpose may be unsuitable for another image or for another purpose. In addition, image enhancement is conducted without regard for the integrity of the original data: the original brightness values will be altered in the process of improving their visual qualities and they will lose their relationships to the original brightnesses on the ground. Therefore, enhanced images should not be used as input for additional analytical techniques; rather, any further analysis should use the original values as input.

Contrast Enhancement

Contrast refers to the range of brightness values present on an image. Contrast enhancement is required because, digital data usually have brightness ranges that do not match the capabilities of the human visual system nor those of photographic films. Therefore, for analysts to view the full range of information conveyed by digital images, it is usually necessary to re-scale image brightnesses to ranges that can be accommodated by human vision, photographic films and computer displays.

For example, if the maximum possible range of values is 0 to 255 (i.e., 8 bits), but the display can show only the range from 0 to 63 (6 bits), then the image will have poor contrast and important detail may be lost in the values that cannot be shown on the display (Fig. 6.19a). Contrast enhancement alters each pixel value in the old image to produce a new set of values that exploits the full range of 256 brightness values (Fig. 6.19b). Several approaches can be applied to enhance contrast.

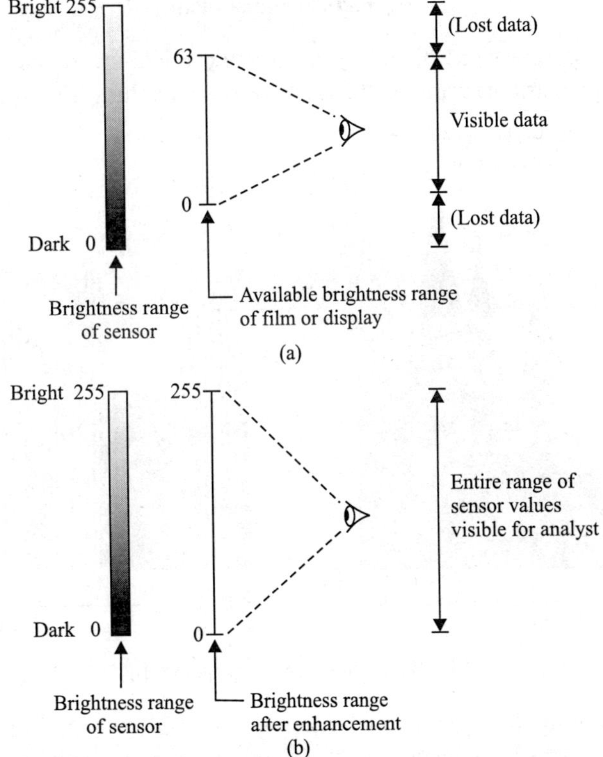

Fig. 6.19. Loss of visual information in display of digital imagery.

Linear stretch converts the original digital values into a new distribution, using new minimum and maximum values specified. The algorithm then matches the old minimum to the new minimum and the old maximum to the new maximum. All of the old intermediate values are scaled proportionately between the new minimum and maximum values (Fig. 6.20). Piecewise linear stretch means that the original brightness range was divided into segments before each segment was stretched individually. This variation permits the analyst to emphasise certain segments of the brightness range that might have more significance for a specific application.

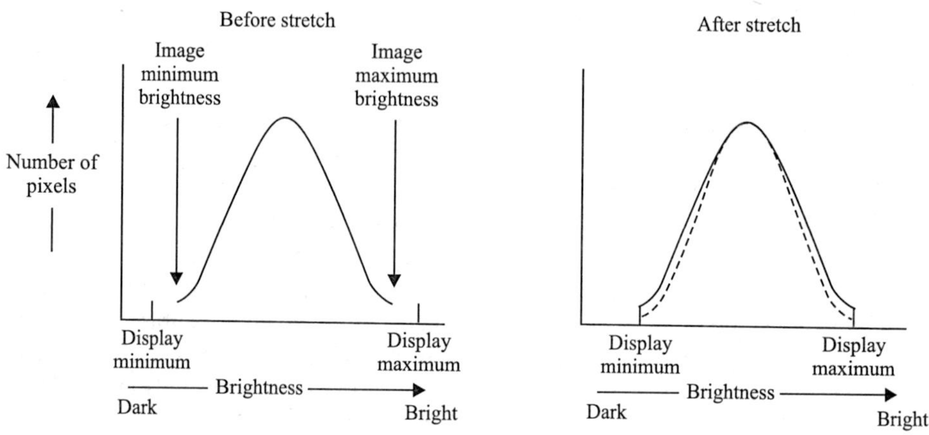

Fig. 6.20. Linear stretch.

Histogram equalisation re-assigns digital values in the original image such that brightnesses in the output image are equally distributed among the range of output values (Fig. 6.21).

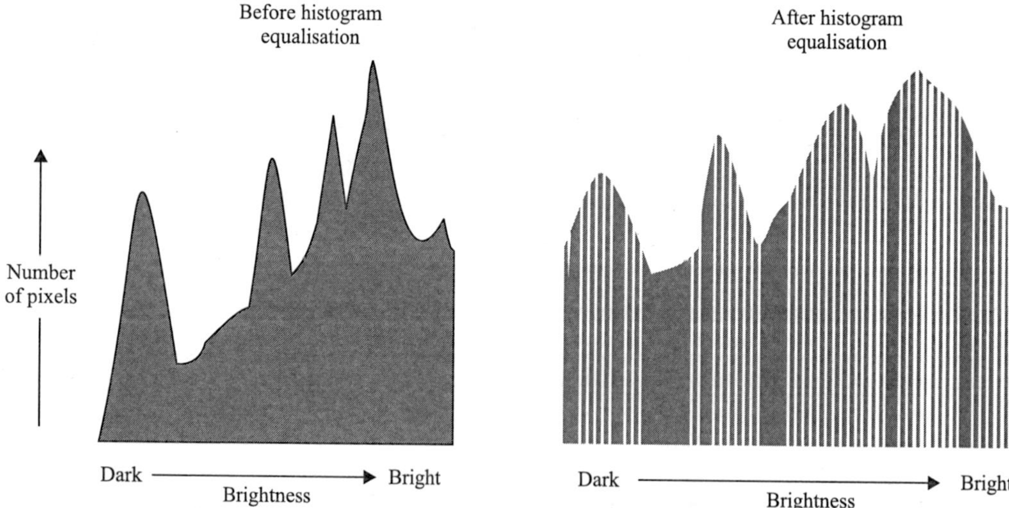

Fig. 6.21. Histogram equalisation.

Unlike contrast stretching, histogram equalisation is achieved by applying a non-linear function to re-assign the brightnesses in the input image such that the output image approximates a uniform distribution of intensities. The histogram peaks are broadened and the valleys are made shallower. Histogram equalisation has been used for image comparison processes (because it is effective in enhancing image detail) and for adjustment of artifacts introduced by digitisers or other instruments.

Density slicing is accomplished by arbitrarily dividing the range of brightnesses in a single band into intervals, then assigning each interval to a colour (Fig. 6.22). Density slicing may have the effect of emphasising certain features that may be represented in vivid colours, but, of course, does not carry any more information than the single image used as the source.

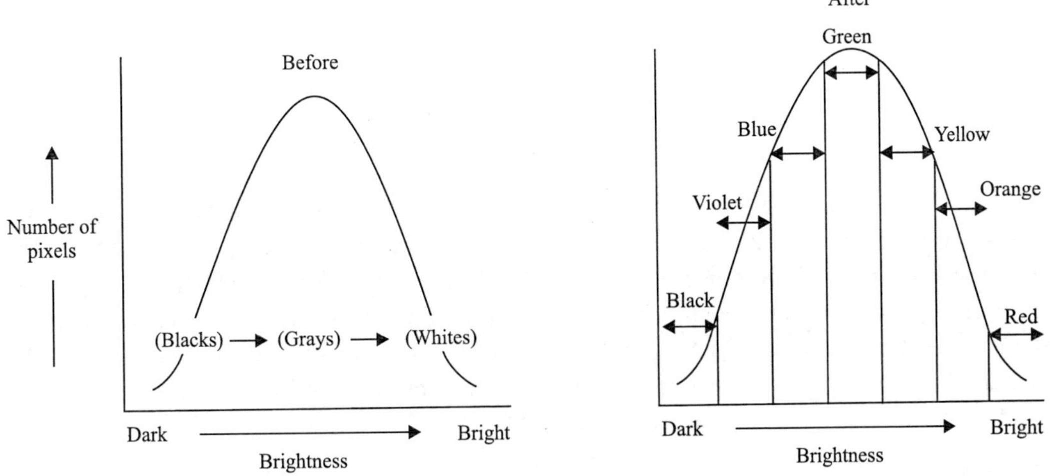

Fig. 6.22. Density slicing.

Edge Enhancement

Edge enhancement is an effort to reinforce the visual boundaries between regions of contrasting brightness. Typically, the human interpreter prefers sharp edges between adjacent parcels, whereas the presence of noise, coarse resolution and other factors often tends to blur or weaken the distinctiveness of these edges. Edge enhancement is in effect the strengthening of local contrast—enhancement of contrast within a local region. A typical edge-enhancement algorithm consists of a window that is systematically moved through the image, centerd successively on each pixel. At each position, it is then possible to calculate a local average of values within the window; the central value can be compared to the averages of the adjacent pixels. If the value exceeds a specified difference from this average, the value can be altered to accentuate the difference in brightness between the two regions. Rohde describe an edge-enhancement procedure used at the EROS Data center. A new (output) digital value is calculated using the original (input) value and the local average of five adjacent pixels. A constant can be applied to alter the effect of the enhancement as necessary to specific situations. The output value is the difference between twice the input value and the local average. The effect is to increase the brightness of those pixels that are already brighter than the local average and to decrease the brightnesses of pixels that are already darker than the local average. Thus the effect is to accentuate differences in brightnesses, especially at places ('edges') where a given value differs greatly from the local average. Note that the use of an average value from adjacent pixels reduces the effect of a single value upon the output values.

Thus, despite the increasing significance of digital analysis in all aspects of remote sensing, image interpretation still forms a key component in the way that human understand images. Analysts must evaluate imagery, either as paper prints or as displays on a computer monitor, using the skills outlined in this chapter.

7

Land Observation Satellites

INTRODUCTION

Today many corporations and national governments operate satellite remote sensing systems specifically designed for observation of the earth's surface to collect information concerning topics such as crops, forests, water bodies, land use, cities and minerals. Satellite sensors offer several advantages over aerial platforms: they can provide a synoptic view (observation of large areas in a single image), fine detail and systematic, repetitive coverage. Such capabilities are well suited to creating and maintaining a worldwide cartographic infrastructure and to monitoring changes in the many broad-scale environmental issues that the world faces today, to list two of many pressing concerns.

SATELLITE REMOTE SENSING

Because of the large number of satellite observation systems in use and the rapid changes in their design, this chapter cannot list or describe all systems currently in use or planned. It can, however, provide readers with the basic framework they need to understand key aspects of earth observation satellites in general as a means of preparing readers to acquire knowledge of specific satellite systems as it becomes available. Therefore, this chapter outlines essential characteristics of the most important systems—past, present and future—as a guide for understanding other systems not specifically discussed here.

Today's land observation satellites have evolved from earlier systems. The first earth observation satellite, the Television and Infrared Observation Satellite (TIROS), was launched in April 1960 as the first of series of experimental weather satellites designed to monitor cloud patterns. TIROS was the prototype for the operational programmes that now provide meteorological data for daily weather forecasts throughout the world. Successors to the original TIROS vehicle have seen long service in several programmes designed to acquire meteorological data. Although data from meteorological satellites have been used to study land resources, this chapter focuses on satellite systems specifically tailored for observation of land resources, mainly via passive sensing of radiation in the visible and infrared regions of the spectrum.

LANDSAT ORIGINS

Early meteorological sensors hand limited capabilities for land resources observation. Although their sensors were1 valuable for observing cloud patterns, most had coarse spatial resolution, so they could provide only rudimentary detail concerning land resources. Today the Landsat system is important both in its own right—as a remote sensing system that has contributed greatly to earth resources studies—and as an introduction to similar land observation satellites operated by other organisations.

Initially, Landsat was known as the 'Earth Resources Technology Satellite,' 'ERTS' for short. The first Landsat sensors recorded energy in the visible and near infrared spectrums. Although these regions of the spectrum had long been used for aircraft photography, it was by no means certain that they would also prove practical for observation of earth resources from satellite altitudes. Scientists and engineers were not completely confident that the sensors would work as planned, that they would prove to be reliable, that detail would be satisfactory or that a sufficient proportion of scenes would be free of cloud cover. Although many of these problems were encountered, the feasibility of the basic concept was demonstrated and Landsat became the model for similar systems now operated by other organisations.

The Landsat system consists of spacecraft-borne sensors that observe the earth and then transmit information by microwave signals to ground stations that receive and process data for dissemination to a community of data users. Early Landsat vehicles carried two sensors systems: the return beam videcon (RBV) and the multispeed scanner sub-system (MSS) (Table 7.1). The RBV was a camera-like instrument designed to provide, relative to the MSS, high spatial resolution and geometric accuracy, but lower spectral and radiometric detail. That is, positions of features would be accurately represented, by without fine detail concerning their colours and brightnesses. In contrast, the MSS was designed to provide finer detail concerning spectral characteristics of the earth, but less positioned accuracy. Because technical difficulties restricted RBV operation, the MSS soon became the primary Landsat sensor. A second generation of Landsat vehicles (Landsat 4 and 5) added the thematic mapper (TM)— a more sophisticated version of the MSS. The current family of Landsats which carry ETM+, an advanced version of the thematic mapper.

Table 7.1. Landsat missions.

Satellite	*Launched*	*End of service*[a]	*Principal sensors*[b]
Landsat 1	23 July 1972	6 January 1978	MSS, RBV
Landsat 2	22 January 1975	25 January 1982	MSS, RBV
Landsat 3	5 March 1978	3 March 1983	MSS, RBV
Landsat 4	16 July 1982	c	TM, MSS
Landsat 5	1 March 1984	–	TM, MSS
Landsat 6	5 October 1993	Destroyed at launch	ETM
Landsat 7	15 April 1999	–	ETM+

[a] Satellite systems typically operate on an intermittent or stand-by basis for considerable periods prior to formal retirement from service.

[b] Sensors are discussed in the text, MSS, multispectral scanner sub-system; RBV, return beam vidicon; TM, thematic mapper; ETM, enhanced TM; ETM+, enhanced TM plus.

[c] Transmission of TM data failed in August 1993.

SATELLITE ORBITS

Satellites are placed into orbits tailored to match the objectives of each satellite mission and the capabilities of the sensors they carry. For simplicity, this section describes normal orbits, based on the assumption that the earth's gravitational field is spherical, although in fact satellites actually follow perturbed orbits, due in part to distortion of the earth's gravitational field by the earth's oblate shape (flattened at the poles and bulging at the equator) and in part to lunar and solar gravity, tides, solar wind and other influences.

A normal orbit forms an ellipse with the center of the earth at one focus, characterised by an apogee (A; point farthest from the earth), perigee (P; point closest to the earth), ascending node (AN; point where the satellite crosses the equator moving south to north) and descending node (DN; point where the satellite crosses the equator passing south to north). For graphical simplicity, the inclination (i) is shown in Fig 7.1 as the angle that a satellite track forms with respect to the equator at the descending node (Fig. 7.1) (More precisely, the inclination should be defined as the angle between the earth's axis at the North Pole and a line drawn perpendicular to the plane of the satellite orbit, viewed such that the satellite follows a counterclockwise trajectory).

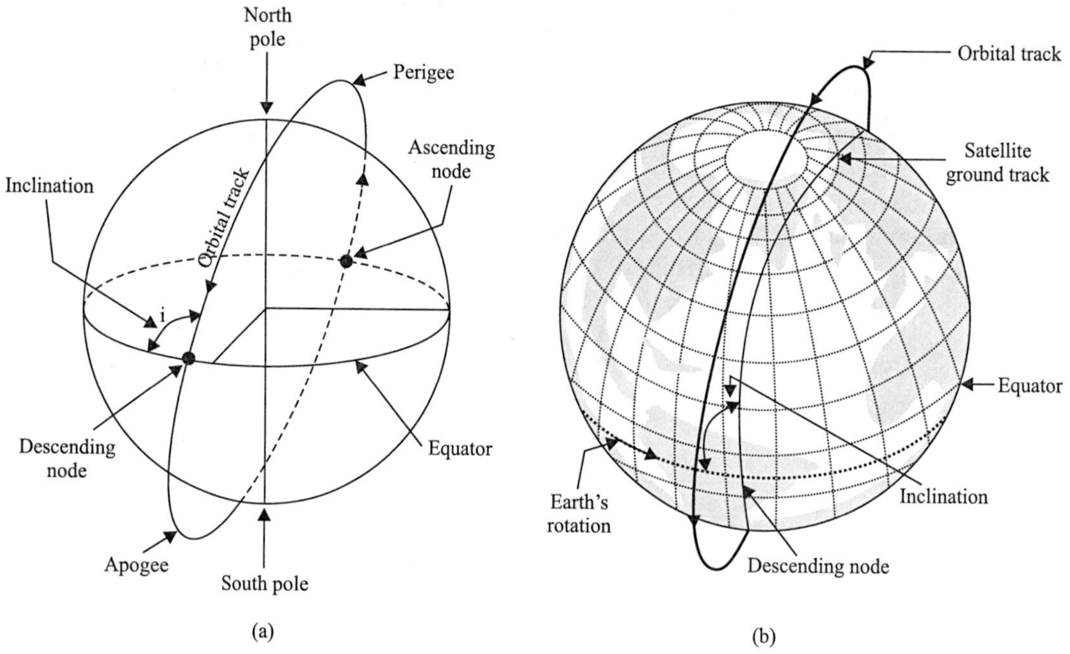

Fig. 7.1. Satellite orbits: (a) definitions; and (b) schematic representation of a sun-synchronous orbit.

The time required for a satellite to complete one orbit (its period) increases with altitude. At an altitude of about 36000 km, a satellite has the same period as the earth's surface, so (if positioned in the equatorial plane) it remains stationary with respect to the earth's surface—it is in a geostationary orbit. Geostationary orbits are ideal for meteorological or communications satellites designed to maintain a constant position with respect to a specific region on the earth's surface. Earth observation satellites, however, are usually designed to satisfy other objectives.

Ideally, all remotely sensed images acquired by satellite would be acquired under conditions of uniform illumination, so that brightnesses of features within each scene would reliably indicate conditions on the ground rather than changes in the conditions of observation. In reality, brightnesses recorded by satellite images are not directly indicative of ground conditions because differences in latitude, time of day and season lead to variations in the nature and intensity of light that illuminates each scene.

Sun-synchronous orbits are designed to reduce one important source of variation in illumination: that caused by differences in time of day, which arises from the fact that the spherical earth rotates inside the solar beam.

LANDSAT SYSTEM

Although the first generation of Landsat sensors is no longer in service, those satellites acquired a large library of images that are available as a baseline reference of environmental conditions for land areas throughout the world.

Support Sub-systems

Although our interest here is primarily focused upon the sensors that these satellites carried, it is important to briefly mention the support sub-systems, units that are necessary to maintain proper operation of the sensors. Although this section refers specifically to the Landsat system, all earth observation satellites require similar support systems. The attitude control sub-system (ACS) maintained orientation of the satellite with respect to the earth's surface and with respect to the orbital path.

The orbit adjust sub-system (OAS) maintained the orbital path within specified parameters after the initial orbit was attained. The OAS also made adjustments throughout the life of the satellite to maintain the planned repeatable coverage of imagery. The power sub-system supplied electrical power required to operate all satellite systems by means of two solar array panels and eight batteries. The batteries were charged by energy provided by the solar panels while the satellite was on the sunlit side of the earth, then provided power when the satellite was in the earth's shadow. The thermal control sub-system controlled the temperatures of satellite components by means of heaters, passive radiators (to dissipate excess heat) and insulation. The communications and data-handling sub-system provided microwave communications with ground stations for transmitting data from the sensors, commands to satellite sub-systems and information regarding satellite status and location.

Data from sensors were transmitted, in digital form, by microwave signal to ground stations equipped to receive and process data. Direct transmission from the satellite to the ground station as the sensor acquired data was possible only when the satellite had direct line-of-sight view of the ground antenna (a radius of about 1800 km from the ground stations). In North America, stations at Greenbelt, Maryland; Fairbanks, Alaska; Goldstone, California; and Prince Albert, Saskatchewan, Canada, provided this capability for most of the United States and Canada.

Elsewhere a network of ground stations has been established over a period of years through agreements with other nations. Areas outside the receiving range of a ground station could be imaged only by use of the two tape recorders onboard each of the early Landsats. Each tape recorder could record about 30 minutes of data; then, as the satellite moved within range of a ground station, the recorders could transmit the stored data to a receiving station. Thus these satellites had, within the limits of their orbits, a capability for worldwide coverage. Unfortunately, the tape recorders proved to be one of the most unreliable elements of the Landsat system and when they failed the system was unable to image areas beyond the range of the ground stations. These unobservable areas became smaller as more ground stations were established, but there were always some areas that Landsat could not observe. Later satellites were able to avoid this problem by use of communications relay satellites.

Return Beam Vidicon

The return beam vidicon (RBV) camera system generated high-resolution television-like images of the earth's surface. On Landsats 1 and 2, the RBV system consisted of three independent cameras that operated simultaneously, with each sensing a different segment of the spectrum (Table 7.2). All three instruments were aimed at the same region beneath the satellite, so the images they acquired registered to one another to form a three-band multispectral representation of a 185 km × 170 km ground area, known as a Landsat scene (Fig. 7.2). This area matched the area represented by the corresponding MSS scene.

Table 7.2. Landsats 1–5 sensors.

Sensor	*Band*	*Spectral sensitivity*
	Landsats 1 and 2	
RBV	1	0.475–0.575 μm (green)
RBV	2	0.58–0.68 μm (red)
RBV	3	0.69–0.83 μm (near infrared)
MSS	4	0.5–0.6 μm (green)
MSS	5	0.6–0.7 μm (red)
MSS	6	0.7–0.8 μm (near infrared)
MSS	7	0.8–1.1 μm (near infrared)
	Landsat 3	
RBV		0.5–0.75 μm (panchromatic response)
MSS	4	0.5–0.6 μm (green)
MSS	5	0.6–0.7 μm (red)
MSS	6	0.7–0.8 μm (near infrared)
MSS	7	0.8–1.1 μm (near infrared)
MSS	8	10.4–12.6 μm (far infrared)
	Landsats 4 and 5[a]	
TM	1	0.45–0.52 μm (blue-green)
TM	2	0.52–0.60 μm (green)
TM	3	0.63–0.69 μm (red)
TM	4	0.76–0.90 μm (near infrared)
TM	5	1.55–1.75 μm (mid infrared)
TM	6	10.4–12.5 μm (far infrared)
TM	7	2.08–2.35 μm (mid infrared)
MSS	1	0.5–0.6 μm (green)
MSS	2	0.6–0.7 μm (red)
MSS	3	0.7–0.8 μm (near infrared)
MSS	4	0.8–1.1 μm (near infrared)

[a] On Landsats 4 and 5 MSS bands were re-numbered although the spectral definitions remain the same.

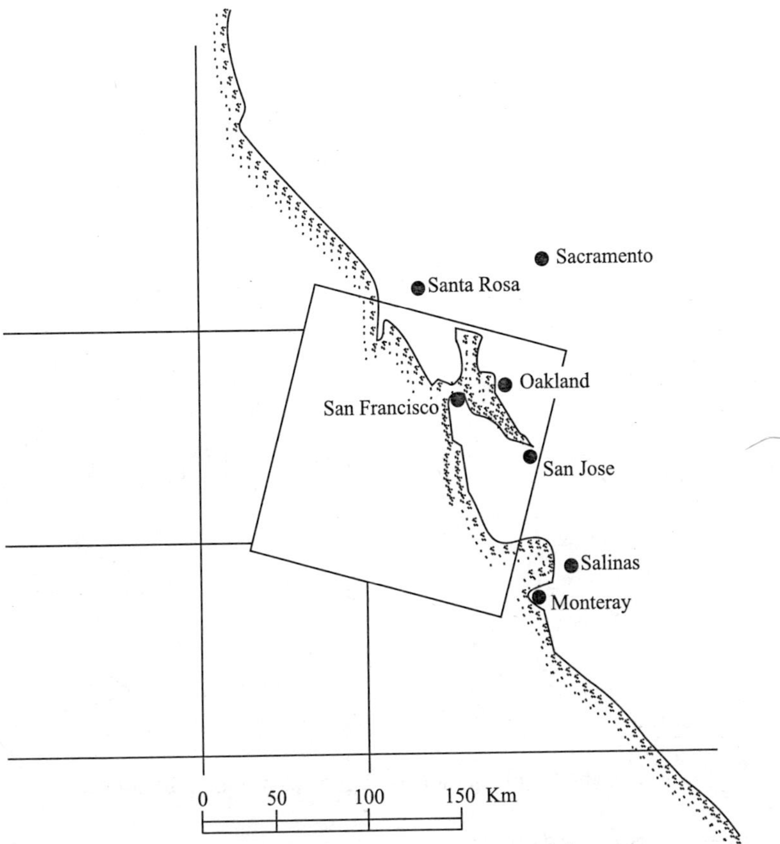

Fig. 7.2. Schematic diagram of a Landsat scene.

The RBV shutter was designed to open briefly, in the manner of a camera shutter, to simultaneously view the entire scene (Fig. 7.3a). Solar radiation reflected from the ground passed through a lens and was focused on the photosensitive surface of the vidicon camera. After the shutter closed, the photosensitive surface was then scanned by an electron beam to convert the scene's reflectance values into a video signal for transmission to a ground station. The RBV design was therefore analogous to that of a camera, but with a photosensitive plate substituted for film in the focal plane position that would normally hold film. The RBV system could acquire one image every 25 seconds, to produce a series of images with a small forward overlap. Because the RBV was designed with an optical geometry analogous to that of a camera, scientists hoped to be able to use RBV imagery as the source of accurate cartographic measurements—much in the same way that aerial photographs had long been used to compile accurate maps. Thus the function of the RBV was primarily to provide data for accurate measurements of position and distance. Because of electrical failures on Landsat 1, the RBV was turned off less than 1 month after launch. A similar malfunction caused the Landsat 2 RBV to be shut down shortly after launch, so the first two satellites acquired relatively little RBV imagery. Some scientists found the increased detail of the Landsat 3 RBV imagery to be of interest, but the sensor experienced technical problems that seemed to preclude routine acquisition of high-quality imagery. As a result, Landsat RBV imagery was not used in the role that was envisioned for it at the start of the Landsat programme.

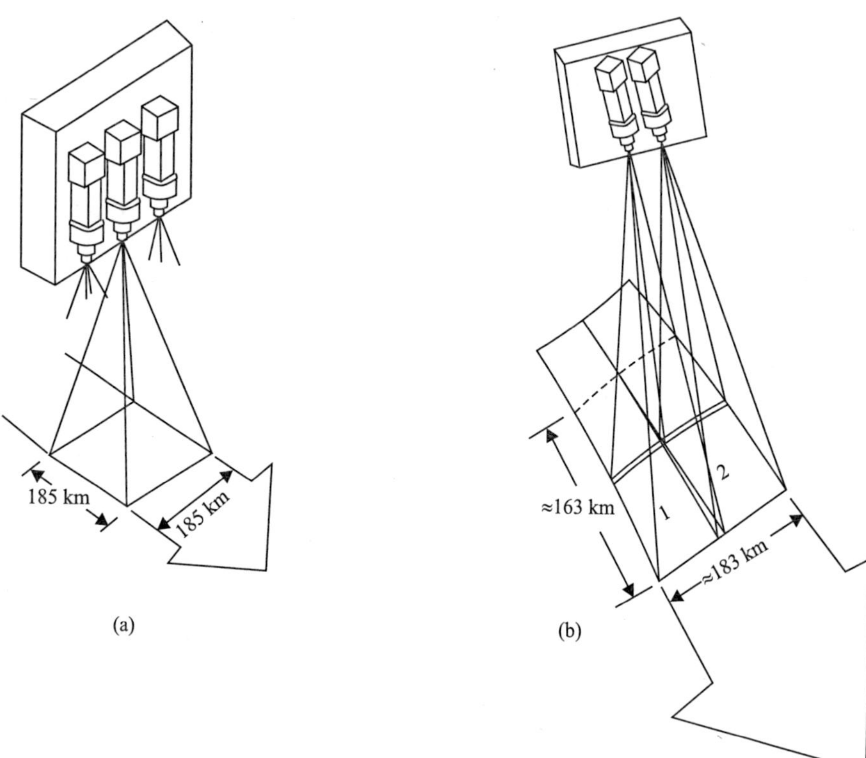

Fig. 7.3. RBV configuration. (a) Landsats 1 and 2. (b) Landsat 3.

Multispectral Scanner Sub-system

As a result of malfunctions in the RBV sensors early in the missions of Landsats 1 and 2, the multispectral scanner sub-system (MSS) became the primary Landsat sensor. Whereas the RBV was designed to capture images with known geometric properties, the MSS was tailored to provide multispectral data without as much concern for positional accuracy. In general, MSS imagery and data were found to be of good quality—indeed, much better than many expected—and clearly demonstrated the merits of satellite observation for acquiring earth resources data. The economical routine availability of MSS digital data has formed the foundation for a sizeable increase in the number and sophistication of digital image processing capabilities available to the remote sensing community. A version of the MSS was placed on Landsats 4 and 5; later systems have been designed with an eye toward maintaining the continuity of MSS data.

The MSS (Fig. 7.4) is a scanning instrument utilising a flat oscillating mirror to scan from west to east to produce a ground swath of 185 km (100 nautical miles.) perpendicular to the orbital track. The satellite motion along the orbital path provides the along-track dimension to the image. Solar radiation reflected from the earth's surface is directed by the mirror to the telescope-like instrument that focuses the energy onto fiber-optic bundles located in the focal plane of the telescope. The fiber-optical bundles then transmit energy to detectors sensitive to four spectral regions (Table 7.2).

Each west-to-east scan of the mirror covers a strip of ground approximately 185 km long in the east-west dimension and 474 m wide in the north-south dimension. The 474 m distance corresponds to the forward motion of the satellite during the interval required for the west-to-east movement of the mirror and its inactive east-to-west retrace to return to its starting position. The mirror returns to start another active scan just as the satellite is in position to record another line of data at a ground position immediately adjacent to the preceding scan line. Each motion of the mirror corresponds to six lines of data on the image because the fibre optics split the energy from the mirror into six contiguous segments.

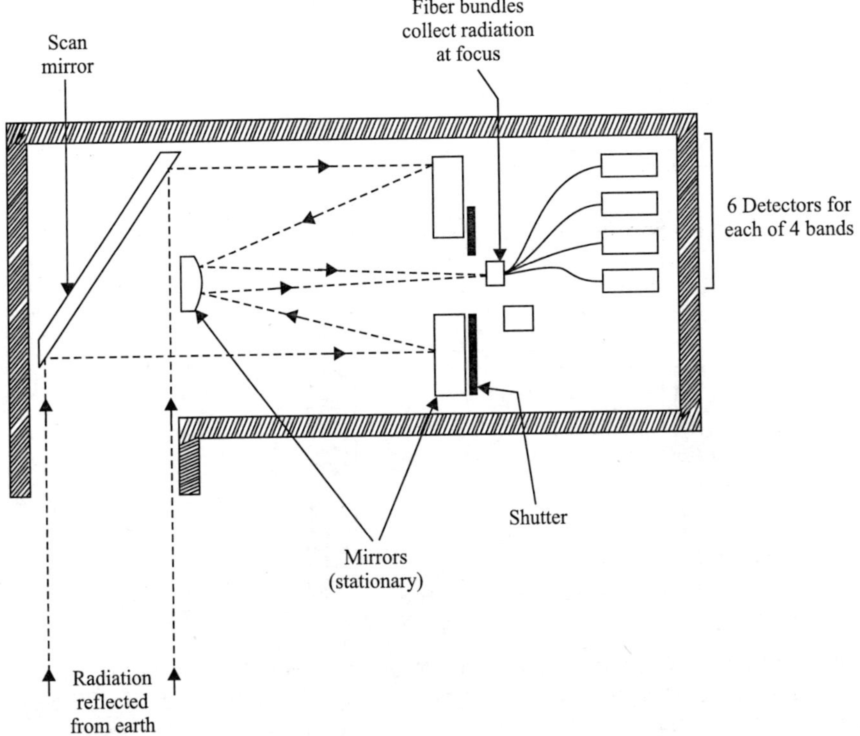

Fig. 7.4. Schematic diagram of a Landsat multispectral scanner.

The instantaneous field of view (IFOV) of a scanning instrument can be informally defined as the ground area viewed by the sensor at a given instant in time. The nominal IFOV for the MSS is 79 m × 79 m. Slater provides a more detailed examination of MSS geometry that shows the IFOV to be approximately 76-m square (about 0.58 ha or 1.4 acres), although differences exist between Landsats 1, 2 and 3 and within orbital paths as satellite altitude varies. The brightness from each IFOV is displayed on the image as a pixel (picture element) formatted to correspond to a round area said to be approximately 79 m × 57 m in size (about 0.45 ha or 1.1 acres). In everyday terms, the ground area corresponding to a MSS pixel can be said to be somewhat less than that of a US football field (Fig. 7.5).

For the MSS instruments onboard Landsat 1 and 2, the four spectral channels were located in the green, red and infrared portions of the spectrum:

1. Band 1: 0.5–0.6 μm (green).
2. Band 2: 0.6–0.7 μm (red).
3. Band 3: 0.7–0.8 μm (near infrared).
4. Band 4: 0.8–1.1 μm (near infrared).

(Originally, the four MSS bands were designated as Bands 4, 5, 6 and 7, to maintain continuity of band designations. Later bands designations were changed, even though the spectral designations of these bands remained consistent).

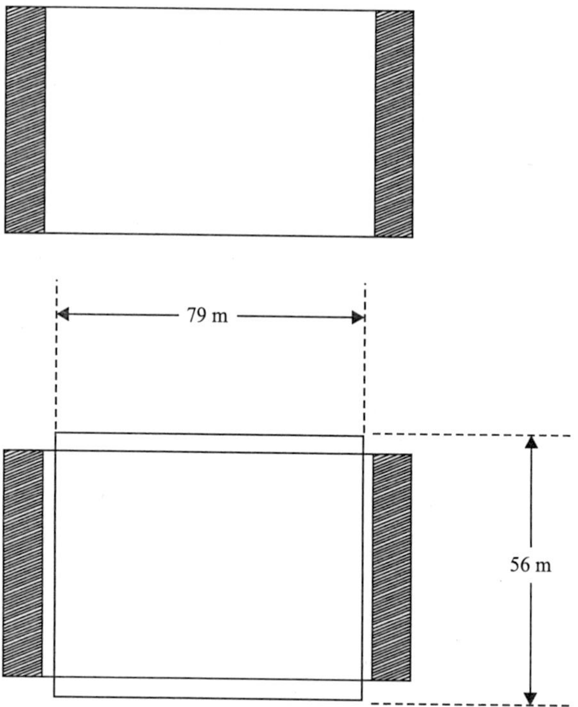

Fig. 7.5. Nominal MSS pixel shown in relation to a football field. (Here the orientation of the pixel is rotated 90° to match to the usual rendition of a football field; on an image, the narrow ends of MSS pixels are oriented approximately north and south).

The Landsat 3 MSS included an additional band in the far infrared from 10.4 to 12.6 μm. Because this band included only two detectors, energy from each scan of the mirror was sub-divided into only two segments, each 234 m wide. Therefore, the IFOV for the thermal band was 234 × 234 m, much coarser than MSS images for the other bands.

MULTISPECTRAL SCANNER SUB-SYSTEM IMAGES

Multispectral Scanner Sub-system Scene

The MSS scene is defined as an image representing a ground area approximately 185 km in the east–west (across-track) direction and 178 km in the north-south (along-track) direction (Fig. 7.6). The across-track dimension is defined by the side-to-side motion of the MSS; the along-track dimension is defined by the forward motion of the satellite along its orbital path. If the MSS were operated continuously for an entire descending pass, it would provide a continuous strip of imagery representing an area 185 km wide. The 178 km north-south dimension simply divides this strip into segments of convenient size.

The MSS scene, then, is an array of pixel values (in each of four bands) consisting of about 2400 scan lines, each composed of 3240 pixels (Fig. 7.6). Although centerpoints of scenes acquired at the same location at different times are intended to register with each other, there is often in fact a noticeable shift from one date to another (known as the temporal registration problem) in ground locations of center points due to uncorrected drift in the orbit.

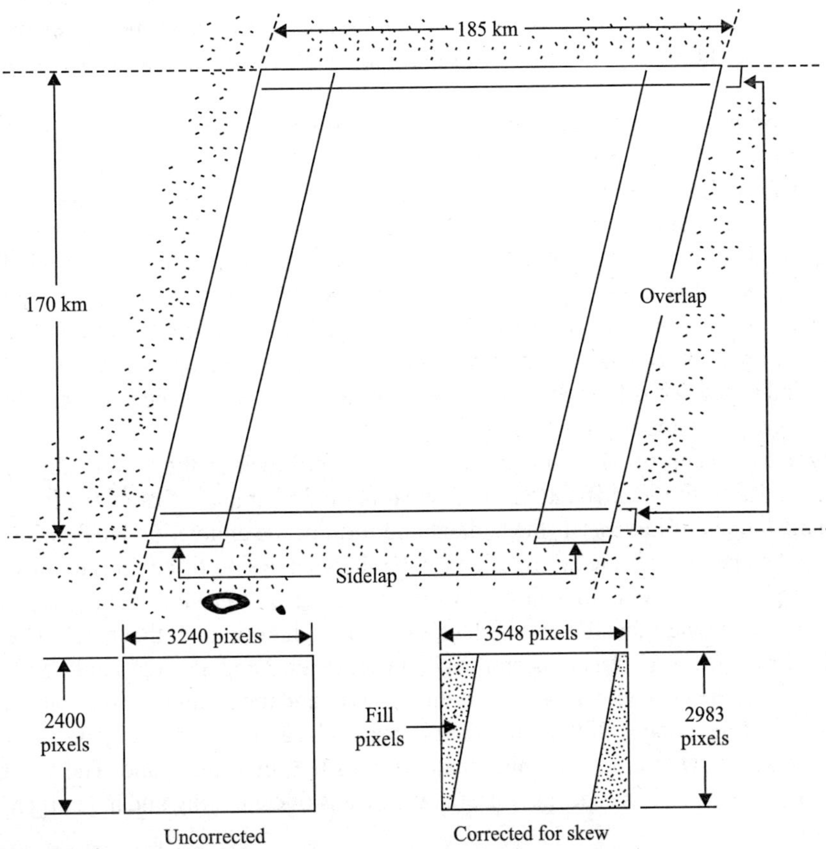

Fig. 7.6. Diagram of an MSS scene.

There is a small overlap (about 5 per cent or 9 km) between scenes to the north and south of a given scene. This overlap is generated by repeating the last few lines from the preceding image, not by stereoscopic viewing of the earth. Overlap with scenes to the east and west depends upon latitude; sidelap will be a minimum of 14 per cent (26 km) at the equator and increases with latitude to 57 per cent at 60°, then to 85 per cent at 80° N and S latitude. Because this overlap is created by viewing the same area of the earth from different perspectives, the area within the overlap can be viewed in stereo. At high latitudes, this area can constitute an appreciable portion of a scene.

Image Format

MSS data are available in several image formats that have been subjected to different forms of processing to adjust for geometric and radiometric errors. The following section describes some of the basic forms for MSS data, which provide a general model for other kinds of satellite imagery, although specifics vary with each kind of data.

In its initial form a digital satellite image consists of a rectangular array of pixels in each of four bands (Fig. 7.6). In this format, however, no compensation has been made for the combined effects of spacecraft movement and rotation of the earth as the sensor acquires the image (this kind of error is known as skew). When these effects are removed, the image assumes the shape of a parallelogram (Fig. 7.6). For convenience in recording data, fill pixels are added to preserve the correct shape of the image. Fill pixels, of course, convey no information, as they are simply assigned values of zero as necessary to attain the desired shape.

Each of the spectral channels of a multispectral image forms a separate image, each emphasising landscape features that reflect specific portions of the spectrum. These separate images, then, record in black-and-white form the spectral reflectance in the green, red and infrared portions of the spectrum, for example. The green, red and infrared bands can be combined into a single colour image, known as a false-colour composite. The near infrared band is projected onto colour film through a red filter, the red band 2 through a green filter and the green band through a blue filter. The result is a false-colour rendition that uses the same assignment of colours used in conventional colour infrared aerial photography. Strong reflectance in the green portion of the spectrum is represented as blue on the colour composite, red as green and infrared as red. Thus living vegetation appears as bright red, turbid water as a blue colour and urban areas as a gray or sometimes pinkish-gray.

On photographic prints of MSS images, the annotation block at the lower edge gives essential information concerning the identification, date, location and characteristics of the image. During the interval since the launch of Landsat 1, the content and form of the annotation block have been changed several times, but some of the basic information can be shown in a simplified form to illustrate key items (Fig. 7.7). The data has obvious meaning. The format center and ground nadir give, in degrees and minutes of latitude and longitude, the ground location of the center point of the image. The spectral band is given in the form 'MSS 1' (meaning multispectral scanner, band 1). Sun angle and sun elevation designate, in degrees, the solar elevation (above the horizon) and the azimuth of the solar beam from true north at the center of the image. Of the remaining items on the annotation block, the most important for most users is the scene ID, a unique number that specifies the scene and band. The scene ID uniquely specifies any MSS scene, so it is especially useful as a means of cataloging and indexing MSS images as explained below.

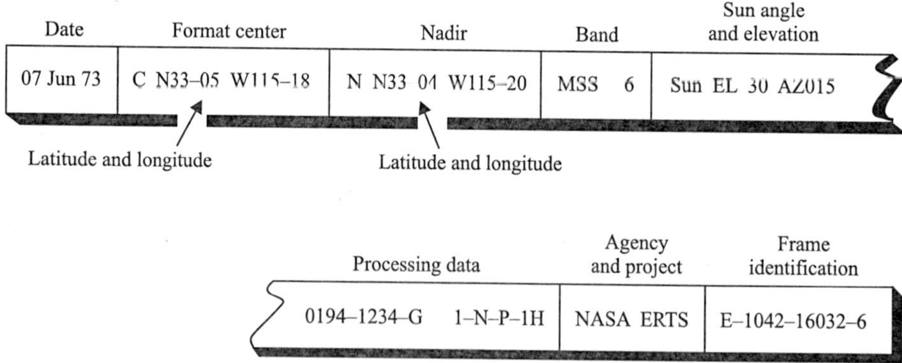

Fig. 7.7. Landsat annotation block. The annotation block has been changed several times, but all show essentially the same information.

Worldwide Reference System

The worldwide reference system (WRS), a concise designation of nominal center point of Landsat scenes, is used to index Landsat scenes by the location. The reference system is based upon a coordinate system in which there are 233 north-south paths corresponding to orbital tracks of the satellite and 119 rows representing latitudinal centre lines of Landsat scenes. The combination of a path number and a row number uniquely identifies a nominal scene center (Fig. 7.8). Because of the drift of satellite orbits over time, actual scene centers may not match exactly to the path-row locations but the method does provide a convenient and effective means of indexing locations of Landsat scenes. To outline concept in its most basic form, this discussion has presented the Landsat 1–3 WRS; note that Landsats 4 through 7 each have WRS systems analogous to those described here, though they differ with respect to detail. Therefore, investigate the specifics of the WRS system you expect to use.

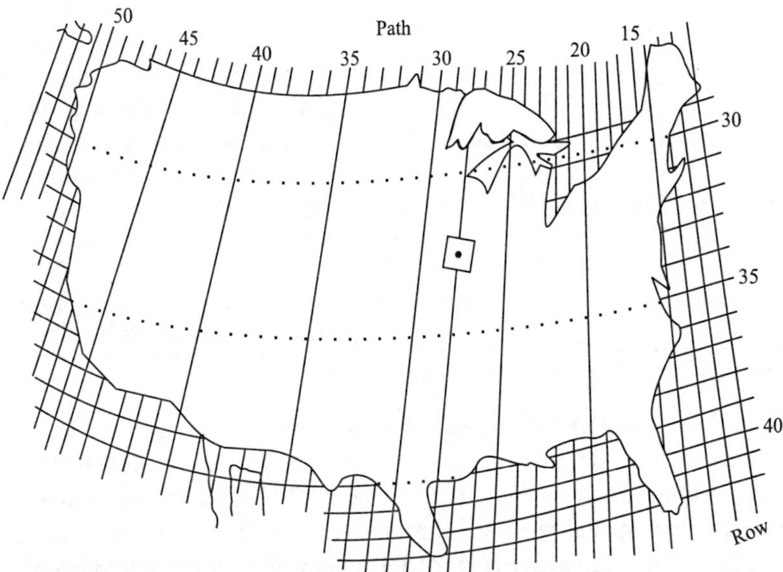

Fig. 7.8. WRS path-row coordinates for the Unites States.

LANDSAT THEMATIC MAPPER

Even before Landsat 1 was launched, it was recognised that existing technology could improve the design of the MSS. Efforts were made to incorporate improvements into a new instrument modelled on the basic design of the MSS. Landsats 4 and 5 carried a replacement for MSS known as the thematic mapper (TM), which can be considered as an upgraded MSS. In these satellites, both the TM and a MSS were carried on an improved platform that maintained a high degree of stability in orientation as a means of improving geometric qualities of the imagery. TM was based upon the same principles as the MSS, but had a more complex design. It provides finer spatial resolution, improved geometric fidelity, greater radiometric detail and more detailed spectral information in more precisely defined spectral regions. Improved satellite stability and an orbit adjust sub-system were designed to improve positional and geometric accuracy. The objectives of the second generation of Landsat instruments were to assess the performance of the TM, to provide ongoing availability of MSS data and to continue foreign data reception.

Despite the historical relationship between the MSS and the TM, the two sensors are distinct. Whereas the MSS has four broadly defined spectral regions, the TM records seven spectral bands (Table 7.3). TM band designations do not follow the sequence of the spectral definitions (the band with the longest wavelengths is band 6, rather than band 7) because band 7 was added so late in the design process that it was not feasible to relabel bands to follow a logical sequence.

Table 7.3. Summary of TM sensor characteristics.

Band	*Resolution*	*Spectral definition*	*Some applications*[a]
1	30 m	Blue-green, 0.45–0.52 μm	Penetration of clear water; bathymetry; mapping of coastal water; chlorophyll absorption; distinction between coniferous and deciduous vegetation
2	30 m	Green, 0.52–0.60 μm	Records green radiation reflected from healthy vegetation; assesses plant vigour; reflectance from turbid water
3	30 m	Red, 0.63–0.69 μm	Chlorophyll absorption important for plant-type discrimination
4	30 m	Near infrared, 0.76–0.90 μm	Indicator of plant cell structure; biomass; plant vigour; complete absorption by water facilitates delineation of shorelines
5	30 m	Mid-infrared, 1.55–1.75 μm	Indicative of vegetation moisture content; soil moisture mapping; differentiating snow from clouds; penetration of thin clouds
6	120 m	Far infrared, 10.4–12.5 μm	Vegetation stress analysis; soil moisture discrimination; thermal mapping; relative brightness temperature; soil moisture; plant heat str ess
7	30 m	Mid-infrared, 2.08–2.35 μm	Discrimination of rock types; alteration zones for hydrothermal mapping; hydroxyl ion absorption

[a]Sample applications listed here; these are not the only applications.

TM spectral bands were tailored to record radiation of interest to specific scientific investigations, rather than the more arbitrary definitions used for the MSS. Spatial resolution is about 30 m (about 0.09 ha or 0.22 acre), compared to the 76 m IFOV of the MSS (TM band 6 had coarser spatial resolution of about 120 m). The finer spatial resolution provided a noticeable increase (relative to the MSS) in spatial detail recorded by each TM image (Fig. 7.9). Digital values are quantised at 8 bits (256 brightness levels), which provide (relative to the MSS) a much larger range of brightness values. These kinds of changes produced images with much finer detail than those of the MSS.

Each scan of the TM mirror acquired 16 lines of data. Unlike the MSS, the TM scan acquires data as it moves in both the east-west and west-east directions. This feature permitted engineers to design a slower speed of mirror movement, thereby improving the length of time the detectors can respond to brightness in the scene. However, this design required additional processing to reconfigure image positions of pixels to form a geometrically accurate image. TM detectors are positioned in an array in the focal plane (it does not use the fibre optics employed in the MSS to ensure perfect spatial registration of the MSS bands); as the result, there may be a slight misregistration of TM bands.

TM imagery is analogous to MSS imagery with respect to areal coverage and organisation of data into several sets of multispectral digital values that overlay to form an image. In comparison with MSS images, TM imagery has a much finer spatial and radiometric resolution, so TM images show relatively fine detail of patterns on the earth's surface.

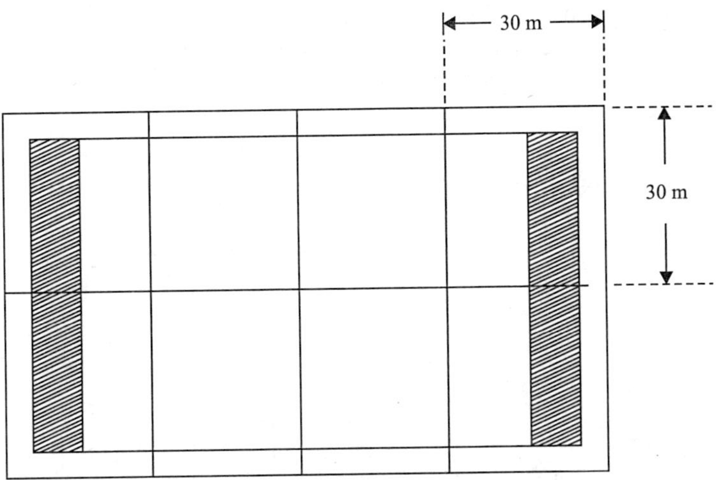

Fig. 7.9. Nominal size of a TM pixel.

Use of seven rather than four spectral bands and use of a smaller pixel size within the same image area, means that TM images consist of many more data values than do MSS images. As a result, each analyst must determine those TM bands that are most likely to provide the required information. Because the 'best' combinations of TM bands vary according to the purpose of each study, season, geographic region and other factors, a single selection of bands is unlikely to be equally effective in all circumstances.

A few combinations of TM bands appear to be effective for general-purpose use. Use of TM bands 2, 3 and 4 creates an image that is analogous to the usual false-colour aerial photograph. TM bands 1 (blue-green), 2 (green) and 3 (red) form a natural colour composite, approximately equivalent to a colour aerial photograph in its rendition of colours. Experiments with other combinations have shown that Bands 2, 4 and 5; 2, 4 and 7; and 2, 4 and 5 are also effective for visual interpretation. Of course, there are many other combinations of the seven TM bands that may be useful in specific circumstances.

Orbit and Ground Coverage: Landsats 4 and 5

Landsats 4 and 5 were placed into orbits resembling those of earlier Landsats. Sun-synchronous orbits brought the satellites over the equator at about 9:45 a.m., thereby maintaining approximate continuity of solar illumination with imagery from Landsats 1, 2 and 3. Data were collected as the satellite passed north-east to south-west on the sunlight side of the earth. The image swath remained at 185 km. In these respects, coverage was compatible with that of the first generation of Landsat systems.

However, there were important differences. The finer spatial resolution of the TM was achieved in part by a lower orbital altitude, which required several changes in the coverage cycle. Earlier Landsats produced adjacent image swaths on successive days. However, Landsats 4 and 5 acquired coverage of adjacent swaths at intervals of 7 days. Landsat 4 completed a coverage cycle in 16 days. Successive passes of the satellite were separated at the equator by 2752 km; gaps between successive passes were filled in over an interval of 16 days. Adjacent passes were spaced at 172 km. At the equator, adjacent passes overlapped by about 7.6 per cent; overlap increased as latitude increased.

A complete coverage cycle was achieved in 16 days—233 orbits. Because this pattern differs from earlier Landsat systems, Landsats 4 and later required a new WRS indexing system for labelling paths and rows (Fig. 7.10). Row designations remained the same as before, but a new system of numbering paths were required. In all there are 233 paths and 248 rows, with row 60 positioned at the equator. Communications for Landsats 4 and 5 were linked with a network of tracking and data relay satellites (TDRS).

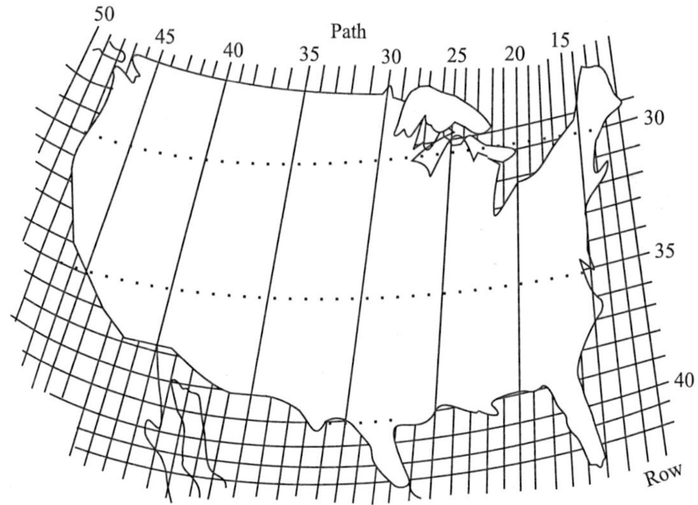

Fig. 7.10. WRS for Landsats 4 and 5.

ADMINISTRATION OF THE LANDSAT PROGRAMME

Landsat was originally operated by NASA as a part of its mission to develop and demonstrate applications of new technology related to aerospace engineering. Although NASA had primary responsibility for Landsat, other federal agencies, including the USGS and National Oceanographic and Atmospheric Administration (NOAA) contributed to several aspects of the programme.

Land Remote Sensing Policy Act of 1992 and related agreements has many provisions, including steps to maintain continuity in the collection of data, establishment of the basis for a pricing policy for image data and an outline of the nature of additional instruments to be designed for future satellites. The act outlines four options for continued development of the system:

1. Private funding and management.
2. Management by an international consortium.
3. Funding and management by the government.
4. Joint operation between the government and private industry.

CURRENT SATELLITE SYSTEMS

This outline of early Landsat systems sets the stage for examination of the more advanced systems now in use or scheduled for deployment in the near future. In recent years the number of such systems has increased so rapidly that it is impractical to list them, let alone describe all of their characteristics. Understanding this wide range of satellite systems can be easier if we consider them as members of three families of satellites.

The first group consists of Landsat-like systems, designed for acquisition of rather broad geographic coverage at moderate levels of detail. Data from these systems have been used for an amazingly broad range of applications, which can be generally described as focused on survey and monitoring of land and water resources. A second group is formed by those satellite observation systems designed to acquire very-broad scale images at coarse resolutions, intended in part to acquire images that can be aggregated to provide continental or global coverage. Such images enable scientists to monitor broad-scale environmental dynamics. Finally, a third family of satellite systems provides fine detail for small regions, to acquire imagery that might assist in urban planning or design of highway or pipeline routes, for example. Although this categorisation is imperfect, it does provide a rough framework that helps us understand the capabilities of a very large number of satellite systems now available.

Landsat-Class Systems

The success of Landsat in the early 1970s stimulated interests in other nations. For example, Laidet reported that French users were 'strongly impressed' with the Landsat system and that 'the French space programme has been strongly under the influence' of the US programme as they designed their own system. Much later, Lauer listed 33 separate Landsat or Landsat-like systems launched or planned for launch between 1972 and 2007. This number attests to the value of observational systems designed to acquire regional overviews at moderate-to-coarse levels of spatial detail. Landsat has formed the model for these systems with respect to their essential characteristics: technological design, data management and overall purpose. For example, Landsat established the value of digital data for the general community of remote sensing practitioners, set the expectation that imagery would be available for all customers and established a model for organising, archiving and cataloging imagery. Related systems have followed Landsat's lead in almost every respect.

Landsat 7 and the enhanced thematic mapper plus

Landsat's current flagship sensor, the enhanced thematic mapper plus (ETM+), was placed in orbit in April 1999, with the successful launch of Landsat 7. This system was designed by NASA and is operated by NOAA and USGS. ETM+ is designed to extend the capabilities of previous TMs by adding modest improvements to the TM's original design. In the visible, near infrared and mid-infrared, its spectral channels duplicate those of earlier TMs (Table 7.4). The thermal channel has 60 m resolution, improved from the 120-m resolution of earlier TMs. The ETM+ also has a 15 m panchromatic channel. Swath width remains at 185 km and the system is characterised by improvements in accuracy of calibration, data transmission and other characteristics.

Table 7.4. Spectral characteristics of ETM+.

Band	*Spectral range*	*Ground resolution*
1	0.450–0.515 μm	30 m
2	0.525–0.605 μm	30 m
3	0.630–0.690 μm	30 m
4	0.75–0.90 μm	30 m
5	1.55–1.75 μm	30 m
6	10.4–12.5 μm	60 m
7	2.09–2.35 μm	30 m
Pan	0.52–0.90 μm	15 m

Note: See Table 7.3.

ETM+ extends the continuity of earlier Landsat data (from both MSS and TM) by maintaining consistent spectral definitions, resolutions and scene characteristics, while taking advantage of improved technology, calibration and efficiency of data transmission.

SPOT

SPOTs 1, 2 and 3

SPOT—Le Système pour 1'Observation de la Terre (Earth Observation System)—began operations in 1986, with the launch of SPOT 1. SPOT was conceived and designed by the French Centre National d'Etudes Spatiales (CNES) in Paris, with the cooperation of other European organisations. SPOT 1, launched on 22 February 1986, was followed by SPOT 2 (22 January 1990), SPOT 3 (26 September 1993) and SPOT 4 (24 March 1998), all of which carry sensors identical to those of SPOT 1. SPOT 5 (planned for launch in late 2002) is designed to carry sensors modified from those used on the earlier systems.

The SPOT system is designed to provide data for land-use studies, assessment of renewable resources, exploration of geologic resources and cartographic work at scales of 1:50000 to 1:1,00,000. It is the first commercial remote sensing satellite designed to provide high-quality service and data for an operational user community worldwide. SPOT data, like those from Landsat, promise to meet the needs of a wide variety of customers with diverse technical, scientific and commercial needs. Design requirements included provision for complete world coverage, rapid dissemination of data, stereo capability, high spatial resolution and sensitivity in spectral regions responsive to reflectance from vegetation.

The SPOT bus is the basic satellite vehicle, designed to be compatible with a variety of sensors (Fig. 7.11). The bus provides basic functions related to orbit control and stabilisation, reception of commands, telemetry, monitoring of sensor status and the like. The bus, with its sensors, is placed in a sun-synchronous orbit at about 832 km, with a 10:30 a.m. equatorial crossing time. For vertical observation, successive passes occur at 26-day intervals, but because of the ability of SPOT sensors to be pointed off-nadir, successive imagery can be acquired, on the average, at 2½ day intervals (The exact interval for repeat coverage varies with latitude).

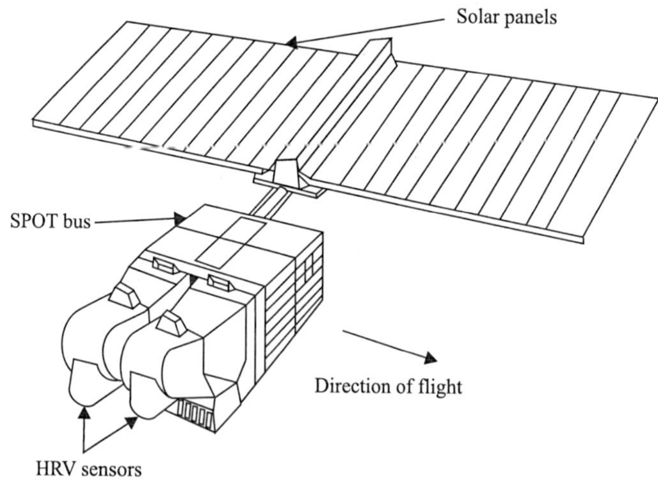

Fig. 7.11. SPOT bus.

The SPOT payload consists of two identical sensing instruments, a telemetry transmitter and magnetic tape recorders. The two sensors are know as HRV ('high resolution visible') instruments. HRV sensors use pushbroom scanning, based upon CCDs, that simultaneously images an entire line of data in the cross-track axis. SPOT linear arrays consist of 6000 detectors for each scan line in the focal plane; the array is scanned electronically to record brightness values (8 bits; 256 brightness values) in each line. Radiation from the ground is reflected to the two arrays by means of a moveable plane mirror. An innovative feature of the SPOT satellite is the ability to control the orientation of the mirror by commands from the ground—a capability that enables the satellite to acquire oblique images, as described below.

The HRV can be operated in either of two modes. In panchromatic (PN) mode, the sensor is sensitive across a broad spectral band from 0.51 to 0.73 μm. It images a 60 km swath with 6000 pixels per line, for a spatial resolution of 10 m (Fig. 7.12a). In this mode the HRV instrument provides fine spatial detail, but records a rather broad spectral region. In the panchromatic mode, the HRV instrument provides coarse spectral resolution but fine (10 m) spatial resolution.

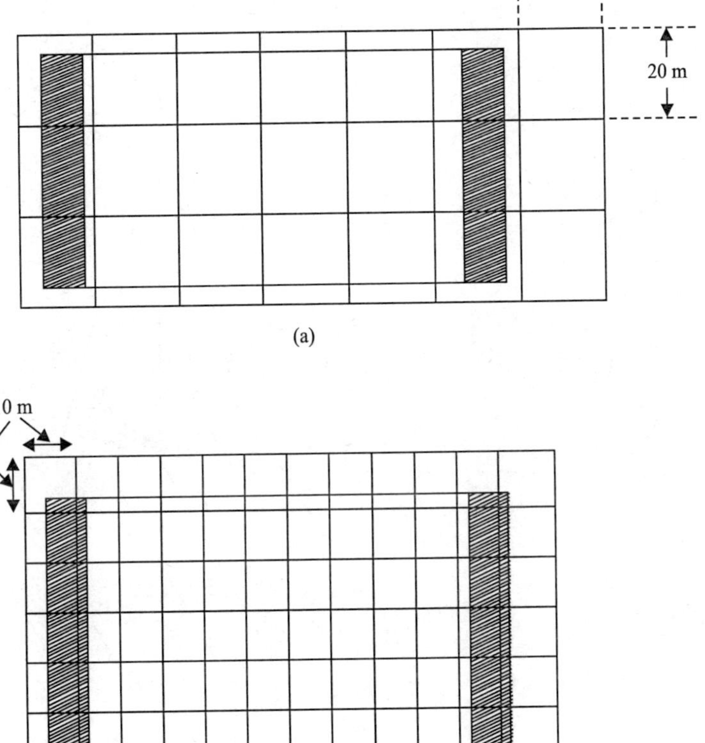

Fig. 7.12. Nominal sizes of SPOT HRV pixels. The top diagram (a) depicts the pixel size of the HRV employed in the multispectral mode. The panchromatic mode (b) achieves finer resolution.

In the other mode, the multispectral (XS) configuration, the HRV instrument senses three spectral regions:

1. Band 1: 0.50–0.59 μm (green).
2. Band 2: 0.60–0.68 μm (red; chlorophyll absorption).
3. Band 3: 0.79–0.89 μm (near infrared; atmospheric penetration).

In this mode the sensor images a strip 60 km width using 3000 samples for each line, at a spatial resolution of about 20 m (Fig. 7.12b). Thus, in the multispectral mode, the sensor records fine spectral resolution but coarse spatial resolution. The three images from the multispectral mode can be used to form false-colour composites, in the manner of CIR, MSS and TM images. In some instances, it is possible to 'sharpen' the lower spatial detail of multispectral images by superimposing them on the fine spatial detail of high-resolution panchromatic imagery of the same area.

With respect to sensor geometry, each of the HRV instruments can be positioned in either of two configurations (Fig. 7.13). For nadir viewing (Fig. 7.13a), both sensors are oriented in a manner that provides coverage of adjacent ground segments. Because the two 60 km swaths overlap by 3 km, the total image swath is 117 km. At the equator, center of adjacent satellite tracks are separated by a maximum of only 108 km, so in this mode the satellite can acquire complete coverage of the earth's surface.

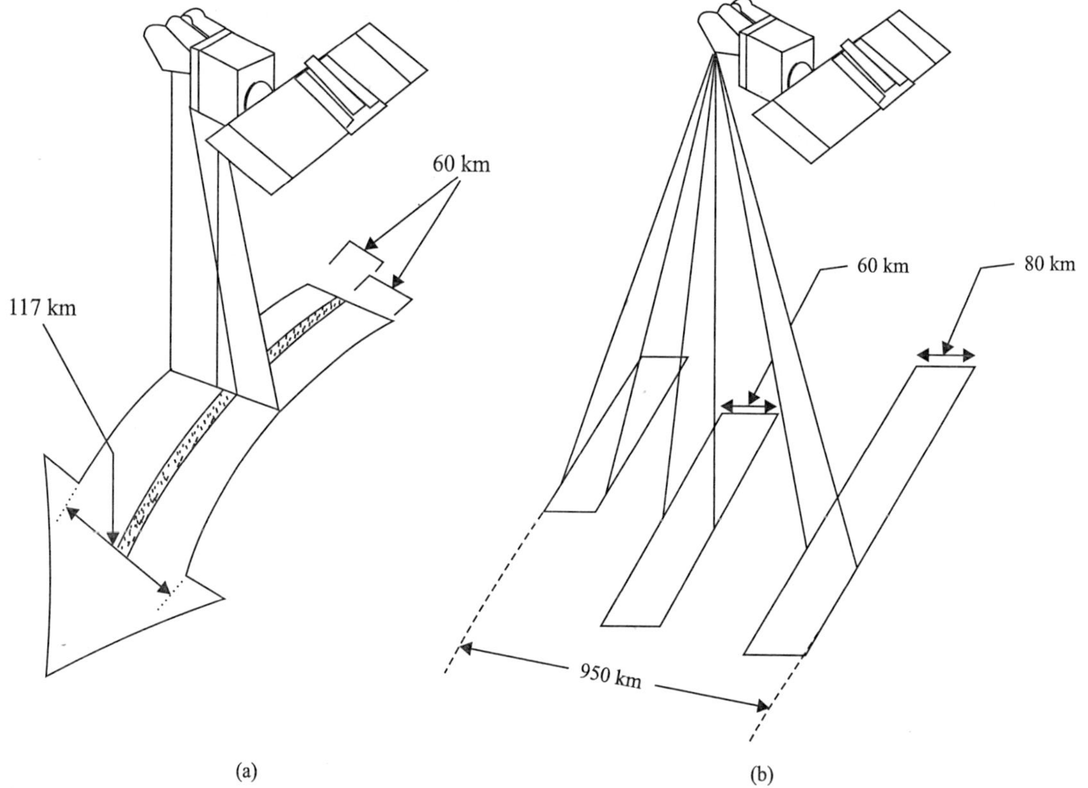

Fig. 7.13. Geometry of SPOT imagery: (a) Nadir viewing; and (b) Off-nadir viewing.

An off-nadir viewing capability is possible by pointing the HRV field of view as much as 27° relative to the vertical in 45 steps of 0.6° each (Fig. 7.13b) in a plane perpendicular to the orbital path. Off-nadir viewing is possible because the sensor observes the earth through a pointable mirror that can be controlled by command from the ground. (Note that although mirror orientation can be changed upon command, it is not a scanning mirror, as used by the MSS and the TM). With this capability, the sensors can observe any area within a 950 km swath centered on the satellite track. The pointable mirror can position any given off-nadir scene center at 10 km increments within this swath.

When SPOT uses off-nadir viewing, the swath width of individual images varies from 60 to 80 km, depending upon viewing angle. Alternatively, the same region can be viewed from separate positions (from different satellite passes) to acquire stereo coverage. (Such stereo coverage depends, of course, upon cloud-free weather during both passes). The twin sensors are not required to operate in the identical configuration; that is, one HRV can operate in the vertical mode while the other images obliquely. Using its off-nadir viewing capability, SPOT can acquire repeat coverage at intervals of 1 to 5 days, depending upon latitude.

Ground control is provided by a station in Toulouse, France, with a number of ground stations around the world providing relay and back-up capability as required. Direct reception of image data is possible within a 2600 km radius of participating ground receiving stations. In addition, the tape recorders provide the capability for recording data acquired beyond this range. An onboard computer provides the capability for programming a sequence of viewing modes and angles for later execution. Reception of SPOT data is possible at a network of ground stations positioned throughout the world.

CNES processes SPOT data in collaboration with the Institute Geographique National (IGN); image archives are maintained by the Centre de Rectification des Images Spatiales (CRIS), also operated by CNES and IGN. Four levels of processing are listed below in ascending order of precision:

1. Level 1: Basic geometric and radiometric adjustments.
   (a) Level 1a: Sensor normalisation.
   (b) Level 1b: Level 1a processing, with the addition of sample geometric corrections.
2. Level 2: Use of GCPs to correct image geometry; no correction for relief displacement.
3. Level 3: Further corrections using digital elevation models.

SPOTs 4 and 5

SPOT 4, launched in March 1998 and SPOT 5, launched in 2002, continue the SPOT programme. A principal feature of the SPOT 4 mission is the high-resolution visible and infrared (HRVIR) instrument, a modification of the HRV used for SPOTs 1, 2 and 3. HRVIR resembles the HRV, with the addition of a mid-infrared band (1.58–1.75 μm), designed to provide capabilities for geological reconnaissance, for vegetation surveys and for survey of snow cover. Whereas the HRV's 10 m resolution band covered a panchromatic range of 0.51–0.73 μm, the HRVIR's 10 m band is positioned to provide spectral coverage identical to band 2 (0.61–0.68 μm). In addition, the 10 m band will be registered to match data from band 2, facilitating use of the two levels of resolution in the same analysis.

SPOT 4 carries two identical HRVIR instruments, each with the ability to point 27° to either side of the ground track, providing a capability to acquire data within a 460 km swath for repeat coverage or stereo. In its monospectral (M) mode, HRVIR will acquire four bands of data (1, 2, 3 and mid-infrared) at 20 m resolution. Both M and X data are compressed onboard the satellite, then decompressed on the ground to provide 8 bits.

SPOT 5 will carry an upgraded version of the HRVIR, which will acquire data at 5 m resolution and provide a capability for along-track stereo imagery. Stereo imagery at 5 m resolution is intended to provide data for compilation of large-scale topographic maps and data. The new instrument, the high-resolution geometrical (HRG), will also have the flexibility to acquire data using the same bands and resolutions as the SPOT 4 HRVIR, thereby providing continuity with earlier systems.

India Remote Sensing

After operating two coarse-resolution remote sensing satellites in the 1970s and 1980s, India began to develop multispectral remote sensing programmes in the style of the Landsat system. During the early 1990s, two India remote sensing (IRS) satellites were in service. IRS-1A, launched in 1988 and IRS-1B, launched in 1991, carried the LISS-I and LISS-II pushbroom sensors (Tables 7.5 and 7.6).

Table 7.5. Spectral characteristics for LISS-I and LISS-II sensors (IRS-1A and IRS-1B).

		Resolution	
Band	*Spectral limits*	*LISS-I*	*LISS-II*
1	Blue-green (0.45–0.52 μm)	72.5 m	36.25 m
2	Green (0.52–0.59 μm)	72.5 m	36.25 m
3	Red (0.62–0.68 μm)	72.5 m	36.25 m
4	Near infrared (0.77–0.86 μm)	72.5 m	36.25 m

Table 7.6. Spectral characteristics of a LISS-III sensor (IRS-1C and IRS-1D).

Band	*Spectral limits*	*Resolution*
1[a]	Blue	–
2	Green (0.52–0.59 μm)	23 m
3	Red (0.62–0.68 μm)	23 m
4	Near infrared (0.77–0.86 μm)	23 m
5	Mid-infrared (1.55–1.70 μm)	70 m

[a]Band 1 is not included in this instrument, although the numbering system from earlier satellites is maintained to provide continuity.

These instruments collect data in four bands: blue (0.45–0.52 μm), green (0.52–0.59 μm), red (0.62–0.68 μm) and near infrared (0.77–0.86 μm), creating images of 2400 lines in each band. LISS-I provides resolution of 72.5 m in a 148 km swath and LISS-II has 36.25 m resolution. Two LISS-II cameras acquire data from 74 km-wide swaths positioned within the field of view of LISS-I (Fig. 7.14), so that four LISS-II images cover the area imaged by LISS-I, with an overlap of 1.5 km in the cross-track direction and of about 12.76 km in the along-track direction. Repeat coverage is 22 days at the equator, with more frequent re-visit capabilities at higher latitudes. Image data can be acquired within range of receiving stations in Shadnagar, India and Norma, Oklahoma.

The LISS-III instrument is designed for the IRS-1C and IRS-1D missions, launched in 1995 and 1997, respectively. These systems use tape recorders, permitting acquisition of data outside the range of the receiving stations mentioned above. They acquire data in four bands: green (0.52–0.59 μm), red (0.62–0.68 μm), near infrared (0.77–0.86 μm) and short-wave infrared (1.55–1.70 μm). LISS-III provides 23 m resolution for all bands, except for the short-wave infrared, which will have 70-m resolution (Table 7.5). Swath width is 142 km for bands 2, 3 and 4 and 148 km in band 5. The satellite provides a capability for 24-day repeat coverage at the equator.

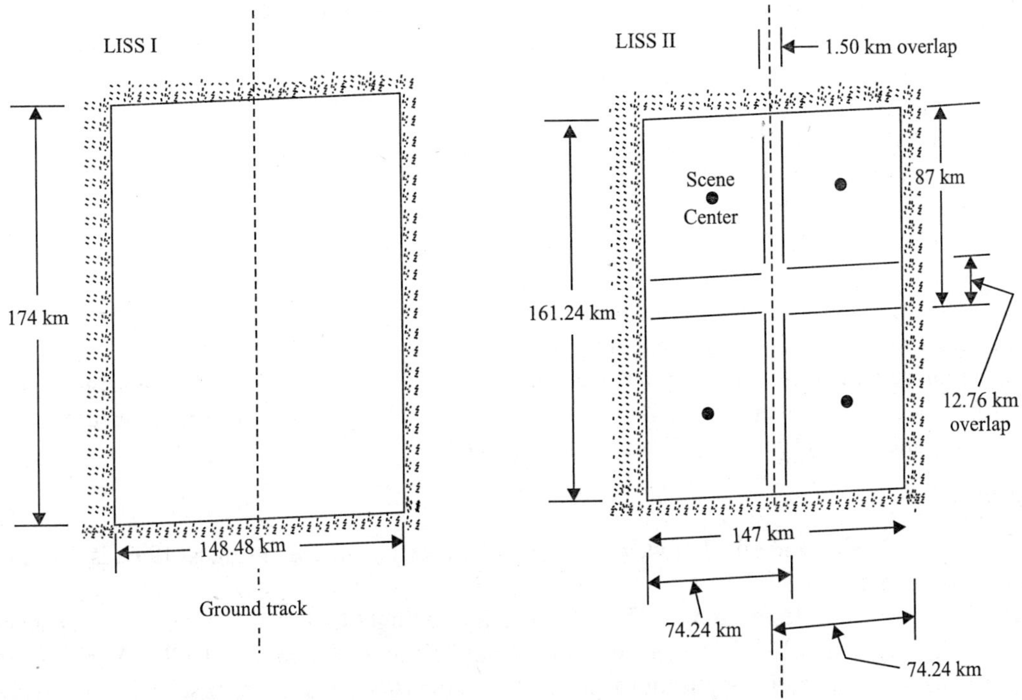

Fig. 7.14. Coverage diagram for the IRS LISS-II sensor. Sub-scenes gathered by the LISS-II sensors combine to cover the area imaged by the coarser resolution of the LISS-I instrument.

Broad-Scale Coverage

This class of systems includes satellite systems that provide coarse levels of detail for very large regions. Images collected over a period of several weeks can be used to generate composites that represent large areas of the earth without the cloud cover that would be present in any single scene. These images have opened a new perspective for remote sensing by allowing scientists to examine topics that require examination at continental or global scale that previously were outside the scope of direct observation.

AVHRR

AVHRR (advanced very-high-resolution radiometer) is a scanning system carried on NOAA's Polar Orbiting Environmental Satellites. The first version was placed in service in 1978, primarily as a meteorological satellite to provide synoptic views of weather systems and to assess the thermal balance of land surfaces in varied climate zones.

The satellite makes 14 passes each day, viewing a 2399 km swath. Unlike many other systems described here, the system provides complete coverage of the earth from pole to pole.

At nadir, the system provides an IFOV of about 1.1 km. Data presented at that level of detail are referred to as local area coverage (LAC). In addition, a global areal coverage (GAC) data set is generated by onboard averaging of the full-resolution data. GAC data are formed by the selection of every third line of data in the full-resolution data set; for each of these lines, four out of every five pixels are used to compute an average value that forms a single pixel in the GAC data set. This generalised GAC coverage provides pixels of about 4 km × 4 km resolution at nadir. A third AVHRR image product, HRPT (high-resolution picture transmission) data, is created by direct transmission of full-resolution data to a ground receiving station as the scanner collects the data. Like LAC data, the resolution is 1.1 km (LAC data are stored onboard for later transmission when the satellite is within line of sight of a ground receiving station; HRPT data are directly transmitted to ground receiving stations).

For recent versions of the AVHRR scanner, spectral channels are:

1. Band 1: 0.58–0.68 μm (red; matches TM Band 3).
2. Band 2: 0.725–1.10 μm (near infrared; matches TM Band 4).
3. Band 3: 3.55–3.93 μm (mid-infrared).
4. Band 4: 10.3–11.3 μm (thermal infrared).
5. Band 5: 11.5–12.5 μm (thermal infrared).

Data from several passes are collected to create georeferenced composites that show large regions of the earth without cloud cover. Scientists interested in broad-scale environmental issues can use such data to examine patterns of vegetation, climate and temperature.

SeaWiFS

SeaWiFS (sea-viewing wide field of view sensor) (Orbview 2) launched in August 1997, is designed to observe the earth's oceans.

The instrument was designed by NASA-Goddard Space Flight Center and was built and is operated by ORBIMAGE. ORBIMAGE is an affiliate of Orbital Sciences Corporation (Dulles, Viginia), which retains rights for commercial applications, but sells data to NASA in support of scientific and research applications. Under this data-sharing agreement, most data are held privately for a 2-week interval to preserve their commercial value, then released for more general distribution to the scientific community.

SeaWiFS's primary mission is to observe ocean colour. The colour of the ocean surface is sensitive to changes in abundance and types of marine phytoplankton, which indicate the rate that marine organisms convert solar energy into biomass (i.e., basic production of food for other marine organisms). Estimation of this rate leads to estimates of primary production of marine environments, an important consideration in the study of global marine systems. SeaWiFS data also contribute to studies of meteorology, climatology and oceanography (e.g., currents, upwelling, sediment transport, shoals) and, over land bodies, to studies of broad-scale vegetation patterns. To accomplish these objectives, SeaWiFS provides broad-scale imagery at coarse spatial resolution, but at fine spectral and radiometric resolution. That is, it is designed to survey very broad regions, but make fine distinctions of brightness and colour within those regions. It provides imagery at a spatial resolution of 1.1 km, with a swath width of 2800 km. The satellite is positioned in a sun-synchronous orbit (with a noon equatorial crossing) that can observe a large proportion of the earth's oceans every 48 hours.

SeaWiFS uses eight spectral channels:

1. Band 1: 0.402–0.422 μm (blue; yellow pigment/phytoplankton).
2. Band 2: 0.433–0.453 μm (blue; chlorophyll).
3. Band 3: 0.480–0.500 μm (blue-green; chlorophyll).
4. Band 4: 0.500–0.520 μm (green; chlorophyll).
5. Band 5: 0.545–0.565 μm (red; yellow pigment/phytoplankton).
6. Band 6: 0.660–0.680 μm (red; chlorophyll).
7. Band 7: 0.745–0.785 μm (near infrared; land-water contact, atmospheric correction, vegetation).
8. Band 8: 0.845–0.855 μm (near infrared; land-water contact, atmospheric correction, vegetation).

VEGETATION

SPOT 4, launched in March 1998, carries an auxiliary sensor, the VEGETATION (VGT) instrument, a joint project of several European nations. VGT is a wide-angle radiometer designed for high radiometric sensitivity and broad areal coverage to detect changes in spectral responses of vegetated surfaces. The swath width is 2200 km, with repeat coverage on successive days at latitudes above 35° and at the equator, coverage for 3 out of every 4 days.

The VGT instrument has a CCD linear array sensitive in four spectral bands designed to be compatible with the SPOT 4 HRVIR mentioned above:

1. Band 1: 0.45–0.50 µm (blue).
2. Band 2: 0.61–0.68 µm (red).
3. Band 3: 0.79–0.89 µm (near infrared).
4. Band 4: 1.58–1.75 µm (mid-infrared).

VEGETATION concurrently provides data in two modes. In direct (regional observation mode, VGT provides a resolution of 1 km at nadir. In recording (worldwide observation) mode, each pixel corresponds to four of the 1 km pixels, aggregated by onboard processing. In worldwide observation mode, VGT can acquire data within the region between 60° N and 40° S latitude. Data from HRVIR and VGT can be added or mixed, using onboard processing, as required to meet requirements for specific projects.

The system provides two products. VGT-P offers full radiometric fidelity, with minimal processing, for researchers who require data as close as possible to the original values. VGT-S data have been processed to provide geometric corrections composites generated to filter out cloud cover. These images are designed for scientists who require data prepared to fit directly with applications projects.

Fine-Resolution Satellite Systems

The third class of land observation satellites consist of those systems designed to provide very detailed coverage of very small regions. Landsat, SPOT and other systems established the technical and commercial value of the land observations satellite concept in the 1970s and 1980s, but they also revealed the high costs and technical challenges of designing and operating a system intended to provide general-purpose data for a broad community of users who may have diverse requirements. During the late 1980s and early 1990s, interest increased among those who believed it would be feasible to operate smaller, special-purpose, earth observations satellites focused on the requirements of very specific groups of users.

For example, the broad areal and multispectral coverage of Landsat and SPOT data might be sacrificed for much finer resolution in a single panchromatic band focused on a small area selected by specific customer. In addition, it might be possible to link imaging technology with GPS and data relay systems to integrate image data with observations acquired directly in the field. This kind of approach to satellite remote sensing generated a multitude of proposals for small commercial satellite systems tailored for specific markets and purposes.

The ancestors of these systems are the military reconnaissance satellites employed for strategic surveillance during the cold war era, designed to provide detailed images of very specific regions. At the end of the cold war, some of the older defense-related images were released to the public as a historical archive. In 1994 governmental restrictions on the commercial applications of high-resolution satellite imagery were relaxed. These changes in policy, linked with advances in technology, have opened opportunities for deployment of satellites designed to provide high-resolution data for rather small areas.

These characteristics separate them clearly from the design of other systems described here, which have been specifically tailored to produce coarse-resolution data for very large regions.

Today, several commercial firms have exploited this opportunity by designing systems based upon linear array imaging technology to provide spatial detail in the range of 1–4 m. Routine availability of imagery at this level of detail opens a new arena for applications of satellite data, especially in fields such as urban planning, transportation analysis, utility management and precision agriculture that require levels of detail that are not available from broader scale satellite systems.

Imagery from these systems, used in combination with GPSs and GISs will clearly have profound impacts on the ways that spatial data are used throughout the economies of developed nations. They will provide fine-detail digital imagery in a format compatible with existing software systems that will promote routine applications of remotely sensed imagery in areas such as real estate, marketing, urban mapping, transportation and pipeline planning, local land-use surveys and precision agriculture and forestry—to mention only some of the more obvious opportunities.

Imagery at fine levels of detail seems likely to generate new users of the technology, users with interests that differ noticeably from those who use the broad-scale systems. Images will cover much more specific geographic regions, so will be of interest to a much more distinct pool of customers, who will differ in numbers and interests from users of Landsat data, for example. Users of fine-detail imagery are likely to have an interest in observation of specific regions in fine detail rather than large regions in coarse detail.

IKONOS

The IKONOS satellite system (named from the Greek word for 'image'), launched in September 1999 (an earlier launch in April 1999 failed), is operated by Space Imaging, Denver, Colorado.

In panchromatic mode, IKONOS provides spatial resolution at 1 meter, in the spectral range 0.45–0.90 μm. In multispectral mode, it provides imagery at 4 m spatial resolution in four spectral bands:

1. Band 1: 0.45–0.52 μm (blue).
2. Band 2: 0.52–0.60 μm (green).
3. Band 3: 0.63–0.69 μm (red).
4. Band 4: 0.76–0.90 μm (near infrared).

The image swath is 11 km at nadir; imagery is acquired from a sun-synchronous orbit, with a 10:30 a.m. equatorial crossing. The re-visit interval varies with latitude; at 40°, repeat coverage can be acquired at about 3 days in the multispectral mode and at about 1½ days in the panchromatic mode.

OrbView 3 and 4

Orbimage plans to launch two satellite systems. OrbView 3 will provide 1 m resolution in a panchromatic band and 4-m resolution in four multispectral bands:

1. Band 1: 0.45–0.52 μm.
2. Band 2: 0.52–0.60 μm.
3. Band 3: 0.625–0.695 μm.
4. Band 4: 0.76–0.90 μm.

It will provide a swath width of 8 km.

Warfighter (OrbView 4) is intended to acquire hyperspectral data from satellite altitudes. It will sense 200 spectral channels in the range of 0.45–2.5 μm, at a spatial resolution of about 8 m, over a 5 km swath width. It will also collect 4 m multispectral data and 1 m panchromatic images in the same manner as OrbView 3. The re-visit interval will be 3 days or less.

QuickBird

In October 2001, EarthWatch Inc. launched Quickbird, a satellite designed to acquire fine-detail imagery using a panchromatic band with detail at 61 cm resolution and four multispectral bands with 2.44 m detail at:

1. Band 1: 0.45–0.52 μm (blue).
2. Band 2: 0.52–0.60 μm (green).
3. Band 3: 0.63–0.69 μm (red).
4. Band 4: 0.76–0.890 μm (near infrared).
5. Band 5: 0.76–0.890 μm (panchromatic).

Quickbird will acquire data using a swath width of 16.5 km (An earlier system, Earlybird, was lost just after launch in 1996).

COMPUTER SEARCHES

Because of the unprecedented amount of data generated by earth observation satellite systems, from the very beginning computerised databases formed the principal means of indexing satellite imagery. Each satellite system mentioned above is supported by an electronic catalogue that characterises each scene by area, date, quality, cloud cover and other qualities. Although in the past customers could submit requests by mail, FAX, phone or e-mail, many organisations have now begun to implement systems that permit customers to search their achieves and order their products online. An example in Earth Explorer, offered by the USGS as an index for USGS and Landsat imagery and cartographic data.

Users can specify a geographic region by using geographic coordinates, by outlining a region on a map or by entering a place-name. Subsequent screens allow users to select specific kinds of data, specify desirable dates of coverage and indicate the minimum quality of coverage. The result is a computer listing that provides a tabulation of coverage meeting the constraints specified by the user. Some organisations can provide quick-look images: simplified versions of specific images that permit customers to verify, prior to ordering data, the coverage, quality and cloud cover of specific scenes. Earth Explorer and similar systems provide Internet access to quick look, with opportunities to establish user accounts that permit placing of electronic orders to purchase image data using the www.

A list of results of a search of the image database will vary in length according to the nature of the user's request. A conservative, restrictive request closely tailored to the user's needs will result in a much shorter listing than will a loosely defined, very broad request. Unless the user suspects that there is very little coverage of an area, it is usually best to define the request to closely match his or her needs, as it can be very tedious to search through a long list to identify the best images.

Because it is usually necessary to make compromises between competing qualities (e.g., date, coverage, quality, etc.), it is important that an analyst be innately familiar not only with the technical qualities of the satellite system, but also with the purposes and objectives of the specific project for which its images will be used. Note that to prepare the request for a geographic computer search and to interpret the resulting computer listing, it is necessary to have access to medium or large-scale maps with accurate representation of latitude and longitude.

Because tabulations of image data are difficult to interpret, the analyst must examine information displaying the outline of image coverage plotted on a map (the image footprint) that shows basic reference features, to permit as assessment of coverage with respect to project requirements and coverage of other imagery (Fig. 7.15). Earth Explorer and similar systems provide this capability as part of their indexing and cataloging functions. Another easily accessible example is the USGS Landsat 7 Image Viewer.

Descriptive records describing coverages of satellite data are examples of a class of data known as metadata. Metadata consist of descriptive summaries of other data sets (in this instance, the satellite images themselves). As increasing large volumes of remotely sensed data are accumulated, the ability to search, compare and examine metadata has become increasingly significant. In the context of remote sensing, metadata usually consists of text describing images: dates, spectral regions, quality ratings, cloud cover, geographic coverage and so on. An increasing number of efforts are underway to develop computer programs and communication systems that will link databases together to permit searches of multiple archives.

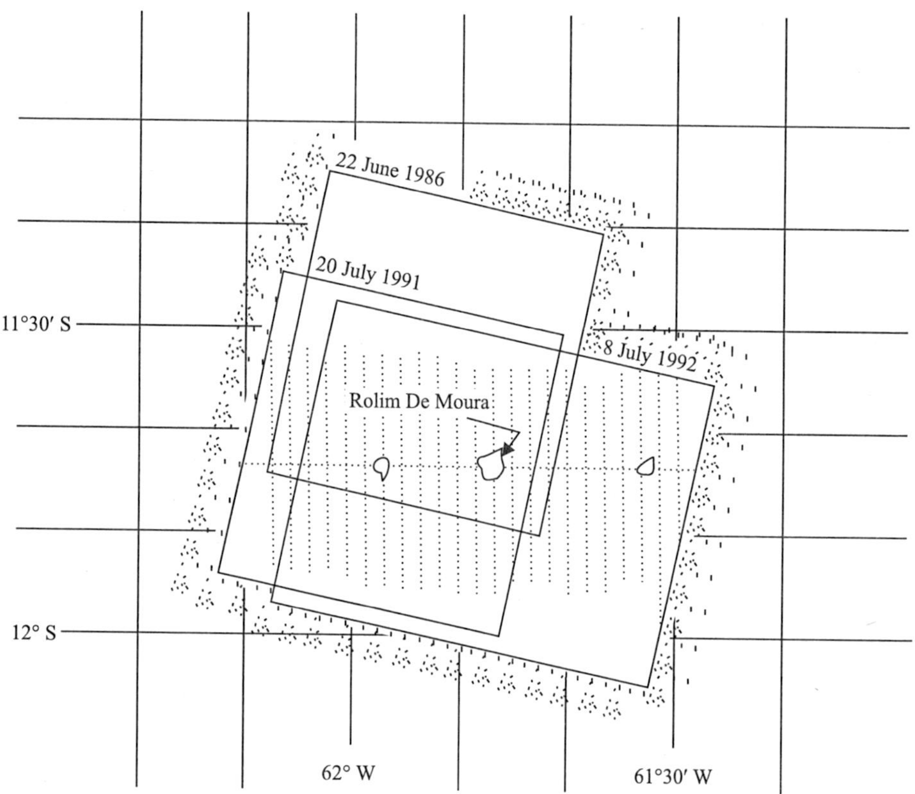

Fig. 7.15. Example of map plot of image coverage from a computer search.

Thus satellite observation of the earth has greatly altered the field of remote sensing. Since the launch of Landsat 1, a larger and more diverse collection of scientists than ever before have conducted remote sensing research and used its applications. Public knowledge of and interest in, remote sensing has increased. Digital data for satellite images has contributed greatly to the growth of image processing, pattern recognition and image analysis. Satellite observation systems have increased international cooperation through joint construction and operation of ground receiving stations and through collaboration in the training of scientists.

The history of the US Landsat system, as well as the histories of comparable systems of other nations, illustrate the continuing difficulties experienced in defining structures for financing the development, operation and distribution costs required for satellite imaging systems. The large initial investments and high continuing operation costs (quite unlike those of aircraft systems) resemble those of a public utility. Yet there is no comparable shared understanding that such systems generate widespread public benefits, so users must contribute substantially to supporting their costs. But if such systems were to pass their full costs on to customers, the prices of imagery would be too high for development of new applications and growth of the market. In the United States, as well as in other nations, there has been increasing interest in development of policies and encourage governmental agencies, military services and private corporations to share costs of development and operation of satellite systems. This approach (dual use) may represent an improvement over previous efforts to establish long-term support of satellite remote sensing, but it is now too early to determine if it constitutes a real solution to the long-term problem.

Another concern that will attract more and more public attention is the issue of personal privacy. As systems provide more-or-less routine availability of imagery with submeter resolution, governmental agencies and private corporations will have direct access to information that could provide very detailed information about specific individuals and their property. Although this imagery would not necessarily provide information not already available through publicly available aerial photography, the ease of access and the standardised format open new avenues for use of such information. The real concern should focus not so much on the imagery itself, but upon the effects of combining such imagery with other data from marketing information, census information and the like. The combination of these several forms of information, each in itself rather benign, could develop capabilities that many people would consider to be objectionable or even dangerous.

A third issue concerns reliable public access to fine-resolution imagery. For example, news organisations might wish to maintain their own surveillance systems to provide independent sources of information regarding military, political and economic developments throughout the world. Will governments, as investors and/or operators of satellite imaging systems, feel that they are in a position to restrict access when questions of national security are at stake?

This chapter forms an important part of the foundation necessary to develop topics presented in subsequent chapters. The specific systems described here are significant in their own right, but they also provide the foundation for understanding other satellite systems that operate in the microwave and far infrared.

8

Active Microwave and Lidar

INTRODUCTION

This chapter describes active microwave and lidar (Light Detection and Ranging) sensors, two sensor systems that would seem to differ greatly because they use energy in widely separated regions of the spectrum—the microwave and visible light spectra, respectively—and record contrasting properties of the earth's surface.

However, they share a significant characteristic that distinguishes them from other instruments. Active microwave and lidar sensors are the two best examples of active sensors, sensors that broadcast a directed pattern of energy to illuminate a portion of the earth's surface, then receive the portion scattered back to the instrument. This energy forms the basis for the imagery we interpret.

Because passive sensors (e.g., photography) are sensitive to variations in solar illumination, their use is constrained by time of day and atmospheric conditions. In contrast, active sensors generate their own energy, so their use is subject to fewer constraints and they can be used under a wider range of operational conditions. Further, because active sensors use energy generated by the sensor itself, its properties are known in detail. Therefore, it is possible to compare transmitted energy with received energy to judge with more precision than is possible with passive sensors the characteristic of the surfaces that have scattered the energy.

ACTIVE MICROWAVE

The microwave region of the electromagnetic spectrum extends from wavelengths of about 1 mm to about 1 m. This region is, of course, far removed from those in and near the visible spectrum, where our direct sensory experience can assist in our interpretation of images and data.

Thus formal understanding of the concepts of remote sensing are vital to understanding imagery acquired in the microwave region. As a result, the study of microwave imagery is often a difficult subject for beginning students and requires more attention than is usually necessary for study of other regions of the spectrum.

The family of sensors discussed here (Fig. 8.1) includes active microwave sensors (imaging radars carried by either aircraft or satellites). These are active sensors because they illuminate the ground with their own energy, then record a portion of that energy reflected back to themselves.

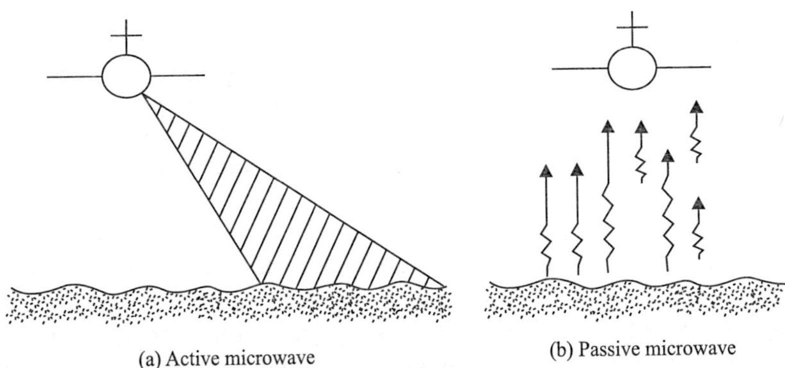

Fig. 8.1. Active and passive microwave remote sensing. (a) Active microwave sensing, using energy generatedby the sensor; and (b) passive microwave sensing, which detects energy emitted by the earth's surface.

Active Microwave Sensors

Active microwave sensors are radar devices, instruments that transmit a microwave signal, then receive its reflection as the basis for forming images of the earth's surface. The rudimentary components of an imaging radar system include a transmitter, a receiver, an antenna array and a recorder (Fig. 8.2). A transmitter is designed to transmit repetitive pulses of microwave energy at a given frequency. A receiver accepts the reflected signal as received by the antenna, then filters and amplifies it as required. An antenna array transmits a narrow beam of microwave energy. Such an array is composed of waveguides, devices that control the propagation of an electromagnetic wave, such that waves follow a path defined by the physical structure of the guide (A simple waveguide might be formed from a hollow metal tube). Usually the same antenna is used both to transmit the radar signal and to receive its echo from the terrain. Finally, a recorder records and/or displays the signal as an image. Numerous refinements and variations of these basic components are possible; a few are described below in greater detail.

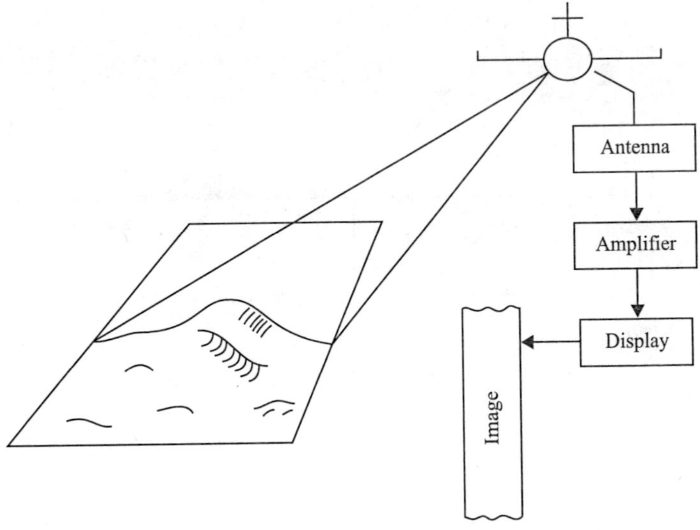

Fig. 8.2. Schematic overview of an imaging radar system.

Side-Looking Airborne Radar

Radar is an acronym for 'radio detection and ranging.' The 'ranging' capability is achieved by measuring the time delay between the time a signal is transmitted toward the terrain and the time its echo is received. Through its ranging capability, possible only with active sensors, radar can accurately measure the distance from the antenna to features on the ground. A second unique capability, also a result of radar's status as an active sensor, is its ability to detect frequency and polarisation shifts. Because the sensor transmits a signal of known wavelength, it is possible to compare the received signal with the transmitted signal. From such comparisons imaging radars detect changes in frequency that give them capabilities not possible with other sensors.

Side-looking airborne radar (SLAR) imagery is acquired by an antenna array aimed to the side of the aircraft, so that it forms an image of strip of land parallel to and at some distance from the ground track of the aircraft (Fig. 8.3). The resulting image geometry differs greatly from that of other remotely sensed images. These qualities establish radar imagery as a distinctive form of remote sensing imagery. One of SLAR's most unique and useful characteristics is its ability to function during inclement weather. SLAR is often said to possess an 'all-weather' capability, meaning that it can acquire imagery in all but the most severe weather conditions. The microwave energy used for SLAR imagery is characterised by wavelengths long enough to escape interference from clouds and light rain (although not necessarily from heavy rainstorms). Because SLAR systems are independent of solar illumination, missions using SLAR can be scheduled at night or during early morning or evening hours when solar illumination might be unsatisfactory for acquiring aerial photography. This advantage is especially important for imaging radars carried by the earth-orbiting satellites described later in this chapter.

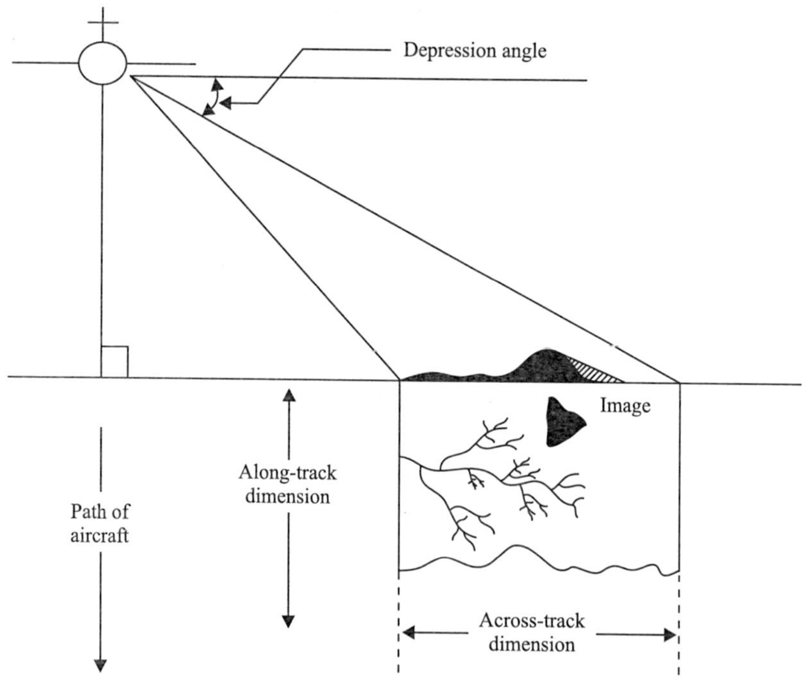

Fig. 8.3. Schematic diagram of a radar image.

Radar images typically provide crisp, clear representations of topography and drainage. Despite being subject to geometric errors described below, radar images typically provide good positional accuracy; in some areas they have provided the data for small-scale base maps depicting major drainage and terrain features. Analysts have registered TM and SPOT data to radar images to form composites of the two quite different kinds of information. Some of the most successful operational applications of SLAR imagery have occurred in tropical climates, where persistent cloud cover has prevented acquisition of aerial photography and where shortages of accurate maps create a context in which radar images can provide cartographic information superior to that on existing conventional maps. Another important characteristic of SLAR imagery is its synoptic view of the landscape. SLAR's ability to clearly represent the major topographic and drainage features within relatively large regions at moderate image scales makes it a valuable addition to our repertoire of remote sensing imagery. Furthermore, because it acquires images in the microwave spectrum, SLAR it may show detail and information that differ greatly from that of sensors operating in the visible and near infrared spectra.

Origins and History

The foundations for imaging radars were laid by scientists who first investigated the nature and properties of microwave and radio energy. James Clerk Maxwell first defined essential characteristics of electromagnetic radiation; his mathematical descriptions of the properties of magnetic and electrical fields prepared the way for further theoretical and practical work. In Germany, Heinrich R. Hertz confirmed much of Maxwell's work and further studied properties and propagation of electromagnetic energy in microwave and radio portions of the spectrum. The Hertz, the unit for designation of frequencies is named in his honor. Hertz was among the first to demonstrate the reflection of radio waves from metallic surfaces and thereby begin research that led to development of modern radios and radars.

In Italy, Guilielmo M. Marconi continued the work of Hertz and other scientists, in part by devising a practical antenna suitable for transmitting and receiving radio signals. In 1895 he demonstrated the practicability of the wireless telegraph. After numerous experiments over shorter distances, he demonstrated in 1991 the feasibility of long-range communications by sending signals across the Atlantic; in 1909 he shared the Nobel Prize in Physics. Later he proposed that ships could be detected by using the reflection of radio waves, but there is no evidence that his suggestion influenced the work of other scientists.

The formal beginnings of radar date from 1922, when A. H. Taylor and L. C. Young, civilian scientists working for the U.S. Navy, were conducting experiments with high-frequency radio transmissions. Their equipment was positioned near the Anacostia River near Washington, DC., with the transmitter on one bank of the river and the receiver on the other. They observed that the passage of a river steamer between the transmitter and the receiver interrupted the signal in a manner that clearly revealed the potential of radio signals as a means for detecting the presence of large objects (Fig. 8.4). Taylor and Young recognised the significance of their discovery for marine navigation in darkness and inclement weather and in a military context, its potential for detection of enemy vessels. Initial efforts to implement this idea depended upon the placement of transmitters and receivers at separate locations, so that a continuous microwave signal was reflected from an object, then recorded by a receiver placed some distance away. Designs evolved so that a single instrument contained both the transmitter and the receiver at a single location, integrated in a manner that permitted use of a pulsed signal that could be reflected from the target back to the same antenna that transmitted the signal. A British inventor, Sir Robert Watson-Watt, is sometimes given credit as the inventor of the first radar system, although Young and Taylor have been credited by other historians.

Fig. 8.4. Beginnings of radar. Schematic diagram of the situation that led to the experiments by Young and Taylor.

Subsequent improvements were based mainly upon refinements in the electronics required to produce high-power transmissions over narrow wavelength intervals, to carefully time short pulses of energy and to amplify the reflected signal. These and other developments led to rapid evolution of radar systems in the years prior to World War II. Due to the profound military significane of radar technology, World War II prompted radar's sophistication. The postwar era perfected imaging radars. Experience with conventional radars during World War II revealed that radar reflection from ground surface (ground clutter) varied greatly according to terrain, season, settlement patterns and so on and from ocean surfaces was modified by winds and waves. Ground clutter was undesirable for radars designed to detect aircraft and ships, but later systems were designed specifically to record the differing patterns of reflection from ground and ocean surfaces. The side-looking characteristic of SLAR was desirable because of the experiences of reconnaissance pilots during the war, who often were required to fly low-level missions along predictable flight paths in lightly armed aircraft to acquire the aerial photography required for battlefield intelligence. The side-looking capability provided a means for acquiring information at a distance using an aircraft flying over friendly territory.

Later, the situation posed by the emergence of the cold war in Europe, with clearly defined frontiers and strategic requirements for information within otherwise closed borders, also provided an incentive for development of sensors with SLAR's capabilities. The experience of the war years also must have provided an intense interest in development of SLAR's all-weather capablities, because allied intelligence efforts were several times severely restricted by the absence of aerial reconnaissance during inclement weather. Thus the development of imaging radars is linked to military and strategic reconnaissance, even though many current applications focus upon civilian requirements.

GEOMETRY OF RADAR IMAGE

The basics of the geometry of a SLAR image are illustrated in Fig. 8.5. Here the aircraft is viewed head-on, with the radar beam represented in vertical cross section as the fan-shaped figure at the side of the aircraft. The upper edge of the beam forms an angle with a horizontal line extended from the aircraft; this angle is designated as the depression angle of the far edge of the image. Upper and lower edges of the beam, as they intersect with the ground surface, define the edges of the radar image; the forward motion of the aircraft (toward the reader, out of the plane of the illustration) forms what is usually the 'long' dimension of the strip of radar imagery. The smallest depression angle forms the far-range side of the image. The near-range region is the edge nearest to the aircraft. Intermediate regions between the two edges are sometimes referred to as midrange portions of the image. Steep terrain may hide areas of the imaged region from illumination by the radar beam, causing radar shadow. Note that radar shadow depends upon topographic relief and the direction of the flight path in relation to topography. Within an image, radar shadow depends also upon depression angle, so that (given equivalent topographic relief) radar shadow will be more severe in the far-range portion of the image (where depression angles are smallest) or for those radar systems that use shallow depression angles. (A specific radar system is usually characterised by a fixed range of depression angles.

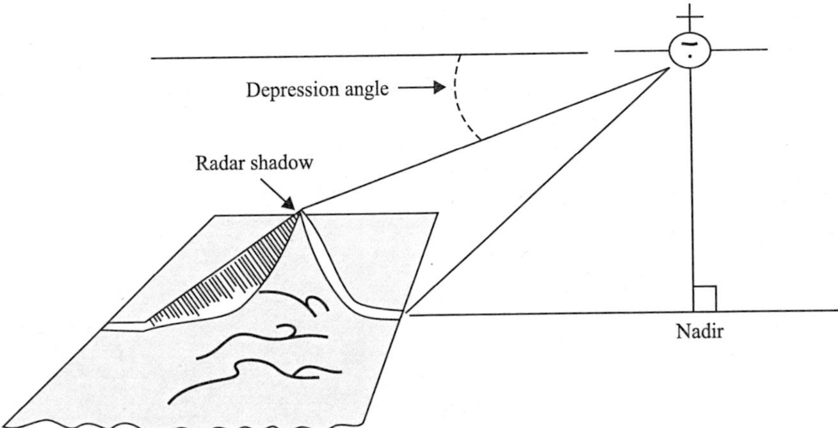

Fig. 8.5. Geometry of an imaging radar system. The radar beam illuminates a strip of ground parallel to the flight path of the aircraft; the reflection and scattering of the microwave signal from the ground forms the basis for the image.

Radar systems measure distance to a target by timing the delay between a transmitted signal and its return to the antenna. Because the speed of electromagnetic energy is a known constant, the measure of time translates directly to a measure of distance from the antenna. Microwave energy travels in a straight path from the aircraft to the ground—a path that defines the slantrange distance, as if one were to stretch a length of string from the aircraft to a specific point on the ground as a measure of distance (Fig. 8.6). Image interpreters prefer images to be presented in ground-range format, with distances portrayed in their correct relative positions on the earth's surface.

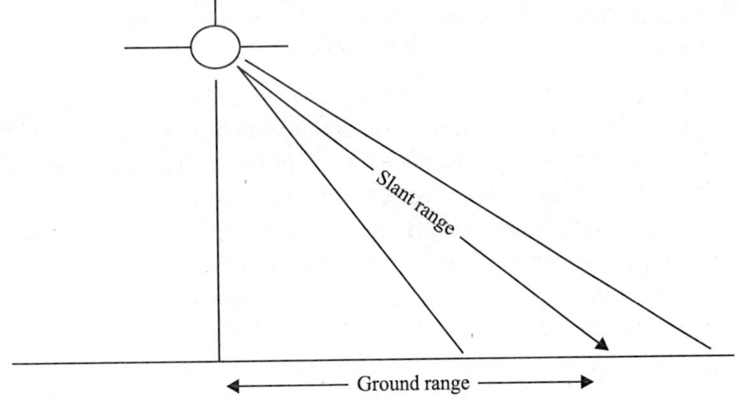

Fig. 8.6. Slant range and ground range. Slant range is the direct distance from the antenna to an object on the ground, as measured by the time delay from transmission of the signal to reception of its echo. Ground range represents the correct scaling of distances as we would measure them on a map.

Because radars collect all information in the slant-range domain, radar images inherently contain geometric artifacts, even though the image display may ostensibly appear to match a ground-range presentation. One such error is radar layover (Fig. 8.7). At near range, the top of a tall object is closer to the antenna than its base. As a result, the echo from the top of the object reaches the antenna before the echo from the base. Because radar measures all distances with respect to time elapsed between transmission of a signal and the reception of its echo, the top of the object appears (i.e., in the slant-range domain) to be closer to the antenna than does its base. Indeed, it is closer, if only the slant-range domain is considered. However, in the ground-range domain (the context for correct positional representation and for accurate measurement), both the top and the base of the object both occupy the same geographic position. In the slant-range domain of the radar image, they occupy different image positions—a geometric error analogous perhaps to relief displacement in the context of aerial photography.

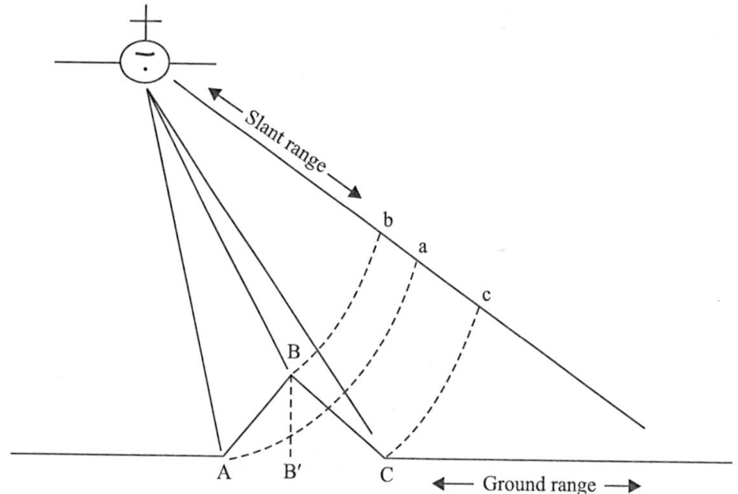

Fig. 8.7. Radar layover. In the ground-range domain AB and BC are equal. Because the radar can measure only slant-range distances, AB and BC are projected onto the slant-range domain, represented by the line *bac*. The three points are not shown in their correct relationship because the slant-range distance from the antenna to the points does not match to their ground-range distances. Point B is closer to the antenna than is point A, so it is depicted on the image as closer to the edge of the image.

Radar layover is depicted in Fig. 8.7. Here the topographic feature ABC is shown with AB = BC in the ground-range representation. However, because the radar can position A, B and C only by the time delay with relation to the antenna, it must perceive the relationships between A, B and C as shown in the slant rage (image plane). Here A and B are reversed from their ground-range relationships, so that ABC is now *bac*, due to the fact that the echo from B must be received before the echo from A.

A second form of geometric error, radar foreshortening, occurs in terrain of modest-to-high relief depicted in the mid-to far-range portion of an image (Fig. 8.8). Here the slant-range representation depicts ABC in their correct relationships abc, but the distances between them are not accurately shown. Whereas AB = BC in the ground-range domain, ab < bc when they are projected into the slant range. Radar foreshortening tends to cause images of a given terrain feature to appear to have steeper slopes than they do in nature on the near-range side of the image and to have shallower slopes than they do in nature on the far-range side of the feature. Thus a terrain feature with equal fore and back slopes may be imaged to have shorter, steeper and brighter slopes than it would in a correct representation and the image of the back slope would appear to be longer, shallower and darker than it would in a correct representation. Because depression angle varies with position on the image, the amount of radar foreshortening in the image of a terrain feature depends not only upon the steepness of its slopes, but also upon its position on the radar image. As a result, apparent terrain slope and shape on radar images are not necessarily accurate representations of their correct character in nature. Thus care should be taken when interpreting these features.

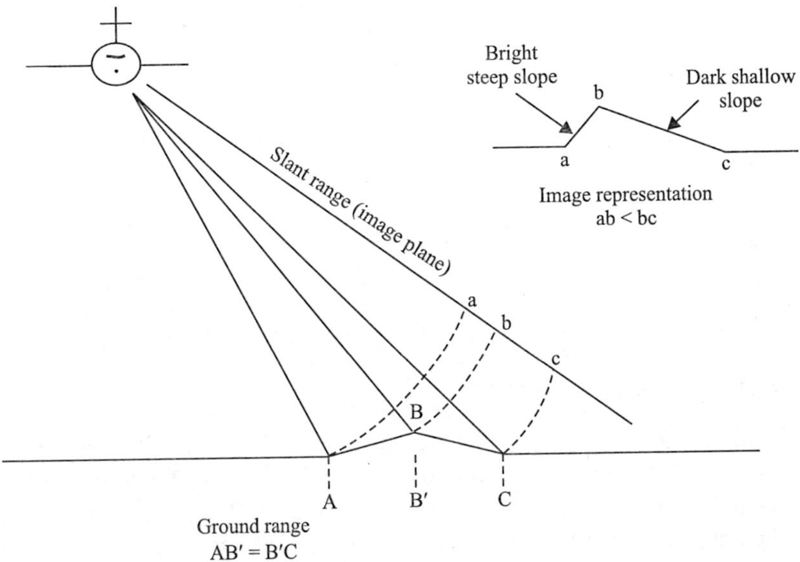

Fig. 8.8. Radar foreshortening. Projection of A, B and C into the slant-range domain distorts the representations of AB and BC, so that ab appears shorter, steeper and brighter than it should be in a faithful rendition and bc appears longer, shallower in slope and darker than it should be.

WAVELENGTH

Imaging radars normally operate within a small range of wavelengths with the rather broad interval defined at the beginning of this chapter. Table 8.1 lists primary sub-divisions of the active microwave region, as commonly defined in various countries. These divisions and their designations have an arbitrary, illogical flavour that is the consequence of their origin during the development of military radars, when it was important to conceal the use of specific frequencies for given purposes. To preserve military security, the designations were designed as much to confuse unauthorised parties as to provide convenience for authorised personnel. Eventually these designations became established in everyday usage and they continue to be used even though there is no longer a requirement for military secrecy.

Although experimental radars can often change frequency or sometimes even use several frequencies (for a kind of 'multispectral radar'), operational systems are generally designed to use a single wavelength band. Airborne imaging radars have frequently used. C-, K- and X-bands, however, imaging radars used for satellite observation often use L-band frequencies.

The choice of a specific microwave band has several implications for the nature of the radar image. For real aperture imaging radars, spatial resolution improves as wavelength becomes shorter with respect to antenna length (i.e., for a given antenna length, resolution is finer with use of a shorter wavelength).

Penetration of the signal into the soil is in part a function of wave length—for given moisture conditions, penetration is greatest at longer wavelengths. The longer wavelengths of microwave radiation (e.g., relative to visible radiation) mean that imaging radars are insensitive to the usual problems of atmospheric attenuation—usually only very heavy rain will interfere with transmission of microwave energy.

Table 8.1. Radar frequency designations.

Band	*Wavelengths*
P-band	107–77 cm
UHF	100–30 cm
L-band	30–15 cm
S-band	15–7.5 cm
C-band	7.5–3.75 cm
X-band	3.75–2.40 cm
Ku-band	2.40–1.67 cm
K-band	1.67–1.18 cm
Ka-band	1.18–0.75 cm

PENETRATION OF THE RADAR SIGNAL

In principle, radar signals are capable of penetrating what would normally be considered solid features, including vegetative cover and the soil surface. In practice, it is very difficult to assess the existence or amount of radar penetration in the interpretation of specific images. Penetration is assessed by specifying the skin depth, the depth to which the strength of a signal is reduced to 1/e of its surface magnitude or about 37 per cent. Separate features are subject to differing degrees of penetration; specification of the skin depth, measured in standard units of length, provides a means of designating variations in the ability of radar signals to penetrate various substances.

In the absence of moisture, skin depth increases with increasing wavelength. Thus optimum conditions for observing high penetration would be in arid regions, using long-wavelength radar system. Penetration is also related to surface roughness and to incidence angle; penetration is greater at steeper angles and decreases as incidence angle increases. We should therefore expect maximum pentration at the near-range edge of the image and minimum penetration at the far-range portion of the image.

The difficulties encountered in the interpretation of an image that might record penetration of the radar signal would probably prevent practical use of any information that might be conveyed to the interpreter. There is no clearly defined means by which an interpreter might be able to recognise the existence of penetration or to separate its effects from the many other variables that contribute to radar backscatter. For radar systems operating near X-band and K-band, empirical evidence suggests that the radar signal is generally scattered from the first surface it strikes, probably foliage in most instances. Even at L-band, which is theoretically capable of a much higher degree of penetration, the signal is apparently scattered from the surface foliage in densely vegetated regions, as reported by Sabins after examining L-band imagery of forested regions in Indonesia.

POLARISATION

The polarisation of a radar signal denotes the orientation of the field of electromagnetic energy emitted and received by the antenna. Radar systems can be configured to transmit either horizontally or vertically polarised energy and to receive either horizontally or vertically polarised energy as it is scattered from the ground. Unless otherwise specified, an imaging radar usually transmits horizontally polarised energy and receives horizontally polarised echo from the terrain. However, some radars are designed to transmit horizontally polarised signals, but to separately receive the horizontally and vertically polarised reflections from the landscape. Such systems produce two images of the same landscape. One is the image formed by the transmission of a horizontally polarised signal and the reception of a horizontally polarised return signal. This is often referred to as the HH image or the like-polarised mode. A second image is formed by the transmission of a horizontally polarised signal and the reception of the vertically polarised return; this is the HV image or the cross-polarised mode.

By comparing the two images, the interpreter can identify features and areas that represent regions on the landscape that tend to depolarise the signal. Such areas will reflect the incident horizontally polarised signal back to the antenna as vertically polarised energy—That is, they change the polarisation of the incident microwave energy. Such areas can be identified as bright regions on the HV image and as dark or dark gray regions on the corresponding HH image. Their appearance on the HV image is much brighter due to the effect of depolarisation—the polarisation of the energy that would have contributed to the brightness of the HH image has been changed, so it creates instead a bright area on the HV image. Comparison of the two images therefore permits detection of those areas that are good depolarisers.

This same information can be restated in a different way. A surface that is an ineffective depolariser will tend to scatter energy in the same polarisation in which it was transmitted; such areas will appear bright on the HH image and dark on the HV image. In contrast, a surface that is a 'good' depolariser will tend to scatter energy in a polarisation different from that of the incident signal; such areas will appear dark on the HH image and bright on the HV image.

Causes of depolarisation are related to physical and electrical properties of the ground surface. A rough surface (with respect to the wavelength of the signal) may depolarise the signal. Another cause of depolarisation is volume scattering from an inhomogeneous medium; such scatter might occur if the radar signal is capable of penetrating beneath the soil surface (as might conceivably be possible in some desert areas where vegetation is sparse and the soil is dry enough for significant penetration to occur), where it might encounter sub-surface inhomogenities, such as buried rocks or indurated horizons.

LOOK DIRECTION AND LOOK ANGLE

Look Direction

Look direction, the direction at which the radar signal strikes the landscape, is important in both natural and man-made landscapes. In natural landscapes, look direction is especially important when terrain features display a preferential alignment. Look directions perpendicular to topographic alignment will tend to maximise radar shadow, whereas look directions parallel to topographic orientation will tend to minimise radar shadow. In regions of small or modest topographic relief, radar shadow may be desirable as a means of enhancing microtopography or revealing the fundamental structure of the regional terrain. The extent of radar shadow depends not only upon local relief, but also upon orientations of features relative to the flight path; those features positioned in the near-range portion (other factors being equal) will have the smallest shadows, whereas those at the far-range edge of the image will cast larger shadows (Fig. 8.9). In areas of high relief, radar shadow is usually undesirable, as it masks large areas from observation. In landscapes that have been heavily altered by human activities, the orientation of structures and land-use patterns are often a significant influence on the character of the radar return and therefore upon the manner in which given landscapes appear on radar imagery. For instance, if an urban area is viewed at a look direction that maximises the scattering of the radar signal from structures aligned along a specific axis, it will have an appearance quite different from that of an image acquired at a look direction that tends to minimise reflection from such features.

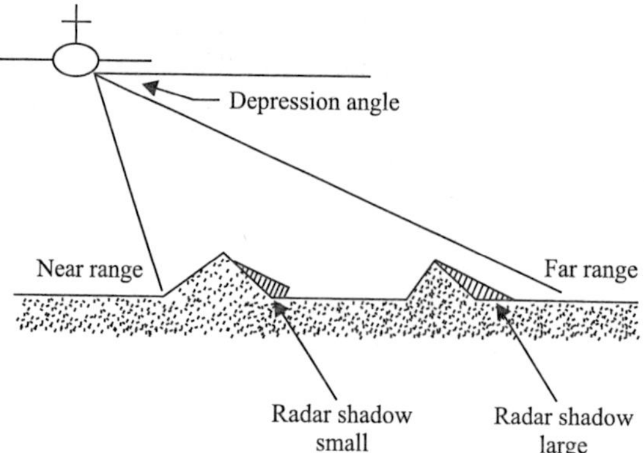

Fig. 8.9. Radar shadow.

Look Angle

Look angle, the depression angle of the radar, varies across an image, from relatively steep at the near-range side of the image to relatively shallow at the far-range side (Fig. 8.10). The exact values of the look angle vary with the design of specific radar systems, but some broad generalisations are possible concerning the effects of varied look angles.

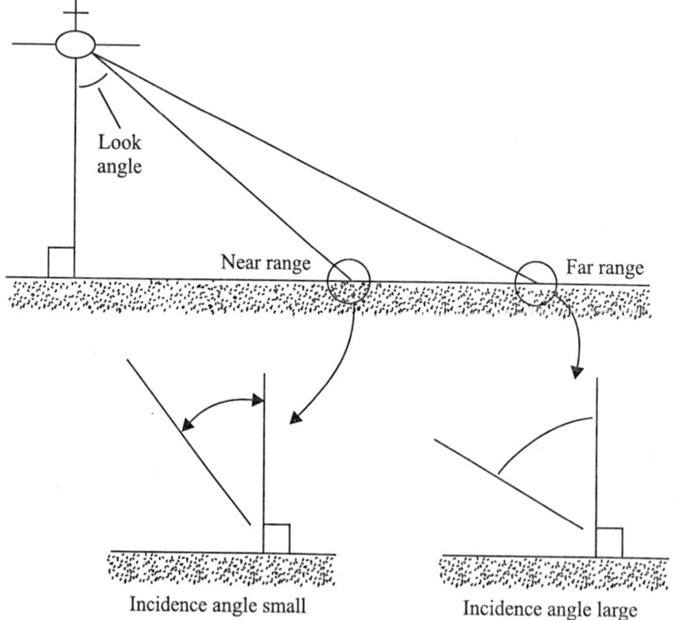

Fig. 8.10. Look angle and incidence angle.

First, the basic geometry of a radar image ensures that the resolution of the image must vary with look angle; at steeper depression angles, a radar signal illuminates as smaller area than does the same signal at shallow depression angles. Therefore, the spatial resolution, at least in the across-track direction, varies with respect to depression angle.

It has been shown that the sensitivity of the signal to ground moisture is increased as depression angle becomes steeper. Furthermore, the slant-range geometry of a radar image means that all landscapes are viewed (by the radar) at oblique angles. As a result, the image tends to record reflections from the sides of features. The obliqueness and therefore the degree to which we view sides, rather than tops, of features varies with look angle. In some landscapes, the oblique view may be very different form the overhead view to which we are accustomed in the use of other remotely sensed imagery (Fig. 8.11). Such variations in viewing angle may contribute to variations in the appearance on radar imagery of otherwise similar landscapes.

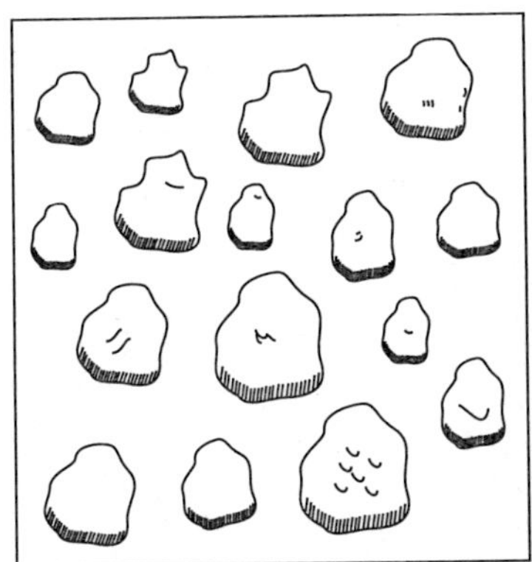

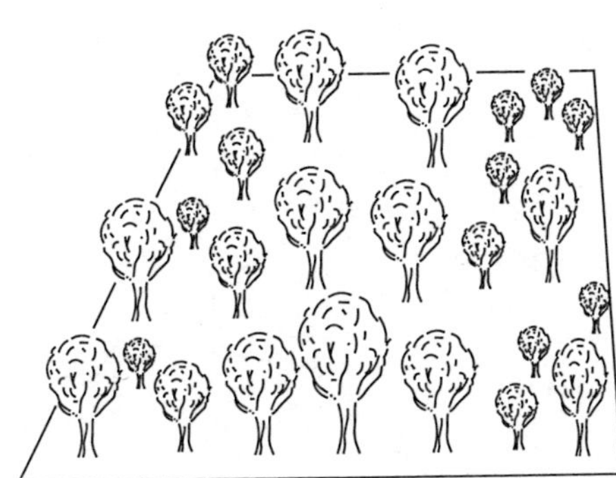

Fig. 8.11. Perspective as related to depression angle. The side-looking nature of imaging radars means that radars tend to view the landscape from an oblique angle, which means that the image tends to portray the sides of objects, rather than the overhead view that we are accustomed to in aerial photography.

REAL APERTURE SYSTEMS

Real aperture SLAR systems (sometimes referred to as brute force systems), one of the two strategies for acquiring radar imagery, are the oldest, simplest and least expensive of imaging radar systems. They follow the general model described earlier for the basic configuration of a SLAR system (Fig. 8.2). The transmitter generates a signal at a specified wavelength and of a specified duration. The antenna directs this signal toward the ground and then receives its reflection. The reflected signal is amplified, filtered, then displayed on a cathode ray tube, where a moving film records the radar image line by line as it is formed by the forward motion of the aircraft.

The resolution of such systems is controlled by several variables. One objective is to focus the transmitted signal to illuminate as small an area as possible on the ground, as it is the size of this areas that determines the spatial detail recorded on the image. If the area illuminated is large, then reflections from diverse features may be averaged together to form a single graytone value on the image and their distinctiveness is lost. If the area is small, individual features are recorded as separate features on the image and their identities are preserved.

The size of the area illuminated is controlled by several variables. One is antenna length in relation to wavelength. A long antenna length permits the system to focus energy on a small ground area. Thus real aperture systems require long antennas in order to achieve fine detail; limits on the ability of an aircraft to carry long antennas forms a practical limit to the resolution of radar images. This restriction on antenna length forms a barrier for use of real aperture systems on spacecraft: small antenna would provide very coarse resolution from spacecraft altitudes, but practical limitations prevent use of large antenna.

The area illuminated by a real aperture SLAR system can be considered analogous to the spot illuminated by a flashlight aimed at the floor. As the flashlight is aimed straight down, the spot of light it creates small and nearly circular in shape. As the flashlight beam is pointed toward the floor at increasingly further distances, the spot of light becomes larger, dimmer and assumes a more irregular shape. By analogy, the near-range portions of a radar image will have finer resolution than the far-range portions. Thus antenna length in relation to wavelength determines the angular resolution of real aperture system—the ability of the system to separate two objects in the along-track dimension of the image (Fig. 8.12).

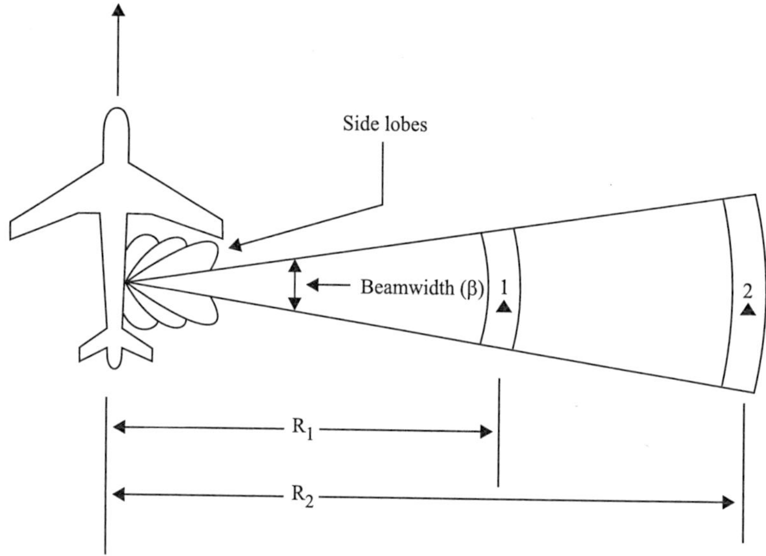

Fig. 8.12. Azimuth resolution. For real aperture radar, the ability of the system to acquire fine detail in the long-track axis derives from its ability to focus the radar beam to illuminate a small area. A long antenna, relative to wavelength, permits the system to focus energy on a small strip of ground, improving detail recorded in the along-track dimension of the image. The beamwidth (β) measures this quality of an imaging radar. Beamwith, in relation to range (R) determines detail—region 1 at range R_1 will be imaged in greater detail than region 2, at greater range R_2. Also illustrated here are side lobes, smaller beams of microwave energy created because the antenna cannot be perfectly effective in transmitting a single beam of energy.

The relationship between resolution and antenna length and wavelength is given by the Equation:

$$\beta = \lambda/A \quad \text{... (8.1)}$$

where β is the beamwidth, λ is the wavelength and A is the antenna length. Real aperture systems can be designed to attain finer along-track resolution by increasing the length of the antenna and by decreasing wavelength. Therefore, these qualities form the design limits on the resolution of real aperture systems—antenna length is constrained by practical limits of aeronautical design and operation.

Radar systems have another, unique, means of defining spatial resolution. The length of the radar pulse determines the ability of the system to resolve the distinction between two objects in the cross-track axis of the image (Fig. 8.13). Long pulses strike two nearby features at the same time, thereby recording the two objects as a single reflection and as a single feature on the image. Shorter pulses are each reflected separately from adjacent features and can record the distinctive identities and locations of the two objects.

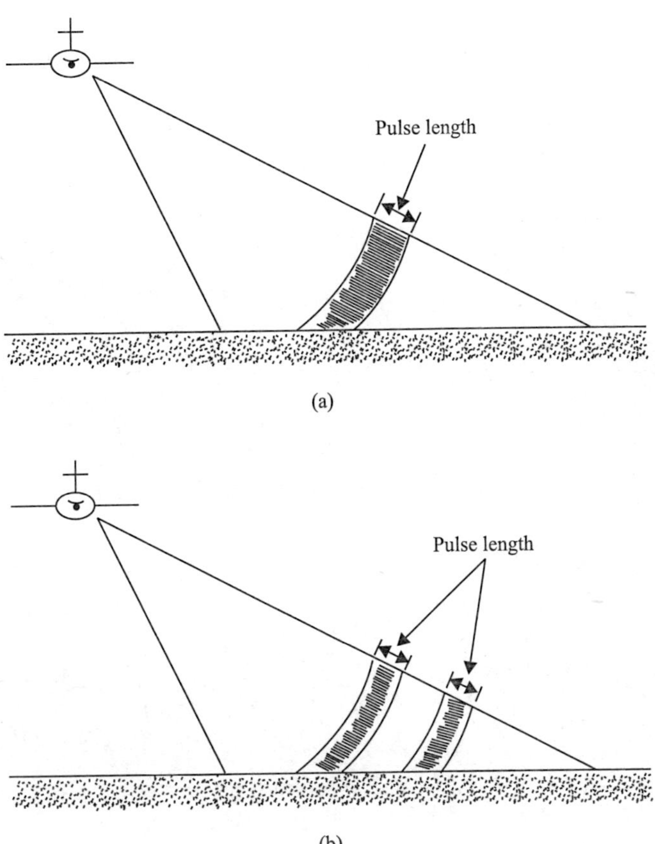

Fig. 8.13. Effect of pulse length. (a) Longer pulse length means that the two objects shown here are illuminated by a single burst of energy, creating a single echo that cannot reveal the presence of two separate objects; and (b) shorter pulse length illuminates the two objects with separate pulses, creating separate echoes for each object. Pulse length determines resolution in the cross-track dimension of the image.

SYNTHETIC APERTURE SYSTEMS

The alternative design is the synthetic aperture radar (SAR), which is based upon principles and technology differing greatly from those of real aperture radars. Although SAR systems have greater complexity and are more expensive to manufacture and operate than are real aperture systems, they can overcome some of the limitations inherent to real aperture systems and therefore can be applied in a wider variety of applications, including observation from earth orbiting satellites.

Consider a SAR that images the landscape as depicted in (Fig. 8.14). At 1, the aircraft is positioned so that a specific region of the landscape is just barely outside the region illuminated by the SAR. At 2, it is fully within the area of illumination. At 3, it just at the trailing edge of the illuminated area. Finally, at 4, the aircraft moves so that the region falls must outside the area illuminated by the radar beam. A synthetic aperture radar operates on the principal that objects within a scene are illuminated by the radar over an interval of time, as the aircraft moves along its flight path. A SAR system receives the signal scattered from the landscape during this interval and saves the complete history of reflections from each object. Knowledge of this history permits later reconstruction of the reflected signals as though they were received by a single antenna occupying physical space abc, even though they were in fact received by a much shorter antenna that was moved in a path along distance 1 2 3 4. (Thus the term 'synthetic aperture' denotes the artificial length of the antenna, in contrast to the 'real' aperture based upon the actual physical length of the antenna used with real aperture systems.

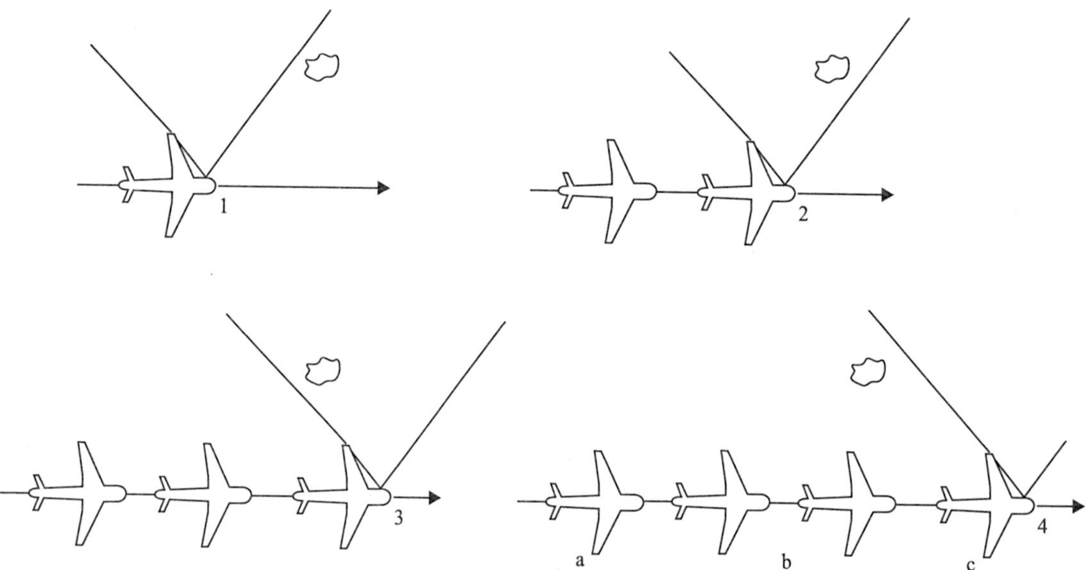

Fig. 8.14. Synthetic aperture imaging radar. Synthetic aperture systems accumulate a history of backscattered signals from the landscape as the antenna moves along path abc.

In order to implement this strategy, it is necessary to define a practical means of assigning separate components of the reflected signal to their correct positions as the spatial representation of the landscape is re-created on the image. This process is, of course, extraordinarily complicated if each such assignment must be considered an individual problem in unravelling the complex history of the radar signal at each of a multitude of antenna positions.

Fortunately, this problem can be solved in a practical manner because of the systematic changes in frequency experienced by the radar signal as it is scattered from the landscape. Objects within the landscape experience different frequency shifts in relation to their distances from the aircraft track. At a given instant, objects at the leading edge of the beam reflect a pulse with an increase in frequency (relative to the transmitted frequency) due to their position ahead of the aircraft and those at the trailing edge of the antenna experience a decrease in frequency (Fig. 8.15). This is the Doppler effect, often explained by analogy to the change in pitch of a train whistle heard by a stationary observer as a train passes by at high speed. As the train approaches, the pitch appears higher than that of a stationary whistle due to the increase in frequency of sound waves. As the train passes the observer, then recedes into the distance, the pitch appears lower, due to the decrease in frequency. Radar, as an active remote sensing system, is operated with full knowledge of the frequency of the transmitted signal. As a result, it is possible to compare the frequencies of transmitted and reflected signals to determine the nature and amount of frequency shift. Knowledge of frequency shift permits the system to assign reflections to their correct positions on the image and to synthesise the effect of a long antenna.

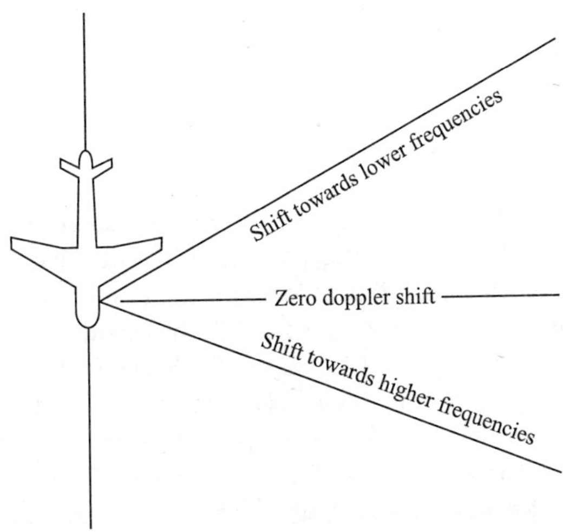

Fig. 8.15. Frequency shifts experienced by features within the field of view of the radar system.

INTERPRETING BRIGHTNESS VALUES

Each radar image is composed of many image elements of varying brightness. Variations in image brightness correspond, at least in part, to place-to-place changes within the landscape; through knowledge of this correspondence, the image interpreter has a basis for making predictions or inferences, concerning landscape properties.

Unlike passive remote sensing systems, active systems illuminate the land with radiation of known and carefully controlled properties. Therefore, in principle, the interpreter should have a firm foundation for deciphering the meaning of the image because the only 'unknowns' of the many variables that influence image appearance are the ground conditions—the object of study.

However, in practice, the interpreter of a radar image faces many difficult obstacles in making a rigorous interpretation of a radar image. First, most imaging radars are uncalibrated in the sense that image brightness values on an image cannot be quantitatively matched to backscattering values in the landscape. Typically, returned signals from a terrain span a very broad range of magnitudes from very low to very high; the ranges in values are often so large that they exceed the ability of photographic emulsions to accurately portray the actual range of values. Very dark and very bright landscape elements may be portrayed in the non-linear portions of the characteristic curve and therefore lack consistent relationships with their representations on the image. Furthermore, the features that compose even the simplest landscape have complex shapes and arrangements and are formed from diverse materials of contrasting electrical properties.

As a result, there are often few detailed models of the kinds of backscattering that should in principle be expected from separate classes of surface materials. Direct experience and intuition are not always reliable guides to interpretation of images acquired outside the visible spectrum. In addition, many SLAR images observe the landscape at very shallow depression angles. Since interpreters gain experience from their observations at ground level or from studying overhead aerial views, they may find the oblique radar view from only a few degrees above the horizon difficult to interpret.

Radar Equation

The fundamental variables influencing the brightness of a region on a radar image are formally given by the radar equation:

$$P_r = \frac{\sigma G^2 P_t \lambda^2}{(4\pi)^3 R^4} \qquad \text{... (8.2)}$$

Here P_r designates the power returned to the antenna from the ground surface; R specifies the range to the target from the antenna; P_t is the transmitted power; λ is the wavelength of the energy; and G is the antenna gain (a measure of the system's ability to focus the transmitted energy). All of these variables are determined by the design of the radar system and are therefore known or controlled quantities. The one variable in the equation not thus far identified is σ, the backscattering coefficient; σ is, of course, not controlled by the radar system, but by the specific characteristics of the terrain surface represented by a specific region on the image. Whereas σ is often an incidental factor for the radar engineer, it is the primary focus of study for the image interpreter, as it is this quantity that carries information about the landscape.

The value of σ conveys information concerning the amount of energy scattered from a specific region on the landscape as measured by $\sigma°$, the radar cross section. It specifies the corresponding area of an isotropic scatterer that would return the same power as does the observed signal. The backscattering coefficient ($\sigma°$) expresses the observed scattering from a large surface area as a dimensionless ratio between two areal surfaces; it measures the average radar cross section per unit area. $\sigma°$ varies over such wide values that it must be expressed as a ratio rather than as an absolute value.

Ideally, radar images should be interpreted with the objective of relating observed $\sigma°$ (varied brightnesses) to properties within the landscape. It is known that backscattering is related to specific system variables, including wavelength, polarisation and azimuth, in relation to landscape orientation and depression angle. In addition landscape parameters are important, including surface roughness, soil moisture, vegetative cover and microtopography. Because so many of these characteristics are interrelated, making detailed interpretations of individual variables is usually very difficult, in part due the extreme complexity of landscapes, which normally are intricate compositions of diverse natural and man-made features. Often many of the most useful landscape interpretations of radar images have attempted to recognise integrated units defined by assemblages of several variables rather than to separate individual components. The notion of 'spectral signatures' is very difficult to apply in the context of radar imagery because of the high degree of variation in image tone as incidence angle and look direction change.

Moisture

Moisture in the landscape influences the backscattering coefficient through changes in the dielectric constant of landscape materials. (The dielectric constant is a measure of the ability of a substance to conduct electrical energy—an important variable determining the response of a substance that is illuminated with microwave energy). Although natural soils and minerals vary in their ability to conduct electrical energy, these properties are difficult to exploit as the basis for remote sensing because the differences between dielectric properties of separate rocks and minerals in the landscape are overshadowed by the effects of even very small amounts of moisture, which greatly change the dielectric constant. As a result, the radar signal is sensitive to the presence of moisture both in the soil and in vegetative tissue; this sensitivity appears to be greatest at steep depression angles.

The presence of moisture also influences effective skin depth; as the moisture content of surface soil increases, the signal tends to scatter from the surface. As moisture content decreases, skin depth increases and the signal may be scattered from a greater thickness of soil.

Roughness

A radar signal that strikes a surface will be reflected in a manner that depends both upon characteristics of the surface and properties of the radar wave, as determined by the radar system and the conditions under which it is operated. The incidence angle (θ) is defined as the angle between the axis of the incident radar signal and a perpendicular to the surface that the signal strikes (Fig. 8.16). If the surface is homogeneous with respect to its electrical properties and 'smooth' with respect to the wavelength of the signal, then the reflected signal will be reflected at an angle equal to the incidence angle, with most of the energy directed in a single direction (i.e., specular reflection).

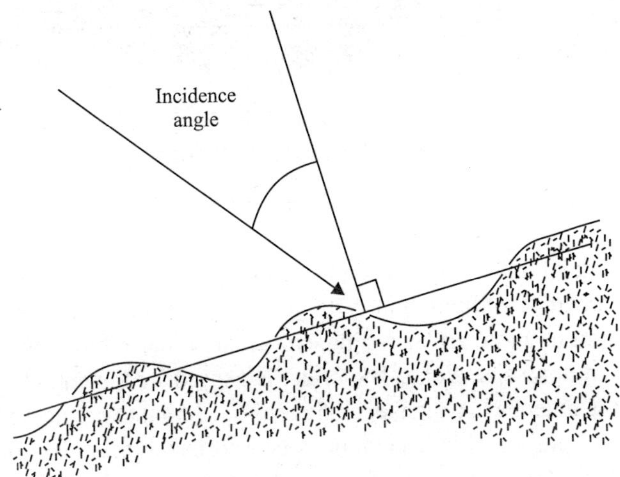

Fig. 8.16. Incidence angle.

For 'rough' surfaces, reflection will not depend as much upon incidence angle and the signal will be scattered more or less equally in all directions (i.e., diffuse or isotropic, scattering). For radar systems, the notion of a rough surface is defined in a manner considerably more complex than that familiar from everyday experience, as roughness depends not only upon the physical configuration of the surface, but also upon the wavelength of the signal and its incidence angle (Table 8.2.). Consider the physical configuration of the surface to be expressed by the standard deviation of the heights of individual facets (Fig. 8.17). Although definitions of surface roughness vary, one common definition defines a rough surface as one in which the standard deviation of surface height (S_h) exceeds one-eight of the wavelength (λ) divided by the cosine of the incidence angle ($\cos\theta$):

$$S_h > \lambda/(8 \cos \theta) \qquad \text{... (8.3)}$$

where h is the average height of the irregularities. In practice, this definition means that a given surface appears rougher as wavelengths become shorter. Also, for a given wavelength, surfaces will act as smooth scatterers as incidence angle becomes greater (i.e., equal terrain slopes will appear as smooth surfaces as depression angle becomes smaller, as occurs in the far-range portions of radar images).

Table 8.2. Surface roughness defined for several wavelengths.

Roughness category	*K-band (λ = 0.86 cm)*	*X-band (λ = 3 cm)*	*L-band (λ = 25 cm)*
Smooth	h < 0.05 cm	h < 0.17 cm	h < 1.41 cm
Intermediate	h = 0.05–0.28 cm	h = 0.17–0.96 cm	h = 1.41–8.04 cm
Rough	h > 0.28 cm	h > 0.96 cm	h > 8.04 cm

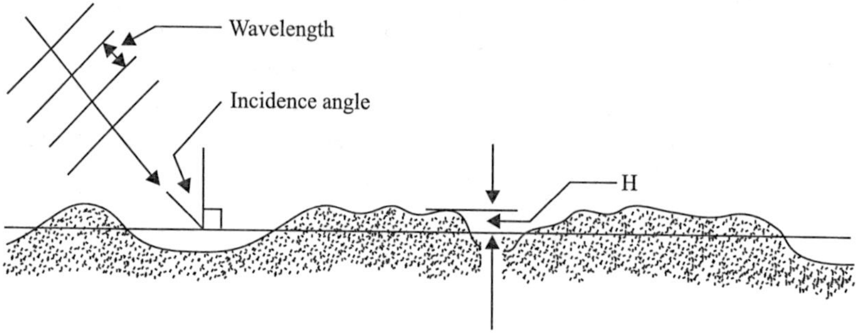

Fig. 8.17. Surface roughness.

Corner Reflectors

The return of the radar signal to the antenna can be influenced not only by moisture and roughness, but also by the broader geometric configuration of targets. Objects that have complex geometric shapes, such as those encountered in an urban landscape, can create radar returns that are much brighter than would be expected based upon size alone. The effect is caused by the complex reflection of the radar signal directly back to the antenna in a manner analogous to a ball that bounces from the corner of a pool table directly back to the player. This behaviour is caused by objects classified as corner reflectors, which often are in fact corner-shaped features (such as the corners of buildings and the alleyways between them in a dense urban landscape), but are also formed by other objects of complex shape.

Corner reflectors are common in urban areas due to the abundance of concrete, masonry and metal surfaces constructed in complex angular shapes (Fig. 8.18). Corner reflectors can also be found in rural areas, formed sometimes by natural surfaces, but more commonly by metallic roofs of farm buildings, agricultural equipment and items such as powerline pylons and guardrails along divided highways.

Corner reflectors are important in interpretation of the radar image. They form a characteristic feature of the radar signatures of urban regions and identify other features such as powerlines, highways and railroads. It is important to remember that the image of a corner reflector is not shown in proportion to its actual size: the returned energy forms a star-like burst of brightness that is proportionately much larger than the size of the object that caused it. Thus they can be valuable in interpreting the radar image, but do not appear on the image in their correct relative sizes.

SATELLITE IMAGING RADARS

Scientists working with radar remote sensing have been interested for years in the possibility of observing the earth by means of imaging radars carried by earth satellites. Whereas real aperture systems cannot be operated at satellite altitudes without unacceptably coarse spatial resolution (or use of impractically large antennas), the synthetic aperture principle permits compact radar systems to acquire imagery of fine spatial detail at high altitudes. This capability, combined with the ability of imaging radars to acquire imagery in darkness, through cloud cover and during inclement weather, provides the opportunity for development of a powerful remote sensing capability, with potential to observe large areas of the earth's ocean and land areas that might otherwise be unobservable because of remoteness and atmospheric conditions.

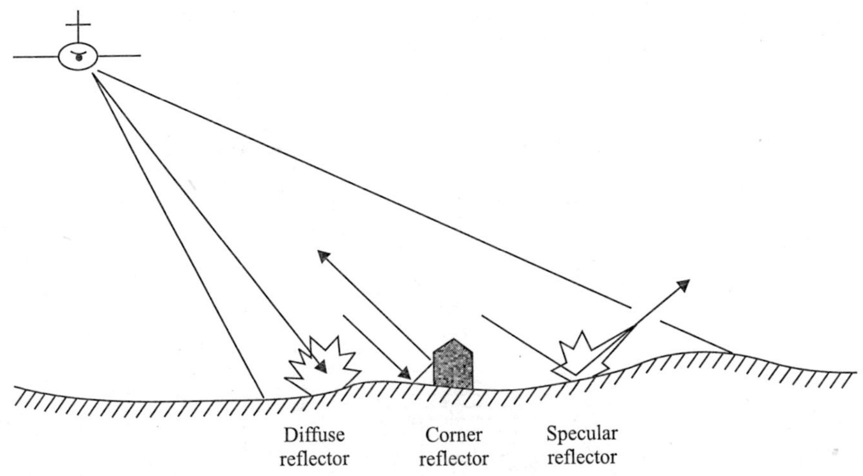

Fig. 8.18. Three classes of features important for interpretation of radar imagery.

Several satellite missions have used imaging radars; all have been experimental programmes to further develop the concepts and experience necessary for longer term efforts. These satellite imaging radars have been designed primarily to acquire a library of imagery representative of diverse terrains and to promote more experience and knowledge of the interpretation and analysis of radar images. In addition, it may be possible to further develop our ability to combine information derived from radar imagery from that collected by satellites observing the visible and near infrared wavelengths to enhance the capabilities of both kinds of sensors.

Seasat Synthetic Aperture Radar

Seasat (Fig. 8.19) was specifically tailored to observe the earth's oceans by means of several sensors designed to monitor winds, waves, temperature and topography. Many of the sensors detected active and passive microwave radiation, although one radiometer operated in the visible and near infrared spectrum. (Seasat carried three microwave radiometers, one imaging radar and a radiometer that operated both in the visible and in the infrared). Some sensors were capable of observing 95 per cent of the earth's oceans every 36 hours. Specifications for the Seasat SAR are as follows:

Launch	28 June 1978
Electrical system failure	10 October 1978
Orbit	Nearly circular at 108° inclination; 14 orbits each day

Frequency	L-band (1.275 GHz)
Wavelength	23 cm
Look direction	Looks to starboard side of track
Swath width	100 km, centered 20° off-nadir
Ground resolution	25 m × 25 m
Polarisation	H H

Our primary interest here is the synthetic aperture radar (SAR), designed to observe ocean waves, sea ice and coastlines. The satellite orbit was designed to provide optimum coverage of oceans, but its track did cross land areas, thereby offering the opportunity to acquire radar imagery of the earth's surface from satellite altitudes. The SAR, of course, had the capability for operation during both daylight and darkness and during inclement weather, so (unlike most other satellite sensors) the Seasat SAR could acquire data on both ascending and descending passes.

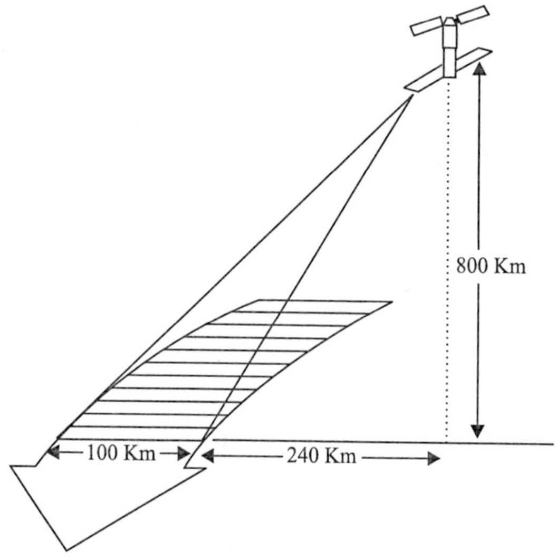

Fig. 8.19. Seasat SAR geometry.

The high transmission rates required to convey data of such fine resolution meant that Seasat SAR data could not be recorded onboard for later transmission to ground stations; instead the data was immediately transmitted to a ground station. Therefore, data could be acquired only when the satellite was within line of sight of one of the five ground stations equipped to receive Seasat data; these were located in California, Alaska, Florida, Newfoundland and England. The SAR was first turned on in early July 1978 (Day 10); it remained in operation for 98 days. During this time, it acquired some 500 passes of data. The average duration of each pass was about 5 minutes, but the longest SAR track covered about 4000 km in ground distance. Data are available in digital form, as either digitally or optically processed imagery. All land areas covered are in the Northern Hemisphere, including portions of North America and Western Europe. Seasat SAR data have been used for important oceanographic studies. In addition, Seasat data have provided a foundation for the study of radar applications within the earth sciences and for the examination of settlement and land-use patterns. Because Seasat data were acquired on both ascending and descending passes, the same ground features can be observed from differing look angles under conditions that hold most other factors constant or almost constant.

Shuttle Imaging Radar-A

The Shuttle Imaging Radar (SIR) is a synthetic aperture imaging radar carried by the Shuttle Transportation System. (NASA's space shuttle orbiter has the ability to carry a variety of scientific experiments; the SIR is one of several.) SIR-A, the first scientific payload carried on board the shuttle, was operated for about 54 hours during the flight of Columbia in November 1981. Although the mission was reduced in length from original plans, SIR-A was able to acquire images of almost 4,000,000 square miles^{-2} of the earth's surface. Additional details of SIR-A are given below:

Launch	12 November 1981
Land	14 November 1981
Altitude	259 km
Frequency	1.278 GHz (L-band)
Wavelength	23.5 cm
Depression angle	40°
Swath width	50 km
Polarisation	H H
Ground resolution	about 40 m × 40 m

SIR-A's geometric qualities were fixed, with no provision for changing depression angle. All data were recorded on magnetic tape and signal film onboard the shuttle; after the shuttle landed, it was physically carried to ground facilities for processing into image products. First-generation film images were typically 12 cm (5 inch) in width at a scale of about 1:5,250,000. About 1400 ft. of film were processed; most has been judged to be of high quality.

SIR-A completed five passes over the United States (during which SIR-A was in operation for about 50 minutes). Portions of all continents (except Antarctica) were imaged, to provided images of a wide variety of environments differing with respect to climate, vegetation, geology, land use and other qualities. Analyses of these data have led to important scientific studies of several subjects, including the geology of remote areas and further knowledge of the capabilities of radar imagery.

Shuttle Imaging Radar-B

The Shuttle Imaging Radar-B (SIR-B) was the second imaging radar experiment for the space shuttle. It was similar in design to SIR-A, except that it provided greater flexibility in acquiring imagery at varied depression angles, as shown below:

Orbital altitude	225 km
Orbital inclination	57°
Frequency	1.28 GHz
Wavelength	23 cm
Resolution	about 25 m × 17 m (at 60° depression) or about 25 m × 58 m (at 15° depression)
Swath width	40–50 km

SIR-B used horizontal polarisation at L-band (23 cm). Azimuth resolution was about 25 m; range resolution varied from about 17 m at an angle of 60° to 58 m at 15°. The shuttle orbited at 225 km; the orbital track drifted eastward 86 km each day (at 45° latitude). In contrast to the fixed geometric configuration of the Seasat SAR and SIR-A, the radar pallet onboard the shuttle permitted control of the angle of observation, which thereby enabled operation of the SIR in several modes. A given image swath of 40–50 km could be imaged repeatedly, at differing depression angles, by changing the orientation of the antenna as spacecraft position changed with each orbit. This capability provided the ability to acquire stereo imagery. Also, the antenna could be oriented to image successive swaths and thereby build up coverage of a larger region than could be covered in any single pass. A mosaic composed of such images would be acquired at a consistent range of depression angles, although angles would, of course, vary within individual images. The shuttle orbit also provided the opportunity to examine a single study area at several look directions. Varied illumination directions and angles permit imaging of a single geographic area at varied depression angles and azimuths and thereby enable (in concept) derivation of information concerning the influence of surface roughness and moisture content upon the radar image and information concerning the interactions of these variables with look direction and look angle. Thus a important function of SIR-B was its ability to advance understanding of the radar image itself and its role in remote sensing of the earth's landscapes.

The significance of SIR imagery arises in part from the repetitive nature of the orbital coverage, with an accompanying opportunity to examine temporal changes in such phenomena as soil moisture, crop growth, land use and the like. Because of the all-weather capability of SAR, the opportunities to examine temporal variation with radar imagery may be even more significant than it was with Landsat imagery. Second, costs of the SIR are said to be very low relative to those of a satellite dedicated specifically to acquiring radar imagery. And third, the flexibility of the shuttle platform and the SIR experiment permit examination of a wide range of configurations for satellite radars, over a broad range of geographic regions, by many subject areas in the earth sciences. Therefore, a primary role for SIR-B was to investigate specific configurations and applications for the design of other satellite systems tailored to acquire radar imagery of the earth's surface.

Shuttle Imaging Radar-C/X-Synthetic Aperture Radar System

In August 1994 the space shuttle conducted a third imaging radar experiment. The Shuttle Imaging Radar-C (SIR-C) is an SAR operating at both L-band (23 cm) and C-band (6 cm), with the capability for transmitting and receiving both horizontally and vertically polarised radiation. SIR-C, designed and manufactured by the Jet Propulsion Laboratory (Pasadena, California) and Ball Communications Systems Division, is one of the largest and most complex items ever built for flight on the shuttle. In addition to the use of two microwave frequencies and its dual polarisation, the antenna has the ability to electronically aim the radar beam, to supplement the capability of the shuttle to aim the antenna by maneuvering the spacecraft. Data from SIR-C can be recorded onboard using tape storage or it can be transmitted by microwave to the Tracking and Data Releay Satellite System (TDRSS) link to ground stations.

The X-synthetic aperture radar (X-SAR) was designed and built in Europe as a joint German–Italian project for flight on the shuttle, to be used independently or in co-ordination with SIR-C. X-SAR was an L-band SAR (VV polarisation) with the ability to create highly focused radar beams. It was mounted in a manner that permits it to be aligned with the L- and C-band beams of the SIR-C. Together, the two systems had the ability to gather data at three frequencies and two polarisation. The SIR-C/X-SAR experiment was co-ordinated with field experiments that collected ground data at specific sites devoted to studies of ecology, geology, hydrology, agriculture, oceanography and other topics. These instruments continue the effort to develop a clearer understanding of the capabilities of SAR data to monitor key processes at the earth's surface.

X-SAR characteristics can be briefly summarised as under:

Frequencies	X-band (3 cm)
	C-band (6 cm)

	L-band (23 cm)
Ground swath	15–90 km, depending upon orientation of the antenna
Resolution	10–200 m

European Resource Satellite Synthetic Aperture Radar

The European Space Agency (ESA), a joint organisation of several European nations, designed a remote sensing satellite with several sensors configured to conduct both basic and applied research. Here our primary interest is the SAR for European Resource Satellite-1 (ERS-1) and (ERS-2). One of the satellite's primary missions is to use several of its sensors to derive wind and wave information from 5 km × 5 km SAR scenes positioned within the SAR's 80-km swath width. Nonetheless, the satellite has acquired a library of images of varied land and maritime scenes.

Because of the SAR's extremely high data rate, SAR data cannot be stored onboard, so it must be acquired within range of a ground station. Although the primary ground control and receiving stations are located in Europe, receiving stations throughout the world are equipped to receive ERS-1 data. ERS-1 has a sun-synchronous, nearly polar orbit that crosses the equator at about 10:30 a.m. local sun time. Other characteristic include:

Frequency	5.3 GHz
Wavelength	C-band (6 cm)
Incidence angle	23° at midrange (20° near range; 26° far range)
Polarisation	V V
Altitude	785 km
Spatial resolution	30 m
Swath width	100 km

ERS data are available from space Imaging (800–425–2997) and from RADARSAT International.

RADARSAT Synthetic Aperture Radar

RADARSAT is a joint project of the Canadian federal and provincial governments, the United States government and private corporation. The United States, through NASA, provides launch facilities and the services of a receiving station in Alaska. Canada has special interests in use of radar sensors because of its large territory, the poor illumination prevailing during much of the year at high latitudes, unfavourable weather conditions, interest in monitoring sea ice in shipping lanes and many other issues arising from assessing natural resources, especially forests and mineral deposits. Radar sensors, particularly those carried by satellites, provide capabilities tailored to address many of these concerns.

The RADARSAT's C-band radar was launched on 4 November 1995 into a sun-synchronous orbit at 98.6° inclination, with equatorial crossings at 6:00 a.m. and 6:00 p.m. An important feature of the RADARSAT SAR is the flexibility it offers to select among a wide range of trade-offs between area covered and spatial resolution and to use a wide variety of incidence angles (Fig. 8.20). This flexibility increases opportunities for practical applications. Critical specifications include:

Frequency	5.3 GHz
Wavelength	5.6 cm (C-band)
Incidence angle	varies, 10° to 60°
Polarisation	H H
Altitude	793 to 821 km
Spatial resolution	varies, 100 × 100 m to 9 × 9 m

Swath width varies, 45 to 510 km
Repeat cycle 24 days

Applications of RADARSAT SAR imagery include geological exploration and mapping, sea ice mapping, rice crop monitoring, flood delineation and mapping, coastal zone mapping and oil spill/seep detection. Because superstructure of ships form good corner reflectors, SAR data are effective in detecting ships at sea and RADARSAT imagery has been used in the monitoring of shipping lanes.

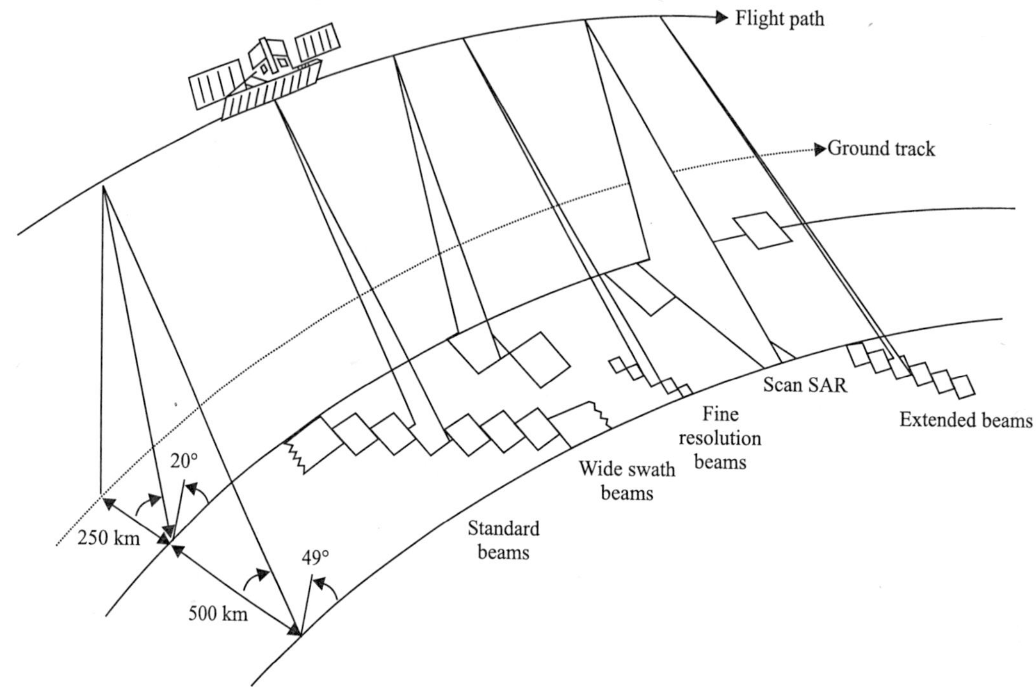

Fig. 8.20. RADARSAT SAR geometry.

Japanese Earth Resources Satellite-1

The Japanese Earth Resources Satellite-1 (JERS-1) is a satellite launched in February 1992 by the National Space Development Agency of Japan carrying a C-band SAR. In addition, it carries an optical CCD sensor sensitive in seven spectral regions from 0.52 to 2.40 μm, with resolution of about 18 m. One band in the near infrared is collected with a forward-looking sensor; when combined with data from the nadir-aimed instruments, it can provide as stereo capability.

The JERS-1 SAR has the following characteristics:

Altitude	568 km
Orbit	sun-synchronous
Wavelength	23 cm (L-band) (1.3 GHz)
Incidence angle	35°
Swath width	75 km
Spatial resolution	18 m
Polarisation:	H H

Radar Interferometry

It is possible to derive accurate topographic information from multiple SAR images of a single region. In a broad sense, SAR interferometry is comparable to the use of stereo photography to determine topography of a region by observation from two different perspectives. However, SAR interferometry is applied not in the optical domain of photogrammetry, but in the realm of radar geometry, to exploit radar's ranging capability. Because SARs can accurately measure differences in slant-range distances to the same feature from separate observation points, the technique can provide very accurate topographic information.

If two images are acquired from the same track at different times (e.g., if two antennas are mounted before and after in the same aircraft or if images are acquired at different times within the same orbital track), it is possible to establish a temporal baseline, which provides an image pair that can reveal changes that occurred during the interval between the acquisition of the two images. This precise record of change permits recognition of changes in position. In a military context, the objects in motion might be vehicles; in a scientific context, the motion might record ocean currents, ice flow in glaciers or ice floes in polar oceans. The sensitivity of such analyses depends upon the nature of the temporal baseline, so that very short temporal baselines can record rather rapid motion (such as vehicular motion), whereas longer baselines can detect slower speeds, such as movement of surface ice in glaciers. Paired antennas operated from a single platform are sensitive to velocities of centimeters per second (e.g, suitable for observing moving vehicles or ocean waves). Longer temporal baselines (e.g., separate passes within the same orbital path) are effective in recording slower speeds, perhaps centimeters per day, such as the motion of glacial ice.

A more widespread use of SAR interferometry depends upon the acquisition of pairs of images of the same region acquired by imaging radars following separate tracks. The separation in distance of the two instruments establishes a spatial baseline, which permits measurement of topographic relief. The most favourable case arises when two images are acquired on parallel tracks, although analysis is possible with nonparallel tracks provided that the angle of intersection is small.

Shuttle Radar Topography Mission

The most striking application of SAR interferometry was the Shuttle Radar Topography Mission (SRTM) (STS-99 Shuttle Endeavour), launched 11 February 2000, landed 22 February 2000, for a duration of about 11 day, 5½ hours.

SRTM was designed to use C-band and X-band interferometric synthetic aperture radars to acquire topographic data over 80 per cent of earth's land mass (between 60° N and 56° S). One antenna was mounted, as in previous shuttle SAR missions, in the shuttle's payload bay; another antenna was mounted on a 60-m (200-ft.) mast extended after the shuttle attained orbit (Fig. 8.21). The configuration was designed for single-pass interferometry using C-band and X-band SAR imagery.

The interferomic data have been used to produce digital topographic data for very large portions of the world at unprecedented levels of detail and accuracy—for the first time, there will be consistent, high-quality, cartographic coverage for most of the earth's land areas. SRTM data cover approximately 80 per cent of the earth's landmass.

SRTM data have been used for a broad range of practical applications in geology and geophysics, hydrologic modeling, aircraft navigation, transportation engineering, land-use planning, siting of communications facilities and military training and logistical planning. Furthermore, they will support other remote sensing applications by facilitating rectification of remotely sensed data and registration of remotely acquired image data. (SRTM data are consistent with U.S. National Map Accuracy Standards, at 30 m × 30 m spatial sampling with less than 16-m absolute vertical height accuracy, less than 10-m relative vertical height accuracy and less than 20-m absolute horizontal circular accuracy. All accuracies are quoted at the 90 per cent level, consistent with US National Map Accuracy Standards.) SRTM was sponsored by the U.S. National Imagery and Mapping Agency (NIMA), NASA, the German aerospace center (Deutsches Zentrum fur Luft-und Raumfart [DLR]), the Italian space agency (Agenzia Spaziale Italiana [ASI]) and managed by the Jet Propulsion Laboratory, Pasadena, California.

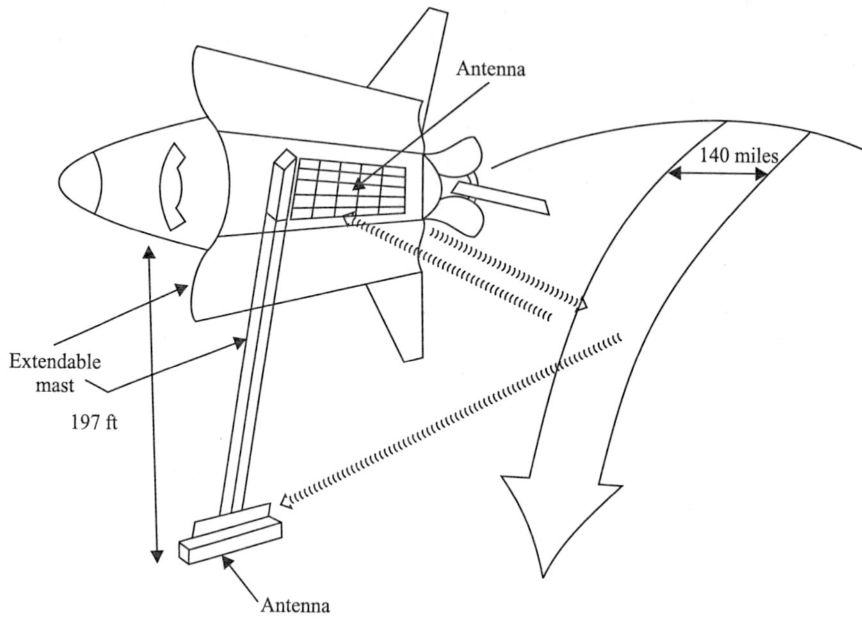

Fig. 8.21. Radar interferometry.

LIDAR

Lidars ('light detection and ranging') are active sensors that transmit carefully timed pulses of light and measure the time delay for a portion of the pulse to return to the instrument. Lidars differ in many ways from the microwave radars described in this chapter. However, lidars and radars resemble each other much more than they do other sensors, despite the fact that they operate in different regions of the spectrum. Lidars have also been considered to be 'laser radars', some prefer the term 'ladar' (laser detection and ranging).

'Laser' is itself an acronym for 'light amplification by stimulated emission of radiation.' Lasers create highly directional beams of radiation in the visible or near infrared regions of the spectrum. Lidars use lasers that generate very precisely defined beams of light ('coherent' light), in very carefully timed pulses. Because characteristics of these pulses are known in detail, it is possible to employ them very effectively as sensors. After the first development of optical lasers in the 1960s, they found a wide range of applications in industry and communications. Initial applications for remote sensing focused upon measurement of atmospheric clarity—lidars were used as meteorological instruments to be aimed at the atmosphere rather than at the ground surface. Initial applications of lidar to remote sensing of the earth's surface were based upon airborne lidars designed to collect single lines of data beneath the aircraft.

These instruments provided an accurate profile of topography along the aircraft's flight track but did not create 'images' in the sense of our discussion here.

It is only relatively recently that lidars could be considered remote sensing instruments that collect images of the earth's surface. Imaging lidars are based upon improvements in applications of inertial measurement units (IMUs), which precisely record the orientation of the instrument and GPS, which precisely records geographic location to accurately record the position and attitude of an aircraft as it gathers lidar data. A rapidly oscillating or rotating mirror scans a laser beam side to side along the cross-track axis of the image, recording many thousands of returns each second. Imaging lidars usually use visible (e.g., 5.32 μm, green for penetration of water bodies) or near infrared regions (e.g., 1.64 μm, for sensitivity to vegetation and freedom from atmospheric scattering).

One family of lidars uses continuous wave lasers that generate a continuously modulated beam of light, then examine phase differences between the transmitted and reflected radiation. Another family uses pulsed lasers that generate very carefully timed bursts of light. These lidars generate range information by measuring the time delay (travel time) for emitted and received pulses. Because light travels at a known constant velocity, the time for a pulse to return to the sensor translates directly to a distance or range, to the ground beneath the aircraft. The forward motion of the aircraft moves the field of view forward to create the along-track dimension.

Resolutions of different systems vary widely. The detail available depends upon system design and operation, including flying height and the beam divergence. The area the sensor illuminates at a given instant is known as the system's 'footprint.' Sometimes imaging lidars are designated as small footprint ('discrete return lidars') or large footprint ('waveform lidars'). Small-footprint systems might acquire data from areas as small as 0.5 to 2 ft. in diameter. Large-footprint systems might view areas as large as 5 m or larger.

Because the instrument can accurately record the angle of individual pulses, the attitude of the aircraft (using inertial navigational systems) and the position of the aircraft (using GPS), a lidar system can create an image-like array representing variation of elevation within the areas under observation (i.e., each pulse can be associated with a scan angle and data describing the position and orientation of the aircraft) (Fig. 8.22). Depending upon the design of a specific lidar system, the positions of individual returns (known as 'postings') are irregularly spaced in their original, unprocessed, form. These irregular positions are later interpolated to form a regular grid that provides a more coherent representation of the terrain. Thus each return from the ground surface can be precisely positioned in xyz space to provide an array that records both position and elevation. For small footprint lidars, horizontal accuracy might be in the range of 20 to 30 cm and vertical accuracy in the range between 15 and 20 cm. Therefore, the array or image, forms a detailed digital elevation model (DEM). With the addition of ground control (points of known location that can be accurately located within the imaged region, often found using GPS), lidar can provide data comparable in detail and positional accuracy to those acquired by photogrammetric analysis of aerial photographs.

A lidar can record different kinds of returns from the terrain. Some returns, known as primary returns, originate from the first objects a lidar pulse encounters—often the upper surface of a vegetation canopy (Fig. 8.23). In addition, portions of a pulse pass through gaps in the canopy into the interior structure of leaves and branches, to lower vegetation layers and the ground surface itself. This energy creates echoes known as secondary or partial, returns. Therefore, for complex surfaces, such as forests with multiple canopies, some portions of a pulse might be reflected from upper and middle portions of the canopy and other portions from the ground surface at the base.

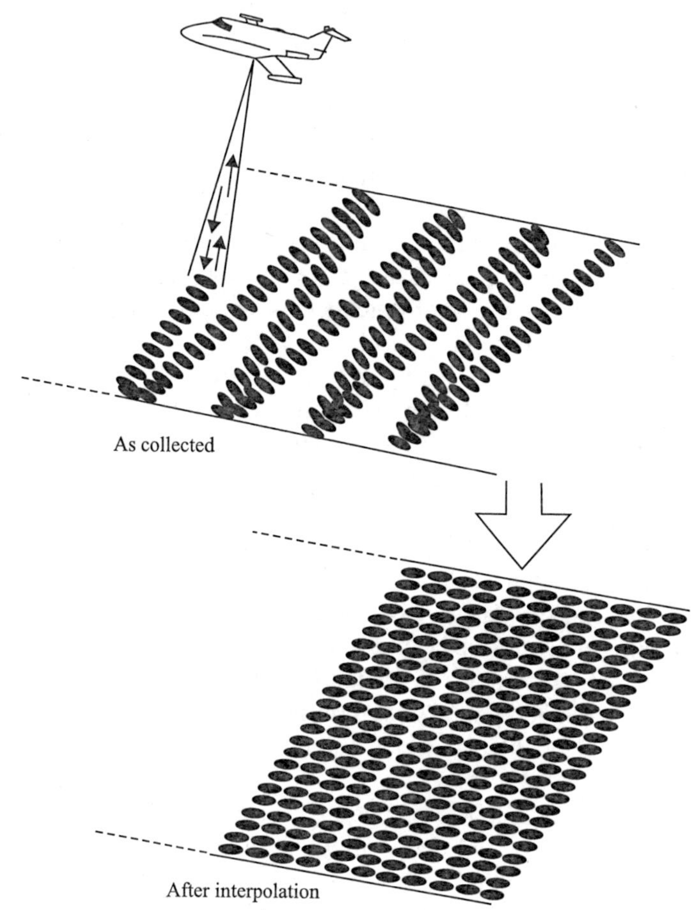

Fig. 8.22. Acquisition of lidar data. Lidar systems acquire data by scanning in the pattern suggested by the top diagram; details vary according to specific systems. The pattern of returns is then interpolated to generate the regular array that forms the lidar image.

The total collection of lidar returns for a region can be examined to separate those returns that originate above a specified level from those that originated below that level. This kind of approach can then form a kind of filtering process to separate ground returns from non-ground returns and with additional analysis, thereby separate the terrain surface from overlying vegetation cover and structures. Lidars are unique in being the only sensors that can reliably differentiate between multiple imaged layers.

Lidar data provide detailed, spatial data of high accuracy and precision. Lidar data provide direct measurement of surface elevation, with detail and accuracy usually associated only with photogrammtric surveys. Principal applications have focused on urban regions, which experience continuing needs for detailed information concerning building densities, urban structures and building footprints. Lidar data are used for highway planning, pipeline routing planning, route planning and for designing wireless communication systems in urban regions. Lidar data have also been used to study forest structure, as the detailed and accurate information describing canopy configuration and structure may permit accurate mapping of timber volume.

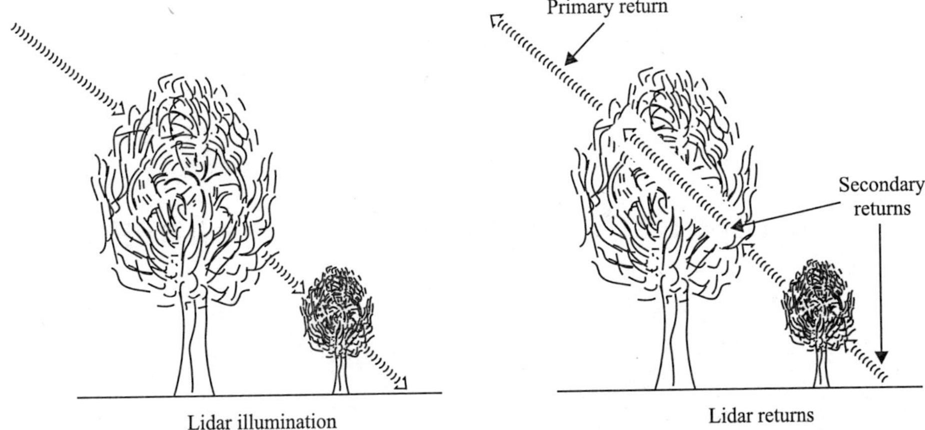

Fig. 8.23. Primary and secondary lidar returns.

Thus radar and lidar imagery are especially useful because they complement characteristics of images acquired in other portions of the spectrum. Aerial photography, for example, provides excellent information concerning the distribution and status of the earth's vegetation cover. The information it conveys is derived from biological components of plant tissues. However, from aerial photography we learn little direct information about the physical structure of the vegetation. In contrast, although active microwave and lidar provide no data about the biological component of the plant cover, they do provide detailed information concerning the physical structure of plant communities. We would not expect to replace aerial photography or optical satellite data with radar or lidar imagery, but we could expect to be able to combine information from both sources to acquire a more complete understanding of the character of the vegetation cover. Thus the value of any sensor must be assessed not only in the context of its specific capabilities, but also in the context of its characteristics relative to other sensors.

9

Thermal Radiation and Infrared Images

INTRODUCTION

In order to interpret thermal infrared (IR) images, one must understand the basic physical processes that control the interactions between thermal energy and matter, as well as thermal properties of matter that determine the rate and intensity of the interactions.

The literal meaning of 'infrared' is 'below the red', indicating that its frequencies are lower than those in the red portion of the visible spectrum. With respect to wavelength, however, the infrared spectrum is 'beyond the red', having wavelengths longer than those of red radiation. The infrared is often defined from about 0.76 µm to about 1000 µm (1 mm) and there are great differences between properties of radiation within this range, as noted below.

Foucault demonstrated that infrared radiation has optical properties similar to those of visible light with respect to reflection, refraction and interference patterns.

The infrared portion of the spectrum extends beyond the visible region to wavelengths about 1 mm (Fig. 9.1). The shorter wavelengths of the infrared spectrum, near the visible, behave in a manner analogous to visible radiation—this region forms the reflective infrared spectrum (sometimes known as the 'near infrared'), extending from about 0.7 µm to 3.0 µm. Many of the same kinds of films, filters, lenses and cameras that we use in the visible portion of the spectrum can also be used, with minor variations, for imaging in the near infrared. The very longest infrared wavelengths are in some respects similar to the shorter wavelengths of the microwave region.

This chapter discusses use of radiation from about 7 to 18 µm for remote sensing of landscapes. This spectral region is often referred to as the emissive or the thermal infrared. Of course, emission of thermal energy occurs over many wavelengths, so some prefer to use the term far infrared for this spectral region. In addition, this chapter also considers passive remote sensing of shorter microwave radiation, which resembles thermal remote sensing in some respects.

Remote sensing in the mid and far infrared is based upon a family of imaging devices that differ greatly from the cameras and films used in the visible and near infrared. The mid and far infrared's interaction with the atmosphere is also quite different from that of shorter wavelengths. The far infrared regions are free from the scattering that is so important in the ultraviolet and visible regions, but absorption by atmospheric gases restricts uses of mid and far infrared spectrum to specific atmospheric windows. Also, the kinds of information acquired by sensing the far infrared differ from those acquired in the visible and near infrared. Variations in emitted energy in the far infrared provide information concerning surface temperature and thermal properties of soils, rocks, vegetation and man-made structures. Inferences based upon thermal properties lead to inferences about the identities of surface materials.

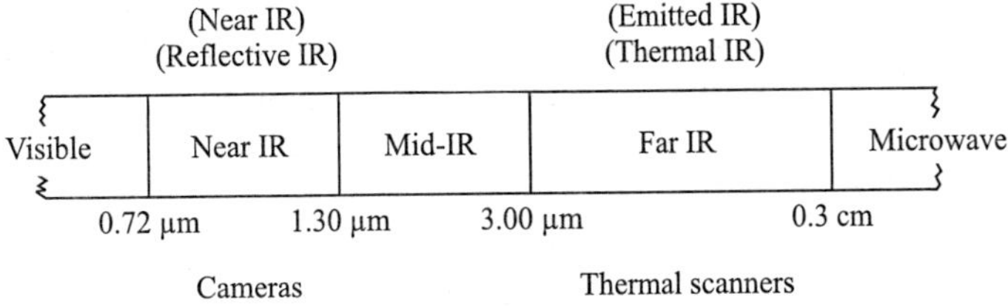

Fig. 9.1. Infrared spectrum.

THERMAL DETECTORS

Before the 1940s, the absence of suitable instruments limited use of thermal infrared radiation for aerial reconnaissance. Aerial mapping of thermal energy depends upon use of a sensor that is sufficiently sensitive to thermal radiation that variations in apparent temperature can be detected by an aircraft moving at considerable speed high above the ground. Detectors in use prior to the 1940s, known as thermal detectors, responded to differences in thermal radiation through changes in electrical resistance or in other physical properties of the object under study by the detector. Such instruments are widely used in the laboratory setting, but are not sufficiently sensitive for use in the context of remote sensing. They respond slowly to changes in temperature and cannot be used at distances required for remote sensing applications. During the 1940s the development of photo detectors provided a practical means for use of the thermal portion of the spectrum in remote sensing. Such detectors are capable of responding directly to incident photons by changes in electrical resistance, providing a sensitivity and speed of response suitable for use in reconnaissance instruments. Since the 1940s a family of photo detectors has been developed to provide the basis for electro-optical instruments used in several portions of the spectrum.

Detectors are devices formed from substances known to respond to energy over a defined wavelength interval, generating a weak electrical signal with a strength related to the radiances of the features in the field of view of the sensor. The electrical current is amplified, then used to generate a digital signal that can be used to form a pictorial image, roughly similar in overall form to an aerial photograph (Fig. 9.2).

Detectors have been designed with sensitivities for many of the spectral intervals of interest in remote sensing, including regions of the visible, near infrared and ultraviolet spectra. Detectors sensitive in the thermal portion of the spectrum are formed from rather exotic materials, such as *indium antimonide* (InSb) and mercury-doped germanium (Ge:Hg). InSb has a peak sensitivity near 5 μm, in the mid-infrared and Ge:Hg has a peak sensitivity near 10 μm, in the far infrared spectrum (Fig. 9.3). Mercury cadmium telluride (MCT) is sensitive over the range 8 to 14 μm. To maintain maximum sensitivity, such detectors must be cooled to very low temperatures (–196°C or –243°C) using liquid nitrogen or liquid helium.

The sensitivity of the detector is a significant variable in the design and operation of the system. Low sensitivity means that only large differences in brightness are recorded ('coarse radiometric resolution') and most of the finer detail in the scene is lost. High sensitivity means that finer differences in scene brightness are recorded ('fine radiometric resolution'). The signal-to-noise ratio (SNR or S/N ratio) expresses this concept. The 'signal' in this context refers to differences in image brightness caused by actual variations in scene brightness. 'Noise' designates variations unrelated to scene brightness. Such variations may be the result of unpredictable variations in the performance of the system. (There may also be random elements contributed by the landscape and the atmosphere, but here 'noise' refers specifically to that contributed by the sensor.) If noise is large relative to the signal, the image does not provide a reliable representation of the feature of interest. Clearly, high noise levels will prevent imaging of subtle features. Even if noise levels are low, there must be minimum contrast between a feature and its background (i.e., a minimum magnitude for the signal) for the feature to be imaged. Also, note that increasing fineness of spatial resolution decreases the energy incident upon the detector, with the effect of decreasing the strength of the signal. For many detectors, noise levels may remain constant even though the level of incident radiation decreases; if so, the increase in spatial resolution may be accompanied by decreases in radiometric resolution.

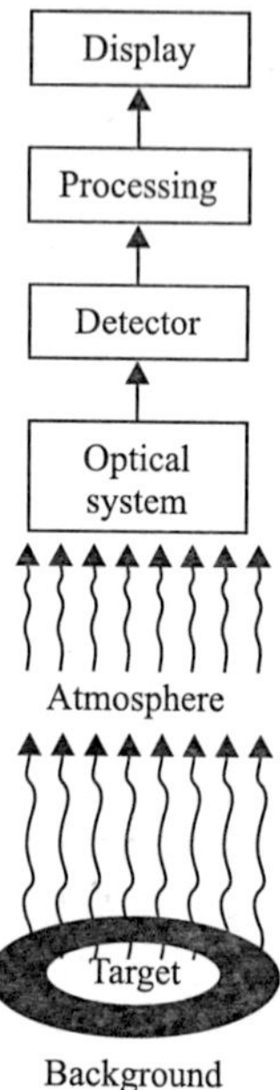

Fig. 9.2. Use of thermal detectors.

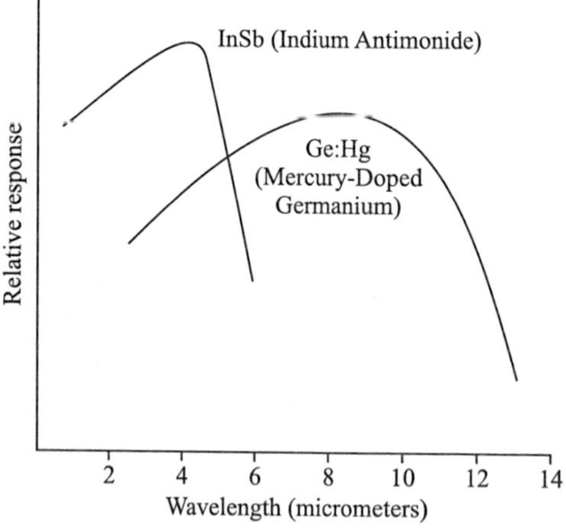

Fig. 9.3. Sensitivity of some common thermal detectors.

THERMAL RADIOMETRY

A radiometer is a sensor that measures the intensity of radiation received within a specified wavelength interval and within a specific field of view. Figure 9.4 gives a schematic view of a radiometer. A lens or mirror gathers radiation from the ground, then focuses it upon a detector positioned in the focal plane. A field stop may restrict the field of view and filters may be used to restrict the wavelength interval that reaches the detector. A characteristic feature of radiometers is that radiation received from the ground is compared to a reference source of known radiometric qualities.

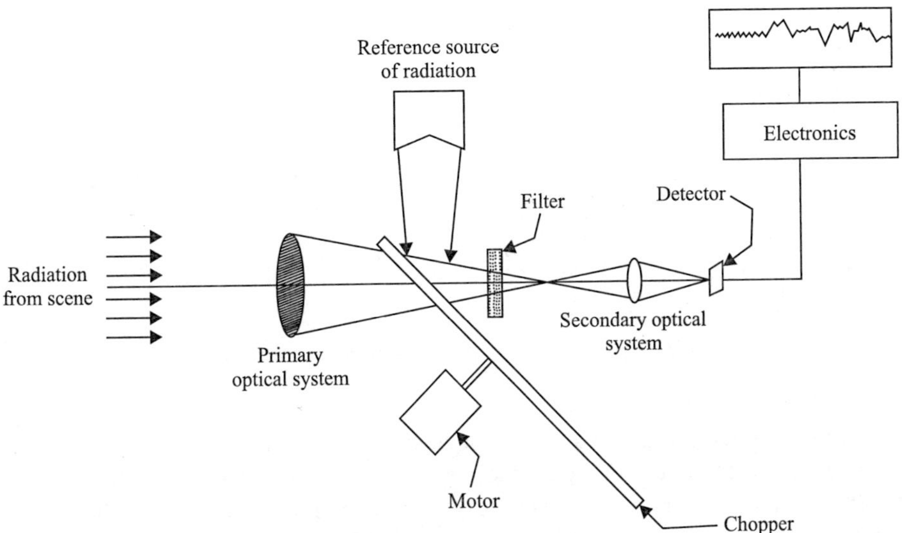

Fig. 9.4. Schematic diagram of a radiometer.

A device known as a chopper is capable of interrupting the radiation that reaches the detector. The chopper consists of a slotted disk or similar device rotated by an electrical motor so that as the disk rotates it causes the detector to alternately view the target, then the reference source of radiation. Because the chopper rotates very fast, the signal from the detector consists of a stream of data that alternately measures the radiance of the reference source, then radiation from the ground. The amplitude of this signal can be used to determine the radiance difference between the reference and the target. Because the reference source has known radiance, radiance of the target can then be estimated.

Although there are many variations on this design, this description identifies the most important components of radiometers. Related instruments include photometers, which operate at shorter wavelengths and often lack the internal reference source and spectrometers, which examine radiance over a range of wavelengths. Radiometers can be designed to operate at different wavelength intervals, including portions of the infrared and ultraviolet spectra. By carefully tailoring the sensitivity of radiometers, scientists have been able to design instruments that are very useful in studying atmospheric gases and cloud temperatures. Radiometers used for earth resource study are often configured to view only a single trace along the flight path; the output signal then consists of a single stream of data that varies in response to differences in radiances of features along the flight line (Fig. 9.5). A scanning radiometer can gather data from corridor beneath the aircraft; output from such a system resembles those from some of the scanning sensors discussed in earlier chapters.

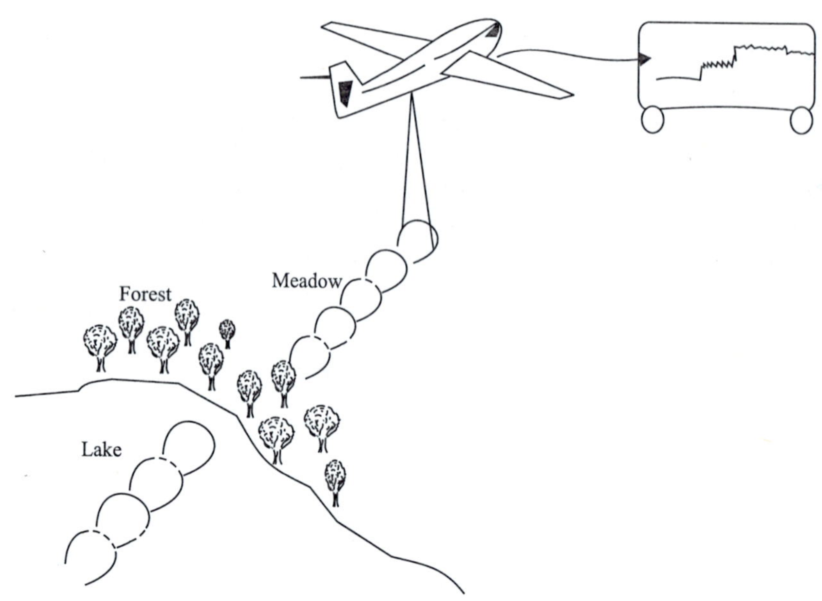

Fig. 9.5. Single stream of data from a radiometer.

Spatial resolution of a radiometer is determined by an instantaneous field of view (IFOV), which is in turn controlled by the sensor's optical system, the detector and flying altitude. Radiometers often have relatively coarse spatial resolution—for example, satellite-borne radiometers may have spatial resolution of 60 m to 100 km or more—in part because of the desirability of maintaining high radiometric resolution. To assure that the sensor receives enough energy to make reliable measurements of radiance, the IFOV is defined to be rather large; a smaller IFOV would mean that less energy would reach the detector, that the signal would be much too small with respect to system noise and that the measure of radiance would be much less reliable.

The IFOV can be informally defined as the area viewed by the sensor if the motion of the instrument were to be suspended so that it records radiation from only a single patch of ground. The IFOV can be more formally expressed as the angular field of view (β) of the optical system (Fig. 9.6). The projection of this field of view onto the ground surface defines the circular area that contributes radiance to the sensor. Usually β for a particular sensor is expressed in radians (r); to determine the IFOV for a particular image, it is necessary to know the flying altitude (H) and to calculate the size of the circular area viewed by the detector.

From elementary trigonometry it can be seen that the diameter of this area (D) is given as

$$D = H\beta \qquad \text{... (9.1)}$$

as illustrated by Fig. 9.6. Thus, for example, if the angular field of view is 1.0 milliradians (mr) (1 mr = 0.001 r) and the flying altitude (H) is 400 m above the terrain, then:

$$D = H\beta$$

$$D = 400 \times 1.0 \times 0.001$$

$$D = 0.40 \text{ m}$$

Because a thermal scanner views a landscape over a range of angles as it scans from side to side, the IFOV varies in size depending upon the angle of observation (θ). Near the nadir (ground track of the aircraft), the IFOV is relatively small; near the edge of the image, the IFOV is large. This effect is beneficial in one sense because it compensates for the effects of the increased distances from the sensor to the landscape, thereby providing consistent radiometric sensitivity across the image. Other effects are more troublesome. Equation 9.1 defines the IFOV at nadir as Hβ. At angle θ, the IFOV measures H sec θβ in the direction of flight and H $\sec^2$ θβ along the scan axis. Thus, near the nadir the IFOV is small and symmetrical; near the edge of the image, it is larger and elongated in the direction of flight. The variation in the shape of the IFOV creates geometric errors in the representations of features—a problem discussed in subsequent sections. The variation in size means that radiance from the scene is averaged over a larger area and can be influence data for IFOVs of any size, the impact is more severe when the IFOV is large.

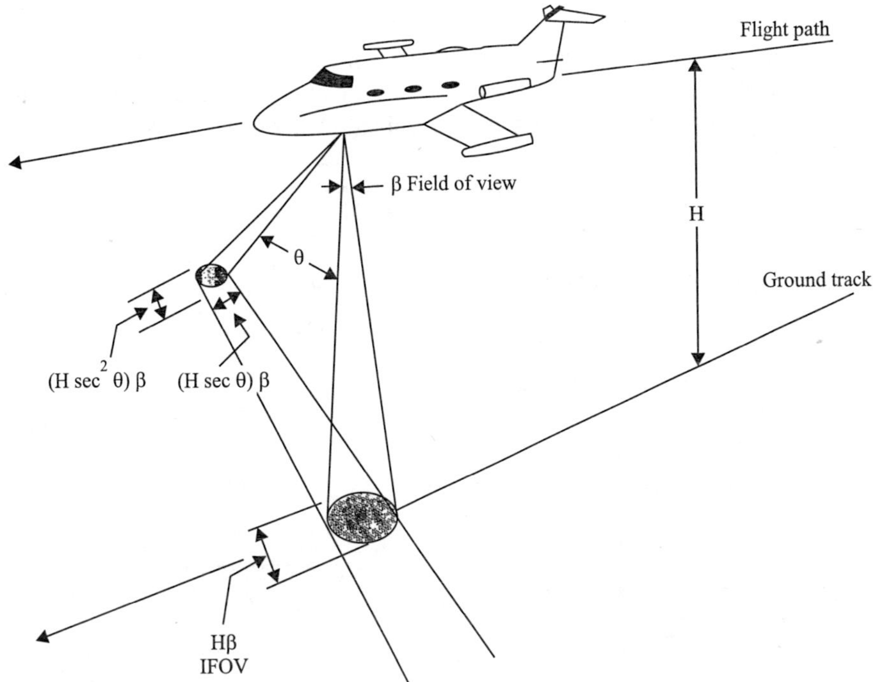

Fig. 9.6. Instantaneous field of view (IFOV). At nadir, the diameter of the IFOV is given by flying altitude (H) and the instrument's field of view (β). As the instrument scans to the side, it observes at angle θ; in the off-nadir position, the IFOV becomes larger and unevenly shaped.

MICROWAVE RADIOMETERS

Microwave emissions from the earth convey some of the same information carried by thermal (far infrared) radiation. Even though their wavelengths are much longer than those of thermal radiation, microwave emissions are related to temperature and emissivity in much the same manner as is thermal radiation. Microwave radiometers are very sensitive instruments tailored to receive and record radiation in the range from about 0.1 mm to 3 cm. The imaging radars are active sensors that illuminate the terrain with their own energy, microwave radiometers are passive sensors that receive microwave radiation naturally emitted by the environment. The strength and wavelength of such radiation is largely a function of the temperature and emissivity of the target. Thus, although microwave radiometers, like radars, use the microwave region of the spectrum, they are functionally most closely related to the thermal sensors discussed in this chapter.

In the present context, we are concerned with microwave emissions from the earth, which indirectly provide information pertaining to vegetation cover, soil moisture status and surface materials. Other kinds of studies, peripheral to the field of remote sensing, derive information from microwave emissions from the earth's atmosphere or from extra-terrestrial objects. In fact, the field of microwave radiometry originated with radio astronomy and some of its most dramatic achievements have been in the reconnaissance of extraterrestrial objects.

A microwave radiometer consists of a sensitive receiving instrument typically in the form of a horn or dish-shaped antenna that observes a path directly beneath the aircraft or satellite; the signal gathered by the antenna is electronically filtered and amplified and then displayed as a stream of digital data or in the instance of scanning radiometers, as an image (Fig. 9.7). As with thermal radiometers, microwave radiometers have a reference signal from an object of known temperature. The received signal is compared with the reference signal as a means of deriving the radiance of the target.

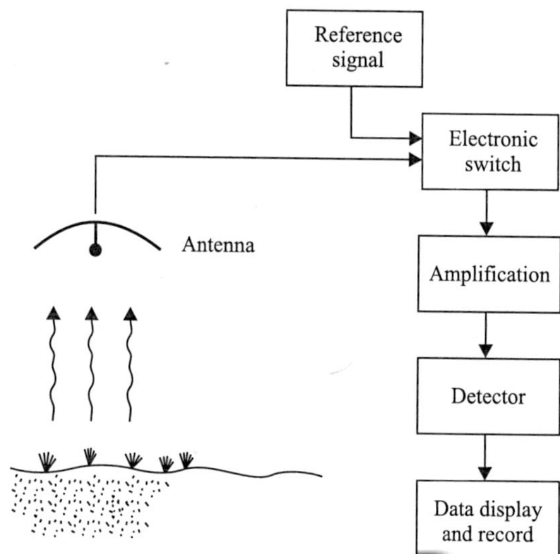

Fig. 9.7. Microwave radiometer.

Examination of data from a microwave radiometer can be very complex due to many factors that contribute to a given observation. The component of primary interest is usually energy radiated by the features within the IFOV; of course, variations within the IFOV are lost, as the sensor can detect only the average radiance within this area. The atmosphere also radiates energy, so it contributes radiance, depending upon moisture content and temperatures. In addition, solar radiation in the microwave radiation can be reflected from the surface to the antenna.

THERMAL SCANNERS

The most widely used imaging sensors for thermal remote sensing are known as thermal scanners. Thermal scanners sense radiances of features beneath the aircraft flight path and produce digital and/or pictorial images of that terrain. There are several designs for thermal scanners. Object-plane scanners view the landscape by means of a moving mirror that oscillates at right angles to the flight path of the aircraft, generating a series of parallel (or perhaps overlapping) scan lines that together image a corridor directly beneath the aircraft. Image-plane scanners use a wider field of view to collect a more comprehensive image of the landscape; this images is then moved, by means of a moving mirror, relative to the detector. In either instance, the instrument is designed as series of lenses and mirrors configured to acquire energy from the ground and to focus it on the detector.

An infrared scanning system consists of a scanning unit, with gyroscopic roll connection unit, infrared detectors (connected to a liquid nitrogen cooling unit) and an amplification and control unit (Fig. 9.8). A magnetic tape unit records data for later display as a video image; some systems may provide film recording of imagery as it is acquired. Together these units might weigh about 91 kg (200 lbs.) and are usually mounted in an aircraft specially modified to permit the scanning unit to view the ground through an opening in the fuselage.

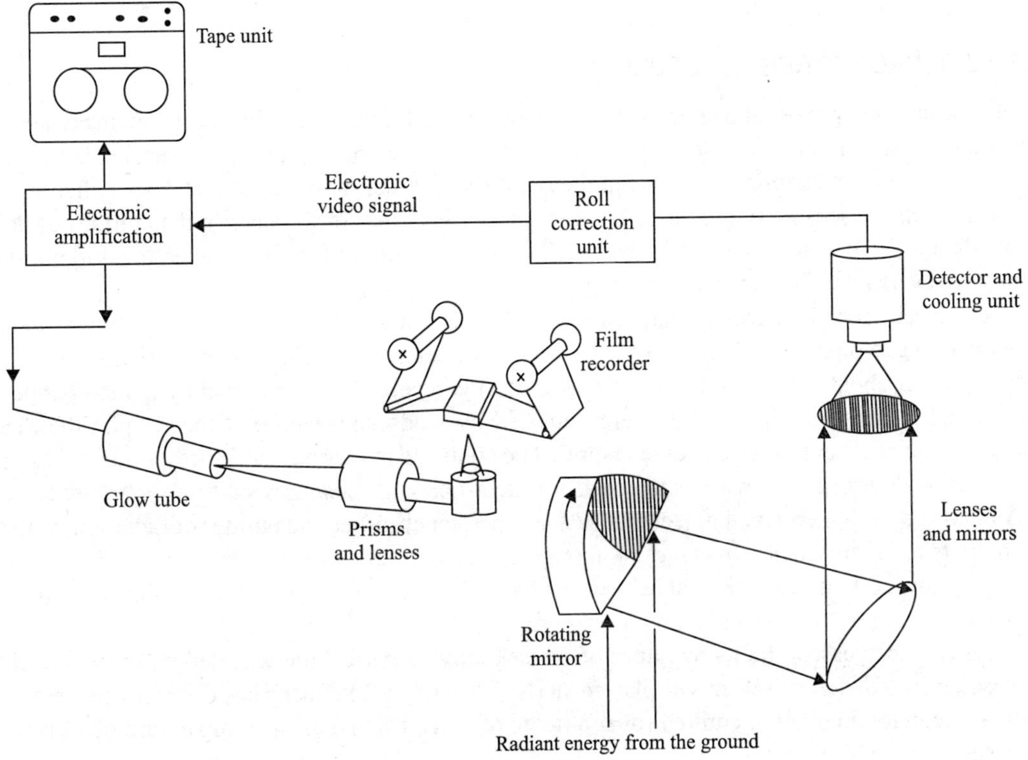

Fig. 9.8. Thermal scanner.

Infrared energy is colleted by a scanning mirror that scans side to side across the flight path, in a manner similar to that described earlier for the Landsat MSS. The typical field of view might be as wide as 77°, so an aircraft flying at an altitude of 300 m (1000 ft.) could record a strip as wide as 477 m (1564 ft.). The forward motion of the aircraft provides the long dimension of the imagery. The mirror might make as many as 80 scans per second, with each scan representing a strip of ground about 46 cm (18 inch) in width (assuming the 300 m altitude mentioned above).

Energy collected by the scanning mirror is focused first on a parabolic mirror and then on a flat, stationary mirror that focuses energy on the infrared detector unit. The infrared detector unit consists of one of the detectors mentioned above, confined in a vacuum container cooled by liquid nitrogen (to reduce electronic noise and enhance sensitivity of the detector). On some units the detector can be easily changed by removing a small unit, then replacing it with another. The detector generates an electrical signal that varies in strength in proportion to the radiation received by the mirror and focused on the detector. The signal from the detector is very weak, however, so it must be amplified before it is recorded by the magnetic tape unit that is connected to the scanner. A role correction unit, consisting in part of a gyroscope, senses side-to-side motion of the aircraft and sends a signal that permits the electronic control unit to correct the signal to reduce geometric errors caused by aircraft instability.

After the aircraft has landed, the magnetic tape from the sensor is removed from the aircraft, then taken to a specially equipped laboratory. There data from the tape can be displayed on a cathode ray tube; brightnesses on the screen are proportional to infrared energy received by the scanning mirror. Photographic representations of such image are prepared to form the scenes used for interpretation or often the digital data may be analysed directly.

THERMAL PROPERTIES OF OBJECTS

All objects at temperatures above absolute zero emit thermal radiation, although the intensity and peak wavelength of such radiation varies with the temperature of the object. For remote sensing in the visible and near infrared, we examine contrasts in the abilities of objects to reflect direct solar radiation to the sensor. For remote sensing in the far infrared spectrum, we sense differences in the abilities of objects and landscape features to absorb shortwave visible and near infrared radiation, then to emit this energy as longer wavelengths in the far infrared region.

Thus, except for geothermal energy, man-made thermal sources and range and forest fires, the immediate source of emitted thermal infrared radiation is shortwave solar energy. Direct solar radiation (with a peak at about 0.5 μm in the visible spectrum) is received and absorbed by the landscape. The amount and spectral distribution of energy emitted by landscape features depend upon the thermal properties of these features, as discussed below. The contrasts in thermal brightness, observed as varied gray tones on the image, are used as the basis for identification of features.

A blackbody is a theoretical object that acts as a perfect absorber and emitter of radiation; it absorbs and reemits all energy that it receives. Although the blackbody is theoretical concept, it is useful in describing and modelling the thermal behaviour of actual objects. Moreover, it is possible to approximate the behaviour of blackbodies in laboratory experiments.

As already discussed, the temperature of a blackbody increases, the wavelength of peak emission decreases in accordance with Wien's displacement law. The Stefan-Boltzmann law describes mathematically the increase in total radiation emitted (over a range of wavelengths) as the temperature of a blackbody increases.

Emissivity (ε_λ) is a ratio between emittance of an object in relation to emittance of a blackbody at the same temperature:

$$\varepsilon_\lambda = \frac{\text{Radiant emittance of an object}}{\text{Radiant emittance of a blackbody at the same temperature}} \qquad \text{... (9.2)}$$

The subscript (λ) sometimes used with ε signifies that ε has been measured for specific wavelengths. Emissivity therefore varies from 0 to 1 signifying a substance with a thermal behaviour identical to that of a blackbody. Table 9.1 lists emissivities for some common materials. Note that many of the substances commonly present in the landscape (e.g., soil, water) have emissivities rather close to 1. Note, however, that emissivity can vary with temperature, wavelength and angle of observation.

Table 9.1. Emissivities of some common materials.

Material	*Temperature (°C)*	*Emissivity*[a]
Polished copper	50–100	0.02
Polished brass	200	0.03
Polished silver	100	0.03
Steel alloy	500	0.35
Graphite	0–3600	0.7–0.8
Lubricating oil (thick film on nickel base)	20	0.82
Snow	–10	0.85
Sand	20	0.90
Wood (planed oak)	20	0.90
Concrete	20	0.92
Dry soil	20	0.92
Brick (red common)	20	0.93
Glass (polished plate)	20	0.94
Wet soil (saturated)	20	0.95
Distilled water	20	0.96
Ice	–10	0.96
Carbon lamp black	20–400	0.96
Lacquer (matte black)	100	0.97

[a] Measured at normal incidence over a range of wavelengths.

Graybodies

An object that has an emissivity less than 1.0 but has constant emissivity over all wavelengths is know as a graybody (Fig. 9.9). A selective radiator is an object with emissivity that varies with respect to wavelength. If two objects in the same setting are at the same temperature, but have different emissivities, the one having the higher emissivity will radiate more strongly. Because the sensor detects radiant energy (apparent temperature) rather than the kinetic ('true') temperature, precise interpretation of an image requires knowledge of emissivities of features shown on the image.

Heat

Heat is the internal energy of a substance arising from the motion of its component atoms and molecules. Temperature measures the relative warmth or coolness of a substance. It is the kinetic temperature or average thermal energy of molecules within a substance. Kinetic temperature, sometimes known as the true temperature, is measured using the usual temperature scales, most notably the Fahrenheit, Celsius (Centigrade) and Kelvin (absolute) scales. Radiant (or apparent) temperature measures the emitted energy of an object. Photons from the radiant energy are detected by the thermal scanner.

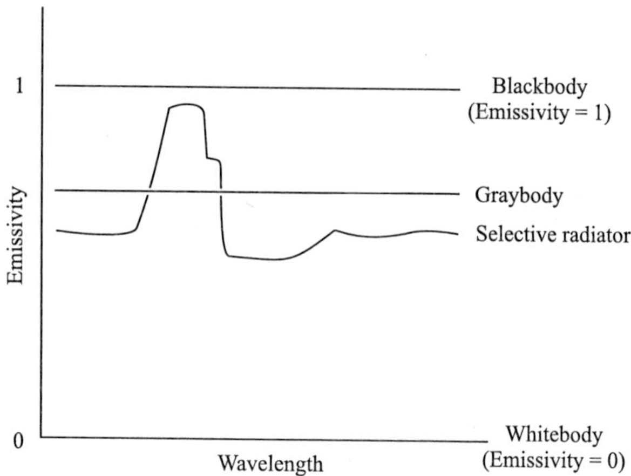

Fig. 9.9. Blackbody, graybody, whitebody.

Heat capacity is the ratio of the change in heat energy per unit mass to the corresponding change in temperature (at constant pressure). For example, we can measure the heat capacity of pure water to be 1 calorie (cal) per gram (g), meaning that 1 cal is required for each gram to raise its temperature by 1°C. The specific heat of a substance is the ratio of its heat capacity to that of a reference substance. Because the reference substance typically is pure water, specific heat is often numerically equal to its heat capacity. Because a calorie is defined as the amount of heat required to raise by 1°C the temperature of 1 gram of pure water, use of water as the reference means that heat capacity and specific heat will be numerically equivalent. In this context, specific heat can be defined as the amount of heat (measured in calories) required to raise the temperature of 1 gram of a substance 1°C.

Thermal conductivity is a measure of the rate that a substance transfers heat. Conductivity is measured as calories per centimeter per second per degree Celsius, so it measures calories required to transfer a change in temperature over specified intervals of length and time.

Some of these variables can be integrated into a single measure, called thermal inertia (P), defined as

$$P = \sqrt{KC\rho} \qquad \text{... (9.3)}$$

where K is the thermal conductivity ($cal \cdot cm^{-1} \cdot sec^{-1} \cdot {}^\circ C^{-1}$); C is the heat capacity ($cal \cdot gm^{-1} \cdot {}^\circ C^{-1}$); and ρ is the density ($gm \cdot cm^{-3}$). Thermal inertia, P, is then measured in $cal \cdot cm^{-2} \cdot {}^\circ C^{-1} \cdot sec^{-1/2}$. Thermal inertia measures the tendency of a substance to resist changes in temperature or more precisely, the rate of heat transfer at the contact between two substances. Table 9.2 gives thermal inertia values for a number of common materials. A substance with low thermal inertia is one with low density, low conductivity and low specific heat, such that it resists changes in temperature. Such substances (e.g., wood, glass or cork) are insensitive to changes in temperature. In contrast, substances with high values of P will heat and cool quickly. Such substances, such as silver, copper and lead, have high densities, high conductivity and high specific heat. These measures and the terminology, are established by long-standing convention, even though they cause misunderstanding. Many people find it confusing to find that a low value for thermal inertia indicates high resistance to temperature change, since they interpret 'low inertia' to mean the opposite. Therefore, the thermal parameter, P^{-1}, is perhaps easier to interpret, as high values indicate high resistance to change and low values indicate low resistance to thermal change.

Table 9.2. Thermal properties of some common substances.

	K	*ρ*	*C*	*P*	P^{-1}
Basalt	0.0050	2.8	0.20	0.053	19
Clay soil (moist)	0.0030	1.7	0.35	0.042	24
Dolomite	0.012	2.6	0.18	0.075	13
Granite	0.0065	2.6	0.16	0.052	19
Limestone	0.0048	2.5	0.17	0.045	22
Sandy soil	0.0014	1.8	0.24	0.024	41
Shale	0.0030	2.3	0.17	0.034	29
Slate	0.0050	2.8	0.17	0.049	21
Aluminium	0.538	2.69	0.215	0.544	1.81
Copper	0.941	8.93	0.092	0.879	1.14
Pure iron	0.18	7.86	0.107	0.389	2.57
Lead	0.083	11.34	0.031	0.171	5.86
Silver	1.00	10.42	0.056	0.764	1.31
Carbon steel	0.150	7.86	0.110	0.360	2.78
Glass	0.0021	2.6	0.16	0.029	34
Wood	0.0005	0.5	0.327	0.009	–

Thermal conductivity, K, measured in $cal{\cdot}cm^{-1}{\cdot}sec^{-1}{\cdot}{}^{\circ}C^{-1}$; density, ρ, measured in $g{\cdot}cm^{-3}$; thermal inertia, P, measured in $cal{\cdot}cm^{-2}{\cdot}{}^{\circ}C^{-1}{\cdot}sec^{-1/2}$, thermal parameter symbolised by P^{-1}.

GEOMETRY OF THERMAL IMAGES

Thermal scanners, like all remote sensing systems, generate geometric errors as they gather data. These errors mean that representations of positions and shapes of features depicted on thermal imagery do not match to their correct planimetric forms. Therefore, images cannot be directly used as the basis for accurate measurements.

Some errors are caused by aircraft or spacecraft instability (Fig. 9.10). As the aircraft rolls and pitches, the scan lines lose their correct positional relationships and of course, the features they portray are not accurately represented in the image.

Thermal imagery also exhibits relief displacement, analogous to that encountered in aerial photography (Fig. 9.11). Thermal imagery, however, does not have the single central perspective of an aerial photograph, but rather a separate nadir for each scan line. Thus, the focal point for relief displacement is the nadir for each scan line or in effect the trace of the flight path on the ground. Thus, relief displacement is projected from a line that follows the center of the long axis of the image. At the center of the image, the sensor views objects from directly overhead and planimetric positions are correct. However, as distance from the centerline increases, the sensor tends to view the sides rather than only the tops of features and relief displacement increases. The effect increases toward the edges of the image and other geometric qualities of thermal line scan imagery.

At nadir, the sensor is closer to the ground than it is at the edge of the image; in a given interval of time, the sensor scans a shorter distance at nadir than it does at the edge of the image. Therefore, the scanner produces a geometric error that tends to compress features along an axis oriented perpendicular to the flight line and parallel to the scan lines. This effect, known as tangential scale distortion, is visible in the shapes of the cylindrical storage tanks. The images of those nearest the flight line are more circular, whereas the shapes of those furthest from the flight line (nearest the edge of the image) are compressed along an axis perpendicular to the flight line. Sometimes the worst effects can be removed by corrections applied as the film image is generated, although it is often necessary to avoid use of the extreme edges of the image.

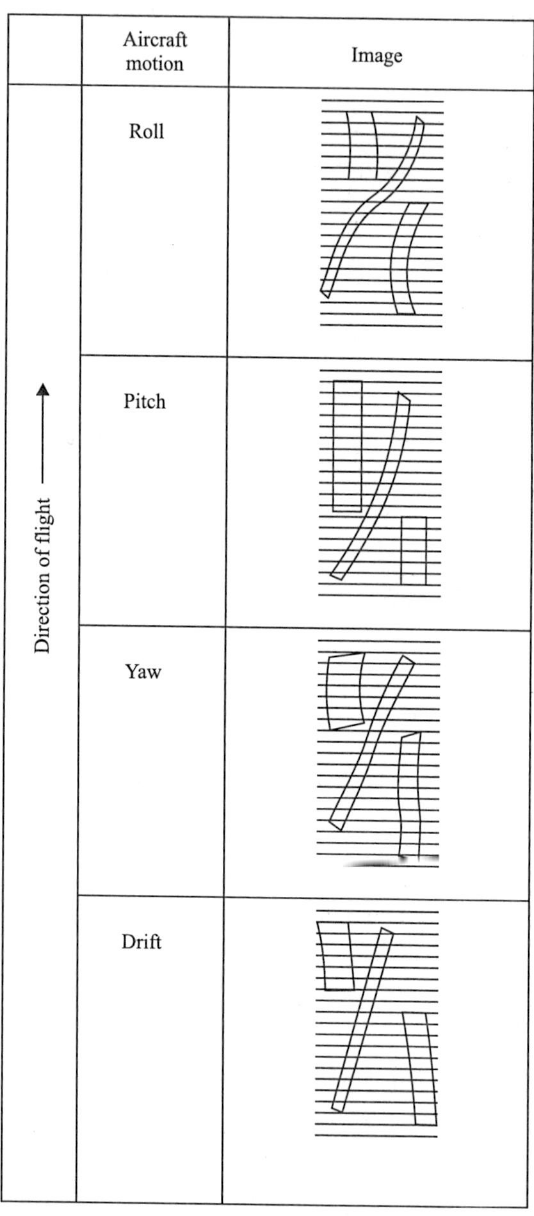

Fig. 9.10. Geometric errors caused by aircraft instability.

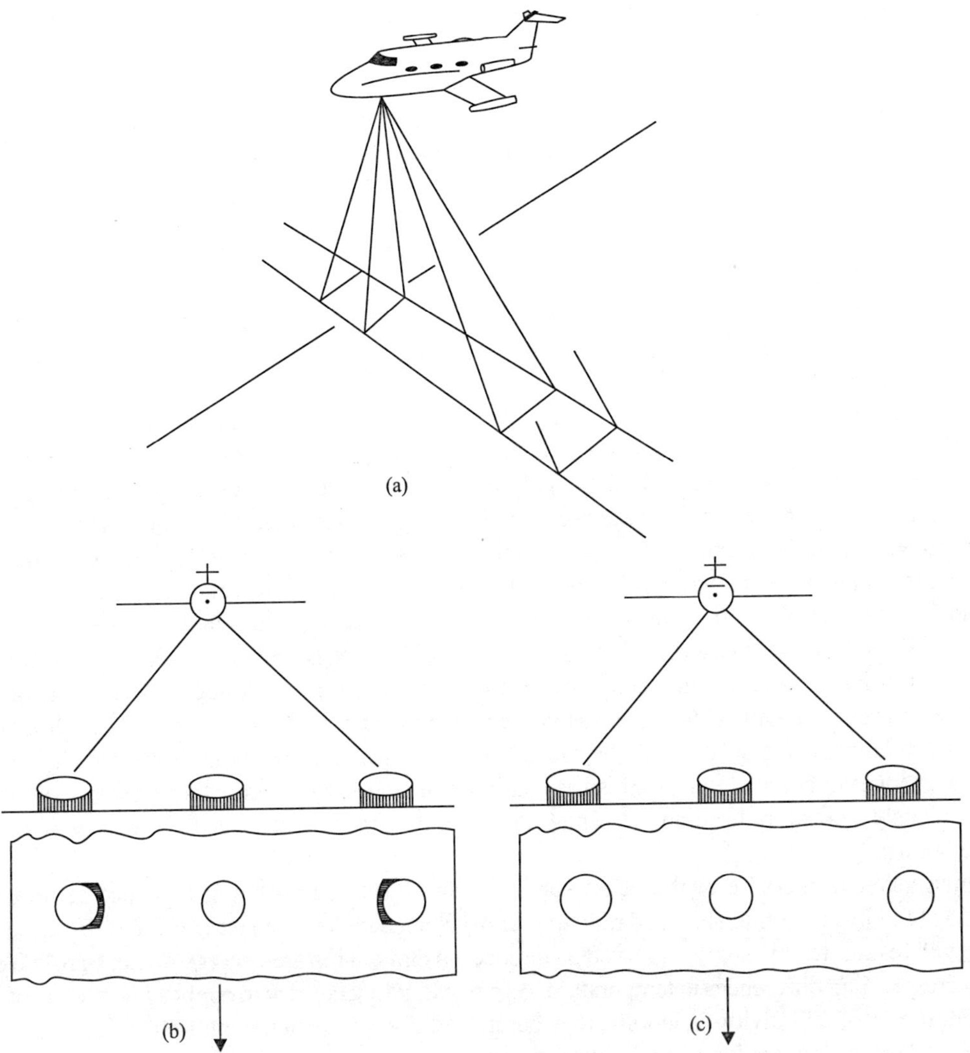

Fig. 9.11. Relief displacement and tangential scale distortion.

THERMAL IMAGE AND ITS INTERPRETATION

The image generated by a thermal scanner is a strip of black-and-white film depicting thermal contrasts in the landscape as variations in gray tones. Usually brighter tones (whites and light grays) represent warmer features; darker tones (dark grays and blacks) represent cooler features. In some applications the black-and-white image may be subjected to level slicing or other enhancements that assign distinctive hues to specific gray tones as an aid for manual interpretation. Often it is easier for the eye to separate subtle shades of colour than the variations in gray on the original image. Such enhancements are simply manipulations of the basic infrared image; they do not represent differences in means of acquisition or in the quality of the basic information available for interpretation.

For any thermal infrared image, the interpreter must always determine: (i) if the image at hand is a positive or a negative image; and (ii) the time of day that the image was acquired. Sometimes it may not be possible to determine the correct time of day from information within the image itself; misinterpretation can alter the meaning of gray tones on the image and render the resulting interpretation useless.

As the sensor views objects near the edge of the image, the distance from the sensor to the ground increases. This relationship means that the IFOV is larger nearer the edges of the image than it is near the flight line. Thermal scanners are generally uncalibrated, so they show relative radiances rather than absolute measurements of radiances. However, some thermal scanners do include reference sources that are viewed by the scanning system at the beginning and end of each scan. The reference sources can be set at specific temperatures that are related to those expected to be encountered in the scene. Thus, each scan line includes values of known temperature that permit the analyst to estimate temperature of objects within the image.

In addition, errors caused by the atmosphere and by the system itself prevent precise interpretation of thermal imagery. Typical system errors might include recording noise, variations in reference temperatures and detector errors. Full correction for atmospheric conditions, requires information not usually available in detail, so often it is necessary to use approximations or value-based samples acquired at a few selected times and places, then extrapolated to estimate values elsewhere. Also, the atmospheric path travelled by radiation reaching the sensor varies with angle of observation, which changes as the instrument scans the ground surface. These variations in angle lead to errors in observed values in the image.

Even when accurate measures of radiances are available, it is difficult to derive data for kinetic temperatures from the apparent temperature information within the image. Derivation of kinetic temperatures requires knowledge of emissivities of the materials. In some instances, such knowledge may be available, as the survey may be focused on a known area that must be repeatedly imaged to monitor changes over time (e.g., as moisture conditions change). But many other surveys examine areas not previously studied in detail and information regarding surface materials and their emissivities may not be known.

Emissivity is a measure of the effectiveness of an object in translating temperature into emitted radiation (and in converting absorbed radiation into a change in observed temperature). Because objects differ with respect to emissivity, observed differences in emitted infrared energy do not translate directly into corresponding differences in temperature. As a result, it is necessary to apply a knowledge of surface temperature or of emissivity variations, to accurately study surface temperature patterns from thermal imagery. Because knowledge of these characteristics assumes a very detailed prior knowledge of the landscape, such interpretation should be considered as appropriate for examination of a distribution known already in some detail rather than for reconnaissance of an unknown pattern, (e.g., one might already know the patterns of soils and crops at an agricultural experiment station, but wish to use the imagery to monitor temperature patterns). Often estimated values for emissivity are used or assumed values are applied to areas of unknown emissivity.

Also, it should be recognised that the sensor records radiances of the surfaces of objects. Because radiance may be determined at the surface of an object by a layer perhaps as thin as 50 μm, a sensor may record conditions that are not characteristic of the sub-surface mass, which is probably the object of the study. For example, evaporation from a water body or a moist soil surface may cool the thin layer of moisture at the contact point with the atmosphere. Because the sensor detects radiation emitted at this surface layer, the observed temperature may differ considerably from that of the remaining mass of the soil or water body.

Leckie estimates the calibration error and other instrument errors are generally rather small, although they may be important in some instances. Errors in estimating emissivity and in attempts to correct for atmospheric effects are likely to be the most important sources of error in quantitative studies of thermal imagery.

In most instances, a thermal image must be interpreted to yield qualitative rather than quantitative information. Although some applications do require interpretations of quantitative information, there are many others for which qualitative interpretation is completely satisfactory. An interpreter who is well informed about the landscape represented on the image, the imaging system, the thermal behaviour of the various materials and the timing of the flight is prepared to derive considerable information from an image, even though it may not be possible to derive precise temperatures from the image.

The thermal landscape is a composite of the familiar elements of surface material, topography, vegetation cover and moisture. Various rocks, soils and other surface materials respond differently to solar heating. Thus, in some instances the differences in thermal properties tabulated in Table 9.1 can be observed in thermal imagery. However, the thermal behaviour of surface materials is also influenced by other factors. For example, slopes that face the sun will tend to receive more solar radiation than slopes that are shadowed by topography. Such differences are, of course, combined with those arising from different surface materials. Also, the presence and nature of vegetation alters the thermal behaviour of the landscape. Vegetation tends to heat rather rapidly, but can also shade areas, creating patterns of warm and cool.

Water tends to retain heat, to cool slowly at night and to warm slowly during daytime. In contrast, many soils and rocks (if dry) tend to release heat rapidly at night and to absorb heat quickly during the daytime. Even small or modest amounts of moisture can greatly alter the thermal properties of soil and rock. Therefore, thermal sensors can be very effective in monitoring the presence and movement of moisture in the environment. In any given image, the influences of surface materials, topography, vegetation and moisture can combine to cause very complex image patterns. However, often it is possible to isolate the effect of some of these variables and therefore to derive useful information concerning, for example, movement of moisture or the patterns of differing surface materials.

Timing of acquisition of thermal imagery is very important. The optimum times vary according to the purpose and subject of the study, so it is not possible to specify universally applicable rules. Since the greatest thermal contrast tends to occur during the daylight hours, sometimes thermal images are acquired in the early afternoon to capture differences in thermal properties of landscape features. However in the 3 to 6 μm range the sensor may record reflected as well as emitted thermal radiation, so daytime missions in this region may not be optimum for thermal information. Also during daytime, the sensor may record thermal patterns caused by topographic or cloud shadowing; although shadows may sometimes be useful in interpretation, they are more likely to complicate analysis of a thermal image, so it is usually best to avoid acquiring heavily shadowed images. In a daytime image, water bodies typically appear as cool relative to land and bare soil, meadow and wooded areas appear as warm features.

Some of the problems arising from daytime images are avoided by missions planned just before dawn. Shadows are absent and sunlight, of course, cannot cause reflection (at shorter wavelengths) or shadows. However, thermal contrast is lower, so it may be more difficult to distinguish between broad classes of surfaces based upon differences in thermal behaviour. On such an image, water bodies would appear as warm relative to land. Forested areas may also appear to be warm. Open meadows and dry, bare soil are likely to appear as cool features.

The thermal images of petroleum storage facilities show thermal contrasts that are especially interesting. The image clearly shows the sharp contrast in temperature as the warm water flows into the main channel, then disperses and cools as it is carried downstream. Note the contrast between the full and partially full tanks and the warm temperatures of the pipelines that connect the tanker with the storage tanks.

Thermal imagery has obvious significance for studies of heat loss, thermal efficiency and effectiveness of insulation in residential and commercial structures.

If imagery or data for two separate times are available, it may be possible to employ knowledge of thermal inertia as a means of studying the pattern of different materials at the earth's surface. Figure 9.12 illustrates the principles involved. Two images are acquired at times that permit observation of extremes of temperature, perhaps near noontime and again just before dawn. These two sets of data permit estimation of the ranges of temperature variation for each region on the image. Because these variations are determined by the thermal inertias of the substances, they permit interpretation of features represented by the images. Leckie notes that misregistration can be a source of error in comparisons of day and night images, although such errors are thought to be small relative to other errors.

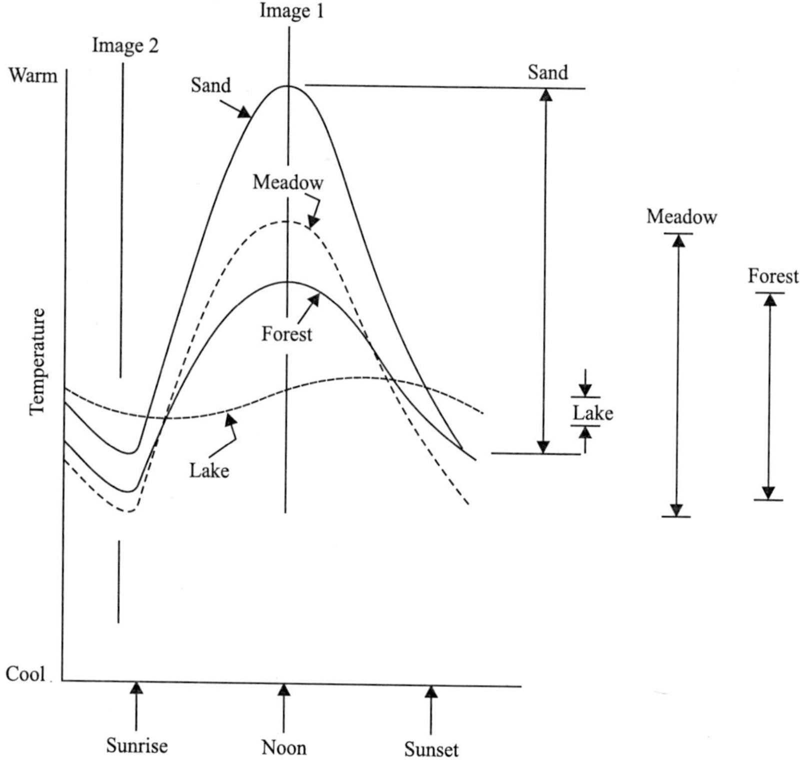

Fig. 9.12. Schematic illustration of diurnal temperature variation of several broad classes of land cover. The two solid vertical lines depict timing of two thermal images acquired at an interval timed to maximise thermal contrast over a 24 hour period. The vertical bars at the right are projections from the diagram on the left, so that the lengths of the bars represent thermal variation of each class of land cover.

In Fig. 9.12 images are acquired at noon, when temperatures are high and again just before dawn, when temperature are lowest. By observing the differences in temperature, it is possible to estimate thermal inertia. Thus the lake, composed of a material that resists changes in temperature, shows rather small changes in temperature, whereas the surface of open sand displays little resistance to thermal changes and exhibits a wider range of temperature.

HEAT CAPACITY MAPPING MISSION

The heat capacity mapping Mission (HCMM) was a satellite system specifically designed to evaluate the concept that orbital observations of temperature differences at the earth's surface at different points in the daily heating/cooling cycle might provide a basis for estimation of thermal inertia and other thermal properties of surface materials. The satellite was in a sun-synchronous orbit, at an altitude of 620 km, bringing it over the equator at 2:00 p.m. local sun time. At 40°N latitude the satellite passed overhead at 1:30 p.m., then again about 12 hours later at 2:30 a.m. These times provided observations at two points on the diurnal heating/cooling cycle (Fig. 9.13). (It would have been desirable to use a time later in the morning just before sunrise, in order to provide higher thermal contrast, but orbital constraints dictated the time differences between passes). The repeat cycle varied with latitude—at mid-latitude locations the cycle was 5 days. The 12 hour repeat coverage was available for some locations at 16 day intervals, but other locations received only 36 hour coverage. The HCMM radiometer used two channels. One, in the reflective portion of the spectrum (0.5 to 1.1 μm), had a spatial resolution of about 500 m × 500 m. A second channel was available in the thermal infrared region, from 10.5 to 12.5 μm and had a spatial resolution of 600 m × 600 m. The image swath was about 716 km wide.

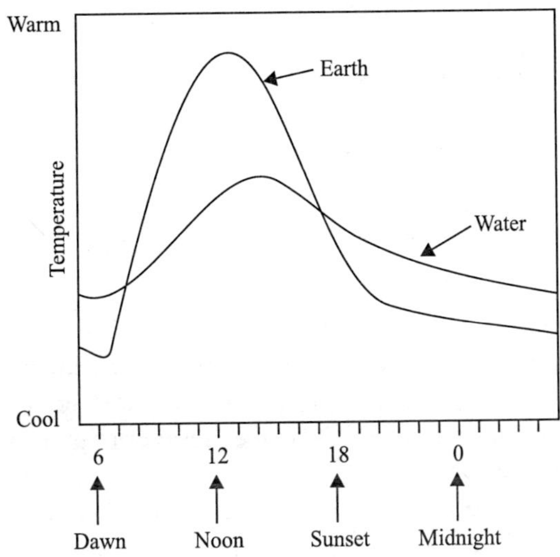

Fig. 9.13. Diurnal temperature cycle.

Estimation of thermal inertia requires that two HCMM images be registered to observe apparent temperatures at different points on the diurnal heating/cooling cycle. Because the day and night images must be acquired on different passes with different inclinations (Fig. 9.14), the registration of the two images is often much more difficult than might be the case with similar images. The rather coarse resolution means that normally distinct landmarks are not visible or are more difficult to recognise.

NASA's Goddard Space Flight Center received and processed HCMM data, calibrating the thermal data and performing geometric registration, when possible, for the two contrasting thermal images. Ideally, these two images permit reconstruction of a thermal inertia map of the imaged area. In fact, atmospheric conditions varied during the intervals between passes and the measured temperatures were influenced by variations in cloud cover, wind, evaporation at the ground surface and atmospheric water vapour. As a result, the measured differences are apparent thermal inertia (ATI) rather than a true measure of thermal inertia. Due to the number of approximations employed and scaling of the values, the values for ATI are best considered to be measures of relative thermal inertia.

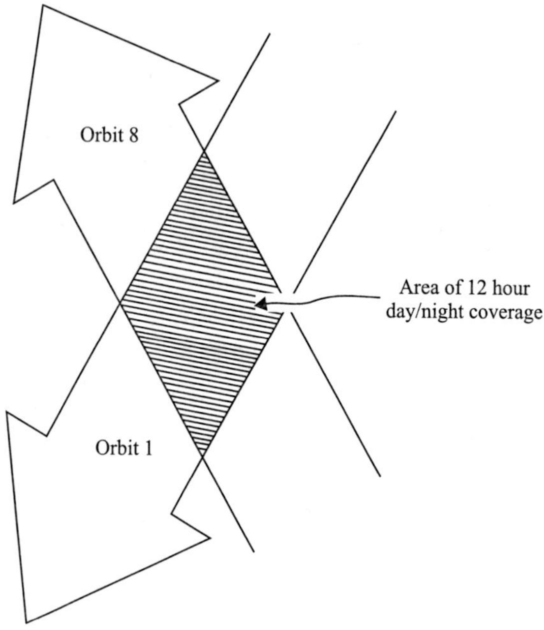

Fig. 9.14. Overlap of two HCMM passes at 40° latitude.

Thus, thermal imagery is a valuable asset for remote sensing because it conveys information not easily derived from other forms of imagery. The thermal behaviour of different soils, rocks and construction materials can permit derivation of information not present in other images. The thermal properties of water contrast with those of many other landscape materials, so that thermal images can be very sensitive to the presence of moisture in the environment. And the presence of moisture is itself often a clue to the differences between different classes of soil and rock.

Of course, use of data from the far infrared region can present its own problems. Like all images, thermal imagery has geometric errors. Moreover, the analyst cannot derive detailed quantitative interpretations of temperatures unless detailed knowledge of emissivity is at hand. Timing of image acquisition can be critical. Atmospheric effects can pose serious problems, especially from satellite altitudes. Because the thermal landscape differs so greatly from the visible landscape, it may often be necessary to use aerial photography to locate familiar landmarks while interpreting thermal images. Existing archives of thermal imagery are not comparable in scope to those for aerial photography or satellite data (such as those of Landsat or SPOT), so it may be difficult to acquire suitable thermal data unless it is feasible to purchase custom-flown imagery.

10

Image Resolution

INTRODUCTION

In very broad terms, resolution refers to the ability of a remote sensing system to record and display fine spatial and radiometric detail. A working knowledge of resolution is essential for understanding both practical and conceptual aspects of remote sensing. Our understanding or lack of understanding of resolution may be the limiting factor in our efforts to use remotely sensed data, especially at coarse spatial resolution.

For scientists with an interest in instrument design and performance, measurement of resolution is of great significance in determining the optimum design and configuration of individual elements (e.g., specific lenses, detectors or photographic emulsions) of a remote sensing system. Here our interest focuses upon understanding image resolution in terms of the entire remote sensing system, regardless of our interests in specific elements of the landscape. Whether our focus concerns soil patterns, geology, water quality, land use or vegetation distribution, a knowledge of image resolution is a pre-requisite for understanding the information recorded on the image we examine.

The purpose of this chapter is to discuss image resolution as a separate concept in recognition of its significance throughout the field of remote sensing. Thus it is primarily an effort to outline generally applicable concepts, but it does not ignore special and unique factors that apply in certain instances.

This chapter also highlights the significance of image resolution as a concept that extends across many aspects of remote sensing. Although the special and unique elements of any image must always be recognised and understood, many of the general aspects of image resolution can assist us in understanding how to interpret remotely sensed images.

Although there has long been an intense interest in measuring image resolution, especially in photographic systems, it is clear that much of our more profound understanding has been developed through work with satellite scanning system such as the Landsat MSS. Such data were of much coarser spatial resolution than any studied previously. As more and more attention was focused upon their analysis and interpretation, it was necessary to develop a better understanding of image resolution and its significance for specific tasks. Now much finer resolution data are available, but we can continue to develop and apply our knowledge of image resolution to maximise our ability to understand and interpret these images.

Estes and Simonett define resolution as 'the ability of an imaging system to record fine detail in a distinguishable manner. This definition includes several key concepts. The emphasis upon the imaging system is significant because in most practical situations it makes little sense to focus attention upon the resolving power of a single element of the system (e.g., the film) if another element (e.g., the camera lens) limits the resolution of the final image. 'Fine detail' is, of course, a relative concept, as is the specification that detail be recorded in a 'distinguishable' manner. Both of these aspects of the definition emphasise that resolution can be clearly defined only by operational definitions applicable under specified conditions.

For the present, it is sufficient to note that there is a practical limit to the level of detail that can be acquired from a given aerial or satellite image. This limit we define informally as the 'resolution' or the remote sensing system, although it must be recognised that image detail also depends upon the character of the scene that has been imaged, atmospheric conditions, illumination and the experience and ability of the image interpreter.

Most individuals think of resolution as spatial resolution, the fineness of the spatial detail visible in an image. 'Fine detail' in this sense means that small objects can be identified on an image. But other forms of resolution are equally important. Radiometric resolution can be defined as the ability of an imaging system to record many levels of brightness. Coarse radiometric resolution would record a scene using only a few brightness levels or a few bits (i.e., at very high contrast), whereas fine radiometric resolution would record the same scene using many levels of brightness. Spectral resolution denotes the ability of a sensor to define fine wavelength intervals. Hyperspectral sensors generate images composed of 200 or more narrowly defined spectral regions—these data represent an extreme of spectral data relative to thematic mapper of Landsat MSS images, which convey spectral information in only a few rather broad spectral regions.

Finally, temporal resolution is an important consideration in many applications. Remote sensing has the ability to record sequence of images, thereby representing changes in landscape patterns over time. The ability of a remote sensing system to record such a sequence at relatively close intervals generates a data set with fine temporal resolution. In contrast, systems that can record images of a given region only at infrequent intervals produce data at coarse temporal resolution. In some applications, such as flood or disaster mapping, temporal resolution is a critical characteristic that might override other desirable qualities. Clearly, those applications that attempt to monitor dynamic phenomena such as news events, range fires, land-use changes, traffic flows or weather-related events, will have an interest in temporal resolution.

In many situations, there are clear trade-offs between different forms of resolution. For example, in traditional photographic emulsions, increases in spatial resolving power are based upon decreased size of film grain, which produces accompanying decreases in radiometric resolution (i.e., the decreased sizes of grains in the emulsion portray a lower range of brightnesses). In other systems there are similar trade-offs. Increasing spatial detail requires, in scanning systems, a smaller instantaneous field of view (i.e., energy reaching the sensor has been reflected from a smaller ground area). If all other variables have been held constant, this must translate into decreased energy reaching the sensor; lower levels of energy mean that the sensor may record less 'signal' and more 'noise,' thereby reducing the usefulness of the data. This effect can be compensated for by broadening the spectral window to pass more energy (i.e., decreasing spectral resolution) or by dividing the energy into fewer brightness levels (i.e., decreasing radiometric resolution). Of course, overall improvements can be achieved by improved instrumentation or by altering operating conditions (e.g., flying at a lower altitude). The general situation, however, seems to demand costs in one form of resolution for benefits achieved in another.

TARGET VARIABLES

Observed spatial resolution in a specific image depends greatly upon the character of the scene that has been imaged. In complex natural landscapes, identification of the essential variables influencing detail observed in the image may be difficult, although many of the key factors can be enumerated. Contrast is clearly one of the most important influences upon spatial and radiometric resolution. Contrast can be defined as the difference in brightness between an object and its background. If other factors are held constant, high contrast favours recording of fine spatial detail; low contrast produces coarser detail. A black automobile imaged against a black asphalt background will be more difficult to observe than a white vehicle observed under the same conditions.

The significance of contrast as an influence on spatial resolution illustrates the interrelationships between the various forms of resolution and emphasises the reality that no single element of system resolution can be considered in isolation from the others. It is equally important to distinguish between contrast in the original scene and that recorded on the image of that scene; the two may be related, but not necessarily in a direct fashion. Also, it should be noted that contrast in the original scene is a dynamic quality that, for a given landscape, varies greatly from season to season (with changes in vegetation, snow cover, etc.) and within a single day (as angle and intensity of illumination change).

The shape of an object or feature is significant. Aspect ratio refers to the length of a feature in relation to its width. Usually long thin features, such as highways, railways and rivers, tend to be visible on aerial imagery, even in circumstances when their widths are much less than the nominal spatial resolution of the imagery. Regularity of shape favours recording of fine detail. Features with regular shapes, such as cropped agricultural fields, tend to be recorded in fine detail, whereas complex shapes with be imaged in coarser detail. The number of objects in a pattern also influences the level of detail recorded by a sensor. For example, the pattern formed by the number and regular arrangement of tree crowns in an orchard favours the imaging of the entire pattern in fine detail. Under similar circumstances, the crown of a single isolated tree might not be visible on the imagery.

Extent and uniformity of background contributes to resolution of fine detail in many distributions. For example, a single automobile in a large, uniform parking area or a single tree positioned in a large cropped field will be imaged in detail not achieved under other conditions.

SYSTEM VARIABLES

Remember that the resolution of individual sensors depends in part upon the design of that sensor and in part upon its operation at a given time. In any specific situation these considerations must be acknowledged. Studies to determine their roles in defining resolution should be performed. For example, resolution of an aerial photograph is determined by the quality of the camera lens, the choice of film, flying altitude, scale and the design of the aerial camera. For scanning systems such as the Landsat MSS/TM or thermal scanners, the IFOV determines many of the qualities of image resolution. The IFOV depends, of course, upon the optical system (the angular field of view) and operating altitude. Speed of the scanning motion and movement of the vehicle that carries the sensor will also have their effects upon image quality. For active microwave sensors, image resolution is determined by beamwidth (antenna gain), angle of observation, wavelength and other factors discussed previously.

OPERATING CONDITIONS

For all remote sensing systems, the operating conditions, including flying altitude and ground speed, are important elements influencing the level of detail in the imagery. Atmospheric conditions can be included as important variables, especially for satellite and high-altitude imagery.

MEASUREMENT OF RESOLUTION

Ground Resolved Distance

Perhaps the simplest measure of spatial resolution is ground resolved distance (GRD), defined simply as the dimensions of the smallest objects recorded on an image. One might speak of the resolution of an aerial photograph as being '2 m,' meaning that objects of that size and larger could be detected and interpreted from the image in question. Smaller objects presumably would not be resolved and therefore would not be interpretable.

Such measures of resolution may have utility as a rather rough suggestion of usable detail, but must be recognised as having only a very subjective meaning. The objects and features that compose the landscape vary greatly in size, shape, contrast with background and pattern. Usually we have no means of relating a given estimate of GRD to a specific problem of interest. For example, the spatial resolution of US Department of Agriculture (USDA) 1:20000 black-and-white aerial photography is often said to be 'about 1 m,' yet typically one can easily detect on these photographs the painted white lines in parking lots and highways; these lines may be as narrow as 6 to 9 inch.

Does this mean that the resolution of this photography should be assessed as 6 inch rather than 1 m? Only if we are interested in the interpretation of long thin features that exhibit high contrast with their background could we accept such an estimate as useful. Similarly, the estimate of 1 m may be inappropriate for many applications.

Line Pairs Per Millimeter

Line pairs per millimeter (LPM) is a means of standardising the characteristics of targets used to assess image resolution. Essentially, it is a means of quantifying, under controlled conditions, the estimate of GRD by using a standard target, positioned on the ground, that is imaged by the remote sensing system under specified operating conditions.

Although many targets have been used, the resolution target designed by the US Air Force has been a standard for a variety of studies (Fig. 10.1). This target consists of parallel black lines positioned against a white background. The width of spaces between lines is equal to that of the lines themselves; their length is five times their width. As a result, a block of three lines and the two white spaces that separate them from a square. This square pattern is reproduced at varied sizes to form an array consisting of bars of differing widths and spacings. Sizes are controlled to produce changes in spacing of the bars (spatial frequency) of 12 per cent. Repetition of the pattern at differing scales assures that the image of the pattern will include at least one pattern so small that individual lines and their spaces will not be fully resolved. If image of two objects are visually separated, they are said to be 'spatially resolved.' Images of the resolution target are examined by an interpreter to find that smallest set of lines in which the individual lines are all completely separated along their entire length.

The analyst measures the width of the image representation of one 'line pair,' (i.e., the width of the image of one line and its adjacent white space) (Fig. 10.2). This measurement provides the basis for the calculation of the number of line pairs per millimeter (or any other length we may choose; 'line pairs per millimeter' [LPM] is standard for many applications). For example, in Fig. 10.2 the width of a line and its adjacent gap is measured to be 0.04 mm. From 1 line pair/0.04 mm we find a resolution of 25 LPM.

For aerial photography, this measure of resolution can be translated into GRD by the relationship;

$$\text{GRD} = \frac{H}{(f)(R)} \qquad \text{... (10.1)}$$

where GRD is ground resolved distance, in meters; H is the flying altitude above the terrain, in meters; f is the focal length, in millimeters; and R is the system resolution, in line pairs per millimeters.

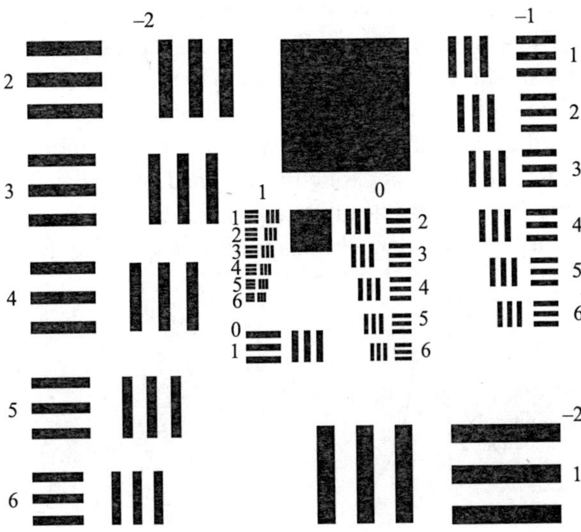

Fig. 10.1. Bar target used in resolution studies.

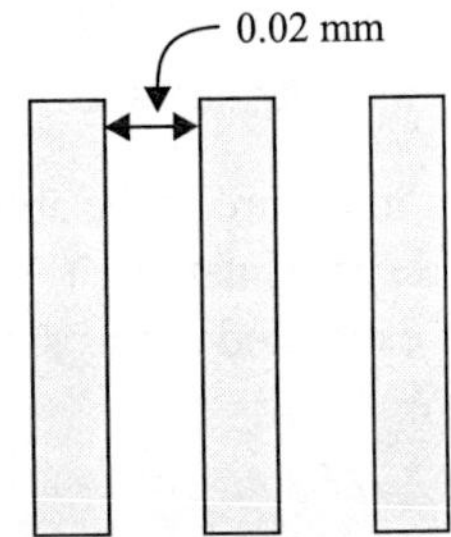

Fig. 10.2. Use of bar target to find LPM.

Such measures have little predictable relationship to the actual size of landscape features that might be interpreted in practical situations because seldom will the features of interest have the same regulatrity of size, shape and arrangement and the high contrast of the resolution target used to derive the measures. They are, of course, valuable as comparative measures for assessing the performance of separate systems under the same operating conditions or of a single system under different conditions.

Although the US Air Force target has been widely used, other resolution targets have been developed. For example, a coloured target has been used to assess the spectral fidelity of colour films and bar targets have been constructed with contrast ratios somewhat closer to conditions observed during actual applications. The USGS target is a large array; painted on the roof the USGS national Center, in Reston, Virginia, as a means of assessing aerial imagery under operational conditions from high altitudes. The array is formed from large bar targets, about 100 ft. in length, of known contrast and a star target about 140 ft. in diameter designed for assessment of the resolution of non-photographic sensors.

Modulation Transfer Function

The modulation transfer function (MTF) records system response to a target array with elements of varying spatial frequency (i.e., unlike the bar targets described above, targets used to find MTFs are spaced at varied intervals). Often the target array is formed from bars of equal length spaced against a white background at intervals that produce a sinusoidal variation in image density along the axis of the target.

Modulation refers to changes in the widths and spacings of the target. Transfer denotes the ability of the imaging system to record these changes on the image—that is, to 'transfer' these changes from the target to the image. Because the target is explicitly designed with spatial frequencies too fine to be recorded on the image, some frequencies (the high frequencies at the closest spacings) cannot be imaged. The 'function' then shows the degree to which the image records specified frequencies (Fig. 10.3).

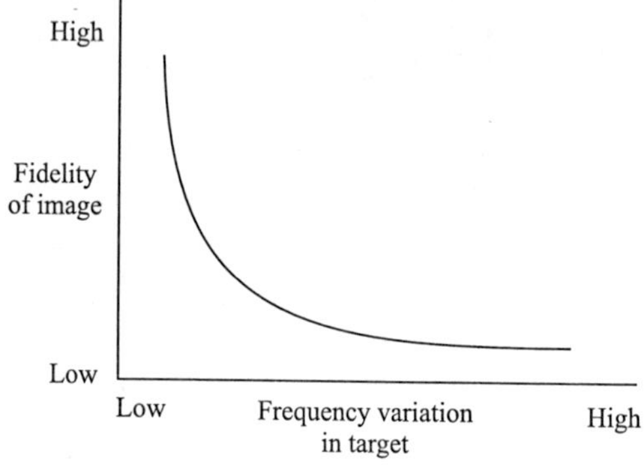

Fig. 10.3. Modulation transfer function.

Although the MTF is probably the 'best' measure of the ability of an imaging system as a whole or of a single component of that system to record spatial detail, the complexity of the method prevents routine use in many situations. The MTF can be estimated using simpler and more readily available targets, including the USAF target described above.

MIXED PIXELS

As spatial resolution interacts with the fabric of the landscape, a special problem is created in digital imagery by those pixels that are not completely occupied by a single, homogeneous category. The sub-division of a scene into discrete pixels acts to average brightnesses over the entire pixel area. If a uniform or relatively uniform land area occupies the pixel, then similar brightnesses are averaged and the resulting digital value forms a reasonable representation of the brightnesses within the pixel. That is, the average value does not differ greatly from the value that contribute to the average. However, when a pixel area is composed of two or more areas that differ greatly with respect to brightness, then the average is composed of several very different values and the single digital value that represents the pixel may not accurately represent any to the categories present (Fig. 10.4).

An important consequence of the occurrence of mixed pixels is that pure spectral responses of specific features are mixed together with the pure responses of other features. The mixed response sometimes known as a composite signature does not match the pure signatures that we wish to use to map the landscape. Note, however, that sometimes composite signatures can be useful because they permit us to map features that are too complex to resolve individually.

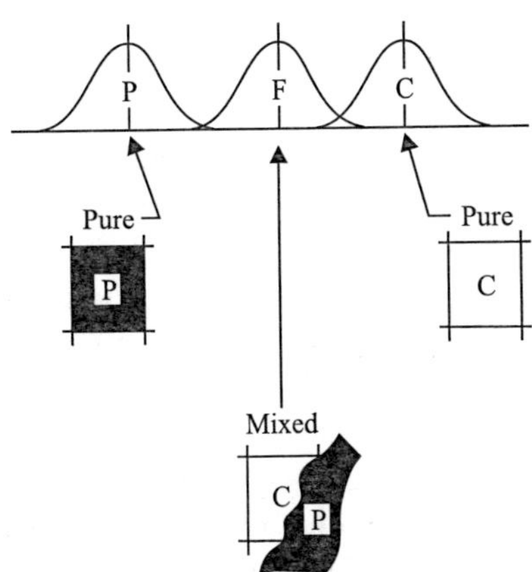

Fig. 10.4. False resemblance of mixed pixels to a third category.

Nonetheless, mixed pixels are also a source of error and confusion. In some instances, the digital values from mixed pixels may not resemble any of the several categories in the scene; in other instances, the value formed by a mixed pixel may resemble those from other categories in the scene but not actually present within the pixel—an especially misleading kind of error.

Mixed pixels occur often at the edges of large parcels or along long linear features, such as rivers or highways, where contrasting brightnesses are immediately adjacent to one another (Fig. 10.5). The edge or border, pixels then form opportunities for errors in digital classification. Scattered occurrences of small parcels (such as farm ponds observed at the resolution of the Landsat MSS) may produce special problems because they may be represented only by mixed pixels and the image analyst may not be aware of the presence of the small areas of high contrast because they occur at sub-pixel sizes. An especially difficult situation can be created by landscapes composed of many parcels that are small relative to the spatial resolution of the sensor. A mosaic of such parcels will create an array of digital values, all formed by mixed pixels (Fig. 10.6).

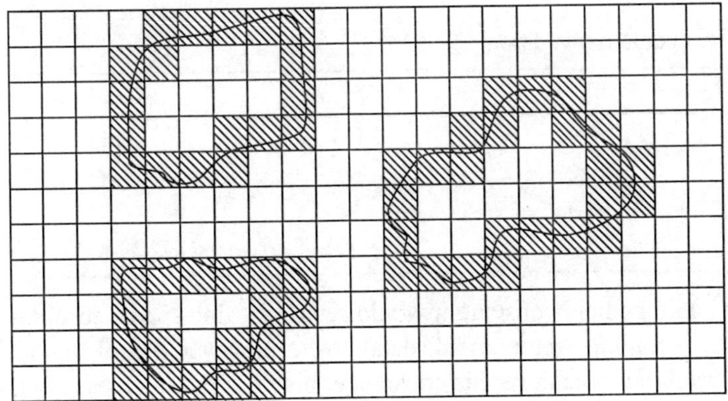

Fig. 10.5. Edge pixels.

It is interesting to examine the relationships between the numbers of mixed pixels in a given scene and the spatial resolution of the sensor. Studies have documented the increase in numbers of mixed pixels that occurs as spatial resolution decreases. Because the numbers, sizes and shapes of landscape parcels vary greatly with season and geographic setting, there can be no generally applicable conclusion regarding this problem. Yet examination of a few simple examples may help us understand the general character of the problem.

Consider the same contrived scene that is examined at several different spatial resolutions (Fig. 10.7). This scene consists of two contrasting categories with two parcels of one superimposed against the more extensive background of the other. This image is then examined at four levels of spatial resolution; for each level of detail, pixels are categorised as 'background,' 'interior,' or border.' (Background and interior pixels consist only of a single category; border pixels are those composed of two categories.) A tabulation of proportions of the total in each category revals a consistent pattern (Table 10.1). As resolution becomes coarser, the number of mixed pixels increases (naturally) at the expense of the number of pure background and pure interior pixels. In this example, interior pixels experience the larger loss, but this result is the consequence of the specific circumstances of this example and is unlikely to reveal any generally applicable conclusions.

'Mosiac' pixels
All pixels are mixed pixels

Worst case situation: Feature represented only by mixed pixels

Fig. 10.6. Mixed pixels generated by image of landscape composed of small parcels.

Table 10.1. Summary of data derived from Fig. 10.7.

Spatial resolution		*Total*	*Mixed*	*Interior*	*Background*
Fine	A	900	109	143	648
	B	225	59	25	141
	C	100	34	6	60
Coarse	D	49	23	1	25

If other factors could be held constant, it would seem that fine spatial resolution would offer many practical advantages, including capture of fine detail. Note, however, the substantial increases in the total numbers of pixels required to achieve this advantage; note too that increases in the numbers of pixels produce compensating disadvantages, including increased costs. Also, this example does not consider another important effect often encountered as spatial resolution is increased: the finer detail may resolve features not recorded at coarser detail, thereby increasing, rather than decreasing, the proportions of mixed pixels. This effect may explain some of the results observed by Sadowski and Sarno, who found that classification accuracy decreased as spatial resolution became finer.

Marsh and others have reviewed strategies for resolving the percentages of components that compose the ground areas with mixed pixels. The measured digital value for each pixel is determined by the brightnesses of distinct categories within that pixel area projected on the ground, as integrated by the sensor over the area of the pixel. For example, the projection of a pixel on the earth's surface may encompass areas of open water (W) and forest (F). Assume that we know that (a) the digital value for such a pixel is 'mixed,' not 'pure'; (b) the mean digital value for water in all bands is i (W_i) (c) the mean digital value for forest in all bands is (F_i); and (d) the observed value of the mixed pixel in all spectral bands is (M_i). We wish then to find the areal percentages P_W and P_F that contribute to the observed value M_i.

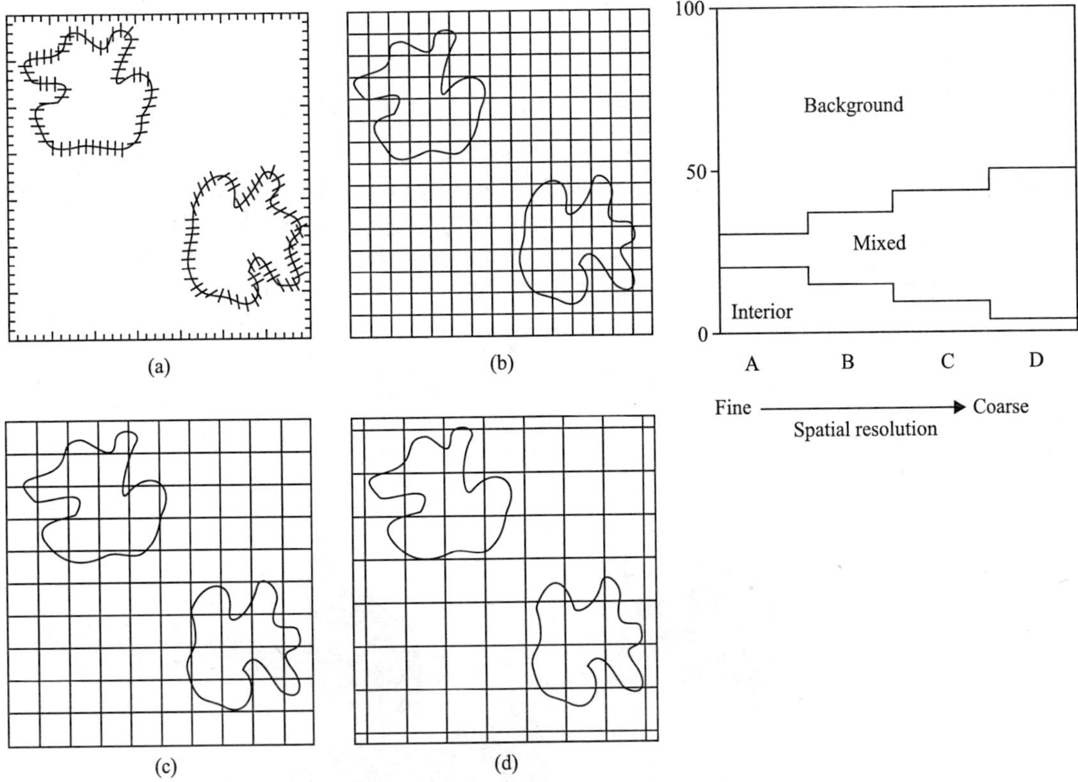

Fig. 10.7. Influence of spatial resolution on proportions of mixed pixels.

Marsh outline several strategies for estimating P_W and P_F under these conditions; the simplest, if not the most accurate, is the weighted average methods:

$$P_W = (M_i - F_i)/(W_i - F_i) \qquad \text{... (10.2)}$$

An example can be shown using the following data:

	Band			
	1	*2*	*3*	*4*
Means for the mixed pixel (M_i):	16	12	16	18
Means for forest (F_i):	23	16	32	35
Means for water (W_i):	9	8	0	1

Using Equation 10.2, the areal proportion of the mixed pixel composed of the water category can be estimated as follows:

Band 1: $P_W = (16 - 23)/(9 - 23) = -7/-14 = 0.50$

Band 2: $P_W = (12 - 16)/(8 - 16) = -4/-8 = 0.50$

Band 3: $P_W = (16 - 32)/(0 - 32) = -16/-32 = 0.50$

Band 4: $P_W = (18 - 35)/(1 - 35) = -17/-34 = 0.50$

Thus, the mixed pixel is apparently composed of about 50 per cent water and 50 per cent forest. Note that in practice we may not know which pixels are mixed and may not know the categories that might contribute to the mixture. Note also that this procedure may yield different estimates for each band. Other procedures, too lengthy for concise description here, may give more suitable results in some instances.

SPATIAL AND RADIOMETRIC RESOLUTION: A SIMPLE EXAMPLE

Some of these effects can be illustrated by an artificial example. The contrived scene in Fig. 10.8 is composed of two water bodies (W), several areas of forest (F), a large area of pasture (P) and a cultivated region (A) composed of a pattern of agricultural fields, some with mature crops, others composed of plowed bare ground. A digital representation of this scene might resemble Fig. 10.9, the product of an imaginary sensor with fine spatial and radiometric resolution operating in the near infrared portion of the spectrum.

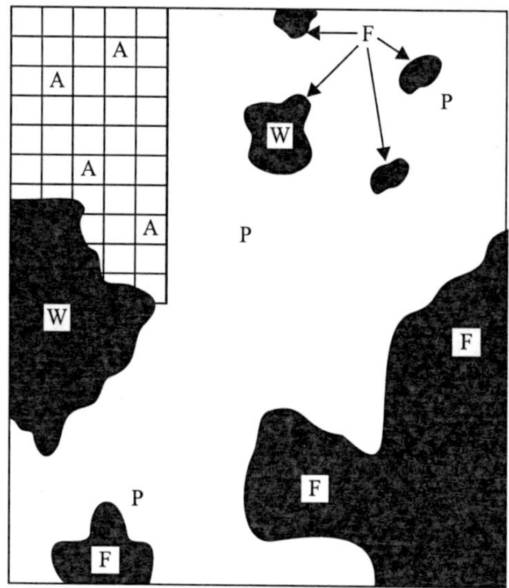

Fig. 10.8. Hypothetical landscape.

This hypothetical sensor records the scene at 10 brightness levels, from '0' (very dark) to '9' (very bright). In digital representation, the water bodies are very dark mainly '0s' and '1s'; forest is brighter, '3s' and '5s'. Pasture has an intermediate brightness of '2'. Agricultural land is represented either as '0' (the dark areas of bare soil) or '9' (the brighter areas of living vegetation).

Figure 10.10a. represents the same scene as portrayed at high spatial resolution, but very low radiometric resolution; the sizes of the pixels are the same as in Fig. 10.10, but only two levels of brightness are used. (Pixels darker than 5 in Fig. 10.9 are coded 0 in Fig. 10.10a; those brighter than 5 are coded 1.) At such coarse radiometric resolution few features in the original scene can be recognised, even though the spatial resolution remains constant from one to the other.

```
0 9 0 9 9 2 2 2 3 2 2 3 2 2 2 2
9 9 9 9 9 3 2 2 2 2 2 2 3 2 2 2
9 0 0 9 9 2 2 2 0 2 3 2 2 2 2 2
9 9 9 9 0 3 2 2 0 0 2 2 3 2 3 2
9 8 9 9 9 3 2 2 2 2 2 2 2 2 2 2
8 6 9 8 0 3 2 2 2 2 2 2 2 3 2 2
1 0 0 6 9 2 2 2 2 2 2 2 2 3 2 5
1 0 1 9 8 2 2 2 2 2 2 2 2 5 5 5
0 0 0 0 7 2 2 2 2 2 2 2 5 5 5 5
0 1 0 1 0 2 2 2 2 2 2 2 3 5 5 5
0 0 0 0 2 2 2 2 2 2 2 2 5 3 5 3
0 0 0 2 2 2 2 2 5 5 2 2 5 5 3 3
2 1 2 2 2 2 2 2 3 5 5 5 5 3 5 3
2 2 2 3 2 2 2 2 5 5 5 3 5 5 3 5
2 2 3 5 5 2 2 2 2 2 2 2 5 3 3 3
2 2 2 5 5 3 2 2 2 2 2 2 3 5 5 5
```

Fig. 10.9. Digital representation of Fig. 10.8.

```
0 1 0 1 1 0 0 0 0 0 0 0 0 0 0 0
1 1 1 1 1 0 0 0 0 0 0 0 0 0 0 0
1 0 0 1 1 0 0 0 0 0 0 0 0 0 0 0
1 1 1 1 1 0 0 0 0 0 0 0 0 0 0 0
1 1 1 1 1 0 0 0 0 0 0 0 0 0 0 0
1 1 1 1 0 0 0 0 0 0 0 0 0 0 0 0
0 0 0 1 1 0 0 0 0 0 0 0 0 0 0 1
0 0 0 1 1 0 0 0 0 0 0 0 0 1 1 1
0 0 0 0 1 0 0 0 0 0 0 0 1 1 1 1
0 0 0 0 0 0 0 0 0 0 0 0 0 1 1 1
0 0 0 0 0 0 0 0 0 0 0 0 1 0 1 0
0 0 0 0 0 0 0 0 1 1 0 0 1 1 0 1
0 0 0 0 0 0 0 0 0 1 1 1 1 0 1 0
0 0 0 0 0 0 0 0 1 1 1 0 1 1 0 1
0 0 0 1 1 0 0 0 0 0 0 0 1 1 1 1
0 0 0 1 1 0 0 0 0 0 0 0 1 1 1 1
```

(a)

```
0 2 0 2 2 0 0 0 1 0 0 1 0 0 0 0
2 2 2 2 2 1 0 0 0 0 0 0 1 0 0 0
2 0 0 2 2 0 0 0 0 0 0 1 0 0 0 0
2 2 2 2 0 1 0 0 0 0 0 0 1 0 1 0
2 2 2 2 2 0 0 0 0 0 0 0 0 0 0 0
2 1 2 2 0 0 0 0 0 0 0 0 0 1 0 0
0 0 0 1 2 0 0 0 0 0 0 0 0 0 0 1
0 0 0 2 2 0 0 0 0 0 0 0 0 1 1 1
0 0 0 0 2 0 0 0 0 0 0 0 1 1 1 1
0 0 0 0 0 0 0 0 0 0 0 0 1 1 1 1
0 0 0 0 0 0 0 0 0 0 0 0 1 1 1 1
0 0 0 0 0 0 0 0 1 1 0 0 1 1 1 1
0 0 0 0 0 0 0 0 1 1 1 1 1 1 1 1
0 0 0 1 0 0 0 0 1 1 1 1 1 1 1 1
0 0 0 1 1 0 0 0 0 0 0 0 1 1 1 1
0 0 0 1 1 0 0 0 0 0 0 0 1 1 1 1
```

(b)

```
7 7|7 7|6 6|2 2|2 2|2 2|2 2|2 2
7 7|7 7|6 6|2 2|2 2|2 2|2 2|2 2
7 7|7 7|4 4|2 2|3 3|2 2|2 2|2 2
7 7|7 7|4 4|2 2|3 3|2 2|2 2|2 2
8 8|9 9|4 4|2 2|2 2|2 2|2 2|2 2
8 8|9 9|4 4|2 2|2 2|2 2|2 2|2 2
0 0|4 4|5 5|2 2|2 2|2 2|3 3|4 4
0 0|4 4|5 5|2 2|2 2|2 2|3 3|4 4
0 0|0 0|3 3|2 2|2 2|2 2|4 4|5 5
0 0|0 0|3 3|2 2|2 2|2 2|4 4|5 5
0 0|0 0|2 2|2 2|4 4|2 2|4 4|4 4
0 0|0 0|2 2|2 2|4 4|2 2|4 4|4 4
2 2|2 2|2 2|2 2|4 4|4 4|4 4|4 4
2 2|2 2|2 2|2 2|4 4|4 4|4 4|4 4
2 2|4 4|4 4|2 2|2 2|3 3|4 4|4 4
2 2|4 4|4 4|2 2|2 2|3 3|4 4|4 4
```

(c)

```
7 7 7 7|3 3 3 3|2 2 2 2|2 2 2 2
7 7 7 7|3 3 3 3|2 2 2 2|2 2 2 2
7 7 7 7|3 3 3 3|2 2 2 2|2 2 2 2
7 7 7 7|3 3 3 3|2 2 2 2|2 2 2 2
5 5 5 5|4 4 4 4|2 2 2 2|3 3 3 3
5 5 5 5|4 4 4 4|2 2 2 2|3 3 3 3
5 5 5 5|4 4 4 4|2 2 2 2|3 3 3 3
5 5 5 5|4 4 4 4|2 2 2 2|3 3 3 3
0 0 0 0|2 2 2 2|2 2 2 2|4 4 4 4
0 0 0 0|2 2 2 2|2 2 2 2|4 4 4 4
0 0 0 0|2 2 2 2|2 2 2 2|4 4 4 4
0 0 0 0|2 2 2 2|2 2 2 2|4 4 4 4
2 2 2 2|2 2 2 2|4 4 4 4|4 4 4 4
2 2 2 2|2 2 2 2|4 4 4 4|4 4 4 4
2 2 2 2|2 2 2 2|4 4 4 4|4 4 4 4
2 2 2 2|2 2 2 2|4 4 4 4|4 4 4 4
```

(d)

Fig. 10.10. Fig 10.9 represented at (a) coarse radiometric resolution; (b) at modest radiometric resolution; (c) at a modest level of spatial resolution; and (d) at coarse spatial resolution.

Figure 10.10b shows the original scene recorded at finer radiometric resolution. Three brightness levels are formed by representing the original 0's, 1's and 2's as 0's; the original 3's, 4's, 5's and 6's as 1's; and the original 7's, 8's and 9's, as 2's. In this image the distinction between pasture and forest is evident, but the contrast between water and pasture is insufficient for these two categories to be represented as separate features.

Figures 10.10c and 10.10d show the effects of changing spatial resolution while retaining essentially the same level of radiometric resolution. In Fig. 10.10c spatial resolution has been decreased to show one-fourth of the detail visible in Fig. 10.9; each pixel is formed by the average of four of the smaller original pixels. Here many of the major features in the original scene are recognisable, although sizes, shapes and positions are indistinct. Figure. 10.10d shows the scene at extremely coarse spatial resolution; these values are formed by averaging brightness values over areas 16 times as large as those of the original pixels. Many of the major difference in brightness are distinguishable, although the pattern is greatly altered from the original distribution in Fig. 10.9.

INTERACTIONS WITH THE LANDSCAPE

Although most discussions of image resolution tend to focus upon sensor characteristics, understanding the significance of image resolution in the application sciences requires assessment of the effect of specific resolutions upon images of specific landscapes or classes of landscapes. For example, relatively low resolution may be sufficient for recording the essential features of landscapes with rather coarse fabrics (e.g., the broad-scale patterns of the agricultural fields of the North American Great Plains), but inadequate for imaging complex landscapes composed of many small parcels with low contrast.

Podwysocki's studies of field sizes in the major grain-producing regions of the world is an excellent example of the systematic investigation of this topic. His research can be placed in the context of the widespread interest in accurate forecasts of world wheat production in the years that followed large international wheat purchases by the erstwhile Soviet Union in 1972. Computer models of biophysical processes of crop growth and maturation could provide accurate estimates of yields (given suitable climatological data), but estimates of total production also require accurate estimates of planted acreage. Satellite imagery would seem to provide the capability to derive the required estimates of area plowed and planted. Podwysocki attempted to define the extent to which the spatial resolution of the Landsat MSS would be capable of providing the detail necessary to provide the required estimates.

He examined Landsat MSS scenes of the United States, China, the erstwhile Soviet Union, Argentina and other wheat-producing regions, sampling fields for measurements of length, width and area. His data are summarised by frequency distributions of field sizes for samples of each of the world's major wheat-producing regions. (He used his samples to find the Gaussian distributions for each of his samples, so he was able to extrapolate the frequency distributions to estimate frequencies at sizes smaller than the resolution of the MSS data). Cumulative frequency distributions for his normalised data reveal the percentages of each sample that equal or exceed specific areas (Fig. 10.11). For example, the curve for India reveals that 99 per cent (or more) of this sample were at least 1 ha in size and that all were smaller than about 100 ha (247 acres) and that we can expect the Indian wheat fields to be smaller than those in Kansas. These data and others presented in his study, provide the basis for evaluating the effectiveness of a given resolution in monitoring features of specified sizes. This example is especially instructive because it emphasises not only the differences in average field size in the different regions (shown in Fig. 10.11 by the point where each curve crosses the 50 per cent line), but also the differences in variation of field size between the varied regions (shown in Fig. 10.11 by the slopes of the curves).

In a different analysis of relationships between sensor resolution and landscape detail, Simonett and Coiner examined 106 sites in the United States, each selected to represent a major land-use region. Their study was conducted prior to the launch of Landsat 1 with the objective of assessing the effectiveness of MSS spatial resolution in recording differences between major land-use regions in the United States. Considered as a whole, their sites represent a broad range of physical and cultural patterns in the 48 co-terminous states.

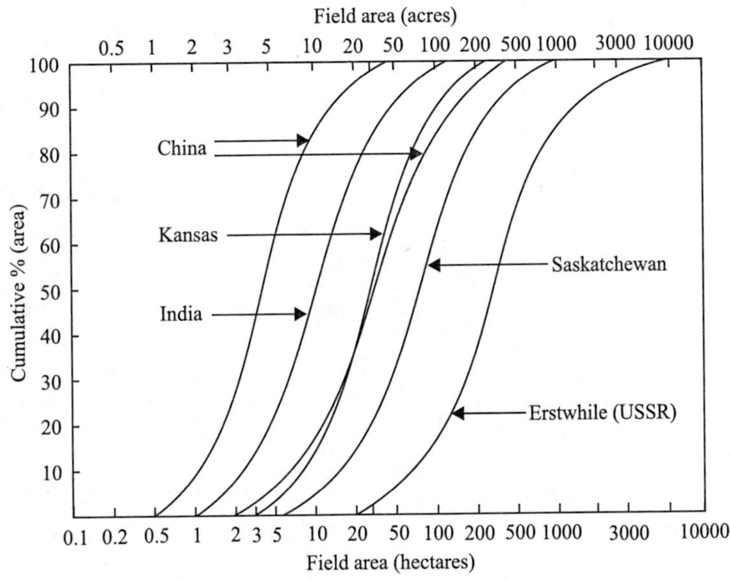

Fig. 10.11. Field size distributions for selected wheat-producing regions.

For each site they simulated the effects of imaging with low-resolution imagery by superimposing grids over aerial photographs, with grid dimensions corresponding to ground distances of 800, 400, 200 and 100 ft. Samples were randomly selected within each site. Each sample consisted of the number of land-use category within cells of each size and thereby formed a measure of landscape diversity, as considered at several spatial resolutions. For example, those landscapes that show only a single land-use category at the 800-ft. resolution have a very coarse fabric and would be effectively imaged at the low resolution of satellite sensors. Those landscapes that have many categories, within the 100 ft. grid are so complex that very fine spatial resolution would be required to record the pattern of landscape variation. Their analysis grouped sites according to their behaviour at various resolutions. They reported that natural landscapes appeared to be more susceptible than man-made landscapes to analysis at the relatively coarse resolution of the Landsat MSS.

Welch and Pannell examined Landsat MSS (bands 2 and 4) and Landsat 3 RBV images (in both pictorial and digital formats) to evaluate their suitability as sources of landscape information at levels of detail consistent with a map scale of 1:2,50,000. Images of three study areas in China provided a variety of urban and agricultural landscapes for study, representing a range of spatial detail and a number of geographical settings. Their analysis of modulation transfer functions reveals that the RBV imagery represents an improvement in spatial resolution of about 1.7 over the MSS imagery and the Landsat 4 TM provided an improvement of about 1.4 over the RBV (for target: background contrasts of about 1.6:1).

Features appearing on each image were evaluated with corresponding representations on 1:2,50,000 maps in respect to size, shape and contrast. A numerical rating system provided scores for each image based upon the numbers of features represented and the quality of the representations on each form of imagery. MSS images portrayed about 40 to 50 per cent of the features shown on the usual 1:2,50,000 topographic maps. MSS band 2 was the most effective for identification of airfields; band 4 performed very well for identification and delineation of water bodies. Overall, the MSS images achieved scores of about 40 to 50 per cent. RBV images attained higher overall scores (50 to 80 per cent), providing considerable improvement in representation of high-contrast targets, but little improvement in imaging of detail in fine-textured urban landscapes. Welch and Pannell concluded that spatial resolution of MSS and RBV images were inadequate for compilation of usual map detail at 1:2,50,000.

11

Pre-processing

INTRODUCTION

In the context of digital analysis of remotely sensed data, pre-processing refers to those operations that are preliminary to the main analysis. Typical pre-processing operations could include: (i) radiometric pre-processing to adjust digital values for the effect of a hazy atmosphere; and (ii) geometric pre-processing to bring an image into registration with a map or another image.

Once corrections have been made, the data can then be subjected to the primary analyses described in subsequent chapters. Thus pre-processing forms a preparatory phase that, in principle, improves image quality as the basis for later analyses that will extract information from the image.

It should be emphasised that, although certain pre-processing procedures are frequently used, there can be no definitive list of 'standard' pre-processing steps because each project requires individual attention and some pre-processing decisions may be a matter of personal preference. Furthermore, the quality of image data vary greatly, so some data may not require the pre-processing that would be necessary in other instances. Pre-processing changes data.

We assume that such changes are beneficial, but the analyst should remember that pre-processing may create artifacts that are not immediately obvious. As a result, the analyst should tailor pre-processing to the data at hand and the needs of specific projects, using only those pre-processing operations essential to obtain a specific result.

Pre-processing includes a wide range of operations, from the very simple to extremes of abstractness and complexity. Most can be categorised into one of the three groups:

1. Feature extraction.
2. Radiometric corrections.
3. Geometric corrections.

Although there are far too many pre-processing methods to discuss in detail here, we will illustrate some of the principles important for each group.

FEATURE EXTRACTION

In the context of image processing, the term feature extraction (or feature selection) has specialised meaning. 'Features' are not geographical features, visible on an image, but are rather 'statistical' characteristics of image data: individual bands or combinations of band values that carry information concerning systematic variation within the scene. Thus feature extraction could also be known as 'information extraction,' isolation of components within multispectral data that are most useful in portraying the essential elements of an image. In theory, discarded data contain noise and errors present in original data. Thus feature extraction may increase accuracy. In addition, feature extraction reduces the number of spectral channels or bands, that must be analysed, thereby reducing computational demands. After feature selection is complete, the analyst works with fewer but more potent channels. The reduced data set may convey almost as much information as does the complete data set. Feature selection may increase speed and reduce cost of analysis.

Multispectral data, by their nature, consist of several channels of data. Although some images may have as few as 3, 4 or 7 channels, other image data may have many more, possibly 200 or more channels. With so much data, processing of even modest-sized images requires considerable time. In this context, feature selection assumes considerable practical significance, as image analysts wish to reduce the amount of data while retaining effectiveness and/or accuracy.

Our examples here are based on TM data, which provide enough channels to illustrate the concept, but are compact enough to be reasonably concise (Table 11.1). A variance-co-variance matrix shows interrelationships between pairs of bands; some pairs show rather strong correlations—for example, bands 1 and 3 and 2 and 3 both show correlations above 0.9. High correlation between pairs of bands means that the values in the two channels are closely related. Thus, as values in channel 2 rise or fall, so do those in channel 3; one channel tends to duplicate information in the other. Feature selection attempts to identify, then remove, such duplication so that the data set can include maximum information using the minimum number of channels.

Table 11.1. Similarity matrices for seven bands of a TM scene.

	Co-variance matrix						
	1	*2*	*3*	*4*	*5*	*6*	*7*
1	48.8	29.2	43.2	50.0	76.5	0.9	44.9
2	29.2	20.3	29.0	48.6	65.4	1.5	32.8
3	43.2	29.0	46.4	59.9	101.2	0.6	53.5
4	49.9	48.6	59.9	327.8	325.6	12.4	104.32
5	76.5	65.4	101.2	325.6	480.5	10.2	188.5
6	0.9	1.5	0.6	12.5	10.2	14.0	1.1
7	45.0	32.8	53.5	104.5	188.5	1.1	90.8

	Co-variance matrix						
	1	*2*	*3*	*4*	*5*	*6*	*7*
1	1.00						
2	0.92	1.00					
3	0.90	0.94	1.00				
4	0.39	0.59	0.48	1.00			
5	0.49	0.66	0.67	0.82	1.00		
6	0.03	0.08	0.02	0.18	0.12	1.00	
7	0.67	0.76	0.82	0.60	0.90	0.02	1.00

For example, for data represented by Table 11.1, bands 3, 5 and 6 might include almost as much information as the entire set of seven channels because band 3 is closely related to bands 1 and 2, band 5 is closely related to bands 4 and 7 and band 6 carries information largely unrelated to any others. Therefore, the discarded channels (1, 2, 4 and 7) each resemble one of the channels that have been retained. So a simple approach to feature selection discards unneeded bands, thereby reducing the number of channels. Although this kind of selection can be used as a kind of rudimentary feature extraction, typically feature selection is a more complex process based upon statistical interrelationships between channels.

A common approach to feature selection applies a method of data analysis called principal components analysis (PCA). This text will offer only a superficial description, as more complete explanation requires the level of detail provided by Davis and others. In essence, PCA identifies the optimum linear combinations of the original channels that can account for variation of pixel values in an image. Linear combinations are of the form

$$A = C_1X_1 + C_2X_2 + C_3X_3 + C_4X_4 \quad \text{... (11.1)}$$

where X_1, X_2, X_3 and X_4 are pixel values in four spectral channels and C_1, C_2, C_3 and C_4 are coefficients applied individually to the values in the respective channels. 'A' represents a transformed value for the pixel. Assume, as an example, that $C_1 = 0.35$, $C_2 = -0.08$, $C_3 = 0.36$ and $C_4 = 0.86$. For a pixel with $X_1 = 28$, $X_2 = 29$, $X_3 = 21$, $X_4 = 54$, the transformation assumes a value of 61.48. Optimum values for coefficients are calculated by a procedure that ensures that the values they produce account for maximum variation within the entire data set. Thus this set of coefficients provides the maximum information that can be conveyed by any single channel formed by a linear combination of the original channels. If we make an image from all the values formed by applying this procedure to an entire image, we generate a single band of data that provides an optimum depiction of the information present within the four channels of the original scene.

Effectiveness of this procedure depends, of course, upon calculation of the optimum coefficients. Here our description must be, by intention, abbreviated because calculation of the coefficients is accomplished by methods requiring full explanations, such as those given by upper-level statistics texts or discussions such as those of Davis and Gould. For the present, the important point is that PCA permits identification of a set of coefficients that concentrates maximum information in a single band.

The same procedure also yields a second set of coefficients that will yield a second set of values (we could represent this as the B set or B image) that will be a less effective conveyor of information, but will still represent variation of pixels within the image. In all, the procedure will yield seven sets of coefficients (one set for each band in the original image) and therefore will produce seven sets of values or bands (here denoted as A, B, C, D, E, F and G), each in sequence conveying less information than the preceding band. Thus in Table 11.2 transformed channels I and II (each formed from linear combinations of the seven original channels) together account for about 93 per cent of the total variation in the data, whereas channels III-VII together account for only about 7 per cent of the total variance. the analyst may be willing to discard the variables that convey 7 per cent of the variance as a means of reducing the number of channels. The analyst still retains 93 per cent of the original information in a much more concise form. Thus feature selection reduces the size of the data set by eliminating replication of information.

The effect is easily seen in Fig 11.1, which shows transformed data for a subset of a Landsat TM scene. Image PC I and PC II are the most potent; PC III, PC IV, PC VI and PC VII show the decline in information content, such that the final images record (one assumes) artifacts of system noise, atmospheric scatter and other undesirable contributions to image brightness. If these two channels are excluded from subsequent analysis, it is likely that accuracy can be retained (relative to the entire set of four channels) while also reducing costs.

Table 11.2. Results of principal components analysis of data in Table 11.1.

	Component						
	I	*II*	*III*	*IV*	*V*	*VI*	*VII*
				Eigenvectors			
% var.:	82.5%	10.2%	5.3%	1.3%	0.4%	0.3%	0.1%
EV:	848.44	104.72	54.72	13.55	4.05	2.78	0.77
	0.14	0.35	0.60	0.07	–0.14	–0.66	–0.20
	0.11	0.16	0.32	0.03	–0.07	–0.15	–0.90
	0.37	0.35	0.39	–0.04	–0.22	0.71	–0.36
	0.56	–0.71	0.37	–0.09	–0.18	0.03	–0.64
	0.74	0.21	–0.50	0.06	–0.39	–0.10	0.03
	0.01	–0.05	0.02	0.99	0.12	0.08	–0.04
	0.29	0.42	–0.08	–0.09	0.85	0.02	–0.02
				Loadings			
Band 1	0.562	0.519	0.629	0.037	–0.040	–0.160	–0.245
Band 2	0.729	0.369	0.529	0.027	–0.307	–0.576	–0.177
Band 3	0.707	0.528	0.419	–0.022	–0.659	–0.179	–0.046
Band 4	0.903	–0.401	0.150	–0.017	0.020	0.003	–0.003
Band 5	0.980	0.098	–0.166	0.011	–0.035	–0.008	–0.001
Band 6	0.144	–0.150	0.039	0.969	0.063	0.038	–0.010
Band 7	0.873	0.448	–0.062	–0.033	0.180	0.004	–0.002

This method is not the only means for feature selection, but it does illustrate the objectives of this step: to reduce the number of channels to be examined while simultaneously retaining as much information as possible and reducing contributions of noise and error.

SUBSETS

Because of the very large sizes of many remotely sensed images, analysts typically work with those segments of full images that specifically pertain to the task at hand. Therefore, to minimise computer storage and the analyst's time and effort, one of the first tasks in each project is to prepare subsets, portions of larger images selected to show only the region of interest.

Although selecting subsets would not appear to be one of remote sensing's most challenging tasks, it is more difficult than one might first suppose. Often subsets must be 'registered' (matched) to other data or to other projects, so it is necessary to find distinctive landmarks in both sets of data to assure that coverages coincide spatially. Second, since time and computational effort devoted to matching images to maps or other images (as described below) increase with large images, it is often convenient to prepare subsets before registration. Yet if the subset is too small, then it may be difficult to identify sufficient landmarks for efficient registration. Therefore, it may be useful to prepare a preliminary subset, large enough to conduct the image registration effectively, before selecting the final, smaller, subset for analytical use (Fig. 11.1).

The same kinds of considerations apply in other steps of an analysis. Subsets should be large enough to provide context required for the specific analysis at hand. For example, it may be important to prepare subsets large enough to provide sufficient numbers of training fields for image classification or a sufficient set of sites for accuracy assessment.

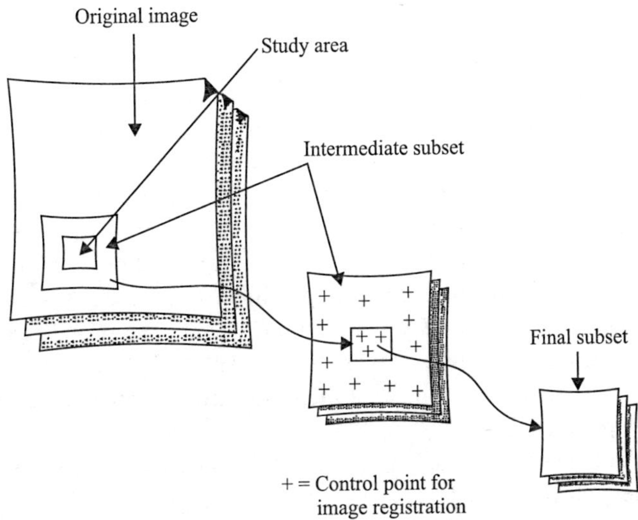

Fig. 11.1. Subsets. Sometimes a subset of a particular area is too small to encompass sufficient points to allow the subset to be accurately matched to an accurate map. Selection of an intermediate temporary subset permits accurate registration using an adequate number of control points. After the temporary subset has been matched to the map, the study area can be more precisely subset without concern for the distribution of control points.

Radiometric Pre-processing

Many pre-processing operations fall into the category of image restoration, the effort to remove the undesirable influence of atmospheric interference, system noise and sensor motion. By applying a knowledge of the nature of these effects, it is possible to estimate their magnitude, then to remove or minimise their influence upon the data used in later steps of the analysis. After removing these effects, the data are said to be 'restored' to their (hypothetical) correct condition, although we can, of course, never know what the correct values might be and must always remember that attempts to correct data may themselves introduce errors. So the analyst must decide if the errors removed are likely to be greater than those that might be introduced. Typically, image restoration includes efforts to correct for both radiometric and geometric errors.

Radiometric pre-processing influences the brightness values of an image to correct for sensor malfunctions or to adjust the values to compensate for atmospheric degradation. Any sensor that observes the earth's surface using visible or near visible radiation will record a mixture of two kinds of brightnesses. One brightness is due to the reflectance for the earths's surface—the brightnesses that are of interest for remote sensing. But the sensor also observes the brightness of the atmosphere itself—the effects of scattering. Thus an observed digital brightness value (e.g., '56') might be in part the result of surface reflectance (e.g., '45') and in part the result of atmospheric scattering (e.g., '11'). Of course we cannot immediately distinguish the two brightnesses, so one objective of atmospheric correction is to identify and separate these two components so the main analysis can focus upon examination of correct surface brightness (the '45' in this example). Ideally, atmospheric correction should find separate correction for each pixel in the scene; in practice, we may apply the same correction to an entire band or apply a single factor to a local region within the image.

Pre-processing operations to correct for atmospheric degradation fall into three rather broad categories. First are those procedures based upon efforts to model the physical behaviour of the radiation as it passes through the atmosphere. Application of such models permits observed reflectances to be adjusted to approximate true values that might be observed under a clear atmosphere, thereby improving image quality and accuracies of analyses. Physical models (i.e., models that attempt to model the physical process of scattering at the level of individual particles and molecules) have important advantages with respect to rigour, accuracy and applicability to a wide variety of circumstances. But they also have significant disadvantages. Often they are very complex, usually requiring use of intricate computer programmes. A more important limitation is the requirement for detailed meteorological information pertaining to atmospheric humidity and the concentrations of atmospheric particles. Such data may be difficult to obtain in the necessary detail and may apply only to a few points within a Landsat scene, for example. Also, atmospheric conditions vary with altitude and the radiosonde data that depict changes with altitude are routinely collected only at a few locations. Although the availability of data collected by meteorological satellites offers the possibility for increased use of such methods, routine application of such models is not now practicable.

Among the most widely used and widely available of the physical models are the LOWTRAN 7 and MODTRAN models developed by the U S Air Force.

LOWTRAN calculates atmospheric transmittance and atmospheric background radiance for a variety of atmospheric conditions (Fig. 11.2). LOWTRAN applies relatively low spectral resolution (2.0 cm, in increments as small as 0.50 cm, beginning at 0.2 μm), whereas MODTRAN uses somewhat finer spectral resolution (0.2 cm). These programmes estimate atmospheric absorption and emission by atmospheric gasses (H_2O, NO_2, O, O_3, CH_4, CO_2, N_2O, CO, O_2, NH_3 and SO_2). These models accommodate differing atmospheric conditions, including seasonal and geographic variations, cloud conditions, rain and haze. The model considers all possible atmospheric paths.

A—second group of atmospheric correction procedures is based upon examination of reflectances from objects of known or assumed brightness recorded by multispectral imagery. From basic principles of atmospheric scattering, it is known that scattering is related to wavelength, sizes of atmospheric particles and their abundance. If a known target is observed using a set of multispectral measurements, the relationships between values in the separate bands can help assess atmospheric effects.

Ideally, the target consists of a natural or man-made feature that can be observed with airborne or ground-based instruments at the time of image acquisitions, so the analyst could know from measurements independent of the image the true brightness of the object when the image was acquired. However, in practice we seldom have such measurements and therefore we must look for features of known brightness, that commonly or fortuitously, appear within an image. In its simplest form, this strategy can be implemented by identifying a very dark object or feature within the scene. Such an object might be a large water body or possibly shadows cast by clouds or by large topographic features. In the infrared portion of the spectrum both water bodies and shadows should have brightness at or very near zero because clear water absorbs strongly in the near infrared spectrum and because very little infrared energy is scattered to the sensor from shadowed pixels. Analysts who examines such areas or the histograms of the digital values for a scene, can observe that the lowest values (for dark area, such as clear water bodies) are not zero, but some larger value. Typically, this value will differ from one band to the next, so, for example, for Landsat band 1 the value might be 12, for band 2 the value is 7, for band 3 the value is 2 and for band 4 the value is 2 (Fig. 11.3). These values, assumed to represent the value contributed by atmospheric scattering for each band, are then subtracted from all digital values for that scene and that band. Thus the lowest value in each band is set to zero, the dark black colour assumed to be the correct tone for a dark object in the absence of atmospheric scattering. This procedure forms one of the simplest, most direct methods for adjusting digital values for atmospheric degradation, known sometimes as the histogram minimum method (HMM).

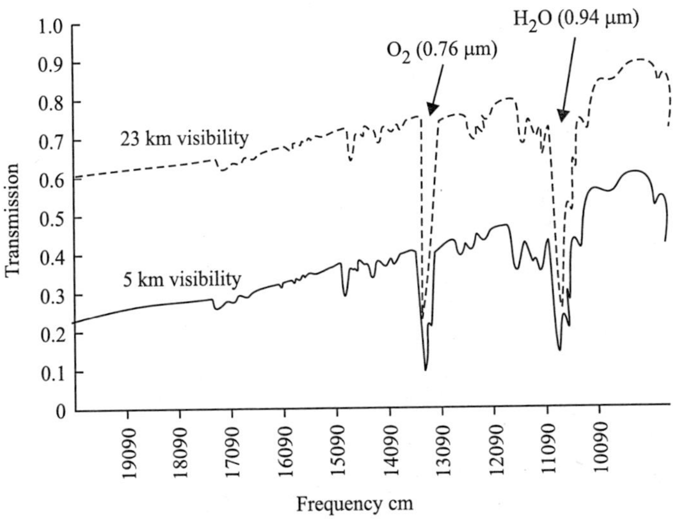

Fig. 11.2. LOWTRAN output.

This procedure has the advantages of simplicity, directness and almost universal applicability, as it exploits information present within the image itself. Yet it must be considered as an approximation; atmospheric effects change not only the position of the histogram on the axis, but also its shape (i.e., not all brightnesses are affected equally). Already explained that the atmosphere can cause dark pixels to become brighter and bright pixels to become darker, so application of a single correction to all pixels will provide only a rough adjustment for atmospheric effects. In addition, in arid regions observed at high sun angles, shadows, clouds and open water may be so rare or of such small areal extent that the method cannot be applied.

A more sophisticated approach retains the idea of examining brightness of objects within each scene, but attempts to exploit knowledge of interrelationships between separate spectral bands. Chavez devised a procedure that paired values from each band with values from band 7. The Y intercept of the regression line is then taken as the correction value for the specific band in question. Whereas the HMM procedure is applied to entire scenes or to very large areas, the regression technique can be applied to local areas (of possibly only 100 to 500 pixels each), assuring that the adjustment is tailored to conditions important within specific regions. An extension of the regression technique is to examine the variance–co-variance matrix, the set of variances and co-variance between all band pairs on the data. (This is the co-variance matrix method [CMM].) Both procedures assume that within a specified image region, variations in image brightness are due to topographic irregularities and reflectivity is constant (i.e., land-cover reflectivity in several bands is uniform for the region in question). Therefore, variations in brightness are caused by small-scale topographic shadowing (Fig. 11.3) and the dark regions reveal the scattering mentioned previously. Although these assumptions may not always be strictly met, the procedure, if applied with care and with knowledge of the local geographic setting, seems to be robust and often satisfactory. Campbell and Liu modified this strategy by using an automatic grouping procedure to ensure that regions are defined in such a way that their reflections are in fact uniform.

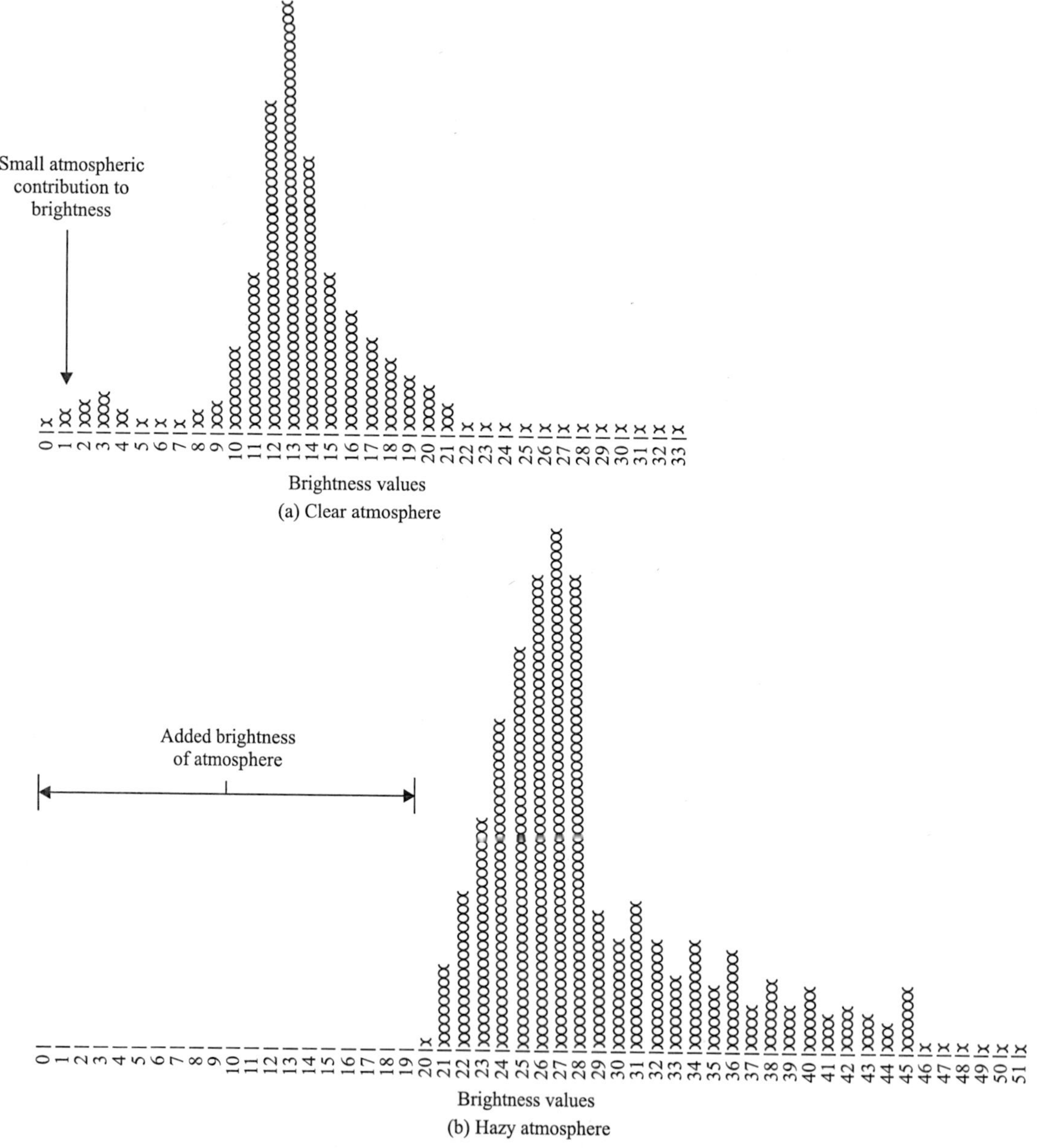

Fig. 11.3. Histogram minimum method for correction of atmospheric effects. The lowest brightness value in the scene is assumed to reveal the added brightness of the atmosphere and is then subtracted from all pixels in a specific band.

How can the analyst decide if atmospheric corrections are necessary? This may be a difficult decision, as effects of atmospheric degradation are not always immediately obvious from causal inspection. The analyst should always examine summary statistics for each scene, inspecting means, variances and frequency histograms for suggestions of poor image quality and the absence of dark values, especially if the image is known to show large water bodies (Fig. 11.4).

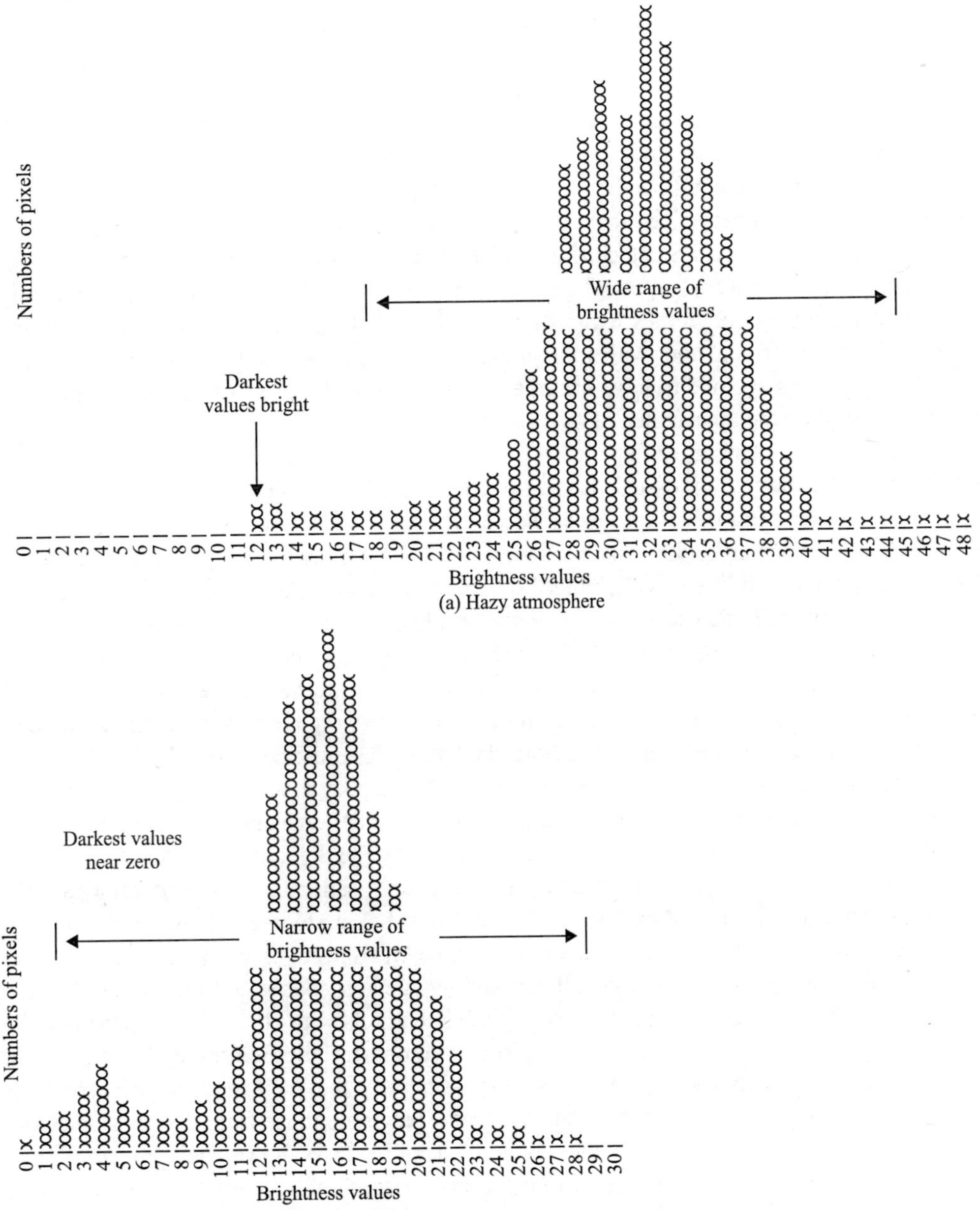

Fig. 11.4. Inspection of histogram for evidence of atmospheric degradation.

Of course, inspection of the image may reveal evidence suggesting a requirement for correction. Loss of resolution and low contrast may indicate poor atmospheric conditions. Sometimes the image date may itself suggest the nature of atmospheric quality. In the central United States, summer dates often imply high humidity, haze and poor visibility, whereas autumn, winter and spring dates are often characterised by clearer atmospheric conditions. Thus the image date may provoke further investigation by the analyst to determine if corrections are necessary. Finally, the analyst should examine summary statistics for the scene and especially the frequency histograms for each band.

Destriping

Landsat MSS data sometimes exhibit a kind of radiometric error known as sixth-line striping, caused by small differences in the sensitivities of detectors within the sensor. Within a given band, such differences appear on images as a horizontal banding or 'striping,' because individual scan lines exhibit unusually brighter or darker brightness values that contrast noticeably with the background brightnesses of the 'normal' detectors. Because MSS detectors are positioned in arrays of six lines. Striping may appear on only one or two bands of a multispectral image or may be severe for only a portion of a band. Other forms of digital imagery sometimes exhibit similar effects, all caused by difficulties in maintaining consistent calibration of detectors with in a single sensor. Campbell and Liu found that striping and paneling in digital data seemed to have minimal impact on the character of the data—much less than might be suggested by the appearance of the imagery.

Although sixth-line striping is often clearly visible as an obvious banding it may also be present in a more subtle form that may escape casual visual inspection. Destriping refers to the application of algorithms to adjust incorrect brightness values to values thought to be near the correct values. Some image-processing software provides special algorithms to detect striping. Such procedures search through an image line by line to look for systematic differences in average brightnesses of lines spaced at intervals of six; examination of the results permits the analyst to have objective evidence of the existence or absence of sixth-line striping (Table 11.3). If striping is present, the analyst must make a decision. If no correction is applied, the analysis must proceed with brightness values that are known to be incorrect. Conversely, efforts to correct for such serious errors may yield rather rudimentary approximations of the (unknown) true values. Often striping may be so severe that it is obvious the band lines must be adjusted.

A variety of destriping algorithms have been devised. All identify the values generated by the defective detectors by searching for lines that are noticeably brighter or darker than the lines in the remainder of the scene. These lines are presumably the bad lines caused by the defective detectors (especially if they occur at intervals of six lines). Then the destriping procedure estimates corrected values for the band lines. There are many different estimation procedures; most belong to one of two groups. One approach is to replace bad pixels with values based upon the average of adjacent pixels not influenced by striping; this approach is based upon the notion that the missing value is probably quite similar to the pixels that are nearby (Fig. 11.5a). A second strategy is to replace bad pixels with new values based upon the mean and standard deviation of the band in question or upon statistics developed for each detector (Fig. 11.5b). This second approach is based upon the assumption that the overall statistics for the missing data must, because there are so many pixels in the scene, resemble those from the good detectors.

The algorithm described by Rohde combines elements of both strategies. Their procedure attempts to bring all values in band to a normalised mean and variance, based on overall statistics for the entire band. Because brightnesses of individual regions within the scene may vary considerably from these overall values, a second algorithm can be applied to perform a local averaging to remove the remaining influences of striping. Some destriping algorithms depend entirely on local averaging; because they tend to degrade image resolution and introduce statistical dependencies between adjacent brightness values, it is probably best to be cautious in their application if alternatives are available.

Table 11.3. Results of a sixth-line striping analysis.

	Mean	*Standard deviation*
Entire image:	19.98	7.06
Detector 1:	19.07	6.53
Detector 2:	19.50	6.97
Detector 3:	19.00	6.78
Detector 4:	22.03	7.60
Detector 5:	21.09	7.34
Detector 6:	19.17	6.51

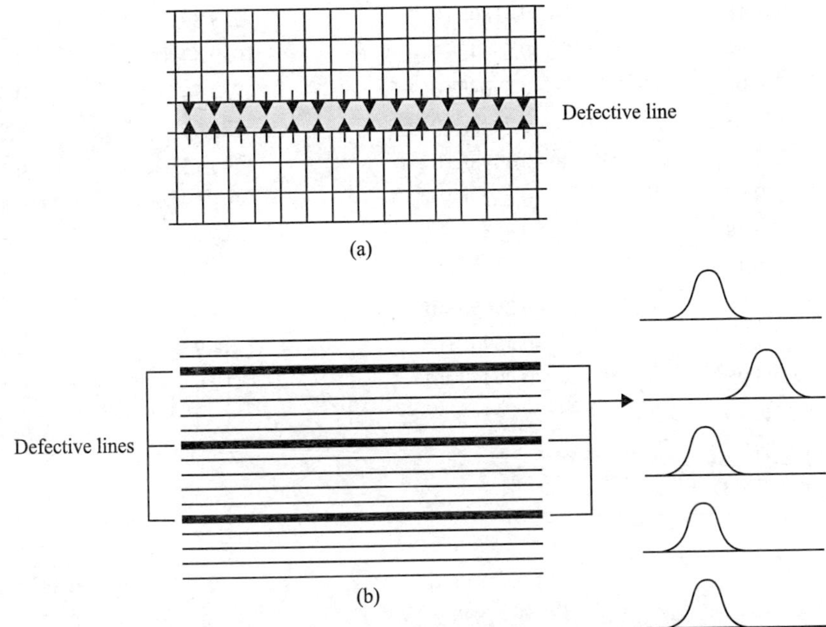

Fig. 11.5. Two strategies for destriping. (a) Local averaging. (b) Normalisation.

Table 11.4 shows the results for an analysis of striping in a Landsat MSS scene. The tabulation provides means and standard deviations of lines organised such that all lines collected by detector 1 are grouped together, all those collected by detector 2 are grouped together and so on. All the lines collected by the first detector are found by starting at the first line, then skipping to line 7, then to line 13 and so on. All the lines collected by the second detractor are found by starting at line 2, then skipping to line 8, then to line 14 and so on. For the image reported in Table 11.4, it is clear that detectors 4 and 5 are producing results that differ from the others—the means and standard deviations of the pixels collected by these detectors are higher than those of pixels collected by other detectors. The differences seem rather small—only two or three brightness values—yet the effect is usually quiet obvious to the eye probably because the brightness differences are organised in distinct linear patterns which attract the attention of the observer's visual system.

Table 11.4. Sample tabulation of data for GCPs.

Point No.	*Image X pixel*	*X pixel residual*	*Image Y pixel*	*Y pixel residual*
1	1269.75	–0.2471E+00	1247.59	0.1359E+02
2	867.91	–0.6093E+01	1303.90	0.8904E+01
3	467.79	–0.1121E+02	1360.51	0.5514E+01
4	150.52	0.6752E+02	1413.42	–0.8580E+01
5	82.20	–0.3796E+01	163.19	0.6189E+01
6	260.89	0.2890E+01	134.23	0.5234E+01
7	680.59	0.3595E+01	70.16	0.9162E+01
8	919.18	0.1518E+02	33.74	0.1074E+02
9	1191.71	0.6705E+01	689.27	0.1127E+02
10	1031.18	0.4180E+01	553.89	0.1189E+02
11	622.44	–0.6564E+01	1029.43	0.8427E+01
12	376.04	–0.5964E+01	737.76	0.6761E+01
13	162.56	–0.7443E+01	725.63	0.8627E+01
14	284.05	–0.1495E+02	1503.73	0.1573E+02
15	119.67	–0.8329E+01	461.59	0.4594E+01
16	529.78	–0.2243E+00	419.11	0.5112E+01
17	210.42	–0.1558E+02	1040.89	–0.1107E+01
18	781.85	–0.2915E+02	714.94	–0.1521E+03
19	1051.54	–0.4590E+00	1148.97	0.1697E+02
20	1105.95	0.9946E+01	117.04	0.1304E+02

X rms error = 18.26133

Y rms error = 35.33221

Total rms error = 39.77237

Point No.	*Error*	*Error contribution by point*
1	13.5913	0.3417
2	10.7890	0.2713
3	12.4971	0.3142
4	68.0670	1.7114
5	7.2608	0.1826
6	5.9790	0.1503
7	9.8416	0.2474
8	18.5911	0.4674
9	13.1155	0.3298
10	12.6024	0.3169

(Contd...)

Point No.	Error	Error contribution by point
11	10.6815	0.2686
12	9.0161	0.2267
13	11.3944	0.2865
14	21.6990	0.5456
15	9.5121	0.2392
16	5.1174	0.1287
17	15.6177	0.3927
18	154.8258	3.8928
19	16.9715	0.4267
20	16.3982	0.4123

Image Matching

Image matching is the process of superimposing two images of the same area, then moving them to find the position at which they best match. Visually, two transparencies have a registration point where the image detail matches. Digitally, there are many separate procedures; some are very complex. One of the simplest and most widely used strategies is to digitally overlay the two images, then calculate a correlation for the area where the two images overlap (or for some smaller zone). Matched positions are systematically shifted, pixel by pixel, until all possible matches have been attempted. At each position a new correlation value is calculated, then saved. The optimum position, presumably the correct registration, is the position that yields the highest correlations. This kind of image-matching procedure is important in many automated processes, including matching of digital stereo images.

A much more common problem is the registration of two images, meaning that two images are brought to registration, but one is usually altered using one of the procedures described below. (In image matching, the two images are not changed—we simply find the position at which the two match.) Typically, we wish to register a Landsat image to a planimetrically correct map or to register to images from different dates or to register Landsat and Seasat images of the same area. In each instance, we have the same problem: we must rearrange pixels to match to the new map or we must estimate pixel values at points that match the new distribution.

The most difficult but most rigorous approach to image registration is to apply knowledge of sensor geometry and motion to derive accurate coordinates for each pixel. To apply this approach, which we will designate as the analytical approach, the analyst must know the satellite altitude, its trajectory, the shape of the earth's surface, its motion relative to the satellite and the motion of the sensor scanner. Although for satellites such as Landsat factors are known with some precision, analytical image correction can correct only some of the geometric errors in images.

GEOMETRIC CORRECTION BY RE-SAMPLING

A second approach to image registration treats the problem in a completely different manner. No effort is made to apply our knowledge of system geometry; instead, the images are treated simply as an array of values that must be manipulated to create another array with the desired geometry.

This can be seen essentially as an interpolation problem similar to those routinely considered in cartography and other disciplines. In Fig. 11.6, the input image is represented as an array of open dots, each representing the center of a pixel in the uncorrected image. Superimposed over this image is a second array, symbolised by the solid dots, which shows the centers of pixels in the image transformed to have the desired geometric properties (the 'output' image). The locations of the output pixels are derived from locational information provided by ground control points (GCPs), locations on the input image that can be located with precision on the ground and on planimetrically correct maps. (If two images are to be registered, GCPs must be easily recognised on both images.) The locations of these points establish the geometry of the output image and its relationship to the input image. Thus this first step establishes the framework of pixel positions for the output image using the GCPs.

Fig. 11.6. Re-sampling. Open circles represent the reference grid of known values in the input image. Black dotes represent the regular grid of points to be estimated to form the output image. Each re-sampling method employs a different strategy to estimate values at the output grid, given known values for the input grid.

The next step is to decide how to best estimate the values of pixels in the corrected image, based upon information in the uncorrected image. The simplest strategy from a computational perspective is simply to assign each 'corrected' pixel the value from the nearest 'uncorrected' pixel. This is the nearest-neighbour approach to re-sampling (Fig. 11.7).

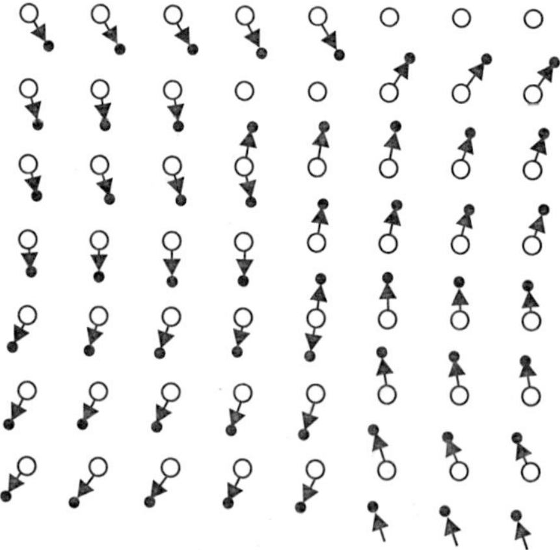

Fig. 11.7. Nearest neighbour re-sampling. Each estimated value (•) receives its value from the nearest points on the reference grid (○).

It has the advantages of simplicity and the ability to preserve original values in the unaltered scene. On the other hand, it may creates noticeable positional errors, which may be severe in linear features where the re-alignment of pixels is obvious. In Kovalick's study the nearest-neighbour method was computationally the most efficient of the three methods studied.

A second, more complex, approach to re-sampling is bilinear interpolation (Fig. 11.8). Bilinear interpolation calculates a value for each output pixel based upon a weighted average of the four nearest input pixels. In this context, 'weighted' means that nearer pixel values are given greater influence in calculating output values than are more distant pixels. Because each output value is based upon several input values, the output image will not have the unnaturally blocky appearance of some nearest-neighbour images. The image therefore has a more 'natural' look. Yet there are important changes. First, because bilinear interpolation creates new pixel values, the brightness values in the input image are lost. The analyst may find that the range of brightness values in the output image differs from those in the input image. Such changes to digital brightness values may be significant in later processing steps. Second, because the re-sampling is conducted by averaging over areas (i.e., blocks of pixels), it decreases spatial resolution by a kind of 'smearing' caused by averaging small features with adjacent background pixels.

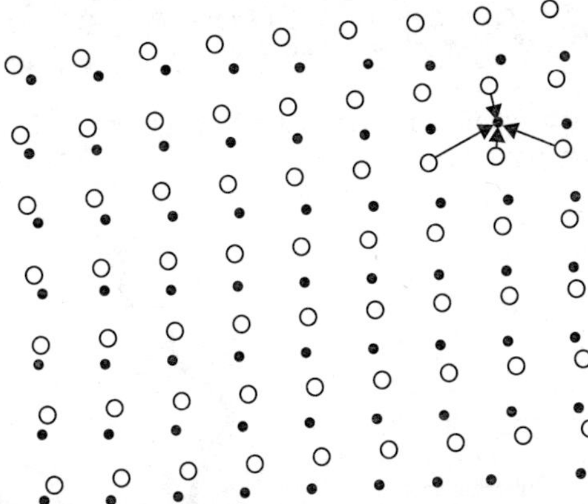

Fig. 11.8. Bilinear interpolation. Each estimated value in the output image is formed by calculating a weighted average of the four nearest neighbours in the input image. Each estimated value is weighted according to its distance from the known values in the input image.

Finally, the most sophisticated, most complex and (possibly) most widely used re-sampling method is cubic convolution (Fig. 11.9). Cubic convolution uses a weighted average of values within a neighbourhood that extends about two pixels in each direction, usually encompassing 16 adjacent pixels. Typically, the images produced by cubic convolution re-sampling are much more attractive than those of other procedures, but the data are altered more than those of nearest-neighbour or bilinear interpolation, the computations are more intensive and the minimum number of GCPs is larger. Images altered in this manner by re-sampling should be examined carefully before they are used for subsequent analyses.

Identification of ground control points

A practical problem in applying image registration procedures is the selection of control points (Fig. 11.10). GCPs are features that can be located with precision and accuracy on accurate maps yet are also easily located on digital images. Ideally, GCPs could be as small as a single pixel, if one could be easily identified against its background. In practice, most GCPs are likely to be spectrally distinct areas as small as a few pixels. Examples might include intersections of major highways, distinctive water bodies, edges of land-cover parcels, stream junctions and similar features. Although identification of such points may seem to be an easy task, in fact, difficulties that might emerge during this step can form a serious roadblock to the entire analytical process, as another procedure may depend on completion of an accurate registration.

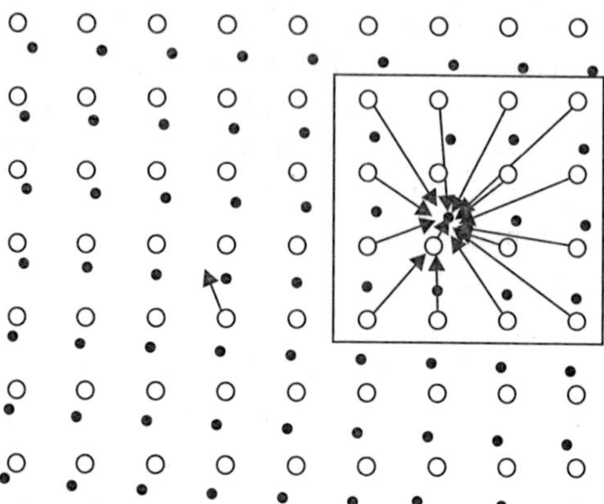

Fig. 11.9. Cubic convolution. Each estimated value in the output matrix is found by assessing values within a neighbourhood of 16 pixels in the input image.

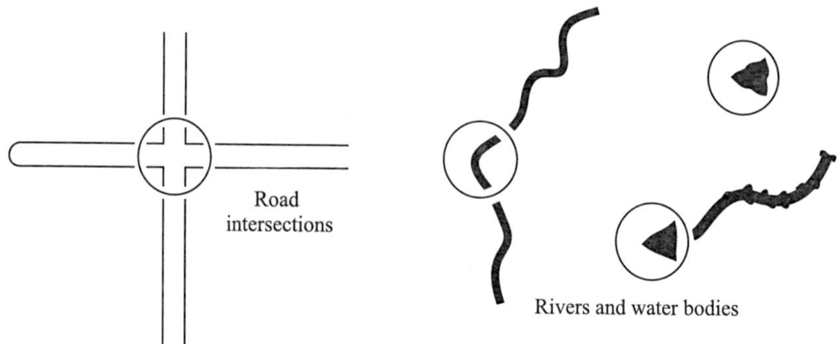

Fig. 11.10. Selection of ground control points.

Typically, it is relatively easy to find a rather small or modest-sized set of control points. However, in some scenes, the analyst finds it increasingly difficult to expand this set, as one has less and less confidence in each new point added to the set of GCPs. Thus there may be a rather small set of 'good' GCPs, points that the analyst can locate with confidence and precision both on the image and on an accurate map of the region. The locations may also be a problem. In principle, GCPs should be dispersed throughout the image, with good coverage near edges. Obviously, there is little to be gained from a large number of GCPs if they are all concentrated in a few regions of the image. Analysts who attempt to expand a real coverage to ensure good dispersion are forced to consider points in which it is difficult to locate GCPs with confidence. Therefore the desires to select 'good' GCPs and to achieve good dispersion may work against each other such that the analyst finds it difficult to select a judicious balance. Analysts should anticipate difficulties in selecting GCPs as they prepare subsets early in the analytical process. If subsets are too small or if they do not encompass important landmarks, the analysts may later find that the subset region of the image does not permit selection of a sufficient number of high-quality GCPs.

Bernstein present information that shows how registration error decreases as the number of GCPs is increased. Obviously, it is better to have more rather than fewer GCPs. But as explained above, the quality of GCP accuracy may decrease as their number increases because the analyst usually picks the best points first. Bernstein recommend that 16 GCPs may be a reasonable number if each can be located with an accuracy of one-third of a pixel. This number may not be sufficient if the GCPs are poorly distributed or if the nature of the landscape prevents accurate placement.

Many image-processing programmes permit the analyst to anticipate the accuracy of the registration by reporting errors observed at each GCP if a specific registration has been applied. The standard measure of the location error is the root mean square (rms) error, which is the standard deviation of the difference between actual positions of GCPs and their calculated positions (i.e., after registration). These differences are known as the residuals. Usually rms is reported in units of image pixels for both north-south and east-west directions (Table 11.4). Note that this practice reports locational errors among the GCPs, which may not always reflect the character of errors encountered at other pixels. Nonetheless, it is helpful to be able to select the most use ful GCPs. If analysts wish to assess the overall accuracy of the registration, some of the GCPs should be withheld from the registration procedure, then used to assess its success.

MAP PROJECTIONS FOR REPRESENTING SATELLITE IMAGES AND GROUND TRACKS

Mapping of any distribution on the earth's surface requires use of a map projection whenever the area considered exceeds a few square miles. This requirement arises from the fundamental problem of projecting locations on the earth's spherical surface onto the flat surface of the map. A map projection is a system of transformations that enables locations on the spherical earth to be represented systematically on a flat map. Because of the inherent difference between the two surfaces, there is always some sacrifice in accurate representation of area, shape, scale or direction on maps relative to globes. However, such errors may be confined to a few of these characteristics or may be very small in certain portions of a map.

Continuous mapping of a region viewed by Landsat or other earth observation satellites present serious problems for those using conventional map projections. Both the satellite and the earth's surface are moving as imagery is acquired, so at best the usual maps are very inconvenient. Therefore, users of early Landsat data encountered problems in representing coverage of Landsat scenes on conventional maps. The ground tracks of sun-synchronous satellites trace curved lines on the usual map projections, greatly complicating the representation of satellite paths and coverage. Snyder addressed this problem by devising projections specially designed to represent ground tracks of sun-synchronous satellites as straight lines. For global tracking, his map is based upon a cylindrical projection; for larger scale maps of continents or areas of similar size, he uses a map based upon a conic projection. To show the ground track as a straight line, it is, of course, necessary to sacrifice other map qualities, so these maps cannot show accurate shape and area everywhere.

Furthermore, representation of Landsat data as a rectangular array of pixels does not place them in their correct positions relative to the earth's surface. Convenient representation of correct positions of pixels requires projects specifically designed to capture the complex geometry of the Landsat image.

Alden P. Colvocoresses is credited with defining the Space Oblique Mercator (SOM) projection tailored for use with Landsat data, although others contributed to its development and mathematical definition. Research to develop the SOM was conducted by the USGS specifically for the purpose of defining a map projection to provide constant scale for the ground track of an earth observation satellite for the entire coverage cycle. Although the SOM was designed for use with Landsat, it is equally applicable to other land observation satellites, if tailored to their specific orbital characteristics. For Landsat, the projection must depict coverage from 81° N to 81° S, through a coverage cycle of 251 orbits. The projection shows only a narrow strip parallel to the ground track of the satellite—essentially that area subject to view by the MSS.

The SOM is based upon the map projection devised by Gerhard Kramer, a Dutch scholar and cartographer who used the Latinised version of his name, Gerhardus Mercator. His name has been given to the map projection he devised for an atlas he published in 1569. The Mercator projection was the first projection to attain widespread use, primarily because of its utility for marine navigation.

The Mercator projection can be envisioned as a transformation of the network of lines of latitude and longitude (known as the graticule) onto a flat surface such that the meridians of longitude form equally spaced vertical lines and the parallels of latitude form horizontal lines intersecting the meridians at right angles. The creation of this projection is envisioned as wrapping a transparent global in a cylinder tangent at the equator with a light inside the globe projecting the graticule onto the cylinder, which is then opened up to form a flat, map-like, surface.

On a globe, lines of latitude are parallel to one another, but lines of longitude converge near the poles. The Mercator projection differs significantly from a globe because it shows the converging meridians as parallel lines. But, simply described, the essence of Mercator' projection is that this error is (in part) compensated for by his method of spacing lines of latitude. Although the globe shows lines of latitude as equally spaced, Mercator's map increases this spacing so that as distance from the equator increases and as divergence of the meridians from their true spacing increases, so does spacing between lines of latitude. Thus the interval between lines of latitude increases dramatically toward the poles, to compensate for converging meridians near the poles. This compensation preserves correct shape in cartographic representation of the earth's features. The poles cannot be shown on the classic (i.e., centered on the equator). Mercator as parallels of latitude would have to be spaced at an infinite distance from one another at the poles.

If a Mercator projection is centered on the equator, the portion nearest the equator (where the hypothetical cylinder is tangent to the globe) is correct in representation of distance, shape, area and direction; all are shown accurately or with only minor errors (Fig. 11.11a). As distance from the equator increases, errors become increasingly severe. Area, in particular, is shown with large errors at high latitudes. However, shape is shown accurately throughout the map. Furthermore, this projection has an important feature that has been especially valuable throughout its history. A line of constant compass bearing (known as a loxodrome) is shown on a Mercator projection as a straight line—a feature that has made the projection especially valuable for navigational use, both now and in the past.

For our present concerns, the Mercator projection is significant in its modified forms, the transverse Mercator and the oblique Mercator projections. The transverse Mercator can be visualised as a cylinder tangent not at the equator, but at a meridian of longitude (Fig. 11.11b). When the cylinder is unfolded, only the most accurate strip centered at the meridian of tangency is selected for use—the outer sections of the map where the map is inaccurate, are discarded. If the process is repeated successively for different meridians, each time retaining only the accurate center strip, very accurate maps of large areas of the earth can be constructed. This process forms the basis for the Universal Transverse Meracator (UTM) geographic reference system, which is based upon such a projection.

For the oblique Mercator projection, the line of tangency is shifted from a meridian to a great circle on the earth oriented at some angle (other than 90°) to the meridians (Fig. 11.11c). On oblique Mercator projections the graticule appears as a set of curved lines. For the SOM (Fig. 11.12), the line of tangency is defined not as a circle on the earth's surface, but as a curve that follows the ground track of the satellite. For Landsat and other satellites in sun-synchronous orbits, this line is a nearly sinusoidal curve.

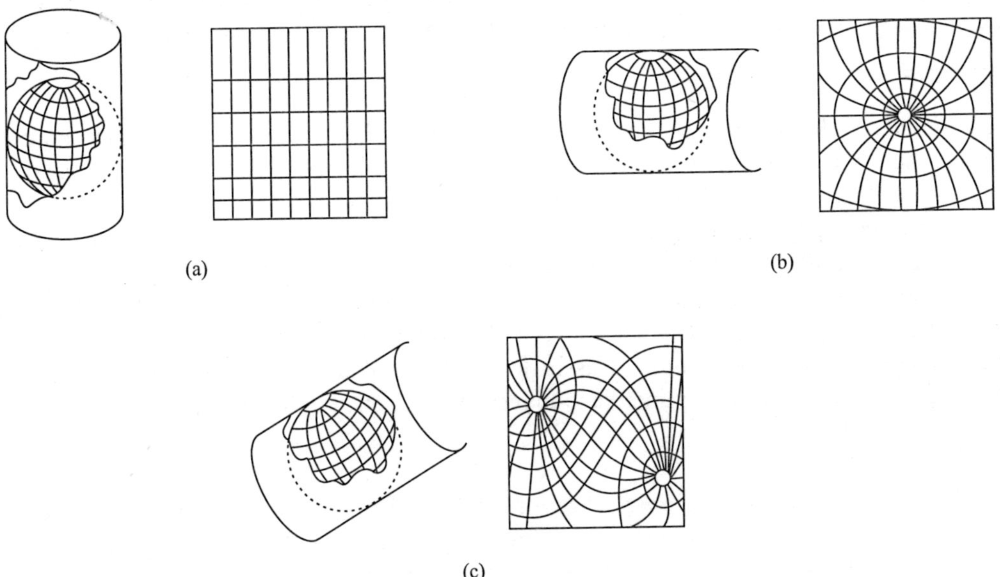

Fig. 11.11. Mercator projection. (a) Projection centered on equator; (b) Transverse Mercator projection; and (c) Oblique Mercator.

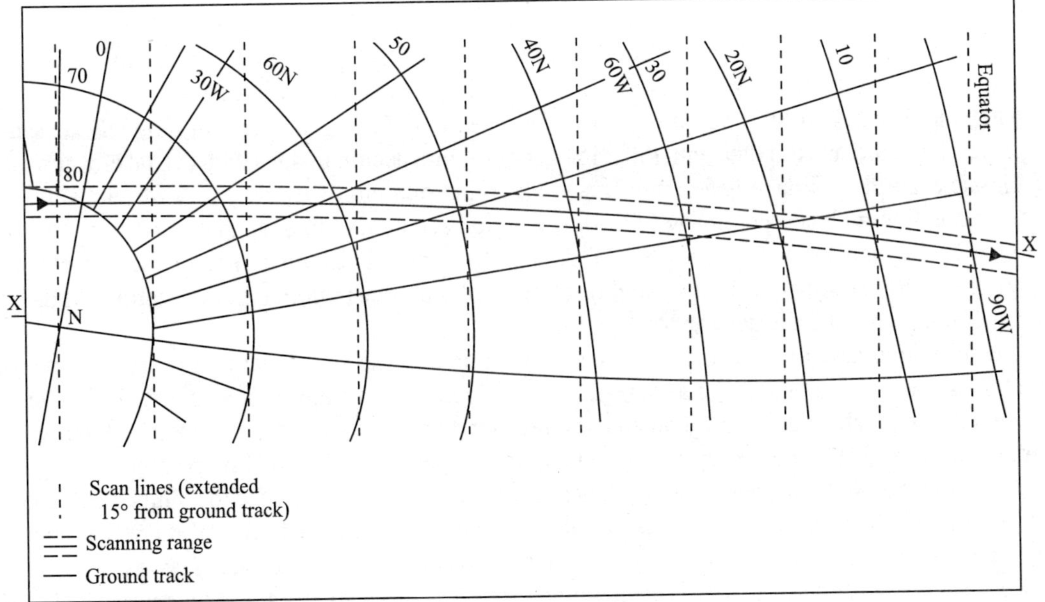

Fig. 11.12. Space oblique Mercator.

The scan lines, representing the area depicted by MSS imagery, intersect the ground track at 86° degrees at the equator, but at 90° where the track is closest to the poles. The differentce is caused by variations in skew (0 to 4°) caused by interaction of mirror scan motion with movement of the earth's surface as it rotates beneath the moving satellite. Like other mercator projections, the SOM has errors in representation of distance and area, but errors are very small near the ground track.

EFFECT OF PRE-PROCESSING

There is indirect evidence that pre-processing operations sometimes have unwanted effects upon digital values and therefore upon the accuracies of classification based upon such data. It seems clear from a basic understanding of the pre-processing operations that the data are in fact altered from their original values and that such operations alter the mean values for each band as well as the variances and covariance. Presumably other qualities, such as cor-relations between bands, are also influenced. Yet few studies have systematically examined actual effects or pre-processing operations upon final results of analyses. Kovalick examined a Landsat MSS scene of a forested wetland in North Carolina to study the effects of re-smpling and destriping upon accuracies of image classification. He found that re-sampling tended to reduce class means (of the training data he examined) and to increases variances relative to the original data.

DATA FUSION

Data fusion refers to processes that bring images of varied resolution into a single image that incorporates, for example, the high spatial resolution of a panchromatic image with the multispectral content of a multiband image at coarser resolution. Because of the broad range of characteristics of imagery collected by varied sensors and the routine availability of digital data, there has been increasing incentive to bring data from varied systems together into a single image. Such products are often valuable because they can integrate several independent sources of information into a single image (Because image fusion prepares data for visual interpretation rather than for digital analysis, it differs from the other pre-processing techniques discussed in this chapter. However, placement of this topic in this unit permits development of concepts in a more progressive sequence than would otherwise be possible).

Although data fusion can be applied to a varied selection of different forms of remotely sensed data (e.g., merging multispectral data with radar imagery or multispectral images with digital elevation data), the classic example of image fusion involves the merging of a multispectral image of relatively coarse spatial resolution with another image of the same region acquired at finer spatial resolution. Examples, might include fusing multispectral SPOT data (20 m spatial resolution) with the corresponding panchromatic SPOT scene (at 10 m spatial resolution) of the same region or multispectral TM data with corresponding high-altitude aerial photography.

The technique assumes that the images are compatible in the sense that they were acquired on or about the same date and that the images register to each other. The analyst must rectify the images to be sure that they both share the same geometry and register them to be sure that they match spatially. In this context, the basic task of image fusion is to substitute the spatial detail of the fine-resolution image detail to replace one of the multispectral bands, then apply a technique to restore the lost multispectral content of the discarded band for the coarse-resolution multispectral image. Specifics of these procedures are beyond the scope of this discussion. Briefly stated, the techniques fall into three classes.

Spectral domain procedures project the multispectral bands into spectral data space, then find the new (transformed) band most closely correlated with the panchromatic image. That spectral content can then be assigned to the high-resolution panchromatic image.

The intensity-hue-saturation (IHS) technique is one of the spectral domain procedures. Intensity-hue-saturation refers to the three dimensions of multispectral data that we know in the everyday context as 'colour'. Intensity is equivalent to brightness, hue refers to dominant wavelength (what we regard as 'colour') and saturation specifies purity, the degree to which a specific colour is dominated by a single wavelength. For the IHS fusion technique, the three bands of the lower resolution image are transformed from normal red-green-blue (RGB) space into IHS space. The high-resolution image is then stretched to approximate the mean and variance of the intensity component. Next, the stretched high-resolution image is substituted for the intensity component of the original image and then the image is projected back into RGB data space. The logic of this strategy lies in the substitution of the intensity component by the high-resolution image, which is characterised by an equivalent range of intensity, but superior spatial detail.

The principal components transformation (PCT) conducts a principal components analysis of the raw low-resolution image. The high-resolution image is then stretched to approximate the mean and variance of the first principal component. Next, the stretched high-resolution image is substituted for the first principal component of the low-resolution image and then the image is reconstructed back into its usual appearance using the substituted high-resolution image as the first principal component. The logic of this PCT approach rests on the fact that the first principal component of a multispectral image often coveys most of the brightness information in the original image.

Spatial domain procedures extract the high-frequency variation of a fine-resolution image and then insert it into the multispectral framework of a corresponding coarse-resolution image. The high-pass filter technique (HPF) is an example. A high-pass filter is applied to the fine-resolution image to isolate and extract the high-frequency component of the image. It is this high-frequency information that conveys the scene's fine spatial detail. This high-frequency element is then introduced into the low-resolution image (with compensation to preserve the original brightness of the scene) to synthesise the fine detail of the high-resolution image. The ARSIS technique proposed by Ranchin and Wald applies the wavelet transform as a method of simulating the high-resolution detail within the coarse-resolution image.

Algebraic procedures operate on image at the level of the individual pixel to proportion spectral information among the three bands of the multispectral image, so that the replacement (high-resolution) image used as a substitute for one of the band can be assigned correct spectral brightness. The Brovey Transform finds proportional brightnesses conveyed by the band to be replaced and assigns it to the substitute. Its objective of preserving the spectral integrity of the original multispectral image is attained if the panchromatic image has a spectral range equivalent to the combined range of the three multispectral bands. Because this assumption is often not correct for many of the usual multispectral images, this procedure does not always preserve the spectral content of the original image.

The multiplicative model (MLT) multiplies each multispectral pixel by the corresponding pixel in the high-resolution image. To scale the brightnesses back to an approximation of their original ranges, the square root of the combined brightness are calculated. The result is a combined brightness than requires some sort of weighting to restore some approximation of the relative brightnesses of the individual bands. Although these weights are selected arbitrarily, many have found the procedure to produce satisfactory results.

Composite images created by image fusion are intended for visual interpretation. Comparative evaluations of the different approaches have examined different combinations of fused data that the HPF technique was superior to the IHS and PCT methods for fused TM and high-altitude photographic data. Carter found that the IHS and HPF methods produced some of the best result. Wald proposed a framework for evaluating the quality of fused images and emphasised that the character of the scene recorded by the imagery is an important consideration. Because fused images are composites derived from arbitrary manipulations of data, the combined images are suited for visual interpretation but not for further digital classification or analysis.

Thus it is important to recognise that many of the pre-processing operations used today have been introduced into the field of remote sensing from the related fields of pattern recognition and image processing. In such disciplines, the emphasis if usually upon detection or recognition of objects as portrayed on digital images. In this context, the digital values have much different significance than they do in remote sensing. Often, the analysis requires recognition simply of contrasts between different objects or the study of objects against their backgrounds, detection of edges and reconstruction of shapes from the configuration of edges and lines. Digital values can be manipulated freely to change image geometry or to enhance images without concern that their fundamental information content will be altered.

However, in remote sensing we usually are concerned with much more subtle variations in digital values and we are concerned when pre-processing operation after the digital values. Such changes may alter spectral signatures, contrasts between categories or variance and co-variances of spectral bands.

12

Image Classification

INTRODUCTION

This chapter describes a few specific classifiers as a means of introducing the student to the variety of different classification strategies that are available today. Possibly the student may have the opportunity to use some of these procedure, so these descriptions may form the first step in a more detailed learning process. Nonetheless, those procedures that are available for student use are likely to be based upon the same principles outlined here using specific classifiers as examples.

Therefore, this chapter should not be regarded as complete catalogue of image classification methods, but rather as an effort to illustrate some of the primary methods of image classification. Specific details and methods will vary greatly, but if the student has mastered the basic strategies and methods of image classification, he or she will recognise unfamiliar methods as variations on the fundamental approaches described here.

Digital image classification is the process of assigning pixels to classes. Usually each pixel is treated as an individual unit composed of values in several spectral bands. By comparing pixels to one another and to pixels of known identity, it is possible to assemble groups of similar pixels into classes that are associated with the informational categories of interest to users of remotely sensed data. These classes form regions on a map or an image, so that after classification the digital image is presented as a mosaic of uniform parcels, each identified by a colour or symbol (Fig. 12.1). These classes are, in theory, homogeneous: pixels within classes are spectrally more similar to one another than they are to pixels in other classes. In practice, of course, each class will display some diversity, as each scene will exhibit some variability within classes.

Image classification is an important part of the fields of remote sensing, image analysis and pattern recognition. In some instances, the classification itself may be the object of the analysis. For example, classification of land use from remotely sensed data produces a map-like image as the final product of the analysis. In other instances, the classification may be only an intermediate step in a more elaborate analysis, in which the classified data form one of several data layers in a GIS. For example, in a study of water quality, an initial step may be to use image classification to identify wetlands and open water within a scene. Later steps may then focus upon more detailed study of these areas to identify influences upon water quality and to map variations in water quality. Image classification therefore forms an important tool for examination of digital images—sometimes to produce a final product, other times as one of several analytical procedures applied to derive information from an image.

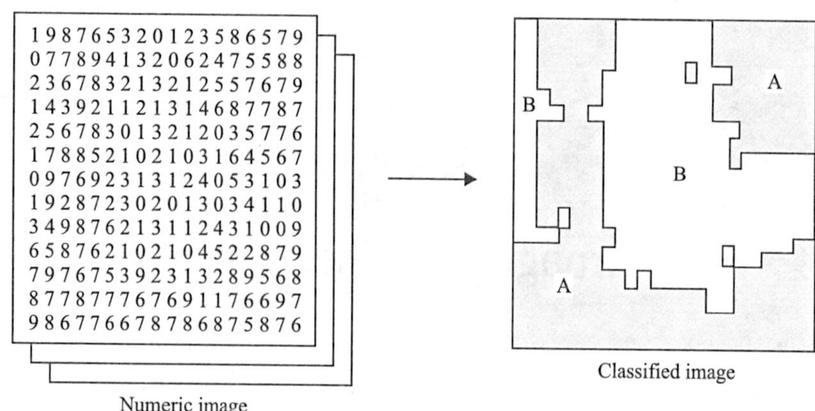

Fig. 12.1. Numeric image and classified image. The classified image (right) is defined by examining the numeric image, then grouping together those pixels that have similar spectral values. Here class 'A' is formed from bright pixels (values of 6, 7, 8 and 9) and class 'B' is formed from dark pixels (values of 0, 1, 2 and 3). Usually there are many more classes and at least three or four spectral bands.

The term classifier refers loosely to a computer program that implements a specific procedure for image classification. Over the years scientists have devised many classification strategies. The analyst must select a classification method that will best accomplish a specific task. At present it is not possible to state that a given classifier is 'best' for all situations because the characteristics of each image and the circumstances for each study vary so greatly. Therefore, it is essential that each analyst understand the alternative strategies for image classification so that he or she may be prepared to select the most appropriate classifier for the task at hand.

The simplest form of digital image classification is to consider each pixel individually, assigning it to a class based upon its several values measured in separate spectral bands (Fig. 12.2). Sometimes such classifiers are referred to as spectral or point classifiers because they consider each pixel as a 'point' observation (i.e., as values isolated from their neighbours).

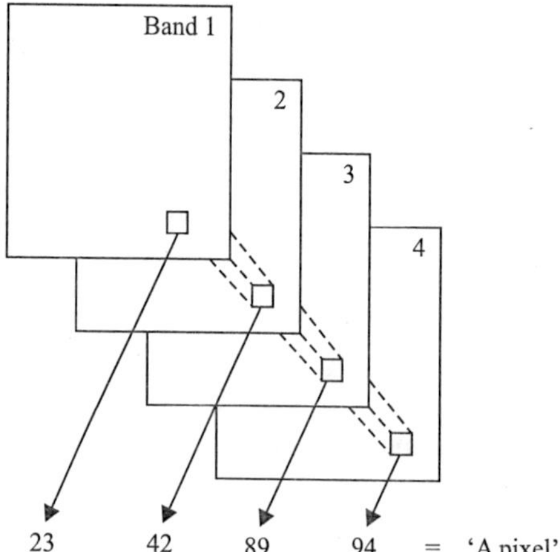

Fig. 12.2. Point classifiers operate upon each pixel as a single set of spectral values considered in isolation from its neighbours.

Although point classifiers offer the benefits of simplicity and economy, they are not capable of exploiting the information contained in relationships between each pixel and those that neighbour it. Human interpreters, for example, could derive little information using the point-by-point approach, because humans derive less information from the brightnesses of individual pixels than they do from the context and the patterns of brightnesses, of groups of pixels and from the sizes, shapes and arrangements of parcels of adjacent pixels. These are the same qualities that we discussed in the context of manual image interpretation. As an alternative, more complex classification processes consider groups of pixels within their spatial setting within the image as a means of using the textural information so important for the human interpreter. These are spatial or neighbourhood, classifiers, which examine small areas within the image using both spectral and textural information to classify the image (Fig. 12.3). Spatial classifiers are typically more difficult to programme and much more expensive to use than point classifiers. In some situations spatial classifiers have demonstrated improved accuracy, but few have found their way into routine use for remote sensing image classification.

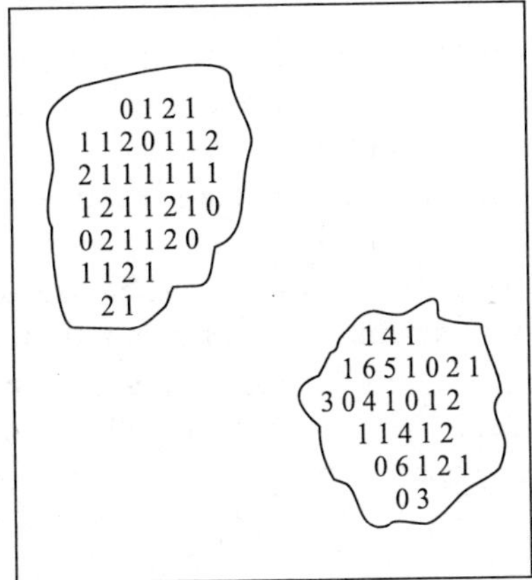

Fig. 12.3. Image texture, the basis for neighbourhood classifiers. A neighbourhood classifier considers values within a region of the image in defining class membership. Here two regions within the image differ with respect to average brightness and also with respect to 'texture', the uniformity of pixels within a small neighbourhood.

Another kind of distinction in image classification separates supervised classification from unsupervised classification. Supervised classification procedures require considerable interaction with the analyst, who must guide the classification by identifying areas on the image that are known to belong to each category. Unsupervised classification, on the other hand, proceeds with only minimal interaction with the analyst, in a search for natural groups of pixels present within the image. The distinction between supervised and unsupervised classification is useful, especially for students who are first learning about image classification. But the two strategies are not as clearly distinct as these definitions suggest, for some methods do not fit neatly into either category. These so-called hybrid classifiers share characteristics of both supervised and unsupervised methods.

INFORMATIONAL CLASSES AND SPECTRAL CLASSES

Informational classes are the categories of interest to the users of the data. Informational classes are, for example, the different kinds of geological units, different kinds of forest or the different kinds of land use that convey information to planners, managers, administrators and scientists who use information derived from remotely sensed data. These classes are the information that we wish to derive from the data—they are the object of our analysis. Unfortunately, these classes are not directly recorded on remotely sensed images; we can derive them only indirectly, using the evidence contained in brightnesses recorded by each image. For example, the image cannot directly show geological units, but rather only the differences in topography, vegetation, soil colour, shadow and other factors that lead the analyst to conclude that certain geological conditions exist in specific areas. Spectral classes are groups of pixels that are uniform with respect to the brightnesses in their several spectral channels. The analyst can observe spectral classes within remotely sensed data; if it is possible to define links between the spectral classes on the image and the informational classes that are of primary interest, then the image forms a valuable source of information.

Thus, remote sensing classification proceeds by matching spectral categories to informational categories. If the match can be made with confidence, then the information is likely to be reliable. If spectral and informational categories do not correspond, then the image is unlikely to be a useful source for that particular form of information. Seldom can we expect to find exact one-to-one matches between informational and spectral classes. Any informational class includes spectral variations arising from natural variations within the class. For example, a region of the informational class 'forest' is still 'forest', even though it may display variations in age, species composition, density and vigour, which all lead to differences in the spectral appearance of a single informational class. Furthermore, other factors, such as variations in illumination and shadowing, may produce additional variations even within otherwise spectrally uniform classes.

Thus, informational classes are typically composed of numerous spectral sub-classes, spectrally distinct groups of pixels that together may be assembled to form an informational class (Fig. 12.4). In digital classification, we must often treat spectral sub-classes as distinct units during classification, but then display several spectral classes under a single symbol for the final image or map to be used by planners or administrators (who are, after all, interested only in the informational categories, not in the intermediate steps required to generate them).

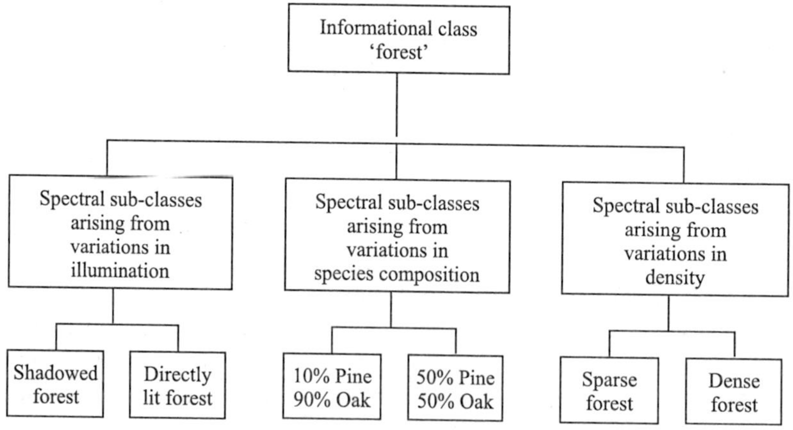

Fig. 12.4. Spectral subclasses.

For each band, each class is characterised by a mean or average, value that of course represents the typical brightness of each class.

In nature, all classes exhibit some variability around their mean values: some pixels are darker than the average, others a bit brighter. These departures from the mean are measured as the variance or sometimes by the standard deviation (the square root of the variance).

Often we wish to assess the distinctiveness of separate spectral classes, perhaps to determine if they really are separate classes or if they should be combined to form a single, larger class. A crude measure of the distinctiveness of two classes is simply the difference in the mean values; presumably classes that are very different should have big differences in average brightness, while classes that are similar to one another should have small differences in average brightness. This measure is a bit too simple because it does not take into account the differences in variability between classes.

Another simple measure of distinctiveness is the normalised difference (ND), found by dividing the difference in class means by the sum of their standard deviations. For two classes A and B, with means $\bar{x}_a$ and $\bar{x}_b$ and standard deviations s_a and s_b, the ND is defined as:

$$ND = \frac{|\bar{x}_a - \bar{x}_b|}{s_a + s_b} \qquad \text{... (12.1)}$$

As an example, Table 12.1 summarises properties of several classes, then uses these properties to show the normalised difference between these classes in several spectral channels. Note that some pairs of categories are very distinct relative to others. Also note that some spectral channels are much more effective than others in separating categories from one another.

Table 12.1. Normalised difference.

	MSS band				*MSS band*			
	4	*5*	*6*	*7*	*4*	*5*	*6*	*7*
	Water				Forest			
$\bar{x}$	37.5	31.9	22.8	6.3	26.9	16.6	55.7	32.5
s	0.67	2.77	2.44	0.82	1.21	1.49	3.97	3.12
	Crop				Pasture			
$\bar{x}$	37.7	38.0	52.3	27.3	28.6	22.0	53.4	32.9
s	3.56	5.08	4.13	4.42	1.51	5.09	13.16	3.80

$$\text{Water forest (band 6): } \frac{55.7 \quad 22.8}{2.44+3.97} = \frac{32.9}{6.41} = 5.13$$

$$\text{Crop-pasture (band 6): } \frac{52.3 \quad 53.4}{4.13+13.16} = \frac{1.1}{17.29} = 0.06$$

UNSUPERVISED CLASSIFICATION

Unsupervised classification can be defined as the identification of natural groups or structures, within multispectral data. The notion of the existence of natural, inherent groupings of spectral values within a scene may not be intuitively obvious, but it can be demonstrated that remotely sensed images are usually composed of spectral classes that are reasonably uniform internally in respect to brightnesses in several spectral channels. Unsupervised classification is the definition, identification, labelling and mapping of these natural classes.

Advantages

The advantages of unsupervised classification (relative to supervised classification) can be enumerated as follows:

1. No extensive prior knowledge of the region is required: Or, more accurately, the nature of knowledge required for unsupervised classification differs from that required for supervised classification. To conduct supervised classification, detailed knowledge of the area to be examined is required to select representative examples of each class to be mapped. To conduct unsupervised classification, no detailed prior knowledge is required, but knowledge of the region is required to interpret the meaning of the results produced by the classification process.
2. The opportunity for human error is minimised: To conduct unsupervised classification, the operator may perhaps specify only the number of categories desired (or possibly, minimum and maximum limits on the number of categories) and sometimes constraints governing the distinctness and uniformity of groups. Many of the detailed decisions required for supervised classification are not required for unsupervised classification, so the analyst is presented with less opportunity for error. If the analyst has inaccurate pre-conceptions regarding the region, they will have little opportunity to influence the classification. The classes defined by unsupervised classification are often much more uniform, with respect to spectral composition, than those generated by supervised classification.
3. Unique classes are recognised as distinct units: Such classes, perhaps of very small areal extent, may remain unrecognised in the process of supervised classification and could inadvertently be incorporated into other classes, generating error and imprecision throughout the entire classification.

Disadvantages and Limitations

The disadvantages and limitations of unsupervised classification arise primarily from a reliance upon 'natural' groupings and difficulties in matching these groups to the informational categories that are of interest to the analyst.

1. Unsupervised classification identifies spectrally homogenous classes within the data that do not necessarily correspond to the informational categories that are of the interest to the analyst: As a result, the analyst is faced with the problem of matching spectral classes generated by the classification to the informational classes that are required by the ultimate user of the information. Seldom is there a simple one-to-one correspondence between the two sets of classes.
2. The analyst has limited control over the menu of classes and their specific identities: If it is necessary to generate a specific menu of informational classes (e.g., to match to other classifications for other dates or adjacent regions), the use of unsupervised classification may be unsatisfactory.
3. Spectral properties of specific informational classes will change over time (on a seasonal basis, as well as over the years): As a result, relationships between information classes and spectral classes are not constant and relationships defined for one image cannot be extended to others.

Distance Measures

Some of the basic elements of unsupervised classification can be illustrated using data presented in Tables 12.2 and 12.3. These values can be plotted on simple diagrams constructed using brightnesses of two spectral bands as orthogonal axes (Figs. 12.5 and 12.6). Plots of band pairs 4 and 5 and band pairs 5 and 6 are sufficient to illustrate the main points of significance here. These two-dimensional plots illustrate principles that can be extended to include additional variables (e.g., to analyse Landsat ETM + bands 1 through 5 simultaneously). The additional variables create three or four-dimensional plots of points in multidimensional data space, which are difficult to depict in a diagram, but can be envisioned as groups of pixels represented by swarms of points with depth in several dimensions (Fig. 12.7).

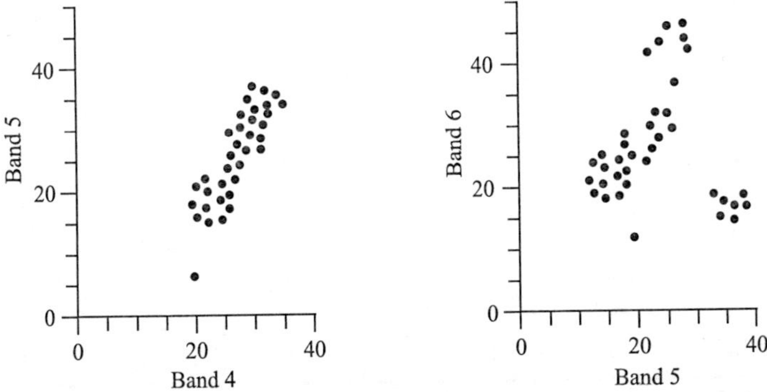

Fig. 12.5. Two-dimensional scatter diagrams, February (Table 12.2). Compare with Fig. 12.6.

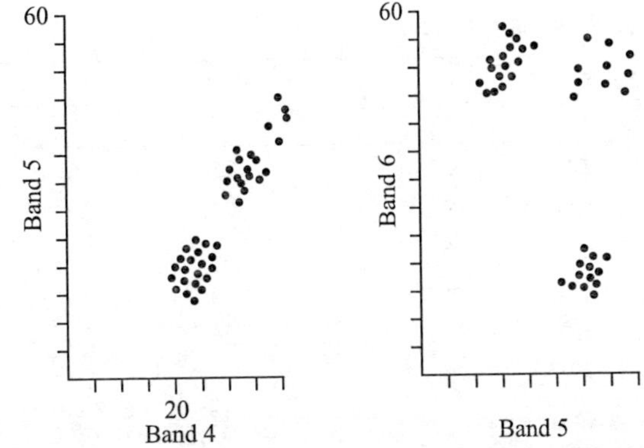

Fig. 12.6. Two-dimensional scatter diagrams, May (Table 12.3). These pixels represent the same categories shown in Fig. 12.5 but have different brightnesses because of difference in date.

Table 12.2. Landsat MSS Digital Values for February.

	MSS band					*MSS band*			
	4	*5*	*6*	*7*		*4*	*5*	*6*	*7*
1.	19	15	22	11	21.	24	24	25	11
2.	21	15	22	12	22.	25	25	38	20
3.	19	13	25	14	23.	20	29	19	3
4.	28	27	41	21	24.	28	29	18	2
5.	27	25	32	19	25.	25	26	42	21
6.	21	15	25	13	26.	24	23	41	22
7.	21	17	23	12	27.	21	18	12	12
8.	19	16	24	12	28.	25	21	31	15

(Cont'd...)

	MSS band					MSS band			
	4	5	6	7		4	5	6	7
9.	19	12	25	14	29.	22	22	31	15
10.	28	29	17	3	30.	26	24	43	21
11.	28	26	41	21	31.	19	16	24	12
12.	19	16	24	12	32.	30	31	18	3
13.	29	32	17	3	33.	28	27	44	24
14.	19	16	22	12	34.	22	22	28	15
15.	19	16	24	12	35.	30	31	18	2
16.	19	16	25	13	36.	19	16	22	12
17.	24	21	35	19	37.	30	31	18	2
18.	22	18	31	14	38.	27	23	34	20
19.	21	18	25	13	39.	21	16	22	12
20.	21	16	27	13	40.	23	22	26	16

Note. These are raw digital values for a forested area in central Virginia as acquired by the Landsat 1 MSS in February 1994. These values represent the same area as those in Table 12.3, although individual pixels do not correspond.

Table 12.3. Landsat MSS digital values for May.

	MSS band					MSS band			
	4	5	6	7		4	5	6	7
1.	34	28	22	6	21.	26	16	52	29
2.	26	16	52	29	22.	30	18	57	35
3.	36	35	24	6	23.	30	18	62	28
4.	39	41	48	23	24.	35	30	18	6
5.	26	15	52	31	25.	36	33	24	7
6.	36	28	22	6	26.	27	16	57	32
7.	28	18	59	35	27.	26	15	57	34
8.	28	21	57	34	28.	26	15	50	29
9.	26	16	55	30	29.	26	33	24	27
10.	32	30	52	25	30.	36	36	27	8
11.	40	45	59	26	31.	40	43	51	27
12.	33	30	48	24	32.	30	18	62	38
13.	28	21	57	34	33.	28	18	62	38
14.	28	21	59	35	34.	36	33	22	6
15.	36	38	48	22	35.	35	36	56	33
16.	36	31	23	5	36.	42	42	53	26
17.	26	19	57	33	37.	26	16	50	30
18.	36	34	25	7	38.	42	38	58	33
19.	36	31	21	6	39.	30	22	59	37
20.	27	19	55	30	40.	27	16	56	34

Note. These are raw digital values for a forested area in central Virginia as acquired by the Landsat 1 MSS in May 1994. These values represent the same area as those in Table 12.2, although individual pixels do not correspond.

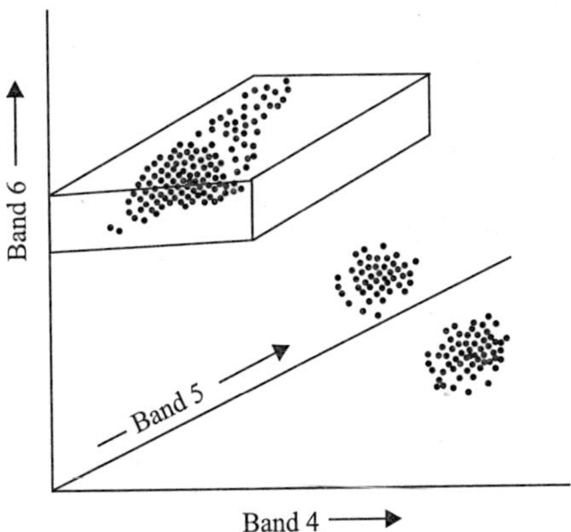

Fig. 12.7. Sketch illustrating multidimensional scatter diagrams. Here three bands of data are shown.

The general form for such diagrams is illustrated by Fig. 12.8. A diagonal line of points extends upward from a point near the origin. This pattern occurs because a pixel that is dark in one band will often tend to be dark in another band and as brightness increases in one spectral region, so does it tends to increase in others. (This relationship often holds for spectral measurements in the visible and near infrared; it is not necessarily observed in data from widely separated spectral regions.) Forty values are plotted in each of the diagrams in Fig. 12.6. Specific groupings or clusters, are evident; these clusters may correspond to informational categories of interest to the analyst. Unsupervised classification is the process of defining such clusters in multidimensional data space and (if possible) matching them to informational categories.

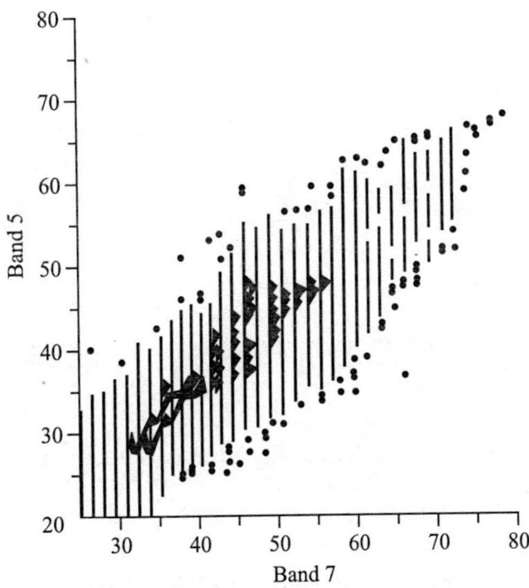

Fig. 12.8. Scatter diagram. Data from two Landsat MSS bands illustrate the general form of the relationship between spectral measurements in continuous regions of the spectrum. This diagram shows several hundred points; when so many values are shown, the distinct clusters visible in Fig. 12.6 are not visible. The groups may still be present, but they can only be detected by application of classification algorithms that can simultaneously consider values in many spectral bands.

When we consider large numbers of pixels, the clusters are not usually as distinct because pixels of intermediate values tend to fill in the gaps between groups (Fig. 12.8). We must therefore apply a variety of methods to assist us in the identification of those groups that may be present within the data but may not be obvious to visual inspection.

Over the years image scientists and statisticians have developed a wide variety of procedures for identifying such clusters—procedures that vary greatly in complexity and effectiveness. The general model for unsupervised classification can, however, be illustrated using one of the simplest classification strategies, that can serve as the foundation for understanding more complex approaches. Figure 12.9 shows two pixels, each with measurements in several spectral channels, plotted in multidimensional data space in the same manner as those illustrated in Fig. 12.6. For ease of illustration, only two bands are shown here, although the principles illustrated extend to as many bands as may be available.

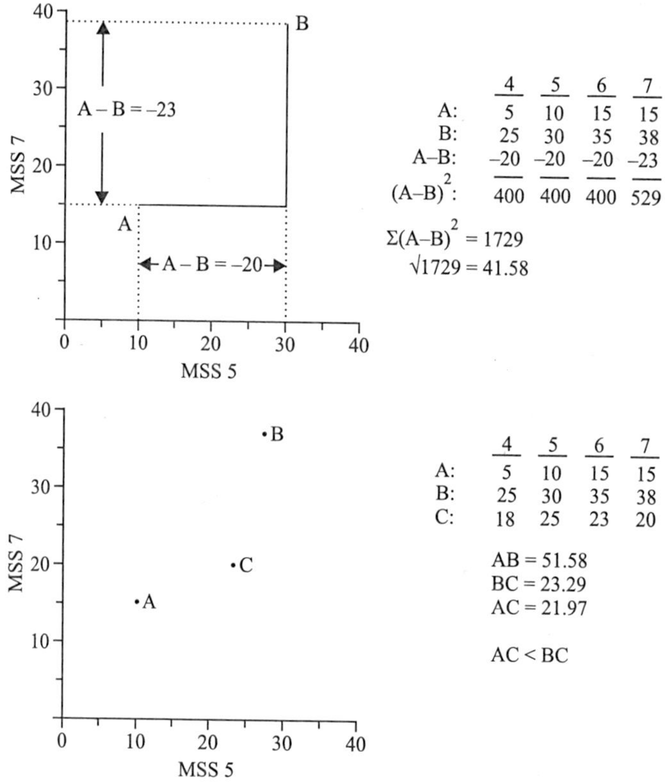

Fig. 12.9. Illustration of Euclidean distance measure.

Unsupervised classification of an entire image must consider many thousands of pixels. But the classification process is always based upon the answer to the same questions: 'Do the two pixels belong to the same group'? For this example, the question is, 'Should pixel C be grouped with A or with B'? (See the lower part of Fig. 12.9.) This question can be answered by finding the distance between pairs of pixels. If the distance between A and C is greater than that between B and C, then B and C are said to belong to the same group and A may be defined as a member of a separate class.

There are thousands of pixels in a remotely sensed image; if they are considered individually as prospective members of groups, the distances to other pixels can always be used to define group membership. How can such distances be calculated? A number of methods for finding distances in multidimensional data space are available. One of the simplest is *Euclidean distance*:

$$D_{ab} = \left[\sum_{i=1}^{n} (a_i - b_i)^2 \right]^{1/2} \qquad \text{... (12.2)}$$

where i is one of n spectral bands, a and b are pixels and D_{ab} is the distance between the two pixels. The distance calculation is based upon the Pythagorean theorem (Fig. 12.10):

$$c = \sqrt{a^2 + b^2} \qquad \text{... (12.3)}$$

In this instance we are interested in distance c; a, b and c are measured in units of the two spectral channels.

$$c = D_{ab} \qquad \text{... (12.4)}$$

To find D_{ab}, we need to find distances a and b. Distance a is found by subtracting values of A and B in MSS channel 7 (a = 38 – 15 = 23). Distance b is found by finding the difference between A and B with respect to channel 6 (b = 30 – 10 = 20).

$$D_{ab} = c = \sqrt{20^2 + 23^2}$$

$$D_{ab} = \sqrt{400 + 529} = \sqrt{929}$$

$$D_{ab} = 30.47$$

This measure can be applied to as many dimensions (spectral channels) as might be available, by addition of distances. For example:

	Landsat MSS band			
	1	*2*	*3*	*4*
Pixel A	34	28	22	6
Pixel B	26	16	52	29
Difference	8	12	–30	–23
(Difference)^2	64	144	900	529
	Total of (differences)^2 = 1637			
		$\sqrt{\text{Total}}$ = 40.5		

The lower part of Fig. 12.9 shows another worked example.

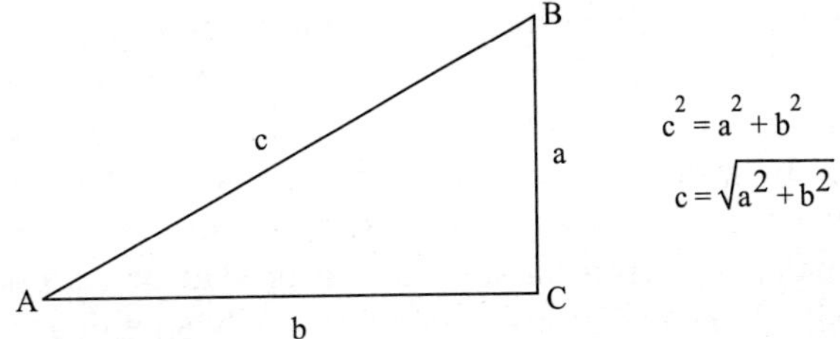

Fig. 12.10. Definition of symbols used for Euclidean distance.

Thus, the Euclidean distance between A and B is equal to 40.45 distance units. This value in itself has little significance, but in relation to other distances it forms a means of defining similarities between pixels. For example, if we find that distance ab = 40.45 and that distance ac = 86.34, then we know that pixel A is closer (i.e., more nearly similar) to B than it is to C and that we should form a group from A and B rather than A and C.

Unsupervised classification proceeds by making thousands of distance calculations as a means of determining similarities for the many pixels and groups within an image. Usually the analyst does not actually know any of these many distances that must be calculated for unsupervised classification, as the computer presents only the final classified image without the intermediate steps necessary to derive the classification. Nonetheless, distance measures are the heart of unsupervised classification.

But not all distance measures are based upon Euclidean distance. Another simple measure of determining distance is the L_1 distance, the sum of the absolute differences between values in individual bands. For the example given above, the L_1 distance is 73 (73 = 8 + 12 + 30 + 23). Other distance measures have been defined for unsupervised classification; many are rather complex methods of scaling distances to promote effective groupings of pixels.

Unsupervised classification often proceeds in an interactive fashion to search for an optimal allocation of pixels to categories, given the constraints specified by the analyst. A computer program for unsupervised classification includes an algorithm for calculation of distances as described above (sometimes the analyst might be able to select between several alternative distance measures) and a procedure for finding, testing, then revising classes according to limits defined by the analyst. The analyst may be required to specify limits upon the number of clusters to be generated, to constrain the diversity of values within classes or to require that classes exhibit a specified minimum degree of distinctness with respect to neighbouring groups. Specific classification procedures may define distances differently; for example, it is possible to calculate distances to the centroid of each group or to the closest member of each group or perhaps to the most densely occupied region of a cluster. Such alternatives represent refinements of the basic strategy outlined here and each may offer advantages in certain situations. Also, there are many variations in the details of how each classification programme may operate; because so many distance measures must be calculated for classification of a remotely sensed image, most programmes use variations of these basic procedures that accomplish the same objectives with improved computational efficiency.

Sequence for Unsupervised Classification

A typical sequence might begin with the analyst specifying minimum and maximum numbers of categories to be generated by the classification algorithm. These values might be based upon the analyst's knowledge of the scene or upon the user's requirements that the final classification display a certain number of classes. The classification starts with a set of arbitrarily selected pixels as cluster centers; often these are selected at random to ensure that the analyst cannot influence the classification and that the selected pixels are representative of values found throughout the scene. The classification algorithm then finds distances (as described above) between pixels and forms initial estimates of cluster centers as permitted by constraints specified by the analyst. The class can be represented by a single point, known as the 'class centroid', which can be thought of as the center of the cluster of pixels for a given class, even though many classification procedures do not always define it as the exact center of the group. At this point, classes consist only of the arbitrarily selected pixels chosen as initial estimates of class centroids. In the next step, all the remaining pixels in the scene are assigned to the nearest class centroid. The entire scene has now been classified, but this classification forms only an estimate of the final result, as the classes formed by this initial attempt are unlikely to be the optimal set of classes and may not meet the constraints specified by the analyst.

To begin the next step, the algorithm finds new centroids for each class, as the addition of new pixels to the classification means that the initial centroids are no longer accurate. Then the entire scene is classified again, with each pixels assigned to the nearest centroid. And again new centroids are calculated; if the new centroids differ from those found in the preceding step, then the process repeats until there is not significant change detected in locations of class centroids and the classes meet all constraints required by the operator.

Throughout the process the analyst generally has no interaction with the classification, so it operates as an 'objective' classification within the constraints provided by the analyst. Also, the unsupervised approach identifies the 'natural' structure of the image in the sense that it finds uniform groupings of pixels that form distinct classes without the influence of pre-conceptions regarding their identities or distributions. The entire process, however, cannot be considered to be 'objective', as the analyst has made decisions regarding the data to be examined, the algorithm to be used, the number of classes to be found and (possibly) the uniformity and distinctness of classes. Each of these decisions influences the character and the accuracy of the final product, so it cannot be regarded as a result isolated from the context in which it was made.

Many different procedures for unsupervised classification are available; despite their diversity, most are based upon the general strategy just described. Although some refinements are possible to improve computational speed and efficiency, this approach is in essence a kind of wearing down of the classification problem by repetitive application assignment and re-assignment of pixels to groups. Key components to any unsupervised classification algorithm are effective methods of measuring distances in data space, identifying class centroids and testing the distinctness of classes. There are many different strategies for accomplishing each of these tasks.

AMOEBA

The AMOEBA classification operates in the manner of usual unsupervised classification, with the addition of a contiguity constraint that considers the location of values as spectral classes are formed. The analyst specifies a tolerance limit that governs the diversity permitted as classes are formed. As a class if formed by a group of neighbouring pixels, adjacent pixels belonging to other classes are considered as prospective members of the class if it occurs as a small region within a larger, more homogeneous, background (Fig. 12.11). If the candidate pixel has values that fall within the tolerance limits specified by the analyst, the pixel is accepted as a member of the class despite the fact that it differs from other members. Thus, locations as well as spectral properties of pixels form classification criteria for AMOEBA and similar algorithms. Although this approach increases the spectral diversity of classes—normally an undesirable quality—the inclusion of small areas of foreign pixels as members of a more extensive region may satisfy our notion of the proper character of a geographic region. Often, in the manual preparation of maps, the analyst will perform a similar form of generalisation as a means of eliminating small inclusions within larger regions. This kind of generalisation presents cartographic data in a form suitable for presentation at small scale. The AMOEBA classifier was designed for application to scenes composed primarily of large homogeneous regions, such as the agricultural landscapes of the North American prairies. For such scenes, it seems to work well, although it may not be as effective in more complex landscapes composed of smaller parcels.

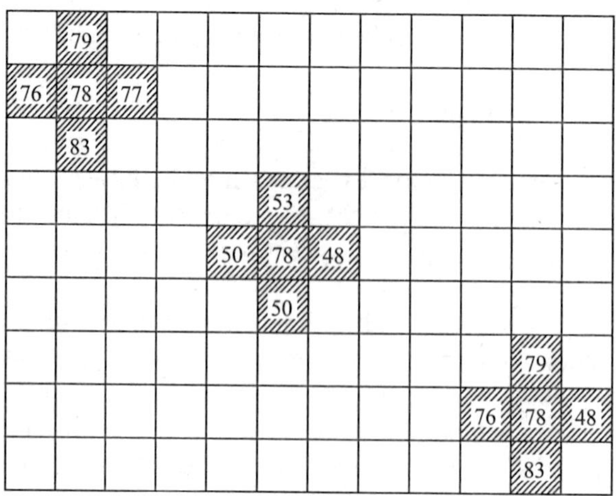

Fig. 12.11. AMOEBA spatial operator. This contrived example shows AMOEBA as it considers classification of three pixels, all with the same digital value of '78'. Upper left: The central pixels has a value similar to those of all its neighbours; it is classified together with the surrounding pixels. Center: The central pixel differs from its neighbours, but due to its position within a background of contrasting but homogenous pixels, it is classified with the darker pixels. Lower left: The central pixel is classified with the darker pixels at the top, left and bottom. In all three situations, classification is based upon values adjacent locations.

Assignment of Spectral Categories to Informational Categories

The classification result described thus far provide uniform groupings of pixels—classes that are uniform with respect to the spectral values that compose each pixel. These spectral classes are significant only to the extent that they can be matched to one or more informational classes that are of interest to the user of the final product. These spectral classes may sometimes correspond directly to informational categories. For example, in Fig. 12.12 the pixels that compose the group closest to the origin correspond to 'open water'. This identification is more or less obvious from the spectral properties of the class—few other classes will exhibit such dark values in both spectral channels. However, seldom can we depend upon a clear identification of spectral categories from spectral values alone. Often it is possible to match spectral and informational categories by examining patterns on the image; many informational categories are recognisable by the positions, sizes and shapes of individual parcels and their spatial correspondence with areas of known identity.

Often, however, spectral classes do not match directly to informational classes. In some instances, informational classes may occur in complex mixtures and arrangements. Perhaps forested patches are scattered in small areas against a more extensive background of grassland. If these forested areas are small relative to the spatial resolution of the sensor, then the overall spectral response for such an area will differ from either 'forest' or 'grassland', due to the effect of mixed pixels upon the spectral response. This region may be assigned then to a class separate from either the forest or the grassland classes. It is the analyst's task to apply his or her knowledge of the region and the sensor to identify the character of the problem and to apply an appropriate remedy.

Or, because of spectral diversity, even nominally uniform informational classes may manifest themselves as a set of spectral classes. For example, a forested area may be recorded as several spectral clusters, due perhaps to variations in density, age, aspect, shadowing and other factors that alter the spectral properties of a forested region, but do not alter the fact that the region belongs to the informational class 'forest'. The analyst must therefore examine the output to match spectral categories from the classification with the informational classes of significance to those who will use the results.

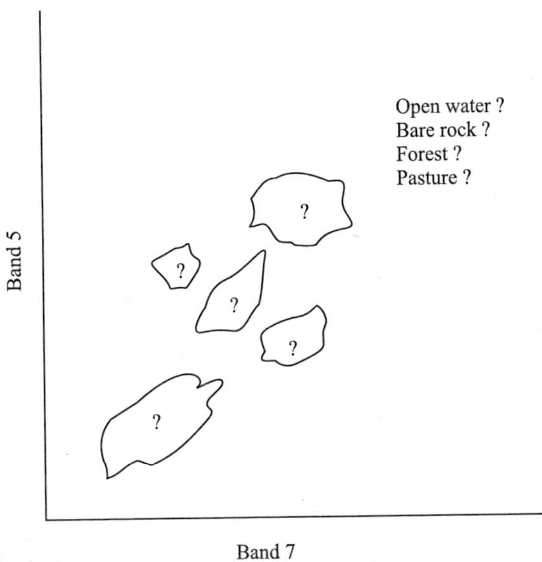

Fig. 12.12. Assignment of spectral categories to image categories. Unsupervised classification defines the clusters defined schematically on the scatter diagram. The analyst must decide which, if any, match to the list of informational categories that form the object of the analysis.

Thus, a serious practical problem with unsupervised classification is that clear matches between spectral and informational classes are not always possible; some informational categories may not have direct spectral counterparts and vice versa. Furthermore, the analyst does not have control over the nature of the categories generated by unsupervised classification. If a study is conducted to compare results with those from an adjacent region or from a different date, for example, it may be necessary to have the same set of informational categories on both maps or the comparison cannot be made. If unsupervised classification is to be used, it may be difficult to generate the same sets of informational categories on both images.

SUPERVISED CLASSIFICATION

Supervised classification can be defined informally as the process of using samples of known identity (i.e., pixels already assignment to informational classes) to classify pixels of unknown identity (i.e., to assign unclassified pixels to one of several informational classes). Samples of known identity are those pixels located within training areas or training fields. The analyst defines training areas by identifying regions on the image that can be clearly matched to areas of known identity on the image. Such areas should typify spectral properties of the categories they represent and of course, must be homogeneous in respect to the informational category to be classified. That is, training areas should not include unusual regions, nor should they straddle boundaries between categories. Size, shape and position must favour convenient identification both on the image and on the ground. Pixels located within these areas form the training samples used to guide the classification algorithm to assign specific spectral values to appropriate informational classes. Clearly, the selection of these training data is a key step in supervised classification.

Advantages

The advantages of supervised classification, relative to unsupervised classification, can be enumerated as follows. First, the analyst has control of a selected menu of information categories tailored to a specific purpose and geographic region. This quality may be vitally important if it becomes necessary to generate a classification for the specific purpose of comparison with another classification of the same area at a different date or if the classification must be compatible with those of neighbouring regions. Under such circumstances, the unpredictable (i.e., with respect to number, identity, size and pattern) qualities of categories generated by unsupervised classification may be inconvenient or unsuitable. Second, supervised classification is tied to specific areas of known identity, determined through the process of selecting training areas. Third, the analyst using supervised classification is not faced with the problem of matching spectral categories on the final map with the informational categories of interest (this task has, in effect, been addressed during the process of selecting training data). Finally, the operator may be able to detect serious errors in classification by examining training data to determine if they have been correctly classified by the classification procedure—inaccurate classification of training data indicates serious problems in the classification or selection of training data, although correct classification of training data does not always indicate correct classification of other data.

Disadvantages and Limitations

The disadvantages of supervised classification are numerous. First, the analyst, in effect, imposes a classification structure upon the data (recall that unsupervised classification searches for 'natural' classes). These operator-defined classes may not match the natural classes that exist within the data and therefore may not be distinct or well defined in multidimensional data space. Second, training data are often defined primarily with reference to informational categories and only secondarily with reference to spectral properties. A training area that is '100 per cent forest' may be accurate with respect to the 'forest' designation, but may still be very diverse with respect to density, age, shadowing and the like and therefore form a poor training area. Third, training data selected by the analyst may not be representative of conditions encountered throughout the image. This may be true despite the best effects of the analyst, especially if the area to be classified is large, complex or inaccessible.

Fourth, conscientious selection of training data can be a time-consuming, expensive and tedious undertaking, even if ample resources are at hand. The analyst may experience problems in matching prospective training areas as defined on maps and aerial photographs to the image to be classified. Finally, supervised classification may not be able to recognise and represent special or unique categories not represented in the training data, possibly because they are not known to the analyst or because they occupy very small areas on the image.

Training Data

Training fields are areas of known identity delineated on the digital image, usually by specifying the corner points of a square or rectangular area using line and column numbers within the co-ordinate system of the digital image. The analyst must of course, know the correct class for each area. Usually the analyst begins by assembling and studying maps and aerial photographs of the area to be classified and by investigating selected sites in the field. (Here we assumes that the analyst has some field experience with the specific area to be studied, is familiar with the particular problem the study is to address and has conducted the necessary field observations prior to initiating the actual selection of training data). Specific training areas are identified for each informational category, following the guidelines outlined below. The objective is to identify a set of pixels that accurately represent spectral variation present within each informational region (Fig. 12.13).

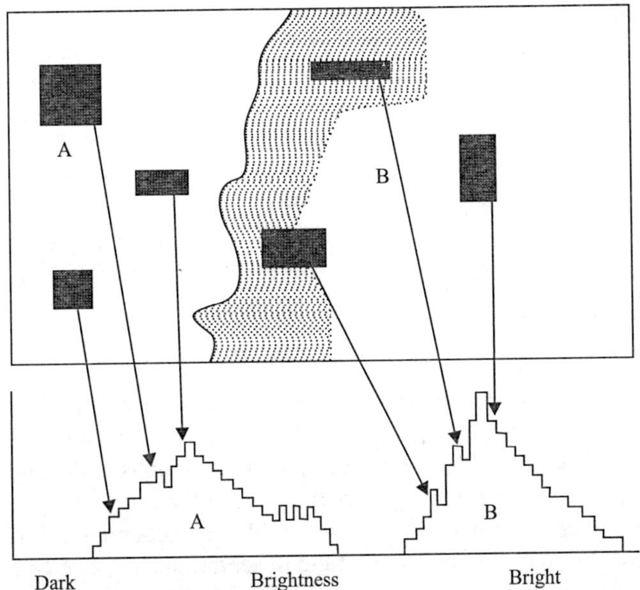

Fig. 12.13. Training fields and training data. Training fields, each composed of many pixels, sample the spectral characteristics of informational categories. Here the shaded figures represent training fields, each positioned carefully to estimate the spectral properties of each class, as represented by the histograms. This information provides the basis for classification of the remaining pixels not within the training fields.

Key Characteristics of Training Areas

Numbers of pixels

An important concern is the overall number of pixels selected for each category; as a general guideline, the operator should ensure that several individual training areas for each category provide a total of at least 100 pixels for each category.

Size

Sizes of training areas are important. Each must be large enough to provide accurate estimates of the properties of each informational class. Therefore, they must as a group include enough pixels to form reliable estimates of the spectral characteristics of each class (hence, the minimum figure of 100 suggested above). Individual training fields should not, on the other hand, be too big, as large areas tend to include undesirable variation. (Because the total number of pixels in the training data for each class can be formed from many separate training fields, each individual area can be much smaller than the total number of pixels required for each class.) Joyce recommends that individual training areas be at least 4 ha (10 acres) in size at the absolute minimum and preferably include about 16 ha (40 acres). Small training fields are difficult to locate accurately on the image. To accumulate an adequate total number of training pixels, the analyst must devote more time to definition and analysis of the additional training fields. Conversely, use of large training fields increases the opportunity for inclusion of spectral inhomogeneities. Joyce suggests 65 ha (160 acres) as the maximum size for training fields.

Joyce specifically refers to Landsat MSS data. So in terms of numbers of pixels, he is recommending from 10 to about 40 pixels for each training field. For TM or SPOT data, of course, his recommendations would specify different numbers of pixels, as the resolutions of these sensors differ from that of the MSS. Also, since the optimum sizes of training fields vary according to the heterogeneity of each landscape and each class, each analyst should develop his or her own guidelines based on experience acquired in specific circumstances.

Shape

Shapes of training areas are not important, provided that shape does not prohibit accurate delineation and positioning of correct outlines of regions on digital images. Usually it is easiest to define square or rectangular areas; such shapes minimise the number of vertices that must be specified, usually the most bothersome task for the analyst.

Location

Location is important, as each informational category should be represented by several training areas positioned throughout the image. Training areas must be positioned in locations that favour accurate and convenient transfer of their outlines from maps and aerial photographs to the digital image (Fig. 12.14). As the training data are intended to represent variation within the image, they must not be clustered in favoured regions of the image that may not typify conditions encountered throughout the image as a whole. It is desirable for the analyst to use direct field observations in the selection of training data, but the requirement for an even distribution of training fields often conflicts with practical constraints, as it may not be practical to visit remote or inaccessible sites that may seem to form good areas for training data. Often aerial observation, or use of good maps and aerial photographs, can provide the basis for accurate delineation of training fields that cannot be inspected in the field. Although such practices are often sound, it is important to avoid development of a cavalier approach to selection of training data that depends completely upon indirect evidence in situations when direct observation is feasible.

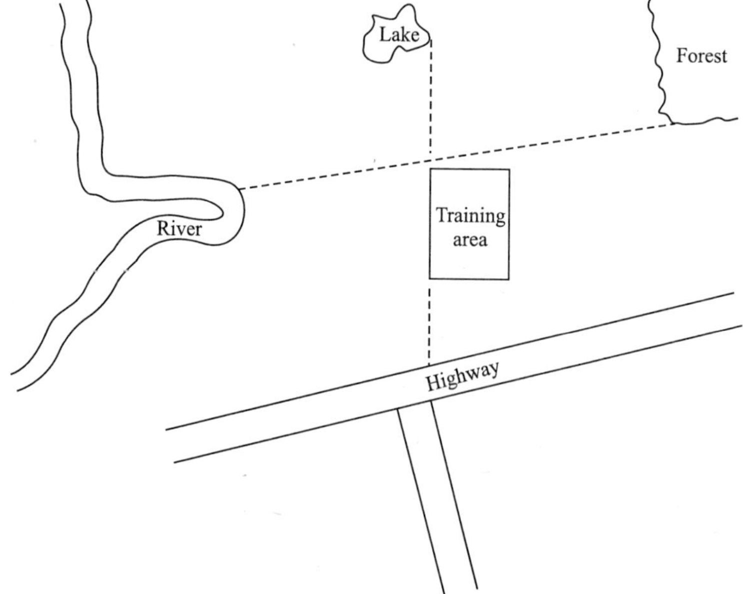

Fig. 12.14. Location of training fields with reference to landmarks. Training fields must be positioned with reference to features easily recognisable on the ground, on maps and aerial photographs and on the digital imagery.

Number

The optimum number of training areas depends upon the number of categories to be mapped, their diversity and the resources that can be devoted to delineating training areas. Ideally, each informational category or each spectral sub-class should be represented by a number (5 to 10 at a minimum) of training areas to ensure that the spectral properties of each category are represented. Because informational classes are often spectrally diverse, it may be necessary to use several sets of training data for each informational category, due to the presence of spectral sub-classes. Selection of multiple training areas is also desirable because later in the classification process it may be necessary to discard some training areas if they are discovered to be unsuitable. Experience indicates that it is usually better to define many small training areas than to use only a few large areas.

Placement

Placement of training areas may be important. Training areas should be placed within the image in a manner that permits convenient and accurate location with respect to distinctive features, such as water bodies or boundaries between distinctive features on the image. They should be distributed throughout the image so that they provide a basis for representation of the diversity present within the scene. Boundaries of training fields should be placed well away from the edges of contrasting parcels so that they do not encompass edge pixels (Fig. 12.15).

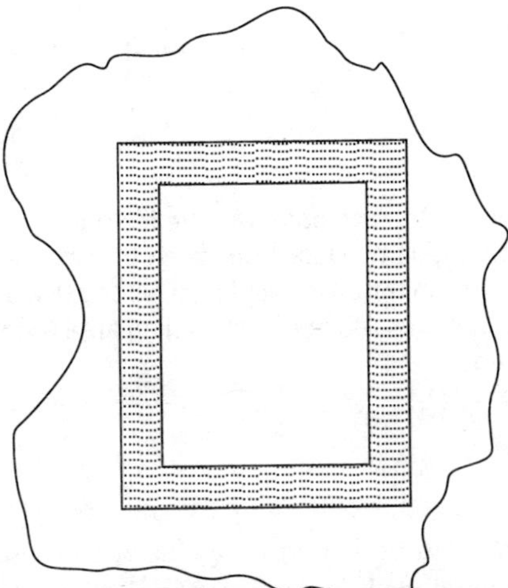

Fig. 12.15. Positioning training fields. Here the irregular line represents the edge of parcel visible on a digital image. The inner rectangle represents the training field surrounded by a 'buffer' of pixels within the parcel, but not included in the training data. These unused pixels help ensure that mixed pixels at the edge of the parcel are not included within the training field (Remember that the analyst may not have absolute confidence in his or her ability to match map or photo information to the digital image).

Uniformity

Perhaps the most important property of a good training area is its uniformity or homogeneity. Data within each training area should exhibit a unimodal frequency distribution for each spectral band to be used (Fig. 12.16). Prospective training areas that exhibit bimodal histograms should be discarded if their boundaries cannot be adjusted to yield more uniformity. Training data provide values that estimate the means, variances and covariances of spectral data measured in several spectral channels. For each class to be mapped, these estimates approximate the mean values for each band, the variability of each band and the interrelationships between bands. As an ideal, these values should represent the conditions present within each class within the scene and thereby form the basis for classification of the vast majority of pixels within each scene that do not belong to training areas. In practice, of course, scenes vary greatly in complexity and individual analysts differ in their knowledge of a region and in their ability to define training areas that accurately represent the spectral properties of informational classes. Moreover, some informational classes are not spectrally uniform and cannot be conveniently represented by a single set of training data.

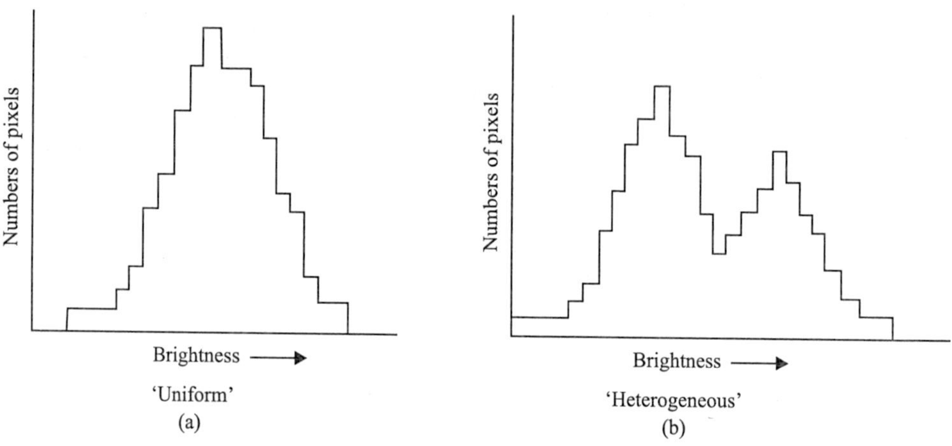

Fig. 12.16. Uniform and heterogeneous training data. (a) The histogram of the training data has a single peak, indicating a degree of spectral homogeneity. Data from such training fields form a suitable basis for image classification. (b) A second set of training data display a bimodal histogram that reveals that this area encompasses two, rather than one, spectral classes. This training area is not satisfactory for image classification and must be discarded or re-defined.

Significance of Training Data

Scholz and Hixson discovered that selection of training data may be as important as or even more important than choice of classification algorithm in determining classification accuracies of agricultural areas in the central United States. They concluded that differences in the selection of training data were more important influences upon accuracy than were differences among some five different classification procedures.

The results of their studies show little difference in the classification accuracies achieved by the five classification algorithms that were considered, if the same training statistics were used. However, in one part of the study, a classification algorithm given two alternative training methods for the same data produced significantly different results. This finding suggests that the choice of training methods, at least in some instances, is as important as the choice of classifier. Scholz concluded that the most important aspect of training fields is that all cover types in the scene must be adequately represented by a sufficient number of samples in each spectral sub-class.

A study by Campbell examined the character of the training data as it influences accuracy of the classification. His examples showed that adjacent pixels within training fields tended to have similar values; as a result, the samples that compose each training field may not be independent samples of the properties within a given category. Training samples collected in continuous blocks may tend to underestimate the variability within each class and to overestimate that distinctness of categories. His examples also show that the degree of similarity varies between land-cover categories, from band to band and from date to date. If training sample are selected randomly within classes, rather than as blocks of continuous pixels, effects of high similarity are minimised and classification accuracies improve. Also, his results suggests that it is probably better to use a rather large number of small training fields rather than a few large areas.

Idealised Sequence for Selecting Training Data

Specific circumstances for conducting supervised classification vary greatly, so it is not possible to discuss in detail the procedures to follow in selecting training data, which will be determined in part by the equipment and software available at a given facility. However, it is possible to outline and idealised sequence as a suggestion of the key steps in the selection and evaluation of training data.

1. Assemble information, including maps and aerial photographs of the region to be mapped.
2. Conduct field studies, to acquire first-hand information regarding the area to be studied. The amount of effort devoted to field studies varies depending upon the analyst's familiarity with the region to be studied. If the analyst is intimately familiar with the region and has access to up-to-date maps and photographs, additional field observations may not be necessary. However, in the vast majority of situations at least some field work will be required.
3. Carefully plant collection of field observations and choose a route designed to observe all regions of the study region. Maps and images should be taken into the field in the form that permits the analyst to annotate them as he or she makes observations in the field (e.g., images may be prepared with overlays; photocopies of maps can be marked with coloured pens). Although time and access may be limited, it is important to observe all classes of terrain encountered within the study area, as well as all regions. Observations should not be limited to a few easily observed segments of the area. The analyst should keep good notes, carefully keyed to annotations on the image. He or she may find it useful to take photographs as a permanent record of conditions observed. In very remote areas aerial observation may be the only practical means of observing the study region. Ideally, field observations should be timed to coincide with image acquisition; when this is not possible, they should at least be made during the season images were acquired.
4. Conduct a preliminary examination of the digital scene. Determine landmarks that may be useful in positioning training fields. Assess image quality. Examine frequency histograms of the data and determine if pre-processing is necessary.
5. Identify prospective training areas, using guidelines proposed by Joyce and outlined here. Sizes of prospective areas must be assessed in the light of scale differences between maps or photographs and the digital image. Locations of training areas must be defined with respect to features easily recoganisable on the image and on the maps and photographs used as collateral information.
6. Display the digital image, then locate and delineate training areas on the digital image. Be sure to place training area boundaries well inside parcel boundaries to avoid including mixed pixels within training areas. At the completion of this step, all training areas should be identified with respect to row and column co-ordinates within the image.

7. For each training field, display and inspect frequency histograms of all spectral bands to be used in the classification. If possible, examine means, variance, divergence measures, covariances and so on, to assess the usefulness of training data.
8. Modify boundaries of the training fields to eliminate bimodal frequency distributions or if necessary, discard those areas that are not suitable. If necessary, return to Step 1 to define new areas to replace those that have been eliminated.
9. Incorporate training data information into a form suitable for use in the classification procedure and proceed with the classification process as described in subsequent sections of this chapter.

Specific Methods for Supervised Classification

A variety of different methods have been devised to implement the basic strategy of supervised classification. All use information derived from the training data as a means of classifying those pixels not assigned to training fields. The following sections outline only a few of the many methods of supervised classification.

Parallelepiped classification

Parallelepiped classification, sometimes also known as box decision rule or level-slice procedures, are based on the ranges of values within the training data to define regions within a multidimensional data space. The spectral values of unclassified pixels are projected into data space; those that fall within the regions defined by the training data are assigned to the appropriate categories.

An example can be formed from data presented in Table 12.4. Here Landsat MSS bands 5 and 7 are selected from larger data set to provide a concise, easily illustrated example. In practice, four or more bands can be used. The ranges of values with respect to band 5 can be plotted on the horizontal axis in Fig. 12.17. The extremes of values in band 7 training data are plotted on the vertical axis, then projected to intersect with the ranges from band 5. The polygons thus defined (Fig. 12.17) represent regions in data space that are assigned to categories in the classification. As pixels of unknown identity are considered for classification, those that fall within these regions are assigned to the category associated with each polygon, as derived from the training data. The procedure can be extended to as many bands or as many categories, as necessary. In addition, the decision boundaries can be defined by the standard deviations of the values within the training areas rather than their ranges. This kind of strategy is useful because fewer pixels will be placed in an 'unclassified' category (a special problem for parallelepiped classification), but it also increases the opportunity for classes to overlap in spectral data space.

Table 12.4. Data for example shown in Fig. 12.17.

Group A Band				*Group B Band*			
4	*5*	*6*	*7*	*4*	*5*	*6*	*7*
34	28	22	3	28	18	59	35
36	35	24	6	28	21	57	34
36	28	22	6	28	21	57	30
36	31	23	5	28	14	59	35
36	34	25	7	30	18	62	28
36	31	21	6	30	18	62	38

(Cont'd)

	Group A Band				*Group B Band*			
	4	*5*	*6*	*7*	*4*	*5*	*6*	*7*
	35	30	18	6	28	16	62	36
	36	33	24	2	30	22	59	37
	36	36	27	10	27	16	56	34
High	34	28	18	10	27	14	56	28
Low	36	36	27	3	30	22	62	38

Note. These data have been selected from a larger data set to illustrate parallelepiped classification.

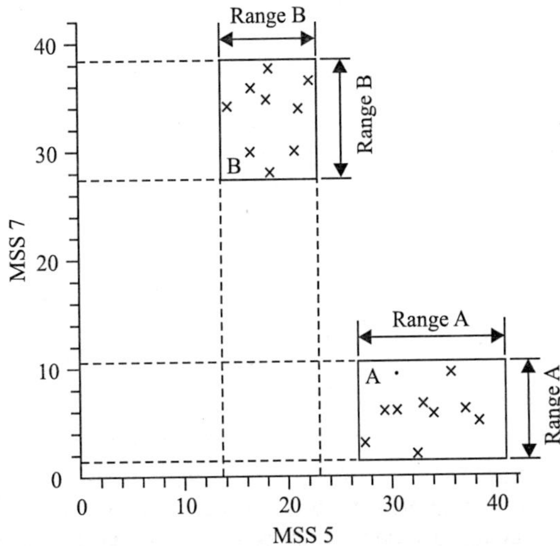

Fig. 12.17. Parallelepiped classification. Ranges of values within training data (Table 12.4) define decision boundaries. Here only two bands are shown, but the principle extends to several spectral bands. Other pixels, not from the training fields, are classified as a given category if their positions fall within the polygons defined by the training data.

Although this procedure for classification has the advantages of accuracy, directness and simplicity, some of its disadvantages are obvious. Spectral regions for informational categories may intersect. Training data may underestimate actual ranges of classification and leave large areas in data space and on the image unassigned to informational categories. Also, the regions as defined in data space are not uniformly occupied by pixels in each category; those pixels near the edges of class boundaries may belong to other classes. Also, if training data do not encompass the complete range of values encountered in the image (as is frequently the case) large areas of the image remain unclassified or the basic procedure described here must be modified to assign these pixels to logical classes. This strategy was among the first used in the classification of Landsat data and is still used, although it may not always be the most effective choice for image classification.

Minimum distance classification

Another approach to classification uses the central values of the spectral data that form the training data as a means of assigning pixels to informational categories. The spectral data from training fields can be plotted in multidimensional data space in the same manner illustrated previously for unsupervised classification. Values in several bands determine the positions of each pixels within the clusters that are formed by training data for each category (Fig. 12.18). These clusters may appear to be the same as those defined earlier for unsupervised classification. However, in unsupervised classification, these clusters of pixels were defined according to the 'natural' structure of data. Now, for supervised classification, these groups are formed by values of pixels within the training fields defined by the analyst.

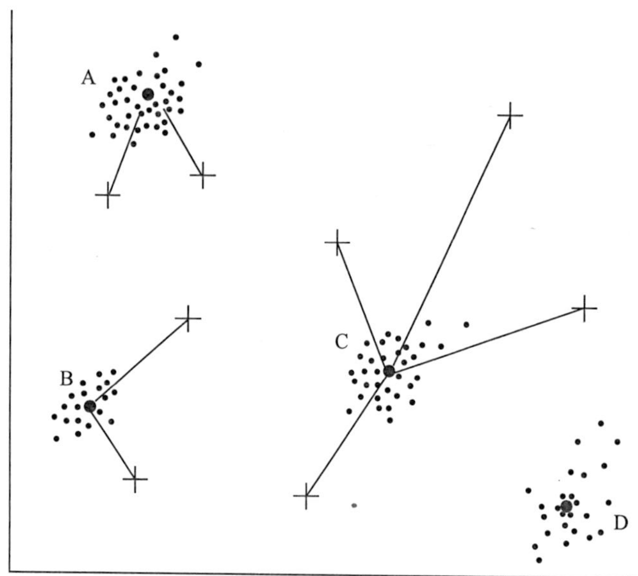

Fig. 12.18. Minimum distance classifier. Here small dots represent pixels from training fields and crosses indicate the large unclassified pixels from elsewhere in the image; each of these pixels is assigned to the class with the closest centroid, as measured using the distance measures discussed in the text.

Each cluster can be represented by its centroid, often defined as its mean value. As unassigned pixels are considered for assignment to one of the several classes, the multidimensional distance to each cluster centroid is calculated and the pixel is then assigned to the closest cluster. Thus, the classification proceeds by always using the 'minimum distance' from a given pixel to a cluster centroid defined by the training data as the spectral manifestation of an informational class

Minimum distance classifiers are direct in concept and in implementation, but are not widely used in remote sensing work. In its simplest form, minimum distance classification is not always accurate; there is no provision for accommodating differences in variability of classes and some classes may overlap at their edges. It is possible to devise more sophisticated versions of the basic approach just outlined by using different distance measures and different methods of defining cluster centroids.

ISODATA

The ISODATA classifier is a variation on the minimum distance method; however, it produces results that are often considered to be superior to those derived from the basic minimum distance approach. ISODATA is often seen as a form of supervised classification, although it differs appreciably from the classical model of supervised classification presented at the beginning of this chapter. It is a good example of a technique that shares characteristics of both supervised and unsupervised methods (i.e., 'hybrid' classification) and provides evidence that the distinction between the two approaches is not as clear as idealised descriptions imply.

ISODATA starts with the training data selected, as previously described; these data can be envisioned as clusters in multidimensional data space. All unassigned pixels are then assigned to the nearest centroid. Thus, far the approach is the same as described previously for the minimum distances classifier. Next, new centroids are found for each group and the process of allocating pixels to the closest centroids is repeated if the centroid changes position. The process is repeated until there is no change or only a small change, in class centroids from one iteration to the next. A step-by-step description is as follows:

1. Choose initial estimates of class means. These can be derived from training data; in this respect, ISODATA resembles supervised classification.
2. All other pixels in the scene are assigned to the class with the closest mean, as considered in multidimensional data space.
3. Class means are then re-computed to include effects of those pixels that may have been re-assigned in step 2.
4. If any class mean changes in value from step 2 to step 3, then the process returns to step 2 and repeats the assignment of pixels to the closest centroid. Otherwise, the result at the end of step 3 represents the final results.

Steps 2, 3 and 4 use the methodology of unsupervised classification, although the requirement for training data identifies the method essentially as supervised classification. It could probably best be considered as a hybrid rather than as a clear example of either approach.

Maximum likelihood classification

In nature the classes that we classify exhibit natural variation in their spectral patterns. Further variability is added by the effects of haze, topographic shadowing, system noise and the effects of mixed pixels. As a result, remote sensing images seldom record spectrally pure classes; more typically, they display a range of brightnesses in each band. The classification strategies considered thus far do not consider variation that may be present within spectral categories and do not address problems that arise when frequency distributions of spectral values from separate categories overlap. For example, for application of a parallelepiped classifier, the overlap of classes is a serious problem because spectral data space cannot then be neatly divided into discrete units for classification. This kind of situation arises frequently because often our attention is focused upon classifying those pixels that tend to be spectrally similar rather than those that are distinct enough to be easily and accurately classified by other classifiers.

As a result, the situation depicted in Fig. 12.19 is common. Assume that we examine a digital image representing a region composed of three-fourths forested land and one-fourth cropland. The two classes 'Forest' and 'Cropland' are distinct with respect to average brightness, but extreme values (very bright forest pixels or very dark crop pixels) are similar in the region where the two frequency distributions overlap. (For clarity, Fig. 12.19 shows data for only a single spectral band, although the principle extends to values observed in several bands and to more than the two classes shown here.) Brightness value '45' falls into the region of the overlap, where we cannot make a clear assignment to either 'Forest' or to 'Cropland'. Using the kinds of decision rules mentioned above, we cannot decide which group should receive these pixels unless we place the decision boundary arbitrarily.

In this situation, an effective classification would consider the relative likelihoods of '45 as a member of Forest' and ' 45 as a member of Cropland'. We could then choose the class that would maximise the probability of a correct classification, given the information in the training data. This kind of strategy is known as maximum likelihood classification—it uses the training data as a means of estimating means and variances of the classes, which are then used to estimate the probabilities. Maximum likelihood classification considers not only the mean or average, values in assigning classification, but also the variability of brightness values in each class.

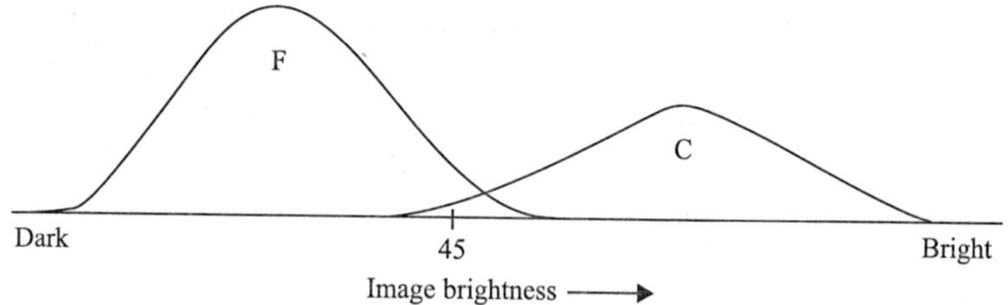

Fig. 12.19. Maximum likelihood classification. These frequency distributions represent pixels from two training fields; the zone of overlap depicts pixel values common to both categories. The relations of the values within the overlap region to the overall frequency distribution for each class forms the basis for assigning pixels to classes.

The maximum likelihood decision rule, implemented quantitatively to consider several classes and several spectral channels simultaneously, forms a powerful classification technique. It requires intensive calculations, so it has the disadvantage of requiring more computer resources than do most of the simpler techniques mentioned above. Also, it is sensitive to variation in the quality of training data—even more so than most other supervised techniques. Computation of the estimated probabilities is based on the assumption that both training data and the classes themselves display multivariate normal (Gaussian) frequency distributions. (This is one reason that training data should exhibit unimodal distributions, as discussed above.) Data from remotely sensed images often do not strictly adhere to this rule, although the departures are often small enough that the usefulness of the procedure is preserved. Nonetheless, training data that are not carefully selected may introduce error.

TEXTURAL CLASSIFIERS

Image classification presents special problems for digital analysis because of the diverse spectral characteristics of the landscape. Idealised landscape regions consist of spectrally homogeneous patches on the earth's surface. Accurate mapping of such regions could be accomplished by the relatively straightforward process of matching spectral categories to the spectral 'signatures' of information categories, as described above.

Actual landscape regions are, of course, usually formed by assemblages of spectrally diverse features. Low-density residential land, for example, as viewed from above in detail, is composed largely of tree crowns, rooftops, lawns and paved streets, driveways and parking lots. We are interested in classification of the composite of these many features rather than in making an inventory of the many components that in themselves may be of little interest. Thus, in the ideal, the classification should focus upon the overall pattern of variation that characterises each category, rather than upon the average brightness, which may not reveal much about the essential differences between categories. Although human interpreters can intuitively recognise such complex patterns, many digital classification algorithms encounter serious problems in accurate classification of such scenes because they are designed to classify each separate spectral region as a separate informational category.

Textural classifiers attempt to measure image texture: distinctive spatial and spectral relationships between neighbouring pixels. For example, the standard deviation of brightness values within a neighbourhood of specified size, systematically moved over the entire image, may provide a rough measure of the spectral variability over short distances as a measure of image texture. Such a measure may permit the analyst to classify composite categories such as the one mentioned above.

Usually more sophisticated measures of texture are required to produce satisfactory results. For example, other textural measures examine relationships between brightness values at varying distances and directions from a central pixel, which is systematically moved over the image.

Jensen found that the use of textural measures improved his classification of Level II and III sub-urban and transitional land using band 5 of the Landsat MSS. Improvements were confined to certain categories and were perhaps of marginal significance when considered in the context of increases costs.

Textural measures seem to work best when relatively large neighbourhoods are defined (perhaps as large as 64 × 64 pixels). Such large neighbourhoods may cause problems when they straddle the boundaries between categories. In addition, such large neighbourhoods may decrease the effective spatial resolution of the final map, as they must form its smallest spatial elements.

ANCILLARY DATA

Ancillary or collateral, data can be defined as data acquired by means other than remote sensing that are used to assist in the classification or analysis of remotely sensed data. For manual interpretation, ancillary data have long been useful in the identification and delineation of features on aerial images. Such uses may be an informal, implicit application of an interpreter's knowledge and experience or may be more explicit reference to maps, reports and data. For digital remote sensing, uses of ancillary data are quite different. Ancillary data must be incorporated into the analysis in a structured and formalised manner that connects directly to the analysis of the remotely sensed data. Ancillary data may consist, for example, of topographic, paedologic or geologic data. Primary requirements are (i) that the data be available in digital form; (ii) that the data pertain to the problem at hand; and (iii) that the data be compatible with the remotely sensed data.

In fact, a serious limitation to practically applying digital ancillary data is incompatibility with remotely sensed data. Physical incompatibility (matching digital formats, etc.) is of course one such incompatibility, but logical incompatibility is more subtle, but equally important. Seldom are ancillary data collected specifically for use with a specific remote sensing problem; usually they are data collected for another purpose, perhaps as a means of reducing costs in time and money. For example, digital terrain data gathered by the USGS and by the National Imagery and Mapping Agency (NIMA), are frequently used as ancillary data for remote sensing studies. A remote sensing project, however, is not likely to be budgeted to include the resources for digitising, then editing and correcting, these data and therefore the data would seldom be compatible with the remotely sensed data with respect to scale, resolution, date and accuracy. Some differences can be minimised by pre-processing the ancillary data to reduce effects of different measurement scales, resolutions and so on, but without that, unresolved incompatibilities, possibly quite subtle, would detract from the effectiveness of the ancillary data.

Choice of ancillary variables is critical. In the mountainous regions of the western United States, elevation data have been very effective as ancillary data for mapping vegetation patterns with digital MSS data, due in part to the fact that there is dramatic variation in local elevation there and change in vegetation is closely associated with change in elevation, slope and aspect. In more level settings, elevation differences have subtle influences on vegetation distributions; therefore, elevation data would be less effective as ancillary variables. Although some scientists advocate the use of any and all available ancillary data, in the hope of deriving whatever advantage might be possible, common sense would seem to favour careful selection of variables with conceptual and practical significance to the mapped distributions.

The conceptual basis for the use of ancillary data is that the additional data, collected independently of the remotely sensed data, increase the information available for separating the classes and for performing other kinds of analysis. To continue the example from above, in some regions, vegetation patterns are closely related to topographic elevation, slope and aspect. Therefore the combination of elevation data with remotely sensed data forms a powerful analytical tool because the two kinds of data provide separate, mutually supporting contributions to the subject being interpreted. Some techniques for working with ancillary data are outlined below.

Stratification refers to the subdivision of an image into regions that are easy to define using the ancillary data, but might be difficult to define using only the remotely sensed data. For example, topographic data regarding elevation, slope and aspect would be hard to extract from the spectral information in the remotely sensed image. But, ancillary topographic data would provide a means of restricting the classes that would be necessary to do when using the spectral data.

The stratification is essentially an implementation of the layered classification strategy to be discussed in next section. Some analysts have treated each strata as completely separate, selecting training data separately for each strata and classifying each strata independent of the others. The several classifications are then merged so as to present the final results as a single image. Hutchinson emphasised the dangers of ineffective stratification and warns of unpredictable, inconsistent effects of classification algorithms across different strata.

Ancillary data have also been used to form an additional channel. For example, digital elevation data could be incorporated with SPOT or Landsat MSS data as an additional band, in the hope that the additional data, independent of the remotely sensed data, would contribute the effective image classification. In general, it appears that this use of ancillary data has not been proven effective in producing substantial improvements in classification accuracy. Strahler implemented another approach, using ancillary data as a means of modifying prior probabilities in maximum likelihood classification. Digital elevation data, as an additional band of data, were used to refine the probabilities of observing specific classes of vegetation in Southern California mountains. For example, the probability of observing a specific class, such as 'lodgepole pine', varies with topography and elevation. Therefore, a given set of spectral values can have a different meaning, depending on the elevation value in the which a given pixel is situated. This approach appears to be effective, at least for how it has been used and studied thus far.

Finally, ancillary data can be used after the usual classifications have been completed, in a process known as post-classification sorting. Postclassification sorting examines the confusion matrix derived from a traditional classification. Confused classes are the candidates for post-classification sorting. Ancillary data are then used in an effort to improve discrimination between pairs of classes, thereby improving the overall accuracy by focusing on the weakest aspects of the classification. Hutchinson encountered several problems with his application of post-classification sorting, but in general favours it for being simple, inexpensive and convenient to implement.

On the whole, ancillary data, despite their benefits, present numerous practical and conceptual problems for the remote sensing analyst. Sometimes it may be difficult to select and acquire the data that may be most useful for a given problem. The most useful data might not be available in digital form; the analyst might be forced to invest considerable effort in identifying, acquiring, then digitising the desired information. Therefore, many if not most uses of ancillary data rely on those data that can be acquired 'off-the-shelf', from a library of data already acquired and digitised for another purpose. This presents a danger that the ancillary data may be used much because of their availability as for their appropriateness for a specific situation.

Because ancillary data is generally acquired for a purpose other than the one at hand, the problem of compatibility can be important. Ideally, ancillary data should posses compatibility with respect to scale, level of detail, accuracy, geographic reference system and in instances where time differences are important, the date of acquisition. Because analysts are often forced to use off-the-shelf data, incompatibilities form one of the major issues in use of ancillary data. To be useful, ancillary data must be accurately registered to the remotely sensed data. Therefore, the analyst may be required to alter the geometry or the level of detail, in the ancillary data to bring them into registration with the remotely sensed data. Efforts to alter image geometry or the resample data change the values and therefore are likely to influence the usefulness of that data.

Sometimes ancillary data may already exist in the form of discrete classes—that is, as specific geologic or paedologic classes, for example. Such data are typically represented on maps as discrete parcels, with abrupt changes at the boundaries between classes. Digital remote sensor data are continuous and therefore differences between the discretely classed and continuous remote sensor data may influence the character of the results, possibly causing sharp changes where only gradual transitions should occur.

To summarise, ancillary data are non-image information used to aid in classification of spectral data. There is a long tradition of both implicit and explicit use of such information in the process of manual interpretation of images, including data from maps, photographs, field observations, reports and personal experience. For digital analysis, ancillary data often consist of data available in formats consistent with the digital spectral data or in forms that can be conveniently transformed into usable formats. Examples include digital elevation data or digitised soil maps.

Ancillary data can be used in either of two ways. They can be 'added to' or 'superimposed' over the spectral data to form a single multiband image; the ancillary data are treated simply as additional channels of data. Or, the analysis can proceed in two steps using a layered classification strategy (as described below); the spectral data are classified in the first step, then the ancillary data form the basis for reclassification and refinement of the initial results.

LAYERED CLASSIFICATION

Layered classification refers to use of a hierarchical process in which two or more steps form the basis for classification. The usual single-step classification algorithm uses all available information in a single process to produce the entire menu of informational categories. Layered classification uses subsets of data in a series of separate steps, presumably by applying each form of information in its most effective context. The hierarchical structure permits the most difficult classification decisions to be made in a context that isolates the problem categories from others and focuses the most effective variables upon the classification decision. This approach represents another example of digital classification strategies modelled to imitate selected characteristics of manual image interpretation methods.

For example, Jensen devised a layered classification strategy that separated vegetated and non-vegetated regions early in the classification by using vegetation indices, as a measure of extend of living biomass with each pixel. This basic distinction separated built-up and heavily vegetated regions at an early point in the classification, preventing confusion between categories later in the classification process.

Layered classification can be useful only if the classification logic can be structured in a way that minimises errors at the upper levels of the decision tree. If errors are made at the first stage, they are carried to lower levels and will appear in the final product regardless of the soundness of subsequent decisions.

13

Field Data

INTRODUCTION

Every application of remote sensing must apply, if only implicitly, field observations in one form or another. Each analyst must define relationships between image data and conditions at corresponding points on the ground. Although use of field data appears, at first glance, to be self-evident, there are numerous practical and conceptual difficulties to be encountered and solved in the course of even the most routine work.

Field data consist of observations collected at or near ground level in support of remote sensing analysis. Although it is a truism that characteristics of field data must be tailored for the specific study at hand, the inconvenience and expense of collecting accurate field data often lead analysts to apply field data collected for one purpose to other, perhaps different, purposes. Therefore, a key concern is not only to acquire field data but to acquire data suitable for the specific task at hand. Accurate field data permit the analyst to match points or areas on the imagery to corresponding regions on the ground surface and thereby to establish with confidence relationships between the image and conditions on the ground. In their simplest form, field data may simply permit an analyst to identify a specific region as forest. In more detailed circumstances, field data may identify a region as a specific form of forest or specify height, volume, leaf area index, photosynthetic activity or other properties according to specific purposes of a study.

KINDS OF FIELD DATA

Field data typically serve one of three purposes. First, they can be used to verify, to evaluate or to assess the result of remote sensing investigations. Second, they can provide reliable data to guide the analytical process, such as creating training fields to support supervised classification. This distinction introduces the basic difference between the realms of qualitative (nominal labels) and quantitative analyses, discussed later in this chapter. Third, field data can provide information used to model the spectral behaviour of specific landscape feature (e.g., plants, soils or water bodies). For example, analyses of the spectral properties of forest canopies can be based on quantitative models of the behaviour of radiation within the canopy—models that require detailed and accurate field observations.

Despite its significance, development of sound procedures for field data collection has not been discussed in a manner that permits others to easily grasp the principles that underlie them.

Discussions of field data collection procedures typically include some combination of the following components:

1. Data to record ground-level or low-level, spectral data for specific features and estimates of atmospheric effects.
2. Broad guidelines for collection of data for use with specific kinds of imagery.
3. Discipline-specific guidelines for collection and organisation of data.
4. Guidelines for collection of data for use with specific digital analyses.
5. Highlighting of special problems arising from methodologies developed in unfamiliar ecological settings.
6. Evaluation of relative merits of quantitative biophysical data in relation to qualitative designations.

The work by Joyce probably comes the closest to defining field data collection as a process to be integrated into a study's analytical plan. He outlined procedures for systematic collection of field data for digital classification of multispectral satellite data. Although his work focused on specific procedures for analysis of Landsat MSS data, he implicitly stressed the need for the data collection plan to be fully compatible with the resolution of the sensor, the spatial scale of the landscape and the kinds of digital analyses to be employed. Further, his recognition of the need to prepare a specific document devoted to field data collection itself emphasised the significance of the topic.

Field data must include at least three kinds of information. The first consists of attributes or measurements that describe ground conditions at a specific place. Examples might include identification of a specific crop or land use or measurements of soil moisture content. Second, these observations must be linked to locational and size (e.g., slope, aspect and elevation) information so the attributes can be correctly matched to corresponding points in image data. And third, observations must also be described with respect to the time and date. These three elements—attributes, location, time—form the minimum information for useful field data. Complete field data also include other information, such as records of weather, illumination, identities of the persons who collected the data, calibration information for instruments and other components as required for specific projects.

NOMINAL DATA

Nominal labels consist of qualitative designations applied to regions delineated on imagery that convey basic differences with adjacent regions. Simple examples include forest, urban land, turbid water and so on. Despite their apparent rudimentary character, accurate and precise nominal labels convey significant information. Those that are most precise—for example, evergreen forest, single-family residential housing, maize, winter wheat—convey more information than broader designations and therefore are more valuable.

Nominal labels originate from several alternative sources. One is an established classification system, such as that proposed by Anderson and comparable systems established in other disciplines. These offer the advantage of acceptance by other workers, comparability with other studies, established definitions and defined relationships between classes. In other instances, classes and labels have origins in local terminology or in circumstances that are specific to a given study. These may have the advantage of serving well the immediate purposes of the study, but limit comparison with other studies. Collection of data in the field is expensive and inconveninet, so there are many incentives to use a set of field data for as many purposes as possible; this effect means that it is often difficult to anticipate the ultimate application of a specific set of data. Therefore, adhoc classifications that are unique to a specific appliciation often prove unsatisfactory if the scope of the study expands beyond its initial purpose. Nonetheless, analysts must work to address the immediate issues at hand without attempting to anticipate every potential use of their data—the objective should be to maintain flexibility rather than to cover every possibility.

In the field, nominal data are usually easy to collect at points or for small areas; difficulties arise as one attempts to apply the labelling system to larger areas. For these reasons, it is usually convenient to annotate maps or aerial photographs in the field as a means of relating isolated point observations to areal units. As the system is applied to broader regions, requiring the work of several observers, it becomes more important to train observers in the consistent application of the system and to evaluate the results to detect inconsistencies and errors at the earliest opportunity. Because physical characteristics of some classes vary seasonally, it is important to ensure that the timing of field observations match those of the imagery to be examined.

DOCUMENTATION OF NOMINAL DATA

The purpose of field data is to permit reconstruction, in as much detail as possible, of ground and atmospheric conditions at the place and time that imagery was acquired. Therefore, field data require careful and complete documentation because they may be required later to answer questions that had not been anticipated at the time they were collected. Nominal data can be recorded as field sketches or as annotated aerial photographs or maps. The inherent variability of landscapes within nominal labels means that careful documentation of field data is an important component of the field data collection plan. Field observations should be collected using standardised procedures designed specifically for each project to ensure that uniform data are collected at each site (Fig. 13.1). Reliable documentation includes careful notes, sketches, ground photographs and even videotapes. Workers must keep log to identify photographs in relation to field sites and to record dates, times, weather, orientations and related information. Photographs must be cross-indexed to field sketches and notes. In some instances, small-format aerial photographs might be useful if feasible within the constraints of the project.

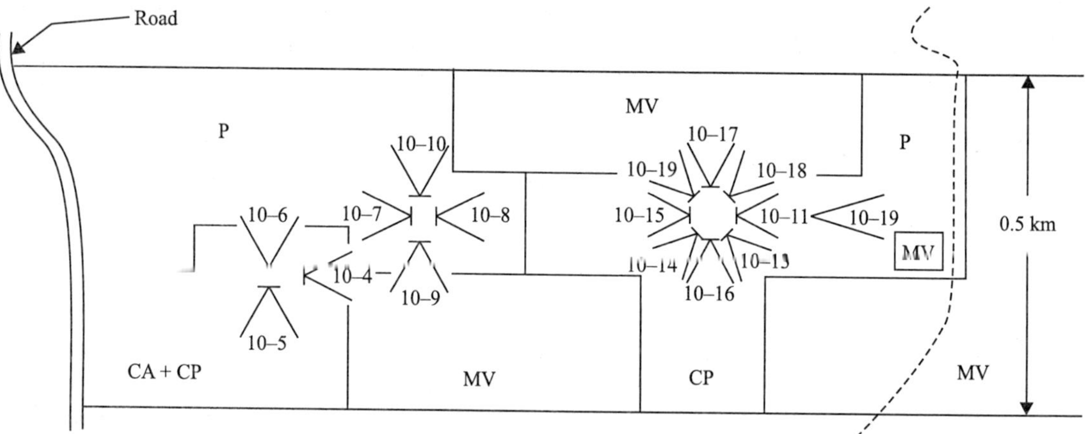

Fig. 13.1. Field sketch illustrating collection of data for nominal labels. The V-shaped symbols represent the fields of view of photographs documenting land cover within cadastral units.

BIOPHYSICAL DATA

Biophysical data consist of measurements of physical characteristics collected in the field describing, for example, the type, size, form and spacing of plants that form the vegetative cover. Or, as another example, biophysical data might record the texture and mineralogy of the soil surface. The exact character of biophysical data collected for a specific study depends on the purposes of the study, but typically data might include such characteristics as leaf area index (LAI), biomass, soil texture and soil moisture. Many such measurements vary over time, so they often must be coordinated with image acquisition; in any event, careful records must be made of time, date, location and weather.

Biophysical data typically apply to points, so often they must be linked to areas by averaging of values from several observations within an area. Further, biophysical data must often be associated with nominal labels, so they do not replace nominal data but rather document the precise meaning of nominal labels. For example, biophysical data often document the biomass or structure of vegetation within a nominal class rather than completely replacing a nominal label. In their assessment of field data recording forest sites, Congalton and Biging found that purely visual assessment provided accurate records of species present, but that plot and field measurements were required for accurate assessment of dominant-size classes.

FIELD RADIOMETRY

Radiometric data permit the analyst to relate brightnesses recorded by an aerial sensor to corresponding brightnesses near the ground surface. A field spectroradiometer consists of a measuring unit with a hand-held probe connected to the measuring unit by a fiber-optic cable. The measuring unit consists of an array of photosensitive detectors, with filters or diffraction gratings to separate radiation into several spectral regions. Radiation received by the probe can therefore be separated into separate spectral regions and then projected onto detectors. Brightnesses can usually be presented either as radiances (absolute physical values) or reflectances (proportions).

Direct measurements can be recorded in physical units, although spectra are often reported as reflectances to facilitate comparisons with other data. Reflectance (relative brightness) can be determined with the aid of a reference target of known reflectance/transmittance over the range of brightnesses examined. Such a target is essentially a pure white surface. Everyday materials, despite their visual appearance, do not provide uniform brightness over a range of non-visible wavelengths, so reference panels must be prepared from materials with well-known reflectance properties, such as barium sulphate ($BaSO_4$) or proprietary materials, such as Spectralon images, that have been specifically manufactured to present uniform brightness over a wide range of wavelengths. If readings are made from such targets just before and just after readings are acquired in the field, then the field measurements can be linked to measurements of the reference target under the same illumination conditions. Usually, a reported field reading is derived from the average of a set of 10 or more spectroradiometer readings collected under specified conditions, to minimise the inevitable variations in illumination and field practice.

Readings from a reflectance standard form the denominator in calculating the relative reflectance ratio:

$$\text{Relative refectance ratio} = \frac{\text{Measured radiation, sample}_{(\lambda)}}{\text{Measured brightness, reference source}_{(\lambda)}} \quad \text{... (13.1)}$$

where λ signifies a specific wavelength interval. Because reflectance is an inherent characteristic property of a feature (unlike radiance, which varies according to illumination and weather conditions), it permits comparisons of samples collected under different field conditions.

Some instruments have the ability to match their spectral sensitivities to specific sensors, such as SPOT HRV, MSS or TM. The results can be displayed as spectral plots or as an array of data. Many units interface to notebook computers, which permit the analyst to record spectra in the field and write data to minidisks, which can then be transferred to office or laboratory computers for analysis or incorporation into databases. Typically, a field spectroradiometer fits within a portable case designed to withstand inclement weather and other rigours of use in the field.

Analysts can select from several designs for probes with differing fields of view or for immersion in liquids (e.g., to record radiation transmitted by water bodies). Sometimes measuring units are situated on truck-mounted booms that can be used to acquire overhead views that simulate the viewing perspective of airborne or satellite sensors.

Field spectroradiometers must be used carefully with specific attention devoted to the field of view in relation to the features to be observed, background surfaces, direction of solar illumination and the character of diffuse light from nearby objects (Fig. 13.2). The field of view for the field unit is determined by the foreoptic, a removable attachment that permits the operator to carefully aim the field of view for the instrument. Foreoptics might have fields of view between 1° and 10°; some have pistol grips and sighting scopes. Diffuse light is influenced by surrounding features, so measurements should be acquired at sites well clear of features of contrasting radiometric properties. Likewise, the instrument may record indirect radiation reflected from the operator's clothing, so special attention must be devoted to orientation of the probe with respect to surrounding objects.

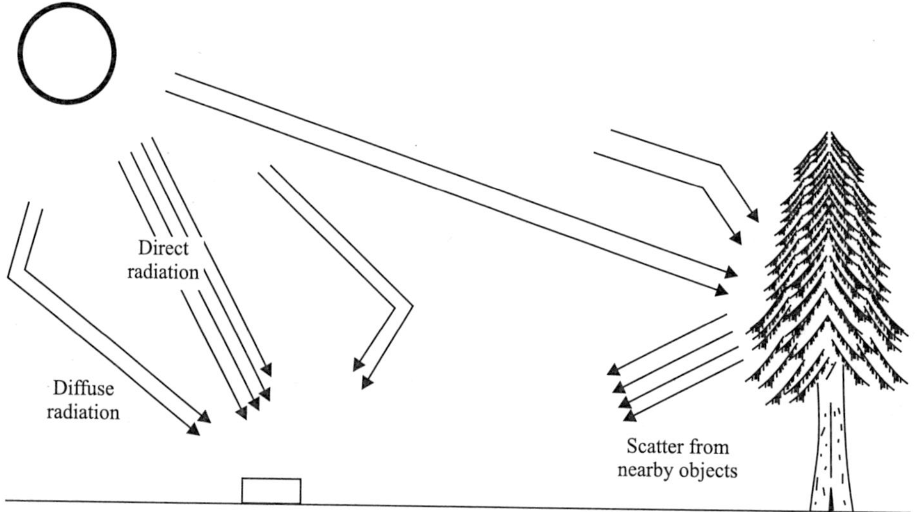

Fig. 13.2. Careful use of the field radiometer with respect to nearby objects.

The most useful measurements are those coordinated with simultaneous acquisition of aircraft or satellite data. Operators must carefully record the circumstances of each set of measurements to include time, date, weather, conditions of illumination and location. Some instruments permit the analyst to enter such information through the laptop's keyboard as annotations to the radiometric data. As data are collected, the operator should supplement spectral data with photographs or videos to permit clear identification of the region represented by the radiometric observations.

In the field it is often difficult to visualise the relationship between ground features visible at a given location and their representations in multispectral data. Not only it is sometimes difficult to relate specific points in the field to the areas visible in overhead views, but often it is equally difficult to visualise differences between representations in visible and non-visible regions of the spectrum and at the coarse resolutions of some sensors. Therefore, analysts must devote effort to matching point observations to the spectral classes that will be of interest during image analysis.

UNMANNED AIRBORNE VEHICLES

Unmanned airborne vehicles (UAVs) are remotely piloted light aircraft that can carry cameras or other sensors in support of remote sensing applications. Current UAVs extend design concepts originally developed by hobbyists for recreation and by military services for reconnaissance under difficult or dangerous conditions. Although the basic concept of designing small remotely piloted aircraft has been pursued for decades, recent advances in miniaturisation, communications, strengths of lightweight materials and power supplies have recently permitted significant advances in UAV design. This discussion outlines applications of UAVs in support of civil remote sensing operations. There is a much larger body of knowledge and experience that pertains specifically to military UAVs.

UAVs are powered either by small gasoline engines or by electric motors. Smaller UAVs typically have wingspans of perhaps of a meter or so, wingspans of larger vehicles might reach several meters. Navigation is controlled by remote radio signals, usually given by an operator who can directly observe the UAV in flight or use remote television images to view the terrain observed by the UAV.

Although it may seem incongruous to consider aerial imagery as constituting a form of field data, such imagery can provide detailed data that permits interpretation of other imagery collected at coarser levels of detail. UAVs can carry cameras, digital cameras or video cameras, as required. Images can be recorded on film, tape or disk for retrieval after the UAV has landed or can be transmitted by telemetry to a ground receiver.

Because UAVs can fly close to the surfaces they observe, they can collect ancillary data such as temperature, CO_2 concentrations, humidity or other information related to the subject under investigation. Furthermore, because they can be deployed in the field at short notice, they have the ability to monitor sites more often than would be possible with other systems and to respond quickly to unexpected events. Their value resides in the opportunity they provide for investigators to closely co-ordinate UAV operations with those of broader scale imagery acquired by aircraft or satellite systems.

Despite their potential, there are still obstacles to the use of UAVs for routine remote sensing applications. For example, in rugged terrain or densely vegetated regions, suitable landing surfaces may not be within range of the areas to be observed. Piloting may be difficult and experienced UAV pilots may not always be at hand. Accidents can destroy expensive equipment, perhaps in inaccessible terrain. Local weather conditions at or near the ground surface may limit flight operations.

UAVs are unlikely to replace more conventional remote sensing platforms, but they do offer advantages as means of supplementing conventional field data, especially by providing data that can be coordinated with broad-scale imagery from aircraft and satellite platforms. Civilian applications of UAVs for remote sensing are still under development, principally for applications in agriculture, forestry and related areas. A classic difficulty encountered in the collection of field data for such applications is assuring that variable data can be collected simultaneously with image data. For example, measurements such as temperature, humidity or illumination can vary over the time and space so rapidly that the values vary as data are collected throughout a large region. Therefore, an investigator who desires to capture a snapshot of temperature conditions, for example, simultaneously with the acquisition of an aircraft or satellite image may find that the temperature values may be changing even as they are being collected. UAVs can assist with this kind of data collection task by facilitating the reliable acquisition of such data rapidly over rather large regions.

LOCATIONAL INFORMATION

Locational data permit attributes or measurements gathered in the field to be matched to imagery of the same region. Traditionally, many of the principal problems in collection of field data for remote sensing analysis have focused on the difficulty of acquiring locational information that permits field observations to be matched to corresponding points on imagery. Accurate observations have little use unless they can be confidently placed in their correct locations. Because of the difficulty and inaccuracies of deriving absolute locational information (e.g., latitude and longitude or comparable coordinates) in the field, most field data have been positioned with reference to distinctive landmarks (e.g., water bodies, road intersections, topographic features) visible on imagery. Such methods, of course, can introduce positional errors that negate the effort invested in accurate measurement of other qualities. In well-mapped regions of developed nations, it is often possible to acquire accurate maps to use in positioning of field data, but in unmapped or poorly mapped regions the absence of reliable positional information is a major difficulty for the use of field observations.

In some situations, locational information can be acquired by positioning easily recognised targets within the area to be imaged. If positions of these targets are know with precision and if they are easily recognised on the imagery, then it is possible to derive an accurate network of GCPs within an image. For photogrammetric surveys, high-contrast (e.g., black figures against white backgrounds) cloth targets are often employed to mark positions of known locations. For radar imagery, portable corner reflectors can be positioned in the field to form a network of easily recognisable points within an image.

Global Positioning System

The availability of global positioning system (GPS) technology has permitted convenient, inexpensive and accurate measurement of absolute location. GPS has greatly enhanced the usefulness of remote sensing data, especially when it is necessary to integrate image data with field data. These instruments now are inexpensive, easy to use and can be employed in almost any area on the earth's surface.

A GPS receiver consists of a portable receiving unit sensitive to signals transmitted by a network of earth-orbiting satellites. These satellites are positioned in orbits such that each point on the earth's surface will be in view of at least four and perhaps as many as twelve, satellites at any given time. A system of 24 satellites is positioned at an altitude of about 13500 miles, to circle the earth at intervals of 12 hours, spaced to provide complete coverage of the earth's surface (Fig. 13.3).

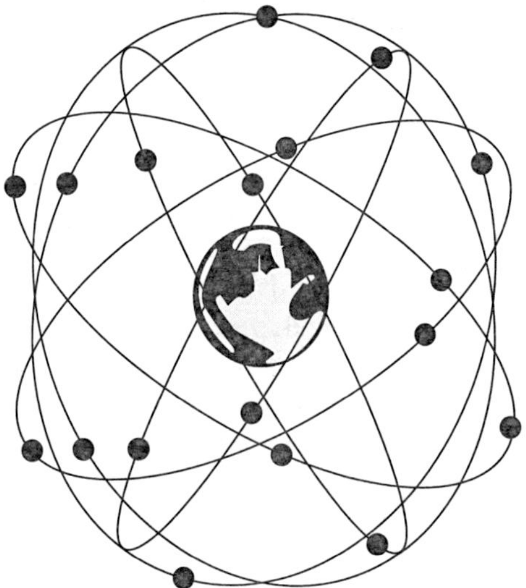

Fig. 13.3. GPS satellites.

These satellites continuously broadcast signals to two carrier frequencies within the L-band region of the microwave spectrum. Although at ground level these signals are very weak, they are designed so that they can be detected even under adverse conditions (e.g., severe weather or interference from other signals). The frequency of each of these carrier signals is modulated in a manner that both (i) identifies the satellite that broadcasts the signal; and (ii) gives the exact time that the signal was broadcast. A receiver therefore can calculate the time delay for the signal to travel from a specific satellite and then accurately estimate the distance from the receiver to a specific satellite.

One reason that it is possible to employ such a weak signal is that the time and identification information each satellite transmits is very simple and the receiver can listen for long periods to acquire it accurately. Because a receiver is always within range of multiple satellites, it is possible to combine positional information from three or more satellites to accurately estimate geographic position on the earth's surface. A network of ground stations periodically re-computes and uploads new positional data to the GPS satellites.

GPS Receivers

A GPS receiver consists of an antenna, power supply, electronic clock and circuitry that can translate signals into positional information. Hand-held receivers, intended for recreational or leisure use, typically are about the size of a wireless phone. Survey-grade GPS units, designed for scientific or commercial use, are larger, use large antenna and include connections to permit use of a keypad and a computer (such as the usual laptop or notebook models). Survey-grade units are usually designed to be carried in a small backpack. Smaller units achieve portability by conserving power or using less accurate clocks. More sophisticated GPS receivers use very accurate clocks and employ more substantial power suppliers. Both hand-held and survey-grade units can permit the analyst to enter coding information in the field and to download information to laboratory or office computers for use with GIS or image processing systems. Other GPS units have been specifically designed as miniaturised circuits (about the size of a credit card) to be used as components in digital cameras or related equipment. Images or data acquired with such instruments can be referenced directly to maps or images.

Pseudoranging

Pseudoranging is one of two ways that GPS signals can be used to estimate location. Pseudoranging is based on the use of time differences to estimate distances. GPS satellites are equipped with accurate clocks. The system maintains its own time standard, with the capability to update times as signals are received from five ground stations. GPS receivers simultaneously generate codes that match codes generated by GPS satellites. As GPS receivers receive coded signals from satellites, they estimate the temporal displacement required to synchronise the two codes. The amount of displacement forms the basis for an estimate of distances between the receiver and each of the satellites within range. Pseudoranging is less accurate than other methods, but its simplicity, convenience and cost effectiveness mean that it is widely used for determining positions of fixed points—the kind of information usually required for applications in remote sensing and GIS.

Carrier Phase Measurement

An alternative strategy for using GPS signals to estimate distance is known as carrier phase measurement, which is based on a detailed examination of signals broadcast by the satellites. GPS receivers detect either or both of the two L-band signals and add them to a signal generated by the receiver. This process is, in essence, the application of the Doppler principle, using observed frequency shifts to derive positional information. If a receiver can acquire data from as many as four satellites, it is possible to estimate both vertical and horizontal positions. Survey-grade GPS units often are based upon the use of carrier-phase measurement.

Precise Positioning Service

Because of the implications for national security of universal availability of quick, accurate, locational data, some aspects of the satellite signal were encrypted. Exploitation of the system's full accuracy required access to a cryptographic key, provided only to authorised users. The system's most accurate data, known as precise positioning service (PPS), is provided to military services and to other governmental agencies with requirements for high levels of positional accuracy.

GPS Accuracy

GPS errors arise from combination of several sources:

1. Orbital position (*ephmeris*).
2. Clock error.
3. Ionosphereic effects (atmospheric effects encountered in the high atmosphere).
4. Tropospheric effects (atmospheric effects in the lower atmosphere).
5. Noise contributed by the GPS receiver itself.
6. Multipath error (reflection of GPS signals from nearby surfaces).

In addition, designers of the GPS system deliberately added errors to create selective availability (SA), to preserve the advantage of full precision of the GPS system for authorised users, while allowing the civil community access to the degraded signal. SA introduced deliberate errors in both the ephemeris and the clock to significantly increase positional errors. Access to the signal's full accuracy was provided by a cryptographic key that allowed friendly military services and other authorised users to receive the undegraded signal.

On 1 May 2002 the US government announced the decision to turn off SA, allowing the civil GPS community to receive the undegraded GPS signal. This decision leaves ionospheric effects as the largest source of positional error. This policy recognised the growing significance of accurate GPS signals for civil applications and the potential impact if foreign governments were to build competing systems using different technical specifications. The removal of SA opens the possibility that foreign systems would be compatible with the US system, thereby increasing the accuracy of both.

Conservative estimates of GPS accuracy suggest that horizontal errors should be within about 22 m 95 per cent of the time and vertical errors should be about 33 m 95 per cent of the time. However, observed accuracies suggest that performance is usually superior to these estimates, perhaps 10 m or less in some instances.

Local Differential GPS

When a GPS receiver can be stationed at a fixed position of known location, it becomes possible to derive estimates of some of the errors that influence GPS accuracy and then to apply these estimates to improve the accuracy of GPS positions at unknown locations. This process is known as local differential GPS. Differential GPS requires that a GPS receiver be established at a fixed point for which the geographic location is known with confidence—this location forms the base station. Information from base station can be applied to locational information from GPS receivers to derive more accurate estimates of location.

A carefully established differential network can permit estimates of location to within centimeters of the true position.

Careful use of GPS receivers can provide locational information adequate for use in many if not most remote sensing studies, especially if it is possible to employ differential location. Atmospheric effects constitute one of the major sources of error in GPS measurements. Atmospheric interference can delay transmission of signals from the satellites—the delays can be interpreted by the system as a difference in distance. Electrically charged particles in the ionosphere (30 to 300 miles, 48 to 483 km, above the earth's surface) and unusually severe weather in the troposphere (ground level to about 7.5 miles or 12 km) can combine to cause errors of as much as 1 to 5 m. Some of these errors cancel each other out or can be removed by filtering, while others remain to create errors in the estimated positions.

USING LOCATIONAL INFORMATION

Locational information can serve several purposes. One of the most important is to assist in identification of GCPs that allow analysts to re-sample image data to provide accurate planimetric location and correctly match image detail to maps and other images. Accurate locational information also permits correct positioning of field data with image data so that field data match to the correct regions within the image.

GPS permits analysts to specify coordinates for distinctive landmarks clearly visible both on imagery and on the ground. Examples include highway intersections, water bodies, distinctive terrain features and the like. A network of such points then provides a locational framework that permits specification of locations of other points that might not be so distinctive. In other instances, field teams may acquire data in remote regions, far from distinctive landmarks. Prior to the availability of GPS, these data could be positioned within imagery only approximately, using relative locations from distant landmarks as the basis for rather rough estimates. GPS provides the capability to specify positions of such observations precisely within the imagery, provided that the image itself can be positioned within a coordinate system. That is, even with the accurate information provided by the GPS, it is still important to devote care to establishing the link between the image data and ground observations.

GEOGRAPHIC SAMPLING

Although ideally, it would be useful to acquire complete information concerning a study area, practical constraints require that analysts sample the patterns they study. Even modest-sized images can show such large areas that complete inventories are not feasible and large areas of the study area may be inaccessible. As a result, field data must usually be collected for a sample of pixels from the image. Here the work observation signifies the selection of a specific cell or pixel; a sample is used here to designate a set of observations that will be used to construct an error matrix.

Any effort to sample a map or any other spatial pattern must consider three separate decisions: (i) determination of the number of observations to be used; (ii) choice of the sampling pattern to position observations within an image; and (iii) the selection for a given sampling pattern of the spacing of observations.

Numbers of Observations

Clearly, determination of the number of observations to be collected is fundamental. The issue is much more complex that it might seem to be at first consideration and scientists have employed different strategies to estimate the numbers of observations.

However, it is possible to outline the main considerations:

1. The number of observations determines the confidence interval of an estimate of the accuracy of a classification. Thus, from elementary statistics, we know that a large sample size decreases the width of the confidence interval of our estimate of a statistic—that is, we can have greater confidence that our estimate is close to the actual value when we employ larger numbers of samples.
2. For most purposes, we must consider not only the observations for the entire image, but those that are allocated to each class, as it is necessary to have some minimum number of observations assigned to each class.

Sampling Pattern

Sampling pattern specifies the arrangement of observations. The most commonly used sampling patterns include the simple random sampling pattern, the stratified random pattern, systematic patterns and the systematic stratified unaligned pattern. A simple random sample (Fig. 13.4) positions observations such that the choice of any specific location as the site for an observation is independent of the selection of any other location as an observation. Randomness assures that all portions of a region are equally subject to selection for the sample, thereby yielding data that accurately represent the area examined and satisfying one of the fundamental requirements of inferential statistics.

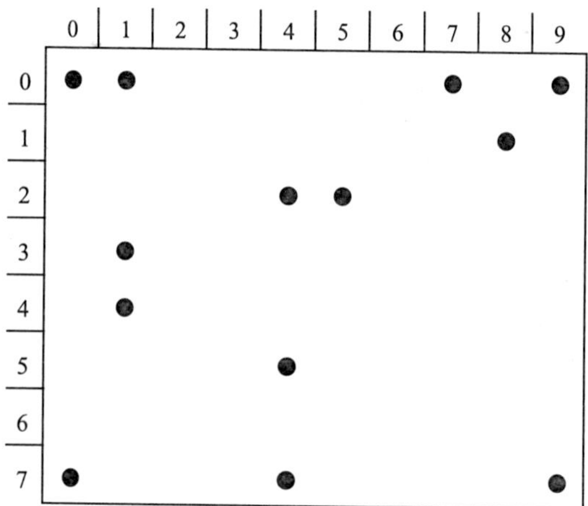

Fig. 13.4. Simple random sampling pattern.

Typically the simple random sample of a geographic region is defined by first dividing the region to be studied into a network of cells. Each row and column in the network is numbered, then a random number table is used to select values that, taken two at a time, form coordinate pairs for defining the locations of observations. Because the coordinates are selected at random, the locations they define should be positioned at random.

The random sample is probably the most powerful sampling strategy available as it yields data that can be subjected to analysis using inferential statistics. However, in a geographic context, it has some shortcomings. Often a random sample is not uniform, but instead positions observations in patterns that tend to cluster together. Also, observations are unlikely to be proportionately distributed among the categories on the image and classes of small areal extent may not be represented at all in the sample. In addition, observations may fall at or near the boundaries of parcels; in the context of accuracy assessment, such observations should probably be avoided, as they may record registration errors rather than classification errors. Thus the pure random sample, despite its advantages in other situations, may not be the best choice for comparing two images. It is, however, important to include an element of randomness in any sampling strategy, as described above.

A stratified sampling pattern assigns observations to sub-regions of the image to ensure that the sampling effort is distributed in a rational manner (Fig. 13.5). For example, a stratified sampling effort plan might assign specific numbers of observations to each category on the map to be evaluated. This procedure would ensure that every category would be sampled. If a purely random pattern is used, on the other hand, many of the smaller categories might escape the sampling effort.

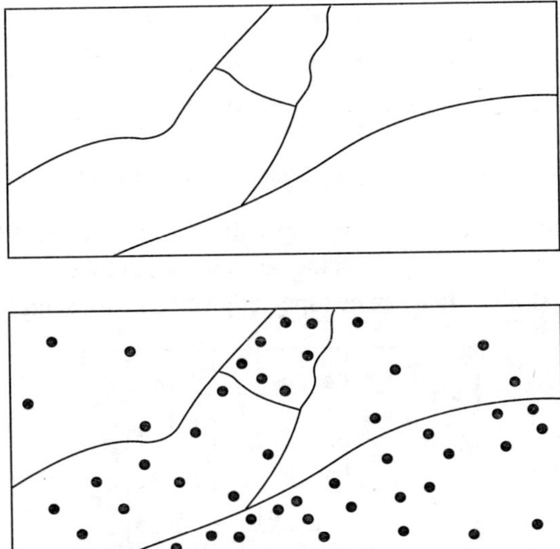

Fig. 13.5. Stratified random sampling pattern. Here a region has been sub-divided into sub-regions (strata) shown at the top. Samples are then allocated to each stratum in proportion to its expected significance to the study, then positioned randomly within each sub-area.

Often the positions of observations within strata are selected at random—a process that yields the stratified random sampling pattern. Thus stratification allocates observations to categories (the strata, in this instance) in proportion to their size or significance; the random element ensures that observations are located within categories by chance, thereby ensuring a representative sample within each class.

Systematic sampling positions observations at equal intervals according to a specific strategy (Fig. 13.6). Because selection of the starting point pre-determines the positions of all subsequent observations, data derived from systematic samples will not meet the requirements of inferential statistics for randomly selected observations.

Another potential problem in the application of systematic samples is the presence of systematic variation in the underlying pattern that is to be sampled. For example, in the central United States, the Township-Range Survey System introduces a systematic component to the sizes, shapes and positions of agricultural fields. Therefore, a purely systematic sample of errors in the classification of such landscape could easily place all observations at the centers of fields, thereby missing errors that might occur systematically near the edges of fields and giving an inflated estimate of accuracy. Or systematic samples could oversample the edges and overestimate errors. There may be other, more subtle periodicities in landscapes that could interact with a systematic pattern to introduce other errors. Systematic sampling may nevertheless be useful if it is necessary to ensure that all regions within a study area are represented; a purely random sample, for example, may place observations in clustered patterns and leave some areas only sparsely sampled.

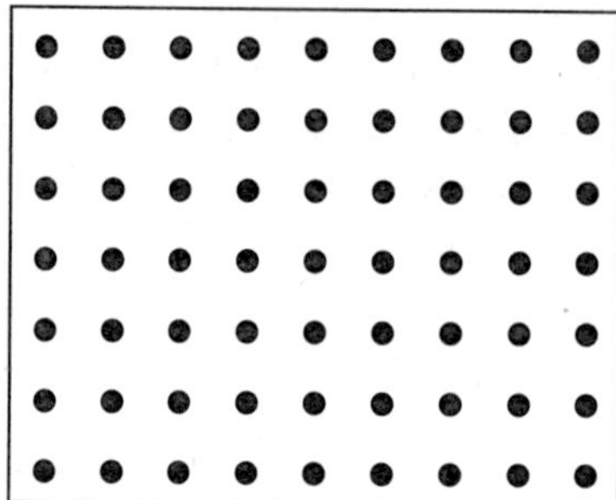

Fig. 13.6. Systematic sampling pattern.

The stratified systematic non-aligned sampling pattern combines features of both systematic and stratified samples while simultaneously preserving an element of randomness (Fig. 13.7). These features combine to form a sampling strategy that can be especially versatile for sampling geographic distributions.

Fig. 13.7. Stratified systematic non-aligned sampling pattern.

The entire study area is divided into uniform cells, usually by means of a square grid. The grid cells, of course, introduce a systematic component of the sample and form the basis for stratification; one observation is placed in each cell. An element of randomness is contributed by the method of placement of observations within each cell. A number is randomly selected as the east-west coordinate for placement of the observation within the first cell; this value forms the east-west coordinate not only within the first cell but for all cells in that column (Fig. 13.7). A second number is randomly selected to define the north-south coordinate within the first cell; this value also specifies the north-south placement of observations within all cells in the first row of cells. Each row and each column is assigned a new random number that is applied to locating observations within each cell.

The resulting placement of observations within the study area has many favourable characteristics. The use of grid cells as the basis for stratification means that observations are distributed evenly within an image; no segment of the area will be unrepresented. The random element destroys the rigid alignment caused by a purely systematic design and introduces an element of chance that increases the probability that the observations will accurately represent the categories within the image. The primary pitfall is that the analyst must specify an appropriate size for the grid, which determines the number of observations and the spacing between them. These factors determine the effectiveness of a given sample in representing a specific pattern. If the analyst knows enough about the region to make a good choice of grid size, the stratified systematic non-aligned sample is likely to be among the most effective.

In some situations, the sampling effort must be confined to certain sites, perhaps because of difficult access to ground observation of remote areas or because financial restrictions confine the analyst's ability to apply the other sampling patterns mentioned above. Cluster sampling selects points within a study area, then uses each point as a center to determine locations of additional 'satellite' observations placed nearby, so that the overall distribution of observations forms the clustered pattern illustrated in Fig. 13.8. Centers can be located randomly or be assigned specifically to certain areas or classes on a reference map. Satellite observations can be located randomly, within constraints of distance. Cluster sampling may be efficient with respect to time and resources devoted to the sampling effort. If the pattern to be sampled is known beforehand, it may provide reasonably accurate results. However, if the distribution to be sampled is not known beforehand, it is probably best not to use a clustered pattern if it is at all possible to employ alternatives. Because observations are constrained to be close to one another, there is a distinct danger that the observations will replicate information rather than provide new information. If so, the analyst receives an inflated confidence in the assessment because the number of observations will suggest that more information is available than is actually the case.

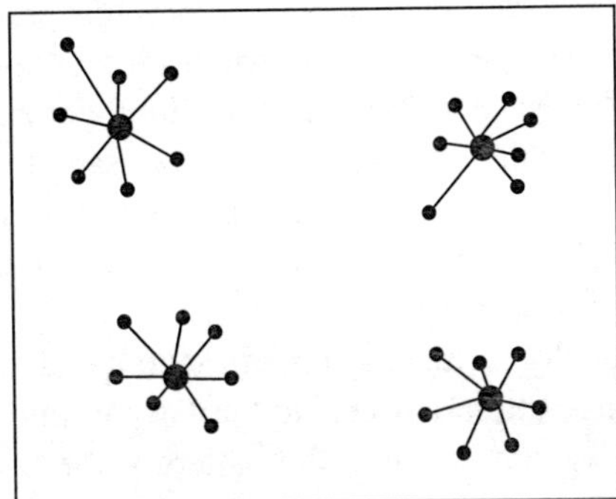

Fig. 13.8. Clustered sampling pattern. Larger dots represent focal points for clusters selected randomly or possibly according to access or availability. Smaller dots represent satellite samples positioned at randomly selected distances and direction from the central point.

Spacing of Observations

All efforts to define geographic sampling patterns must consider the effect of spacing of observations. If observations are spaced too close together, they tend to replicate information already provided by their neighbours and thereby provide the analyst with an unjustified confidence in the reliability of his or her conclusions. Use of 100 observations, if closely spaced, may in fact convey the information of only 50 evenly spaced observations. Closely spaced samples may underestimate variability and provide a poor indication of the number of categories present.

Examination of only a few images should be sufficient to reveal the significance of sample spacing. Some landscapes have a coarse fabric of landscape parcels—for example, the large agricultural fields of the North American plains can be represented by observations spaced at rather large distances. Other landscapes, typically those of complex topography or densely occupied regions, display a finer, more intricate fabric and require more intense sampling patterns.

Spatial autocorrelation describes the tendency of measurements at one location to resemble those at nearby locations. Thus, a measurement of soil moisture at one place is likely to resemble another measurement made 6 inch distant and less likely to resemble one made 6 ft. away. Spatial autocorrelation provides quantitative estimates of the rate that similarities between paired observations change over distance. Spatial autocorrelation assesses the degree to which samples provide independent information.

Without prior knowledge of the pattern to be studied, it is impossible to decide if a given sampling pattern positions observations too close to one another. However, in some instances we can apply the results of experience acquired in similar situations and avoid using clustered samples unless they are dictated by other considerations. Even a purely random sample will often place observations in clusters, so many investigators prefer the systematic stratified non-aligned pattern, which retains a random component but forces a degree of uniformity in spacing samples. Even when the most effective sampling patterns are used for accuracy assessment, it is usually necessary to augment the sample with observations selected at random from the less significant categories (in terms of area) as a means of ensuring that all categories are represented by an adequate number of independent observations.

Sampling Summary

It is difficult to recommend sampling strategies that might prove best for assessing accuracy because there has been little study of the comparative advantages of sampling procedures in the context of accuracy assessment. Congalton evaluated five sampling patterns to assess their performance in representing agricultural, range and forested landscapes. For the agricultural pattern, he concluded that the random sample performed the best. He found that the stratified random sample was best for the rangeland scene and that the systematic random sample provided the most accurate information regarding the forest image. In general, he concluded that the systematic and systematic non-aligned sample performed well on the forest scene but poorly on other scenes.

His results highlight the difficulty in making broad recommendations for application of sampling strategies—the optimum sampling pattern is likely to vary according to the nature of the pattern to be sampled. In some applications, we can examine the pattern to be sampled, then select the sampling strategy likely to provide the best results. However, in many instances we are likely to face situations in which it is difficult or impossible to know beforehand the best sampling strategy and we will be forced to develop experience on a case-by-case basis.

Thus, full exploitation of field data can be considered one of the unexplored topics in the field of remote sensing. In recent years the availability of GPS, field spectroradiometers and laptop computers (among other technological advances) has greatly expanded the nature and accuracy of field data. These developments have provided data that are vastly superior to those of previous era's data with respect to quantity of accuracy by:

1. Effective integration of field data within an image-processing system.
2. Compatibility of varied forms of field data.
3. Coordination of field acquisition with image data.
4. Evaluation and assessment.
5. Questions of efficient and accurate sampling.
6. Access to remote regions.

14

Accuracy Assessment

INTRODUCTION

Accuracy assessment is a very complex process. Research continues and despite agreement on many important aspects of accuracy evaluation, other issues likely to be debated for a long time before they are re-solved. For example, there is no clearly superior method of sampling an image for accuracy assessment and there is disagreement concerning the best way to compare two error matrices. For many problems, there may be no single 'correct' way to conduct the analysis, but we may be able to exclude some alternatives and to speak of the relative merits and shortcomings of others.

This chapter will provide the background to assess the accuracies of the classification using procedures that, if not perfect, are at least comparable in quality to those in common use today. Furthermore, the student should now be prepared to read some of the current research on this topic and possibly to contribute to improvements in the study of accuracy assessment. Many of the problems in this field are difficult, but are not beyond the reach of interested and informed students.

Prospective users of maps and data derived from remotely sensed images quite naturally ask about the accuracy of the information they will use. Yet questions concerning accuracy are surprisingly difficult to address in a convincing manner. This chapter describes how the accuracy of a map or image can be evaluated and identifies some of the difficulties that remain.

Accuracy defines 'correctness'; it measures the agreement between a standard assumed to be correct and a classified image of unknown quality. If the image classification corresponds closely with the standard, it said to be 'accurate.' There are several methods for measuring the degree of correspondence, all described in later sections.

Precision defines 'detail' (Fig. 14.1). The distinction is important because one may be able to increase accuracy by decreasing precision—that is, by being vague in the classification. For example, as the analyst classifies a stand of trees as forest, coniferous forest, pine forest, shortleaf pine forest or mature shortleaf pine forest, detail increases and so too does the opportunity for error. (It is clearly more difficult to be correctly assign detailed classes than to assign general classes.) Evaluation of accuracy seldom explicitly considers precision, yet we must always ask if the precision is appropriate for the purpose at hand. Accuracy of 95 per cent in separating water and forest in unlikely to be useful if we need to know the distributions of evergreen and deciduous categories.

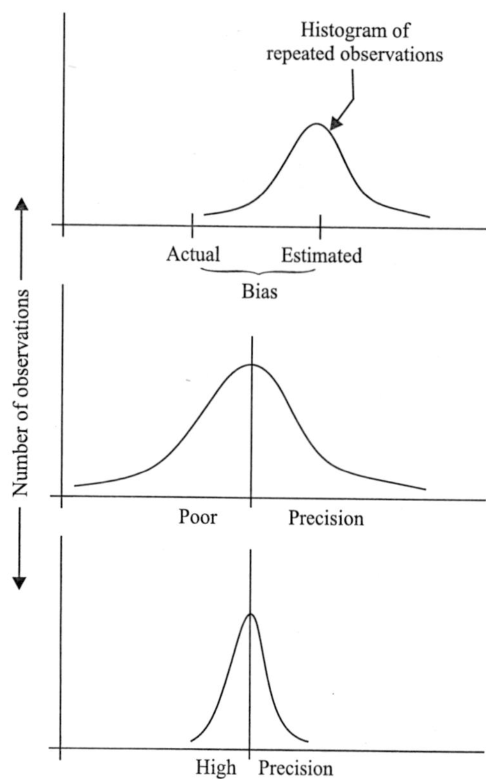

Fig. 14.1. Bias and precision. Accuracy consists of bias and precision. Consistent differences between estimated values and true values create bias (top diagram). The lower diagram illustrates the concept of precision. High variability of estimates lead to poor precision; low variability of estimates creates high precision.

In a statistical context, high accuracy means that bias is low (that estimated values are consistently close to an accepted reference value) and that the variability of estimates is low (Fig. 14.1). The usefulness of a map is related not only to its correctness, but also to the precision with which the user can make statements about specific points depicted on the map. A map that offers only general classes (even if correct) enables users to make only vague statements about any given point represented on the map; one that uses detailed classes permits the user to make more precise statements.

Accuracy has many practical implications: for example, it affects the legal standing of maps and reports derived from remotely sensed data, the operational usefulness of such data for land management and their validity as a basis for scientific research. Analyses of accuracies of alternative classification strategies have significance for everyday uses of remotely sensed data. There have, however, been few systematic investigations of relative accuracies of manual and machine classifications, of different individuals, of the same interpreter at different times, of alternative pre-processing and classification algorithms or of accuracies associated with different images of the same area. As a result, accuracy studies would be valuable research in both practical and theoretical aspects of remote sensing.

Often people assess accuracy from the appearance of a map, from past experience or from personal knowledge of the areas represented. These can all be misleading, as overall accuracy may be unrelated to the map's cosmetic qualities and often personal experience may be unavoidably confined to a few unrepresentative sites. Instead, accuracy should be evaluated through a well-defined effort to assess the map in a manner that permits quantitative measure of accuracy and comparisons with alternative images of the same area.

Evaluation of accuracies of information derived from remotely sensed images has long been of interest, but a new concern regarding the accuracies of digital classifications has stimulated research on accuracy assessment. As digital classifications were first offered in the 1970s as replacements for more traditional products, many found the methods of machine classification to be abstract and removed from the direct control of the analyst; their validity could not be accepted without evidence. This concern prompted much of the research outlined in this chapter.

Users should not be expected to accept at face value the validity of any map, regardless of its origin or appearance, without supporting evidence.

SOURCES OF CLASSIFICATION ERROR

Errors are present in any classification. In manual interpretations, errors are caused by misidentification of parcels, excessive generalisation, errors in registration, variations in detail of interpretation and other factors. Perhaps the simplest causes of error are related to the misassignment of informational categories to spectral categories. Bare granite in mountainous areas, for example, can be easily confused with the spectral response of concrete in urban areas. However, most errors are probably more complex. Mixed pixels occur as resolution elements fall on the boundaries between landscape parcels; these pixels may well have digital values unlike either of the two categories represented and may be misclassified even by the most robust and accurate classification procedures. Such errors may appear in digital classification products as chains of misclassified pixels that parallel the borders of large, homogeneous parcels (Fig. 14.2).

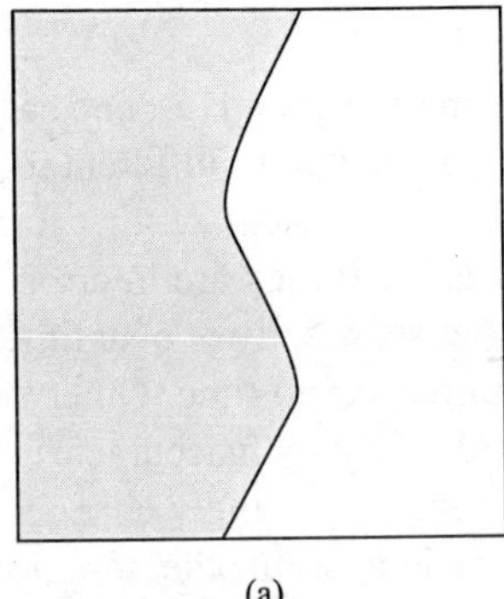

(a)

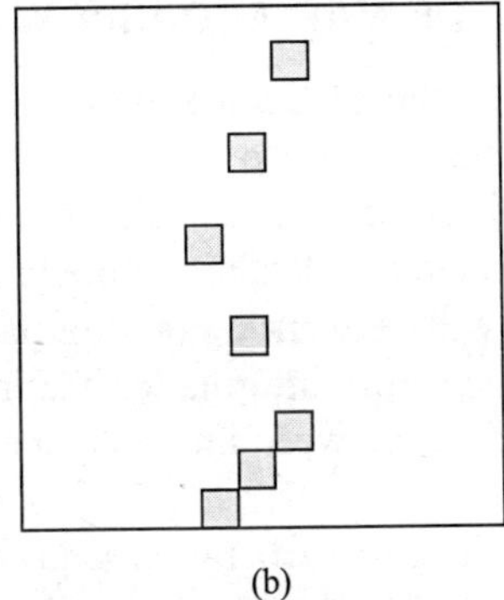

(b)

Fig. 14.2. Incorrectly classified border pixels at the edges of parcels. (a) Map of edge between two contrasting categories. (b) Idealised representation of errors that might occur in a digital classification. The dark cells represent erroneously classified pixels. Usually, of course, we would not be able to know where these errors might occur.

In this manner the character of the landscape contributes to the potential for error through the complex patterns of parcels that form the scene. A very simple landscape composed of large uniform, distinct categories is likely to be easier to classify accurately than one with small, heterogeneous, indistinct parcels arranged in a complex pattern. Key landscape variables are likely to include:

1. Parcel size.
2. Variation in parcel size.

3. Parcel identities.
4. Number of categories.
5. Arrangement of categories.
6. Number of parcels per category.
7. Shapes of parcel.
8. Radiometric and spectral contrast with surrounding parcels.

These variables change from one region to another and within a given region from season to season. As a result, errors present in a given image are not necessarily predictable from previous experience in other regions or on other dates.

ERROR CHARACTERISTICS

Classification error is the assignment of a pixel belonging to one category (as determined by ground observation) to another category during the classification process. There are few if any systematic studies of geographic characteristics of these errors, but experience and logic suggest that errors are likely to possess at least some of the characteristic listed below:

1. Errors are not distributed over the image at random, but display a degree of systematic, ordered occurrence in space. Likewise, errors are not assigned at random to the various categories on the image, but are likely to be preferentially associated with certain classes.
2. Often erroneously assigned pixels are not spatially isolated but occur grouped in areas of varied size and shape.
3. Errors may have specific spatial relationships to the parcels to which they pertain; for example, they may tend to occur at the edges or in the interiors of parcels.

MEASUREMENT OF MAP ACCURACY

The accuracy assessment task can be defined as one of comparing two maps, one based upon analysis of remotely sensed data (the map to be evaluated) and another based upon a different source of information. This second map is designated the reference map, assumed to be accurate, that forms the standard for comparison. The reference data are of obvious of significance; if they are in error, then the attempt to measure accuracy will be in error. For information that varies seasonally or over time, it is important that the reference image shows information that matches with respect to time. Otherwise, the comparison may detect differences between images that are not caused solely by inaccuracies in the classification. For example, some of the differences may not really be errors, but simply changes that have occurred during the interval that elapsed between acquisition of the two images. In other instances, we may examine two images simply to decide if there is a difference, without concluding that one is more accurate than the other. For example, we may compare images of the same area taken by different sensors or classifications made by different interpreters. In such instances, it is not always necessary to assume that one image is more accurate than the other, as the objective is simply to determine if and how the two differ.

Usually, however, the reference map is assumed to be the 'correct' map. Both maps must be in the form of 'parcel' or 'mosaic' maps—that is, maps composed of a network of discrete parcels, each designated by a single label from a set of mutually exclusive categories. To assess the accuracy of one map, it is necessary that the two maps register to one another, that they both use the same classification systems and that they have been mapped at comparable levels of detail. The strategies described here are not appropriate if the two maps differ with respect to detail, number of categories or meanings of the categories.

The simplest method of evaluation is to compare the two maps with respect to the areas assigned to each category. The result of such a comparison is to report the areal proportions of categories (Fig. 14.3). These values report the extent of the agreement between the two maps in respect to total areas in each category, but do not take into account compensating errors in misclassification that cause this kind of accuracy measure to be itself inaccurate. For example, underestimation of 'forest' in one part of the image can compensate for overestimation of 'forest' in another part of the image; serious errors in classification have been made, but are not revealed in the simple report of total areas in each category.

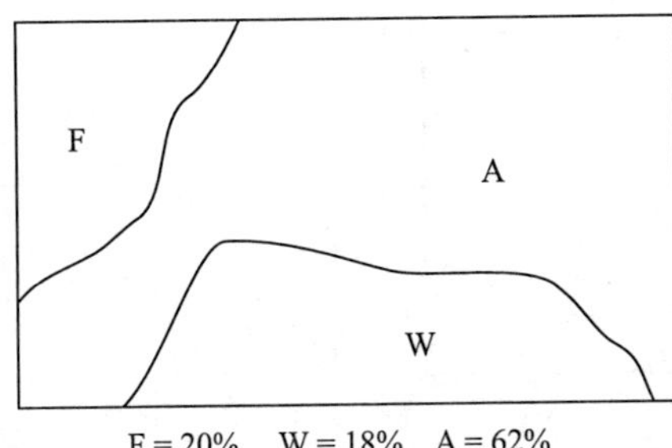

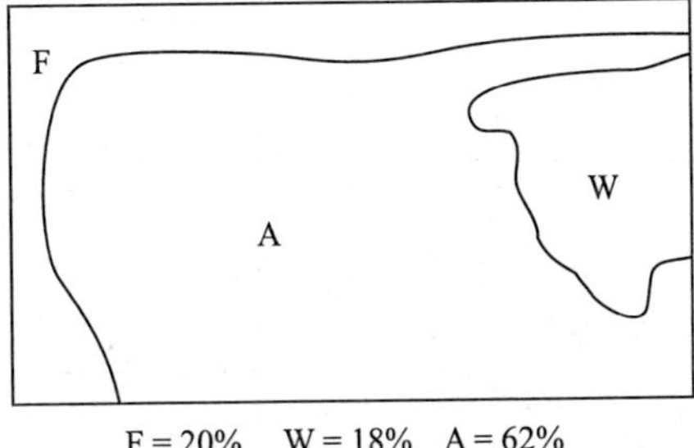

Fig. 14.3. Non-site-specific accuracy. Here two images are compared only on the basis of total areas in each category. Because total areas may be similar even though placement of the boundaries differs greatly, this approach can give misleading results, as shown here.

This form of error assessment is sometimes called non-site-specific accuracy because it does not consider agreement between the two maps at specific locations, but only the overall figures for the two maps. Figure 14.3 illustrates this point. The two patterns are clearly different, but the difference is not revealed by the overall percentages for each category. Gershmehl and Napton refer to this kind of error as inventory error, as the process considers only the aggregate areas for classes rather than the placement of classes on the map.

Site-Specific Accuracy

The second form of accuracy, site-specific accuracy, is based upon the detailed assessment of agreement between two maps at specific locations (Fig. 14.4). Gershmehl and Napton refer to this kind of error as classification error. In most analyses the units of comparison are simply pixels derived from remotely sensed data, although if necessary a pair of matching maps could be compared using any network of uniform cells. Site-specific accuracy has been measured using several alternative strategies. Sometimes, training data for image classification can be sub-divided into two groups, one used to prepare the classification, the other to assess the accuracy of the classification.

Hord and Brooner distinguish between errors in classification and errors in positioning boundaries. Classification errors are misidentifications of the identities of pixels. Boundary errors are caused by misplacement of boundaries between categories. In automated classifications, boundary errors are caused mainly by geometric errors either in the image or in the reference data, so that the correctly classified pixel may be misregistered to the wrong pixel in the reference image and thereby counted as an error.

Error Matrix

The standard form for reporting site-specific error is the error matrix, sometimes referred to as the confusion matrix because it identifies not only overall errors for each category, but also misclassifications (due to confusion between categories) by category. Compilation of an error matrix is required for any serious study of accuracy. It consists of an n × n array, where n represents the number of categories (Table 14.1 and Fig. 14.5).

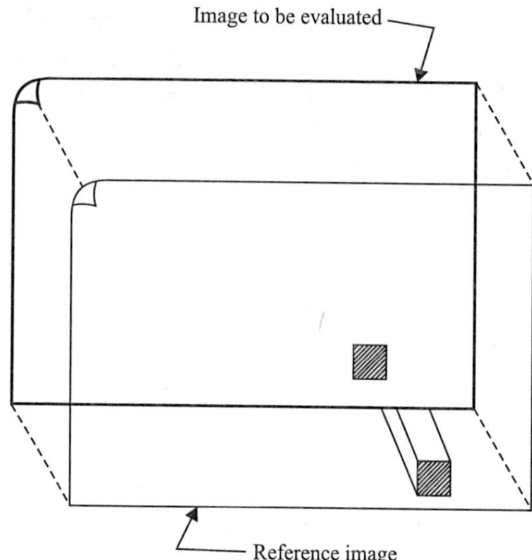

Fig. 14.4. Site-specific accuracy. The two images are compared on site-by-site ('cell-by-cell', or 'pixel-by-pixel') basis to accumulate information concerning the correspondence of the two images. Here only a single pair of cells is shown, although the comparison considers the entire images.

Table 14.1. Example of an error matrix.

	Image to be evaluated						
Reference image	*Urban*	*Crop*	*Range*	*Water*	*Forest*	*Barren*	*Totals*
Urban	150	21	0	7	17	30	225
Crop	0	730	93	14	115	21	973
Range	33	121	320	23	54	43	594
Water	3	18	11	83	8	3	126
Forest	23	81	12	4	350	13	483
Barren	39	8	15	3	11	115	191
Totals	248	979	451	134	555	225	1748

Note. Percentage correct = Sum of diagonal entries/total observations = 1748/2592 = 67.4 per cent.

The left-hand side (y-axis) is labelled with the categories on the reference ('correct') classification; the upper edge (x-axis) is labelled with the same n categories; these refer to those on the map to be evaluated. (Note that the meanings of the two axes can be reversed in some applications, as the convention is not universal.) Here values in the matrix represent numbers of pixels for which the analyst has been able to compare the evaluated and reference images (in some representations, these numbers might constitute the entire image; other times they might only form a sample of the total). Sometimes the matrix is constructed using percentages rather than absolute values, but here we will show absolute values counted directly from the image.

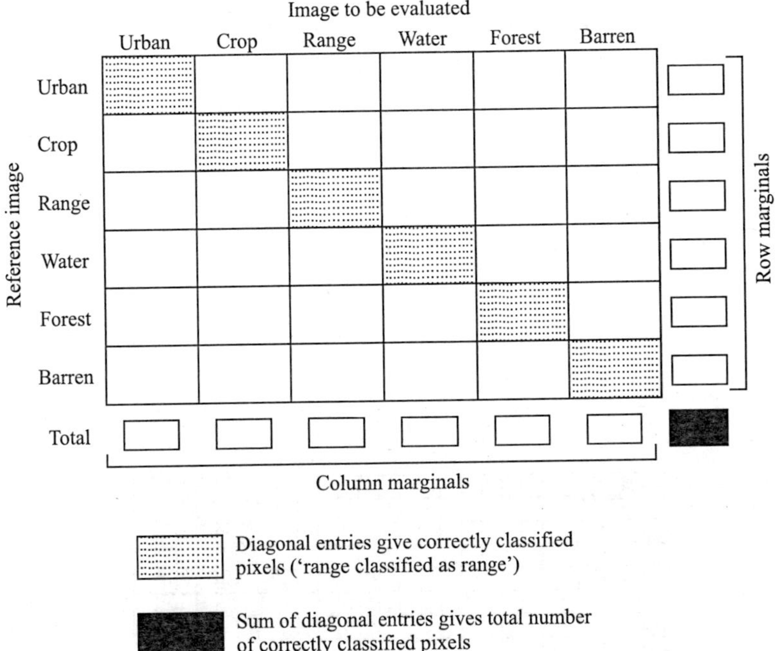

Fig. 14.5. Schematic representation of an error matrix. Here elements of the matrix are represented to correspond to the text and to Table 14.1.

Inspection of the matrix shows how the classification represents actual areas on the landscape. For example, in Table 14.1, there are 225 pixels of urban land (the far right value in the first row). Of the 225 pixels of urban land, 150 were classified as urban (row 1, column 1); these, of course, are the pixels of urban land correctly classified. Reading succeeding values along the first row, we next find incorrectly classified urban pixels and the categories to which they were assigned: crop, 21; range, 0; water, 7; forest, 17 and barren land, 30. Reading across each row, we then learn how the classification assigned pixels identified by their actual classes as they occur on the landscape. The diagonal from upper left to lower right gives numbers of correctly classified pixels.

Further inspection of the matrix reveals a summary of other information. Column totals on the far right give the total number of pixels in each class as recorded on the reference image. The bottom row of totals shows numbers of pixels assigned to each class as depicted on the image to be evaluated.

Compiling the Error Matrix

To construct the error matrix, the analyst must compare two images—the reference image and the image to be evaluated—on a point-by-point basis to determine exactly how each site on the reference image is represented in the classification. In this context, the two 'images' are not necessarily both remotely sensed images—the comparison could include remotely sensed images, maps representing the same region and maps depicting field-verified data. The critical consideration is not the form of the two images, but that they register to one another and use comparable classifications. Errors in registration will appear as errors in classification, so registration problems will create errors in the assessment of accuracy. The analyst must establish a network of uniform cells that form the units of comparison (Fig. 14.6); these cells must be small enough to provide enough cells for a statistically valid sample and also small enough to avoid large numbers of mixed cells (caused by cells that fall on the boundaries between parcels), but large enough to avoid the tedium and expense that accompany use of impractically small units.

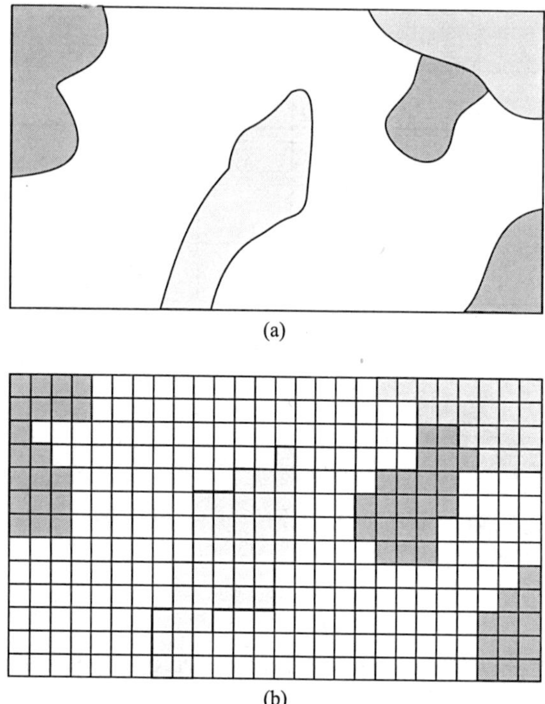

Fig. 14.6. Representation of a category map by uniform cells. The network of uniform cells (bottom) represents the pattern of the original map or image (top). These cells then form the units of comparison for site-specific accuracy assessment.

The two images are then superimposed, either literally if the compilation is to be conducted manually or figuratively if the compilation is conducted digitally, by computer. For manual compilation, the analyst examines the superimposed images systematically on a cell-by-cell basis, tabulating for each cell the predominant category shown on the reference map and the category of the corresponding cell on the image to be evaluated (Table 14.2). The analyst maintains a count of the numbers in each reference category as they are assigned to classes on the map to be evaluated. A summation of this tabulation then forms the basis for construction of the error matrix.

If both images are in digital form, the unit of compilation is likely to be the pixel as defined by the image sensor or a unit formed from even multiples of pixels. Matching of the two images, tabulation of the cross-classification and construction of the error matrix is most difficult when one map, typically the reference map, is in manuscript form and the other, typically the map to be evaluated, is in digital form. It is then necessary to bring them both into the same format, probably by digitising the manuscript map. Digitisation can be time-consuming and expensive and the analyst then faces questions of optimum registration and resampling. Thus, although compilation of the error matrix is straightforward, preparation of maps for comparison may be very difficult.

Table 14.2. Tabulation of data for the error matrix.

	Worksheet	
Cell	*Reference map*	*Classification*
1	F	F
2	F	U
3	W	W
4	W	W
5	C	C
6	C	F
7	C	C
	Summation	
Forest classified as forest		350
Forest classified as urban		23
Forest classified as cropland		81
Forest classified as water		4
Cropland classified as cropland		730
Cropland classified as forest		115
Cropland classified as water		14

Table 14.3 illustrates the significance of compatibility of the classification used for the two images. Ideally, the two images use the same classification system. In practice, the two images may differ with respect to classification. Sometimes different classifications may be compatible—categories can be matched to one another in a manner that permits a valid comparison of the two images. If the differences are simply a matter of detail, often the more detailed categories can be collapsed into more general classes, as illustrated in Table 14.3. In other instances, the two images may be fundamentally incompatible; the categories may be based on different classification logics, so the two sets of classes cannot be matched (Table 14.3). In some instances two classifications may use differing definitions but the same names, so it is important to examine each image and the supporting information very closely before attempting a comparison.

Errors of Omission and Errors of Commission

Examination of the error matrix reveals, for each category, errors of omission and errors of commission (Table 14.3). Errors of omission are, for example, the assignment of errors of forest on the ground to the agriculture category on the map (in other words, an area of 'real' forest on the ground has been omitted from the map). Using the same example, an error of commission would be to assign an area of agriculture on the ground to the forest category on the map. The analyst in this instance has actively committed an error by assigning a region of forest to a wrong category. (This error of commission for one category will, of course, also be tabulated as an error of omission for another category.) The distinction is essential because the interpretation could otherwise achieve 100 per cent accuracy in respect to forest by assigning all pixels to forest. Tabulations of errors of commission reveal such actions to be meaningless because they are balanced by compensating errors.

Table 14.3. Examples of compatible and incompatible classifications.

Reference map	*Image to be evaluated*
	Compatible
Water	Water
Urban and built-up land	Urban residential Urban commercial Urban industrial
Deciduous forest Coniferous forest Mixed forest	Forest
Agricultural land	Cropland Pasture
	Incompatible
Open land	Cropland
Dense settlement	Forest
Strip development	Cities and towns
Water	Lakes and rivers
Rough, uneven land	Disturbed land
Roads and highways	

By examining relationships between the two kinds of errors, the map user gains insight about the varied reliabilities of classes on the map and the analyst learns about the performance of the process that generated the maps. Examined from the user's perspective, the matrix reveals consumer's accuracy (or 'user's accuracy') examined from the analyst's point of view, the matrix reveals producer's accuracy. The difference between the two lies in the base from which the error is assessed. For producer's accuracy, the base is the area in each class on the final map. Thus, for the example in Table 14.4, producer's accuracy for forest is 350/483 or 73 per cent.

Table 14.4. Errors of omission, errors of commission.

	Image to be evaluated									
Reference image	*Urban*	*Crop*	*Range*	*Water*	*Forest*	*Barren*	*Totals*	*PA%*	*EO%*	*EC%*
Urban	150	21	9	7	17	30	234	64.1	35.9	41.9
Crop	0	730	93	14	115	21	973	75.0	25.0	25.6
Range	33	121	320	23	54	43	594	53.9	46.1	23.6
Water	3	18	11	83	8	3	126	65.9	34.1	40.5
Forest	23	81	12	4	350	13	483	72.5	27.5	42.4
Barren	39	8	15	3	11	115	191	60.2	39.8	57.6
Totals	248	979	460	134	555	225	1748			
CA (%):	60.5	74.6	69.6	61.9	63.1	51.1				

Note. CA, consumer's accuracy; PA, producer's accuracy; EO, errors of omission; and EC, errors of commission.

For the same class, consumer's accuracy is 350/555 or 63 per cent. Consumer's accuracy forms a guide to the reliability of the map as a predictive device—it tells the user of the map that, in this example, of the area labelled forest, 63 per cent actually corresponds to forest on the ground. Producer's accuracy informs the analyst who prepared the classification that, of the actual forested landscape, 73 per cent was correctly classified. In both instances the error matrix permits identification of the classes erroneously labelled forest and forested areas mislabelled as other classes.

INTERPRETATION OF THE ERROR MATRIX

Table 14.1 and Fig. 14.5 show an example of an error matrix. Each of the 2592 pixels in this scene was assigned to one of six land-cover classes. The resulting classification was then compared, pixel by pixel, to a previously existing land-use map of the same area and the differences were tabulated, category by category, to form the data for Table 14.1. The total number of pixels reported by the matrix (in this instances 2592) may constitute the entire image or may simply be a sample selected from the image as explained below. Also, the land-use classes here simply form examples; the matrix could be based on other kinds of classes (including forest types, geology, etc.) and could be smaller or larger, depending upon the number of classes examined.

The column of sums on the right-hand edge of the matrix gives total numbers of pixels in each category on the reference image; the row of sums at the bottom shows total pixels in each category in the classified scene. These are known, respectively, as row and column marginals (Fig. 14.5). The sequence of values that extends from the upper left corner to the lower right corner is referred to as the diagonal (here we are not interested in the opposite diagonal). These diagonal entries show the number of correctly classified pixels: rangeland classified as rangeland, urban as urban and so on. Non-diagonal values in each row give errors of omission, for row-labelled categories. For example, as we read across the third row (Table 14.1), we see the numbers of pixels of rangeland that have been placed in other categories; urban land, 33; cropland, 121; water, 23; forest, 54 and barren land, 43. These are 'errors of omission' because the image analyst has erred by omitting true errors of rangeland from the interpreted image. More specifically, we know the rangeland on the reference map is most likely to be misclassified as cropland on the classified image.

In contrast, non-diagonal values along the columns give errors of commission (for labels at the tops of rows). To continue the example with the rangeland category, errors of commission are caused by active misassignment of other categories to the rangeland class. These errors are found by reading down the third column (Table 14.1): urban land, 0; cropland, 93; water, 11; forest, 12; and barren land, 15. These values reveal that the classification of rangeland erred most often by assigning true rangeland to the crop class. Here errors of omission and commission both reveal that rangeland is most often confused with cropland and that the classified map image is likely to confuse these two categories.

Table 14.4 summarises errors of omission and commission for another matrix. For example, there were 234 pixels of urban land in the land-use map; of these, 150 were correctly classified as urban land, for a percentage of about 64 per cent. The remaining 84 pixels (the sum of the off-diagonal entries from row 1, Table 14.4), forming about 36 per cent of the total urban land, were incorrectly classified, mainly as barren land, but also as other categories. These form the errors of omission for urban land.

Errors of omission (equal to about 42 per cent of the total of urban land in this area) consist mainly of urban land classified as barren land and rangeland, as shown in Table 14.4. For this example, it is clear that the classifier's confusion of urban land and barren land is a major source of error in the classification of urban land use.

For a contrasting relationship between errors of omission and commission, note that rangeland tends to be classified as urban land, whereas very seldom is urban land classified as rangeland. Inspection of the error matrix reveals the kinds of errors generated by the classification process, which may in turn permit improved interpretation of the map's reliability and improved accuracy in future classifications.

Percentage Correct

One of the most widely used measures of accuracy is the percentage correct, a report of the overall proportion of correctly classified pixels in the image or in the sample used to construct the matrix. The percentage correct, of course, can be easily found; the number correct is the sum of the diagonal entries. Dividing this value by the total number of pixels examined gives the proportion that have been correctly classified (Table 14.1). This value estimates the unknowable 'true' value; the closeness of this value to the true values depends, in part, on the sampling strategy, as explained below. The percentage correct can be reported with a confidence interval.

Often the percentage correct is used alone, without the error matrix, as a simple measure of accuracy. Reported values vary widely. Anderson state that accuracies of 85 per cent are required for satisfactory land-use data for resource management. Fitzpatrick-Lins reports that accuracies of USGS land-cover maps of the central Atlantic coastal region are about 85 per cent (1:24000), 77 per cent (1:1,00,000) and 73 per cent (1:2,50,000). For automated interpretations of land use in the Denver metropolitan area (six level I categories), Tom achieved 38 per cent accuracy using only MSS data (including band ratios) and about 78 per cent using ancillary data.

By itself, the percentage correct may suggest the relative effectiveness of a classification, but in the absence of an opportunity to examine the full error matrix it cannot provide convincing evidence of the classification's accuracy. A full evaluation must consider the categories used in the classification. For example, it would be easy to achieve high values of percentage correct by classifying in scene composed chiefly of open water—a class that is easy to classify correctly. Furthermore, variations in the accuracies of specific classes should be noted, as should the precision of the classes. A classification that used only broadly defined classes could achieve high accuracies, but would not be useful for someone who required more detail. Finally, later sections of this chapter will show that raw values for the percentage correct can in inflated by chance assignment of pixels to classes—yet another reason for careful inspection of the assessment task.

Hay stated that it is necessary to consider five questions to thoroughly understand the accuracy of a classification:

1. What proportion of the classification decision is correct?
2. What proportion of assignments to a given category is correct?
3. What proportion of a given category is correctly classified?
4. Is a given category overestimated or underestimated?
5. Are errors randomly distributed?

'Percentage correct' can answer only the first of these questions; the others can be answered only by examination of the full error matrix.

Quantitative Assessment of the Error Matrix

After an initial inspection of the error matrix reveals the overall nature of the errors present, there is often a need for a more objective assessment of the classification. For example, we may ask if the two maps are in agreement—a question that is very difficult to answer because the notion of 'agreement' may be difficult to define and implement. The error matrix is an example of a more general class of matrices, known as contingency tables, that summarise classifications analogous to those considered here. Some of the procedures that have been developed for analysing contingency tables can be applied to examination of the error matrix.

Chrisman and Congalton propose application of techniques described by Bishop and Cohen as a means of improving interpretation of the error matrix. A shortcoming of usual interpretations of the error matrix is that even chance assignments of pixels to classes can result in surprisingly good results, as measured by percentage correct. Hord and Brooner and others have noted that the use of such measures is highly dependent upon the samples and therefore upon the sampling strategy used to derive the observations used in the analysis.

κ (kappa) is a measure of the difference between the observed agreement between two maps (as reported by the diagonal entries in the error matrix) an the agreement that might be attained solely by chance matching of the two maps. Not all agreement can be attributed to the success of the classification. κ attempts to provide a measure of agreement that is adjusted for chance agreement. κ is estimated by $\hat{\kappa}$ ('k hat'):

$$\hat{\kappa} = \frac{\text{Observed–expected}}{\text{1–expected}} \quad \text{... (14.1)}$$

This form of the equation, given by Chrisman and others, is a simplified version of the more complete form given by Bishop. Here 'observed' designates the accuracy reported in the error matrix and 'expected' designates the correct classification that can be anticipated by change agreement between the two images.

'Observed' is the overall value for 'percentage correct' defined previously: the sum of the diagonal entries divided by the total number of samples. 'Expected' is an estimate of the contribution of chance agreement to the observed percentage correct. Expected values are calculated using the row and column totals (the 'marginals', as explained above). Products of row and column marginals estimate the numbers of pixels assigned to each cell in the confusion matrix, given that pixels are assigned by chance to each category.

The role of marginals in estimating chance agreement is perhaps clearer if we consider the situation in its spatial context (Fig. 14.7). Then the marginals can be seen to represent areas occupied by each of the categories on the reference map and the image and the chance mapping of any two categories is the product of their proportional extents on the two maps.

In tabular form (Table 14.5), the 'expected' correct, based upon chance mapping, is found by summing the diagonals, then dividing by the grand total of products of row and column marginals. This estimate for 'expected' correct can be compared to the 'percentage correct' or 'observed' value defined above. Table 14.5 shows a worked example for estimating $\hat{\kappa}$.

Table 14.5. Worked example illustrating calculation of $\hat{\kappa}$.

Part 1. Calculation of 'observed correct'			
	Image to be evaluated		
35	14	11	1
4	11	3	0
12	9	38	4

(Contd...)

Part 1. Calculation of 'observed correct'

2	5	12	2

Grand total = 163

Total correct = 86

'Observed correct' = 86/163 = 0.528

(Percentage correct = 53 per cent)

Part 2. Calculation of 'expected correct'

Marginals

				61
				18
				63
				21
53	39	64	7	

Products of row and column marginals

3233	2379	3904	427
954	702	1152	126
3339	2457	4032	441
1113	819	1344	147

$$\text{Expected agreement by change} = \frac{\text{Sum of diagonal entries}}{\text{Grand total}} = \frac{8114}{26569} = 0.305$$

Part 3. Calculation of $\hat{\kappa}$ using data from parts 1 and 2

$$\hat{\kappa} = \frac{\text{Observed} - \text{expected}}{1 - \text{expected}} = \frac{0.528 - 0.305}{1 - 0.305} = \frac{0.223}{0.695} = 0.321$$

$\hat{\kappa}$ in effect adjusts the 'percentage correct' measure by subtracting the estimated contribution of chance agreement. Thus, $\hat{\kappa} = 0.83$ can be interpreted to mean that the classification achieved an accuracy that is 83 per cent better than would be expected from chance assignment of pixels to categories. As the percentage correct approaches 100 and as the contribution of chance agreement approaches 0, the value of $\hat{\kappa}$ approaches +1.0, indicating the perfect effectiveness of the classification (Fig. 14.8). On the other hand, as the effect of chance agreement increases and the percentage correct decreases, the values of $\hat{\kappa}$ assumes a negative values.

$\hat{\kappa}$ and related coefficients have been discussed by Rosenfield and Fitzpatrick-Lins, Foody and Redmond. According to Cohen, any negative value indicates a poor classification, but the possible range of negative values depends upon the specific matrix evaluated. Thus, the magnitude of a negative value should not be interpreted as an indication of the relative performance of the classification. Values near zero suggest that the contribution of chance is equal to the effect of the classification and that the classification process yields no better results than would a chance assignment of pixels to classes. $\hat{\kappa}$ is asymptotically normally distributed.

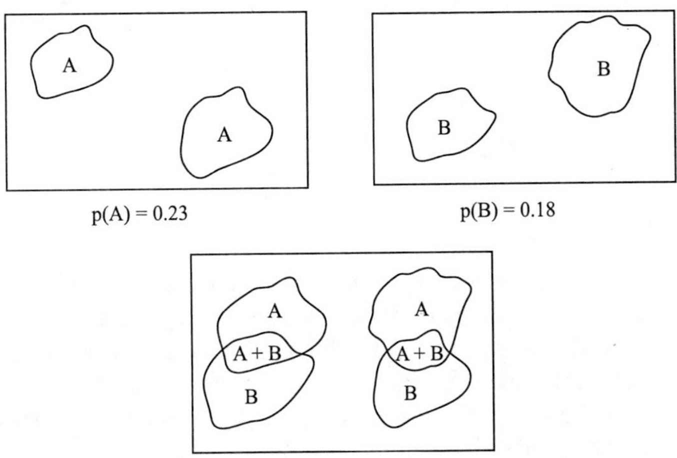

Fig. 14.7. Contrived example illustrating computation of chance agreement of two categories when two images are superimposed. Here p(A) and p(B) would correspond to row and column marginals; their product estimates the agreement expected by chance matching of the two areas.

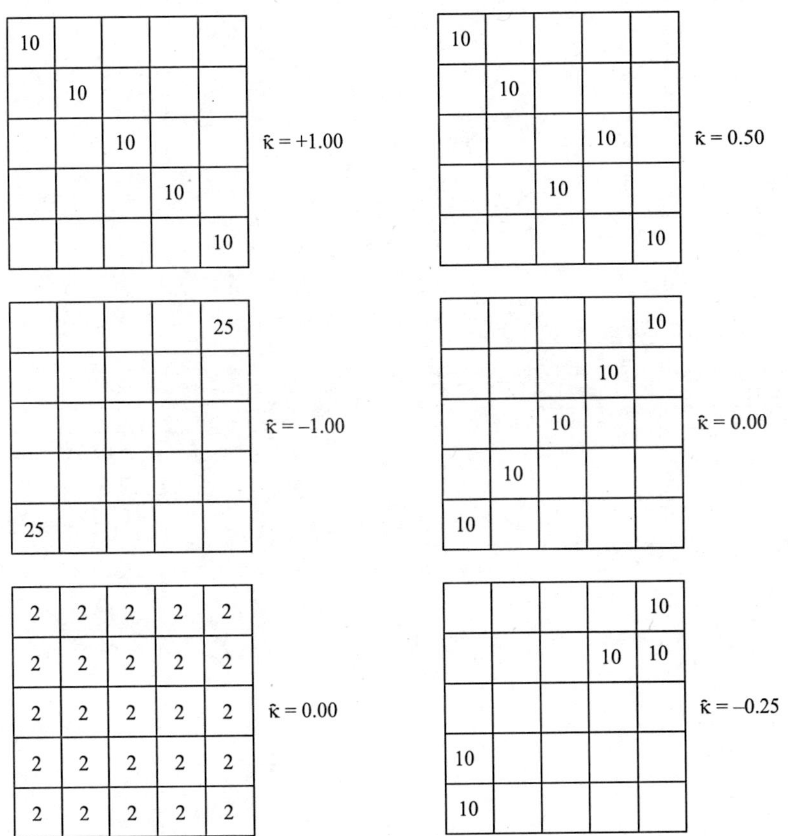

Fig. 14.8. Contrived matrices illustrating $\hat{\kappa}$.

Congalton and Congalton described how the large sample variance can be estimated, then used a Z test to determine if individual $\hat{\kappa}$ scores differ significantly from one another. Congalton provides a FORTRAN computer programme that calculate $\hat{\kappa}$ and the necessary values to conduct the test of significance. Foody and Redmond have advocated use of the tau statistic (τ) as an important improvement over $\hat{\kappa}$. τ is analogous to κ, but is based upon a priori classification probabilities, rather than observed occurrences used in calculation of $\hat{\kappa}$.

Comparisons of Error Matrices

One of the primary purposes of error analyses is to permit comparisons of different interpretations. For a given region, we may have alternative classifications made using images acquired at different dates, classified by different procedures or produced by different individuals. In such instances, we wish to generate error matrices, then ask which classification might be best for a given purpose. Such an analysis can permit identification of the specific imagery, dates, pre-processing procedures and other procedures that might be best for a given purpose.

15

Hyperspectral Remote Sensing

INTRODUCTION

Remote sensing involves examination of features observed in several regions of the electromagnetic spectrum. Conventional remote sensing, as outlined in previous chapters, is based upon use of several rather broadly defined spectral regions. Hyperspectral remote sensing is based upon examination of many narrowly defined spectral channels.

Sensor systems such as SPOT 1 HRV, Landsat MSS and Landsat TM provide 3, 4 and 7 spectral channels, respectively. The hyperspectral sensors described below can provide 200 or more channels, each only 10 nm wide.

In the context of the discussion of image resolution, hyperspectral sensors implement the concept of 'spectral resolution' to the extreme. Although hyperspectral remote sensing applies the same principles and methods discussed previously, it requires such specialised data sets, instruments, field data and software that it forms a specialised field of inquiry.

SPECTROSCOPY

Hyperspectral data have detail and accuracy that permit investigation of phenomena and concepts that greatly extend the scope of traditional remote sensing. For example, analysts can begin to match observed spectra to those recorded in spectral libraries and to closely examine relationships between brightnesses in several channels to estimate atmospheric effects using data within the image itself. Such capabilities present opportunities for much more precise identification of earth surface phenomena than is possible with broad-band sensors, for investigation of phenomena such as the blue shift and the red shift and for correction of data in some bands using other bands that convey information about atmospheric transmission.

These capabilities extend the reach of remote sensing into the field of spectroscopy, the science devoted to the detailed examination of very accurate spectral data. Classical spectroscopy has its origins in experiments conducted by Isaac Newton, who used glass prisms to separate visible light into the spectrum of colours. Later, another English physicist, William Wollaston noted that spectra displayed dark lines when light is projected through a narrow slit. The meaning of these lines was discovered through the work of Joseph Fraunhofer, a German glassmaker who discovered distinctive lines in spectral of light from the sun and from stars. Dark lines (absorption spectra) are observed as radiation passes through gases at low pressure; bright lines (emission spectra) form as heated gases (e.g., in the sun's atmosphere) emit radiation. These lines have origins in the chemical elements present in the gases, a discovery that has permitted astronomers to investigate differences in chemical compositions of stars and planets. The Danish physicist Neils Bohr found that the character of Fraunhofer lines is ultimately determined by the atomic structure of gases.

Instruments used in spectroscopy—spectroscopes, spectrometers, spectrographs—are designed to collect radiation with a lens and to divide it into spectral regions (using a prism or diffraction grating) that are then recorded on film or measured electronically. This form of spectroscopy is now a standard method not only in astronomy, but also for laboratory analyses to characterise unidentified materials.

HYPERSPECTRAL REMOTE SENSING

Hyperspectral remote sensing uses the practice of spectroscopy to examine images of the earth's surface. Although hyperspectral remote sensing sometimes applies the techniques of classical spectroscopy to the study of atmospheric gases and pollutants, for example, more commonly it applies these techniques to the making of precise, accurate, detailed spectral measurements of the earth's surface (imaging spectrometry). Such data have accuracy and detail sufficient to begin to match observed spectra to those stored in databases known as spectral libraries. Instruments for hyperspectral remote sensing differ from those of conventional spectroscopy in that they gather spectra not only for point targets, but for areas—not for stars or laboratory samples, but for regions of the earth's surface. Instruments for hyperspectral remote sensing differ from other remote sensing instruments in terms of their extraordinarily fine spectral, spatial and radiometric resolutions and their careful calibration. Some hyperspectral instruments collect data in 200 or more channels at 10 to 12 bits. Because of their calibration and ability to collect data having fine detail, such instruments greatly extend the reach of remote sensing not only by extending the range of applications but also by defining new concepts and analytical techniques.

Although the techniques of classical spectroscopy can be used in hyperspectral remote sensing to examine, for example, atmospheric gases, hyperspectral remote sensing typically examines very detailed spectra for images of the earth's surface, applies corrections for atmospheric effects and matches them to spectra of known features.

AIRBORNE VISIBLE/INFRARED IMAGING SPECTROMETER (AVIRIS)

One of the first airborne hyperspectral sensors was designed in the early 1980s by the Jet Propulsion Laboratory. The airborne imaging spectrometer (AIS) greatly extended the scope of remote sensing by virtue of its number of spectral bands; their fine spatial, spectral and radiometric detail and the accuracy of its calibration. AIS collected 128 spectral channels, each about 10 nm wide in the interval 1.2 to 2.4 μm. The term hyperspectral remote sensing recognises the fundamental difference between these data and those of the usual broad-band remote sensing instruments (Systems with even finer spectral resolution, designed primarily to study atmospheric gases, are known as ultraspectral sensors).

Although several hyperspectral instruments are now in operational use, an important pioneer in the field of hyperspectral remote sensing is the airborne visible/infrared imaging spectrometer. AVIRIS was developed by NASA and JPL from the foundations established by AIS. AVIRIS was first tested in 1987, was placed in service in 1989 and has since been modified at intervals to upgrade its reliability and performance. It has now acquired hundreds of images of test sites in North America and Europe.

Hyperspectral sensors necessarily employ designs that differ from those of the usual sensors systems. An objective lens collects radiation reflected or emitted from the scene; a collimating lens then projects the radiation as a beam of parallel rays through a diffraction grating that separates the radiation into discrete spectral bands (Fig. 15.1). Energy in each spectral band is detected by linear arrays of silicon and indium antimonide. Because of the wide spectral range of AVIRIS, detectors are configured in four separate panels (0.4 to 0.7 μm, 0.7 to 1.3 μm, 1.3 to 1.9 μm and 1.8 to 2.8 μm), each calibrated independently (Fig. 15.2). AVIRIS operates over the spectral range of 400 to 2500 nm (0.4 to 2.45 μm), producing 224 spectral channels, each 10 nm wide (Fig. 15.3). After processing, data consist of 210 spectral channels. At its usual operating altitude each image records a strip 11 km wide, processed to form scenes recording areas about 11 km × 11 km. Each line of data conveys about 614 pixels. If operated at low altitude, pixels might each represent ground areas about 4 m on a side; if operated at higher altitudes, as is common practice, pixels each represent ground areas as large as about 20 m on a side.

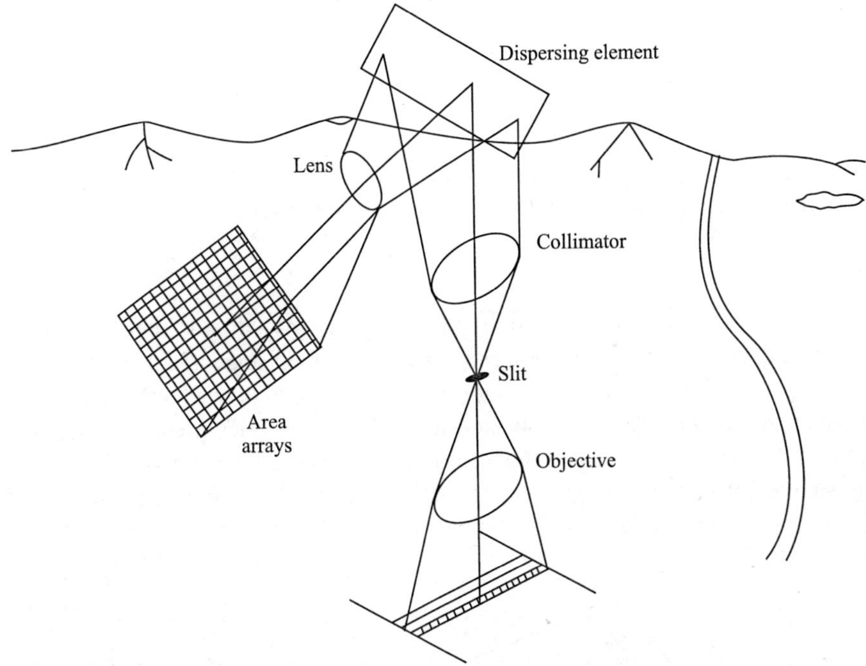

Fig. 15.1. Imaging spectrometer.

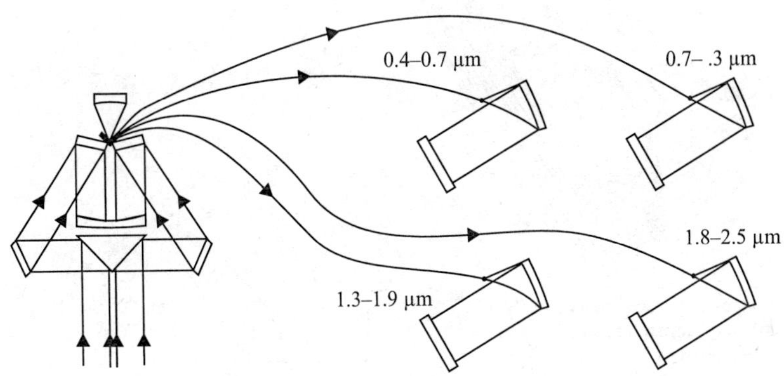

Fig. 15.2. AVIRIS sensor design.

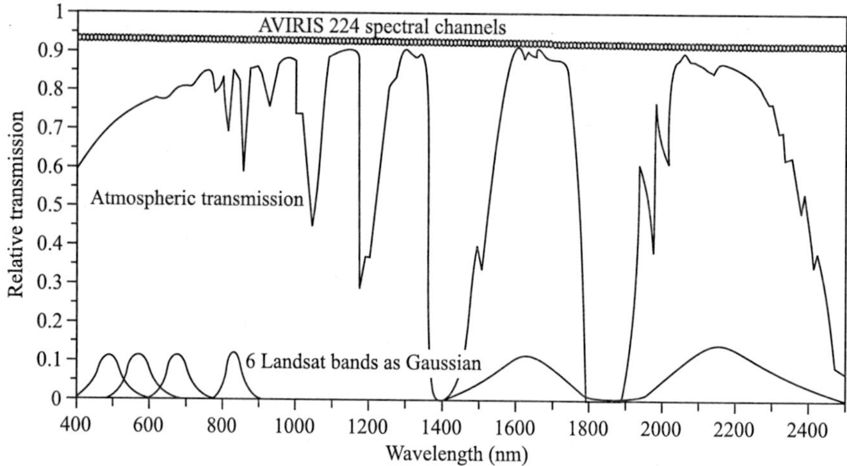

Fig. 15.3. AVIRIS spectral channels compared to Landsat TM spectral channels. The 220 narrow bands at the top represent AVIRIS spectral channels. For comparison, Landsat TM channels are shown at the bottom.

IMAGE CUBE

The image cube refers to the representation of hyperspectral data as a three-dimensional figure, with two dimensions formed by the x and y axes of the usual map or image display and the third (z) formed by the accumulation of spectral data as additional bands are superimposed on each other. In Fig. 15.4., the top of the cube is an image composed of data collected at the shortest wavelength (collected in the ultraviolet) and the bottom of the cube is an image composed of data collected at the longest wavelength (2.5 μm). Intermediate wavelengths are found as slices through the cube at intermediate positions. Values for a single pixel observed along the edge of the cube form a spectral trace describing the spectra of the surface represented by the pixel.

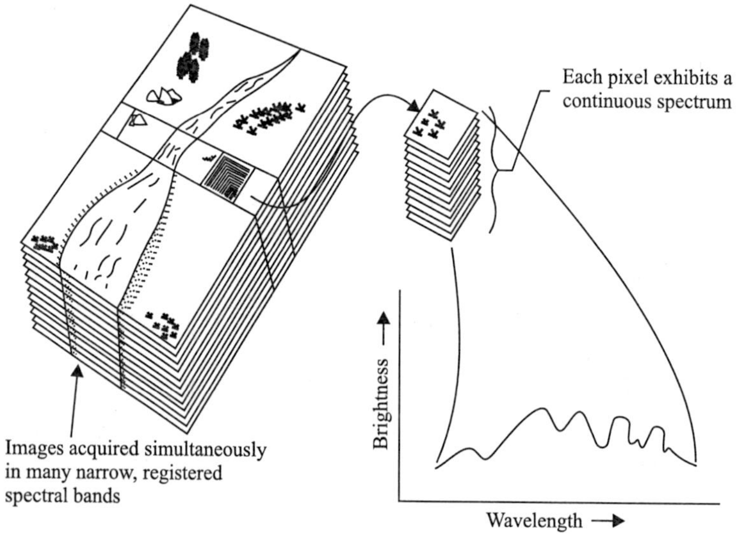

Fig. 15.4. Image cube.

DATA LIBRARIES

The development of hyperspectral remote sensing has been accompanied by the accumulation of detailed spectral data acquired in the laboratory and in the field. These data are organised in spectral libraries, database maintained primarily to governmental agencies, but also by other organisations. These libraries assemble spectra that have been acquired at test sites representative of varied terrain and climate zones, observed in the field under natural conditions. Included also are other data describing, for example, construction materials, minerals, vegetation and fabrics as observed in laboratories under standardised conditions. Such data are publicly available to the remote sensing community and have been incorporated into software designed for use in hyperspectral remote sensing. Maintenance of a spectral library requires specialised effort to bring data into a common format that can be used by a diverse community of users. Spectral data are typically collected by diverse instruments under varied conditions of illumination. These many differences must be resolved to prepare data in a format that permits use by a diverse community.

Because of the fine spectral, spatial and radiometric detail of hyperspectral analysis, identification and cataloging form special problems for design of spectral libraries. Therefore each spectral record must be linked to detailed information specifying the instruments used, meteorological conditions, nature of the surface and the circumstances of the measurement. These kinds of ancillary data are required for successful interpretation and analysis of the image data.

SPECTRAL MATCHING

Figure 15.5, illustrates a sequence of analysis for hyperspectral data. Analysis begins with acquisition and pre-processing (1) to remove known system errors and assure accurate calibration. Any of several methods can be used to correct for atmospheric effects (2). The lower portion of Fig. 15.5 represents the analytical process. Data are organised to permit convenient display and manipulation of specified bands or combinations of bands. Selected bands can be used to prepare colour composites for display. Alarm (5) means that the analyst can place the cursor on the image to mark a specific pixel or region of pixels, then instruct the computer to highlight (alarm) other regions on the image that are characterised by the same spectral response. Then (6) the analyst can attempt to match the alarmed areas to spectra from a spectral library accessible to the image-processing system. If a match can be made, then the analyst can examine another region and attempt to match it to entries from the spectral library.

SPECTRAL MIXING ANALYSIS

Fine spectral resolution, like fine spatial resolution, does not overcome the enduring obstacles to the practice of remote sensing. Surface materials recorded by the sensor are not always characteristic of sub-surface conditions. Atmospheric effects, shadowing and topographic variations contribute to observed spectra to confuse interpretations. Even when observed at fine spatial and spectral detail, surfaces are often composed of varied materials. Therefore, the sensor observes composite spectra that may not clearly match to the pure spectral of spectra libraries. Linear mixing refers to additive combinations of several diverse materials that occur in patterns too fine to be resolved at the resolution of the sensors. As long as the radiation from component patches remains separate until it reaches the sensor, it is possible to estimate proportions of component surfaces from the observed pixel brightness. Linear mixing might occur when components of a composite surface are found in a few compact areas (Fig. 15.6b). Non-linear mixing occurs when radiation from several surfaces combines before it reaches the sensor. Non-linear mixing occurs when component surfaces arise in highly dispersed patterns (Fig. 15.6c). Non-linear mixing cannot be described by the techniques addressed here.

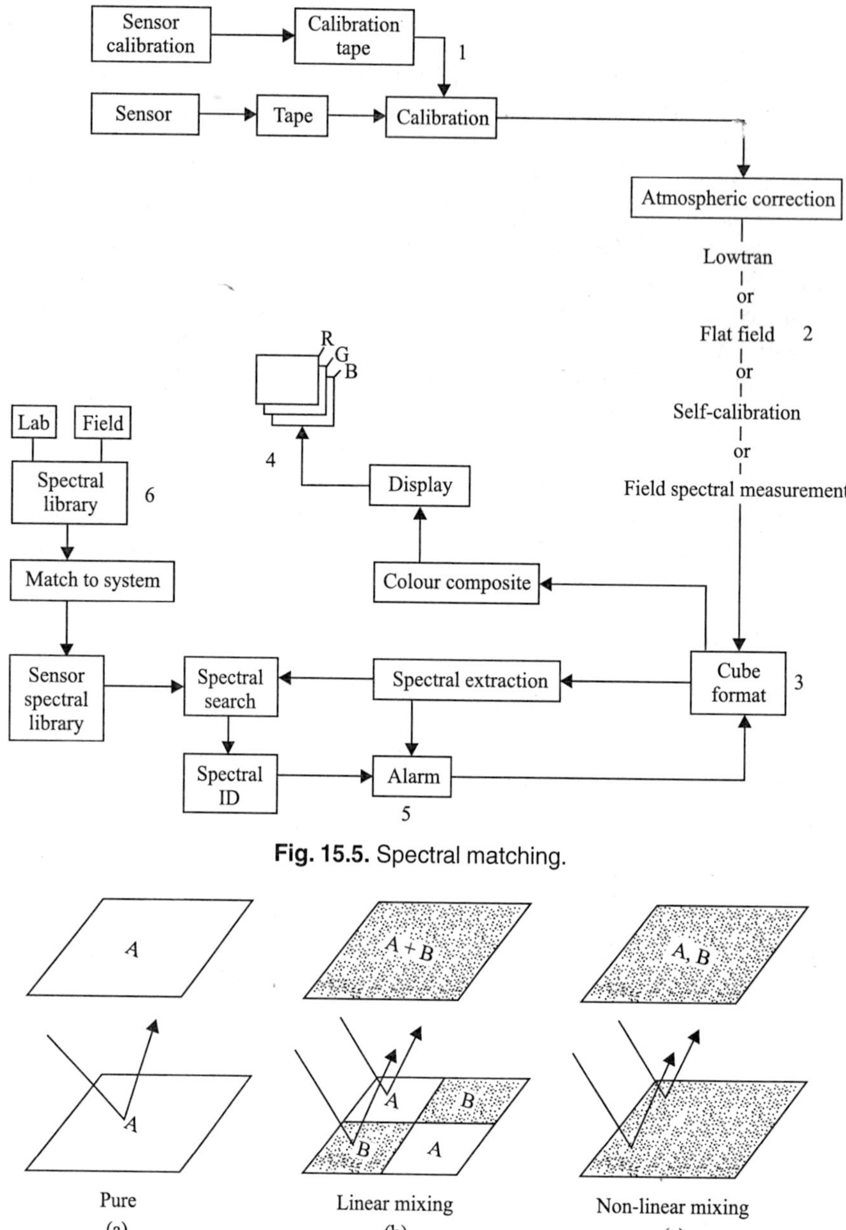

Fig. 15.5. Spectral matching.

Fig. 15.6. Linear and non-linear spectral mixing. (a) If a pixel represents a uniform ground area at the resolution of the sensor, the pixel represents a pure spectrum. (b) If a pixel represents two or more surfaces that occur in patches that are large relative to the sensor's resolution, mixing occurs at the sensor. The pattern of the composite surfaces can never be resolved, but because mixing occurs in a linear manner, proportions of the components can be estimated; and (c) If the composite occurs at a scale that is fine relative to the resolution of the sensor, mixing occurs before radiation reaches the sensor and components of the composite cannot be estimated using methods described here.

Spectral mixing analysis (also known as spectral unmixing) is devoted to extracting pure spectra from the complex composites of spectra that by necessity form each image. It assumes that pixels are formed by linear mixing and further assumes that it is possible to identify the components contributing to the mixture. It permits analysts to define key components of a specific scene and forms an essential component in the process of spectral matching, discussed below. Analysts desire to match data from hyperspectral images to corresponding laboratory data to identify surfaces from their spectral data much more precisely than previously was possible. Whereas conventional images analysis matches pixels to broad classes of features, hyperspectral image matching attempts to make more precise identifications—to specific mineralogies of soils or rocks, for example.

Therefore, spectral matching requires the application of techniques that enable analysts to separate pure pixels from impure pixels. This problem is well matched to the capabilities of convex geometry, which examines multidimensional data envisioned in n dimensions. Individual points (pixels) within this data space can be examined as linear combinations of an unknown number of pure components. Convex geometry can solve such problems provided that the components are linearly weighted, sum to unity and are positive. We assume also that the data have greater dimensionality (more spectral bands) than the number of pure components.

The illustrations here, for convenience and legibility, show only two dimensions, although the power of the technique is evident only with much higher dimensionality. In Fig. 15.7, the three points A, B and C represent three spectral observations at the extreme limits of the swarm of data points, represented by the shaded pattern. That is, the shaded pattern represents values of all the pixels within a specific image or sub-image, which is simplified by the triangle shape (Other shapes can be defined as appropriate to approximate the shape of data swarm, although an objective is to define the simplest shape [simplex] that can reasonably approximate the pattern of the data swarm).

These three points (for the example in Fig. 15.7a) form endmembers, defined as the pure pixels that contribute to the varied mixtures of pixels in the interior of the data swarm. Once the simple form is defined, the interior pixels can be defined as linear combinations of the pure endmembers. In general, interior points can be interpreted as positive unit-sum combinations of the pure variable represented by endmembers at the vertices. In general, a shape defined by $n + 1$ vertices is the simplest shape that encompasses interior points (i.e., for two dimensions [$n = 2$], the simplex is a triangle (i.e., $3 = n + 1$). The faces of the shape are facets and the exterior surface is a convex hull. In Fig. 15.7, A, B and C are the observed approximations of the idealised spectra A′, B′ and C′ that may not be observed on any specific image. In the application of convex geometry to hyperspectral data, it is first necessary to define the dimensionality of the data. An image is typically subset to define a region of relative homogeneity and to remove bands with high variance (assumed to include high levels of error). The original hyperspectral data are converted to ground-level reflectances (from radiances) using atmospheric models. The data are condensed by applying a version of principal components analysis (PCA). Although hyperspectral data may include many bands (224 for AVIRIS), duplication from one channel to another means that inherent dimensionality is much less (perhaps as few as 3 to 10), depending upon the specifics of each scene.

The analyst then examines the transformed data in a data space to define the smallest simplex that fits the data. This process defines the $n + 1$ facets that permit identification of the n endmembers (Fig. 15.7a). These vertices, when projected back into the original spectral domain, estimate the spectra of the endmembers. These spectra are represented by Fig. 15.7b. The objective is to match these endmembers to spectra from spectral libraries, then to prepare maps and images that reveal the varied mixtures of surfaces that contribute to the observed spectra in each image.

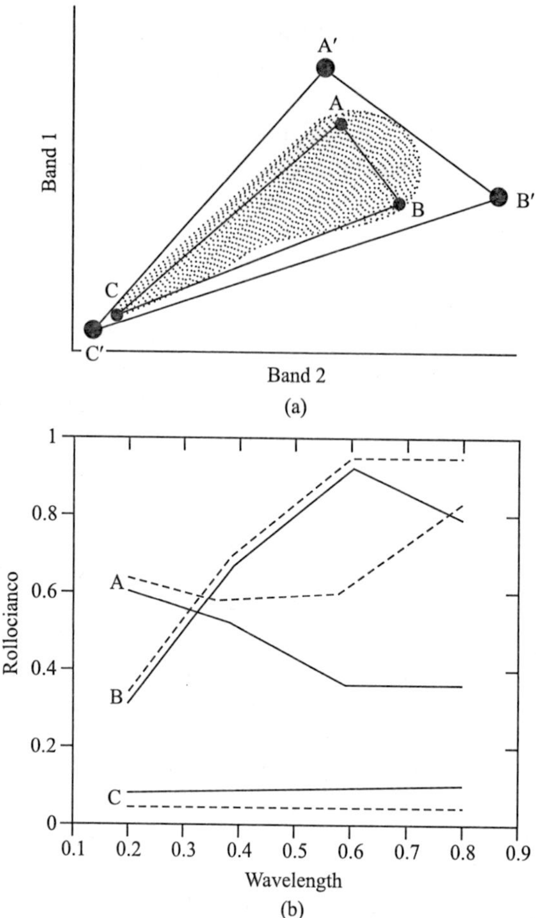

Fig. 15.7. Spectral mixing analysis. (a) Simplex; and (b) Endmembers.

Typical endmembers in arid regions have included bare soil, water, partially vegetated surfaces, fully vegetated surfaces and shadows. Endmembers can be investigated in the field to confirm or revise identifications made by computer. Software for hyperspectral analysis often includes provisions for accessing spectral libraries (and for importing additional spectra as acquired in the field or laboratory) and the ability to search for matches with endmembers identified. Although it may not always be possible to uniquely identify matches in spectral libraries, such analyses can narrow the range of alternatives. In some instances mathematical model can assist in defining poorly established endmembers.

ANALYSES

Other investigations have attempted to understand relationships between spectral data and specific physical or biological processes. For example, Curran reviews efforts to use hyperspectral data to monitor botanical variables, such as the chlorophyll, lignin, cellulose, water and nitrogen content of plant tissues. Others have examined, at high levels of spectral, radiometric and spatial resolution, observed spectra of laboratory samples of plant tissues influenced by atomic and molecular structures of water and by specific concentrations of organic compounds (such as chlorophyll, lignin and cellulose). These relationships have formed the basis for research devoted to the examination of hyperspectral data of vegetation canopies, to derive estimates of foliar chemistry of plant tissues *in situ*. Such estimates would support agricultural, forestry and ecological studies by providing indications of nutrient availability, rates of productivity and rates of decomposition. Green and Rivard and Arvidson report some of the applications of hyperspectral data to lithological and mineralogic analyses.

Thus, the vast amounts of data collected by hyperspectral systems and the problems they present for both collection and analysis, prevent routine use of hyperspectral data in the same way that we might collect TM or SPOT data on a regular basis. More likely, hyperspectral data will provide a means for discovering and refining the knowledge needed to develop improved sensors and analytical techniques that can be applied on a more routine basis.

A second important role for hyperspectral data lies in the monitoring of long-term research sites, especially those devoted to study of biophysical processes and other phenomena that change over time. The fine detail of hyperspectral data will provide enhanced data for ecological monitoring and for understanding patterns recorded on lower resolution data of the same sites.

Several plans to deploy hyperspectral sensors for the satellite observation are underway. One is NASA's EO–1 satellite, launched in November 2000 and designed as a vehicle to test the feasibility of advanced imaging systems. One of EO–1's sensors is the Hyperion, a high-resolution hyperspectral sensor capable of resolving 220 spectral bands from 0.4 to 2.5 μm at a 30 m resolution. The instrument can image a 7.5 km × 100 km land area to provide detailed spectral mapping across all 220 channels with high radiometric accuracy. EO–1 has been placed in an orbit that permits both Landsat 7 and EO–1 to image the same ground area at least once a day, permitting both systems to collect images under identical viewing conditions. The paired images are then available for evaluation of the imaging technology.

ORBIMAGE has developed other plans for hyperspectral observation from space, using its Orb View-4 satellite, which was designed to carry sensors capable of continuing acquisition of the detailed panchromatic and multispectral imagery. In addition, Orbimage plans to use OrbView-4 as the platform for a 200-channels hyperspectral sensor operating in the spectral region from 450 to 2500 nm, designed to image a swath width of 5 km at a spatial resolution of 8 m. The 8 m data is to be released to US agencies with military and national security missions; other customers could purchase the same data at a resolution of 20 m. The satellite will re-visit each location on earth in less than 3 days with an ability to acquire off-nadir views to 45° from its polar orbital path.

16

Geographic Information Systems

INTRODUCTION

The concept of the geographic information system (GIS), although implemented in many different forms, is ideally one that permits full utilisation of the goals of remote sensing. Remote sensing achieves its maximum usefulness when images from one date or formed from one part of the spectrum can be integrated with those acquired at a different date or from a different portion of the spectrum. Although this kind of integration can be accomplished by many means, the GIS provides maximum flexibility in both display and analysis.

The concept of the GIS has also been important in remote sensing because it has formed a focal point for scientists who work in sub-fields of remote sensing and diverse disciplines. By its nature, a GIS requires expertise from many fields of knowledge, so GIS research has brought scientists from diverse backgrounds together to work on common issues.

GIS research has emphasised the need for further development of capabilities of significance both to GIS and to remote sensing. Image matching, image registration and related topics are important both for remote sensing and for GISs and both fields can benefit from improvements. Future developments in remote sensing are likely to address topics such as data compatibility, improvements in image geometry and other subjects that may improve the usefulness of remotely sensed data for GISs.

Geographic information systems (GISs) are specialised computer programs designed to analyse spatially referenced data. A computer provides storage, manipulation and display of large amounts of geospatial data that have been encoded in digital form. Broadly stated, geospatial data describe attributes accurately associated with positions on the earth's surface, including everyday examples such as highways maps, property records, census surveys or remotely sensed images.

The theory and practice of designing and using GISs forms a body of knowledge known as geographic information science, which is relevant not only to GISs, but also to remote sensing, cartography and spatial statistics.

In essence, a GIS consists of a series of map overlays for a specific geographic region. These overlays may depict raw data (e.g., topographic elevation) or may show thematic information (e.g., soils, land use or geology), but they must share common geographic qualities (including a common geographic co-ordinate system) that permit them to be merged so that one can identify and analyse interrelationships between the data. These data can be visualised as a set of superimposed images (Fig. 16.1).

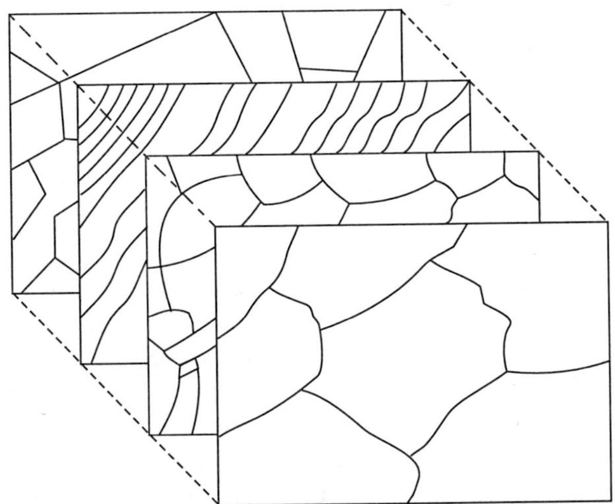

Fig. 16.1. A GIS portrayed as a series of overlays.

Ideally, a GIS consists of several kinds of information. A detailed planimetric base accurately records the positions of primary features on the landscape. This base serves as the locational framework that permits accurate positioning and registration of the varied overlays of thematic data (e.g., forest types, rivers, highways and power lines) that form the GIS. Some systems may also include a cadastre, a record of land parcels that depicts each unit of land, defined by its legal description of ownership. A third element consists of the varied thematic overlays that describe physical and cultural features such as stream and rivers, topography, soils, geology, highways, political boundaries and structures.

Sometimes the term land information system (LIS) describes the cadastre and the planimetric base and the term geographic information system is reserved for those systems that focus on resource information (e.g., vegetation, soils or geology) and/or demographic and economic data. Further, the term automated mapping/facilities management (AM/FM) is reserved for systems devoted to mapping of utilities, transportation networks and similar infrastructure at large scale, primarily in urban areas. In concept, there is no reason that a single system could not include these varied kinds of information, but as a practical matter, the constraints of costs, the varied expertise required to administer and maintain these systems and the fact that each tends to be used by different kinds of organisations means that they often are separate. However, it is still possible for separate systems within an organisation to be co-ordinated and networked, such that information can be shared and passed from one system to another.

Superficially, a GIS may resemble computer-aided design and display (CADD) or computer-aided mapping (CAD/CAM) systems, which are designed to prepare technical graphics by computer. Quite naturally, CAD/CAMs could be applied not only to prepare engineering diagrams, but also to produce maps and diagrams. However, the defining characteristic of a GIS is not its graphic capability, but rather its ability to conduct analytical operations based on the thematic and geographic characteristics of the data. Therefore, despite the similarity in appearance of the display used for both GIS and CAD/CAM, there is a fundamental difference in purpose and capability. Although CAD/CAM systems were originally intended specifically for graphic design, in recent years they have included more and more GIS-related capabilities that blur the previously distinct differences between the two kinds of systems.

Many of the basic concepts for GIS originated in the 1950s and 1960s, but recent innovations in computer technology have greatly increased the numbers and kinds of applications of GIS. Especially important are decreases in computer costs and improvements in their reliability and efficiency that have increased availability of computers for businesses and governmental agencies. Such widespread availability of computer equipment has stimulated interest in applications of GIS not only among large organisations, but also among small businesses and governmental units that previously would not have been able to purchase such equipment. In the United States, the increasing use of 911 emergency telephone systems and the requirement that such systems be based on systematic records of addresses and locations has promoted the introduction of GIS into local governments throughout the nation.

GISs have evolved side by side with remote sensing systems, so there are many close relationships between the two. First, remote sensing systems contribute data to GIS. Remotely sensed data can provide timely information at low cost and in a form that is compatible with the requirements of a GIS. Second, both GIS and digital remote sensing systems use similar equipment and similar computer programs for analysis and display. Therefore, investment of funds and expertise in one field tends to form the foundation for work in the other. Third, the non-remote sensing data from a GIS can be used to assist in the analysis of remotely sensed images. Thus, remote sensing and GIS have natural, mutually supporting, relationships to each another. Nonetheless, the links between GIS and remote sensing are incomplete and imperfectly formed and much more research is necessary to fully exploit the benefits of their interrelationships.

A GIS must include at least three main elements: (i) computer hardware; (ii) computer programs; and (iii) data. Computer hardware can vary in capabilities from the inexpensive personal computers that can easily fit on an office desk to more sophisticated workstations with massive storage capacities and complex peripheral equipment. A computer's capabilities for storage and analysis, of course, are closely related to its size and computing capabilities and its ability to input, display and output, data are determined by computer hardware. For purposes of discussion in this chapter we assume that the GIS is supported by a substantial workstation and by peripheral devices for digitising, plotting and colour display of data.

EQUIPMENT FOR A GEOGRAPHIC INFORMATION SYSTEM

Much of the equipment required for a GIS resembles that required for image analysis. The heart of the GIS is a computer. Because of the requirement of work with large data sets and with complex programs, the capabilities of a GIS are greatly enhanced if the computer has a large memory capacity and can access large volumes of mass storage.

Because a GIS often depends on data that may have been gathered by other organisations, it is important for the GIS to have access to mass storage (e.g., tape units, CD-ROM drives) and to computer network communications for data transfer from other computer systems. A digitising table (Fig. 16.2) or scanning system forms another method for data entry. Individual digitising tables vary in size from perhaps 10 inch × 12 inch (digitising tablets) to tables as large as 4 ft. × 8 ft. The table consists of a fine grid of thin wires or a printed circuit board encased in a dense, stable substance such as fiberglass. By this means the table can sense the x–y positions of a cursor that is moved over the surface of the table. The finer the spacing of the grid within the table, the more precise the data generated by the digitiser. The analyst tapes a map or aerial photograph to the surface of the digitiser and after establishing a co-ordinate systems, traces the outlines of areas or marks positions of points and lines with the cursor. As the cursor moves, the digitiser creates a digital record of its successive positions, usually as a sequence of co-ordinate pairs.

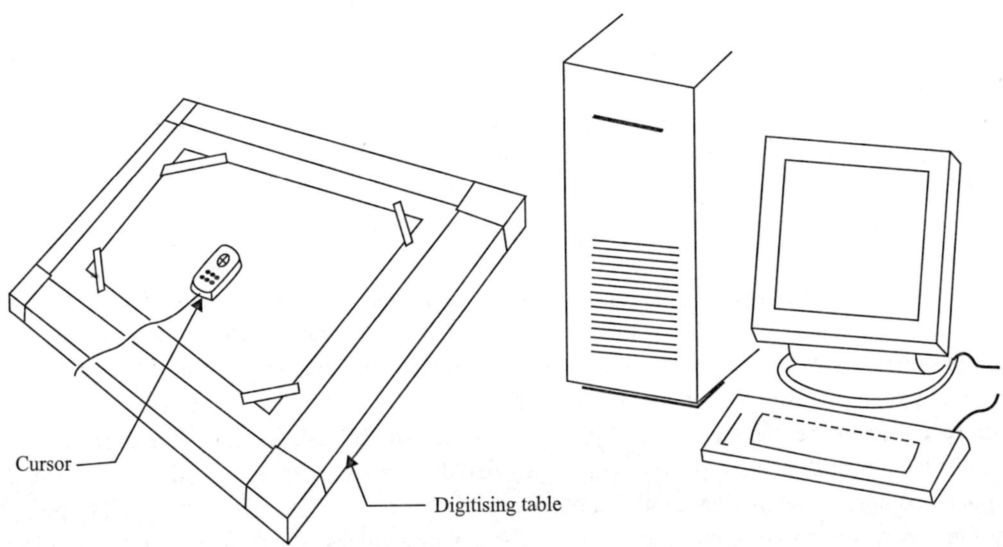

Fig. 16.2. Equipment for a GIS.

Usually the digitiser is supported by a computer that allows the analyst to record data with separate codes (e.g., to identify lines that record streams, highways or power lines) and to perform geometric transformations (to correct positional errors). A display permits the analyst to see the digitised line on a computer screen as it is traced, to permit prompt identification of errors and their correction as they occur.

Scanning, another method of data entry, uses a sensor such as a charge-coupled device (CCD) to systematically record patterns depicted on images or maps. Although high-quality scanners are expensive, even inexpensive scanners are often accurate enough for many purposes. A principal concern is often the process of editing scanned data to remove errors and assure logical consistency. For some kinds of data, scanning is the principal form of data entry.

GEOGRAPHIC INFORMATION SYSTEMS SOFTWARE

A GIS requires specialised programs tailored for manipulation of geographic data. Other kinds of databases may have very large volumes of data, but do not need to retain locational information for data. Therefore, GIS software must satisfy the special needs of the analyst who needs to reference data by geographic location. Furthermore, the GIS must provide the analyst with the capability to solve the special problems that arise whenever maps or images are examined—the problems of changing co-ordinate systems, matching images, bringing different images into registration and so on. A GIS must be supported by the ability to perform certain operations related to the geographic character of the data. For example, it must be capable of identifying data by location or by specified areas in order to retrieve and to display data in map-like image. Thus, the GIS permits the analyst to display data in a map-like format so that geographic patterns and interrelationships are visible to him or her.

Furthermore, software for a GIS must be able to perform operations that relate values at one location to those at neighbouring locations. For example, to compile slope information from elevation data, it is necessary to examine not only specific elevation values but also those at neighbouring locations in order to calculate the magnitude and direction of the topographic gradient.

A GIS is not a single data set. It consists of two or more data sets that together show several kinds of information (themes) for the same geographic area. Thus, a GIS may include data for topographic elevation, streams and rivers, land use, political and administrative boundaries, power lines and other variables. This combined data set is useful only if the themes register to one another exactly. Therefore, the several kinds of the data must share a common co-ordinate system. Because separate variables are likely to be derived from quite different sources, it is common for different variables to have different scales, different reference systems and different cartographic projections. Thus, a GIS must have special programs to bring input data into registration by changing the scale and geometric qualities of the data.

Aside from problems with data acquisition, the capabilities of a GIS are determined largely by the ability it gives the analyst to ask questions concerning the geographic patterns recorded by the data. Although some queries are relatively simple ('How many acres of category A are present'?) and can be addressed by relatively simple conventional programs, many other kinds of queries are special for GIS. Therefore, GISs require special computer programs to perform the tasks essential for GISs (Table 16.1). Image display permits the analyst to present a specified data set as an image on a display screen, then to manipulate colours, scales, orientation and other qualities as desired. An overlay capability permits the analyst to superimpose two or more data sets for display or analysis. Visual overlay refers to the ability to superimpose two overlays on the screen so that the two patterns can be seen together in a single image (Fig. 16.3a). Logical overlay and arithmetic overlay means that the analyst can define new variables or categories based upon the matching of different overlays at each point on the map (Fig. 16.3b).

Table 16.1. Operations for GISs.

Data input	Spatial interpolation
Display	Raster-to-vector conversion
Subset	Data output
Overlay	Data storage and retrieval
Projection conversion	Buffering
Registration/image matching	Network operations
Re-sampling	Data manipulation
Logical operations	Data reporting
Arithmetic operations	Statistical generation
Vector-to-raster conversion	Models

The ability to overlay different images depends, of course, upon the ability to manipulate the geometric qualities of data sets. Projection conversion provides the ability to change from one map projection or geographic reference system to another. For example, geographic position in one overlay may be specified using state plane co-ordinates, whereas others may be based upon the Universal Transverse Mercator (UTM) grid system. Unless the GIS has the capability to translate data from one reference system to another, it is not possible to match the separate overlays that form the GIS and the GIS cannot perform one of the most basic functions; superimposing and comparing different data sets. Thus, the GIS must have programs to perform image registration and re-sampling; these capabilities permit the analyst to bring two images into registration. These capabilities are among the most important of all those required for a GIS and among the most difficult to perform accurately.

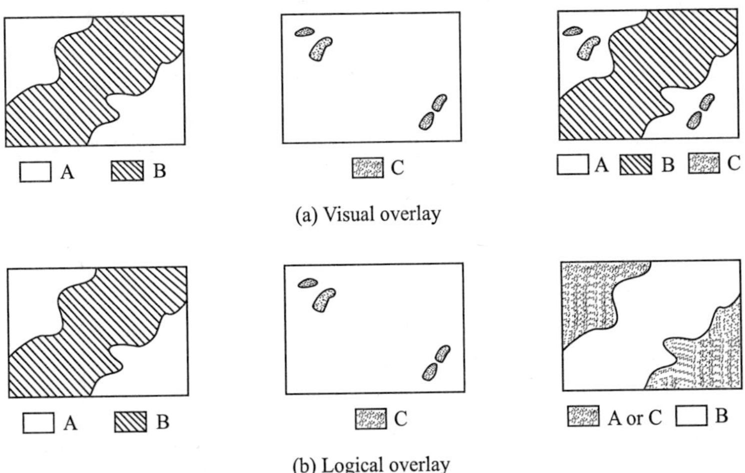

Fig. 16.3. (a) Visual overlay; and (b) logical overlay.

Other operations permit the analyst to examine individual overlays or combinations of individual overlays using logical rules. For example, the analyst may wish to delineate all areas above a certain elevation or to define all areas within a certain soil category that have a certain slope or elevation. Thus, the analyst must be able to use the elevation matrix to define a slope overlay; then he or she must be able to find the appropriate soil category within the soil overlay and match it to the elevation and slope overlays to find the slopes and elevations within soil classes. Such operations require a variety of general-purpose programs that permit the analyst to perform operations such as selecting regions from an image, registering images, registering two images to identify regions where specific regions match or calculating slopes from elevations. GIS software should also permit the analyst to define 'tailor-made' geographic regions—for example, to delineate all areas within a specified distance of a particular class of stream or highway.

There are a wide range of software packages for GIS analysis, each with its own advantages and disadvantages.

DATA AND DATA ENTRY

A GIS consists of information depicting geographic distributions of significance to those who use the GIS. Examples include topographic elevation, streams, highways, water bodies, soils and census data regarding population and economic status. Although such data are widely available as lists and tabulations, the purpose of a GIS requires that data must be coded by geographic locations so that each item of information can be associated with a specific geographic location. The analyst therefore, for example, can determine not only the total population for a state, but can display an image that shows the pattern of population variation within the state and can relate the population pattern to other variables within the database or to population distribution at earlier dates.

A GIS retains locational identity by means of a co-ordinate system (Fig. 16.4). The fineness of the co-ordinate system relative to actual ground distances determines the resolution of the GIS or of the variable coded at a particular level of detail. Obviously, it would be desirable to encode locations at very fine levels of detail to provide high precision in specification of location. But remember that fine detail means that it is more difficult and more time-consuming to enter a given amount of data and remember too that as detail increases the amount of memory and storage required for a given mass of data must rapidly increase. For example, doubling the number of rows and columns increases the number of locations by a factor of 4 and tripling the number of rows and columns increases the number of locations by a factor of 9. In practice the decision to use a given level of resolution is a compromise that balances factors such as: (i) the need to preserve detail and accuracy of the source documents; (ii) resources available for digitisation and data storage; and (iii) requirements of the user.

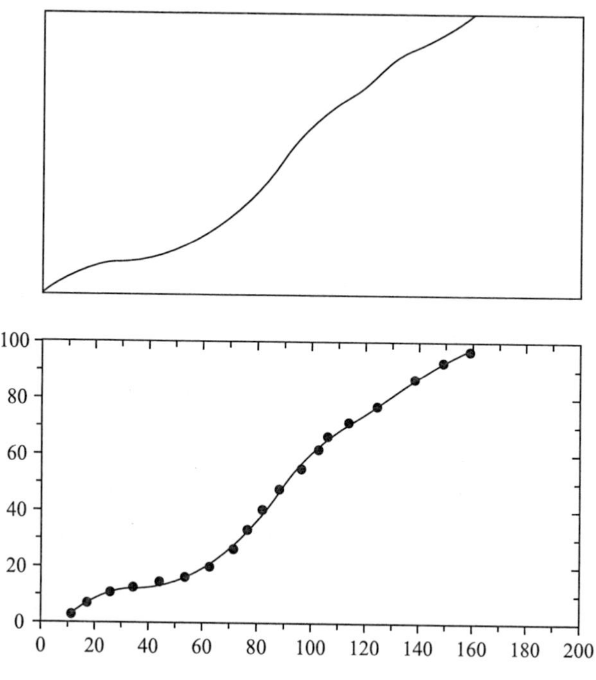

Fig. 16.4. Co-ordinate systems.

Data for a GIS can be derived from many sources. It is, of course, desirable to gather data directly in the field by an original survey tailored specifically for the purposes of the GIS. The availability of inexpensive, accurate and easy-to-use GPS receivers has greatly increased the feasibility of gathering, verifying and updating field collection of geospatial data. Nonetheless, it is likely that most data for GIS will be derived from a source that is already generally available. For example, topographic data can be derived from topographic maps, which also can provide information concerning streams, highways and forested areas. Within the United States, such information is often easily available from federal or state governmental agencies via the Internet. Other data must be prepared for entry into the GIS by digitisation, described below. Although data can also be derived from sources such as aerial photographs or other images, the analyst must devote extra effort to scaling the data to specified level of detail and to correcting geometric errors inherited from the aerial images.

A third class of data is derived from digital data files generated in digital form, archived data. Examples include the data from the US Census, available in digital form for urban areas, topographic elevation data provided by the USGS and the National Imagery and Mapping Agency (NIMA), land-use data provided by the USGS and remotely sensed data gathered by Landsat and other systems. Although some of these data are digitised from source documents (as described above), they are available at modest cost in digital form, thereby providing the analyst with digital data at a small fraction of the cost and effort required for digitisation locally.

ALTERNATIVE DATA STRUCTURES

Data for a GIS must be represented in a form that preserves the locational identities of each unit of information so that it is possible to retrieve data by location and therefore to depict and analyse geographic patterns. Because data are frequently derived from a 'conventional' (non-digital) map or image, it is necessary to convert them into digital form suitable for use by a GIS. This process, known as geocoding, records the pattern on each map in a form that can be accepted and manipulated by computers. Geocoding is one of the most expensive and time-consuming aspects of GIS management because it requires considerable manual labour for coding and entering data and for checking and editing errors.

Two alternative GIS data structures offer contrasting advantages and disadvantages. Raster (or cellular) data structures consist of cell-like units, analogous to pixels of an MSS scene. The region of interest is sub-divided into a network of such cells of uniform size and shape; each unit is then encoded with a single category or values (attribute) (Fig. 16.5). Raster structures offer ease of data storage and manipulation and therefore permit use of relatively simple computer programs. Also, raster structures lend themselves to use with remotely sensed data because digital remotely sensed data are already presented in a raster format. Disadvantages are primarily related to losses in accuracy and detail due to the coding of each cell with a single category even though several may be present (Fig. 16.6) (This is the same kind of error caused by mixed pixels).

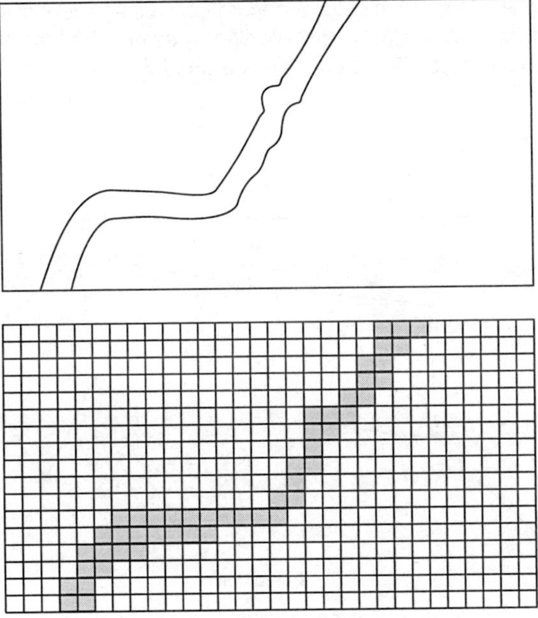

Fig. 16.5. Raster data structure.

The alternative format is the vector (or polygon) format, which records the boundaries or outlines, of parcels on the source document by listing the co-ordinates of the boundaries or the co-ordinates of the vertices of polygons (Fig. 16.7). Vector format tends to provide more efficient use of computer storage than does the raster format, finer detail and more accurate representation of shapes and sizes. Its main disadvantages are (in some instances) the higher costs of encoding data and the greater complexity required for the computer programs that must manipulate data. Today most GIS are designed to use vector format, although most accommodate raster data or may use raster structures for selected analyses. Raster-to-vector conversations and vector-to-raster conversions permit mixing of the two kinds of data, although unnecessary conversions can create errors.

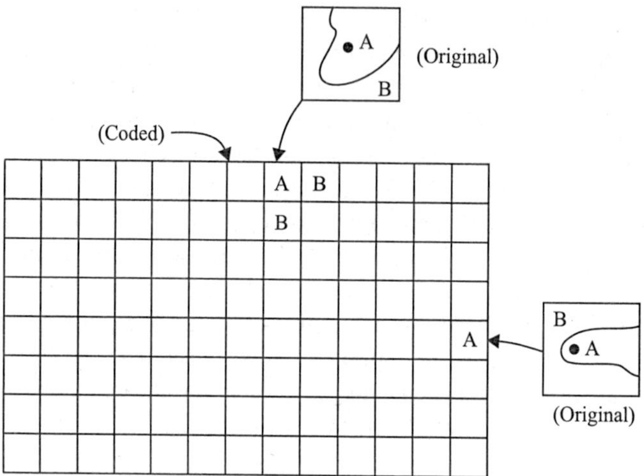

Fig. 16.6. Errors in encoding cell data. Each cell can record only a single identifier, so cells cannot record the fine detail of the original pattern. Here cells illustrate coding by selection of the single class positioned at the center of each cell. The two examples show how cells assigned the same label can correspond to different ground conditions.

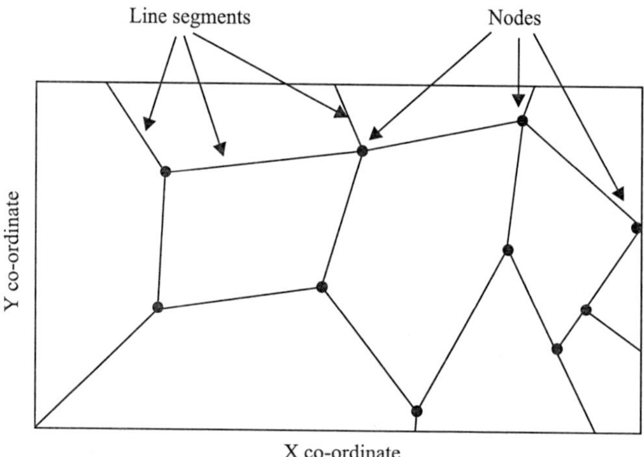

Fig. 16.7. Polygon ('vector') data structure.

Cellular Data Structures

Raster databases establish a uniform network of units as the locational framework for the database. Sometimes the network of cells is completely arbitrary and has no meaning outside the context of a particular GIS. However, many GISs use pre-existing geographic reference systems as the basis for locational coding of information. The UTM grid system, for example, provides a worldwide locational reference that can be applied at any level of detail that may be appropriate (Fig. 16.8). Or, in the western United States, some GISs use the US Public Land Survey (Township-Range Survey System) as the basis for encoding information (Fig. 16.9). Despite its faults, the Township-Range System has been useful in this context because it forms the basis for legal descriptions of land holdings and because many roads, highways and field patterns follow its boundaries, it is often visible on aerial imagery as distinct locational references (Of course, it can be used only in that region of the United States for which it forms the legal reference for land ownership).

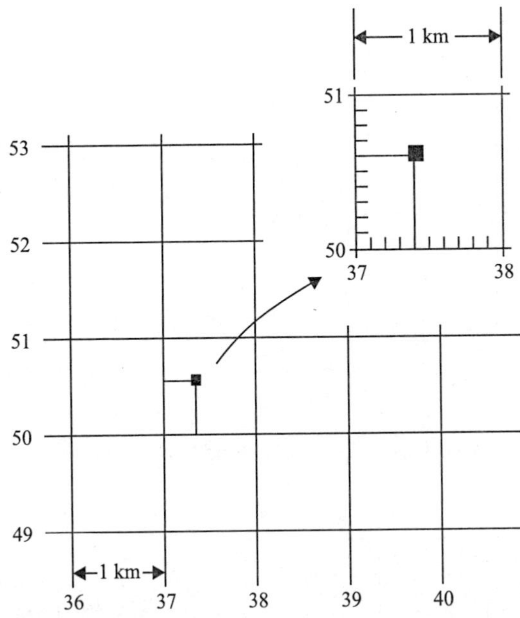

Fig. 16.8. Universal transverse mercator reference system.

Each cell in a GIS theme must be encoded with a single value or a single category that represents a condition at that location (Fig. 16.10). For continuously varying information, such as topographic elevation, the single values could be the elevation at the center of the cell or possibly the average value of elevation within the cell. However, once a choice is made, the same procedure is applied uniformly to all cells within the GIS. A cell can also encode nominal data, such as land-cover class or a geologic or paedologic category. Because a given cell may include several categories, it is necessary to define a rule to consistently select which category represents the cell in the database. The predominant category rule selects the single category that occupies the majority of the cell (Fig. 16.10a). It is easy to understand the major problems inherent to the raster-based GIS. Variation within cells cannot be represented. Sometimes errors are insignificant, but often there are systematic errors due to the fact that some categories occur only as small parcels or as long, narrow shapes that do not occupy large areas within cells and therefore are systematically excluded from the GIS. Raster-based GISs therefore tend to exaggrate the importance of categories that occur in large, regular parcels, whereas small, linear or widely dispersed units tend to be under-represented. Although using a smaller cell size can reduce these problems, they become insignificant only when a cell size is very small in relation to the pattern to be studied. For this reason, costs of using such a small cell size are often prohibitive.

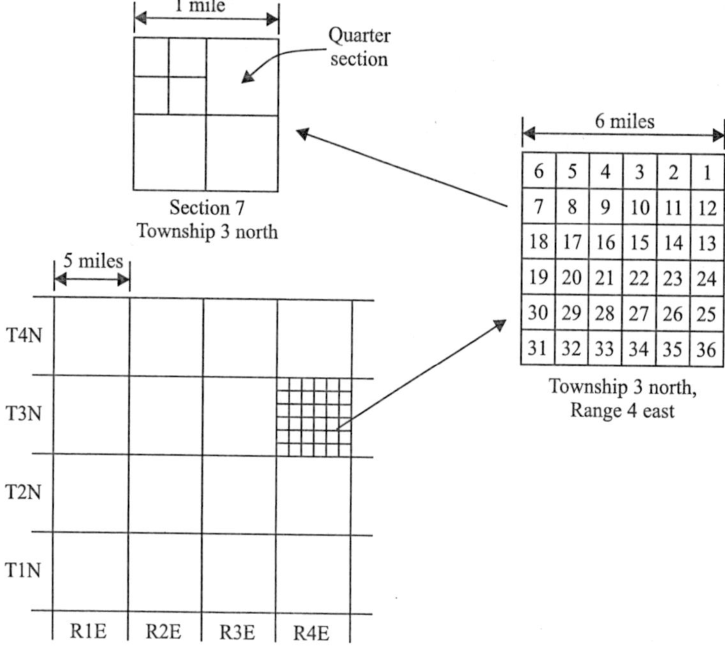

Fig. 16.9. Township-Range survey system.

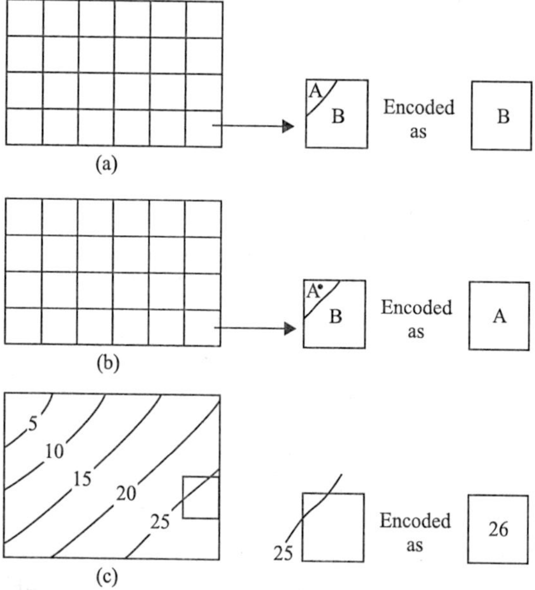

Fig. 16.10. Data entry for a cell-based GIS.

An alternative procedure selects the category by means of a dot in the center of each cell; the category that falls beneath the dot is entered as the category for the cell (Fig. 16.10b). A third procedure uses a dot randomly positioned within each cell (Fig. 16.10c). (Of course, for a given data set, only a single method will be used.) Relative to the predominant category rule, these procedures improve the accuracy of the database as a whole, but the error at each cell can be quite large.

Gersmehl and Napton studied these two kinds of errors. Inventory error is error for the database as a whole in reporting total areas occupied by specific categories. Inventory error is important for users of the GIS who are interested in a regional overview, that is, who wish to learn about the character of specific regions rather than small sites within the region. Use of the dot randomly positioned within each cell reduces inventory error; for large areas, inventory errors may be quite small.

In contrast, classification error is the error in reporting the contents of each cell. Classification error is important for uses that require detailed information concerning specific sties. Gersmehl and Napton found that classification error is usually larger than inventory error (Fig. 16.11). Clearly, classification error increases with use of the random dot method, even though the randomised selection may reduce inventory error. Both kinds of errors can be reduced if cell size is small relative to the pattern to be studied, as illustrated in Fig. 16.5. However, even modest decreases in cell size greatly increase the numbers of cells; as a result, costs and practicality soon limit efforts to reduce cell size. Therefore, selection of cell size must be made with great care, because once a GIS is committed to a specific cell size, the costs and inconvenience of changes preclude conversion to smaller cell size.

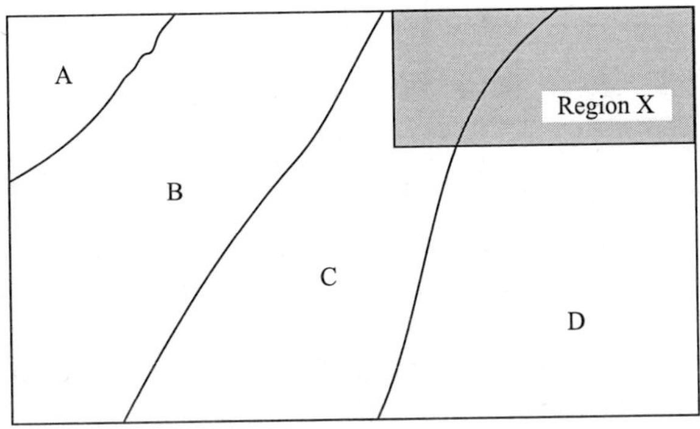

Inventory:
'Report total area of category A'
(Location is not important)

Classification:
'Report categories present within region X'
(Location is important)

Fig. 16.11. Inventory error and classification error.

It should be noted that it is possible to interpolate data from one cell size to another (Fig. 16.12). Data encoded at a 1 km grid size can be represented, for example, at a 4 km grid, as long as the analyst consistently applies a rule for deciding how to encode data for the larger cell (Fig. 16.12a). However, interpolation from larger to smaller cells is a different matter. It is operationally possible to create 1 km cells for data encoded at 4 km cells, but the change cannot improve the level of detail in the data—it simply creates a false impression of finer detail (There can be no method for assigning values for the smaller cells except by replicating information of the larger cells. The visual detail has been improved, but the logical detail remains the same [Fig. 16.12b]).

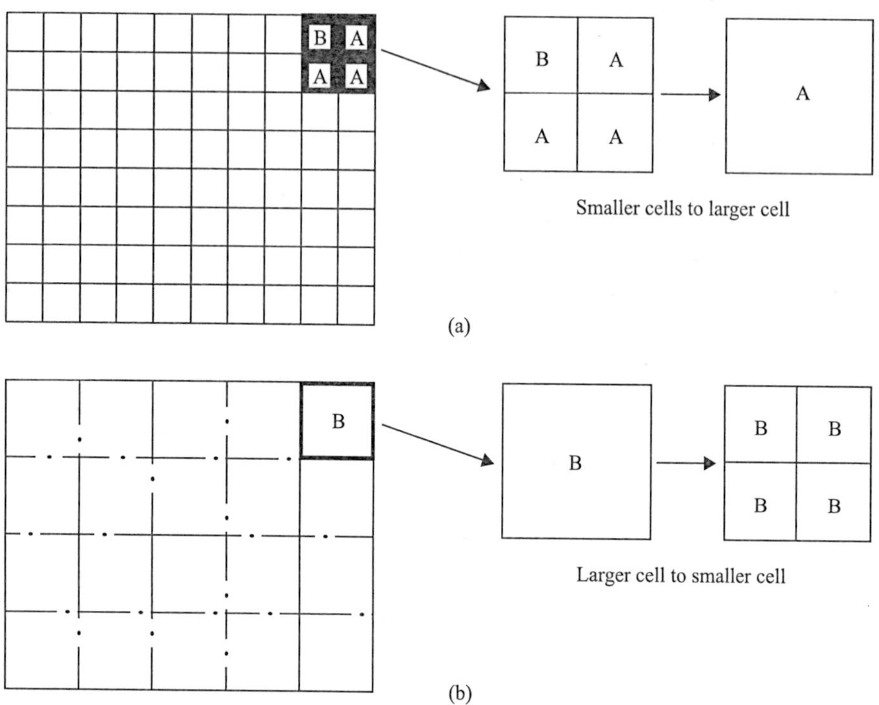

Fig. 16.12. Interpolation from one cell size to another. (a) Smaller cell to larger cell. (b) Larger cell to smaller cell.

Data for raster data systems are entered from paper maps, aerial images or similar documents depicting the pattern to be encoded. Often a template showing the grid system is superimposed and registered to the map. The spacing of the grid must be appropriate for the scale of the map. For example, to encode 1 km cells from a map at 1:24000, the template should show cells 4.17 cm in size, whereas the encode from a map at 1:15840 the template must have cells of 6.31 cm. The analyst then can read the value or category for each cell in sequence (using the specific method adopted for use), recording the information on a special form or possibly reading them to another operator who enters them directly using a computer keyboard. Remotely sensed data and data for GIS can differ in many important respects, so not all concepts from the discussion of image resolution apply directly, but student can benefit from a careful comparison and contrast of the two subjects.

Vector Data Structures

Numerous alternative formats designed by different governmental and commercial organisations exist for organisation of vector data. Essentially each format represents a different way to establish a spatial framework of non-overlapping spatial divisions (known as tesselation) and to use this framework to systematically organise the points, lines and areas that represent geographic features. The challenge is to organise this information in such a way that it is simultaneously effective to store and retrieve this information in computer storage and to retain the positions and geographic meanings of the lines, points and areas. That is, to assure that the computer representation of a map is not simply a network of lines, but a network in which the computer can distinguish between lines that represent roads, those that represent streams and those that are political boundaries. This task is very difficult to accomplish effectively, so there are many alternative strategies for organising vector data that have been designed to optimise a given quality at the expense of another.

Some of the most common vector data formats illustrate different strategies for digitally encoding the boundaries that form a geographic pattern. All depend upon use of a geographic reference system that permits definition of locations at a fine level of detail relative to the sizes of polygons. The reference system may be arbitrarily defined or may be tied to an established geographic reference system, such as latitude and longitude, state plane co-ordinates or the UTM grid system.

Location list data structures (LLS) (Fig. 16.13) simply encode the co-ordinates of the polygons that record the geographic pattern. Each polygon is encoded individually, so interior boundaries are encoded twice. Thus, although LSS is simple and convenient to use, it makes inefficient use of computer storage and creates boundary slivers that must be removed.

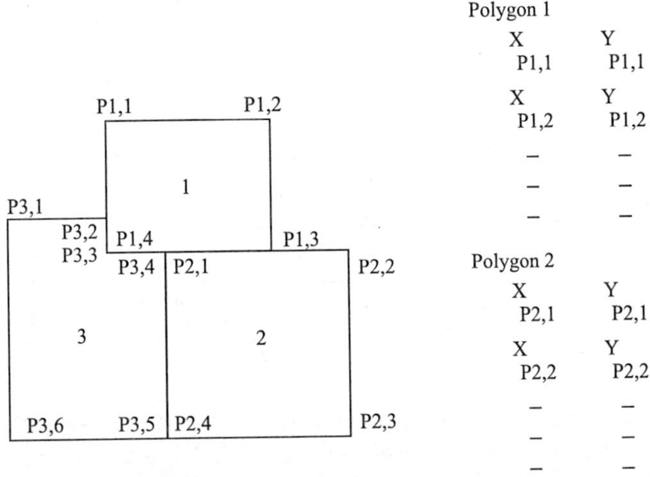

Fig. 16.13. Location list file. Each polygon is treated as a separate unit; many points must be encoded several times.

The point dictionary structure (PDS) (Fig. 16.14) records each vertex of each polygon only once. One file is used to record a list of co-ordinates of all vertices, with a label for each. A second file then identifies each polygon in location list form using labels of points that define its outline. PDS usually provides a great improvement in efficiency over LLS at only a small cost in program complexity.

The dual independent map encoding (DIME) structure (Fig. 16.15) was once one of the most widely used formats for vector data. The basic unit for the DIME format is not the polygon itself, but rather the line segments that form boundaries between polygons. The DIME format encodes a stream of co-ordinates for each line segment, with end points in each stream forming the vertices of polygons. Each segment is labelled with the identities of the polygons on either side of the line segment. The complete pattern is formed by plotting all line segments, using a computer program that can organise line segments into a network of polygons. The DIME format was once the primary method for encoding polygons that form the collection units for US Census data. It is no longer used for that purpose, but its simplicity and familiarly have led to applications for encoding other kinds of vector data.

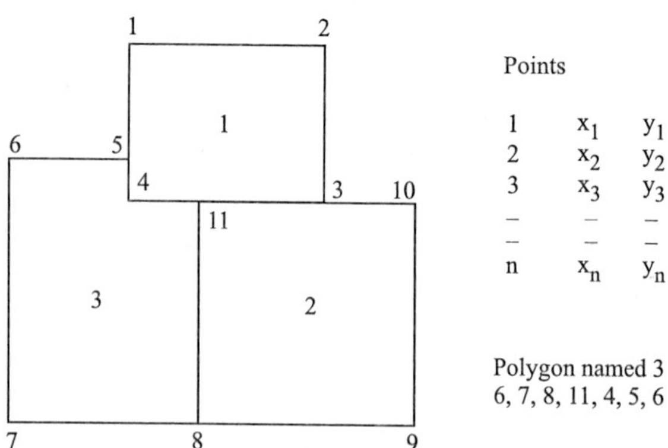

Fig. 16.14. Point dictionary file. Locations of vertices are encoded independently of polygons; the 'dictionary' lists then defines each polygon by the points that form its perimeter.

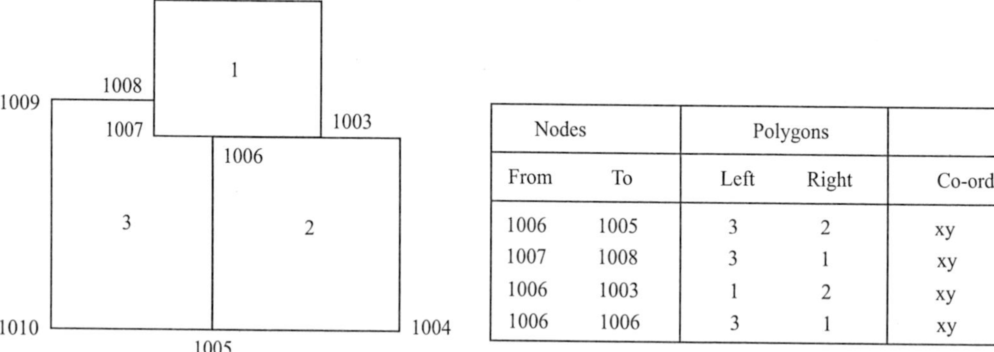

Nodes		Polygons			
From	To	Left	Right	Co-ordinates	
1006	1005	3	2	xy	xy
1007	1008	3	1	xy	xy
1006	1003	1	2	xy	xy
1006	1006	3	1	xy	xy

Fig. 16.15. Dual independent map encoding (DIME). Lines are encoded as separate entities, with polygons identified as areas on either side of each line segment.

The chain file structure (CFS) is organised around 'chains' of line segments that connect key nodes within the network of boundaries (Fig. 16.16). A 'chain' is simply a sequence of locations that defines the boundary between two polygons. Each chain of points has an identifying label, a sequence of points and line segments that define its shape and labels that define the identity of polygons on either side of the chain. This forms an important improvement over the DIME format, as less coding is required during data entry.

Digital line graphs (DLGs) are used for digital representations of the USGS's topographic map series at 1:24000, 1:1,00,000 and 1:2,00,0000 (Fig. 16.17). Each theme (e.g., streams and water bodies, topography and forest cover) is represented by a separate file with the co-ordinates that describe the placement of each line. A complete map can be represented only by combining all of the files.

Topologically integrated geographic encoding and referencing (TIGER) files, an elaboration of the DIME structure, although treated as a single file, is in fact formed from four different file types (Fig. 16.18): (i) TIGER county partition files; (ii) GEO-CAT (GEOgraphic CATalog of Political and Statistical Areas) files; (iii) the national partition file; and (iv) temporary work files. The national partition files consists of boundary outlines of and identifiers for all counties, used to define county data required to represent any specific area to be mapped. The GEO-CAT files include current data and labels for political and statistical units within the system. When a specific area is to be mapped, the system refers to this file to find the correct names, populations and so on. TIGER county partition files hold the boundaries and relationships to other units required to represent any specific region. The work files form temporary work areas to assemble data from each of the other kinds of files as specific map is prepared.

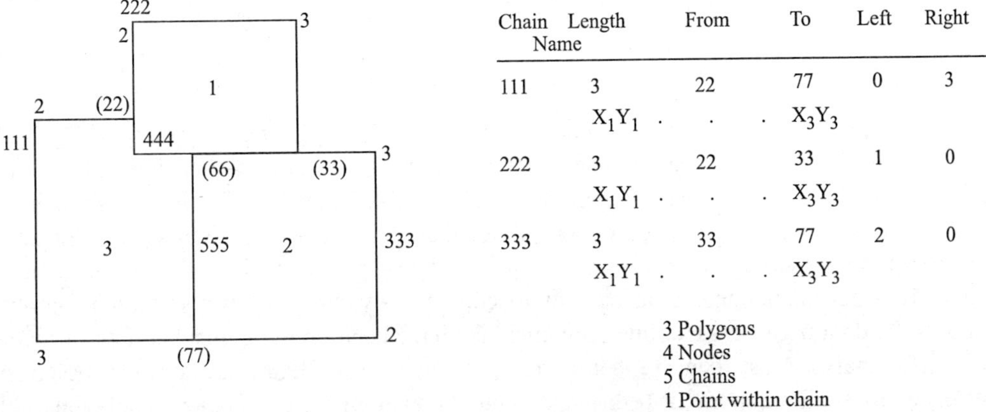

Chain Name	Length	From	To	Left	Right
111	3	22	77	0	3
	X_1Y_1 .	.	. X_3Y_3		
222	3	22	33	1	0
	X_1Y_1 .	.	. X_3Y_3		
333	3	33	77	2	0
	X_1Y_1 .	.	. X_3Y_3		

3 Polygons
4 Nodes
5 Chains
1 Point within chain

Fig. 16.16. Chain code file. Every line is defined by a chain, consisting of a label, a string of co-ordinates that form its inner path, two limiting nodes (i.e., two end points), a length (number of co-ordinate pairs) and polygons on either side.

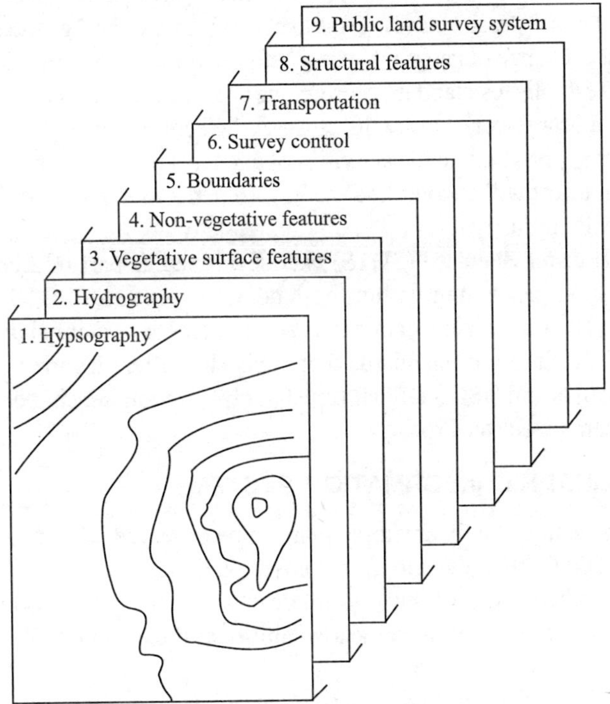

Fig. 16.17. Digital line graph.

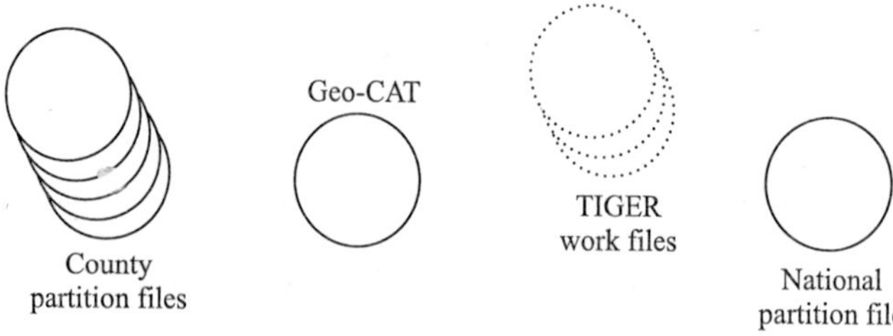

Fig. 16.18. TIGER file structure.

Data for vector systems are usually encoded by scanning or by digitising. Polygons are digitised from paper or mylar copies of maps or aerial images that have been attached to the digitising table. The analyst moves the cursor over the document, tracing the outlines of polygons and labelling each line segment with the identities of the polygons on either side of the line. Usually the digitiser is connected to a computer, so the analyst can enter information at a keyboard and store the digitised information in a computer file. After the document has been digitised, the analyst must carefully edit the computer file that records the data because some line segments may have been omitted, misidentified or incorrectly recorded. The analyst must identify, then correct, all such errors before the data can be considered completely digitised. Equipment has been manufactured for automated digitisation of polygons, although it is expensive and data still require extensive editing.

National Spatial Data Infrastructure

The National Spatial Data Infrastructure (NSDI) (Co-ordinating Geographic Data Acquisition and Access: The National Spatial Data Infrastructure), established by an executing order, is intended to form a framework for efficient exchange of geographic data between different organisations and between different computing systems. It establishes standards for geographic data and a plan for establishing a National Digital Geospatial Data Framework before the close of the century.

The executive order applies only to the activities of agencies of the federal government. However, the existence of the federal effort will encourage state governments to implement similar programs and lead to participation by private industry.

The Spatial Data Transfer Standard (SDTS) was developed as part of a broader effort to establish guidelines for information processing within the federal government. SDTS is intended to minimise problems encountered in transferring data between agencies by establishing common formats and standards. It consists of a family of standards that apply the different forms of spatial data, including Topological Vector Profiles and USGS Digital Line Graphs. Remote sensing data, as well as other raster data, are included within the Raster Profile.

DATA FOR A GEOGRAPHIC INFORMATION SYSTEM

Data for a GIS can represent virtually any topic that can be observed within the area of interest. Typical topics might include topographic elevation, land cover, soils, census information, highways, streams, power lines and many others. Almost any variable can be useful in some context, so the decision to include specific variables often is based on the availability of the data in digital form and on issues such as accuracy and compatibility, discussed below.

Point data consist of observations that occur only at points or occupy very small areas in relation to the scale of the database (Fig. 16.19). Features such as wells, for example, illustrate data that occupy a single point even at the largest levels of detail. In contrast, features such as buildings sometimes occupy significant areas, even though they may be represented as points in the database. A polygon database can depict point data as points and can position them accurately. In contrast, a cellular database can depict point data only at the level of detail of a single cell, so, for example, a cell can show the presence of a well within the cell but cannot show the placement of the well within the cell. Some point observations may represent quantitative measurements, such as the amount of rainfall observed at a specific point or the depth of a specific geological unit below the surface.

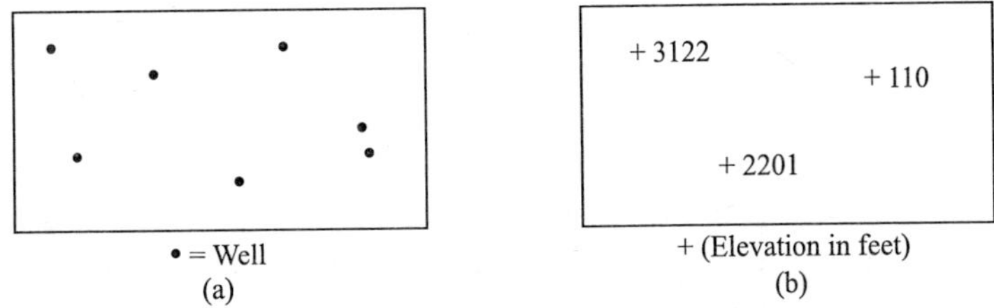

Fig. 16.19. Point data: (a) nominal; and (b) quantitative.

Line data are exemplified by features such as highways, rivers, pipelines or power lines. Vector polygon systems can show line data in fine detail, whereas cellular systems can show linear data only at the resolution of the cell. Thus, a raster database can depict a linear feature only as a series of adjacent cells with a common code that shows the presence or absence of a specific feature (Fig. 16.20). Both raster and vector systems can depict different classes of linear features. For example, a GIS can encode different classes of highways or streams that permit the analyst to examine not only the entire highway or stream network, but also to select only specified classes of highways or streams for analysis.

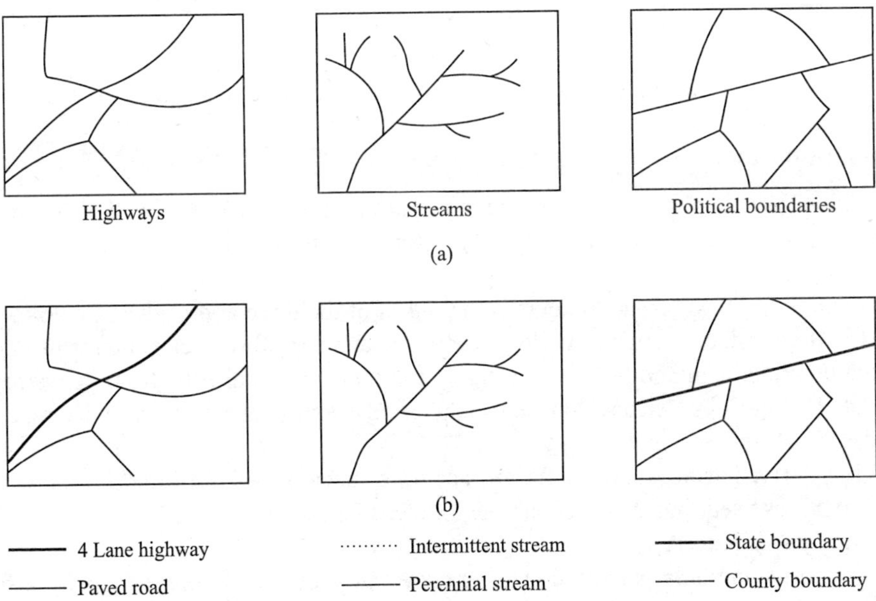

Fig. 16.20. (a) Line data; and (b) line data, illustrating different levels within a hierarchy.

The significance of certain forms of linear data may not be immediately appreciated. Boundaries, including political and administrative boundaries, do not necessarily form physical features on the landscape, yet often they are extremely important in determining the usefulness of a GIS. Many of the queries and tasks that must be addressed by the GIS concern political or administrative units. Therefore, to respond to questions such as 'How many acres of farmland are present within Washington County'?, it is necessary to have accurately entered not only the data concerning land use and agriculture, but also the information that positions the county boundary. Likewise, the boundaries of census units, drainage basins and other features may be very important in determining the usefulness of the GIS.

Examples of areal data (Fig. 16.21) include distributions such as soil, land cover, vegetation classes and other patterns that occupy area at the scale of the GIS. Areal patterns often involve a nominal classification, such as land cover, in which the classes are based upon distinctions in kind rather than differences in quantity. As mentioned above, vector GIS systems provide detailed delineation of the boundaries between nominal classes; use of raster systems inevitably involves loss of information as the data are encoded at each cell. Quantitative data that are grouped by areal units, such as census units, are depicted in finer detail by polygon structures. However, continuous data, such as topographic elevation, where a continuous surface is represented by a network of equally spaced observations, are probably most directly represented by the raster data structure.

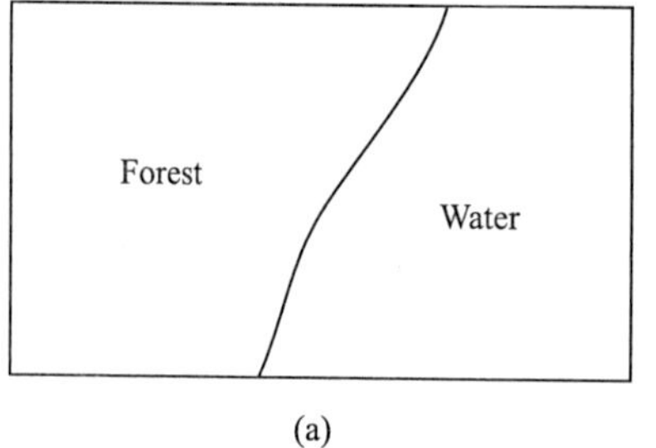

(a)

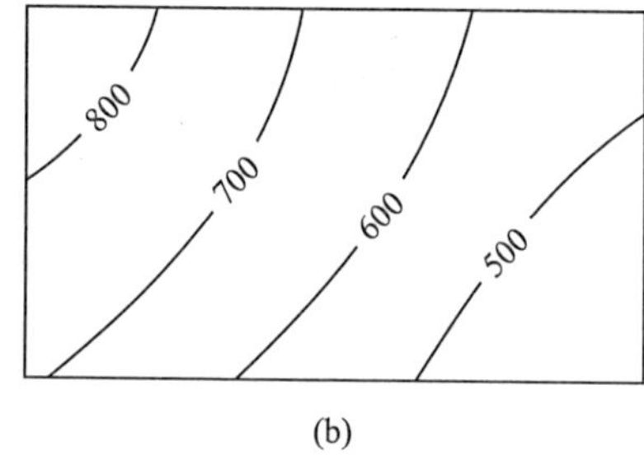

(b)

Fig. 16.21. Areal data: (a) nominal; and (b) continuous.

Digital Elevation Data

Digital elevation data, also referred to as digital elevation models (DEMs) or digital terrain data, are digital representations of the shape of the earth's surface. Data for DEMs are compiled from one of three alternative sources.

1. Derivation of DEMs from contours is the oldest of the three approaches. Contours from maps can be digitised, converted to vector files, edited and tagged with elevation values.
2. Photogrammetric methods derive the digital elevation matrix directly from stereoscopic images. Related methods under development include radar and lidar altimetry and synthetic aperture radar (SAR) interferometry.
3. DEMs derived from survey data are accurate, because of the intensive network of field observations used, but they also are very expensive and time-consuming. They exist only for relatively small areas.

DEMs are most commonly organised in raster data structures, which offer simplicity, efficiency and compatibility with remotely sensed data. In this format, a DEM is represented as an array of values that record topographic elevations observed at equal intervals on the earth's surface (Fig. 16.22). Such data can be considered analogous to digital remote sensing images, except that each pixel represents an elevation measurement, rather than a brightness value. DEMs in this format can be manipulated, classified, analysed and displayed in many of the same ways that we use for digital remote sensing data. An alternative data structure for DEMs, the triangulated irregular network (TIN), forms a network of connected triangles with irregularly spaced points with x and y co-ordinates and z values. The major advantages of TINs relative to raster structures is their ability to represent more variation in areas of complex relief, while avoiding redundant data in regions with even terrain.

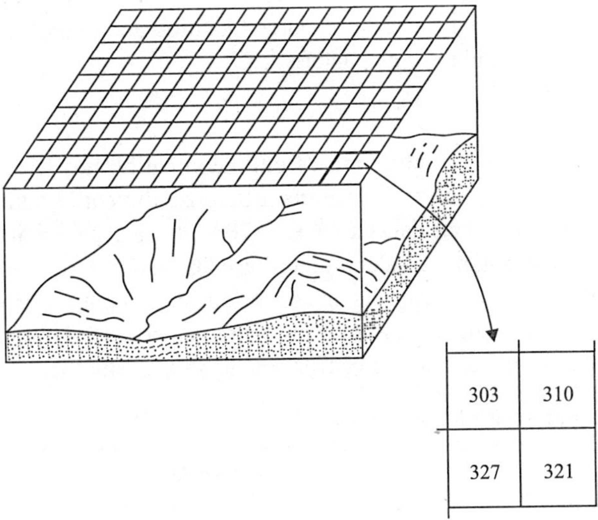

Fig. 16.22. Digital elevation data.

Digital global elevation data or DEMs are available in a variety of formats at a range of scales. These formats typically are either a simple rectangular grid of evenly spaced elevation values or a vector structure consisting of irregular point values or contours. The range of scales varies from 10 minute elevation grids to a 3 second elevation grid. In the United States (and some other nations), more detailed grids are available locally.

Other Digital Data for a Geographic Information System

The National Geospatial Data Clearinghouse is a collection of over 200 spatial data sources that provide digital geographic data primarily for use in GISs and image-processing systems. These collections can be searched through a gateway interface based on their descriptions or 'metadata'.

Examples of data available from these sources include:

1. The National Wetlands Inventory (NWI) of the US Fish and Wildlife Service produces information on the characteristics, extent and status of the nation's wetlands and deepwater habitats. The Emergency Wetland Resources Act of 1986 directs the Service to map the wetlands of the United States. The NWI has mapped 89 per cent of the lower 48 states and 31 per cent of Alaska. The act also requires the Service to produce a digital wetlands database for the United States. About 39 per cent of the lower 48 states and 11 per cent of Alaska are digitised.
2. The USDA Natural Resources Conservation Service has established three soil geographic databases: The Soil Survey Geographic (SSURGO) database, the State Soil Geographic

(STATSGO) database and the National Soil Geographic (NATSGO) database. Components of map units in each database are generally phases of soil series that enable the most precise interpretation. Interpretations are displayed differently for each geographic database to be consistent with differing levels of detail. Attributes for approximately 18000 soil series recognised in the United States are available, to provide physical and chemical soil properties for mapping units.

The SSURGO database is compiled from digital soil data mapped at from 1:12000 to 1:63360. SSURGO is the most detailed level of soil mapping done by the Natural Resources Conservation Service (NRCS). SSURGO digitising duplicates the original soil survey maps. This level of mapping is designed for use by landowners, townships and county natural resource planning and management. The user should be knowledgeable about soils data and their characteristics.

Data Compatibility

One of the major limitations to use of GISs arise from incompatibilities within and between data sets within a GIS (Table 16.2). Compatibility is important because the entire concept of the GIS assumes logical and physical compatibility of the data within each GIS. Physical compatibility refers to the physical form of the data, which, in the instance of a computer-based GIS, is determined largely by data formats. Although incompatibilities in data formats can cause serious practical problems in entering data and in transferring data among different GISs, many such problems can be solved by special computer programs that convert data from one format to another or from one system to another.

Table 16.2. Elements of data quality.

Age	Thematic accuracy
Areal coverage	Thematic detail
Scale	Accessibility
Detail	Costs
Format	Origins
Cartographic projection	Continuity with past and future data
Positional accuracy	Compatibility with other thematic data

Much more serious are logical incompatibilities among data within a GIS, as these are inherent to the data and cannot be easily corrected. For example, consider an ostensibly very simple issue: the recording of data concerning the distinction between open and forested land for a large region, perhaps a state or a large portion of a state. Although the problem seems very straightforward, the issue of compatibility raises many troublesome problems. If we start by gathering data that may have already been collected by county or local governments, we may find that they used different definitions for open and forested land, that the data have variable levels of detail and accuracy and that they were collected at different dates. After encountering these problems, we conclude that it may be better to collect the information directly, for the specific purpose of the GIS, to be sure that the data are internally consistent. Yet even if we use aerial photography, we may find that the available photography, although complete for the area of interest, was flown at several dates, that it has several different scales and that some areas have much higher quality photography than others. If the area is large, we may even have difficulty acquiring Landsat coverage of the same date or season for our region. Therefore, even for the very simplest of matters, compatibility can be surprising difficult to achieve.

Compatibility among different data sets can be an even more difficult problem. Because of the great cost of acquiring and digitising data specifically for a GIS, it is often necessary to use data that were collected or digitised for another purpose. For example, the USGS DEMs mentioned above, US Census Data and the USGS Land Use and Land Cover data are each internally consistent and available at rather low cost in a digital format. Therefore, these data and many others of a similar nature, are often included in GIS. Yet use of off-the-shelf or archival data means that the GIS is formed, in part, of data of differing levels of detail, differing levels of accuracy, differing dates, differing classification systems and differing collection units. Often these kinds of problems can greatly limit the usefulness of the data and prevent the GIS from being able to perform the function for which it was designed: rapid convenient analysis and comparison of data for large regions.

RELATIONSHIPS BETWEEN REMOTELY SENSED DATA AND GEOGRAPHIC INFORMATION SYSTEMS

It is easy to see some of the advantages for using remotely sensed data in a GIS. Satellite systems such as Landsat or SPOT acquire data for very large areas in a short time period, thereby providing essentially uniform coverage with respect to date and level of detail. Furthermore, these data are available for almost all of the earth's land areas and are inexpensive relative to alternative sources. Although satellite data are not planimetrically correct, pre-processing can often bring data to acceptable levels of geometric accuracy with only modest effort. Images formed by analysis or interpretation of the raw data register to the original data. Thus, remotely sensed data have the potential to address some of the difficult problems encountered in the formation of GISs.

Nonetheless, there are still numerous problems and difficulties. Data are not always available for desired dates or seasons. If a large area is to be examined, there may be problems in mosaicking data for separate dates. Accuracies of classification and analytical methods required to process the data prior to entry in the GIS may not be consistently reliable. Furthermore, the levels of detail in the satellite data may not match to those from other sources.

There are several avenues for incorporating remotely sensed data into the GIS. The most satisfactory procedure depends upon the specific requirements of a particular project and the kinds of equipment and financial resources that may be available.

1. Manual interpretation of aerial images or satellite images, often viewed on a computer screen in digital form, produces a map or a set of maps that depicts boundaries between a set of categories (e.g., soil or land-use classes). Onscreen digitising can then provide the digital files suitable for entry into the GIS.
2. Digital remote sensing data are analysed or classified using automated methods to produce conventional (paper) maps and images, which are then digitised for entry into the GIS.
3. Digital remote sensing data are analysed or classified using automated methods, then are retained in digital format for entry into the GIS, using reformatting or geometric corrections as required.
4. Digital remote sensing data are entered directly in their raw form as data for the GIS.

MOBILE GEOGRAPHIC INFORMATION SYSTEMS

Recent decreases of the sizes and increases in the computational power of laptop computers and personal data assistants (PDAs) have enabled analysts to develop field-portable GISs (or mobile GISs). Such units can be easily transported in motor vehicles or carried on foot in the field. Use of GISs in the field permits analysts to enter new data as it is directly observed or to verify or update information already in the system. In some instances, the GIS runs on a laptop as a self-contained unit; in other cases, it is linked by wireless communications to a GIS maintained in a central location (Use of PDAs for this purpose requires wireless communications to connect to a central GIS; the PDA can download a small portion of the GIS at a specific time).

The increasing portability of GPS receivers has enabled laptops and PDAs to link precise, real-time, locational information to a GIS. Such systems are especially valuable when a GIS includes registered digital images or satellite imagery which permits analysts to display GIS layers against a background that shows recognisable structures or landmarks. Workers can then match their location on the ground with representations of the same location in the GIS as they enter new information.

Mobile GISs is especially valuable for utility systems or other organisations that require workers to have immediate on-site access to spatial data in the field. For example, mobile GISs permits workers to ascertain the position of buried utility lines or boundaries of lots without use of outdated, often incompatible paper maps and diagrams. Limitations include the difficulty of viewing computer displays in bright sunlight and difficulties in registering GIS layers with sufficient precision to maintain the integrity of the system at levels of high magnification.

WEB-BASED GEOGRAPHIC INFORMATION SYSTEMS

Often a GIS is administered as part of a large organisation or network of organisations. Examples include the many administrative departments of municipal government, including transportation, water and sewer, fire and rescue, law enforcement, environmental quality, highways and so on. In private industry, organisations might have comparable divisions of responsibility, especially for larger businesses.

Traditional models for organisational use of GISs depend upon each department to update data for the data layers for which they have responsibility, then to forward its data to a central office with responsibility for maintaining the combined data from numerous sources. Revisions and updates are then released to users at appropriate intervals, usually some weeks or months after each department has met a deadline for providing revised data.

Web-based GISs are organised such that each department can post its own data to a common georeferenced database accessible to other departments, other authorised users or possibly the general public. Although there might be administrative reasons for requiring departments to contribute their revisions according to a certain schedule, there would not be a compelling technical reason. Therefore, each department could, if appropriate, publish its revisions as they are noted and posted. Because users access the GIS through the www, they can use the latest versions of overlays as they are updated. This kind of system facilities distribution of the most current information to those who use a GIS. A disadvantage to use of such a dynamic GIS design is that it does not provide an authoritative reference that is stable over time. Users who examine such a system at different times may see different information—a situation that can itself lead to errors and inefficiencies.

17

Plant Sciences

INTRODUCTION

The earth's vegetative cover is often the first surface encountered by the energy we use for remote sensing. So, for much of the earth's land area, remote sensing imagery records chiefly the character of the vegetation at the surface. Therefore, our ability to interpret the earth's vegetation canopy forms the key to knowledge of other distributions, such as geologic and pedologic patterns that are not directly visible but do manifest themselves indirectly through variations in the character and distribution of the vegetation cover.

In other situations, we have a direct interest in the vegetation itself. Remote sensing can be useful for monitoring areas planted to specific crops, for detecting plant diseases and insect infestations and for contributing to accurate crop production forecasts. In addition, remote sensing imagery has been important in mapping forests, including studies of timber volume, insect infestation and site quality.

Further, remote sensing provides the only practical means of mapping and monitoring changes in major ecological regions that, although not directly used for production of food or fiber, have great long-term significance for mankind. For example, the tropical forests that cover significant areas of the earth's surface have never been mapped or studied except in local regions that are unlikely to be representative of the unstudied regions. Yet these regions are of critical importance to mankind due to their role in maintaining the earth's climate and as a source of genetic diversity. Human are rapidly destroying large areas of tropical forests: it is only by means of remote sensing that we are ever likely to understand the nature and locations of these changes.

Similar issues exist with respect to other ecological zones; remote sensing provides a means to observe such regions at global scales and to better understand the interrelationships between the many factors that influence such patterns.

MANUAL INTERPRETATION

Vegetation Classification and Mapping

Vegetation classification can proceed along any of several alternative avenues. The most fundamental is simply to separate vegetated from non-vegetated regions or forested from open lands. Such distinctions, although ostensibly very simple, can have great significance in some contexts, especially when data are aggregated over large areas or are observed over long intervals of time. Thus national or state governments, for example, may have an interest in knowing how much of their territories are covered by forest or may want to make changes in forested land from one 10-year period to the next, even though there may be no data available regarding the different kinds of forest.

However, it is usually important to acquire information at finer levels of detail. Although individual plants can be identified on aerial photographs, seldom if ever is it practical to use the individual plant as the unit for mapping vegetation. Instead, it is more useful to define mapping units that represent groups of plants. A plant community is an aggregation of plants with mutual interrelationships among each other and with the environment. Thus, an oak-hickory forest is a useful designation because we know that communities are not formed by random collections of plants, but by consistent associations of the same groups of plants—plants that tend to prefer the same environmental conditions and to create the environment that permit certain other plants to exit nearby. A community consists of many stands, specific, individual occurrences of a given community (Fig. 17.1)

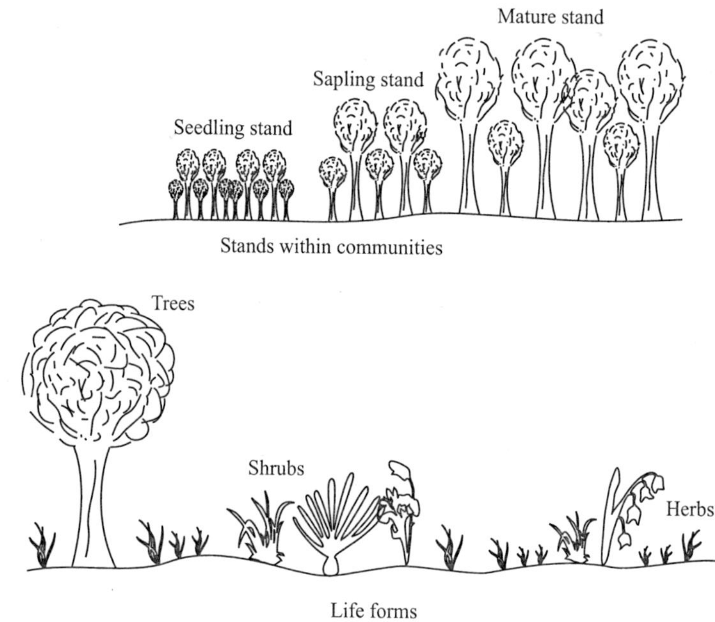

Fig. 17.1. Vegetation communities, stands, vertical stratification and different life forms.

Plants within communities do not occur in equal proportions. Certain species tend to dominate; these species are often used to name communities (e.g., hickory forest), although others may be present. Dominant species may also dominate physically, forming the largest plants in a sequence of layers or strata, that are present in virtually all communities. Stratification is the tendency of communities to be organised vertically, with some species forming an upper canopy, others a middle stratum, then shrubs, mosses, lichens and so on, forming other layers nearer to the ground. Even ostensibly simple vegetation communities in grassland or arctic tundra, for example, can be shown to consist of distinct strata. Specific plants within each community tend to favour distinctive positions within each strata because they have evolved to grow best under the conditions of light, temperature, wind and humidity that prevail in their strata.

Floristics refers to the botanical classification of plants, usually based upon the character of the reproductive organs, using the classification founded by Carolus Linnaeus. Linnaeus, a Swedish botanist, created the binomial system of designating plants by Latin or Latinised names that specify a hierarchical nomenclature, of which the genus and species (Table 17.1) are most frequently used. The Linnaean system provides a distinctive name that places each plant in relationship with others in the taxonomy. Floristic classification reveals the genetic character and evolutionary origin of individual plants.

Table 17.1. Floristic classification.

Level	*Example*[a]
Class	Aangiospermae (broad/general)
Order	Sapindales
Family	Aceraccae
Genus	*Acer*
Species	*Saccharum* (narrow/specific)

[a]Example = sugar maple *(Acer saccharum)*.

In contrast, the life form or physiognomy, describes the physical form of plants (Table 17.2). For example, common physiognomies might include 'tree,' 'shrub,' 'herbaceous vegetation,' and so on. Physiognomy is important because it reveals the ecological role of the plant, the nature of its relationship with the environment and other plants. Floristics and physiognomy often have little direct relationship to one another. Plants that are quite close floristically may have little similarity in their growth form and plants that are quite similar in their ecological roles may by very different floristically. For example, the rose family (Rosaceae) includes a wide variety of trees, shrubs and herbaceous plants that occupy diverse environments and ecological settings. Conversely, a single environment can be home to hundreds of different species, for example, the alpine meadows of New England are composed of some 250 species, including such diverse families as Primulaceae (primrose), Labiatae (mint), Araliaceae (ginseng) and Umbelliferae (parsley). Thus a purely floristic description of plants (e.g., 'the rose family') seldom conveys the kind of information we would like to know about plants, their relationships with one another and their environment.

Table 17.2. Classification by physiognomy and structure.

Woody plants	Broadleaf evergreen
	Broadleaf deciduous
	Needleleaf evergreen
	Leaves absent
	Mixed
	Semi-decidous
Herbaceous plants	Graminoids
	Forbs
	Lichens and mosses
Special life forms	Climbers
	Stem succulents
	Tuft plants
	Bamboos
	Epiphytes

Although it is often possible to identify specific plants and to assign taxonomic designations from large scale imagery, vegetation studies, founded on remotely sensed images typically employ the structure and physiognomy of vegetation for classification purposes. That is, usually we wish to separate forest from grassland, for example or to distinguish between various classes of forest. Although it is important to identify the dominant species for each class, our focus is usually upon separation of vegetation communities based upon their overall form and structure rather than upon floristics alone.

No single approach to vegetation classification can be said to be universally superior to others. At given levels of detail and for specific purposes, each of the approaches mentioned above serves important functions. Floristic classification is useful when scale is large and mapping is possible in fine detail that permits identification of specific plants. For example, analyses for forest management often require a large scale, both for measurement of timber volume and for identification of individual trees. Physiognomy or structure is important whenever image scale is smaller, detail is coarser and the analyst focuses more clearly upon the relationships of plants to environment. Ecological classification may be used at several scales for analyses that require consideration of broader aspects of planning for resource policy, wildlife management or inventory of biological resources.

Another approach to classification of vegetation considers vegetation as the most easily observed component of an environmental complex including vegetation, soil, climate and topography. This approach classifies regions as ecological zones, usually in a hierachical system comparable to that shown in Table 17.3. Bailey defines his units as ecoregions: 'Major ecosystems, resulting from large-scale predictable patterns of solar irradiation and moisture, which in turn affect the kinds of local ecosystems and animals and plants found there.' At the very broadest scales, ecological classification is based on long-term climate and very broad-scale vegetation patterns, traditionally derived from information other than remotely sensed data. However, later sections of this chapter will show how it is now possible to use remotely sensed data to derive these classifications with much more precision and accuracy than was previously possible.

Table 17.3. Bailey's ecosystem classification.

Level	*Example*
Domain	Humid temperate
Division	Hot continental
Province	Eastern deciduous forest
Section	Mixed mesophytic forest
District	
Land-type association	
Land type	
Land-type phase	
Site	

At finer levels of detail, remotely sensed imagery is essential for delineating ecoregions. The interpreter considers not only vegetation cover, but also elevation, slope, aspect and other topographic factors in defining units on the map.

Kinds of Aerial Imagery of Vegetation Studies

Aerial imagery enables the analyst to conduct quick and accurate delineation of major vegetation units, providing at least preliminary identification of their nature and composition. Note, however, that interpretation from aerial images cannot replace ground observations; an accurate interpretation assumes that the analyst has field experience and knowledge of the area to be examined and will be able to evaluate his or her interpretation in the field.

Küchler recommends use of vertical photographs that provide stereoscopic coverage. Optimum choice of image scale, if the analyst has control over such variables, depends upon the nature of the map and the complexity of the vegetation pattern. Detailed studies have been conducted using photography at scales as large as 1:5000, but scales from about 15000 to 1:24000 are probably more typical for general purpose vegetation studies. Of course, if photographs at several different scales, dates or seasons are available, multiple coverage can be used to good advantage to study changes. Small-scale images can be used as the basis for delineation of extents of major regions; the greater detail of large-scale images can be used to identify specific plants and plant associations.

Panoramic photographs have been successfully used for a variety of purposes pertaining to vegetation mapping and forest management. Modern panoramic cameras permit acquisition of high-resolution imagery over very wide regions, such that large areas can be surveyed quickly. Such images have extreme variations in scale and perspective, so they cannot be used for measurements, but their wide areal coverage permits a rapid, inexpensive inventory of wide areas.

Timing of flights, which may not always be under the control of the analyst, can be a critical factor in some projects. For example, mapping the understory in forested areas can be attempted only in the early spring when shrubs and herbaceous vegetation have already bloomed, but the forest canopy has not fully emerged to obscure the smaller plants from overhead views. Because not all plants bloom at the same time, a succession of carefully timed photographic missions in the spring can sometimes record the sequence in which specific species bloom, thereby permitting mapping of detail that could not be reliably determined by a single image showing all trees in full bloom.

Infrared films and colour infrared films have obvious advantages for vegetation studies of all kinds, as emphasised previously. The CIR photography acquired at high altitudes for the United States (usually during leaf-off conditions) is routinely available at modest cost through the NAPP. Custom-flown CIR photography is likely to be considered expensive; many users will find black-and-white photographs satisfactory for many purposes.

Interpretation Procedures

Identification of individual plants can be accomplished by close examination of crown size and shape (Fig. 17.2). At the edges of forested areas, the shadows of trees can form clues to their identification. At smaller scales, individual plants are not recognisable and interpreter must examine patterns formed by the aggregate appearance of individual stands, in which individual crowns form a distinctive tone and texture. Identification may be relatively straightforward if stands are pure or are composed of only a few species that occur in consistent proportions. If many species are present and their proportions vary, then specific identification may not be possible and the use of such broad designations as mixed deciduous forest may be necessary.

At these smaller scales, an interpreter identifies separate cover types from differences in image tone, image texture, site and shadow. Identification of cover type can be considered the interpreter's attempt to implement one of the classification strategies mentioned above in the context of a specific geographic regions, using a specific image. Cover types may not match exactly to the categories in a classification system, but they form the interpreter's best approximation of these categories for a specific set of imagery. Cover classes can be considered as rather broad vegetation classes, based perhaps upon the predominant species present, their age and their degree of crown closure. Thus forest-cover-type classes might include aspen/mixed conifer and Douglas fir, indicating the predominant species without precluding the residence of others. Sub-classes or secondary descriptions could indicate sizes of the trees, crown closure and presence of undergrowth.

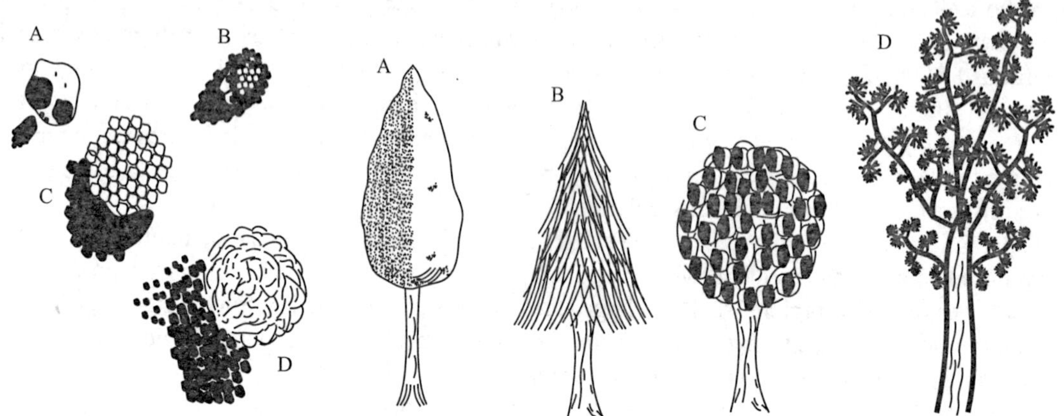

Fig. 17.2. Identification of individual plants by crown size and shape.

Such classifications can be prepared by manual interpretation of aerial photographs if the interpreter has field experience and knowledge of the area to be mapped. Each region has only a finite number of naturally occurring cover types, which usually prefer specific topographic sites, so the interpreter can bring several kinds of knowledge to bear upon the problem of recognition and classification. Image tone, texture, shadow and other photographic features permit separation of major classes. Rather broad classes can be separated using small-scale photography, but finer distinctions require high-quality, large-scale, stereo photography. For example, the classes given in Table 17.4 might be appropriate for information interpreted from aerial photographs at 1:60000, whereas classes in Table 17.4 could be interpreted only from much larger scale photographs, perhaps at 1:15840 to 1:24000. At larger scales, stereoscopic coverage is important for identifying and distinguishing between classes.

Table 17.4. Examples of cover types.

At small scale (1:1,000,000 to 1:50000), cover types must be defined at coarse levels of detail because it will not be possible to distinguish or to delineate classes that are uniform at the species level:
'evergreen forest'
'deciduous forest'
'chaparral'
'mixed broadleaf forest'
'mangrove forest'
At large scale (larger than about 1:20000), cover types may be defined at fine levels of detail. Sometimes, when stands are very uniform, cover types can be mapped at the detail of individual species:
'balsam fir'
'shortleaf pine'
'aspen and white birch'
'oak-hickory forest'

Foresters desire to identify specific stands of timber, areas of forest with uniform species composition, age and density that can be treated as homogeneous units. Stands are the basic unit of forest management, so forest mangers wish to monitor their growth time to detect the effects of disease, insect damage and fire of drought. Even when stands have been planted from seedlings by commercial foresters, aerial photography, by virtue of its map-like perspective and its wealth of environmental information, provides accurate and economical information concerning the condition of the stand at a specific time.

Forest Photogrammetry

If large-scale, high-quality images are available (preferably in stereo), it is possible to apply the principles of photogrammetry to measurement of factors if significance in forestry. Tree height can be measured using lengths of shadows projected onto level, open ground (Fig. 17.3), although there are numerous practical problems that make this method inconvenient for routine use (level, open ground is not often easy to find; it is necessary to determine sun elevations for the latitude, day of the year and time of day and often shadows are too short for reliable measurements). As a result, the parallax bar and the parallax wedge are much more commonly used for routine work.

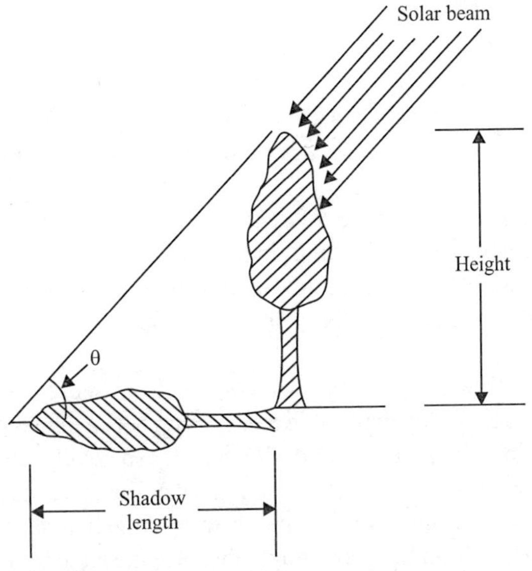

Fig. 17.3. Measurement of tree height from aerial photographs.

Crown diameters can be measured using transparent rules or graticules with tube magnifiers. Crown closure (areal coverage of tree crowns as viewed from above). Figure 17.4 can be estimated by a number of methods, including direct estimation and use of standardised templates that show examples of crown closure classes. The interpreter who uses a template compares the photo with the image on the template to select the closure class nearest to that of the area to be interpreted.

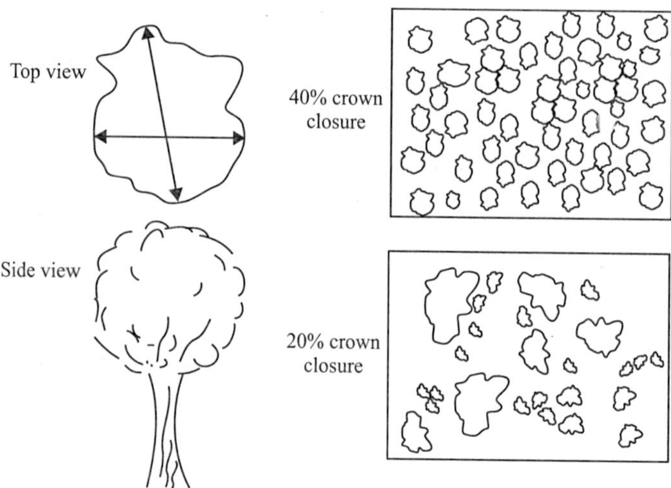

Fig. 17.4. Crown diameter/crown closure.

Timber Volume Estimation

Foresters are routinely interested in estimation of timber volume for a specific stand as a means of monitoring its growth over time, assessing management practices and determining the amount of timber to be obtained at harvest.

Volume measurement consists of estimates of board-foot or cubic-foot volumes to be obtained from a specific tree or more often from a specific stand. In he field, the forester measures the diameter of the tree at breast height (dbh) and the height of the straight section of the trunk (bole) as the two basic components to volume estimation. Measurements made for each tree are summed to give volume estimates for an entire stand.

There are several approaches to estimation of volume from measurements derived from aerial photographs; there can be no universally applicable relationship between photo measurements and timber volume, as species composition, size, age, soil and climate vary so greatly from place to place. Typically, the interpreter must apply a volume table, a tabular summary of the relationship between timber volume and photo-derived measurements such as crown diameter and tree height (Table 17.5). The interpreter can make measurements directly from the photograph, then use the table to find volumes for each tree or for entire stands. New volume tables must be complied as stand composition and the environmental setting change from place to place. Many variations on this basic strategy have been developed, but most rely upon the same kinds of estimates from the photograph.

Crop Identification

Crop identification by manual photo interpretation is accomplished by application of the elements of photointerpretation in the context of knowledge of the local environmental setting and the local crop calendar. In many settings crops are usually observed planted in uniform, distinct fields, with a single crop to a field. In this context, mature crops can often be identified on the basis of photo tone and texture (Fig. 17.5). But precise identification of specific crops may be difficult in the absence of detailed knowledge of the local setting. For example, it is usually easy to separate small grains (e.g., wheat, barley, rye) from large-grain crops (e.g., maize or sorghum), although even experienced photo interpreters may have difficulty distinguishing crops within these classes (e.g., wheat vs. barley). Therefore, careful timing of the date and season of the photographs and knowledge of the crop calendar (e.g., typical dates of planting and harvesting) are essential for derivation of maximum information concerning agricultural crops.

Table 17.5. Example of aerial stand volume table.

Average stand height (ft.)	*Crown cover (%)* 15	35	55	75	95
			8 to 12 ft. crown diameter		
30	15	50	70	95	135
40	35	70	95	125	175
50	50	95	125	170	215
60	90	150	195	235	265
70	160	230	270	300	330
80	250	310	345	380	420
			13 to 17 ft. crown diameter		
30	20	55	80	105	135
40	40	80	100	145	195
50	60	100	135	185	235
60	100	160	205	245	285
70	170	240	275	310	350
80	260	320	360	390	430
90	360	415	450	485	525
100	450	515	555	595	635
			18 to 22 ft. crown diameter		
30	30	70	90	120	160
40	50	90	120	160	200
50	75	120	160	205	245
60	115	180	225	265	305
70	190	255	290	330	370
80	275	330	370	410	450
90	370	430	470	505	550
100	470	530	570	610	650
110	600	660	700	740	780

Note. Volume (tens of cubic feet) per acre, given average stand height, average crown diameter and crown cover, for Rocky Mountain conifer species. Derived from field measurements in test plots.

In some regions crops are planted in very small fields (because of terracing or the requirement to carefully control the timing of irrigation) or many different kinds of plants are planted together in a single field. Under such conditions crop identification may be much more difficult than in the typical mid-latitude situation where fields are large and crops are homogeneous with in fields. In other instances specific crops may tend to be grown in fields with distinctive sizes or shapes, due to the requirements of specialised planting, tilling or harvesting equipment or the need to control movement of irrigation water. Therefore, interpreters may be able to use, along with other information, field size or shape as clues to the identity of crops.

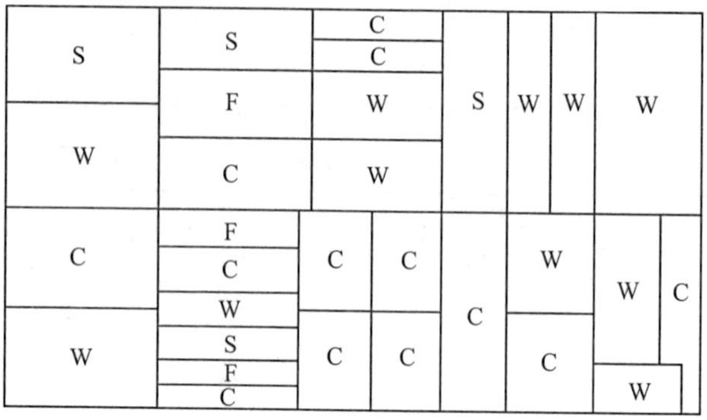

Fig. 17.5. Crop identification. S = sorghum; W = wheat; C = corn; and F = summer fallow.

Although black-and-white photography is usually suitable for crop identification if the interpreter is familiar with the local crop calendar, colour emulsions will usually permit the interpreter to make more subtle distinctions in crop status. If colour or CIR photographs are available, it may be possible to interpret information concerning crop maturity as it approaches time for harvest. In addition, CIR photography may permit interpretation of the presence, location and nature of insect infestations or diseases. Colwell outlined the fundamentals of using CIR photography to detect the progress of crop diseases.

Structure of the Leaf

Many applications of remote sensing to vegetation patterns depend on a knowledge of the spectral properties of individual leaves and plants. These properties are best understood by examining leaf structure at a rather fine level of detail.

The cross-section of a typical leaf reveals its essential elements (Fig. 17.6). The uppermost layer, the upper epidermis, consists of specialised cells that fit closely together without opening or gaps between cells. This upper epidermis is covered by the cuticle, a translucent waxy layer that prevents moisture loss from the interior of the leaf. The underside of the leaf is protected by the lower epidermis, similar to the upper epidermis except that it includes openings called stomates (or stomata), which permit movement of air into the interior of the leaf. Each stomate is protected by a pair of guard cells that can open and close as necessary to facilitate or prevent movement of air to the interior of the leaf. The primary function of stomata is apparently to allow atmospheric CO_2 to enter the leaf for photosynthesis. Although the guard cells and the epidermis appear to be small and inefficient, they are in fact very effective in transmitting gases from one side of the epidermis to the other. Their role in permitting CO_2 to enter the leaf is obviously essential for the growth of the plant, but they also play a critical role in maintaining the thermal balance of the leaf by permitting movement of moisture to and from the interior of the leaf. The guard cells can close to prevent excessive movement of moisture and the thereby economise moisture use by the plant. Apparently the positions of stomata on the lower side of the leaf favour maximum transmission of light through the upper epidermis and minimise moisture loss when stomata are open.

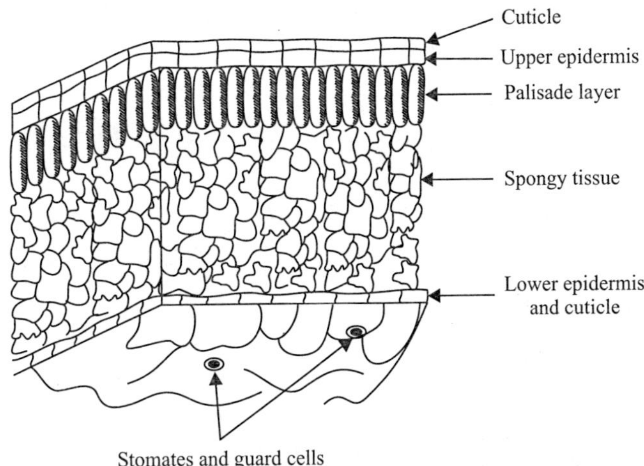

Fig. 17.6. Diagram of a cross-section of a typical leaf.

On the upper side of the leaf, just below the epidermis, is the palisade tissue consisting of vertically elongated cells arranged in parallel, at right angles to the epidermis. Palisade cells include chloroplasts, cells composed of chlorophyll and other ('accessory') pigments active in photosynthesis, as described below. Below the palisade tissue is the spongy mesophyll tissue, which consists of irregularly shaped cells separated by interconnected openings. The surface of that mesophyll has a very large surface area; it is the site for the O_2 and CO_2 exchange necessary for photosynthesis and respiration. Although leaf structure is not identical for all plants, this description provides a general outline of the major elements common to most plants, especially those that are likely to be important in agricultural and forestry studies.

In the visible portion of the spectrum, chlorophyll controls much of the spectral response of the living leaf. Chlorophyll is the green pigment that is chiefly responsible for the green colour of living vegetation. Chlorophyll enables the plant to absorb sunlight, thereby making photosynthesis possible; it is located in specialised lens-shaped structures, known as chloroplasts, found in the palisade layer. Light that passes through the upper tissues of the leaf is received by chlorophyll molecules in the palisade layer, which is apparently specialised for photosynthesis, as it contains the largest chloroplasts, in greater abundance than other portions of the plant. CO_2 (as a component of the natural atmosphere) enters the leaf through stomata on the underside of the leaf, then diffuses throughout cavities within the leaf. Thus photosynthesis creates (in a series of steps) carbohydrates from CO_2 and H_2O, using the ability of chloroplasts to absorb sunlight as a source of energy. Chloroplasts include a variety of pigments, some known as accessory pigments, that can absorb light, then pass its energy to chlorophyll. Chlorophyll occurs in two forms. The most common is chlorophyll a, the most important photosynthetic agent in most green plants. A second form, known as chlorophyll b, has a slightly different molecular structure; it is found in most green leaves, but also in some algae and bacteria.

SPECTRAL BEHAVIOUR OF THE LIVING LEAF

Chlorophyll does not absorb all sunlight equally. The chlorophyll molecules preferentially absorb blue and red light for use in photosynthesis (Fig. 17.7). They may absorb as much as 70 to 90 per cent of incident light in these regions.

Much less of the green light is absorbed and more is reflected, so the human observer, who can see only the visible spectrum, sees the dominant reflection of green light as the colour of light vegetation (Fig. 17.8).

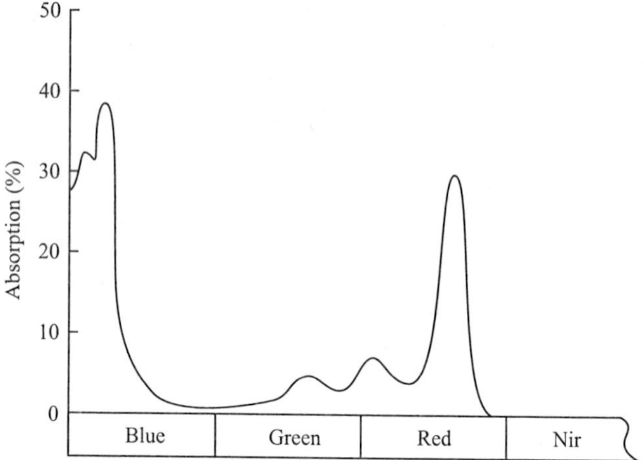

Fig. 17.7. Absorption spectrum for chlorophyll.

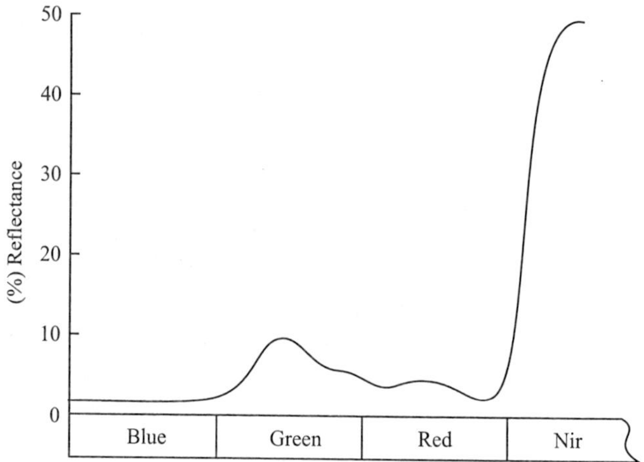

Fig. 17.8. Typical spectral reflectance from a living leaf.

In the near infrared spectrum reflection of the leaf is controlled not by plant pigments but by the structure of the spongy mesophyll tissue. The cuticle and epidermis are almost completely transparent to infrared radiation, so very little infrared radiation is reflected from the outer portion of the leaf. Radiation passing through the upper epidermis is strongly scattered by mesophyll tissue and cavities within the leaf. Very little of this infrared energy is absorbed internally—most (up to 60 per cent) is scattered upward (which we call 'reflected energy') or downward ('transmitted energy'). Some studies suggest that palisade tissue may also be important in infrared reflectance. Thus the internal structure of the leaf is responsible for the bright infrared reflectance of living vegetation.

At the edge of the visible spectrum, as the absorption of red light by chlorophyll pigments begins to decline, reflectance rises sharply (Fig. 17.8). Thus if reflectance is considered not only in the visible but across the visible and the near infrared, peak reflectance of living vegetation is not in the great but in the near infrared (Fig. 17.8). This behaviour explains the great utility of the near infrared spectrum for vegetation studies and facilitates separation of vegetated from non-vegetated surfaces, which are usually much darker in the near infrared. Furthermore, differences in reflectivities of plant species often are more pronounced in the near infrared than they are in the visible, meaning that discrimination of vegetation classes is sometimes made possible by using near infrared reflectance (Fig. 17.9).

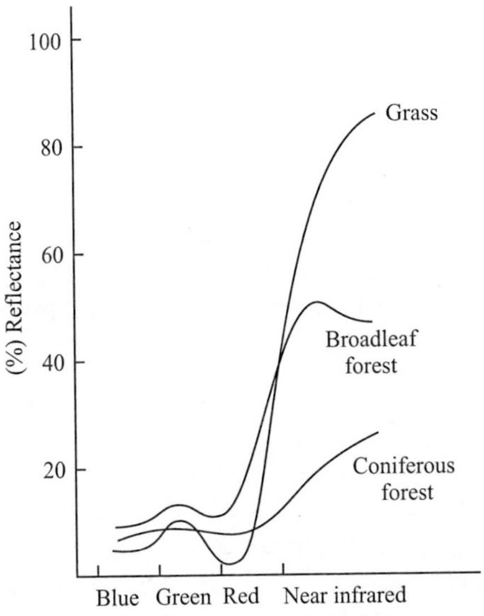

Fig. 17.9. Differences between vegetation classes are often more distinct in the near infrared than in the visible.

As a plant matures or is subjected to stress by disease, insect attack or moisture shortage, the spectral characteristics of the leaf may change. In general, these changes apparently occur more or less simultaneously in both the visible and the near infrared regions, but changes in near infrared reflectance are often more noticeable. Reflectance in the near infrared region is apparently controlled by the nature of the complex cavities within the leaf and internal reflection of infrared radiation within these cavities. Although some scientists suggest that moisture stress or natural maturity of a leaf causes these cavities to 'collapse' as plant wilts, others maintain that it is more likely that decreases in near infrared reflection are caused by deterioration of cell walls rather than physical changes in the cavities themselves. Thus changes in infrared reflectance can reveal changes in vegetative vigour; infrared images have been valuable in detecting and mapping the presence, distribution and spread of crop diseases and insect infestations. Furthermore, changes in leaf structure that accompany natural maturing of crops is subject to detection with infrared imagery, so that it is possible to monitor the ripening of crops as harvest time approaches. CIR film is valuable for observing such changes because of its ability to show spectral changes in both the visible and near infrared regions and to provide clear images that show subtle tonal differences.

In the longer infrared wavelengths (beyond 1.3 μm) leaf water content appears to control the spectral properties of the leaf (Fig. 17.10). The term equivalent water thickness (EWT) has been proposed to designate the thickness of a film of water that can account for the absorption spectrum of a leaf at 1.4 to 2.5 μm.

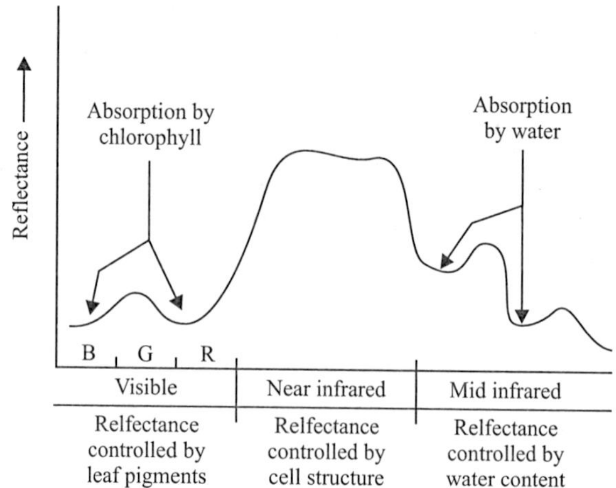

Fig. 17.10. Changes in leaf water content may be pronounced in the near infrared region. This diagram illustrates differences in reflectances between equivalent water thickness of 0.018 cm and 0.014 cm; changes in reflectance are most evident in the infrared region.

Reflection from Canopies

Knowledge of the spectral behaviour of individual leaves is important for understanding the spectral characteristics of vegetation canopies, but cannot itself completely explain reflectance from areas of complete vegetative cover. Vegetation canopies are composed of many separate leaves that may vary in their size, orientation, shape and coverage of the ground surface. In the field, a vegetation canopy (e.g., in a forest or a cornfield) is composed of many layers of leaves; the upper leaves from shadows that mask the lower leaves, creating an overall reflectance created by a combination of leaf reflectance and shadow.

Shadowing tends to decrease canopy reflectance below the values normally observed in the laboratory for individual leaves. Knipling cited the following percentages reported in several previously published studies:

	Per cent reflected	
	Visible	*Near infrared*
Single leaf	10%	50%
Canopy	3–5%	35%

Thus the reflectance values of canopy is considerably lower than the reflectance values measured for individual leaves. But the relative decrease in the near infrared regions is much lower than that in the visible. The brighter canopy reflection for the near infrared is attributed to the fact that plant leaves transmit near infrared radiation, perhaps as much as 50 to 60 per cent. Therefore, infrared radiation is transmitted through the upper layers of the canopy, reflected in part from lower leaves and re-transmitted back through the upper leaves, resulting in bright infrared reflectance (Fig. 17.11). Physicists and botanists have been able to develop mathematical models for canopy reflectances by estimating the optical properties of the leaves and the canopy as a whole. Because some of the transmitted infrared radiation may in fact be reflected from the soil surface below the canopy, such models have formed an important part of the research in agricultural remote sensing.

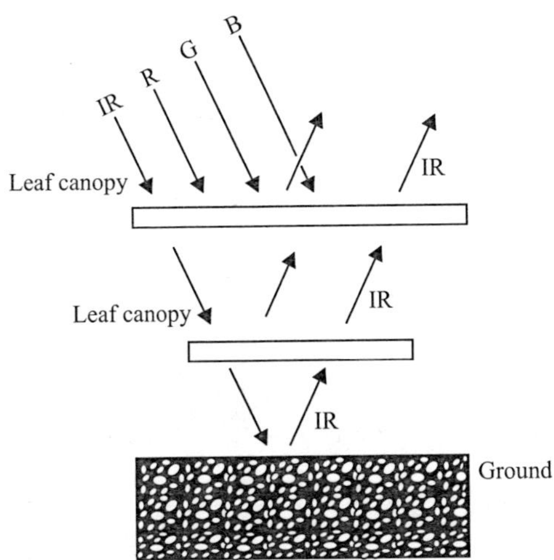

Fig. 17.11. Simplified cross-sectional view of behaviour of energy interacting with a vegetation canopy (See Figs. 17.7 and 17.8). In some portions of the spectrum, energy transmitted through the upper layer is available for reflection from lower layers (or from the soil surface).

Red Shift

Collins reports the results of studies that show changes in the spectral responses of crops as they approach maturity. His research used high-resolution multispectral scanner data of numerous crops at various stages of the growth cycle. Collins's research focused upon examination of the far red region of the spectrum, where chlorophyll absorption decreases and infrared reflection increases (Fig. 17.12). In this zone, the spectral response of living vegetation increases sharply as wavelength increases—in the region from just below 0.7 μm to just above 0.7 μm brightness increases by about 10 times (Fig. 17.8).

Collins observed that as crops approach maturity, the position of the chlorophyll absorption edge shifts toward longer wavelengths, a change he refers to as the 'red shift' (Fig. 17.12). The red shift is observed not only in crops but also in other plants. The magnitude of the red shift varies with crop type (it is a pronounced and persistent feature in wheat).

Collins observed the red shift along the entire length of the chlorophyll absorption edge, although it was most pronounced near 0.74 μm, in the infrared region, near the shoulder of the absorption edge. He suggests that very narrow bands at about 0.745 μm and 0.780 μm would permit observation of the red shift over time and thereby provide a means of assessing differences between crops and the onset of maturity of a specific crop. Causes of the red shift appear to be very complex and are not understood in detail. Chlorophyll 'a' appears to increase in abundance as the plant matures; increased concentrations change the molecular form in a manner that adds absorption bands to the edge of the chlorophyll 'a' absorptions region, thereby producing the red shift.

VEGETATION INDICES

Vegetation indices (VIs), based upon digital brightness values, attempt to measure biomass or vegetative vigour. A VI is formed from combinations of several spectral values that are added, divided or multiplied in a manner designed to yield a single value that indicates the amount or vigour of vegetation within a pixel. High values of the VI identify pixels covered by substantial proportions of healthy vegetation. The simplest form of VI is a ratio between two digital values from separate spectral bands. Some band ratios have been defined by applying knowledge of the spectral behaviour of living vegetation.

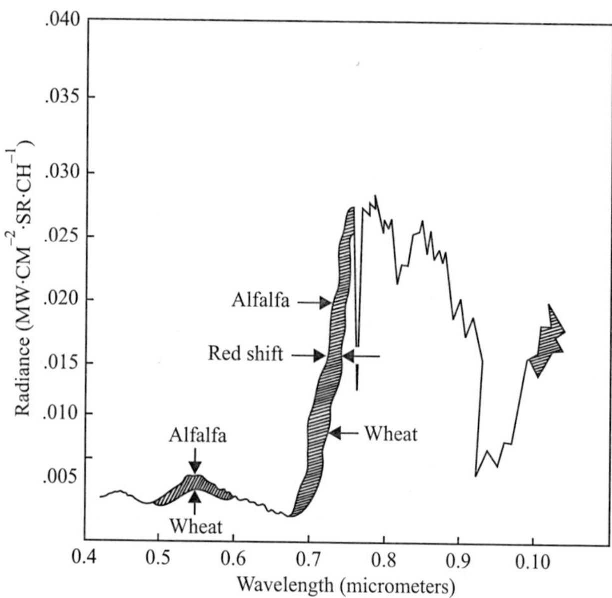

Fig. 17.12. Red shift. The absorption edge of chlorophyll shifts toward longer wavelengths as plants mature. The shaded area represents the magnitude of this shift as the difference between the spectral response of headed wheat and mature alfalfa. Similar but smaller shifts have been observed in other plants. The red shift is important for distinguishing the headed stage of a crop from earlier stages of the same crop and for distinguishing headed grain crops from other green, non-grain, crops.

Band ratios are quotients between measurements of reflectance in separate portions of the spectrum. Ratios are effective in enhancing or revealing latent information when there is an inverse relationship between two spectral responses to the same biophysical phenomenon (Fig. 17.13). If two features have the same spectral behaviour, ratios provide little additional information (Fig. 17.13); but if they have quite different spectral responses, the ratio between the two values provides a single value that concisely expresses the contrast between the two reflectances (Fig. 17.13).

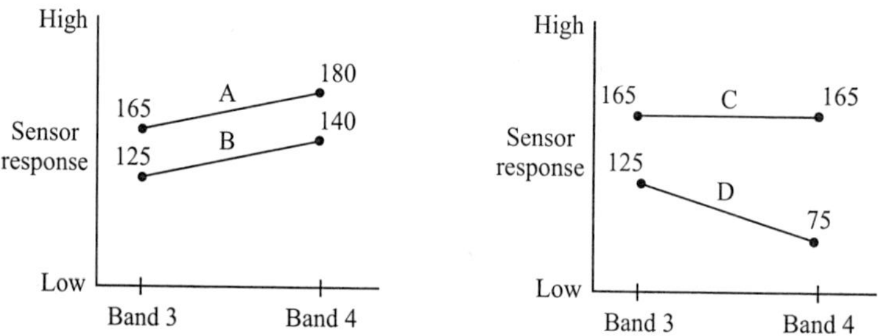

Fig. 17.13. Example of band ratios. Four hypothetical materials are observed in two spectral bands. Materials A and B have similar patterns of response in bands 3 and 4. Ratios therefore reveal little about the differences between them. For A, the ratio of band 3 to band 4 is 0.916 (165/180); for B, it is 0.89 (125/140). The relationship between C and D is quite different and the ratio clearly reveals the contrast between the two materials. For C, it is 1.00 (165/175); and for D, it is 1.67 (125/175).

For living vegetation, the ratioing strategy can be especially effective because of the inverse relationship between vegetation brightness in the red and infrared regions. That is, absorption of red light (R) by chlorophyll and strong reflection of infrared (IR) radiation by mesophyll tissue assures that the red and near infrared values will be quite different and that the ratio (IR/R) of actively growing plants will be high (Fig. 17.14). Non-vegetated surface, including open water, man-made features, bare soil and dead or stressed vegetation will not display this specific spectral response and the ratios will decrease in magnitude. Thus, the IR/R ratio can provide a measure of photosynthetic activity and biomass within a pixel.

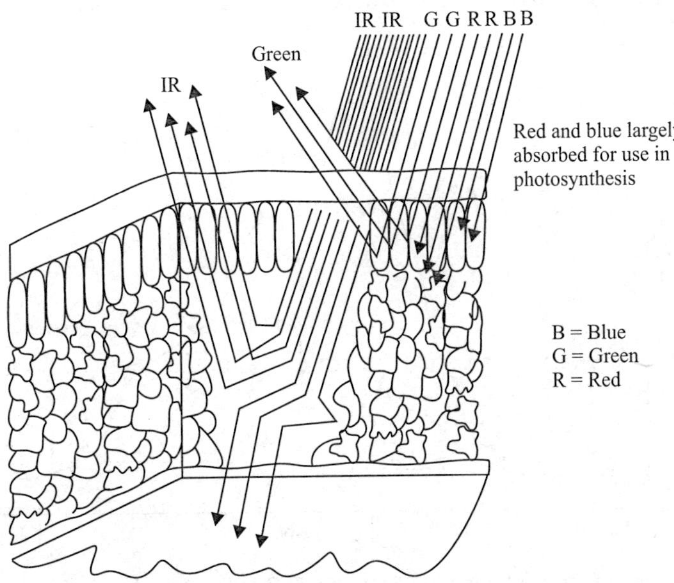

Fig. 17.14. Interaction of leaf structure with visible and near infrared radiation.

The IR/R ratio is only one of many measures of vegetation viguor and abundance. The green/red (G/R) ratio is based upon the same concepts used for the IR/R ratio, although it is considered less effective. Although ratios can be applied with digital values from any remote sensing system, much of the research on this topic has been conducted using Landsat MSS data. In this context, the IR/R ratio is implemented for Landsat 4 and 5 as (MSS 4/MSS 2), although some have preferred to use MSS 3 in place of MSS 4. One of the most widely used VIs is known as the normalised difference vegetation index (NDVI):

$$\text{NIDVI} = \frac{\text{IR} \quad \text{R}}{\text{IR} + \text{R}} = \frac{\text{MSS 4} \quad \text{MSS 2}}{\text{MSS 4} + \text{MSS 2}} \qquad \text{... (17.1)}$$

This index in principle conveys the same kind of information as the IR/R and G/R ratios, but is constrained to vary within limits that provide desirable statistical properties in the resulting values. The studies of Tucker and Perry and Lautenschlager suggest that in practice there are few differences between the many VIs that have been proposed.

Although such ratios have been shown to be powerful tools for studying vegetation, they must be used with care if the values are to be rigorously (rather than qualitatively) interpreted. Values of ratios and VIs can be influenced by many factors external to the plant leaf, including viewing angle, soil background and differences in row direction and spacing in the case of agricultural crops. Ratios may be sensitive to atmospheric degradation. Because atmospheric degradation typically influences some bands much more than other, atmospheric effects can greatly alter the value of the ratio from its true value (Fig. 17.15). Because atmospheric path length varies with viewing angle, values calculated using off-nadir satellite data vary according to position within the image. Clevers and Verhoef found that the relationship between the leaf area index and the VI they studied was very sensitive to differences in leaf orientation. Although pre-processing can sometimes address such problems, it may still be difficult to compare values of VIs over a period of time because of variation in external factors. Price and others have noted that efforts to compare ratios or indices over time or from one sensor to another, should reduce digital values to radiances before calculating ratios, to account for differences in calibration of sensors.

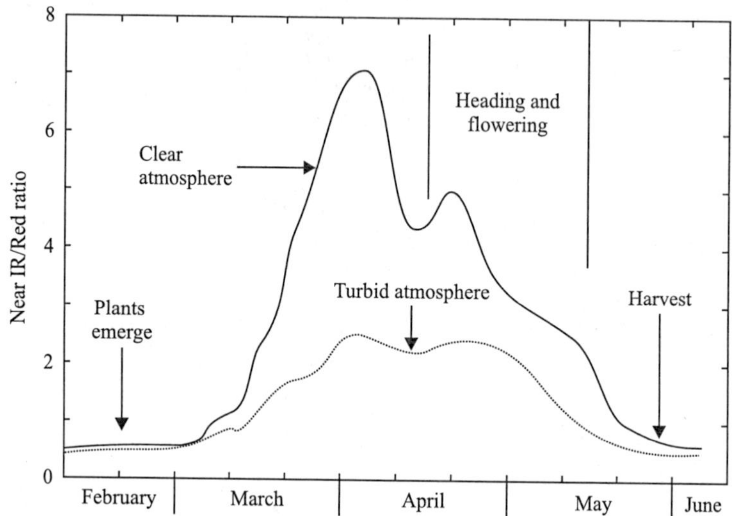

Fig. 17.15. Influence of atmospheric turbidity upon IR/R ratio, as estimated from simulated data.

APPLICATIONS OF VEGETATION INDICES

Vegetation Indices (VIs) have been employed in two separate kinds of research. Many of the first studies defining applications of VIs attempted to 'validate' their usefulness by establishing that values of the VIs are closely related to biological properties of plants. Typically, such studies examined test plots during an entire growing season, then compared values of the VIs, measured throughout the growing season, to samples of vegetation taken at the same times. The objective of such studies is ultimately to establish use of VIs as a means of remote monitoring of the growth and productivity of specific crops or of seasonal and yearly fluctuations in productivity.

Often values of the VIs have been compared to *in situ* measurements of the leaf area index (LAI), which is the areas of leaf surface per unit area of solid surface. LAI is an important consideration in agronomic studies because it measures leaf area exposed to the atmosphere and therefore is significant in studies of nutrient transport and photosynthesis. Values of VIs have also been compared to biomass, the weight of vegetative tissue. A number of VIs appear to be closely related to LAI (at least for specific crops), but not a single VI seems to be equally effective for all plants and all agricultural conditions. Results of such studies have in general confirmed the utility of the quantitative uses of VIs, but details vary with the specific crop considered, atmospheric conditions and local agricultural practices.

A second category of applications uses VIs as a mapping device, that is, much more as a qualitative rather than a quantitative tool. Such applications use VIs to assist in image classification, to separate vegetated from non-vegetated areas, to distinguish between different types and densities of vegetation and to monitor seasonal variations in vegetative vigour, abundance and distribution. Yool studied MSS imagery of a forested area in southern California and concluded that the ratios they examined were not superior to the original MSS values or to simple linear combinations of these values.

PHENOLOGY

Phenology is the study of the relationship between vegetative growth and environment; often phenology refers specifically to seasonal changes in vegetative growth and decline. Many phenological changes can be monitored by means of remote sensing because plants change in appearance and structure during their growth cycle. Of special significance are spectral and physiological changes that occur as a plant matures. Each season, plants experience chemical, physical and biological changes, known as 'senescence', that result in progressive deterioration of leaves, stems, fruit and flowers. In the mid-latitudes, annual plants typically lose most or all of their roots, leaves and stems each year. Woody perennial plants typically retain some or all of their roots, woody stems and branches, but shed leaves. Evergreens, including tropical plants, experience much more elaborate phenological cycles; individual leaves may experience senescence separately (i.e., tress do not necessarily shed all leaves simultaneously) and individual trees or branches of trees may shed leaves on cycles quite distinct from others in the same forest.

During the onset of senescence, deterioration of cell walls in the mesophyll tissue produces a distinctive decline in infrared reflectance; an accompanying increase in visible brightness may be the result of decline in the abundance and effectiveness of chlorophyll as an absorber of visible radiation. Changes in chlorophyll produce the red shift mentioned above. Such changes can be observed spectrally, so remote sensing imagery can be an effective means of monitoring seasonal changes in vegetation.

The phenology of a specific plant defines its seasonal pattern of growth, flowering, senescence and dormancy. Remotely sensed images can expand the scope of study to include overviews of vegetation communities or even of entire biomes. (*Biomes* are broad-scale vegetation regions that correspond roughly to the earth's major climate regions.) Dithier for example, used several forms of imagery and data to observe the geographic spread of the emergence of new growth in spring, as it progressed from south to north in North America. This phenomenon has been referred to as the green wave. Then in late summer, the brown wave sweeps across the continent as plant tissues mature, dry and are harvested.

In an agricultural context, phenology manifests itself through the local crop calendar, the seasonal cycle of plowing, planting, emergence, growth, maturity, harvest and fallow. Each locality and each crop has its own crop calendar, defined by the interaction of the genetic character of the crop, the local climate and local agricultural technology and tradition.

For example, two crop calendars significant in North America are shown in Tables 17.6 and 17.7. Winter wheat (Table 17.6) is grown chiefly in a broad zone in the semi-arid regions that border the western edge of the Great Plains, from west Texas north to western south Dakota. The crop is planted in September or Octrober; during the cool, moist climate of mid to late autumn plants emerge, then grow to a height of a few inches. Growth stops when the severe cold of winter arrives in December, although during winter months the soil receives critical moisture supplies from snow. The wheat crop resumes growth in the spring when temperatures increase, releasing moisture and accelerating biological processes. Wheat grows rapidly in April and May; by mid-June, the crop approaches maturity and is usually harvested in late June or early July.

Table 17.6. Crop Calendar for winter wheat, Western kansas.

Month	Stage
September	Plowing and planting
October	Emergence and early growth
November	
December	
January	
February	Dormancy
March	
April	
May	Growth resumes
June	Heading
July	Harvest
August	

Note: Variations in timing are caused by local differences in weather and climate.

In contrast, the corn crop (Table 17.7) is not planted until spring temperatures have warmed the fields and allowed excess moisture to drain, to permit farm equipment to work the soil. The crop emerges soon after planting in April or May and grows rapidly during May and June, when temperatures are warm and moisture is available. The crop has tasseled by mid-July and matures in August, for harvest in late August or September.

Table 17.7. Crop calendar for corn, Central Mid-Western United States.

Month	Stage
April	Plowing and planting
May	Emergence and early growth
June	
July	Tasseling
August	
September	Maturity and harvest

The spectral characteristics of a given crop, observed over an entire growing season, exhibit distinctive patterns closely related to the local crop calendar. The opportunities for regular coverage provided by earth observation satellites such as Landsat mean that specific areas can be observed over time and that knowledge of the crop calendar can be applied in a manner that is not always practical if there is imagery for only a single data. For example, the winter wheat crop is characterised by bare fields in September and October, then by a mixture of soil and newly emerged vegetation in mid to late autumn. During spring and early summer plant cover increases, completely masking the soil by late May or early June. Then, as the crop matures, spectral evidence of senescence records the approach of harvest in late June or early July. In contrast, the corn crop is not planted until spring, does not attain complete coverage until June and is not mature until August. Thus each crop displays a characteristic signature over time, which permits tracking of the progress of the crop. Knowledge of the local crop calendar permits selection of a single data that will provide maximum contrast between two crops. In the instance of discrimination between corn and wheat, for example, selection of a date in late spring should show complete vegetative cover in wheat field, while the corn fields show only newly emerged plants against a background of bare soil.

ADVANCED VERY-HIGH-RESOLUTION RADIOMETER

Vegetation Indices (VIs) and knowledge of phenology can also be applied in a much different context, using data acquired by a meteorological satellite. The advanced very-high-resolution radiometer (AVHRR) is a multispectral radiometer carried by a series of meteorological satellites operated by NOAA in near-polar, sun-synchronous orbits. They can acquire imagery over a swath width of approximately 2800 km, providing global coverage on a daily basis. Although AVHRR was designed primarily for meteorological studies, it has been successfully used to monitor vegetation patterns over very broad geographic regions. A real coverage is extensive enough that entire biomes or major ecological zones, can be directly observed and monitored in ways that were not previously feasible.

The satellite makes about 14 passes in a 24 hour period, collecting data for each 2800 km swath twice daily, at 12 hour intervals. Resolution at the nadir is about 1.1 km, but an onboard computer can generalise data to 4 km resolution before data are transmitted to ground stations, to permit broader geographic coverage for a given volume of data. Data are recorded at 10 bits. The wide angular view means that areas recorded near the edges of images suffer from severe geometric and angular effects. As a result, AVHRR data selected from the regions near the nadir provide the most accurate information. Although designed initially for much narrower purposes, Tucker report 800 to 900 km of the 2800 km swath are usable (The unusable data are from the edges of the image, where angular effects of perspective and atmospheric path length present problems).

Details of spectral coverage vary with the specific mission, but in general AVHRR sensors have been designed to attain meteorological objectives, including discrimination of clouds, snow, ice, land and open water. Nonetheless, AVHRR has been employed on an adhoc basis for land resource studies. AVHRR collects five channels of data at a spatial resolution of 1.1 km in the visible, near infrared and the thermal infrared (Table 17.8). One channel is in the visible, one in the near infrared and three in the thermal infrared. Channel 1 was originally proposed as 0.55 to 0.90 μm, but after use on the prototypes was re-defined to 0.58 to 0.68 μm to improve separation of snow-free and snow-covered land areas. For agricultural scientists, this change provided the benefit of offering a channel positioned in the red region that permits calculation of vegetation indices.

The visible and near infrared data can be ratioed to form a greenness index of VI similar to those discussed above:

$$\text{NDVI} = \frac{\text{Channel 2} - \text{Channel 1}}{\text{Channel 2} + \text{Channel 1}} \qquad \text{... (17.2)}$$

Although the spectral bands differ from those mentioned earlier, the meaning of the ratio is the same: high values reveal pixels dominated by high proportions of green biomass. The resolution is much coarser than that of Landsat MSS and TM data, but areal coverage is much broader and the opportunity for repeat coverage is much greater. The frequent repeat coverage permits gathering of data for areas that may be obscured by clouds on one date but not the next. Therefore, over time, cloud-free coverage of continental or sub-continental areas can be acquired. Such images do not show the detail of MSS or TM data, but they do give abroad geographic perspective that is not portrayed by other images.

Compiled AVHRR Data

Full-resolution data, at about 1.1 km at nadir, can be acquired during any given day from a restricted region of the earth, usually only when the satellite is within line of sight of a receiving station. This process produces local area coverage (LAC). LAC archives have been compiled for selected regions of the earth. Eidenshink describes the AVHRR data set for the United States derived from 1998 AVHRR data, since repeated for other years. These composites are designed to record phenological variations throughout a growing season. Full-resolution AVHRR scenes were selected to form a set of 19 biweekly composites from March to December. Compositing over the 2 week period permits selection of at least one cloud-free date for each pixel. A special processing programme was designed to select data based upon viewing geometry, solar illumination, sensor calibration and cloud cover and then to prepare geometrically registered NDVI composites. The process produces composite images composed of the original AVHRR bands, NDVI data, describing the compositing process and a statistical summary.

Table 17.8. Spectral channels for AVHRR.

Channel	*Spectral limits*	*Region*
1	0.58–0.68 μm	Visible
2	0.72–1.10 μm	Near infrared
3	3.55–3.93 μm	Thermal infrared
4	10.30–11.30 μm	Thermal infrared
5	11.5–12.5 μm	Thermal infrared

Note. Spectral definitions differ between different AVHRR missions.

Global area coverage (GAC) is complied by onboard sampling and processing, transmitted to ground stations on a daily basis. A GAC pixel is formed by averaging the first four pixels a row, skipping the fifth pixel, averaging the next four pixels, skipping the next, continuing to the end of the line. The algorithm skips the next two lines, then processes the fourth line in the same manner as it did the first line and so on, until the entire scene is processed. These data provide spatial resolution of about 4 km.

Global vegetation index (GVI) data are created from the daily AVHRR data by examining the differences between the red and near infrared channels; the highest values for a 7-day interval are then used to selected the dates for which to calculated an NDVI value that represents a pixel for the entire 7-day period. The preliminary selection using the red-near infrared difference is designed both to select cloud-free pixels (if possible) for the 7 day interval and to minimise atmospheric effects. NDVI data are processed in such a manner that they represent about 15 km resolution. These data have been compiled since 1982, although algorithms and formats have varied considerably during this interval.

AVHRR data have been archived to form a global database and have been processed to provide a variety of products depicting seasonal changes in vegetative cover over areas of continental size.

SEPARATING SOIL REFLECTANCE FROM VEGETATION REFLECTANCE

Digital data collected by satellites, especially at the coarse resolution of the Landsat MSS and AVHRR, mix vegetation reflectance with that of the soil surface. Some mixing of soil and vegetation reflectances occurs because of mixed pixels. In agricultural scenes, however, reflections from individual plants or individual rows of plants are closely intermingled with the bare soil between plants and between rows of plants, so that reflectances are mixed even at the finest resolutions. Of course, this mixing is especially important after plants have emerged because large proportions of soil are exposed to the sensor. But even after leaves have fully emerged, soil can still contribute to reflectance because of penetration of some wavelengths through the vegetation canopy. Mixing of soil and vegetation reflectance can therefore be a serious barrier to implementation of the concepts presented earlier in this chapter. Hutchinson found that vegetation information is difficult to extract when vegetation cover is less than 30 per cent. In arid and semi-arid regions, vegetative cover may always be this low, but even in agricultural settings plant cover is low when crops are emerging early in the growing season.

If many spectral observations are made of surfaces of bare soil, the values of red and near infrared brightnesses resemble those along axis ABC in Fig. 17.16. The soil brightnesses tend to fall on a straight line—as a soil becomes brighter in the near infrared, so does it tend to get brighter in the red. Dry soils tend to be bright in both spectral regions and appear at the high end of the line (C); wet soils tend to be dark and are positioned at the low end (B).

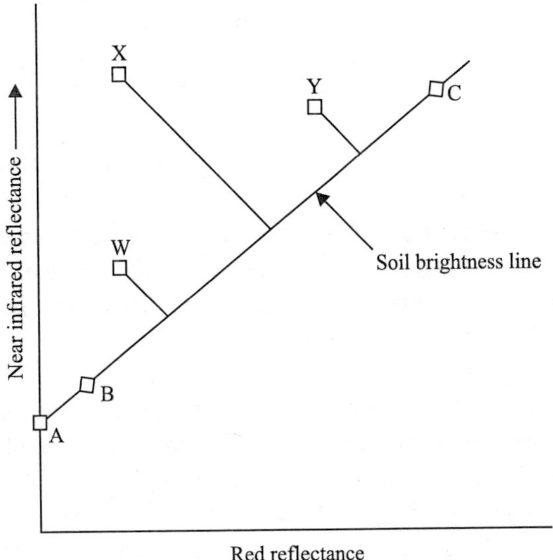

Fig. 17.16. Perpendicular vegetation index.

Richardson and Wiegand defined this relationship, known as the soil brightness line and recognised that the spectral response of living vegetation will always have a consistent relationship to the line. Soils typically have high or modest response in the red and infrared regions, whereas living vegetation must display low values in the red (due to the absorption spectra of chlorophyll) and high values in the near infrared (due to IR brightness of mesophyll tissue). Thus points representing 'pure' vegetation response will be positioned in the upper left of Fig. 17.16, where values on the red axis are low and those on the IR axis are high. Furthermore, Richardson and Wiegand defined an index to portray the relative magnitudes of soil background and vegetative cover to a given spectral response. Thus, point X typifies a 'pure' vegetation pixel, with a spectral response determined by vegetation alone, with no spectral contribution from soil. In contrast point Y typifies a response from a partially vegetated pixel—it is brighter in the red and darker in the near infrared than is X. Richardson and Wiegand quantified this difference by defining the perpendicular vegetation index (PVI) as a measure of the distance of a pixel (in spectral data space) from the soil brightness line. The PVI is simply a Euclidean distance measure:

$$PVI = \sqrt{(S_R \quad V_R)^2 + (S_{IR} \quad V_{IR})^2} \qquad \text{... (17.3)}$$

where S is the soil reflectance, V is the vegetation reflectance, subscript R represents red radiation and subscript IR represents near infrared radiation.

In practice, the analyst must identify pixels known to be composed of bare soil to identify the local soil brightness line and pixels known to be fully covered by vegetation to identify the local value for full vegetative cover (point X in Fig. 17.16). Then, intermediate values of PVI indicate the contributions of soil and vegetation to the spectral response.

Baret and others investigated the soil brightness line from both experimental and theoretical perspectives. They concluded that the theoretical basis for the soil brightness line is sound, although effects of variations in soil moisture and surface roughness are still not well understood. Their experimental data revealed that it is not feasible to define a single, universally applicable soil brightness line, as local variations in soil types lead to spectral variations. However, these variations were found to be minor in the red and infrared regions. They concluded that the use of a single soil brightness line is a reasonable approximation, especially in the context of analysis of course-resolution satellite data.

TASSELED CAP (TC) TRANSFORMATION

The 'tasseled cap' transformation is a linear transformation of landsat MSS data that projects soil and vegetation information into a single plane in multispectral data space—a plane in which the major spectral components of a agricultural scene are displayed in two dimensions. Although defined initially for MSS data, subsequent research has extended the concept to the six non-thermal bands of the TM. The transformation can be visualised as a rotation of a solid multidimensional figure (representing all spectral bands) in a manner that permits the analyst to view the major spectral components of an agricultural scene as a two-dimensional figure.

Tasseled Caps (TC) is consistent from one scene to another, permitting use of a single transformation to monitor crops throughout a growing season. In this context, the analyst should realise that TC transformations may be sensitive to atmospheric turbidity, angle of illumination and other factors not related to vegetation status. These other factors become especially important when changes over time are studied, as it is then necessary to use data that vary greatly with respect to illumination, atmospheric clarity and other factors.

Foliar Chemistry

The development of operational hyperspectral sensors has opened possibilities for application of remote sensing to observation of characteristics of vegetated surfaces not feasible using instruments previously at hand. Hyperspectral data have created the capability to investigate foliar chemistry, the, chemical composition of living leaves. If such a capability could be applied in an operational context, it could assist in the identification of plants at levels of detail not previously feasible and in the monitoring of the growth and health of crops and forests.

Although there is a considerable body of research devoted to remote sensing of foliar chemistry, much of this work is specific to particular sensors, individual test sites or specific processing algorithms and has been acquired by varied means (laboratory analyses, field observations and airborne data). Therefore, much work remains to be completed to develop the suggestion offered by existing studies.

The following points outline some of the efforts investigating hyperspectral sensing of foliar chemistry.

1. Lignin and starch content: Kokaly and Clark applied a normalisation procedure that permitted detection of lignin and cellulose in dried ground leaves in a laboratory setting. Peterson found that the spectral region in the range 1500 nm to 1750 nm in ASI data was linked to levels of lignin and starch content. Martin and Aber reported positive results for predicting lignin using four AVIRIS bands in the range bands 1660 nm to 2280 nm at test sites in the northeastern US.

2. Nitrogen: Card found promising relationships between spectroradiometer data and nitrogen content of ground dried laboratory samples. Wessman investigated forest canopy chemistry using AIS imagery; they found strong relationships between foliar nitrogen and reflectance in bands between 1265 nm and 1555 nm. Martin and Aber examined AVIRIS data (20 m resolution) or a mixed broadleaf forest of oak [*Quercus rubra*] maple, [*Acer rubrum*] and needle-leaved species; they found a relationship between nitrogen content and brightness in the intervals 750 nm and 2140 nm and 950 and 2290 nm.
3. Chlorophyll concentration: Kupiec and Curran examined AVIRIS data to find that brightness at 723 nm was strongly correlated with chlorophyll content in the needles of slash pine (*Pinus elliotti*).

LIDAR DATA FOR FOREST INVENTORY AND STRUCTURE

Because lidar data directly record data characterising the physical structure of a forest (heights, crown closure, crown size, etc.), they provide an opportunity to directly assess the three-dimensional structure of vegetation formations in ways that are not possible with other sensors. For example, Means examined lidar data of Douglas fir (*pseuotsuga taxifolia*) stands in the western Cascades of Oregon using airborne lidar with a footprint of 0.2 m to 0.9 m. He found that lidar data were effective in estimating basal area, height, volume and canopy closure for a range of growth states and concluded that lidar survey should be an effective inventory tool for forest management.

NASA, in collaboration with other organisations, has designed a satellite-borne lidar for the investigation of vegetated surfaces. The vegetation canopy lidar satellite (VCL) is a lidar system designed for operation from satellite altitudes. VCL will use five separate lidars to illuminate five separate tracks, each 25 m in diameter, traversing an 8 km region (Fig. 17.17). A single telescope will be able to receive returns from each laser individually. VCL data are intended as a tool to remotely assess vegetation structure, biomass and other properties that may permit estimation of carbon use within forests. Although this system cannot provide the detail and accuracy mentioned previously for aircraft lidar systems, it is likely that VCL data will find many other applications in other fields.

PRECISION AGRICULTURE

Traditional agricultural practices treat entire fields as single management units. A farmer applies seed, fertiliser and pesticides at the same rate for an entire field. This practice prevails despite inherent variation in natural agronomic components, including soil, solar radiation moisture and drainage, which are known to very markedly within fields. Although farmers understand well that such characteristics vary considerably even within short distances, traditionally they have lacked both the information they need to understand the details and the means to implement any understanding.

Precision agriculture is based on the premise that farmers can control agricultural management practices (e.g., seeding rate, fertilisation, tillage, pesticides, irrigation) at varying rates within fields to optimise production. Thus fertiliser, for example, would be applied at heavier rates where soil conditions requires intense fertilisation, but at lower rates elsewhere within the same field, thereby economising on fuel, materials and labour and minimising unintended environmental effects.

Such measures are possible because of the increased precision and detail of information that can be acquired in part from remotely sensed data and the ability to monitor changes throughout the growing season, as moisture conditions, insect infestations and the like vary within fields and over time, as the growing season progresses. The practice of precision agriculture is based on use of agricultural equipment with GPS to determine accurate position, multispectral imagery to provide current information on crop conditions and agricultural machinery designed to employ varying rates of application and even to sense field conditions on the spot.

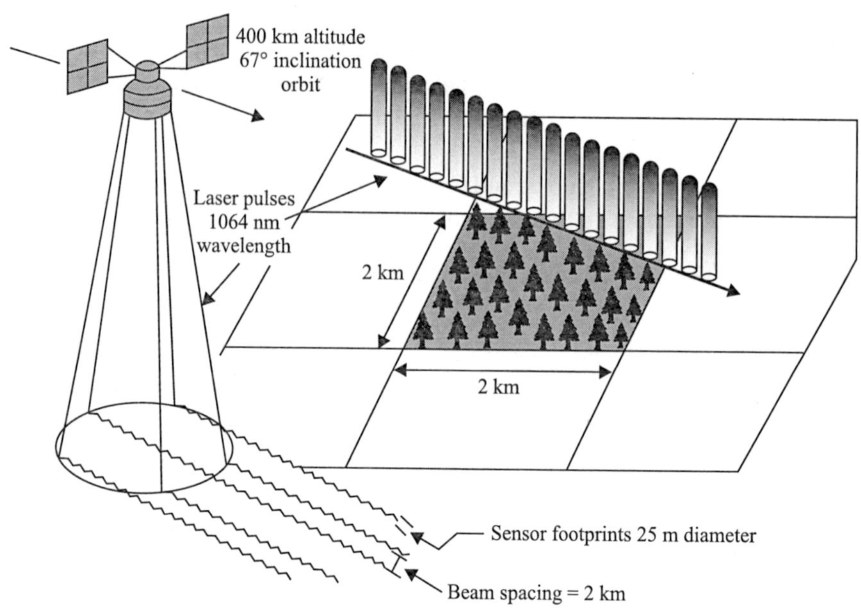

Fig. 17.17. Vegetation canopy lidar (based on a NASA diagram).

Remote sensing forms an important compound of precision agriculture, first because it provides a map-like representation of agricultural landscapes and second, because it can provide information pertaining to growth and health of crops throughout the growing season. Remote sensing can reveal variations in surface soil texture guiding collection of soil samples required to support the precision agriculture effort. Remotely sensed images can detect anomalies, revealing, for example, localised effects of drought or insect infestations. In some instances, data from calibrated instruments can provide direct measurement of physical values, such as brightness in specific portions of the spectrum.

Thus for a large proportion of the earth, vegetation cover forms the surface observed by remote sensing instrument. In some instances, we have a direct interest in examining this vegetative blanket, to map the patterns of different forests, rangelands and agricultural production. In other instances, we must use vegetation as a means of understanding those patterns that may lie hidden beneath the plant cover. In either instance, it is essential that we be able to observe and understand the information conveyed by the vegetated surface.

Given the obvious significance of agriculture and forestry and the immense difficulties of monitoring use of these resources, the techniques outlined in this chapter are likely to form one of the most significant contribution of remote sensing to the well-being of mankind. The ability to examine vegetation patterns using the Vegetation Indices (VIs) described, combined with the synoptic view and repetitive coverage of satellite sensors, provides an opportunity to survey agricultural patterns in a manner that was not possible even a few years ago. If the information gathered by remote sensing systems can be integrated into the decision-making and transportation/distribution systems so important for agricultural production, there is a prospect for improvements in the effectiveness of food production.

18

Remote Sensing for Sustainable Forest Management

INTRODUCTION

Remote sensing has been defined as the detection, recognition or evaluation of objects by means of distant sensing or recording devices. In recent decades, remote sensing technology has emerged to support data collection and analysis methods of potential interest and importance in forest management. In forestry, information extracted visually from aerial photographs is well-understood, well-used and integrated with field surveys. Information extracted from digital remote sensing data, on the other hand, is rarely used in forest management. It is thought that many remote sensing data and methods are complex and are not well understood by those who might best use them.

The technological infrastructure is not in place to make effective use of the data. The characteristics of much remote sensing data are, perhaps, not well suited to the problems that have pre-occupied the forest management community.

But forest management is changing. Today, forest management problems are multiscale and intricately linked to society's need to measure, preserve and manage for multiple forest values. Population growth and climate change appear likely to create continual pressure on forests, making their preservation, even over relatively short time periods, seem largely in doubt. Human activities threaten the continued physical existence, biodiversity and functioning of forests. It is probable that no forest on the planet can survive intact without conscious human decision making and actual on-the-ground treatments and prescriptions that consider ecological processes and functioning.

The forest ecosystem is complex and multifaceted; understanding how forest ecosystems work requires new types of data and data at a range of spatical and temporal scales not often contemplated. Remote sensing information needs to be integrated with other spatical and non-spatial data sets to form the information based upon which sound forest management decisions can be made. The goal is to predict the effects of human activities and natural processes on forests and to promote forest practices that will ensure the world's forests are sustainable.

A major issue facing those with forest management questions is not simply the collection of data, but rather the interpretation of information extracted from those data. Converting remote sensing data to information is no simple task. Remote sensing measurements have a physical or statistical relationship to the forest conditions of interest which may be uneconomical, impractical or impossible to measure directly over large areas.

Even successful conversion of remotely sensed data to forestry information products will not be enough; the process of acquiring vast amounts of new information about forests must be seen as part of the wider responsibility in service of the generation of new knowledge about the current state of the forest and the influences of management and natural processes to further the goal of forest sustainability.

The change has already meant a difference in human interaction with natural forest systems. There is increased emphasis on scientific management and the recognition of the need to understand better ecosystem functioning and patterns over large areas and long periods of time. Such understanding is increasingly required regardless of any philosophical stance assumed on the role of forests, management and continued human use of forests. Sustainable forest management has encouraged continued wide-ranging philosophical discussion within the forest science, applied forestry and ecological communities.

TECHNOLOGICAL APPROACH

Remote sensing has been a valuable source of information over the course of the past few decades in mapping and monitoring forest activities. As the need for increased amounts and quality of information about such activities become more apparent and remote sensing technology continues to improve, it is felt that remote sensing as an information source will be increasingly critical in the future. A powerful line of thought in remote sensing is to consider problems in a technological approach. By this, it is meant that remote sensing can sometimes proceed differently than traditional scientific deductive and inductive approaches. These are considered the pure science approaches and can be contrasted to the scientific technological approach in which the emphasis is shifted to a methodological or applied perspective. A successful remote sensing application proceeds from the design of methodology. In a remote sensing technological approach, the goal is the application of knowledge—the use of what has been learned—to solve problems.

Forest managers are concerned with the spatial distribution of forest resources within their management area and in the surrounding ecosystems; with the timely acquisition of information on conditions and changes to these resources; with the small and large impacts associated with changing patterns and processes at different scales in time and space; with interpretation of the effect of those changes on unmapped components such as wildlife and with economic, social and environmental implications of human activities and impacts on forests. There is a need to have as much relevant information as possible on the conditions of the forest to prescribe treatments, to help formulate policy and to provide insight and predictions on future forest condition and health. Typically, there are few choices in how to acquire all the different types of information. The goal of remote sensing, then, is to help satisfy as many of these multidimensional needs for information as possible. This is the application of knowledge: that is, the applications of remote sensing knowledge in response to forest management questions.

While remote sensing technology must help in providing information to satisfy the needs that forest managers have, remote sensing must be a cost-effective and easily understandable technology.

A methodological design is necessary to show how remote sensing data can be used to determine the spatical distribution of forest resources, can detect changes in those resources and predict changes in other aspects of the forest not captured directly. Remote sensing methodology can be a powerful aspect of a technology to detect changes accurately and to help explain more fully the implications of forest changes and activities. To accomplish this, there must be a series of direct mapping and modelling applications of remote sensing consistent with the needs of forest managers. This is the role of methodological design—to convert data to information in a scientific, understandable and repeatable way. As in all scientific approaches, the hallmark of good science is the use of the knowledge gained to uncover general laws and to predict future conditions; then, the methodological design becomes part of the established scientific method, the analytical approach for the field.

A useful way to consider the diversity of the remote sensing data input to sustainable forest management is to examine the kinds of issues and questions around which sustainable forest management revolves. In Table 18.1 some example questions are listed; each sustainable forest management question is paired with an inferential hypothesis which can be suggestive of the ways in which remote sensing can contribute to providing an answer or generating new insight into the question. All questions of forest value are first rooted in an accurate description of the resource and it is the responsibility of the forest inventory to provide that description.

Table 18.1. Sustainable forest management questions and corresponding remote sensing hypotheses.

Sustainable forest management question driven by human need	*Remote sensing inferential hypothesis driven by technology*
What is the spatial distribution of forest covertypes/ classes? Species composition?	Remote sensing observation can be used to differentiate forest covertypes on the basis of forest structure and species composition
Is there a cost-effective way to map annual changes resulting from harvesting operations and natural disturbances?	Multitemporal remote sensing observations can be used to separate forest management treatments (such as cutovers, thinnings, plantings), new roads, insect damage, windthrow, burned or flooded areas, from surrounding covertypes over time
How can remote sensing data be compared to existing forest inventory data stored in the GIS?	For some attributes (e.g., stand density) over large areas or within forest stands the information content of remote sensing data is consistent with the accuracy and level of confidence that we now possess in the GIS database. For other attributes (e.g., leaf area index) the remote sensing data are superior.
Can we map more detail within each forest stand, but also see the big picture — the ecosystems in which stands are embedded and areas surrounding may management unit?	Remote sensing observations acquired at multiple scales and resolutions can be used to continuously estimate forest conditions from plots to stands to ecosystems
Can habitat fragmentation and connectedness be measured and quantified?	Landscape pattern and structure can be detected and quantified using remote sensing observations.
What is the best way to monitor forest production?	Remote sensing observations can be used to obtain precise estimates of driving variables (e.g., LAI, biomass) for use in initiating and verifying functioning ecosystem process models

REMOTE SENSING DATA AND METHODS

The general role that remote sensing data might play in forest management, within the relatively narrow range of information sources that are available, is probably not well understood. Generally, remote sensing is understood relative to the more familiar aerial photography and of course, field observations.

The field of remote sensing has throughout its development been relatively poorly defined. In remote sensing, one strong focus has always been on methodology; how sensors, computers and human can be used together to solve real-world problems. This situation has persisted since the early days in remote sensing, perhaps leading to or at least not preventing, great creativity and breadth in the emerging field.

An original problem in defining remote sensing can be traced to a fundamental philosophical problem, long since resolved or whether remote sensing was solely the reception of stimuli (data collection) or whether it also include the collective (i.e., analytical) response to such stimuli. But a glance at the titles of early papers in remote sensing journals or at any of the many remote sensing conferences and symposia throughout the 1960s, provides ample evidence that to the pioneers in the field, remote sensing was always much more than simply collection of data—that remote sensing was 'the science of deriving information about an object from measurements at a distance from the object, i.e., without actually coming into contact with it'. Or this one from Avery: 'remote sensing may be defined as the detection, recognition or evaluation of objects by means of distant sensing or recording devices.'

By specifying the key words 'deriving information' and 'detection, recognition or evaluation' these definitions suggested that the most important contribution promised by remote sensing was in the conversion of the collected data to information products; the true value and challenge of remote sensing would be realised in the data interpretation and subsequent applications. The developers of applications of remote sensing data understood from the beginning that remote sensing was both technology and methodology. The term 'remote sensing' has come to be strongly associated with earth-observing satellite technology, but more properly has been understood to include all sensing with distant instruments and that is the meaning that is assumed in this chapter.

Today, remote sensing is usually defined as comprised of two distinct activities:

1. Data collection by sensors designed to detect electromagnetic energy from positions on ground-based, aerial and satellite platforms.
2. The methods of interpreting those data.

Working in those early days of satellites and digital sensors. Avery intended to cover the emerging field of earth-orbiting satellite remote sensing separate from aerial photography. Remote sensing is sometimes now considered to encompass aerial photography or at least occupy a companion, parallel or perhaps not yet fully integrated position. Between 1960 and about 1980, at least, there were always two types of remote sensing:

1. Imagery (or visually)-based remote sensing.
2. Numerically-based remote sensing.

The differences were found in the way the data were acquired, but more significantly, in the way the data were interpreted; in other words, the way information was extracted from the data. To many, this distinction is no longer relevant; the focus has shifted decisively to remote sensing interpretations which best serve the purpose at hand with the available technology. In any given application, a mix of visual and numerical methods is needed.

While the methods and technology of remote sensing have shown tremendous advances, remote sensing is obviously not a completely new idea—having its modern antecedents in the use of cameras and balloons in the nineteenth century. The first known forestry remote sensing application was recorded in the Berliner Tageblatt of September 10, 1887. The notice concerned the experiments of an unnamed German forester who constructed a forest map from photos acquired from a hot-air balloon. Interestingly, the power of the perspective 'from above' was regarded as the principal advantage and many of the same problems that have since preoccupied aerial mapperes and digital image analysts were identified: geometric distortion, spatial coverage, uncertain species identification, within-stand variability, visible indicators of growth and development and so on.

Experimental Method

In many remote sensing applications, the experimental method has been used to better understand the relationship between the forest condition of interest and the information available about that condition from remotely sensed data. In a remote sensing experiment, the remote sensing observation is the dependent variable and the independent variables influencing the dependent variable are the forest conditions of interest. If all of these variables can be controlled, then a precise and accurate predictive model can be created by which the independent variable (the forest condition) can be used to predict the dependent variable (the remote sensing observation). Then, the model can be inverted so that the independent variable can be predicted by the remote sensing observations. In forestry applications, a desirable set of independent variables would include forest vegetative, structural and biophysical conditions such as forest canopy colour, species, density, height, volume age, roughness, leaf area and biochemical or nutrient status.

Extending the knowledge gained through experimental methods of remote sensing to create an actual remote sensing application to predict chlorophyll or nutrient status of forests has proven difficult. The sensitivity of the remote sensing instruments, as measured by the signal-to-noise ratio, has only recently approached the level required for biochemical estimation. Satellite remote sensing instruments are not yet able to acquire data with these characteristics. Airborne (and satellite) remote sensing data are a composite signal from leaves, branches and boles, tree canopies, ground cover and soils and are influenced by shadowing due to height differences and defoliation, sun-target-sensor geometry, topography, leaf orientation, canopy architecture and atmospheric turbidity. These and other factors mean that the relationship between leaf chlorophyll and leaf reflectance obtained under controlled conditions cannot be expected to be found in the same form and strength when those conditions of measurement are allowed to vary in an uncontrolled experiment.

What is important to note is that the experimental approach provides superior understanding of the precise form of the relationship. The point is that the experimental method reveals the nature and exact form of the relationship which, it is understood, will not be found except under ideal conditions.

Normative Method

Because of the difficulty or even the impossibility, of controlling more than a few of the many independent variables during most remote sensing applications, the normative method of scientific procedure is often employed. That is, what is sought in remote sensing is an understanding of the normal relationship (for example, between forest characteristics such as leaf area index, canopy chlorophyll or N content and reflectance or backscatter measured remotely) so that applications of that relationship can be developed to satisfy the practical need for new information. Since not all the independent variables are controlled, the relationships that are found are subject to caveats and constrains that must be carefully documented and described.

An airborne spectrographic image might be acquired to map forest canopy chlorophyll based on the experimental relationship between pigmentation and reflectance. If the optical properties of the atmosphere were not observed and no accounting of the atmosphere was made in the use of the remote sensing measurements, then a description of the effect of the atmosphere on the relationship between remote sensing observation and canopy chlorophyll must accompany the presentation of the relationship. Even if the optical properties of the atmosphere were observed during image acquisition, it is impossible to know all the effects of the atmosphere for every pixel location in the image; assumptions of atmospheric homogeneity are needed to reduce the complexity of the radiative transfer equations through the atmosphere to a manageable level. Alternatively, a number of image processing steps can be taken to simulate control of variables; instead of actual atmospheric measurements and the use of those measurements to correct for the atmospheric contribution to the reflectance, a model or an approximation of the atmosphere conditions can be employed and an estimate of the atmospheric contribution, perhaps based on the image data themselves, is generated and applied *post hoc*. In this way, the observed relationship can be evaluated against the normal form of the relationship or the form of the relationship that would be expected given complete control of all the variables (in this case, the atmospheric contribution).

Use of the normative method does encourage the development and use of relationships developed under less than ideal conditions. The approach can also suffer from a lack of generality that could lead to highly spurious local insights. What is the point in developing a normative relationship between leaf chlorophyll and reflectance on one day in one type of forest, if the moment one leaves those conditions the relationship cannot be used? The point is that, provided the design is sound, estimates of the relationship can be obtained that can be used to solve problems even if the relationship does not generate insight into the 'true' relationship.

CATEGORIES OF APPLICATIONS OF REMOTE SENSING

Applications of remote sensing to sustainable forest management are presented in four categories that include classification of forest cover-type, estimation of forest structure, forest change detection and forest modelling. Each of these categories is further sub-divided for discussion and review into individual and separate issues, variables or model parameters according to the logic shown in Table 18.2. The consideration of each category proceeds from an understanding of the role that specific forest covertype, forest inventory, change detection and forest modelling applications may play in meeting information needs for sustainable forest management.

Table 18.2. Categories of remote sensing applications according to broad categories in forest cover type mapping, inventory variables, change detection and modelling.

	Organisational infrastructure		
Science and technology advancement	Improved understanding	Infrastructure development	
	Covertype mapping		
Physiognomic classification Level I and II classes	Floristic classification Level III classes	Integrated classification Ecological classes	
	Inventory mapping		
Cover, age, DBH, height	Biomass	Volume and growth	
	Change detection		
Harvesting and silviculture	Natural disturbances		
Clearcuts	Defoliation damage		
Partial cuts			
	Forest modelling		
Ecosystem process models	Landscape structure		
	Technological infrastructure		
Acquisition of imagery	Image processing and calibration	Ecological models	Geographical information science

It can be anticipated that these information needs will be identified in stand-level and landscape-level planning generally, to support forest planning there is a need for information related to strategic, tactical and operational activities in forests and to monitor the results of these activities. The criteria and indicators of sustainable forest management can be considered a focus for the monitoring issues and the discussion is tailored to include remote sensing methods and references to examples of the methods that actually work with known error.

The use of remote sensing to estimate some of the more common forest inventory variables—height, age, crown closure—is reviewed before considering other forest information that has potential to be provided by remote sensing technology.

User Adoption of Remote Sensing

Remote sensing has not yet reached a state of maturity; too much research and development remains to be addressed. Potential remote sensing applications can be found in virtually all natural science disciplines and related engineering disciplines and increasingly in the social sciences, but real-world operational examples of remote sensing remain relatively rare. In the forestry application, what can be accomplished operationally with the existing stage of development of the field of remote sensing? A minimal list of most-likely, near-future operational forestry remote sensing applications could include:

1. Forest covertype characterisation.
2. Determination of forest stand conditions and forest health.
3. Site characterisation.
4. Fire monitoring.

Five uses of remote sensing that were considered operational in Asian tropical forest management are given below.

1. Detection of deforestation.
2. Forest covertype mapping.
3. General assessment of volume and cutting rates.
4. Forest stress.
5. Fire monitoring.

In India, Raa and others also provided a list of five uses of remote sensing; but in their view, all required improved data sets and methods before they could be declared fully operational:

1. Plantation inventory and monitoring.
2. Timber volume estimation.
3. Species identification.
4. Estimation of biomass and productivity.
5. Biodiversity monitoring.

And finally, in Oregon, Cohen, focusing not only on the applications but on the fundamental concepts of digital remote sensing, listed three remote sensing applications in forestry that could be considered operational:

1. Mapping forest cover.
2. Measuring and monitoring structure, function and composition of vegetation.
3. Detecting change in these conditions over time.

The common elements in these lists suggest that remote sensing may play a critical role in forest management in many different forest settings around the world—operational forest covertype mapping, forest structure and change analysis and forest inventory assessment. A few additional applications appear on the threshold of operational status—notably, landscape structure modelling, defoliation monitoring and biochemical/biophysical forest inventory. It is expected that rather quickly, in the near future in fact, the appropriate role of remote sensing expressed as a complete set of operational remote sensing applications in forestry, will become increasingly apparent.

Current State of the Technological Infrastructure and Applications

Very few remote sensing applications are conducted in isolation, by a single person, without access to prior history or experience. Users of remote sensing operate within an infrastructure, a framework, an environment; with careful planning, the infrastructure can be designed specifically to accomplish successful remote sensing in support of sustainable forest management goals and objectives. The important questions for a forest manger contemplating remote sensing and for a remote sensing specialist contemplating the forestry applications are:

1. Can remote sensing data be converted to the information that is needed to understand and manage the forest resources of the planet.
2. What are the components of a well-designed remote sensing infrastructure to support sustainable forest management?

At one end of the spectrum, the end-user would buy raw data from a receiving station and perform all data processing and information extraction in-house. At the other end, a number of intermediate informational products could be generated by data providers or value-added consultants. The end-user would then buy only selected information products.

The level of investment in terms of technology, infrastructure, training and knowledge for the end user is vastly different under these different scenarios. Is there a preferred way to operate remote sensing forestry applications? The issue has not yet been re-solved.

One can view the remote sensing infrastructure in terms of both a technological and an organisational infrastructure. An organisational infrastructure is required as the umbrella under which successful remote sensing applications are conducted. An umbrella structure with this wider meaning would perhaps encompass the entire network that is necessary to support a remote sensing facility or laboratory; a remote sensing forestry workstation. Individual components of this workstation or network could include the capital and personnel (and their experience) issues that comprise the institutional response to the increasing importance of remote sensing and GIS in environmental management. In other words how much support for remote sensing can be expected from the institutions in which the remote sensing work is being conducted? Organisational infrastructure issues, such as spatial data standards and accuracy, provision of training materials and opportunities and documentation and distribution of test datasets, are important components of the overarching structures under which specific remote sensing activities occur.

Such issues typically appear to lie beyond the immediate reach of most users of the technology—beyond the remote sensing workstation environment. Progress in dealing with these issues will no doubt come from successful industry consortia, universities and governmental initiatives, supplemented and encouraged by applications specialists and resource managers trying to implement remote sensing in support of forest management. One example is provided by the list of working groups in the Canadian Advisory Council on Remote Sensing (CACRS), a group comprised of industry, university and government representatives formed to help advise the Canada Center for Remote Sensing on the critical issues for funding research (Table 18.3.) None of the issues considered by these groups is basic research; all are aimed at practical applications of remote sensing, bringing the technology to bear on real world problems, applied research issues. The intention is to ensure that the individual remote sensing workstation is supported with progress in these larger issues.

Table 18.3. List of Canadian Remote Sensing advisory groups that have helped create an increasing emphasis on applied remote sensing and the development of the technological approach to environmental and management issues.

Agriculture and land use
Disaster monitoring
Environment
Forestry
Geoinformatics technology
Geoscience
Hydrology
Mapping

Another specific example in which the larger infrastructure issues are addressed in the US focuses on the integration of remote sensing with the enormous resources of data and methods in the realm of geographical information systems. They proceed by recognising a key fact of life in the existence of both remote sensing and GIS analysts; these two technologies need to talk to each other, find ways of synergy and complementarity and work more effectively in tandem. Research priorities to improve remote sensing and GIS integration included three broad categories (Table 18.4):

1. Science and technology advancement.
2. Improved understanding.
3. Infrastructure development.

The list covers only one component of the work in the National Center for Geographic Information and Analysis (NCGIA), but it is clear that even here there is a preponderance of practical, applied research issues. The focus is now on getting the technology into the hands of the users such that benefits can be immediately derived. It is understood that some of the benefits cannot be derived without improvements in the larger infrastructure. A second list, reinforcing this view and the needs expressed, outlines the research priorities in GIS (Table 18.4).

Table 18.4. Broad research priorities in remote sensing GIS integration.

Remote sensing and GIS integration
Science and technology advancement
Advance feature extraction
Spatial analysis and modelling
Visualisation
Lineage or heritage tracking
Improved understanding
Education and training
Data format and structure conversion
Spatial information management
Error and accuracy
Scale
Time

(Contd...)

Infrastructure development
- Standards
- Spatial data catalog
- Test datasets

UCGIS

- Spatial data acquisition and integration
- Distributed computing
- Extensions to geographic representation
- Cognition of geographic information
- Interoperability of geographic information
- Scale
- Spatial analysis in a GIS environment
- The future of spatial information infrastructure
- Uncertainty in spatial data and GIS-based analysis
- GIS and security

The organisational infrastructure is dependent on a link between the research and practice of remote sensing. Numerous attempts have been made and are ongoing to bridge the research and practicing communities. In one recent example, Oderwald and Wynne described a consortium of image suppliers, researchers and potential users. The intent is to provide those engaged in resource assessment and inventory with information on the many potential sources of spatial data, including aerial photographs, digital elevation models, orthophotos and satellite images. The goals of the consortium are:

1. To determine what level of information can be derived given current remote sensing data and methods.
2. Develop methods for obtaining more specific information using the improved imagery becoming available.
3. Disseminate state-of-the-art methods to resource managers through training sessions, research reports and publications.

The problem, as they see it, is that very little use of any of these information sources is made; the use of these data and the many types of newer remote sensing data in actual forest management appears minimal. Apparently, resource management continues to rely almost exclusively on field observations and analogues available through aerial photography. Despite growing recognition of the tremendous potential and an enormous investment in remote sensing and other geospatial information technologies the vast majority of resource assessment and inventory is still performed on the ground.

This situation will change and in fact, is already changing. There appears to be a new vitality in the remote sensing field that is based on a number of powerful trends: the widespread ability to process imagery on the desktop, the long-term and historical availability of satellite data, increased access to new types of airborne and satellite imagery and the enormous growth in GIS and spatial data in general.

One outcome of this activity is the construction and maintenance of a technological infrastructure, the foundation upon which all successful remote sensing applications are built.

The remote sensing infrastructure must allow the trade-offs in acquiring imagery with various combinations of image resolutions. The effect of scale must be addressed for a given application. A complete remote sensing technological infrastructure will have tools that enable the user to test which are the algorithms that work, when do they break down, when are new algorithms needed, where is the focus for new software development. What are the key components that must be in place to get started in remote sensing? What questions can be answered with the technology available now? What questions can be answered with a little more research? And, what are the big research issues still outstanding?

In short, a remote sensing technological infrastructure is necessary to support users in their search for methods and explanation in how best to:

1. Acquire and prepare a remote sensing data set for a forestry application.
2. Understand the implications of not preparing the data set well.
3. Evaluate the selection and performance of certain recommended processes.
4. Consider options when the image processing system available does not support the best procedures.

In other words, the infrastructure is required to present clearly the critical decision points in a remote sensing acquisition and analysis activity.

Acquisition of data, pre-processing systems, image analysis functionality, geographical information systems and forest ecological models can all be considered key pieces of the hardware and software infrastructure—the immediate environment surrounding and supporting successful forestry remote sensing activities. One of the most important but often neglected pieces of technological infrastructure is the image pre-processing system which must support the correction of imagery for variability not related to the target (atmosphere, view angles, etc.) and must provide tasks that can be used to relate imagery to other georeferenced data.

Figure 18.1. Shows graphically the components of these two structures—the technological infrastructure and the organisational infrastructure—which together make up the environment in which remote sensing for sustainable forest management can be optimised. It is not possible to review all available ways of preparing to conduct forestry applications of remote sensing. The idea is to consider the development of various components of the infrastructure that influence individual user's decisions and methods and to summarise the collective experience of the remote sensing community. In more than 30 years of digital remote sensing applications, it is possible to offer suggestions and guidance into what works, what will be enough to get by, when should the line be drawn and what investment might be necessary. At the same time, this review can provide insight into the critical elements of organisational infrastructure that overlie and encompass individual efforts in remote sensing applications.

Three Views of Remote Sensing in Forest Management

To many people—not only to remote sensing scientists, the producers of the technology, but to many familiar with the field and its spectacular growth—the potential role of remote sensing as an information resource to support sustainable forest management appears enormous and immediate based largely on two facts:

1. Sustainable forest management requires synoptic and repetitive biophysical and biochemical vegetation data for large geographic areas over long periods of time.
2. Remote sensing is the only way to acquire such data.

There is no other way. No other technology can possibly provide the data required at reasonable cost, accuracy and effort. No other technology will promote the integration and synergy of analysis for the wide-ranging data types required to address contemporary forestry questions.

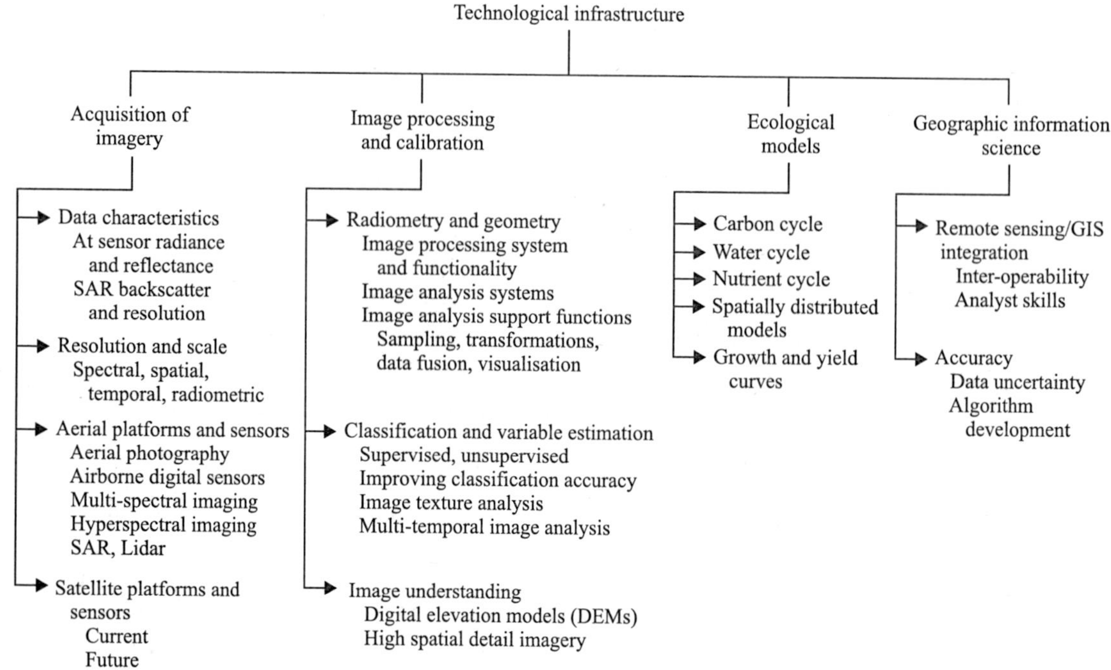

Fig. 18.1. Components of a remote sensing infrastructure. Four broad categories are shown suggesting that remote sensing application in forestry require the combined characteristics and continued development or synergy, in remote sensing image acquisition and analysis, ecological modelling and geographical information science.

Based on these views and an understanding of the extent to which information about the forest continues to limit a sustainable approach, positive scientific assessments reviewing the beneficial role of remote sensing in forest management, forest science and ecological applications are not hard to find in the literature. For example (referring to the contribution of aerial and satellite remote sensing to forest management):

1. 'Synoptic, timely information, which can be provided only with satellite data, is needed to support local, national and global decision-makers in the crucial planning efforts designed to preserve the habitability of this planet for generations to come.'
2. 'Remote sensing and GIS' help give us a better understanding of forest systems, how they function and how to mange them with a holistic view.
3. A strong correlation between stand development and satellite observations would make a valuable contribution to stand development forecasting and thus enable the improvement of forest management strategies.
4. Two time series of satellite images showed the reduction and rapid fragmentation of the giant panda's habitat in China. More than any other factor, it was this perspective provided by satellite imagery that changed the manager's views about the main threats to panda survival.

The idea, that remote sensing can make a substantial contribution to forest management flows from the unique characteristics that remote sensing data provide—synoptic, repetitive, quantitative and spatially explicit capabilities. When these features of remote sensing data are considered in light of the full range of remote sensing methods (including satellite, aerial and field-based methods), there appears to be strong support for the suggestion that remote sensing can satisfy at least some of the projected sustainable forest management information needs.

SUSTAINABLE FOREST MANAGEMENT

Forest management is necessary because of human needs to balance: (i) the flow of values from the forest; and (ii) an unimpaired ability to continue providing those values.

In this present form, forest management adopts a position identical to that of any management activity designed to accommodate a large, open system; forest management is comprised of conscious human actions that lead to a goal. Broadly speaking, the goal of forest management has almost always been stated as the continued flow of benefits from forests to satisfy present and future human needs. In some areas, management is needed to ensure the continued existence and future productivity of the forest in any form. In others, forest management is an ancient practice. Thus, in many forests the results of some of the earliest forest management practices have been known for years; in others, they are only now becoming available to be assessed. In the goal, at least, there seems to exist a remarkable degree of consensus.

The most recent innovations in forest management conform to a sustainable forest management approach. A key facet of this approach is the use of new forestry practices that satisfy the expressed desire or goal that forest management succeed in maintaining forest ecosystems in a sustainable condition; that is, that human activities in the forest do not negatively affect the ability of the forest to continue in virtually the same way as before. Obviously, such a goal is highly idealised; for example, the effect of natural climate change, if it could be discriminated from human-induced climate change, cannot yet be predicted with much confidence. The best information has been obtained from paleoenvironmental records. How can the impact of human activities on the forest be predicted?

Sustainable forest management has been defined by the Food and Agriculture Organisation as a multidisciplinary task, requiring collaboration between government agencies, non-governmental agencies (NGOs) and above all, people, especially rural people. It is of concern at local, regional, national and global scales. The activity of management is presented in terms of the essential management process. Sustainable forest management therefore involves:

1. Planning the production of wood for commercial purposes, as well as meeting local needs for fuelwood, poles, fodder and other purposes.
2. The protection or setting aside of areas to be managed as plant or wildlife reserves or for recreational or environmental purposes.
3. Ensuring that the conversion of forest lands to agriculture and other uses is done in a properly planned and controlled way.
4. Ensuring the regeneration of wastelands and degraded forests, the integration of trees into the farming landscape and the promotion of agroforestry.

While there may be as many definitions and descriptions of sustainable forest management as there are forests and managers responsible for them, most definitions of sustainable forest management are based on two commonsense, easily understood principles:

1. Sustainable forest management must be based on understanding and management of ecosystem processes and patterns over long time frames and large spatial scales.
2. Sustainable forest management must be based on goals that are social, as well as ecological.

What appears to be the main point of contention is not the philosophy, but the practical directions that flow from the two principles of sustainable forest management; for example, how best to balance human use and preservation, to maintain biodiversity and to achieve economic benefits are at the heart of the desired goal of sustainable forest management. How best to proceed with obtaining economic benefits in the light of uncertainty, even ignorance, of the true consequences of our actions. How best to consider the needs of current and future generation. The definition of sustainable forest management is less important than what has come to be understood by managers and the public as a sustainable forest management plan. These plans are where the answers to how best questions can be found. Will the proposed management procedures:

1. Aim to maintain viable population of native species *in situ*?
2. Acknowledge ecological patterns and diversity in terms of the processes and constraints generating them?
3. Sustain ecosystem diversity, health and productivity at different geographic and time scales?
4. Be based on abroad, integrative, interdisciplinary approach?
5. Include public involvement in planning and decision making?
6. Include results of recent scientific research and technology?
7. Be adaptive management techniques (including monitoring and evaluation)?
8. Include educational programmes?
9. Involve setting priorities based on societal demands within the constraints of ecosystem patterns and processes?

Even if the proposed management plan is carefully devised with these aims in mind, there can be problems in implementation and in evaluation. Forest management, like many complex environmental management activities (e.g., consider fisheries management or urban planning), remains an imperfect science with a limited history. Perfecting management through science will continue to be a source of frustration; there will be mistakes, uncertainties and unpalatable tradeoffs. Science is necessary, but not sufficient—broadly speaking, the endeavour is nothing less than human attempting to understand the planet well enough to co-exist sustainably with their environment.

Forestry in Crisis

There is ample evidence for a global failure by society to practice sustainable forest management, regardless of the management paradigm that is invoked to support human activities in forest. By some accounts, almost half of earth's original forest cover is gone, much of it removed within the past 30 years, with only one-fifth remaining in large tracts of relatively undisturbed forest—what the World Resources Institute calls frontier forest. Forests continue to be degraded, damaged, eliminated and converted to non-forest use. Why is this? Perhaps the goal of sustainable forest management can seem futile in the face of the long list of problems facing the world and its forests. Arguably, the list of problems is headed by population growth. Population is certainly not the only issue, although it could be argued that population increases underlay virtually every major human crisis or concern, including climate change; also poverty, hunger, debt, over development, under development and political instability—the list of human travails is virtually endless. Over time, many of these challenges can be seen as intricately linked to the central environmental/population problem—can humanity co-exist sustainably with the environment?

The search for an approach to management of the forests of the world that is sustainable must continue as a top priority for the forest scientists and managers, because there is little doubt that sustainable forest management is a fundamental requirement if human use of natural resources is to continue at anything near the current rate of consumption. Two recent political signposts have been erected that the world's forest community cannot ignore:

1. The United Nations Conference on Environment and Development, the 1992 Earth Summit in Rio de Janeiro, Brazil — This meeting of global leaders and environmental organisations focused intense world scrutiny on a wide array of international environmental issues, including forest conservation and management. In addition, specific conventions were signed concerning world climate change and the conservation of biodiversity. These agreements have led to an emphasis on monitoring criteria and indicators of sustainable forest management and on forest certification. Although the Forest Principles document was voluntary, rather than the binding Forest Conventions document that was originally sought, the net effect of the Rio Earth Summit was that the whole process of forest management was opened up with the consequent healthy questioning of conventional wisdom and practices.
2. The Kyoto Protocol on Climate Change (1997)—created a new, legally binding treaty for industrialised nations to meet the voluntary emissions targets set at Rio de Janeiro. This meeting led to an emphasis on national reporting of carbon budgets and the focus of national contributions to global climate change and has introduced the possibility of international trading of carbon credits. Governments set 2012 as the deadline for reductions of six greenhouse gases. The clean development mechanism (CDM) offered an opportunity to reduce greenhouse gas emissions and forest loss.

Each of these political agreements has given the World's forest scientists and managers much to contend with, not the least of which has been a workable monitoring system to provide key information on local, regional and global performance in managing forests and forest ecosystems.

Role of Remote Sensing

Remote sensing can be designed to support sustainable forest management in the presentation and reporting on the criteria and indicators of sustainable forestry and in the modelling and projections at a variety of scales based on a common understanding of biophysical and ecological principles. Remote sensing, together with GIS and computer simulation models, appear poised to make significant contributions to the way in which the remaining forests of the world are managed. Time and experience will be necessary before the appropriate role of remote sensing and GIS technology is understood in sustainable forest management.

A lack of experience in using GIS and remote sensing in an integrated way is natural; these are emerging technologies, only very recently considered as real tools of use by those concerned with the whole process of forest planning, operations and management. GIS and remote sensing should be viewed in the same way that other emerging technologies in forest management are viewed; their adoption and continued development will be similar to the adoption and development of other emerging technologies in forestry such as technologies for low-impact harvesting, new drying, short-piece and scrap utilisation, scanning, wood hardening, efficient logger programming and fibre and solid wood waste conversion. Why should remote sensing technology be any different? If anything, these other technologies have a more focused purpose and are more readily shown in economic terms to be viable technological improvements over existing procedures.

Few would consider the potential impact on forestry of new scanning or wood hardening technology on a par with the potential impact of remote sensing. What are the potential impacts of remote sensing? This is a large question to which only partial answers are available.

The first step toward sustainable development of the forest rescouses of any country or region is to clarify the status of the resource base; regionally appropriate use of GIS and remote sensing mapping, monitoring and modelling and direct field measurements are requirements of effective forest planning and management. Beyond this inventory requirement there are many operational and research uses of remote sensing in forestry applications, but the role of remote sensing cannot yet be definitively stated. This is simply a result of the extremely wide range of potential applications and the still-rapidly changing technology. Remote sensing and related (e.g., GPS, GIS) technology continues to develop at a rapid pace and the applications continue to be tested and developed, particularly in the research community.

In the meantime, new satellites and airborne sensors have been built, new algorithms to extract information from these images have been added to commercial systems and a continuing research agenda has been pursued worldwide at multiple scales and resolutions. These efforts continue to provide new insights and understanding into the possible role of remote sensing in forestry. But internal developments are not the only source of new knowledge in remote sensing. Externally, things are also moving fast. The field of landscape ecology has shown tremendous growth and a tremendous need for spatially explicit data of the type remote sensing seems ideally suited to provide. Forest management to maintain or enhance biodiversity has emerged as a global theme, requiring new structural data and context for understanding species-richness observation. The whole issue of sustainable forest management certification through monitoring biophysical and social C & I has given remote sensing new demands for information to consider and attempt to meet.

Now, the relevant question for forestry appears to be not whether remote sensing can contribute to forest resource management, but rather, what is the best way for remote sensing to contribute of forest resource management? Routine applications are still rare, but research opportunities have been plentiful and continue to grow in sophistication and planning. General assessments of the role of remote sensing in estimation of criteria and indicators are rapidly being followed by specific indicator assessments.

There are many specific studies in remote sensing of forest condition, productivity, health and change that will lead to quantitative monitoring of value to forest management. The most significant features for forest management offered by remote sensing continue to be the quantitative form of data and the repetitive and synoptic coverage provided by the technology. With multitemporal data acquisitions—and the large historical Landsat database—it is possible to virtually time-travel to review landscapes a (human) generation old. With data acquired in a consistent format over time, a number of previously difficult applications have been made more feasible.

REMOTE SENSING IN INDIAN FOREST MANAGEMENT

Forests are ecological as well as socio-economic resource. These have to be managed judiciously not only for environmental protection and other services but also for various products and industrial raw materials. Considering the crucial role forests play in the country's ecological stability and economic development, the current National Forest Policy in India aims at maintaining a minimum of 33 per cent of country's geographical area under forest and tree cover. This requires periodic monitoring of the forest cover of the country for effective planning and sustainable development. Forest Survey of India (FSI), an organisation under the Ministry of Environment & Forests (Government of India) has been mandated to monitor and map country's forest cover on a biennial basis. Consequently, FSI has been carrying out assessment of forest cover in the country using satellite based remote sensing data and has been publishing its findings in the State of Forest Report (SFR) every two years. Its first assessment of forest cover made in 1987 was published as SFR 1987 and the latest i.e., the eighth one as SFR 2001.

With the improvement in satellite data resolution and adoption of digital image processing by FSI, it has been possible to assess forest cover patches as small as 1 ha. However, there exists a significant tree cover wealth outside conventional forest areas, most of which is less than 1 ha in extent. These include small patches of trees in plantations and woodlands, or scattered trees on farms, homesteads and urban areas or trees along linear features such as roads, canals, bunds etc. and constitute significant area. In a study done in Haryana State by FSI in 1997, it was found that growing stock of trees outside forest was approximately seven times than that from natural forests. Trees outside forests (TOF) are therefore considered an alternative but significant source of fuel, fodder, timber and environmental services to the local people. In 2001 assessment, FSI assessed tree cover (less than 1 ha in extent) in the country using a stratified sampling and field inventory, and estimated it to be 2.48 per cent of country's geographical area. Thereafter, FSI has developed a methodology based on high-resolution satellite data for mapping and stratification of TOF leading to an improved sampling design for field inventory.

In the present section, methodologies of forest cover and tree cover assessments as used by the FSI are discussed.

Forest Cover Assessment

Till recently, FSI was using mostly visual interpretation of satellite data on 1:2,50,000 scale for assessment of forest cover. However, in its latest assessment i.e., 2001 assessment, it used digital interpretation of satellite data on 1:50000 scale for mapping and monitoring forest cover. The present methodology uses digital image processing software and involves the following steps:

Acquisition of satellite data

The digital data of IRS-1C and 1D LISS III is acquired from NRSA in CD. India is covered in about 340 scenes, of IRS-1C and 1D. One scene covers an area of about 20000 km^2, having an overlap of about 10 per cent with adjoining scenes. While procuring the data, care is taken to ensure that it is cloud free (with not more than 10 per cent cloud cover) and therefore data pertaining to the period from October-December is preferred.

Geometric rectification of raw data

After downloading the data into computer, rectification is carried out in each image to provide latitude and longitude information into raw satellite scene using raster based geometric corrections. Rectification carried out in geographic projection is re-projected in shape of polygonal projection and the scene is geo-coded with using SOI toposheets.

Mosaicing of rectified scenes

Different scenes, which are already rectified, may have to be merged together to get one combined FCC (false colour composite). FCC of sheet is extracted from mosaiced scene in a chosen area of interest. Image is displayed in three bands 3, 2, 1. Masking of non-forest areas is done separately to extract forest areas on the basis of ground knowledge, cover map of previous cycles and on the basis of information available through SOI toposheets in the area of interest.

Classification of Forest Cover Using NDVI

Interactive method of display is used for assigning threshold values for each class (open, dense and scrub) on the basis of the ground knowledge to highlight forest/vegetated areas. Density class of forest cover and colour is accordingly allocated. Survey of India toposheets is used for delineating boundaries of each district and classified map of forest cover is generated. Flow chart of methodology of dynamic forest cover mapping using remote sensing is shown in Fig. 18.2.

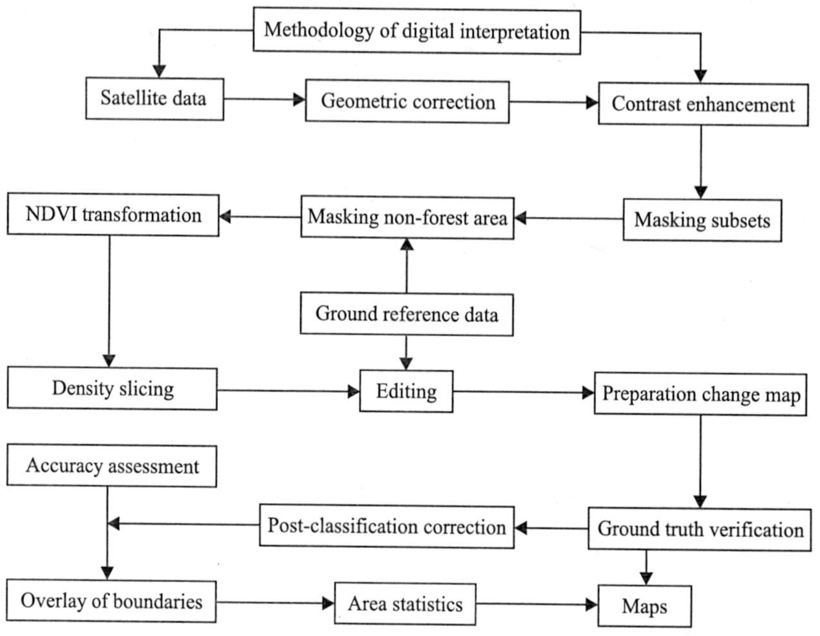

Fig. 18.2. Flow chart of Forest cover mapping using remote sensing.

The output includes forest cover maps on 1:50,000 scale. These maps show forest cover in three classes:

1. Dense forest, having canopy density of more than 40 per cent.
2. Open forests with canopy density between 10-40 per cent.
3. Scrub which are forest areas having less than 10 per cent canopy density.

These maps are also generated for district and States/Union Territories (UT) by overlaying the respective District/State/UT administrative boundary. Area under forest cover at District/State/Country level is then assessed. Change maps are also prepared to depict changes taking place under different land cover classes.

In its latest assessment of 2001, taking advantage of advancements in remote sensing and improvement in digital interpretation qualities, FSI has provided a much more comprehensive status of forest cover in the country than in the previous assessments. Some of the new features incorporated in this assessment are:

1. For the first time FSI has interpreted the satellite data of the entire country digitally. In earlier estimates, interpretation has been largely visual. Digital interpretation has the advantage of overcoming subjectivity prevalent in visual method.
2. Due to absorption of digital image processing technique, it has been possible for FSI to interpret the data on 1:50,000 scale. This has resulted in providing more realistic information on forest cover as areas having forest cover down to 1 ha could be delineated while in earlier assessments, forest cover down to 25 ha could only be delineated. Similarly blanks down to 1 ha within forested areas can be separated. The entire exercise has resulted in new base-line information on forest cover.

3. As perennial woody vegetation (including bamboos, palms, coconut, apple, mango etc.) has been treated as tree and thus all lands with tree crops, such as agro-forestry plantations, fruit orchards, tea and coffee estates with trees etc., have been included in forest cover.
4. Mangrove cover has been classified into dense and open mangrove cover. The area of mangrove cover so assessed has been merged in the respective area figures of dense and open forest cover.
5. A classification is not complete unless its accuracy is assessed. For the first time an independent and systematic assessment of accuracy of satellite data interpretation was made. An error matrix was generated by comparing classified forest cover with the actual forest cover on the ground at 3608 locations spread throughout the country. High resolution PAN data was used as proxy for ground verification. The overall accuracy of forest cover classification was found to be 95.9 per cent.
6. Though forest cover in areas as less as 1 ha in extent could be assessed using satellite data, significant tree cover exists in patches of less than 1 ha and in linear shapes along roads, canals, etc. and scattered trees that can not be assessed using remote sensing. An attempt is made for the first time to assess such tree cover using ground inventory method. Figure 18.3 highlights the forest covers in India.

The abstract of forest cover assessment 2001 is given in Table 18.5.

Table 18.5. Forest cover as per 2001 assessment.

Class	*Area (km²)*	*Per cent of geographic area*
Forest cover		
Dense	4,16,809	12.68
Open	2,58,729	7.87
Total Forest Cover*	6,75,538	20.55
Non-forest		
Scrub	47,318	1.44
Total non-forest**	2,61,1725	79.45
Total geographic area	3,28,7263	100.00

*includes 4482 km^2 under mangroves (0.14 per cent of country's geographic area) **includes scrub.

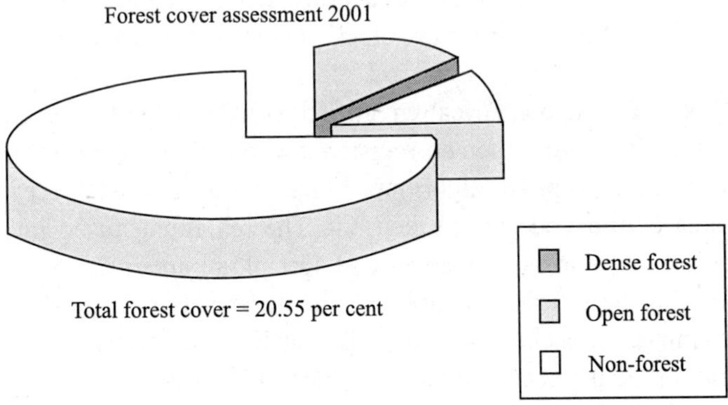

Fig. 18.3. Forest cover in India.

Tree Cover Assessment

Tree outside forest (TOF) is assessed in rural as well as urban areas, although the greater part exists in rural areas. Initially, conventional field method was used for TOF assessment in rural areas. The state or a group of districts is considered as the study area. Since this area is fairly large there is every possibility of heterogeneity of the study variable i.e. growing stock. TOF being planted along with agricultural crops is likely to be influenced by the agro-ecological variables. Therefore, study area is stratified according to agro-ecological zones (AEZ), which has already been demarcated by other agencies. Districts, in India, are the basic planning and administrative units, which influence the TOF and therefore, is considered for further stratification of AEZs. Villages are treated as sampling units. Optimum number of sample villages is selected randomly from different districts proportionate to the TOF area of the same. Complete enumeration of all the trees with diameter of 10 cm and above at breast height in the randomly selected villages in each district is carried out. Data is collected on pre-designed formats following prepared instructions for fieldwork and collected data is processed following appropriate formula. The above-mentioned methodology provided accurate estimates but was very time consuming. It was not able to provide precise information at district level, which is the basic unit for economic planning.

Methodology Using Remote Sensing Data

To do away with these constraints many alternatives were tried and finally a methodology based on digital image processing and GIS analysis using multi spectral and panchromatic data for mapping of trees outside forests (TOF) was devised. The remote sensing data is used to provide stratification of the TOF resources, which is utilised to increase the precision and is time effective. In addition, sometimes the objectives of TOF resource assessment may require spatial distribution of resources on maps along with several other features. This objective can also be appropriately tackled by this methodology.

High-resolution satellite imageries provide information even up to identification of a single tree but these are cost prohibitive. The IRS LISS III data, which is multi spectral and has a resolution of 23.5 m × 23.5 m, provide information on vegetation cover. There are techniques available through which tree vegetated land can be segregated from agriculture land if the tree vegetated patch is about 1 ha and more. However, LISS data cannot be used for smaller patches or scattered trees. The IRS PAN data, which is monochromatic, having resolution of 5.8 m × 5.8 m can identify a tree vegetated land even less than 0.1 ha. Therefore, both LISS III and PAN imageries are used for stratification of TOF resources on the basis of geometrical formation of trees i.e. block plantation (group of trees), linear plantation and scattered trees.

Thereafter, the PAN image is geometrically rectified with the help of Survey of India toposheets on 1:50000 Scale. The LISS III image is then co-registered with the rectified PAN images. PAN and LISS III images are fused using appropriate algorithm. Since mapping of TOF areas is the objective, the boundary of forest area is digitised and masked out. The remaining fused image are classified into settlement, water bodies, burnt areas, tree cover and agriculture area using appropriate classifier viz., maximum likelihood. This classification enables the interpreter to distinguish between tree cover and other classes on fused image. This classified image is visually analysed with respect to fused images for editing and refinement for inclusion and omissions. Since a cluster of trees having 0.1 ha area or more is defined as block plantation, pixels are clumped and cluster of pixels having area less than 0.1 ha are eliminated. After editing of the classified image the final classified map is generated which is done by taking the PAN, LISS-III and the fused images. Incorporating these corrections final classified image is prepared having three classes in TOF areas, namely, block, linear and scattered. From the classified TOF map information pertaining to area under block, linear, scattered and water bodies can be calculated. In addition, such areas, which do not support tree vegetation, like rivers and water bodies, snow covered mountains, marshes,etc. which is termed as culturable non forest area (CNFA)can also be calculated. Such information is very helpful for district level planning.

Sampling Method

Besides generation of TOF maps, the information on block, linear and scattered patches can be used to estimate the number of trees and the corresponding volume (species wise) using appropriate sampling design by laying out optimum number of plots randomly selected in every stratum. Since the variability in each stratum is expected to be different demanding different sample and plot sizes, pilot studies were conducted to ascertain these so that the variability of the stratum can be properly addressed. In this pilot study, 0.1 ha, 0.2 ha and 0.3 ha plots were considered for block stratum. Similarly, strip of size 10 m × 75 m, 10 m × 100 m, 10 m × 125 m, 10 m × 150 m, 10 m ×175 m and 10 m × 200 m were considered for linear stratum. For scattered stratum plot of size 0.5 ha, 1.0 ha, 1.5 ha, 2.0 ha, 2.5 ha and 3.0 ha were considered for non-hilly districts and 0.25 ha, 0.50 ha, 0.75 ha and 1.00 ha were considered for the hilly districts. Twenty concentric plots in each stratum were randomly selected and data were recorded. After analysis it was concluded that optimum plot size for block, linear and scattered stratum are 0.1 ha, 10 × 125 m strip and 3.0 ha respectively for non-hilly districts and 0.1 ha, 10 × 125 m strip and 0.5 ha for hilly district. It was also concluded through pilot study that the sample sizes for block, linear and scattered stratum are 35, 50 and 50 respectively for non-hilly districts and 35, 50 and 95 for hilly district.

Desired number of sample points was randomly generated in each stratum separately and the data on pre-decided variables were collected on designed formats, following Manual for Assessment for Trees Outside Forests. Thereafter, data processing is carried out following appropriate formulae corresponding to sampling design. Table 18.6 indicates the results obtained with regard to stems/ha, total number of stems, volume/ha and total volume of trees outside forests in rural areas of Gurdaspur district of Punjab, India. Likewise, similar results obtained from different districts spread across the country are aggregated to generate national level figures.

Table 18.6. District level estimates Gurdaspur (Punjab) India.

Geographical area	3551 sq.km.
Urban area	76.42 sq.km.
Forest area	368 sq.km.
Water bodies	94.58 sq.km.
CNFA (Rural)	3013 sq.km.
Stems/ha	18.5
Total stems	5,563,798 (5.56 M)
Volume/ha	3.5 cu.m
Total volume	1,054,577 cu.m(1.05 M cu.m)

Accuracy of Classification

Any classification is not complete unless and until its accuracy is assessed. For the present study the accuracy of classification was assessed by taking 53 points in block, 65 in linear and 65 in scattered stratum for a particular district. It is recommended that 50 or more points should be located for ground verification in each class. The accuracy of this classification was high as evident from the following confusion matrix of Kapurthala district of Punjab state.

Table 18.7. Confusion matrix.

Description	*Block*	*Linear*	*Scattered*	*Row total*	*User's accuracy (%)*
Block	41	0	0	41	100
Linear	0	63	0	63	100
Scattered	12	2	65	79	82
Column total	53	65	65	183	–
Producer's accuracy (%)	77	97	100	–	–
Overall accuracy = 92 %					

Thus, the main objective of forest survey of India in mapping and monitoring forest and tree cover of the country on a two-year cycle is to know the dynamic changes of forest resources in terms of quantity and quality over a period of time so that appropriate planning and management interventions can be developed for their conservation and sustainable utilisation. Remote sensing based forest cover mapping and monitoring adopted by FSI has proved to be cost and time effective over traditional forest resource monitoring. The methodology using digital image processing and geographical information system, as explained above can be effectively employed using multi spectral and high-resolution satellite imageries to stratify the TOF resources in such a way that the classification system of TOF resource remains valid. In addition, spatial distribution of TOF resources on maps along with other features will provide information for planning and implementation and utilisation of these resources in a sustainable manner. Since, this methodology enables resource-based stratification, it is expected to provide better estimates of TOF resources than the one generated through field survey alone.

19

Earth Sciences

INTRODUCTION

Aerial photography and remote sensing have long been applied to problems in the earth sciences. Geology, topographic mapping and related topics formed one of the earliest routine applications of aerial photography and today remote sensing, used with other techniques, continues to form one of the most important tools for geologic mapping, exploration and research.

Research for geological remote sensing spans the full range of subjects within the field of remote sensing, including use of additional data in the thermal, near infrared, visible and microwave regions of the spectrum. More than most other subjects, efforts such as geobotanical research are especially interesting because they bring knowledge of so many different disciplines together to bear on a single problem. In addition geological investigations have formed important facets of research and applications programmes for Landsat, SPOT, RADARSAT, ERS–1 and other systems. Geological studies are said to form a major economic component of the practice of remote sensing. Certainly, they form one of the most important elements in both theoretical and practical advances in remote sensing.

This chapter addresses applications of remote sensing in the earth sciences, which are defined here to include geology, geomorphology and soil science. Despite their many differences, these disciplines share a common focus on the earth's shape and structure and on the nature of the soils and sediments at its surface. Applications of remote sensing in the earth sciences are especially difficult. Often the subjects of investigation are geologic structures, soil horizons and other features entirely or partiaclly hidden beneath the earth's surface. Seldom can remotely sensed images directly record such information—instead, we must search for indirect evidence that may be visible at the surface. Thus interpretations of geologic, pedologic and geomorphic information are often based upon inference rather than direct sensing of the qualities to be studied. Furthermore, interpretations of geoscience information are frequently based upon rather small differences in tone, texture and spectral response. Even direct examination on the ground of many geologic and pedologic materials is subject to error and controversy, so it should be no surprise that applications of remote sensing in these fields can be equally difficult. Finally, we must often depend upon composite signatures formed as individual 'pure' signatures of various types of soil, rock and vegetation are mixed together into a single, combined, spectral response that may be unlike any of its components. Field observations are made by necessity at points such as outcrops, soil profiles or boreholes. Because remote sensing instruments record radiation from ground areas rather than from ground points, it may be difficult to relate remotely sensed data to the ground observations with which we traditionally have experience and confidence. Such problems present both practical and conceptual difficulties for applications of remote sensing in the earth sciences.

Remote sensing can, however, provide opportunities not normally available to geoscientists. The ability to observe reflectance and emittance over a range of wavelengths opens the door to the study of subjects that would not otherwise be possible. Also, the synoptic view of satellite images gives a broad-scale perspective of patterns not discernible within the confines of the large-scale, close-up view of ground observation. A single satellite image can record an integrated signature formed of many kinds of information, including shadow, soil, rock and vegetation; although these mixtures may present problems, they also portray subtle differences in terrain that cannot be easily derived from other sources. Although use of remotely sensed images cannot replace direct ground observation or data derived from filed and laboratory studies, they can form valuable supplements to more traditional methods and sometimes provide information and a perspective not otherwise available.

PHOTOGEOLOGY

Geologists study many aspects of the earth's surface in an effort to understand the earth's structure, to guide the search for minerals and fuels and to understand geologic hazards. Remote sensing contributes to several dimensions of the geological sciences by providing information concerning lithology, structure and vegetation patterns. Lithology refers to fundamental physical and chemical properties of rocks, including, for example, the gross distinctions between sedimentary, igneous and metamorphic rocks. Structure defines the kinds of deformation experienced by rocks, including folding, fracturing and faulting. Geobotanical studies focus upon relationships between plant cover at the earths's surface and the lithology of underlying rocks. Photogeology is the derivation of geological information from interpretation of aerial photographs. Photogeology originated early in the development of air photo interpretation. Many of its basic techniques were developed in the 1920s, then refined and applied into the 1950s and 1960s, when they seemed to approach the limits of their capabilities and were assimilated into newly developing research in geological remote sensing. Today photogeology is routinely applied to good effect. However, since aerial photographs now form only one of many forms of aerial images routinely available to the geologist, most research and innovation is now likely to occur in the broader context of geological remote sensing. Many of the techniques of photogeology are the direct application of the principles of image interpretation to geological problems. Image texture, size, shape, tone, shadow and so on, each have special significance in the realm of the geologist's view of the terrain. Likewise, the principles of photogrammetry have special applications in the context of photogeology for calculation of thicknesses of beds and determination of strike and dip from aerial photography. Such measurements permit derivation of structural information from aerial images.

Arid and semi-arid regions, where vegetative cover may be sparse, may be especially favourable for lithologic interpretation of aerial photographs. Bedding in sedimentary rocks, especially those that are exposed at hillsides or by folding or faulting, is one of the strongest clues to lithologic composition. More resistant beds stand out in relief, while less resistant beds are lowered by differential erosion. Differences in image tone of specific beds may reveal differences in lithology. Image tone of strata is often directly influenced by grain size of the rocks, although the relationship between grain size and image tone may vary so widely that it is best not to attempt to establish general rules for interpretation. Nonetheless, guidelines can be defined for specific localities. Examination of drainage density, drainage pattern and vegetation patterns may also provide clues to lithology, even when beds are not directly exposed.

Igneous rocks are usually more difficult to interpret. Extrusive igneous rocks may be recognisable by distinctive landforms, such as cones and flows, especially if they are young and by differences in image tone or by drainage patterns and vegetation distributions. Intrusive igneous rocks can sometimes be easily recognised by their distinctive image tones and by topographic expression through differential erosion, but often their close integration with surrounding sedimentary strata means that they are more subtly expressed on aerial photographs than are extrusive rocks and therefore can be interpreted with less confidence. Information concerning metamorphic rocks can also be interpreted from aerial photographs, but typically only with great difficulty, due to complex local structures induced by metamorphism. Metamorphism may also reduce the differences in resistance to erosion that are so important in inferring lithology.

Manual interpretation for lithological information typically sub-divides an image into distinctive photomorphic regions that show the combined influence of soil colour, vegetation, land use, drainage and shadowing. In the second step, the geologist interprets each region to identify specific lithologies or combinations of lithologies whin each region, using field observations to guide and verify interpretations. The analyst uses areas of known geology as a means of identifying analogous regions elsewhere on the image. Thus, the image provides a map-like perspective and an integrated representation of many different factors that permits separation of regions of differing geology; however, identification of the geological significance of each region usually requires application of other knowledge not visible on the image, knowledge usually derived from field observations.

In some situations geological information can be derived using the techniques of digital classification. Areas of known geological identity can form training areas for the identification of analogous areas elsewhere on the image. In the context of Landsat data, such techniques can be effective only when the composite signatures formed by such elements as soil colour, vegetation, shadowing and other factors form distinctive spectra that are clearly associated with geological patterns. Although such situations exist, they cannot be considered as the typical conditions for geological remote sensing, so other techniques are usually required. In some situations, simple density slicing or band rationing may permit visual recognition of distinctive geological units on remotely sensed images.

LINEAMENTS

Lineaments is the name given by geologists to lines or edges, of presumed geologic origin, visible on remotely sensed images. Such features have also been referred to as linears or lineations. Use of the term lineament in a geological context dates to 1904 and apparently has even earlier analogues in other languages. These early uses, prior to availability of aerial images, applied to specific geologic or geomorphic features, such as topographic features (ridgelines, drainage systems or coastlines), lithologic contacts or zones of fracture.

As early as the 1930s photogeologists studied fracture patterns visible on aerial photographs as a means of inferring geologic structure. These photo features apparently corresponded rather closely to faults and fractures defined in the field. More recently, in the context of geological remote sensing, the term has assumed a broader meaning. Any linear feature visible on an aerial image can be referred to as a lineament. A problem arises because it is difficult to establish a clear link between the features on images and corresponding features, if any, on the ground.

The strength of this link depends in part upon the nature of the imagery. In the instance of interpretations from aerial photographs and mosaics, scales are usually large and ample detail is visible. Linear features visible on such images are likely to match to those that can be confirmed in the field. However, more extensive and subtle features cannot be easily detected on aerial photograph. Each photograph shows only a small area; if mosaics are formed to show larger regions, variations in illumination and shadowing obscure more subtle lineaments that might extend over many photographs. Furthermore, in the era prior to routine availability of CIR films now used for high-altitude photography, high-altitude photographs (which can show large areas under uniform illumination) were not of good visual quality due to effects of atmospheric scatter.

The advent of non-photographic sensors and the availability of the broad-scale view of satellite images changed this situation because it then became possible to view large areas with images of good visual clarity. Early radar images depicted large areas illuminated from a single direction at rather low illumination angles—conditions that tended to increase topographic shadowing in a manner that enhanced the visibility of liner features. Locations of these features did not always match previously known faults or fractures, so the term lineament was evoked to avoid an explicit statement of a geological origin. The detection of lineaments and the interpretation of their meaning has attracted considerable attention and controversy. Because of the broad scale and coarse resolution of such images, the lineaments they show are much more subtly expressed and much more difficult to relate to previously known geological features than were faults and fractures observed previously on aerial photographs.

Lineaments are of course 'real' features if we consider them simply to be linear features detected on aerial imagery. The controversy arises when we attempt to judge the geological significance (if any) of these features. There are sound reasons for assigning a geological meaning to some lineaments, even if they do not always correspond to clearly observable physical features. In the simplest instances, a dip-slip fault may leave a subtle topographic feature that is visible as a linear shadow on aerial photography when illuminated obliquely from elevated side (Fig. 19.1). The axis of a displacement for a dip-slip fault is along the dip of the fault plane, to create a difference in relief, as depicted in Fig. 19.1. In the alternative instance, a strike-slip fault, the axis of the fault displacement follows the strike of the fault (along the trace of the fault on the surface), creating fewer opportunities for surface expression. Of course, a fault that is oriented parallel to the direction of illumination may be indistinct or invisible. Not all faults are expressed topographically, but the fault plane may offer preferred avenues of movement for moisture and for the growth of plant roots (Fig. 19.2.). Therefore, the trace of the fault may be revealed by vegetation patterns even though it has no obvious topographic expression. Faults of any form can alter drainage in a manner that creates linear drainage segments, which are then visible on aerial images. Such features, when clearly expressed, may have structural origins and it may be possible to verify their existence through field observations. However, more subtle features, may be observable only as broad-scale features, not easily verifiable at a given point. Such lineaments may be genuine structural features, but not easily confirmable as such.

Linear features that are clearly of structural origin are significant because they indicate zones of fracturing and faulting. It is often assumed that regions of intersection of lineaments of differing orientation are of special significance, as in theory they might identify zones of mineralisation stratigraphic traps, regions of abundant ground water or zones of structural compression. For this reason, much is often made of the orientation and angles of intersection of lineaments.

Other lineaments may not have structural origins. It is conceivable that some may be artifacts of the imaging system or of pre-processing algorithms. Some linear features may be purely surface features, such as wind-blown sediments, that do not reflect sub-surface structure (Fig. 19.3). Cultural patterns, including land-cover boundaries, edges of land ownership parcels and political borders can all have linear form and can be aligned in a manner that creates the linear features observed on aerial images. Because these features may not be readily distinguished from those of geologic origin and because of the inconsistency of individual delineations of lineaments from the same image, lineament analysis has been regarded with skepticism by a significant proportion of the geological community.

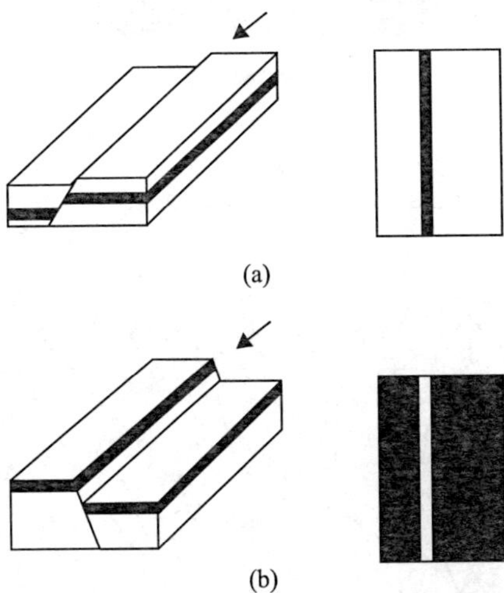

Fig. 19.1. Schematic illustration of a dip-slip fault. (a) Illumination from the elevated side produces a strip-like shadow on the image. (b) Illumination from the downthrust side may produce a bright strip as the sun is reflected from the linear facet that now faces the solar beam.

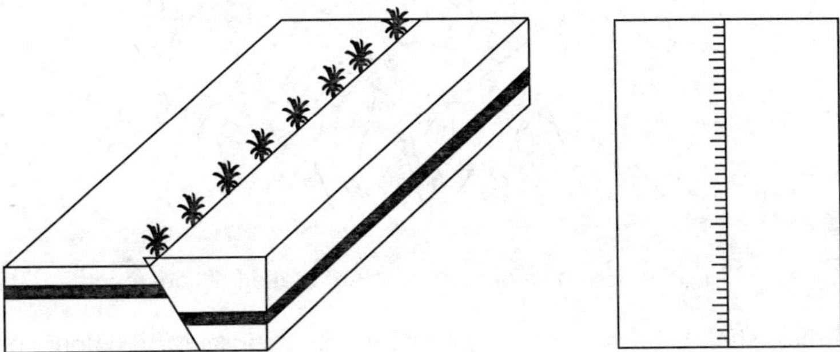

Fig. 19.2. Hypothetical situation in which a fault with little or no surface expression forms a preferred zone of movement for moisture and for the growth of plant roots. Such a zone may create a favourable habitat for certain species or speed the growth of more prevalent plants located near the fault. The linear arrangement of such plants and their shadows may form a linear feature on an image.

Lineaments have been identified by manual image interpretation (Fig. 19.4) and by computer analysis. For manual interpretation, transparencies of prints can be examined using normal equipment and procedures. If multispectral images are available, lineaments may be more distinct on particular bands. For example, interpretations using Landsat MSS images may be easiest using the infrared bands (frequently band 4 is used) because shadows are sharp and vegetation patterns are distinct. Prior to interpretation, images can be enhanced by application of contrast stretch to improve visibility of lineaments.

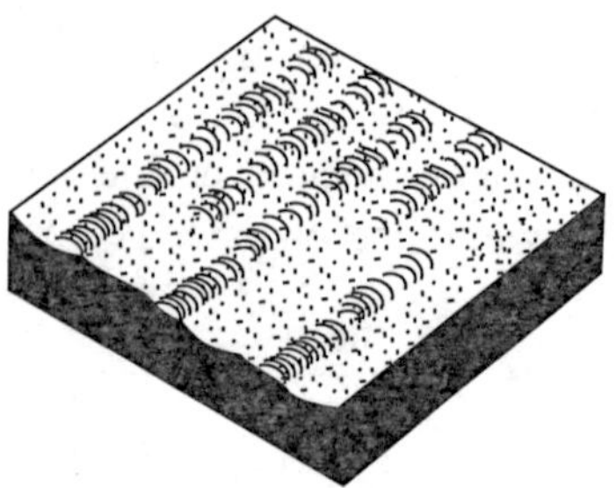

Fig. 19.3. Example of lineaments that do not reflect geologic structure. Wind-blown sand has been aligned in linear ridges that indicte the nature of the surface sediments only.

Fig. 19.4. Example of manual interpretation of lineaments.

Abrams and others studied lineaments interpreted from a Landsat MSS colour composite of a region in southwestern Arizona. Their analysis focused upon the Helvetia-Rosemont area, known to be rich in porphyry copper. They attempted to determine if their techniques would locate previously discovered mineralised zones. Paleozoic limestones, quartzites, shales and dolomites cover Pre-cambrian granites and shists in the study area. The Paleozoic deposits themselves were altered by Mesozoic uplift and erosion, then covered by further deposition. The Laramide orogeny during the late Cretaceous produced intrusion of granitic rocks with thrust faulting along a predominant northeast-southwest trend. This tectonic activity, together with later Paleocene intrusions, caused mineralisation along some of the faults. Tectonic activity continued into the late Tertiary, producing extensive faulting and a complex pattern of lineaments.

Abrams examined orientations of lineaments they interpreted from the Landsat image, then plotted their results in the form of a rose diagram (Fig. 19.5). Each wedge in the circular pattern represents the number of lineaments oriented along specific compass azimuths. Because each lineament has two azimuths (e.g., a 'north–south' line is oriented as much to the south as it is to the north), the diagram is symmetric and some investigators prefer to show only half of the diagram.

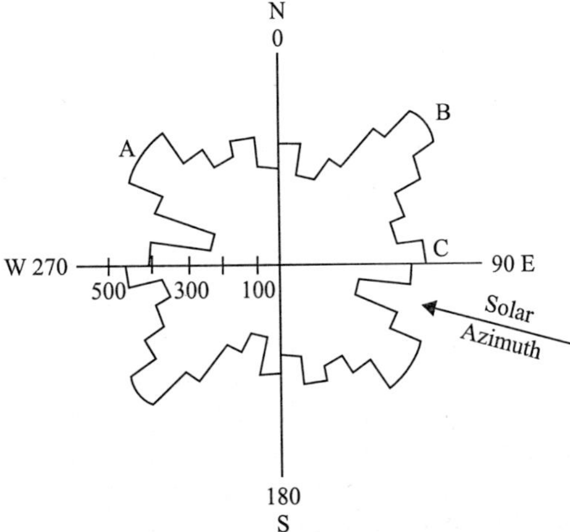

Fig. 19.5. Strike-frequency diagram of lineaments for a region of southeastern Arizona. Features, as discussed in the text, include: A, predominant northwest-southeast orientation; B, predominant northeast-southwest orientation and C, low frequency along the axis that parallels the solar beam at the time of image acquisition.

Several features are noteworthy. First, the low numbers of lineaments oriented at (approximately) 110 (and 290), roughly east-southeast-west-northwest, correspond to the axis that parallels the orientation of the solar beam at the time that the Landsat data were acquired—the lineaments that might have this orientation will not be easily detected because shadowing is minimised. The northeast-southwest trend (B in Fig. 19.5) is said to represent the predominant trend to Pre-cambrian faulting that is observed throughout Arizona. Superimposed over this pattern is the northwest-southeast trend (A) arising from faulting in the Mesozoic rocks mentioned above. Finally, the east-west trend (C) is interpreted as the result of the Laramide faulting known to be associated with the mineralisation that produced the copper deposits present in this region. Abrams and his colleagues counted the frequencies of the lineaments in each cell of a 10-km grid superimposed over the image and concluded that the highest frequencies, which they interpreted to form favourable locations for intrusion of magmas and for mineralisation, correspond to zones of known mineral deposits. This kind of study does not form a conclusive test of the effectiveness of lineament analysis, as it is conducted with foreknowledge of the nature and location of the resources that are to be detected, but it does illustrate the kinds of techniques that can be applied in the study of lineaments in less-well-known regions.

Automated Analysis of Lineaments

Because the human visual system tends to generalise, manual interpretations may identify continuous linear features that are later found to be formed of separate segments of unrelated origin. Lineaments that are found to correspond to geologic features often are extensions of known fault systems rather than completely new systems. Results of manual interpretations vary greatly from interpreter to interpreter—a fact that has detracted from the credibility of lineament analysis. As a result, other research has attempted to automate the interpretation of lineaments. Because detection of edges and lines has long been an important task in the fields of image analysis and pattern recognition, automatic detection of lineaments would seem to be a direct application of an existing methodology.

The first application of digital analysis in the search for lineaments was simply to apply the basic procedures for image enhancement as a means of preparing the image for visual interpretation. In the enhanced images, lineaments are shown with greater clarity and distinctness. Berlin and Chavez applied spatial filtering and both linear and sinusoidal contrast stretch to enhance colour Landsat MSS images of the desert regions of southwestern Jordan. Visual interpretation of these images revealed the presence of lineaments that the scientists judge to correspond to locations of previously undiscovered faults.

Later research takes digital lineament analysis a step further by using enhanced (or otherwise pre-processed) images as input for an algorithm that replaces the manual interpretation by automatically searching for linear features. Moore examined Landsat MSS band 4 by first using a low-pass filter to remove the high-frequency component of the image. Such a filter excludes the short-range image variation that would tend to be noisy, presumably leaving the broader scale variations that would be more likely to portray useful information concerning lineaments. Next they applied a series of directional filters; each filter enhanced features that tended to be linearly oriented in one of eight compass directions. This step produced a set of eight images, each showing the linear features (if any) that tended to be oriented in a specific direction. Then they again applied a smoothing procedure to remove undesirable short-range variation and re-scaled the brightness values to produce a visually sharper image. The final image shows only the linear features detected by this procedure; it can be superimposed on the original image to provide reference to known geographical features.

Vaughn applied a different procedure that relied upon an analogous strategy. He applied filters to isolate the low-frequency component, then sampled every fourth row and column, applied a median filter to isolate major features and re-quantised. He then applied his own algorithm to detect the linear features present within the pre-processed image.

GEOBOTANY

Geologic materials and processes can directly influence the character and amount of nutrients available for plant growth. Weathering of rocks and minerals influences the abundance and nature of clay minerals present in the soil cover, thereby influencing soil fertility and plant growth. Variations in the density, vigour and kinds of plants may then be recorded on remotely sensed images (Fig. 19.6).

Geologic processes may concentrate trace elements in specific strata or regions. Geologic weathering may relases trace elements in a form that can be absorbed by vegetation. Plants that absorb these trace elements at higher than normal levels may display abnormal spectral signatures, thereby signaling the existence and location of the anomalous concentration of elements.

Geobotany depends upon knowledge of how geologic materials release elements into the nutrient pool, how these elements are absorbed by the soil and concentrated in plant tissues and how they can alter the spectral signatures of plants. Because specific kinds of plants may thrive under certain unusual conditions of soil feretility, detailed knowledge of the spectral characteristics of such plants can be very valuable. Geobotanical studies are especially valuable in heavily vegetated regions where soil and rock are not exposed to direct view of the sensor but they may also be useful in sparsely vegetated regions where it may be possible to identify individual plants or where vegetation patterns may be especially sensitive to subtle environmental variations.

The practice of geobotanical reconnaissance is restricted by several factors. First, geobotanical studies may depend upon observations of subtle distinctions in vegetation vigour and pattern, so successful application may require data of very fine spatial, spectral and radiometric resolution—resalution much finer than that of Landsat or SPOT data, for example. Thus some of the concepts of geobotanical exploration cannot be routinely applied with the imagery and data most commonly available. Hyperspectral remote sensing provides the necessary capabilities for developing geobotanical knowledge. This work, now conducted mainly in a research context, may provide the basis for development of sensors and analytical techniques applicable on an operational basis. Second, geology is only one of the many factors that influence plant growth. Site, aspect and distrubance (both by mankind and by nature) influence vegetation distributions in very complex patterns. Effects of these several causes cannot always be clearly separated.

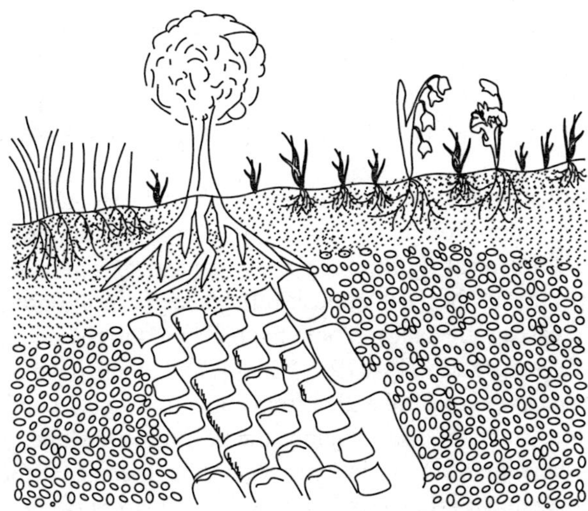

Fig. 19.6. General model for geobotanical studies. Abundance, vigour and patterns of plants are related to the geologic substratum. If geologists can isolate these geologic factors from others that influence vegetation patterns, botanical information can be used (with other data) to contribute to geological knowledge.

Timing of image acquisition is critical. Some geobotanical influences may be detectable only at specific seasons or may be observable as, for example, advances in the timing of otherwise normal seasonal changes in vegetation colouring. The issue of timing may be especially important because the remote sensing analyst may not have control over the timing of image acquisition or may have imagery only for a single date, whereas several may be necessary to observe the critical changes. Finally, many geobotanical anomalies may have a distinctively local character—specific indicators may have meaning only for restricted regions, so intimate knowledge or regional vegetation and geology may be necessary to fully exploit knowledge of geobotany. Geobotanical knowledge can be considered first in the context of the individually plant and its response to the geological substratum. Growth of most plants is sensitive not only to the availability of the major nutrients (phosphorus [P], potassium [K], nitrogen [N]), but also to the micronutrients, those elements (including barium [B], magnesium [Mg], sulphur [S] and calcium [Ca]) that are required in very small amounts. It is well established that growth and health of plants depends upon the availability of elements present in very low concentrations and the sensitivity may be high in some plant species. In contrast, other elements are known to have toxic effects, even at very low concentrations, if present in the soil in soluble form. Heavy metals, including nickel (Ni), copper (Cu), chromium (Cr) and lead (Pb), may be present at sufficient levels to reveal their presence through stunted plant growth or by the localised absence of specific species that are especially sensitive to such elements. From such evidence, it may be possible to indirectly use the concentrations of these elements to reveal the locations of specific geologic formations or zones of mineralisation worthy of further investigation.

Hydrocarbons may significantly influence plant growth if they are present in the root zone. Hydrocarbon gases may migrate from sub-surface locations; at the surface, concentrations may be locally sufficient to influence plant growth. Hydrocarbons may be present in greater concentrations at the surface as petroleum seeps or coal seams. The presence of hydrocarbons in the soil may favour plant growth by increasing soil organic matter, but may also alter soil atmosphere and soil biology in a manner that is toxic to some plants.

Specific geobotanical indicators include the following, which of course may have varied geologic interpretation depending upon the local setting. Variations in biomass, either significantly higher or lower than expected, may indicate geobotanical anomalies. Or the colouring of vegetation may be significant. The term chlorosis refers to a general yellow discolouration of leaves due to a deficiency in the abundance of chlorophyll. Chlorosis can be caused by many of the geologic factors mentioned above, but it is not uniquely of geologic origin, so its interpretation requires knowledge of the local geologic and biologic setting.

Observation of these indicators may be facilitated by use of the vegetation indices and ratios. Manual interpretation of CIR film often provides especially good information concerning the vigour and distribution of vegetation. Of special significance in the context of geobotany is the blue shift in the chlorophyll absorption spectra. In the visible, peak reflectance is in the green region; the absorption spectra of chlorophyll decreases reflectance in both the blue and the red regions. However, in the near infrared, reflectance increases markedly (Fig. 19.7). Collins and others have observed that geochemical stress is most easily observed in the spectral region from about 0.55 to 0.75 μm (which includes portions of the green, red and infrared regions). Most notably, the position and slope of the line that portray the increase in reflectance at the edge of the visible region, although constant for healthy green plants, is especially sensitive to geochemical influences. As geochemical stress occurs, the position of this line shifts toward shorter wavelengths (i.e., toward the blue end of the spectrum; hence the term blue shift) and its slope becomes steeper (Fig. 19.8).

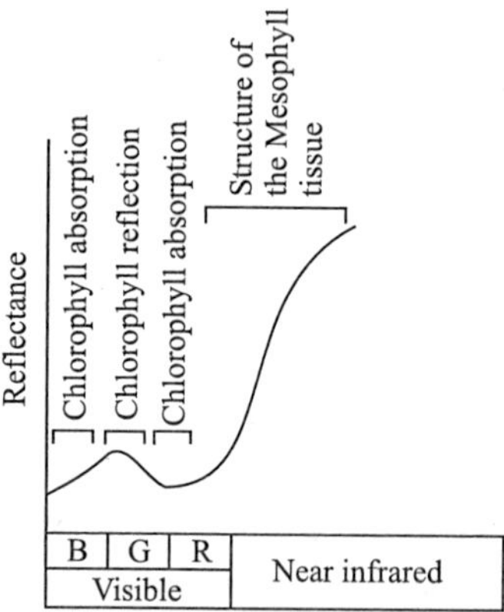

Fig. 19.7. General pattern of spectral reflection from living vegetation. Reflection in the visible spectrum is controlled by leaf pigments, chiefly chlorophyll, which reflects in the green and absorbs in the blue and the red regions. The far edge of the chlorophyll absorption region (where the reflectance rises sharply in the near infrared) is of special interest in geobotanical studies. The high reflectances in the near infrared is controlled largely by cell structure within the leaf; at even longer wavelengths, the water content is the dominant factor.

It must be emphasised that, by everyday standards, the change is very subtle (0.007 to 0.010 μm) and has been observed only in data recorded by high-resolution sensors processed to filter out background reflectance. Such data are not acquired by remote sensing instruments available for routine use, although increased spectral, spatial and radiometric resolution provided by hyperspectral remote sensing opens up opportunities to exploit these kinds of knowledge.

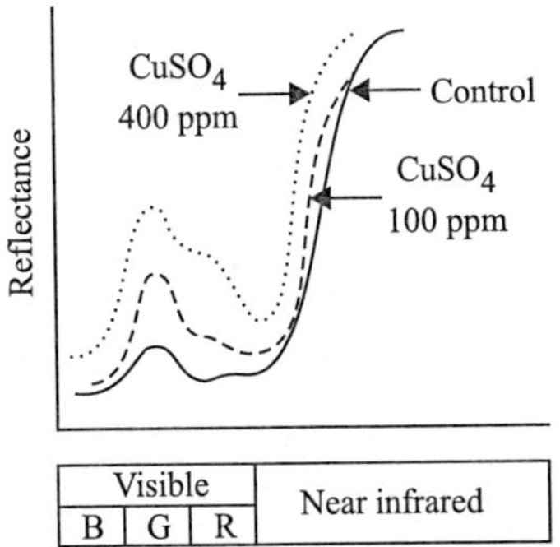

Fig. 19.8. Blue shift in the edge of the chlorophyll absorption band. As heavy mineral concentration in plant tissue increases, the edge of the absorption band shifts toward shorter wavelengths (i.e., toward the blue end of the spectrum). The solid line shows the spectrum for a control plant. The dotted and dashed lines show how the magnitude of the shift increases as concentration of the heavy mineral increases.

Nonetheless, the blue shift has been observed in all plant species studied thus far. Collins and others report that they believe this effect to be 'universal for most green plants' so it is not confined to a few species. The cause of the blue shift is not clearly understood at present. Unusual concentrations of heavy metals in the soil are absorbed by plants and apparently tend to be transported toward the actively growing portions of the plant, including the leaves (Fig. 19.6). Concentrations of such metals can cause chlorosis, often observed by more conventional methods. The relationship between heavy metals and the blue shift is clear, but work by Chang and Collins indicates that the presence of heavy metals in the plant tissues does not alter the chlorophyll itself—the metallic ions apparently do not enter the structure of the chlorophyll. The heavy metals appear to retard the development of chlorophyll, thereby influencing the abundance, but not the quality of the chlorophyll in the plant tissue.

Chang and Collins conducted laboratory and greenhouse experiments to confirm the results of spectral measurements in the field and to study the effects of different metals and their concentrations. Their experiments used oxides, sulphates, sulphides, carbonates and chlorides of copper (Cu), zinc (Zn), iron (Fe), nickel (Ni), manganese (Mn), molybdenum (Mo) and vanadium (V). Selenium (Se), Ni, Cu and Zn produced stress at concentrations as low as 100 ppm. Fe and Pb appeared to have beneficial effects on plant growth; Mo and V produced little effect at the concentrations studied. In combination, some elements counteract each other and some vary in effect as concentrations change.

Regional geobotany focuses upon the study of vegetation patterns as indicators of lithologic variations. Specific plant species may have local significance as indicator species, as they tend to avoid or favour certain lithologic units. In other instances, variations in abundance or vigour may signal the occurrence of certain lithologies (Fig. 19.9).

Direct Multispectral Observation of Rocks and Minerals

A second broad strategy for remote sensing of lithology depends upon accurate observation of spectra from areas of soil and rock exposed to observation. Colour by extension, the spectral characteristics of rocks and minerals can be distinctive identifying features in the direct examination of geologic samples.

Geologists use colour for identification of samples in the field and in the laboratory sensitive instruments are used to measure spectral properties across a range of wavelengths in the ultraviolet, visible and infrared regions. Spectral emittance and reflectance of rocks and minerals is an important property that is often closely related to their physical and chemical properties. In the laboratory, spectral characteristics can be observed in sufficient detail that they can sometimes form diagnostic tests for the presence of specific minerals. In addition, small radiometers can be taken to the field to permit *in situ* observation of rocks and minerals in non-visible portions of the spectrum. As a result, geologists have considerable experience in observing spectral properties of geologic materials and have developed an extensive body of knowledge concerning the spectral properties of rocks and minerals.

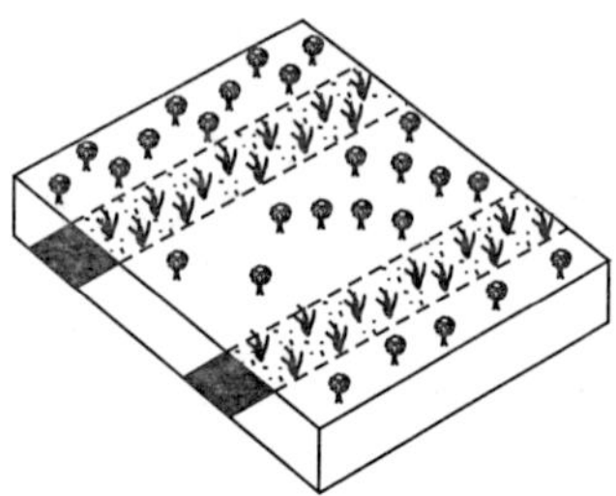

Fig. 19.9. Model for regional geobotany. This diagram depicts a situation in which the geologic difference between two stratigraphic units is not directly observable from surface colour or relief, yet differences in soil and drainage lead to noticeable differences in vegetative cover of the two units.

The application of this knowledge in the context of remote sensing can be very difficult. In the laboratory, spectra can be observed without the contributions of atmospheric attenuation, vegetation or shadowing to the observed spectra. In the laboratory setting, scientists can hold secondary properties (such as moisture content) constant from one sample to the next or can compensate for their effects. In remotely sensed data, the effects of such variables often cannot be assessed. The usual remote sensing instruments do not have the fine spectral and radiometric resolutions required to make any of the subtle distinctions this strategy requires. Furthermore, the relatively coarse spatial resolutions of many remote sensing systems means that the analyst must consider composite signatures formed by the interaction of many landscape variables rather than the pure signatures that can be observed in the laboratory. Whereas photogeology distinguishes between units without attempting to make fine lithologic distinctions, much of the research in multispectral remote sensing in geology is devoted to more precise identification of specific minerals thought both to be spectrally distinctive and to be especially valuable in mineral exploration.

Locations of zones of hydrothermal alteration may be revealed by the presence of limonite at the surface. Limonite refers broadly to minerals bearing oxides and oxyhydrites of ferric iron, including goethite and haematite; such minerals tend to exhibit broad absorption bands in the near infrared, visible and ultraviolet regions. Typically their spectra decline below 0.5 μm, producing a decrease in the ultraviolet not normally observed in other minerals (Fig. 19.10). A broad, shallow, absorption region from 0.85 μm to 0.95 μm is observed in the near infrared. The presence of limonite, either as a primary mineral or secondarily as the product of geologic weathering, may identify the location of a zone of hydrothermal alternation, thereby suggesting the possibility of mineralised zones. However, the identification of limonite is not definitive evidence of hydrothermal activity, as limonite can be present without hydrothermal alteration and hydrothermal activity may occur without the presence of limonite. Thus the observation of these spectra or any spectra, is not uniquely specific and the analyst must always consider such evidence in the context of other information and his or her knowledge of the local geologic setting. Clay minerals often decrease in reflectance beyond 1.6 μm; this behaviour is common to enough minerals and occurs over a spectral region that is broad enough that it has been used to locate zones of hydrothermal alteration by means of the surface materials rich in clay minerals. At finer spectral resolution, these clay minerals and carbonates characterised by AlOH and MgOH structures display spectra with a narrow but distinctive absorption band from 2.1 to 2.4 μm (Fig. 19.10).

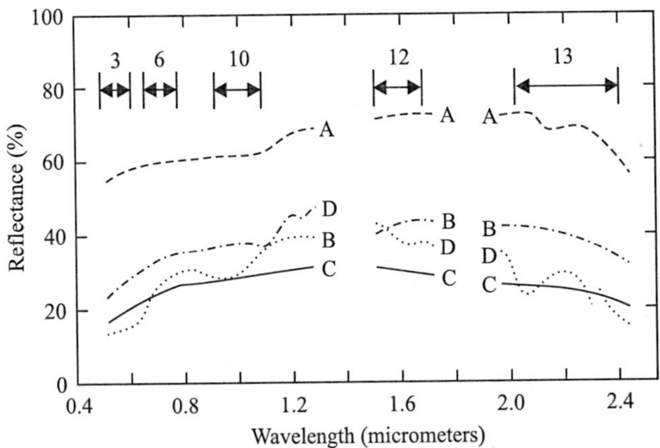

Fig. 19.10. Spectra of some natural geologic surface: A, White Joe Lott Tuff member of Mt. Belkanp volcanics; B, limonitic Joe Lott Tuff member of Mt. Belknap volcanics; C, tan soil on rhyolite; D, orange layered literite. Data were collected in the field near the surface using portable spectroradiometers. Limonitic minerals (B, C, D) show low reflectances at wavelengths below 0.5 μm, relative to non-limonitic materials (A).

Emittance in the spectral region from 8 to 12 μm (in the mid-infrared) permits the identification of some silicate minerals and the separation of silicate minerals from non-silicate minerals. Silicate minerals typically exhibit emittance minima in this region, whereas non-silicate minerals have minima at longer wavelengths.

PHOTOCLINOMETRY

Photoclinometry, loosely defined, is the derivation of topographic information from image brightness. If an irregular surface of uniform reflectance is illuminated at an angle, variations in image brightness carry information concerning the slopes of individual facets on the ground, and therefore the full image, composed of many such pixels, depicts the shape of the earth's terrain.

A diffuse reflector will have a brightness that is predictable from the angle of illumination (Fig 19.11). It is intuitively obvious that as the angle of illumination changes, so also will the brightness of the surface. The relationship between brightness and angle of illumination can be expressed more precisely using Lambert's cosine law:

$$G(x, y) = I \cos \theta (x, y) \qquad \text{... (19.1)}$$

where G is the image gray tone value; (x, y) are the image pixel row and column coordinates; I is the intensity of the solar illumination and θ is the angle of illumination, measured from the zenith.

In the context of remote sensing, the surface and the source of illumination have a fixed geometric relationship, but the scene itself is composed of many individual facets, each with specific orientation with respect to the solar beam. That is, the solar beam illuminates the earth at a fixed angle at any given instant, but topographic irregularities cause the image to be formed of many varied brightnesses. Thus, for a uniform surface type of irregular topography, variations in G portray variations in surface slope and orientation. Here, as a simplification, we will refer to such an image as the topographic image (T).

Although few surfaces on the earth meet the assumption of uniform reflectance, some extraterrestrial surfaces display only small variations in reflectivity, primarily because of the absence of vegetative cover and differences in colour caused by weathering of geologic materials. Photogeologists who have studied the moon's surface and those of the planets have formalised the methods necessary to derive topographic information from images. Photoclinometry encompasses elements of remote sensing, photogrammetry, photometry and radiometry. Although both the theory and practice of photoclinomerty must still deal with many unsolved issues, it has important applications in remote sensing.

Fig. 19.11. Brightnesses of surfaces depend upon the orientation of the surface in relation to the direction of illumination. If these surfaces all have the same surface material and behave in accordance with Lambert's cosine law, their brightnesses are related to the angles at which they are oriented.

In the context of terrestrial remote sensing, photoclinometry must address problems not present in the extraterrestrial case. The varied surface materials that form the earth's surface, such as open water, living vegetation, bare soil and the like contribute to the brightnesses on the image, confusing the purely topographic interpretation of image brightness. (Even though the moon's surface is not completely uniform, its spectral variations are small compared to those of the earth.) Therefore, the equation given above must be modified to include different reflectances (R) of varied surfaces:

$$G = RT \qquad \text{... (19.2)}$$

where R represents the reflectivities of different surface materials that contribute to different brightnesses on the image. Thus brightnesses caused by different reflectivities are mixed together with brightness caused by topography, so it is necessary to separate the two if topographic information is to be derived from the image.

Separation of these two kinds of information is accomplished by means of band ratios and one of fundamental significance in many aspects of remote sensing. In a ratio of two bands, the gray values in the separate bands for a specific pixel are paired, then divided. That is, we take brightness values for the same pixel and divide, using the quotient as a new value for that pixel. The set of all ratio values for a specific image and pair or bands forms a ratio image. (Because the numeric value of the ratio is often a decimal fraction, the quotient is usually multiplied by a constant to scale the values over an appropriate rage of integers).

At each pixel, information pertaining to topography (i.e., cos θ, designated here as T), reflectance of the surface material (R) and diffuse light (D) are combined in the observed gray value. The diffuse light produces another element in the relationship.

$$G = RT + D \qquad \text{... (19.3)}$$

Reflectance and the effects of diffuse light differ greatly from one band to the next, so the value of G at any given pixel varies from one band to the next. For diffuse light, the difference due to separate spectral bands can be approximated by a proportional relationship such that diffuse light in band 2 is estimated by the value in band 1 multiplied by a constant value c:

$$D_{\text{band 2}} = cD_{\text{band 1}} \qquad \text{... (19.4)}$$

Although this relationship is not exactly correct, it can serve as a satisfactory approximation. Note that we can make no such approximation concerning the differences in reflectance between the two bands, so the R components of the relationship are not influenced by this approximation. Thus a ratio between two separate bands can be expressed as:

$$\frac{G_{\text{band 1}}}{G_{\text{band 2}}} = \frac{R_1(T_1 + D_1)}{R_2(T_2 + D_2)} \qquad \text{... (19.5)}$$

Because of the relationship between I_1 and I_2 and between D_1 and D_2, the relationship now becomes

$$\frac{G_{\text{band 1}}}{G_{\text{band 2}}} = \frac{R_1 c(T_2 + D_2)}{R_2(T_2 + D_2)} \qquad \text{... (19.6)}$$

The terms for T and D in the numerator and denominator are now equivalent and cancel out, leaving the reflectance terms as the only components of the ratio image:

$$\frac{G_{\text{band 1}}}{G_{\text{band 2}}} = c\frac{R_1}{R_2} \qquad \text{... (19.7)}$$

This ratio image (R_1/R_2) has several useful properties. First, the relationship holds both for shadowed pixels and for directly illuminated pixels. Therefore, a ratio image shows pure reflectance information without effects of topography. This result permits geologists to examine spectral properties of surfaces without the confusing effects of mixed brightnesses of topography and material reflectances. In the raw image, a difference in pixel brightness can be caused by a difference in slope, by shadowing or by differences in the colour of the surface material. In a ratio image, the geologist knows that differences in brightness are caused by differences in reflectance only.

This result is illustrated by the example given in Fig. 19.12. In the upper diagram the brightness of the scene is caused by combined differences in topography and surface reflectance and the analyst cannot resolve differences between the two effects. In the lower diagram the ratios clearly separate the separate categories of surface reflectance, even though each is present on two different topographic surfaces.

In the context of photoclinometry, ratio images have a special application. An unsupervised classification of the several ratio images derived from a multispectral image permits identification of regions on the earth's surface that have uniform spectral behaviour. Remember that the ratio images convey only spectral, not topographic, information; note also that the classification is performed on the ratio images, not on the original digital values. The classification of the ratio values produces classes with uniform spectral properties, regardless of slope. If the original pixel values for each class are examined, it can be determined that some are light (the directly illuminated pixels), others are dark (the shadowed pixels). Therefore all pixels in the scene, regardless of their spectral class, can be designated as either 'shadow' or 'directly illuminated'.

Because brightnesses of shadowed pixels are determined only by indirect illumination, the values in the shadowed regions provide estimates of the diffuse 'ight present throughout the image. So these values can be subtracted from the entire image to remove the atmospheric influences that remain after pre-processing. Then each pixel is assigned a value determined by the mean value of its spectral cluster (as found by using the ratios, as mentioned above) to produce estimates of the spectral brightness of the terrain. This image is formed from a mosaic of patches, each representing a distinctive class of ground cover. It is not necessary to 'identify' such classes as 'forest, 'water,' 'pasture,' and the like—it is sufficient simply to know that they are spectrally homogeneous, distinctive groups of pixels. This image can be called the reflectance image (Rf). Rf differs from R only in that the estimated reflectance (R) at each pixel has been replaced by the mean value for its spectral class. Because it is formed by averaging together reflectances from many pixels at varied topographic positions, the Rf image approximates the reflectance (R) of each class as if it were observed on level topography, thereby defining an estimate of R that does not include the contribution of T.

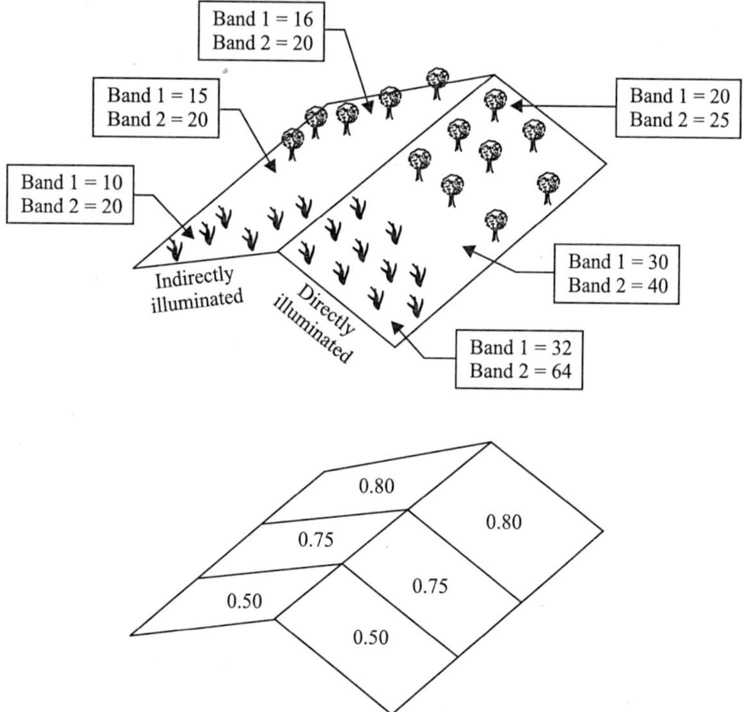

Fig. 19.12. Example illustrating use of band ratios. In this contrived example a topographic surface illuminated from the right side of the illustration consists of three contrasting surface materials, each partially illuminated by the solar beam and on the reverse slope illuminated indirectly by diffuse light. The raw digital values (top) convey the mixed information of surface reflectance and shadowing. Because of shadowing, separate surface materials cannot be clearly separated into their distinctive classes. In the bottom illustration, ratios of the two bands isolate the effects of the different surface materials (removing the topographic effects) to permit recognition of distinct spectral classes. Based on Taranick.

The objective of photoclinometry is the isolation of the purely topographic image. Because the steps described in the preceding paragraphs produce a pure reflectance image, it is possible to separate the original image value into its two components, thereby deriving the topographic content. The final topographic image (Tp) is found simply by dividing values in the dehazed image by the corresponding values in the reflectance image (Rf). This step can be visualised as:

$$Tp = \frac{TR}{Rf} \qquad \text{... (19.8)}$$

Because Rf estimates R, essentially the same term is present in both numerator and denominator and the reflectance component cancels out, leaving only the topographic information. In this final estimate of the topographic image, brightnesses are due solely to differences in topographic slope and it provides clear information concerning the shape of the earth's surface.

BAND RATIOS

Band ratios have further significance in geologic remote sensing. The previous sections illustrate that they convey purely spectral information, so they remove effects of shadowing, which otherwise are mixed with the spectral information necessary to make lithologic discriminations. Furthermore, ratios have other advantages (at least under certain circumstances) because they may minimise differences in brightness between lithologic units (i.e., ratios tend to emphasise colour information, deemphasising absolute brightness) and may facilitate comparisons of data collected on different dates, which will differ in solar angle.

Goetz and others examined rock reflectances in Utah using a portable spectrometer capable of collecting high-resolution spectra for a variety of natural surfaces. They found several ratios to be useful in discriminating between lithologic units. Because their bands are based upon high-resolution data that do not match to familiar sub-divisions of the spectrum, their ratios must be defined using their own designations, given in Fig. 19.10. For example, a ratio between their bands 6 and 10 (roughly, red/near infrared) provided a good distinction between bare rock and vegetation-covered areas. Their $^{12}/_{3}$ ratio (mid-IR/blue) was successful in distinguishing between limonitic and non-limonitic rocks. The spectrum for limonite decrease-sharply in channel 3 (blue) because of the presence of ferric iron, which absorbs strongly in this region, where as non-limonitic rocks tend to be brighter in this region. Thus the $^{12}/_{3}$ ratio tends to accentuate differences between limonitic and non-limonitic rocks. Hydrothermally altered rocks containing clay minerals display absorption bands in channel 13, so the $^{12}/_{3}$ ratio tended to identify hydrothermally altered regions.

Full description of the selection of spectral channels and their interpretation of the image can be presented as follows:

1. The red band in the image is determined by the ratio (0.63–0.69 μm): (0.52–0.60 μm); greater intensity of red indicates high levels of ferric oxide.
2. The green band is a function of the ratio (1.55–1.75 μm): (2.08–2.35 μm); the intensity of green indicates areas where there is high clay content in the surface soil.
3. The blue band is controlled by the value of the ratio (8.20–8.54 μm): (8.60–8.95 μm); the intensity of blue indicates levels of silica at the soil surface.

Thus a yellow colour (both red and green) indicates the presence of both ferric oxide and clay, an indication of hydrothermal alteration and possible presence of a zone of mineralisation. The blue region near the center of the image delineates a region of silification (high silica); it is surrounded by a zone of hydrothermal alternation, marked by yellow regions surrounding the blue center.

This example illustrates the power of using ratios between carefully selected spectral regions as aids for geological investigation. However, it is important to identify aspects of this study that differ from those that might be feasible on a routine basis. Although these data have 30 m resolution, comparable to those of satellite sensors, they were collected at aircraft altitudes, so they are much less affected by atmospheric effects that would be the case for comparable satellite data. Also, this region has a sparsely vegetated even topography, so it favours isolation of geological information that otherwise can be mixed with vegetation, shadowing and topographic effects.

The use of ratio images carries certain risks. In a geologic contest, it is important that data be free of atmospheric effects or that such effects be removed by pre-processing. The significance of the atmosphere can be appreciated by re-examining the earlier discussion, where the diffuse light values in the two band values were estimated to have predictable values that would cancel each other out. If severe atmospheric effects are present, they will differ from one band to the other and the value of the ratio will no longer portray only spectral properties of the ground surface but will have values greatly altered by the varied atmospheric contributions to the separate bands.

SOIL AND LANDSCAPE MAPPING

Soil scientists study the mantle of soil at the earth's surface in an effort to understand soil formation and to map patterns of soil variation. Soil is a complex mixture of inorganic material weathered from the geologic substratum and mixed with decayed organic matter from tissues of plants and animals. Typically, a 'soil' consists of three layers (known as soil horizons) of varying thickness and composition (Fig. 19.13). Nearest the surface is the A horizon, usually dark in colour and rich in decayed organic matter. The A horizon is sometimes known popularly as topsoil—the kind of soil one would like to have for a lawn or garden. In this layer-plant roots are abundant, as are micro-organisms, insects and other animals. Below the A horizon is the second layer, the B horizon, usually lighter in colour and more compact, where plant roots and biologic activity are less abundant. Sometimes the B horizon is known as the sub-soil—the kind of hard infertile soil one would prefer not to have at the surface of a lawn or garden. At even greater depth is the C horizon, the deepest pedologic horizon, which consists of weathered geologic material, decayed or fractured into material that is softer and looser than the unweathered, geologic strata below. This is the material that usually forms the raw material for the A and B horizons. Finally, below the C horizon is the R horizon, consisting of unaltered bedrock.

The exact nature of the horizons at a given place is determined by the interaction between local climatic, topographic, geologic and biologic elements as they act over time. Because varied combination of climate, vegetation and topography produce different soils from similar geologic materials, soil science is distinct from, although closely related to, geology and geomorphology.

The landscape is covered by a mosaic of patches of different kinds of soil, each distinct from its neighbours with respect to character and thickness (Fig. 19.14). Soil surveyors outline on maps those areas covered by specific kinds of soil as a means of soil or when the pattern is very complex, sometimes two or three kinds of soil that occur in an intimate pattern. Soil maps portray distribution of pedologic units, which together with other maps and data convey valuable information concerning topography, geology, geomorphology, hydrology and other landscape elements. In the hands of a knowledgeable reader, they convey a comprehensive picture of the physical landscape. As a result, they can be considered to be among the most practical of all forms of landscape maps and are used by farmers, planners and others who must judge the best locations for specific agricultural activities, for community facilities or for construction of buildings and highways.

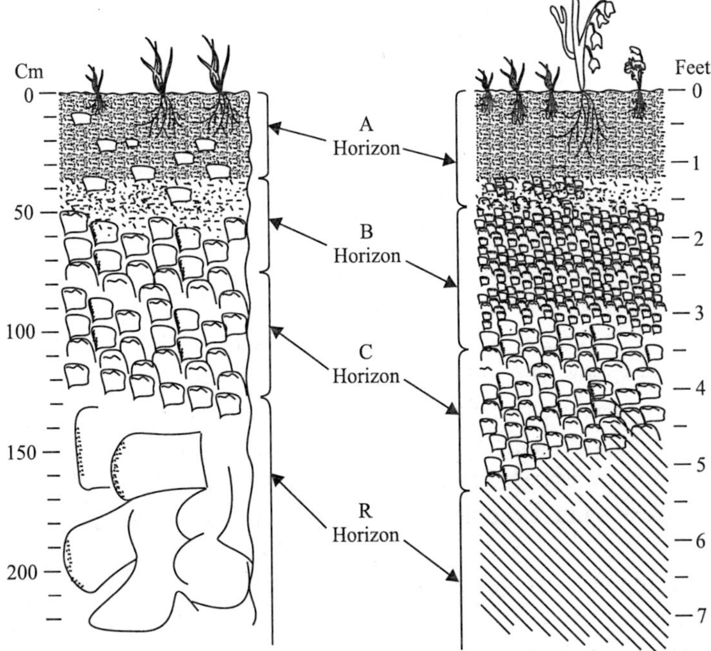

Fig. 19.13. Sketches of two contrasting soil profiles.

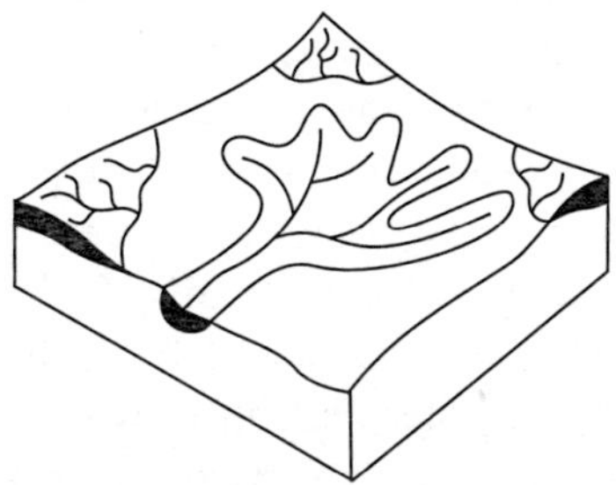

Fig. 19.14. The soil landscape.

Soil mapping is conducted routinely by national soil surveys (or their equivalents) in most countries and by their regional counterparts at lower administrative levels. Details of mapping technique vary from one organisation to another, but the main outlines of the procedure are common to most soil survey organisations. A soil map is formed by sub-dividing the landscape into a mosaic of discrete parcels. Each parcel is assigned to a class of soil—a mapping unit—that is characterised by specific kinds of soil horizons. Each mapping unit is represented on the map by a specific symbol—usually a colour or an alphanumeric designation. In theory, mapping units are homogeneous with respect to pedologic properties, although experienced users of soil maps acknowledge the existence of internal variation as well as the presence of foreign inclusions. Mapping units are usually defined with links to a broader system of soil classification defined by the soil survey organisation, so that mapping units are consistently defined across, for example, county and state borders. For each region, a mapping unit can be evaluated with respect to the kind of agriculture that is important locally, so the map can serve as a guide to select the best uses for each soil. The following paragraphs outline an example of the soil survey process, although details may vary from one organisation to the next.

Compilation of a Soil Map

The first step in the actual preparation of the draft map is the mapping process. The term mapping in this context means specifically to designate the delineation of landscape units on an aerial photograph or map base, rather than in the broader sense that refers to the entire set of activities necessary to generate the map. In the mapping step, the soil scientist examines aerial photographs, often using a stereoscope, to define the major boundaries between classes of soil. The soil scientist has already learned much about the region's soils through field observations, so he or she has a knowledge of the kinds of soils present and their approximate locations. The soil scientist can use this field knowledge in interpretation of the photograph, using breaks in slope, boundaries between vegetation classes and drainage pattern to define boundaries between soil mapping units. Seldom if ever can be soil classes actually be identified from the photographs—identification must be based upon field observations—but in the mapping step, the scientist can sub-divide the landscape into a mosaic of soil parcels, which are then each treated as independent units in the later steps.

Completion of the mapping step requires considerable field experience within the region to be mapped, as the surveyor must acquire knowledge of the numbers and kinds of soils present within a region, their properties and occurrence and their uses and limitations. As a result, completion of this step requires a much longer time than that actually devoted to marking the aerial photographs if we include the time required to learn about the local landscape. Morphological descriptions of each mapping unit are made in the field and mapping units are sampled for later analysis.

The second step is characterisation. Samples are collected from each prospective mapping unit, then subjected to laboratory analysis for physical, chemical and mineralogical properties.

These measurements form the basis for classification, the third step. In the United States, classification is the implementation of the classification criteria specified by Soil Taxonomy, the official classification system of the Soil Conservation Service, US Department of Agriculture. In other countries, classification is conducted by applying the classification criteria established by each national soil survey organisation. Correlation, possibly the most difficult step, matches mapping units within the mapped region to those in adjacent regions and to those in ecologically analogous areas. Whereas the other steps in a soil survey may be conducted largely on a local basis, correlation requires the participation of experienced scientists from adjacent regions and even those from national or international levels in the organisation, to provide the broader experience and perspective often required for successful correlation.

The final step is interpretation, in which each mapping unit is evaluated with respect to prospective agricultural and engineering uses. The interpretation step provides the user of the map with information concerning the likely suitability of each mapping unit to the land uses most common within the region.

Within this rather broad framework there are, of course, many variations in details of technique and in overall philosophy and strategy. The result is a map that shows the pattern of soils within a region and a report that describes the kind of soil that is encountered within each mapping unit. Each mapping unit is evaluated with regard to the kinds of uses that might be possible for the region, so that the map serves as a guide to wise use of soil resources.

Interpretation by Proxy

Remote sensing can be applied to soil studies using either of two approaches: (i) interpretation by proxy or (ii) direct sensing of soil properties. A proxy or surrogate, is a substitute for something else. Proxies are important in soil studies because remotely sensed images cannot show the feature that we wish to study: the soil profile, which is mainly below the ground surface, which is itself often hidden from view by vegetation. As a result, identification of soil units on aerial imagery often must be accomplished indirectly, by means of proxies such as topography, vegetation and drainage patterns that serve as clues for the interpretation of soils (Fig. 19.15).

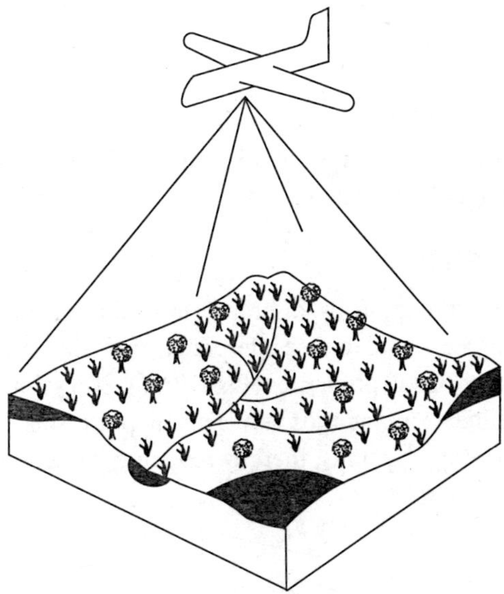

Fig. 19.15. Interpretation by proxy. The analyst uses characteristics such as drainage, topography and vegetative cover to estimate the outlines of the major soil units, while also applying a local knowledge of the geographic setting.

This is the traditional approach used in the mapping step described above, developed over the years for the derivation of soil information from aerial photographs. In essence, the focus is to use the remote sensing image as a base on which to plot the boundaries between mapping units, using evidence on the image to guide correct placement of the boundaries. However, the actual identification of the mapping unit—information concerning the soil profile—is derived from other sources, mainly direct observations in the field.

Although interpretation by proxy is clearly a subjective procedure, it requires systematic and disciplined examination of images. Interpreters perceive image tone and texture; recognise terrain features by their sizes, shapes and locations and employ stereoscopic interpretation to assess slope and relative elevations. These visible features permit the interpreter to estimate the soil pattern, which is not itself visible on the image. Whenever interpretation by proxy is applied, it is necessary to establish the link between the proxy and the mapped distribution using non-image information. Therefore, the soil scientist must make extensive field observations to establish the links between the patterns, visible on the images and the soil profiles hidden beneath the surface. Once a link is established, it can be applied with great effectiveness to speed the otherwise very slow pace of soil survey. However, the link that connects the image pattern to the mapped pattern is valid only for a restricted geographic region (typically 1000 km^2 or so in size), so the interpreters must always check and refine their interpretation procedures based upon field observations.

The interpreter works by drawing lines that separate different mapping units, usually using clues such as breaks in slope, topographic position, vegetation patterns, image tone (if the soil surface is directly visible), drainage lines and other features, to identify positions of boundaries. In the United States, current maps are published on planimetrically correct orthophotomaps. Therefore, such maps can be used as the basis for measurements of distance or area. (Earlier maps had been published on uncorrected photographic images that often exhibited severe positional errors.) Other procedures some-times call for the boundary information to be transferred to a map base, then re-compiled as a separate map.

Sometimes interpreters prepare separate overlays of drainage, slope, vegetation, land use, surficial materials and other topics, then superimpose the overlays so that the coincidence of the several patterns reveals the outlines of the soil pattern. This is the method of interpretive procedures or factor overlays, used by some agencies as a standard procedure.

Direct Sensing of Soil Properties

The alternative strategy for interpretation by inference is to directly sense soil properties. In theory, direct observation of the soil surface would release interpreters from dependence upon proxies and possibly permit quantitative measurements of soil properties (Fig. 19.16). Soil scientists could use remotely sensed images and data not only to delineate boundaries between mapping units, but also to identify some of the properties that characterise the mapping units, thereby reducing the requirement for detailed fieldwork.

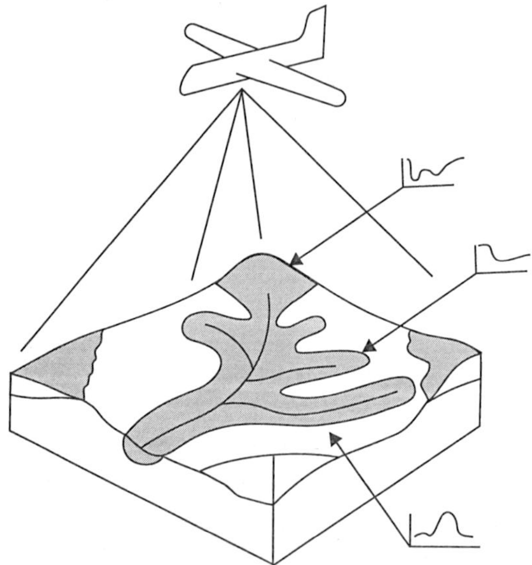

Fig. 19.16. Direct multispectral sensing of soils. The sensor directly observes the soil surface or a partially vegetated soil surface, to derive information concerning soil properties and soil patterns. Soil properties are studied by analysis of their spectral characteristics.

Such a capability could be especially important in remote regions where mapping is very difficult or in the preparation of reconnaissance surveys that might guide the course of more detailed soil surveys. Direct sensing of highly variable properties, such as moisture content at the soil surface, might be especially valuable in contexts unrelated to the mapping effort, such as daily or weekly monitoring of change in soil moisture for agricultural or hydrological purposes. Such data could contribute to more accurate assessment of soil conditions in times of drought or in forecasting floods.

For most practical purposes, spectral characteristics of unvegetated soils are determined by soil characteristics at or very close to the soil surface. In the visible and near infrared, radiation penetrates only 1 to 2 mm in fine-textured materials and 1 to 2 cm in coarse sands. Penetration of longer wavelengths depends upon frequency of the energy and moisture content of the soil. Passive microwave sensors may be sensitive to moisture conditions at depths of 10 cm or more. Active microwave energy (at long wavelengths) is thought to penetrate much deeper (approximately 1 m) under favorable conditions, but few believe that it would be feasible to routinely use such radiation to interpret sub-surface soil properties. Since characteristic of soils are determined at or very near the soil surface, this limits the application of direct sensing of soil properties, as many key differences between soils may reside in sub-surface horizons beneath spectrally similar surface materials and therefore beyond the reach of direct sensing of soil properties. However, these sub-surface differences may be susceptible to indirect interpretation using proxies as described above.

Table 19.1 lists some of the soil properties that have been studied using their spectral properties. It should be noted that this problem is very complex and that in each specific instance it is necessary to consider all of the issues discussed in the following paragraphs. As a very broad generalisation, soils observed in the field display spectra with peak reflectances in or near the red portion of the spectrum and it is in this region that the greatest spectral contrasts are observed. Candit studied spectral properties of 160 soil samples for the United States and found that the spectral properties could be characterised by measurements at only five wavelengths: 0.45 μm (in the blue), 0.54 μm (in the green), 0.67 μm (in the red), 0.74 μm (near infrared) and 0.86 μm (also near infrared).

Table 19.1. Soil properties subject to direct remote sensing.

Property
Mineral content
Texture
Soil moisture
Organic matter
Iron oxide
Albedo
Temperature
Soil structure

Some of the diverse research concerning spectral properties of soils can be summarised by noting the nature of the materials studied and the contributions of the studies to the effort to measure soil properties by remote sensing.

1. Artificial materials: Zwereman and Andrews studied ceramic powders to determine the influence of particle size upon reflectivity. By using identical materials ground to different sizes, the effect of particle diameter upon reflectance could be isolated. Fine-textured particles tend to have

brighter surfaces than coarse particles due to the smoother surface, with less shadowing by particles at the surface. In nature, fine-textured soils are often associated with high moisture or high organic matter content, both of which cause lower reflectivities and therefore counteract the effect of small size alone.

2. Artificial mixtures of natural soil components: Individual components of natural soils can be separated, then reconstituted in desired proportions to create the desired variation in the property to be studied. Gerberman and Neher used this strategy to examine the spectral consequences of varying the proportions of sand and clay, holding other factors constant.
3. Laboratory analyses of natural soils: Bowers and Hanks examined soil samples under laboratory conditions, then used their laboratory spectra to assist in the classification of the same soils observed in the field using an airborne multispectral scanner. Stoner observed differences between spectra of *in situ* soils and those observed in the laboratory.
4. *In situ* soil: Cipra and others examined unvegetated soil surfaces in the field and then compared their results with corresponding spectra acquired by the Landsat MSS. Examination of several soil properties revealed that colour was the property most closely related to spectral variations in the MSS data.

These results emphasise the dichotomy between component and composite signatures. Research devoted to (1) and (2) above attempts to identify component signatures by isolation effects of specific soil properties upon observed spectra.

Thus Mathews specifically excluded variations in organic matter content in a portion of his study. Bowers and Hanks isolated the influence of soil moisture. Such research addresses the question, 'Is it possible to measure the magnitude of soil property X, given spectral information from several soils?

In contrast, naturally occurring soils possess composite signatures, formed by contributions from numerous individual properties interacting in a complex fashion. Thus studies of naturally occurring soils ([3] and [4] above) define, *de facto* signatures for mapping units, without attempting precise measurement of the contributions of specific properties. Such research addresses the question 'Is it possible to distinguish between soil A and soil B?.' A question of this kind is a return to the same kinds of questions that mapping by proxies addresses because it leads to the establishment, then recognition, of classes of soil rather than to measurement of the levels of specific soil properties.

Further obstacles to the application of direct sensing of soil properties can be enumerated briefly. Masking of the soil by vegetation is an obvious problem and one that has unexpected complications. First, vegetative cover is not necessarily opaque in the non-visible portion of the spectrum, so the soil can contribute to the spectral properties in ways that may not be immediately obvious. Second, reflection from partically vegetated surface can be very complex. Siegal and Goetz found that the presence of vegetative cover has the greatest influence upon signatures of dark soil surfaces, which 'may be altered beyond recognition with only ten per cent green vegetative cover'. Signatures of soil surface can vary greatly as angles of illumination and observation vary and in the case of partially vegetated surfaces angular effects can be especially severe. Furthermore, in agricultural landscapes, the effects of cultural practices can be significant. Stoner and Horvath report that 'tillage practices appear to alter greatly the spectral radiance of surface soil. When areas of identical or similar surface practices can be isolated and classified separately, a useful map of certain soil properties can be produced'.

INTEGRATED TERRAIN UNITS

Another approach, definition of integrated terrain units, directly contrasts with the methods described thus far. Direct multispectral recognition of rocks or soils depends on isolation of spectral information pertaining to a general class of data, then defining specific categories within the broader class. For example, the analyst must separate soil spectra from those of other features, then define spectra for various classes of soil, recognising that a single class of soil may have different spectra due to differences in moisture, slope or other factors. This process can present formidable difficulties because of the complexity of the natural landscape and the requirement for fine spatial and spectral resolution. In contrast, the method of integrated terrain units recognises the complex spectral mixtures that are formed as spectral response from vegetation, soil, rock, shadow, moisture and drainage are combined, especially at the coarse resolution of satellite sensors. Thus the method does not attempt, for example, to identify the specific spectral response for a class of soil, but rather to identify a response for the whole ecological setting of which the soil forms one of several elements.

The method of integrated terrain units is based upon the concept that the varied and complex assemblages of soil, terrain, vegetation and so on form distinctive spectral responses that can be recognised and mapped. This general approach has long been applied, under many different names, to the interpretation of resource information from aerial photographs and other forms of imagery. The best known and oldest, of these methods is known as land system mapping.

Land system mapping sub-divides a region into sets of recurring landscape elements based on comprehensive examination of distributions of soils, vegetation, hydrology and physiography. The formalisation of land system mapping procedures dates from the period just after World War II, although some of the fundamental concepts had been defined earlier. Today a family of similar systems are in use; all are based on similar principles and methods, although the terminology and details vary considerably. One of oldest, best known and most formally defined systems is that developed by the Australian CISRO Division of Land Research and Regional Survey; variations have been developed and applied throughout the world.

The method is based on a hierarchical sub-division of landscapes. Land systems are recurring contiguous associations of landforms, soils and vegetation, composed of component land units. The basic units of the system (which are assigned varied definitions and names in alternative versions of this basic strategy) are areas of uniform lithology with relatively uniform soil and drainage. A characteristic feature of all versions of the land system method is a hierarchical spatial organisation, so that sub-categories are nested within the broader categories defined at higher levels. Designation of separate levels within the hierarchy differs among alternative versions. For example, Thomas defines the following sequence: Site (the smallest units), facet, unit landform, landform complex, landform system and landform region. Wendt define a system using landtypes (the smallest regions), landtype associations, landtype phases, sub-sections, sections and provinces. Although many version imply that both land systems and their component elements recur in widely separated geographic regions (although under analogous ecological circumstances), closer examination of the method reveals that land systems are most effective when defined to be local units.

Implicit, if not explicit, in most applications is the use of aerial photography as a primary tool for land system mapping, together with direct observation in the field. Aerial photography provides the broad overview and the map-like perspective favouring convenient definition and delineation of land systems and portrays the complex spatial patterns of topography, vegetation and drainage in an integrated form that is compatible with the assumptions, methods and objectives of this approach to terrain analysis. 'There would be no point in defining any terrain class if its chances of being recognised from the air photographs and background information were small'.

An assumption of the procedure is that easily identified landscape features (e.g., vegetation and physiography) form surrogates for more subtle soil features not as easily defined from analysis of aerial photographs. Although the procedure has been applied at a rage of scales from 1:1,000,000 to 1:25,000, most applications are probably at fairly broad scales, for reconnaissance surveys or mapping of rather simple landscape divisions under circumstances where the ultimate use will be rather extensive.

The method and its many variations have been criticised for their subjectivity and the variability of the results obtained by different analysts. Compared to most large-scale soil surveys, land system mapping presents a rather rough sub-division of the landscape, as the mapping units display much greater internal variability and are not as carefully defined and correlated as one would expect in more intensive surveys. As a result, the procedure may be best suited for application in reconnaissance mapping, where broad-scale, low-resolution mapping is required as the basis for planning more detailed surveys.

The method of integrated terrain units has also been applied to analysis of digital data. At the coarse resolution of satellite sensors, individual spectral responses from many landscape components are combined to form composite responses. In this context, the usual methods of image classification for mapping of individual classes of soil, vegetation or geology may be extraordinarily difficult. Therefore, many analysts have applied the integrated terrain unit strategy to digital classification in an effort to define image classes in a more realistic manner. In the ideal, we might prefer to define pure categories that each show only a single thematic class. But, given the complexity of the natural landscape, composite categories are often well suited to representation of the gradations and mixtures that characterise many environments.

RADAR IMAGERY FOR EXPLORATION

Natural seepage of petroleum from the ocean floor causes a thin film of petroleum floating on the ocean surface (a 'slick'), that creates a locally smooth water surface, that in turn induces conditions that promote spicular reflection over that region of the ocean. Oil slacks occur when molecules of oil reach the sea surface to form a thin layer of petroleum that dampens the ocean-surface capillary waves. SAR technology is sensitive to differences in surface roughness, so it can easily discriminate between the smoother oils slick and the surrounding rough water. Thus oil slacks are regions of little to no backscatter, characterised by distinct areas of darkness on the radar image. Therefore, the dark returns assist in identifying regions where such slacks might originate. Because SAR has the ability to observe such regions day and night and over a wide range of meteorological conditions, SAR data assist in identifying regions where such slacks form on a regular basic. Critical exploration maps can be produced by using a GIS system to overlay other information such as coastline, bathymetry, gravimetric data, shipping lanes and existing oil rigs on the RADARSAT image. These maps allow decision makers to reduce magnetic field exploration risk and increase the cost-effectiveness of off-shore drilling efforts.

20

Hydrospheric Sciences

INTRODUCTION

Open water covers about 74 per cent of our planet's surface. Oceans account for about 95 per cent of the surface area of open water, but freshwater lakes and rivers (about 0.4 per cent) have a significance for mankind that exceeds their small areal extent (Table 20.1). In addition, soil and rock near the earth's surface hold significant quantities of freshwater (but only about 0.1 per cent by volume of the earth's total water), as do the ice and snow of polar regions. Moisture in the form of 'permanent' ice (about 5 per cent of the earth' surface) is largely beyond the reach of mankind, although the seasonal accumulation and melt of snowpack in temperat mountains is an important source of moisture for some agricultural regions in otherwise arid zones. Hydrologists and meteorologists monitor water as it occurs in all these forms, as it changes from liquid to vapour, condenses to rain and snow and moves on and under the earth's surface (Fig. 20.1). In addition, studies of sea ice, movement of pollutants and ocean currents are among the many other important subjects to attract the attention of the many scientists who study hydrology, oceanography and related subjects.

Most traditional means of monitoring the earth's water depend largely upon measurements made at specific points or collections of samples from discrete locations. Oceans, lakes and rivers can be studied by samples collected at the surface or by special devices that fill a collection bottle with water from a specified depth. Ground water can be studied by collection of samples from wells or boreholes. Samples can be subjected to chemical and physical tests to measure levels of pollutants, to detect bacteria and other biological phenomena and to examine oxygen content, sediment content and many other qualities of the water. Such measurements or samples, of course, provide information about discrete points within the water body, whereas the analyst usually is interested in examining entire water bodies or regions within water bodies. Although measurements can be collected at several locations to build up a record of place-to-place variation within the water body, such efforts are at best a piecemeal approach to studying the complex and dynamic characteristics of water bodies that are of interest to hydrologists.

Therefore, remote sensing can provide a valuable perspective concerning broad-scale, dynamic patterns that can be difficult to examine in detail using point measurements only. Careful co-ordination and placement of surface samples permits establishment of the relationship between the sample data and those collected by the remote sensor. Remotely sensed data can be especially valuable in studying phenomena over large areas. Satellite sensors provide the opportunity for regular observation of even very remote regions. Although remotely sensed images seldom replace the usual sources of information concerning water resources, they can provide valuable supplements to field data by revealing broad-scale patterns not recognisable at the surface, recording changes over time and providing data for inaccessible regions.

Table 20.1. Water on earth.

	Percentage	
	By surface area[a]	*By volume*[b]
Oceans	94.90	97.1
Rivers and lakes	0.40	0.02
Ground water	–	0.60
Permanent ice cap	4.69	2.20
Earth's atmosphere	–	0.001

[a] Percentage by area of earth's total water surface.
[b] Percentage by volume of earth's water.

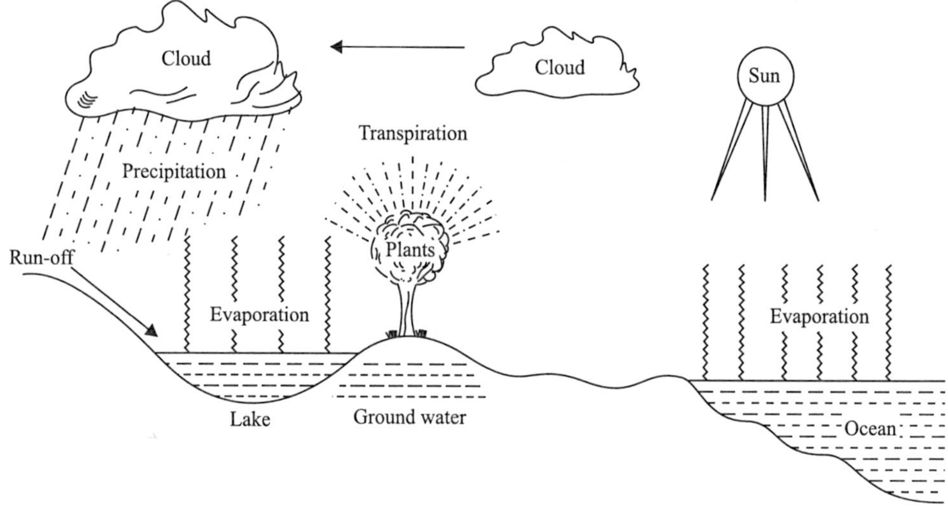

Fig. 20.1. The hydrologic cycle.

SPECTRAL CHARACTERISTICS OF WATER BODIES

Spectral qualities of water bodies are determined by the interaction of several factors, including the radiation incident to the water surface, optical properties of the water, roughness of the surface, angles of observation and illumination and in some instances, reflection of light from the bottom (Fig. 20.2). As incident light strikes the water surface, some is reflected back to the atmosphere; this reflected radiation carries little information about the water itself, although it may convey information about the roughness of the surface and therefore about wind and waves. Instead, the spectral properties (i.e., 'colour') of a water body are determined largely by energy that is scattered and reflected within the water body itself, known as volume reflection because it occurs over a range of depths rather than at the surface. Some of this energy is directed back toward the surface, where it again passes through the atmosphere and then to the sensor (Fig. 20.2). This light, sometimes known as underlight, is the primary source of the colour of a water body.

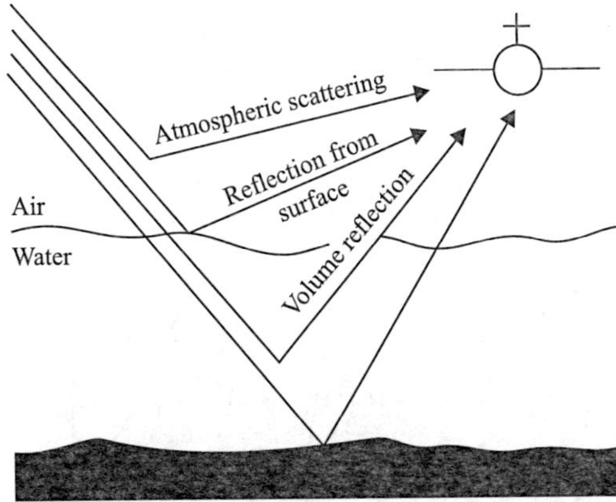

Fig. 20.2. Diagram illustrating major factors influencing spectral characteristics of a water body.

The light that enters a water body is influenced by: (i) absorption and scattering by pure water; (ii) scattering, reflection and diffraction by particles that may be suspended in the water. For pure water, some of the same principles described previously for atmospheric scattering apply. Scattering by particles that are small relative to wavelength (Rayleigh scattering) causes shorter wavelengths to be scattered the most. Thus, for deep water bodies, we expect (in the absence of impurities) water to be blue or blue green in colour (Fig. 20.3). Maximum transmittance of light by clear water occurs in the range 0.44 μm to 0.54 μm, with peak transmittance at 0.48 μm. Because the colour of water is determined by volume scattering, rather than by surface reflection, spectral properties of water bodies (unlike those of land features) are determined by transmittance rather than by surface characteristics alone. In the blue region, light penetration is not at its optimum, but at slightly longer wavelengths, in the blue-green region, penetration is greater. At these wavelengths, the opportunity for recording features on the bottom of the water body are greatest. At longer wavelengths, in the red region, absorption of sunlight is much greater and only shallow features can be detected. Finally, in the near infrared region, absorption is so great that only land-water distinctions can be made.

As impurities are added to a water body, its spectral properties change. Sediments are introduced both from natural sources and by mankind's activities. Such sediments consist of fine-textured silts and clays eroded from stream banks or by water running off disturbed land, that are fine enough to be carried in suspension by moving water. As moving water erodes the land surface or the shoreline, it carries small particles as suspended sediment; faster flowing streams can erode and carry more and larger particles than can slower moving streams. As a stream enters a lake or ocean, the decrease in velocity causes coarser materials to be deposited. But even slow-moving rivers and currents can carry large amounts of fine-textured sediments, such as clays and silts, which can be found even in calm water bodies. Sediment-laden water is referred to as turbid water; scientists can measure turbidity by sampling the water body or by using devices that estimate turbidity by the transparency of the water. One such device is the *Secchi* disk, a white disk of specified diameter that can be lowered on a line from the side of a small boat. Because turbidity decreases the transparency of the water body, the depth at which the disk is no longer visible can be related to sediment content. Another indication of turbidity, nephometric turbidity units (NTU), are measured by the intensity of light that passes through a water sample. A special instrument uses a light beam and a sensor to detect differences in light intensity. Water of high turbidity decreases the intensity of the light in a manner that can be related to sediment content.

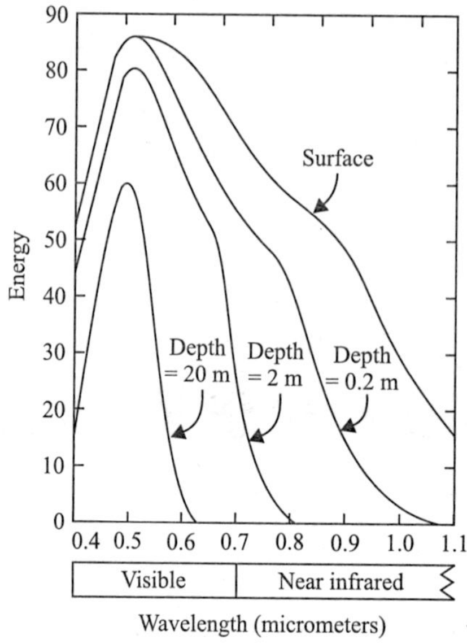

Fig. 20.3. Light penetration within a clear water body.

Thus, as sediment concentration increases, the spectral properties of a water body change. First, its overall brightness in the visible region increases, so the water body ceases to act as a 'dark' object and becomes more and more like a 'bright' object as sediment content increases. Second, as sediment concentrations increase, the wavelength of peak reflectance shifts from a maximum in the blue region toward the green. The presence of larger particles means that the wavelength of maximum scattering shifts toward the blue-green and green regions (Fig. 20.4). Therefore, as sediment content increases there tends to be simultaneous increase in brightness and a shift in peak reflectance toward longer wavelengths and the peak itself becomes broader, so that at high levels of turbidity the colour becomes a less precise indicator of sediment content. As sediment content approaches very high levels, the colour of the water begins to approach that of the sediment itself. The green reflectance of turbid water appear as light blue on the processed CIR film, which provides a sharp contrasts in colour with the dark blue or back of clear water bodies.

SPECTRAL CHANGES AS WATER DEPTH INCREASES

Figure 20.3 shows spectral characteristics of sunlight as it penetrates a clear water body. Near the surface, the overall shape of the curve resembles the spectrum of solar radiation, but the water body increasingly influences the spectral composition of the light as depth increases. At a depth of 20 m, little or no infrared radiation is present because the water body is an effective absorber of these longer wavelengths. At this depth, only blue-green wavelengths remain—these wavelengths are therefore available for scattering back to the surface, from the water itself and from the bottom of the water body.

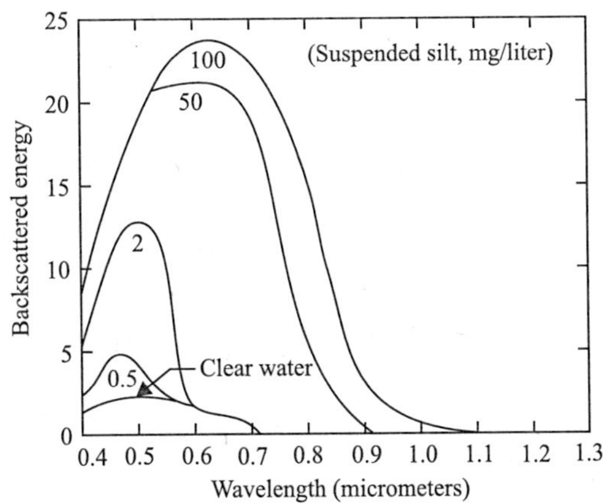

Fig. 20.4. Effects of turbidity on spectral properties of water.

The attenuation coefficient (k) describes the rate at which light becomes dimmer as depth increases. If E_0 is the brightness at the surface, then the brightness at depth z (E_z) is given by:

$$E_z = E_0 e^{-kz} \qquad \text{... (20.1)}$$

In hydrologic studies the influence of the atmosphere can be especially important. The atmosphere, of course, alters the spectral properties of incident radiation and also influences the characteristics of the reflected signal. Although these influences are also present in remote sensing of land surfaces, they assume special significance in hydrologic studies, in part because such studies often depend upon subtle spectral differences (easily lost in atmospheric haze) and also perhaps because much of the hydrologic information is carried by the short wavelengths that are most easily scattered by the atmosphere.

Water bodies are typically dark, so the analyst must work with a rather restricted range of brightnesses relative to those available for study of land surfaces (Fig. 20.5). As a result, analysts who specialise in remote sensing of water bodies must devote special attention to the radiometric qualities of the remotely sensed data. Typically, data to be analysed for hydrologic information are examined carefully to assess their quality, the effects of the atmosphere and sun angle. Geometric pre-processing is used with caution, to avoid unnecessary alteration of radiometric quality of the data. In some instances, analysts calculate average brightness over blocks of contiguous pixels to reduce transient noisy effects of clouds and whitecaps. Sometimes several scenes of the same area, acquired at different times, can be used to isolate permanent features (e.g., shallows and shoals) from temporary features (including waves and atmospheric effects). Also, it is often advantageous to estimate original radiometric brightnesses from digital values as a means of accurately assessing differences in colour and brightness.

LOCATION AND EXTENT OF WATER BODIES

Remote sensing provides a straightforward means to map the extent of water bodies, to inventory area occupied by open water and to monitor changes in water bodies over time. Although such tasks may seem very basic, there are numerous situations in which simple determination of the land-water boundary can be very important. Study of coastal erosion requires accurate determination of shoreline position and configuration at several dates. Likewise, comparisons of shoreline position before and after flooding permits measurement of areas flooded, as well as determination of locations of flooded areas. Such information can be difficult to acquire by conventional means.

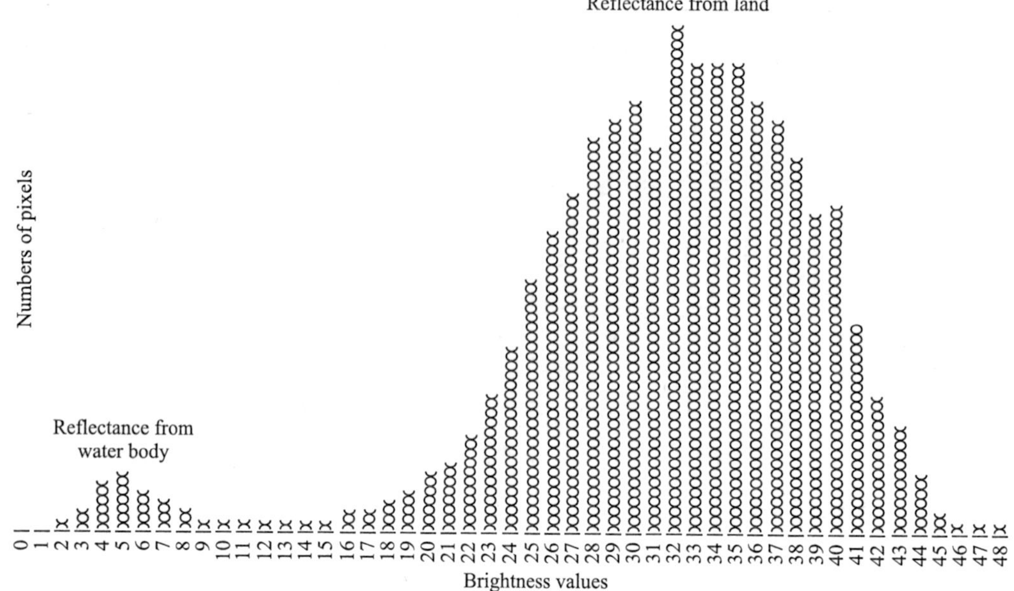

Fig. 20.5. Restricted range of brightnesses in hydrologic setting.

Determination of the land-water body border is usually easiest in the near infrared region, where land, especially if vegetated, is bright and open water dark. Usually it is possible to determine a sharp contact between the two (Fig. 20.6). With Landsat 1–3 MSS data, the contrast is usually clear on bands 6 or 7. With photography, black-and-white infrared film is usually satisfactory. CIR film is suitable if the water is free of sediment. However, because CIR film is sensitive to green light, turbid water will appear bright, thereby preventing clear discrimination of the land-water boundary.

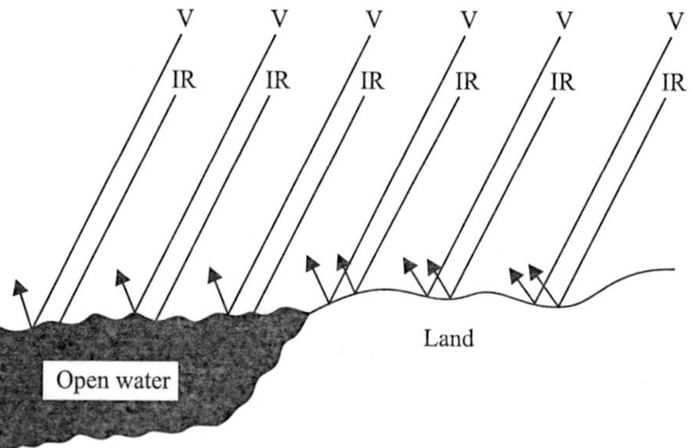

Fig. 20.6. Determining the location and extent of land-water contact.

ROUGHNESS OF THE WATER SURFACE

Figure 20.7 shows spectra for calm and wave-roughened surfaces in the visible and the near infrared. Wave-roughened surfaces are brighter than are smoother surfaces. Calm, smooth water surfaces direct only volume-reflected radiation to the sensor, but rough, wavy water surfaces direct a portion of the solar beam directly to the sensor. As a result, wavy surfaces are much brighter, especially in the visible portion of the spectrum. McKim describe a procedure that uses polarising filters to separate the surface brightness from that of the water body itself, using high-resolution data.

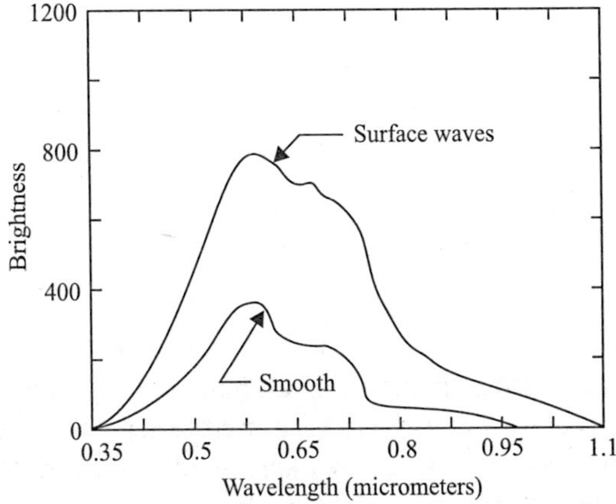

Fig. 20.7. Spectra of calm and wind-roughened water surfaces.

The most intensive studies to study ocean roughness have used active microwave sensors. Sea state refers to the roughness of the ocean surface, which is determined by wind speed and direction, as they interact locally with currents and tides. Sea state is an important oceanographic and meteorological quality because if studied over large areas and over time, it permits inference of wide speed and direction—valuable information for research and forecasts. Radars provide data concerning ocean roughness; the backscattering coefficient increases as wave height increases. Radars therefore provide a means of indirectly observing sea state over large areas and a basis for inferring wind speed and direction at the water's surface. If the imaging radar is carried by a satellite, as is the case with Seasat and the shuttle imaging radar, then the analyst has the opportunity to observe sea state over very large areas at regular intervals. These observations permit oceanographic studies that were impractical or very difficult using conventional data. Furthermore, timely information regarding sea state has obvious benefits for marine navigation and can, in principle, form the basis for inference of wind speed and direction that can contribute to meteorological data. Direct observation of sea state is relatively straightforward, but because ocean areas are so very large and conditions so rapidly changeable, the usual observations from ships in transit are much too sparse to provide reliable data.

Although many experiments have been conducted using a variety of microwave instruments, one of the most important broad-scale sea state experiments was based upon the Seasat A project, which used several instruments to monitor the earth's oceans. The Seasat SAR and RADARSAT have provided an opportunity to observe large ocean areas on a repetitive basis. Calm ocean surfaces, with waves that are small relative to the radar wavelength, act as specular reflectors and appear as dark regions on the image, as energy is reflected away from the antenna. As wind speed increases, the ocean surface becomes rougher and acts more like a diffuse reflector, causing bright regions on the imagery (Fig. 20.7). Because radar wavelength and system geometry are known, the received signal can form the basis for estimates of wave height and velocity. In a test in the Gulf of Alaska, scientists found agreement between data derived from the Seasat SAR and those observed at the ocean surface. Wave direction, height and wavelength were all estimated from the SAR imagery. Waves were most accurately observed when their direction of travel was within 25° of the look direction. Other studies have shown the SAR data to be useful for studying other kinds of ocean swells and currents.

BATHYMETRY

Bathymetry information concerning water depth and configuration of the ocean floor, is one of the most basic forms of hydrographic data. Bathymetry is especially important near coastlines, in harbours and near shoals and banks, where shallow water can present hazards to navigation and where changes can occur rapidly as sedimentation, erosion and scouring of channels alters underwater topography.

Water depth can be measured by instruments carried on vessels, especially by acoustic (sonar) instruments that measure depths directly below the vessel. Ideally, bathometric maps should be compiled from a more or less uniform network of depth measurements rather than from a limited set of data from traverses. Although modern side-scanning sonar can yield a continuous surface of depth information, aerial imagery is an important means of mapping sub-surface topography in shallow water.

Photogrammetry can be applied to bathymetric measurement if high-quality, large-scale, photography is available and if the water is clear. Filters have been used to separate radiation in the spectral region 0.44 to 0.54 μm, where solar energy is most easily transmitted by clear water. As Fig. 20.3 indicates, in principle sunlight can penetrate to depths of about 20 m. Aerial photographs record information only from relatively shallow depths, although depths as deep as 16 m have been mapped using aerial photographs.

Special problems in applications of photogrammetry to bathymetry include estimation of difference in refraction between air and water (Fig. 20.8) and the difficulty in acquiring a good set of underwater control points. Furthermore, mapping is difficult in regions far removed from the shoreline because of the difficulty in extending control across zones of deep water. Nonetheless, photogrammetric methods have been successfully used for mapping zones of shallow water.

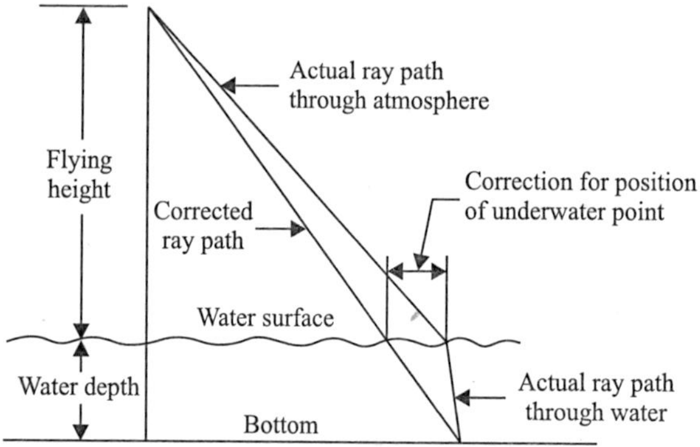

Fig. 20.8. Bathymetry by photogrammetry.

Water depth can also be estimated by observing refraction of waves as they break in shallow water. As a wave approaches the shore, it begins to break at a depth that is determined by its velocity, wavelength and period. If velocities and wavelengths can be measured on successive overlapping photographs, it is possible to calculate an estimate of depth. The method works well only when the water body is large and if the bottom drops slowly with increasing distance from shore. The wave refraction method is not as accurate as other procedures, but it does have the advantage of applicability in turbid water, when other methods cannot be applied.

Multispectral Bathymetry

Depth of penetration of solar energy varies with wavelength. Longer wavelengths are absorbed most strongly; even modest depths—perhaps 2 m or so—of clear water will absorb all infrared radiation, so that longer wavelengths convey no information concerning depth of water or of the nature of the bottom. Visible radiation penetrates to greater depths, but is still influenced by wavelength-dependent factors. For clear water, maximum penetration occurs in the blue-green region, which is approximated by Landsat MSS 1 (using the Landsat 4 and 5 band designation), although TM1 is likely to be more effective for bathymetric studies. Polcyn and Lyzenga report that for their study region in the Bahamas under optimum conditions, maximum penetration for MSS 1 is as deep as 25 m and about 6 m for MSS 2 (For consistency in designation, Landsat 4 and 5 MSS numbering is employed here).

Intensity of radiation decreases exponentially with depth (i.e., brightness decreases as depth increases). Thus use of MSS 4 (or TM 1; both are positioned at or near the spectral region of maximum penetration) should be useful for estimating depth. Dark values suggest that the bottom is deep, beyond the 20 m range represented in Table 20.2. Bright values suggest that the bottom is near the surface (Fig. 20.9). Many depth-extraction algorithms use a logarithmic transformation of MSS 4 brightness as a means of incorporating our knowledge that brightness decreases exponentially with depth.

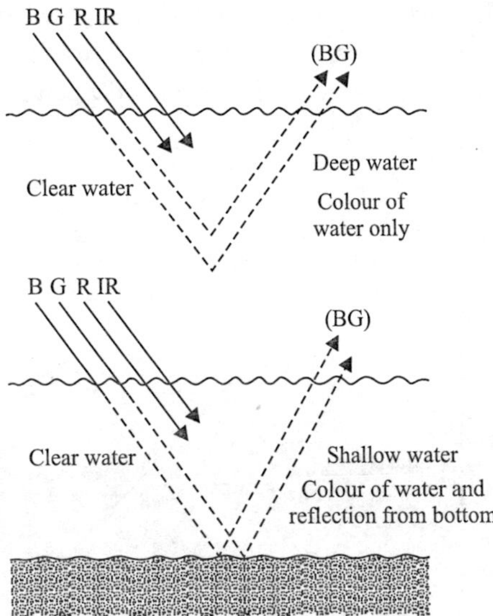

Fig. 20.9. Multispectral bathymetry. Shallow water bodies filter radiation reflected from the bottom; the balance between spectral bands observed at the sensor reveals the approximate depth of the water body.

Table 20.2. Logarithmic transformation of brightnesses.

x	*ln (x)*	*Brightness*	*Depth*
2	0.69	Dim	Deep
6	1.79		
10	2.30		

(Contd...)

x	*ln (x)*	*Brightness*	*Depth*
14	2.64		
18	2.89		
22	3.09		
26	3.26	Bright	Shallow

LANDSAT CHROMATICITY DIAGRAM

Colorimetry, the precise measurement of colour, is of significance in several aspects of remote sensing, but is especially significant in applications of remote sensing to studies of water quality. Even casual observation reveals that water bodies differ significantly in colour, yet it can be very difficult to accurately measure these colour differences and to relate colour to the variables that we wish to study. Specification of colour is not as self-evident as it might seem. Scientists have established several alternative systems for describing colour. Most establish a three-dimensional colour space in which three primaries (red, green and blue) form three orthogonal axes. Unique specification of a colour requires identification of a location within this colour space, giving hue (dominant wavelength), saturation (purity) and value (brightness) or a given colour. These axes define *tristimulus* space, in which any colour can be represented as a mixture of the three primaries—that is, as a location within the coordinate system represented in Fig. 20.10. Such a system defines a colour solid, which in principle permits specification of any colour.

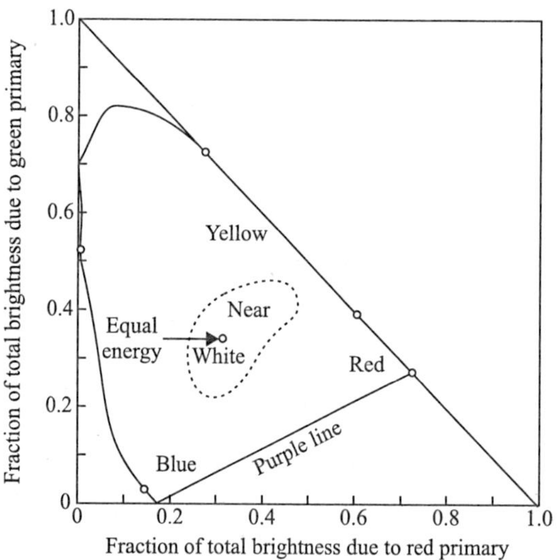

Fig. 20.10. CIE chromaticity diagram.

The Landsat chromaticity coordinates can be used to assess the turbidity of water bodies imaged by the MSS. Figure 20.11 shows the Landsat chromaticity diagram, which is identical to the CIE chromaticity diagram except for the use of MSS bands 4, 5 and 6 as substitutes for the CIE primaries. 'E' signifies the equal radiance point, where radiances in MSS bands 4, 5 and 6 are equal. (Note that the labels in Fig. 20.10 do not apply to the Landsat chromaticity diagram, as it does not use the CIE primaries.) The curved line extending to the right of the equal radiance point is the experimentally defined locus that defines the positions of water pixels as their radiances are plotted on the diagram. Pixels with positions near the right end of this line represent water bodies with clear water. As chromaticity coordinates shift closer to the other end of the line, near the equal radiance point, the spectral properties of the pixels change, indicating increases in turbidity as the pixel position approaches the left-hand end of the line. This line was defined experimentally by Alfoldi and Munday for their study area, using sediment samples collected at the time the imagery was acquired (For detailed studies, it is important to define a specific locus for each individual study region, but for illustrative purposes it is sufficient to use their line as a general-purpose locus).

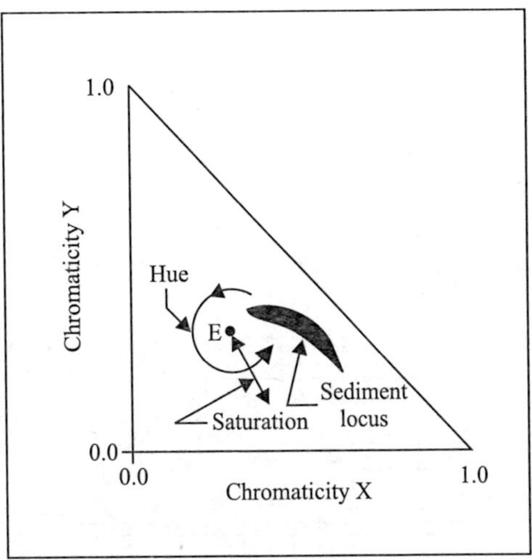

Fig. 20.11. Landsat MSS chromaticity space. The sediment locus is experimentally derived and may vary slightly from region to region or over time within a given region. The radial dimension (outward from E) present spectral purity information and radial shift in the position of the locus are attributed to atmospheric scattering, thin clouds, air pollution or whitecaps.

Thus, in Fig. 20.12, the position of pixel A reveals a clear water body and pixel B represents a turbid water body. As pixels known to represent water bodies drift away from the line (pixel C is an example), so do we suspect that atmospheric haze or thin clouds have altered their radiances. Although our inspection of the chromaticity diagram is essentially a qualitative analysis of pixel positions on the chromaticity diagram, Alfoldi and Munday have conducted more quantitative studies, using observed values of suspended sediment to calibrate the technique.

Drainage Basin Hydrology

A less obvious component of water resources concerns the management of land areas to promote orderly retention and flow of moisture over the land surface and then within the stream system, so that flooding and erosion are minimised and an even steady flow of moisture is maximised. The nature and distribution of land use and land cover within drainage basins influence run-off from the land surface and eventually also influences the flow of water within stream channels. Although there is no set relationship between these elements that can be said to form a universally 'normal' balance, each climatic and ecological situation tends to be characterised by an established pattern of rainfall, evapotranspiration and streamflow. Extensive changes to natural land-cover patterns can disrupt this local balance and cause accelerated soil erosion, flooding and other undesirable consequences. Hydrologists attempt to study such processes by constructing hydrologic models: mathematical simulations that use measurements of local rainfall, together with information concerning patterns of land use, soil, topography and drainage, to predict the nature of the streamflow that might be caused by storms of a given magnitude. Such models provide a means of assessing effects of proposed changes in land use (e.g., new construction, harvesting of timber) or in channel configuration because they can estimate the effects of such changes before they actually occur. Often such models can be evaluated and refined using data from watersheds that have very accurate records of rainfall and streamflow.

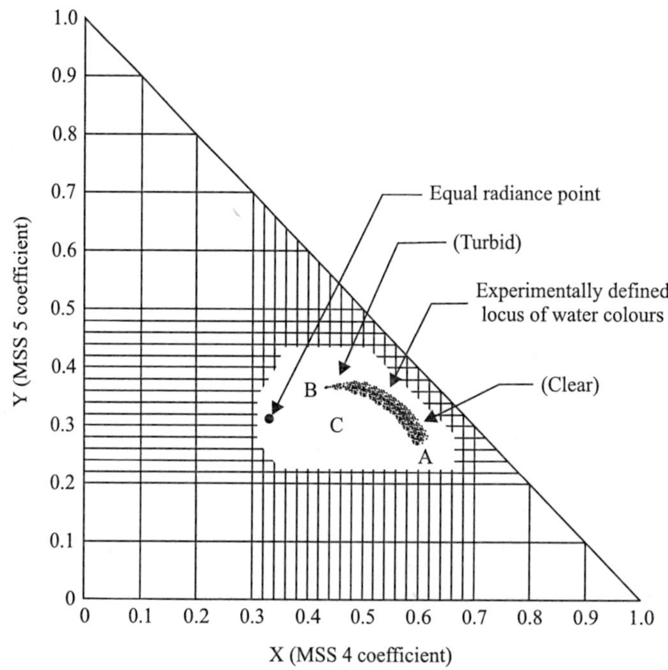

Fig. 20.12. Landsat MSS chromaticity diagram.

Hydrologic models require large amounts of detailed and accurate data, so many of the costs involved in applying a given model to a specific region arise from the effort required to collect accurate information concerning soil and land-cover patterns—two of the important variables required for such models. Some of the information concerning land use can be derived from remotely sensed data.

Manual interpretation of land use and land cover from aerial photographs is a standard procedure and of course, aerial photographs are a source of much of the information regarding topography and soils. Many studies have evaluated the use of image classification of digital remote sensing data as a source of land-cover information for such models.

Advantages include reduced costs and the ability to quickly prepare new information as changes occur. Jackson applied this kind of approach in a study of a small watershed in northern Virginia. His study, using both manual interpretations of aerial photography and computer classification of Landsat MSS data, was able to compare results based upon MSS data with those of conventional estimates. His results indicated that the use of Landsat data was much cheaper than the manual method but tended to produce results of comparable reliability.

EVAPOTRANSPIRATION

Evapotranspiration is defined as combined evaporation, moisture lost to the atmosphere from soil and open water and transpiration, moisture lost to the atmosphere by plants. Evapotranspiration measures the total moisture lost to the atmosphere from the land surface and as such it (together with other variables) forms an important variable in understanding the local operation of the hydrologic cycle.

However, accurate measurement of evapotranspiration is difficult. Reliable data are usually available only for well-equipped meteorological stations and agricultural research facilities that are regularly attended by a trained staff. The vast majority of the earth's land area is not near such installations, so reliable measurements of evapotranspiration are not available. Evapotranspiration can of course, be estimated using measurements of air temperature, wind speed, plant cover, cloudiness and other variables, but such estimates often lack the detail and accuracy required for good environmental studies and also require data that are themselves difficult to obtain.

Remotely sensed data can form the basis for spatially referenced estimates of evapotranspiration—that is, estimates that apply to specific areas of small areal extent. In contrast, estimates based upon meteorological measurements can usually provide only a single estimate for a large region in the vicinity of a climate station. In effect, spatially referenced estimates provide detailed, independent estimates of evapotranspiration for each pixel.

Direct sensing of the soil surface using remote sensing instruments (especially passive) can provide estimates of soil moisture or calculation of such estimates can be based upon digital elevation data that represent topographic elevation as a matrix of values, similar in concept to digital remote sensing images. For the elevation data, each pixel value represents the topographic elevation at the center of each pixel rather than the brightness of the energy reflected from the land at that pixel. From such data a computer programme can calculate the topographic slope at each pixel and can also determine the aspect, the compass direction at which the slope faces.

With the elevation data in hand, it is possible to overlay Landsat data and data from meteorological satellites, such as the AVHRR, so that all three forms of data register to one another. A classification of the Landsat data can provide a map of the major vegetation classes (forest, pasture, bare ground, etc.) present. The data gathered by meteorological satellites can be used to estimate temperature and total solar radiation received during a 24 hours interval. These vary depending upon the slope and aspect of each pixel, as derived from the elevation data. From these separate forms of data, it is then possible to estimate evapotranspiration of each pixel. With independent estimates of evapotranspiration for each pixel within a study area, the analyst can then prepare much more detailed hydrologic data. Jackson describes the estimation of evapotranspiration from remotely sensed data and observes that some difficulties still remain. Atmospheric degradation of the remotely sensed data can cause errors in the estimates and the usual procedures cannot consider effects of factors such as wind speed or surface roughness. Also, estimates apply only to a specific time (when the remotely sensed data were acquired), although usually the requirement is to estimate evapotranspiration over intervals of a day, several days or even longer. Therefore, it in necessary to extend the estimates from a specific time to a longer interval—a process that is likely to introduce error. Nonetheless, it should be emphasised that further development of such procedures is one of the most interesting and practical applications of remote sensing, as they can make major contributions to studies of hydrology, climatology and agriculture in many of the earth's remote and inaccessible regions.

MANUAL INTERPRETATION

The following examples illustrate how techniques of manual image interpretation, applied with a knowledge of films and filters and of the spectral behaviour of water bodies as outlined earlier in this chapter, can be used to derive information concerning water bodies and coastal features.

The islands themselves are long, low, strips of sand shaped by the action of both water and wind. At the edge of the ocean, a long beach slopes toward the water; the lowest sections of the beach are influenced each day by the effects of tides and currents. The upper higher sections are affected only by the highest tides and strongest storms, so these regions may experience major changes only once or twice a year or even less often. Inland from the upper beach ridges is wind-blown sand formed into dunes that are generally above the reach of waves, although very strong storms may alter these regions. The dunes are reshaped by wind, but their general configuration is often stabilised by grasses and small shrubs that cover much of this zone. Inland from the dunes, elevations decrease and water again assumes the dominant influence in shaping the ecosystems. Water from the tidal marshes between the islands and the mainland rises and falls with the tides, but is without the strong waves that characterise the seaward side of the island. These tidal flats are covered with vegetation adapted to the brackish water, experience tidal fluctuations and have poorly drained soils.

Many of these features are clearly visible on the infrared image of this region (Fig. 20.13). The bright white strip along the seaward side of the island contrasts sharply with the cool dark of the open ocean. This bright strip is, of course, the hot surface of the open sandy beach, which has received the direct energy of the solar beam for several hours and now, at mid-day, is very hot. Inland from the beach the dunes are visible as a slightly darker region on the image with darker areas caused by shadowing. The topographic structure of the beach ridges are clearly visible in several regions. In the tidal marshes, the image appearance is controlled largely by vegetative cover, which gives a clear delineation of the edges of the open channel not usually visible on other images. The open water within the tidal lagoons has a lighter tone than that of the open ocean, indicating warmer temperatures. Here the shallow water and the restricted circulation have enabled the water in these areas to absorb the solar radiation it has been receiving now for several hours. Nonetheless, this water is still cooler than water flowing from the land surface; it is possible to see the bright (warm) plumes of water from the streams that flow into the tidal marshes from the mainland. Finally, tidal currents are clearly visible as the bright (warm) stream of water passing between the barrier islands to enter the darker (cooler) water of the open ocean. The tide is now flowing out (ebbing); compare some of the patterns visible on this image with those of a hydrographic chart of the same region (Fig. 20.13).

SEA SURFACE TEMPERATURE

Remote sensing has become one of the most effective means of assessing sea surface temperature (SST), the average temperature of the ocean surface, indicative of temperatures within the upper meter or so of the ocean surface. SST is an important variable for oceanographic studies, including characteristics and dynamics of currents and distributions and movements of marine life. Because SST is major influence for fish and their sources of food, SST maps are important for marine fishing fleets. Commercial services have been successful in providing timely interpretations of satellite data and images for fishing fleets at sea. Because of the significance of oceans for absorbing, radiating and transporting thermal energy, SST has profound meteorological significance not only for marine weather and climate, but also for understanding general atmospheric processes. Therefore, satellite sensing of SST has formed an important component of attempts to models global climate.

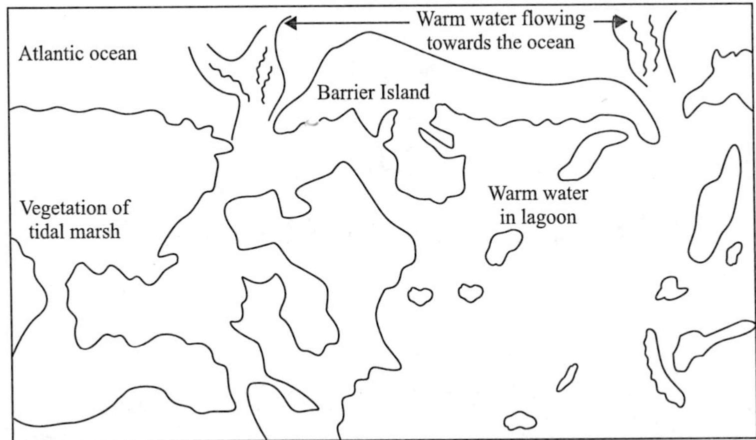

Fig. 20.13. Thermal infrared image of eastern shore of Virginia, 23 July 1992, approximately 12:50 PM.

The radiation detected by sensors is determined by the temperature of the upper 1 mm or so of the ocean surface. Although there is mixing of water in the upper portion of the water column, these values may not accurately represent true temperature of water volume at the upper meter of the ocean. Nonetheless, estimates of SST temperature based on observations from AVHRR and related satellite sensors provide some of the most valuable and widely used sources of SST data.

To reduce or eliminate effects of cloud cover, images with differing patterns of cloud cover or cover acquired at different times (but with in a short interval) are used to create composites that show cloud-free views of the ocean surface. To correct for contributions of atmospheric moisture upon SST estimates, two spectral channels indifferent atmospheric windows are used—the two-channel split-window method. Wavelengths selected for this purpose are positioned close to the peak of the blackbody radiation expected from the earth (roughly, 10 μm) and lie within well-defined atmospheric windows, so the tradition will be transmitted to the atmosphere.

Thus, hydrologic studies in general cover a very broad range of subject matter, from the movement of currents in bodies of open water to the evaporation of moisture from a soil surface. Such studies can be very difficult, especially if the goal is to examine the changes in hydrologic variables as they occur over time and space, because the usual methods of surface observation gather data at isolated points or at specific times. Two of the great advantages of remote sensing in this contest are the synoptic view of the aerial perspective and the opportunity to examine dynamic patterns at frequent intervals.

Yet remote sensing encounters difficulties when applied to hydrologic studies. Many of the standard sensors and analytical techniques have been developed for study of land areas and are not easily applied to the special problems of studying water bodies. Analyses often depend upon detection of rather subtle differences in colour, which are easily lost by effects of atmospheric degradation of the remotely sensed energy. Currents and other dynamic features may change rapidly, requiring frequent observation to record the characteristics of significance to the analyst. Important hydrologic variables, such as ground water, are not usually directly visible and others, such as evapotranspiration, are not at all visible, but must be estimated through other quantities that may themselves be difficult to observe. These problems and others, mean that further development of hydrologic remote sensing is likely to be one of the most challenging research areas in remote sensing.

21

Land Use and Land Cover

INTRODUCTION

Study of land use and land cover reveals the overall pattern of mankind's occupation of the earth's surface and the geographic organisation of its activities. At broad scales, the land-cover map provides a delineation of the broad patterns of climate and vegetation that form the environmental context for our activities. At local and regional scales, knowledge of land use and land cover forms a basic dimension of resources available to any political unit; both the citizens and the leaders of any community must understand the land resources available to them and the constraints that limit uses of land and environmental resources.

Although the formal study of land use and land cover dates from the early 1800s, systematic mapping at large scale was not attempted until the 1920s and aerial photography and remote sensing were not routinely applied until the 1960s. Thus, effective land-use mapping is a relatively recent capability. We have yet to fully assemble and evaluate all of the data that is available and to develop the techniques for acquiring and interpreting imagery.

Without the aerial images acquired by remote sensing, there can be no really practical method of observing the pattern of land cover or of monitoring changes. Systems such as MSS, TM, SPOT and AVHRR have provided a capability for observing land cover at broad scales and at intervals that previously were not practical. Images from such systems have not only provided vital information, but have also presented data at new scales that have changed the intellectual perspective with which we consider the environment by recording broad-scale patterns and relationships that otherwise could not be accurately perceived or analysed.

Land use can be defined as the use of land by human, usually with emphasis on the functional role of land in economic activities. Land use is an abstraction not always directly observable by even the closest inspection. We cannot see the actual use of a parcel of land, only the physical artifacts of that use. Sometimes the implications of the artifacts are quite clear—a steel mill, for example, can be clearly associated with specific economic activities and land-use categories. In contrast, a large extend of forested land may display little if any physical evidence of its varied uses, which might include production of timber, supply of water for distant urban areas, wildlife habitat and space for recreation. In addition, some land areas may be characterised by contrasting activities (belonging perhaps to separate classes of land use) at separate seasons of the year. For example, some farmland might be used alternatively as cropland and as pasture at different times in the agricultural calendar.

In contrast, land cover, in its narrowest sense, often designates only the vegetation, either natural or man-made, on the earth's surface at a specific time of observation (Fig. 21.1). In a much broader sense, land cover designates the visible evidence of land use, to include both vegetative and nonvegetative features. In this meaning, dense forest, plowed land, urban structures and paved parking lots all constitute land cover. Whereas land use is abstract, land cover is concrete and therefore is subject to direct observation.

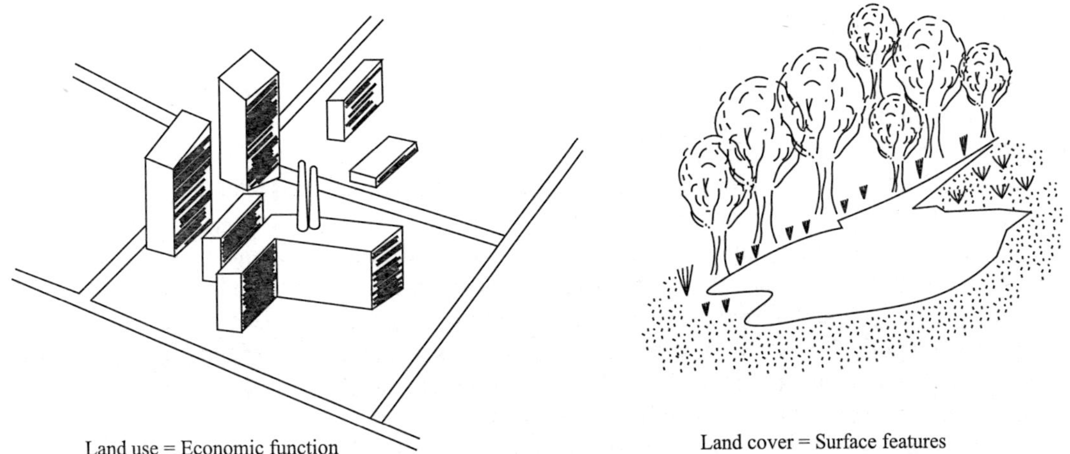

Fig. 21.1. Land use and land cover.

Another distinction is that land cover lacks the emphasis upon economic function that is essential to the concept of land use. A hydrologist can devote his or her interest solely to land cover because of his or her concern only with the physical components of the landscape that pertain to the movement of moisture. But a traffic engineer must use land use as a component of a traffic flow model and must address the economic function of each parcel land as a contributor of automobile traffic to the region's highways. Usually the distinction between land use and land cover becomes more important as the scale of a study becomes larger and its detail becomes finer.

Land-use patterns reflect the character of a society's interaction with its physical environment. This fact become obvious when it is possible to see different economic and social systems occupying the same or similar environment. In the southeastern portion of the scene, the land use pattern is dominated by broad-scale mechanised agriculture practiced by a Mennonite community. The upper right (northeastern) region of the image is a mountainous area occupied by a diminishing population of Indians, who practice a form of slash-and-burn agriculture, visible as dispersed patches of light green. Throughout the northwestern and central portions of the image, the Bolivian government has encouraged broad-scale clearing of forest for agriculture. In the upper left region of the image, these clearings take the form of light green spots aligned northwest to southeast; at the center of the each patch of cleared land is a central facility providing colonists with fertilisers, pesticides and staples. In the southwestern corner of the image, the complex field pattern reflects an established landscape occupied by Japanese immigrants.

SIGNIFICANCE OF LAND USE AND LAND COVER INFORMATION

Almost all governmental units have a continuing requirement to form and implement laws and policies that directly or indirectly involve existing or future land use. If we exclude the possibility of annexation, each community has only a fixed amount of land area to allocate among the varied economic and social activities required to support its citizens. There is increasing recognition that sensible uses of finite or possibly shrinking, resources requires comprehensive planning of community activities to coordinate the amount and placement of private and public facilities with the amounts and locations of human resources. Uncoordinated development can lead to inefficient and undesirable environmental, social and economic consequences. As existing development and increasing population limit options for use of land resources, development may be attracted to sites of marginal suitability or cause displacement of activities from their optimum sites. For example, residential or commercial development on steep slopes, in flood-prone areas or on high-quality agricultural land may inflict long-term damage on the community. In recognition of these problems, many states have legal requirements for local jurisdictions to prepare comprehensive plans outlining the kinds of land-use patterns to be encouraged or discouraged in specific sites and defining favoured locations for specific uses. Land-use information is vital for important decisions made at the state level. For example, traffic flow models used to plan highway development at the state level require land-use data as input to estimate traffic generated by neighbourhoods supplying traffic to specific highways. State legislatures must address issues regarding allocation of land to alternative uses, either in specific geographic regions (e.g., a decision to establish a state park or a scenic reserve) or through general policies tailored for specific statewide goals (e.g., laws to assist in preserving farmland from urbanisation). In either context the availability of accurate information regarding existing uses of the state's land is an important element in making sound decisions.

At national levels, land-use information is an important element in forming policies regarding economic, demographic and environmental issues. In the United States, such policies might pertain to determining the location, extend and character of surface mining; losses of agricultural land to urbanisation; siting of national parks and defense installations; or storage and disposal of hazardous wastes—to mention only a few of today's many controversial issues pertaining to land use.

International requirements for land use data also focus upon many of today's major concerns considered at their broadest possible scales. For example, major changes in land use within the world's major biomes (most notably the tropical forests, but also elsewhere) may have generated as yet unknown effects upon global biochemical cycles and upon the global energy balance. Other issues that require worldwide perspective include changes in global patterns of agricultural and forest lands, settlement patterns within zones of uncertain and variable climate and efforts to control environmentally questionable agricultural practices. Examination of these issues requires collection of data from many diverse sources—data that are compatible with respect to scale, detail, accuracy and categorisation. For example, examination of land use within the selva, considered worldwide, requires data from many diverse areas, separated geographically and with contrasting political and administrative traditions. Existing data, gathered independently by each nation, would probably be of only minimal utility in a serious effort to examine these most important issues from a global perspective.

At the broad scale of a statewide perspective, the character of the required information differs greatly from that needed at local scales. For statewide land-use and land-cover information to be effective, it must be collected for the entire state at comparable levels of detail and accuracy and at comparable dates. If compatible hierarchical classifications have been used, it is perhaps theoretically possible to form a statewide data set from information collected at local levels (assuming the unlikely pre-condition that all component jurisdictions actually collected information). In practice, however, it is unlikely that such an effort could be effective due to the innumerable practical problems of coordination and administration. As a result, discussion of statewide land-use data must assume the availability of a staff administered at the state level to assure compatibility and quality of information.

At local levels, it may be practical to gather data by direct observation or to combine direct observation with the use of remote sensing imagery. At the state level, it would seem to be impractical to rely upon any method except use of aerial photography or other remote sensing imagery.

Significance for Science and Research

Land-use information is, of course, also of great significance in scientific and scholarly research. National and regional land-use patterns reflect the character of the interaction between man and environment and the influence of distance and resource bases upon mankind's basic economic activities. As a result, geographers, economists and others have long regarded knowledge of regional land-use patterns as a fundamental element in their studies of economic systems. Land-use patterns are also recognised as influential element in hydrological and meteorological processes. The importance of land-use theory developed by von Thunen, Losch and others working in the disciplines of regional science, economics and geography is evidence of the fundamental nature of land use in both theoretical and applied research.

APPLICATIONS OF REMOTE SENSING

Remotely sensed images lend themselves to accurate land-cover and land-use mapping in part because land-cover information can be visually interpreted more or less directly from evidence visible on aerial images and objects can be seen in the context of the neighbouring features.

Land-use maps are routinely prepared at a wide variety of scales, typically ranging from 1:12500 and larger to 1:2,50,000 and smaller. At one end of this spectrum (the larger scale maps), remotely sensed imagery may itself contribute relatively little information to the survey; its main role may be to form a highly detailed base for recording data gathered by other means. At such large scales the land-use maps may actually serve as a kind of reference map, having little cartographic generalisation. Such products are often used at the lowest levels of local governments, perhaps mainly urban areas, that have requirements for such detailed information and the financial resources to acquire it.

As the scale of the survey becomes broader (i.e., as map scale becomes smaller), the contribution of the image to the informational content of the map becomes greater, although even at the smallest scales there must always be some contribution from collateral information. Differing scales and levels of detail serve different purposes and different users. For the regional planner, the loss of resolution and detail at smaller scales may actually form an advantage in the sense that there occurs an integration and a simplification of the information that must be examined. For the medium and small-scale land-use surveys that are most often compiled by use of remotely sensed images, the product is a thematic map that depicts the predominant land cover within relatively homogeneous areas, delineated subject to limitations of scale, resolution, generalisation and other constraints accepted (or at least recognised) by both compilers and users of thematic maps.

LAND-USE CLASSIFICATION

Preparation of a land-use map from aerial imagery is in essence a process of segmenting the image into a mosaic of parcels, with each parcel assigned to a land-use class. The novice interpreter is often tempted to devise land-use classes based upon categories easily recognised and delineated from examination of the imagery. For example, 'sub-urban land' may seem to be a reasonable land-use category because of ease of identification and correspondence with informal land-use classes developed from personal experience. In practice, of course, the most useful categories are those that match the information needs of the map user. Typically, categories such as 'sub-urban land' are unsatisfactory for the user who requires division of land into classes such as 'residential', 'commercial' and 'industrial' land. In addition, it is important to use classification systems that are compatible with others that have been used in the past or that are used by neighbouring jurisdictions or by higher levels of government. Compatibility is important if maps and data are to be compared over time (to determine changes), aggregated over counties or states or to be compared with other forms of data. Therefore, although land-use classification is not in itself a task of great difficulty, it requires considerable knowledge and care to prepare a satisfactory land classification scheme and to apply it to a specific landscape.

Because of the unpredictable interplay between image detail, classification detail and map scale, the interpreter must find a balance between the precision of the classification system and the sizes of the parcels that can be interpreted, then portrayed legibly on a map. For example, detailed categories for cemeteries is of no practical value if all cemeteries in the mapped region occur in parcels of land too small to be legibly represented at the scale of the final map or if the image has such coarse resolution that cemeteries cannot be reliably interpreted. As a result, the image interpreter must prepare a classification system that is simultaneously compatible with the needs of the map user and consistent with image detail and map scale.

Although many land-use classification systems have been devised, it is probably best to be familiar with the system that is widely used in the United States (and elsewhere as well); other systems can be used if necessary once the student has gained some experience in the practice of land-use survey. In the early 1970s the USGS began a programme for mapping of the land-use and land-cover of the United States using aerial photography. The land-use and land-cover classification system (Table 21.1) devised for the USGS programme has become one of the most widely used classification systems for land-use maps prepared by interpretation of remotely sensed images.

The USGS system has many useful features. First, it was prepared specifically for use with remotely sensed imagery. Its categories are appropriate for information interpreted from aerial images and it has a hierarchical structure that lends itself to use with images of differing scales and resolutions. Level I, for example, is tailored for use with broad-scale, coarse-resolution imagery (Landsat imagery or high-altitude aerial photography). Levels II and III are composed of more detailed classes that can be interpreted from large-scale, fine-resolution images. Although the USGS system specifies the Level I and II categories, the Level III categories must be defined by the analyst to meet the specific requirements of a particular study and a specific region. As the analyst defines Level III categories, it is, of course, important that he or she use the Level I and II categories as a framework for the more detailed Level III classes.

MAPPING LAND USE BY MANUAL INTERPRETATION

Use of aerial imagery for mapping land cover requires application of skills not normally required in the simple intuitive examination of images for recognition of individual objects. Individual land-cover categories are formed from collections of diverse objects, features and structures that are often not individually resolved on the image; the interpreter's task is not so much one of identifying separate objects as it is the accurate delineation of regions of relatively uniform composition and appearance. The interpreter of land-use information must, then generalise to define the areal units that compose the subject of the interpretation. The goal should be to perform this mental generalisation in a consistent logical manner and to describe the procedures accurately in a written account of the interpretation process.

Image Overlay and the Final Map

The visual interpretation process (Fig. 21.2) begins with the assembling of imagery, collateral information, equipment and materials required to conduct the interpretation. Imagery should be inspected to note defects, holidays (gaps) in coverage and areas obscured by clouds. If there is no index to the coverage of separate frames or images, the interpreter should prepare his or her own index to permit convenient identification of specific images covering in given area. If there are holidays in the coverage, the interpreter should initiate the process of acquiring additional imagery to provide the best possible information for voids in the primary coverage.

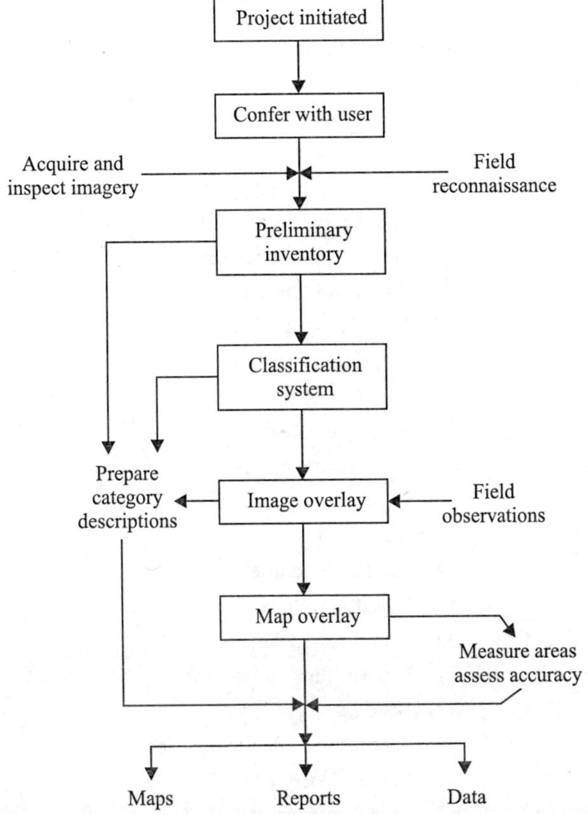

Fig. 21.2. Interpretation process for land-use/land-cover mapping.

For visual interpretation, the process consists of two related but distinct steps. The first consists of constructing an appropriate classification system. Although many different approaches to classification of land-use can be applied, the system proposed by Anderson provides one of the best and the most widely applicable outlines for structuring the classification. Their system (Table 21.1) provides the more general categories, but the interpreter must become involved in the design of the more detailed categories at Levels II and III. The definition and design of these detailed categories must be accomplished in coordination with those who will ultimately use the final maps and data. If it is determined that the users require information or detail not feasible with the use of aerial imagery, then the project must turn to other imagery or to collateral information to supply the needed information. If collateral information is to be used, the interpreter should carefully investigate the alternatives to ensure maximum accuracy and maximum compatibility with the aerial imagery.

Table 21.1. 1976 USGS land use and land cover classification.

Level I	*Level II*
1 Urban or built-up land	11 Residential
	12 Commercial and services
	13 Industrial
	14 Transportation, communications and utilities
	15 Industrial and commercial complexes
	16 Mixed urban or built-up land
	17 Other urban or built-up land
2 Agricultural land	21 Croplands and pasture
	22 Orchards, groves, vineyards, nurseries and ornamental horticultural areas
	23 Confined feeding operations
	24 Other agricultural land
3 Rangeland	31 Herbaceous rangeland
	32 Shrub and brush rangeland
	33 Mixed rangeland
4 Forest land	41 Deciduous forest land
	42 Evergreen forest land
	43 Mixed forest land
5 Water	51 Streams and canals
	52 Lakes
	53 Reservoirs
	54 Bays and estuaries
6 Wetland	61 Forested wetland
	62 Non-forested wetland
7 Barren land	71 Dry salt flats
	72 Beaches
	73 Sandy areas other than beaches
	74 Bare exposed rock
	75 Strip mines, quarries and gravel pits
	76 Transitional areas
	77 Mixed barren land
8 Tundra	81 Shrub and brush tundra
	82 Herbaceous tundra
	83 Bare ground tundra
	84 Wet tundra
	85 Mixed tundra
9 Perennial snow or ice	91 Perennial snowfields
	92 Glaciers

When a tentative outline of the classification is available, the interpreter should then carefully inspect the imagery to compile a list of the categories present, estimate the sizes of parcels likely to result from the application of the classification and in general anticipate problems in identifying or delineating categories. If several interpreters are to work on the same project, all should participate in this process to ensure uniformity of perspective and gain the benefit of independent contributions. A revised list of categories then forms the basis of further discussions with the user before a final classification is accepted for the project. The second step applies the classification system to the imagery. This step is accomplished by marking the boundaries between categories as they occur on the imagery, while consistently following the guidelines outlined below. Each separate parcel is outlined, then identified with a symbol (usually one to three numerals) corresponding the taxa in the classification system (Fig. 21.3). Important considerations include application of standard size for smallest parcels to be shown, as described below and the principles of consistency, clarity and legibility. If several interpreters are to work on separate portions of the same project, special attention must be devoted to coordination of their efforts to ensure uniform application of the guidelines outlined below. Individual interpreters share responsibility for coordination with those working on adjacent areas to be sure that parcel boundaries and labels match at edges of sheets (Fig. 21.4).

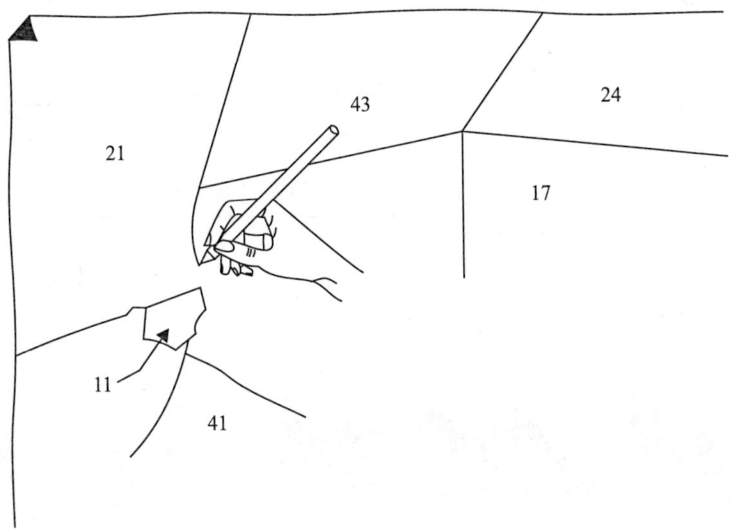

Fig. 21.3. Delineating and labelling land use parcels. Boundaries completely enclose parcels; each parcel is labelled, using leader lines for small parcels.

The results of the interpretation are recorded on a translucent overlay that registers to the image; this image overlay records the boundaries between parcels and identifying symbols (Fig. 21.5). As the interpreter prepares the image overlay, he or she begins to compile the classification table that forms a summary of category definitions and their identifying characteristics. When the image overlay is complete, it will be necessary to generate a map overlay that portrays the land-cover/land-use information on an accurate planimetric base. The map overlay is required because the image overlay inherits from the image the positional errors inherent to all remotely sensed imagery, so measurements of distance or area made directly from the image overlay will be in error.

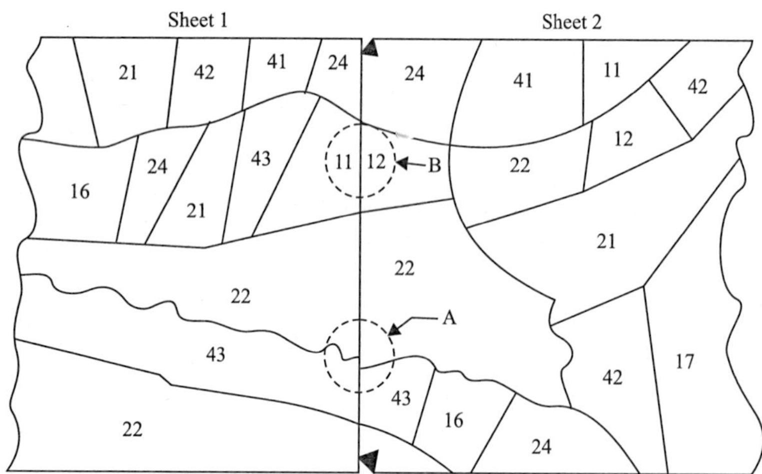

Fig. 21.4. Matching of boundaries and categories at edges of parcels.

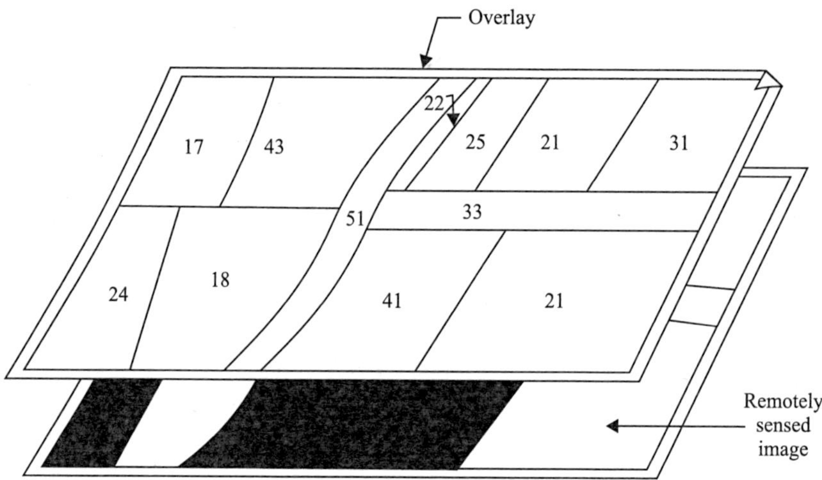

Fig. 21.5. The image overlay.

Another important consideration is recognition that the map cannot stand by itself; a written report must accompany each map so that the map reader has a summary of the interpretation process and a clear definition and description of each mapping unit. Without the written report, the reader cannot understand the classification system or how it has been applied to the imagery. The analyst may well devote as much time to recording and describing the map and its preparation as he does to preparing the map itself.

Preparation of the Image Overlay

The following paragraphs outline some of the essential considerations in preparing the image overlay (Fig. 21.5) and in recording information to appear in the accompanying report. Some of these considerations follow from an obvious interest in visual and logical clarity; others are simply conventions established by long application of rather arbitrary decisions. For the novice, it is probably best to follow the guidelines as outlined below; later, as additional experience is acquired, variations can be devised as required. But always the guiding principles should be attainment of visual and logical clarity and explicit description of the interpretation process.

1. Identification of land cover parcels is based on the elements of image interpretation as discussed previously. Sometimes identification may require a focus on identities of specific objects or facilities, but usually the primary task is one of consistent delineation of uniform parcels that match the classification system. The greater the uniformity of actual land use within areas represented on the map under a single symbol, the greater the usefulness of the map to the user.
2. The classification system must dovetail with categories accepted as useful by the map user. Maps and reports that organise information in a manner inappropriate for user's requirements are of little practical use. The image analyst has responsibility for ensuring that the final product is consistent with user's needs.
3. Sometimes classifications are proposed that tailor categories with respect to ease of recognition on specific forms of imagery. For the user-oriented maps discussed here, such classification systems would not be suitable because they organise informational content of the map around the image, rather than on user's requirements. The analyst should remember that user's requirements may be dictated by legal definitions, by policy of a governing body or by requirements for compatibility with data collected previously or by a neighbouring jurisdiction and therefore are not easily re-defined to meet desires of the image interpreter.
4. As a result, the interpreter should not define categories solely from appearance on the imagery. For example, categories such as 'sub-urban land' and 'strip development' are probably poor categories for most land use maps because they are based largely on ease of recognition of the image rather than correspondence with the land use categories of interest to planners and geographers. Thus, 'sub-urban land' should be re-defined and mapped, as appropriate, into residential and commercial land-use categories accepted in the user's definitions. (Note that any category, if properly defined and tailored to users' needs, may have its merits; as a rule, however, it is best not to devise unconventional categories for the convenience of the interpreter.) In summary, land use categories used in making the map should have a clear meaning to those who will use the map.
5. The beginning interpreter is well advised to use the system proposed by Anderson as a framework for organising the land use classification. The Anderson system (Table 21.1) provides a flexible framework for developing classifications at several levels of detail. Its hierarchical structure provides a capability to permit consistent, compatible classifications using imagery at varied scales and resolutions and the ability for convenient cartographic and statistical generalisation. The USGS publication that describes their classification provides a clear summary of the major issues of significance in the development of land-use classification from aerial imagery. The Anderson system need not be perceived as the ultimate classification, but for most purposes it seems to form a good standard to be accepted unless there is good reason to use another system. Nunnally and Witmer have observed that one of the problems with land-use classification prior to the proposal of the USGS system was the incompatibility of the many systems then in use.
6. Use of collateral material may be necessary if the interpreter is not intimately familiar with the region or if he or she encounters unusual categories. Non-image collateral information might include topographic maps, existing land-cover maps (at scales or dates differing from the one in

preparation) or tabulated economic statistics. Additional imagery at large scale can be used to resolve uncertainties emerging from analysis of small-scale, coarse-resolution imagery.

7. The image overlay records, in manuscript form, the boundaries between land-cover parcels. Each parcel is completely enclosed by a boundary and is labelled with a symbol keyed to the category descriptions in the classification system (Fig. 21.3). As a general rule, the image overlay shows only those features that occupy areas at the scale of the final map; usually point or linear features are not mapped. Thus, a highway would not normally be shown unless publication scale permits legible delineation of both sides of the highway right of way. For example, at very small scale, even four-lane expressways will be represented (if at all) as lines; at somewhat larger scale, the cloverleaf interchanges are large enough to be mapped (Fig. 21.6). And finally, a large-scale land-cover map might be able to show the entire highway as an areal feature. This same rule should be applied to other linear features, such as streams and rivers, railways and power lines. Selected point or linear features may, of course, be useful as landmarks or locational references on the map, but they are not classified as areas.

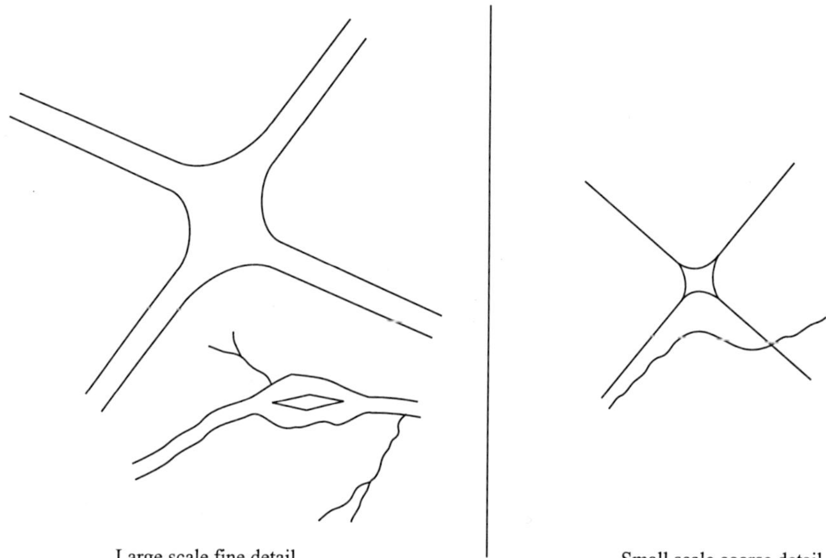

Fig. 21.6. Representation of linear and areal features at different scales.

8. The principle of consistent composition at each category means that the map user can be confident that the map presents a consistent representation of variation present on the landscape. Each parcel will by necessity encompass areas of categories other than that named by the parcel label; these inclusions are permissible, but must be clearly described in the category descriptions and must be consistent throughout the map. The issue of consistency is especially important when several interpreters work on the same project. Individual interpreters must coordinate their work with those working on neighbouring areas and supervisors must check to be sure that detail is uniform throughout the mapped area.
9. The entire area devoted to a specific use is delineated on the overlay (Fig. 21.7). Thus, the delineation of a airfield normally includes not only the runway, but also the hanger, passenger terminals, parking areas, access roads and in general all features inside the limits of the perimeter

fence (i.e., the outline of the parcel encompasses areas occupied by all of these features, even though they are not shown individually on the map). In a similar manner, the delineation of an interstate highway includes not only the two paved roadways, but also the median strip and the right of way.

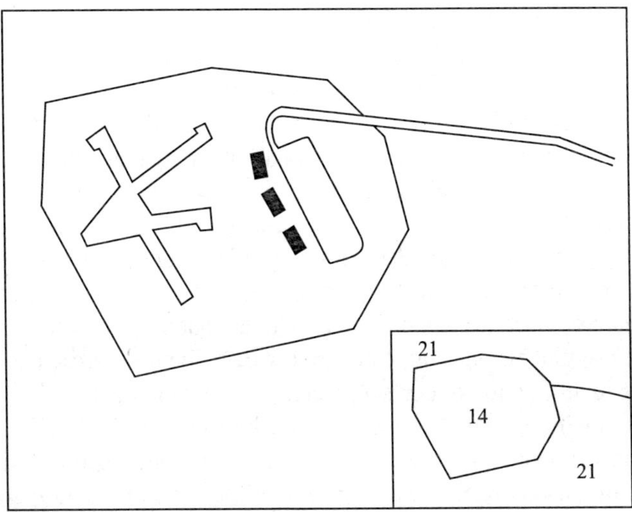

Fig. 21.7. Delineation of the entire area devoted to a given use.

10. The issue of multiple use is discussed in detail by Anderson. In brief, the problem is caused by the practice of assigning parcels to single categories even though we know that there may in fact be several uses. A forested area may simultaneously serve as a source of timber and as a recreational area for hunters and hikers. In general, the interpreter must make a decision, apply it consistently throughout the image and clearly document the procedure in the written report.
11. The interpreter must select an appropriate minimum size for the smallest parcels to be represented on the final map (Fig. 21.8). The interpreter may be able to identify parcels on the image much too small to be legibly represented on the map; therefore, it is necessary to select (as outlined below) a minimum size for the smallest parcels to be shown on the map. If several interpreters are working on the same project, all must apply the same minimum parcel size to assure that the variations in map detail reflect actual variations in parcel size on the ground.
12. In determining an appropriate minimum size for land-cover parcels, it is important to remember that it is the minimum size of parcels on the final map overlay that are of interest to the user, just as it is the legibility of this map (rather than the image overlay) that is of interest to the user. Because the map overlay may be presented at a different scale than that of the image overlay, the interpreter must extrapolate the minimum parcel size from the scale of the final map to the working scale of the image. Because it is difficult to perform this extrapolation mentally, it is sometimes useful to prepare a rough template of the approximate correct size to aid the interpreter in maintaining the correct level of spatial detail on the image overlay.
13. Anderson recommend that parcels on the final map be no smaller than 0.1 inch (2.54 mm) on a side (about 6.5 mm^2 in area). Loelkes presents values for minimum sizes of parcels to be represented on USGS land-use maps. Parcels of urban land, water and certain other specified

categories are to have minimum sizes of 4 ha (10 acres). At 1:1,00,000, such parcels would occupy about 4 mm^2 on the map; at 1:2,50,000, they would require about 0.64 mm^2. For all other categories, the minimum size should be 16 ha (40 acres). At 1:1,00,000, these parcels occupy about 16 mm^2 or about 2.6 mm^2 at 1:2,50,000. These guidelines apply for rather compact parcels; Loelkes proposes additional guidelines governing minimum widths for long narrow delineations. Although these sizes may be appropriate for the USGS land-use maps, they seem too small for routine use by interpreters using less sophisticated equipment and techniques. It should be obvious, however, that any single value proposed as a minimum size for mapped parcels should be interpreted as appropriate for the occasional presence of small parcels; if the interpreter encounters an extremely complex pattern of extremely small units, then an attempt to represent them all at the sizes mentioned above would produce an illegible map. In such a situation, some form of generalisation is clearly required to produce a visually and logically clear map at publication scale.

14. Usually the label of each category identifies the predominant category present within each parcel. Especially at small mapping scales, there may be inclusions of other categories; the mapping effort should aspire to define categories that include relatively consistent mixtures, identities and proportions of such inclusions and to accurately describe their presence within each category.
15. Sometimes the identification or correct placement of boundaries can be a problem, especially if the interpreter can discern a wide transition zone between categories. Usually the interpreter can place the mapped boundary at the center of transition zone, then describe the situation in the written report that accompanies the map. Sometimes wide transition zones occur consistenly within the mapped area; if so, it may be appropriate to define a separate category—for example, '419 Transitional Zone between Evergreen and Deciduous Forest Land'.
16. Mosaics of contrasting categories can present problems if the individual parcels are too small to be represented legibly at the scale of the final map (Fig. 21.9). In these situations, it may be appropriate to create a category tailored to a description of the situation—for example, '215 Mosaic of Cropland and Pasture'. The written category description then specifies the sizes and shapes of the parcels and presents an estimate of the percentages of the areal extent of each member of the mosaic. These composite mapping units are often a necessary departure from the principle of uniform composition of mapping units outlined above, but there is ample precedent for their use.

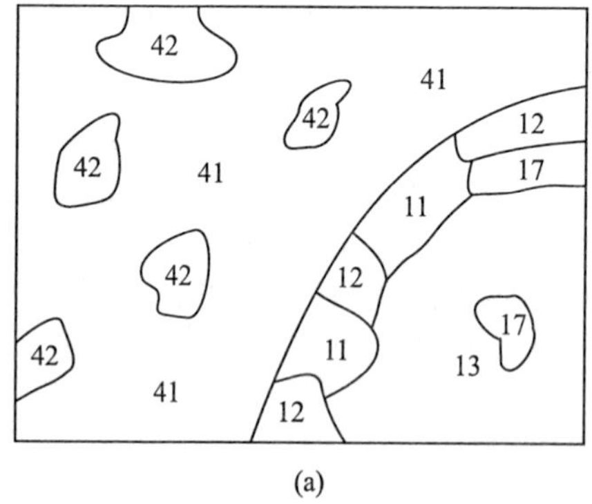

(a)

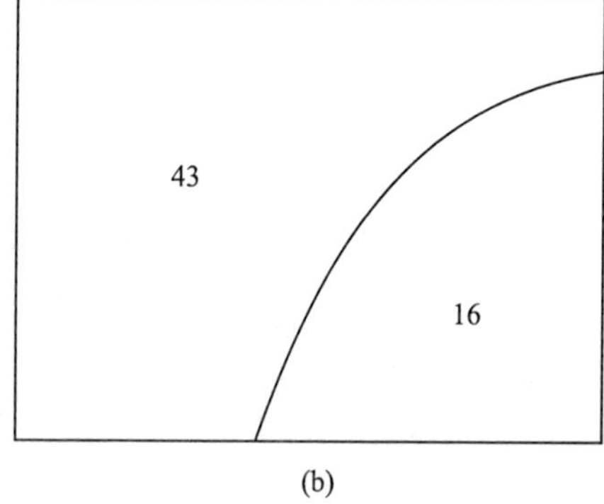

(b)

Fig. 21.8. Minimum parcel size. (a) Small minimum parcel size; and (b) large minimum parcel size.

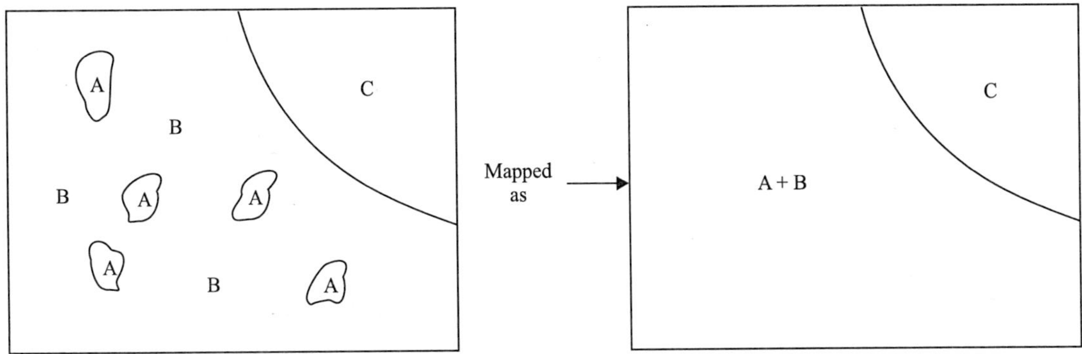

Fig. 21.9. Mosaics.

Field Observations

Even the most thorough, accurate interpretations require use of field observations as confirmation of manuscript maps and as a means of resolving uncertainties in the interpretation process. In the ideal, field observations should be acquired on at least three occasions during preparation of the land-use map: (i) before the interpretation of imagery begins, during preparation of the classification system, as a means of familiarising interpreters with the region and its major land uses; (ii) as the image overlay nears completion, to verify uncertain interpretations and to confirm consistency of the interpretation; and (iii) when the preliminary draft of the map overlay is complete, to detect and resolve any final problems before the final inked copy of the map is prepared. These three excursions to the field serve different purposes, so they may vary in respect to duration, route and intensity.

It is not practical to specify a universally applicable rule for determining the effort to be devoted to field observations. General guidelines can be suggested as follows. The analyst should be sure that field observations are made throughout the study area and that all land-use classes are observed in the field. That is, observations should not be confined to specific regions of the study area or the certain classes of land use. Thus, the analyst must make an effort to systematically observe representative areas of each land use class and each sector of the study region. These rather subjective guidelines must, of course, be applied as appropriate to specific situations. If the field observations are to be used for a quantitative role in the analysis, it may be necessary to apply a more rigorous approach to gathering field data by using the sampling patterns and principles outlined.

Although details of field excursions will depend greatly upon individual preferences and local circumstances, the following observations seem generally applicable:

1. Imagery should be taken to the field, together with manuscript overlays and supporting notes and maps. Provision must be made for annotating images (on overlays) or correcting manuscript overlays in the field. This usually means that maps and overlays should be temporarily clipped to a hardboard or cardboard surface small enough to carry in the field and to use in a vehicle, but large enough to present a sizeable portion of the map for navigation and annotation.
2. The route should be planned carefully to select an efficient itinerary that covers all essential areas. If timing is critical, it is important to allow time for unexpected delays. It may be wise to assign priorities to specific portions of the route, so the most important areas can be visited first.

3. Notes, photographs and sketches should be made in a systematic manner that ensures their usefulness later in the laboratory. If machine (xerox) copies of maps and aerial photographs are made beforehand, they can be used as a medium for making notes and recording locations of photographs and notes. These images will probably not record all detail visible on the original, but they permit the analyst to make annotations and notes without damaging the original.
4. If several interpreters are participating, it is usually best to work in teams, with a division of labour such that each has responsibility for specific tasks. If interpreters have been assigned specific geographic areas, then each is responsible for planning the itinerary for that area.
5. If the project has not already initiated contact with local officials and personnel from local extension services, planning agencies and other offices, these organisations should be solicited for advice and information.
6. At the completion of the trip, a systematic effort must be made to organise all material and information and to be sure that field notes are clearly transcribed into a more formal format while their meaning is still clear to all involved. Notes and annotated maps must be dated and labelled with names of the persons who made the observations.

Checking and Editing

Errors are inevitable. As a result, checking and editing are essential steps in the preparation of a map, equal in significance to the more immediately obvious steps of acquiring imagery and preparation of the image overlay. The search for errors is continuous throughout the preparation of the map, but should be focused at specific stages. Each parcel on the image overlay should be compared to the original image to confirm its identity, correct boundary placement and adhere to the minimum parcel size. On the final draft of the map overlay, a check should be made to confirm the presence and legibility of all boundary segments, to label parcels with their correct symbols and the register land-use boundaries to detail on the base map. For large projects with several map sheets, a check should be made to ascertain that boundaries match at the edges of sheets and the parcel identities match across sheet edges.

There is little benefit to be gained from an attempt to list all the errors that can occur in the preparation of a land-use map from aerial imagery. But we can propose two general principles that can be applied to detect and reduce errors of all kinds. First, checks for errors should be made throughout the preparation of the map; the earlier errors are detected, the easier they are to correct. However, if the check for errors is not focused at specific stages in the production of the map, the search for errors becomes so diffuse that it loses meaning. Therefore, specific steps in the production process (perhaps at the completion of the image overlay, completion of the map overlay, etc.) should be designated as opportunities for checks of the work completed thus far—a hurdle that must be passed before the next step begins. Second, errors are easier to control if specific individuals or groups assume responsibility for specific portions of the project. Checking and editing should be clearly separated from the preparation process by designating individuals to check the work of others or by having individuals check their own work at a time and place different from those of original preparation. These steps assist in promoting a critical attitude during the process of checking work for errors.

Map Overlay

The map overlay is formed by plotting boundaries from the image overlay onto an accurate planimetric base (Fig. 21.10). Parcel boundaries on the image overlay include positional errors inherent to all remotely sensed images. (Sources of such errors include relief displacement [aerial photograph], skew [images generated by electro-optical scanners], radar layover and radar foreshortening [SLAR imagery].) Therefore, the image overlay cannot be used as the basis for accurate measurements of distance or area and as a result must be considered to be a preliminary document. The map overlay registers to an accurate map so that corresponding detail (when present) on the two maps match exactly; it forms the basis for the final land-use map, suitable for use by the planners and administrators who require the land-use data. Even in instances when geometric errors have been minimised by pre-processing of the remotely sensed data, it is often desirable to plot land-use boundaries on a map base familiar to those who will use the map.

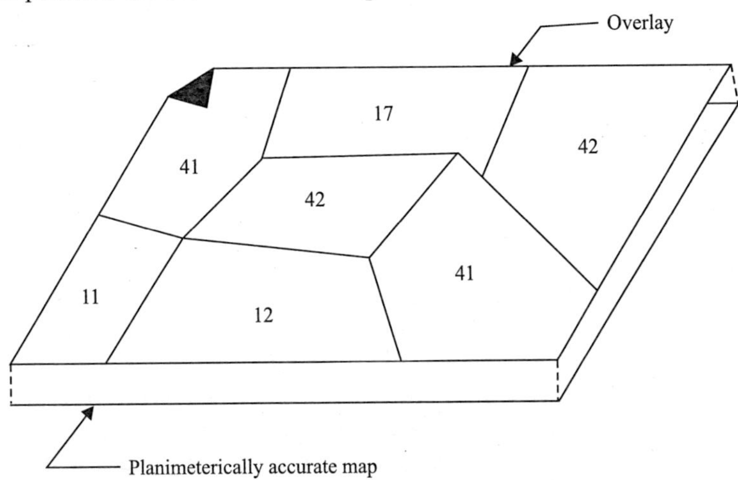

Fig. 21.10. The map overlay registers to an accurate map.

Changes in image scale and geometry can be made using a number of methods, including use of reflecting projectors or image transfer instruments. Often preparation of the map overlay requires not only changes in map scale, but also changes in map geometry necessitated by geometric properties of the remotely sensed images. Image transfer instruments are useful for this purpose because of their ability to permit convenient changes in image geometry—a process that can be accomplished only with difficulty using the usual reflecting projectors.

Regardless of the procedure to be used, the process of matching the two images is easiest when there is ample detail common to both the image and the map. As a result, the image overlay should be prepared to show locations of drainage, topographic and transportation features, for example, visible both on the map and on the remotely sensed image, even if such features do not always correspond to land-use boundaries to be shown on the final map. Such features provide the common detail necessary to permit convenient and accurate registration of the two maps. The map overlay shows land-use boundaries and symbols, plus other features (e.g., major highways, rivers and place-names) that may be useful to the reader in orientation and interpretation of the land-use map. The completed map should include a bar scale, legend, title, north arrow, coverage diagram and other information required for accurate interpretation.

Report

Few if any maps stand alone, to be accepted by readers at face value, without supporting information. The notion of 'supporting information' in this context should be interpreted broadly to include not only formally presented written material that accompanies the map, but also the wider realm of knowledge that the reader uses to examine and evaluate a map.

Some maps include written explanations of mapping technique and mapping unit characteristics, either as text on the map itself or in documents that accompany the map. This kind of information forms explicit information formally presented to the map reader.

Although many maps are without supporting information in such explicit form, the map reader often has the benefit of implicit, informal knowledge derived from experience with similar maps. For example, the reader of a USGS topographic quadrangle is presented with very little explicit information concerning mapping technique if the map itself is considered as the only source of information. However, the reader usually has access to substantial implicit information acquired in the examination of other similar maps and through knowledge of cartographic conventions. As a result, the reader can employ in an interpretation a wide range of knowledge not obvious from inspection of the map itself, pertaining to, for example, symbolisation, accuracy, cartographic conventions and degree of generalisation.

The usual land-use maps, despite many superficial similarities to one another, are characterised by notable diversity with respect to purpose, categorisation, detail, accuracy and symbolisation. Therefore, the reader must depend largely upon explicit information, formally presented in written documents that accompany the map. As a result, careful preparation of supporting documentation assumes an importance possibly equal in significance to that of preparation of the map itself.

Specifically, the reader requires knowledge regarding: (i) the regional setting; (ii) methods and materials used to prepare the map; (iii) definitions of mapping units; and (iv) the summarised results. Emphasis devoted to each of these topics may vary in relation to requirements of the organisation that will use the study, the purposes of the study and the experience of the intended audience. For example, the description of the regional setting may be abbreviated if it is known that the users of the map are already familiar with the area to be mapped. As a general rule, however, each item should be discussed to provide a complete document that can stand by itself.

Regional setting

The regional description outlines the geographic setting of the mapped region with emphasis on those factors most likely to influence the development of land-use patterns (Table 21.2). Unless the area is unusually large and diverse, a brief narrative of a few paragraphs should be sufficient.

Table 21.2. Geographical setting of mapped region likely to influence the development of land use pattern.

Regional setting
This region consists largely of mountainous topography, with valley bottoms at elevations of 150 to 300 meters (500 to 1000 feet), plateaus at 520 to 600 meters (1700 to 2000 feet) and some peaks as high as 1000 meters (3500 feet). Valleys are narrow, with steep sides and even floors. Plateau topography forms rather broad, level, surfaces, with gentle slopes
Climate is characterised by short, cool summers and long, severe winters. Average annual temperature is –3 to 10 degrees Celsius (near 27 to 50 degrees Fahrenheit). Annual precipitation is between 760 and 1000 millimeters (30 to 40 inches). Maximum precipitation falls during the summer months. Much of the winter precipitation falls as snow. Ample precipitation and cool temperatures mean that moisture is plentiful; perennial streams are abundant and moisture deficits are not common
Typical soils are moderately deep, medium-textured and stony. In valleys, slopes are gentle and soils tend to be well drained, although poorly-drained soils are important locally. On the uplands and valley sides slopes are steeper, soils are shallower and stones are more abundant
In valleys, most of the land is in farms, although most farms include sections of mixed hardwood forest. Pasture, hay, small grains and potatoes are among the most important crops. Dairy cattle and poultry are important and some land is devoted to orchards. Abandoned or fallow land is covered with grass and shrubs. Valley sides and uplands are primarily in forest

The reader who requires a detailed description should be directed to longer and more elaborate documents that focus on specific aspects of the region. The purpose of this section is simply to set the stage for subsequent description and analysis of land-use patterns. These patterns can, of course, be best understood in relation to the physical and economic context of the region. The physical setting is described in brief outlines of climate, topography, soils, drainage and natural vegetation. The economic setting is best described in terms of key elements of the industrial, commercial and agricultural life of the region. In most instances, this section should also include a brief description of the regional transportation system, with emphasis on links to other regions. The brevity of the regional description precludes completeness; it should, however, sketch the main features of the regional economic pattern, with emphasis upon interplay of physical and cultural elements that determine the broad features of regional land-use patterns.

Methods and materials

This section is also very brief, consisting of only a few concise paragraphs that describe the imagery and interpretation techniques used in preparing the map and supporting data and documents (Table 21.3). Imagery should be described in detail with respect to scale, resolution, date, quality, format, coverage and source. If it is necessary to use several missions to obtain complete coverage of the study area (due perhaps to holidays, clouds or partial coverage by the primary imagery), a coverage diagram should be prepared to depict respective coverage of each form of imagery (Fig. 21.11). The character and source of collateral information are described. The interpreter also provides an account of the interpretation procedure, with mention of any special equipment used.

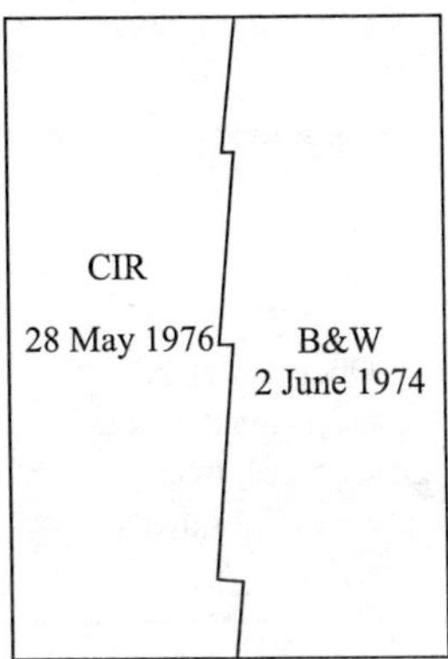

Fig. 21.11. Coverage diagram.

Table 21.3. Imagery and interpretation techniques used in preparing the map.

Methods and materials
Interpretation was made using black and white aerial photography at a scale of about 1:20000. Photography was flown in May of 1987; this imagery is of good quality, free of cloud cover and other defects. Interpretation of urban land use was sometimes aided by the use of large scale photography at 1:12000 dated April 1985, that provided additional detail
Paper prints were examined using magnification and stereoscopes; land cover parcels were then delineated on translucent overlays that registered to the photographs. Information was later transferred, with the aid of Zoom Transfer Scope, to a second overlay that registers to USGS 7.5 minute quadrangles at 1:24000. Land cover parcels are identified by three-digit symbols that match to a classification based upon the land cover classification system defined by Anderson

Mapping unit descriptions

The descriptions of mapping units is the most important part of the written report; they describe each and every category used in making the map, as they have been defined for this specific report and as they have been applied to this specific image. Information should be presented concisely but clearly and in sufficient detail to be of use to the reader in interpreting the map. Each category is described by specifying four separate elements (Table 21.4). First, the name and symbol are presented exactly as they are used in the map legend and on the map itself. Every category used on the map appears in the written report.

Table 21.4. Examples of descriptions of land-cover categories defined from remote sensing imagery.

Symbol	*Name*	*Definition*	*Ground features*	*Image appearance*
111	Single-unit residential	Land occupied primarily by detached dwellings and associated structures	Individual homes Lawns Streets Trees	Tree crowns usually dominant features (medium dark tone, coarse texture) Regular street pattern Driveways, sidewalks, lawns visible Rooftops visible
112	Multiple-unit residential	Dwelling units designed for occupation by several families	Apartment buildings Grassed areas Parking areas	Large buildings, usually rectangular, arranged in clusters Rooftops, parking lots visible Trees usually absent or sparse
211	Cropland	Land used for harvested cash crops	Plowed farmland Land planted in crops Fencelines, hedgerows Farm roads	Fields frequently have straight or even sides Fine, even texture Photo tone usually light (very dark for plowed land) Boundaries sharp Contour plowing, strip cropping frequently found Field size usually small or moderate
212	Pasture	Land used primarily for grazing livestock or for hay	Open grassland Occasional isolated shrubs, trees Fencelines, hedgerows Farm roads	Field frequently large Irregular shape, indistinct boundaries Medium photo tones Texture Mottled appearance

Second, category definitions give precise, clear definitions. The reader may understand the general conceptual definition of, for example, urban land, but cannot be expected to know the specific operational interpretation applied using specific imagery of a specific geographic region. Often the interpreter may be required to make very subtle or arbitrary distinctions in applying the classification to a specific image and these distinctions may vary at differing scales and resolutions and with differing forms of aerial imagery. The reader is entitled to an explanation of the exact procedure used for making the map; without the benefit of the information presented by the interpreter, the map reader has no means of reconstructing the operational meaning of the categories on the map. Descriptions should usually be concise; if elaborate descriptions are required, they probably should be presented in an appendix.

Third, the 'ground features' section presents an inventory of the primary objects and features that occur within each mapping unit. This section serves several purposes. It permits the reader to acquire a very precise understanding of the way that the interpreter has applied the classification to the image; in effect, this section reveals the interpreter has applied the classification to the image; in effect, this section reveals the interpreter's operational definition of each category. It also maintains the interpreter's discipline in defining mapping units; the interpreter who has difficulty in preparing concise inventories for each category discovers in effect that the categories have not been carefully defined or consistently applied to the image. The interpreter discovers earlier rather than later that any efforts include errors.

Fourth, the image appearance section described each category as it appears on the image, using the 'elements of image interpretation' as a framework for description. Table 21.4 lists a suggested vocabulary, with examples, as a means of describing the image appearance of land-use categories, as they appear on black-and-white aerial photography. Variations can be devised to suit other forms of imagery and a range of scales and resolutions. Finally, the most important function of this section is to present an accounting, for each category, of the presence of foreign inclusions. For example, the limitations of mapping scale may require the unmapped parcels of forest be included within areas designated on the map as cropland. If so, the mapping unit description for cropland should specify the presence, identity, proportion and (if possible) the pattern of occurrence of the unmapped inclusions (e.g., 'includes small isolated patches of deciduous forest too small to be mapped up to a total of about 15 per cent of the area mapped as cropland. Size and frequency of these areas decreases toward the southern edge of the mapped region').

The image appearance section does not attempt to describe the ground appearance of the category but the appearance of the category as it is represented on the imagery used for the study. It does not attempt to describe the image appearance at seasons other than the one in question. In brief, it does not form a general, universally applicable description, but merely offers on account of the facts that apply to the specific interpretation at hand.

The mapping unit descriptions can be presented in either of two formats. A brief narrative section, such as that used by Baker, presents each mapping unit description in a few concise sentences, organised to present all of the information outlined above (Table 21.5). Or, it may be appropriate to present the same information in a table (the classification table) organised as illustrated in Table 21.6. The classification table serves two complementary purposes.

Table 21.5. Mapping unit descriptions concisely.

Mapping unit descriptions
Agricultural land
Cropland and pasture
Parcels of varying shapes and sizes often bordered by roads and highways. This category typically appears as a mosaic of parcels of varied tones and textures that occupy valley bottoms in rural regions
Cropland
Areas in cropland are often characterised by straight edges or gently rounded curves, aligned in groups along rural roads. Distinctions between fields of different crops can be made on the basis of image tone and texture and sometimes from field size and shape. Texture are usually smooth to medium; tones are usually light to medium. Textures and tones within fields tend to be uniform. Farm buildings and isolated groves of trees are sometimes recognisable
Pasture and meadow (includes pastures/forest re-growth)
Larger parcels of pasture usually border cropland. Typically, tones vary from light to medium gray, forming a mottled appearance. Textures are smooth to medium. This category is usually positioned on moderate slopes. Often one side of a parcel will border a large tract of forest, while another side borders cropland

Table 21.6. Suggested terminology for written descriptions of land-use categories defined from aerial imagery.

Element of image interpretation	*Some suggested qualitative descriptors*
Size	'Small', 'medium', 'large'; also, is size 'uniform' or 'varied'?
Shape	'Compact', 'regular', 'elongate', 'square', 'irregular', 'rectangular'
Tone	'Light', 'medium', 'dark', 'very light', 'very dark'
Texture	'Coarse' 'medium', 'fine'; also, 'even', 'uneven', 'mottled', 'uniform'
Association	State whether there exists a consistent spatial association with other categories. What is the character of the boundaries with neighbouring categories?
Shadow	Can you determine whether shadow contributes to the appearance of a category? Consider not only objects, but areas as well. For example, scattered bushes in a pasture may be too small to be identified (except perhaps as tiny dots), but often their shadows are large enough to contribute to the photo appearance of the pasture. (Result: a speckled appearance). Or, often the edge of a forest at a pasture may be sharp enough to cause a shadow to fall in the pasture. (Result: an 'enhancement' of the boundary on one side, but not on others)
Site	In some instances, topographic position (site) may be an important means of describing the distinctive characteristics of features or categories
Pattern	Specify whether objects within a specific category are arranged in a distinctive manner. An obvious example: an orchard. Possibly the arrangement of greens and fairways in a golf course could be considered to be a distinctive pattern

Note. Often a precise and accurate description of a manual interpretation of a remote sensing image is rendered difficult by unfamiliarity with appropriate descriptive terms. Here a variety of qualitative descriptive terms are listed as suggestions for your interpretations. These terms are in a sense imprecise and must apply only to specific images, but they do offer a means of specifying image characteristics of land-cover categories. Develop your own modifications as you gain experience.

First, it provides explicit information for the map reader regarding definitions and compositions of categories as they have been defined for this specific study. Second, compilation of the classification table forms a means of the interpreter to evaluate the logic of the interpretation process. If an interpreter attempts to map ill-defined categories or categories that cannot be clearly separated on the basis of image appearance, the problems quickly become evident in the preparation of the mapping unit descriptions.

LAND-COVER MAPPING BY IMAGE CLASSIFICATION

Land cover can be mapped by applying image classification techniques to digital remote sensing images. In principal, the process is straightforward; in practice, many of the most significant factors are concealed among apparently routine considerations:

1. Selection of images: Success of classification for land-cover analysis depends upon the astute selection of images with respect to season and date. Therefore, the earlier discussion of the design and interpretation of searches of image archives, although ostensibly mundane in nature, assumes vital significance for the success of a project. What season will provide the optimum contrasts between the classes to be mapped? Possibly two or more dates might be required to separate all the classes of significance.
2. Pre-processing: Accurate registration of images and correction for atmospheric and system errors are required preliminary steps for successful classification. Sub-setting of the region to be examined requires careful thought.

3. Selection of classification algorithm: Selection of the classification procedure should also be made on the basis of local experience. AMOEBA, for example, tends to be accurate in landscapes dominated by large homogeneous patches, such as the agricultural landscapes of the mid-western United States and less satisfactory in landscape composed of many smaller heterogeneous parcels, such as those found in mountainous regions. Local experience and expertise are likely to be more reliable guides for selection of classification procedures than are universal declarations about their performance. Even when there is comparative information on classification effectiveness, it is difficult to anticipate the balance between effects of the choice of classifier, selection of image data, characteristics of the landscape and other factors.
4. Selection of training data: Accurate selection of training is one process that is universally significant for image classification. Training data for each class must be carefully examined to be sure that it is represented by an appropriate selection of spectral sub-classes, to account for variations in spectral appearance, due to shadowing, composition and the like. Many individual laboratories and image analysis software packages have applied unsupervised classification in various forms to define homogeneous regions from which to select training fields for supervised classification. Another approach to the same question is an algorithm that permits the analyst to select a pixel or group of pixels that forms the focal point for a region that grows outward until a sharp discontinuity is encountered. This process identifies a region of homogenous pixels from which the analyst may select training fields for the class.
5. Assignment of spectral classes to informational classes: Because of the many sub-classes that must be defined to accurately map an area by digital classification, a key process is the aggregation of spectral classes and their assignment to information classes. For example, accurate classification of the informational class deciduous forest may require several spectral sub-classes, such as north-facing forest, south-facing forest, shadowed forest and the like. When the classification is complete, these subclasses should be assigned a common symbol to represent a single informational class.
6. Display and symbolisation: The wide range of colours that can be presented on colour displays and the flexibility in their assignment, provides unprecedented opportunity for effective display of land-cover information. Although unconventional choices of colours can sometimes be effective, it is probably sensible to seek some consistency in symbolisation of land-cover information to permits users to quickly grasp the meaning of a specific map or image without detailed examination of the legend. Therefore, the colour symbols recommended by Anderson (Table 21.7) may be useful guides. Another strategy for assignment of colours to classes is to mimic the colours used for USGS 7.5 minute quadrangles (Table 21.7).

Table 21.7. Colour symbolisation of land-cover classes.

Anderson/USGS level I categories	
Urban or built-up land	Red
Agricultural land	Light brown
Rangeland	Light orange
Forested land	Green
Water	Dark blue

(Contd...)

Anderson/USGS level I categories	
Wetland	Light blue
Barren land	Gray
Tundra	Green-gray
Perennial snow or ice	White
USGS 7.5-minute quadrangles[a]	
Urban or built-up land	Pink
Non-forested land	White
Forested land	Green
Water and wetland	Blue
Exposed soil	Brown
Principal highways	Red
Structures, secondary highways	Black

[a] Offered here as an alternative, for experimentation or for student projects.

Within such general strategies, it is usually effective to assign related colours to related classes to symbolise Level II and Level III categories. For example, sub-classes of agricultural land can be represented in shades of brown (using Anderson strategy as a starting point), water and wetlands in shades of blue, sub-classes of forest in shades of green and so forth.

MAPPING LAND-USE CHANGE

Significance

Land-use patterns change over time in response to economic, social and environmental forces. The practical significance of such changes is obvious. For planners and administrators, they reveal the areas that require the greatest attention if communities are to develop in a harmonious and orderly manner. From a conceptual perspective, study of land-use changes permits identification of long-term trends in time and space and the formation of policy in anticipation of the problems that accompany changes in land use.

Because a given map can show only a single image of the many that form the evolving pattern of land use in a region, any land-use map begins to decrease in accuracy from the time it is completed. Users who are familiar with the mapped region will accumulate an informal knowledge of changes that have occurred after the map was prepared—a mental map of the changes. For systematic study of changes, however, it is necessary to prepare maps that formally document changes in land use between two specific dates. Aerial imagery provides the unique capability to reconstruct previous land-use patterns using archived images and thereby form the basis for a study of former patterns, even though no map was prepared at the time.

Manual Compilation of Land-Use Change Maps

Although in theory preparation of change maps is very simple, a number of practical problems are encountered in practice. Preparation of a change map requires comparison of two separate land-use maps prepared from imagery acquired at two dates; areas that experience changes and land use are noted (usually by superimposition of the two maps), then recorded on a third map (Fig. 21.12). This third map shows only the changes, which can then be tabulated by area and by category to reveal the extent and placement of land-use changes. If imagery for several dates is available, a series of change maps can record the evolution of land-use patterns over time and possibly reveal long-term patterns of change, rates of change in specific areas and intermediate steps in the development of land-use patterns.

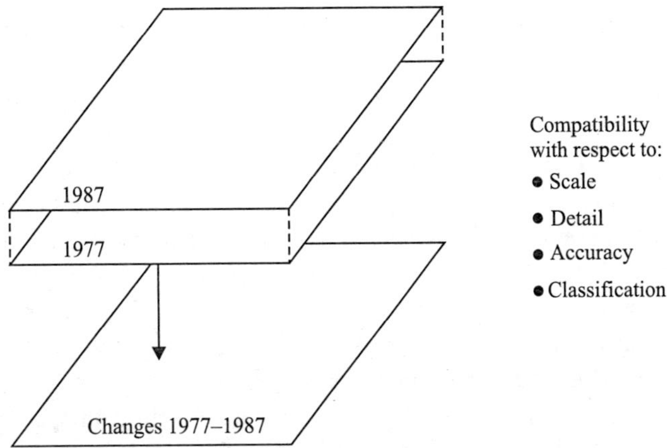

Fig. 21.12. Manual compilation of a land-use change.

Although this procedure is essentially simple and straightforward, a number of practical problems must be anticipated. First, the two maps must share a common base before they can be registered to one another. Even if both maps already use a common base, the interpreter must work carefully because minor differences in placement of boundaries can create differences that do not form evidence of land-use change but are merely artifacts of the interpretation process. Furthermore, the two maps must be prepared at a consistent level of detail so that they change map records true changes rather than differences in interpretation technique. Finally, the two maps must use the same classification system or it will not be possible to compare the two maps. For these reasons, it is important that the same interpreters work on all phases of a change map or that interpreters be supervised by a single individual with overall knowledge of the project. The image interpreter may find that preparation of change map requires examination of imagery at varying scales, resolutions and qualities. Each interpreter must assess the imagery in relation to map scale and classification detail to determine the level of detail most suitable for the change map. As a general guideline, it seems sensible to recommend that all change maps be prepared at a level of detail consistent with that obtained from interpretation of the lowest quality, coarsest resolution imagery that will be used in the project. Otherwise, the interpreter will be faced with the problem of comparing two maps that differ greatly in detail and accuracy.

These considerations lead to the general observation that preparation of change maps requires continuity in technique and in personnel and close coordination throughout the mapping process. Source maps must be compatible with respect to classification, spatial detail and map base. As a result, it would seem unwise to use maps prepared by different individuals or organisations as the basis for change maps.

Digital Compilation of Land-Use Change Maps

The simply logic and mechanical nature of change compilation procedures lend themselves to implementation in the digital domain. Jensen enumerates change detection algorithms and notes that not all land-cover changes are identical. For example, sub-urban land cover typically progresses through several stages, from initial clearing of land, through construction and landscaping—any or all of which may be present on a given image. Because each stage has distinctive spectral characteristics, a given area may appear in different form on each image and the analyst may encounter different levels of difficulty in detection and classification at each stage.

The issue of compatibility retains its significance in the digital domain. Images must register and have comparable levels of spatial, spectral and radiometric resolution. Unless the objective is to compare images from one season to another, the two images typically represent the same season but different years. Jensen lists a selection of pre-processing operations effective in preparing data for use in change detection comparisons. In any specific situation, the analyst must employ an intimate knowledge of the area to be studied, then apply a selection of methods tailored to the specifics of the study area. It seems unlikely that there is any single procedure that can be equally effective in all situations.

Jensen's list of digital change detection procedures includes the following:

1. Image algebra apples arithmetic operations to pixels in each image, then forms the change image from the resulting values. Image differencing, for example, simply subtracts one digital image from another digital image of the same area acquired at a different date. After registration, the two images are compared pixels by pixel to generate a third image composed of numerical differences between paired pixels from the two images. Values at or near zero identify pixels that have similar spectral values and therefore presumably have experienced no change between the two dates. This procedure is typically applied to a single band of a multispectral data set; usually a constant value is added to eliminate negative values. The analyst must select (sometimes by trail and error) a threshold level to separate those pixels that have experienced change from those that have not changed land cover, but may exhibit small spectral variations caused by other factors. Jensen reports that image differencing is among the most accurate change detection algorithms, but that it is not equally effective in detecting all forms of land-use change. Image ratios, another form of image algebra, can be important in change detection because they may assist the analyst in standardising for variations in illumination, thereby isolating spectral changes caused by land-cover changes.
2. Post-classification comparison requires two or more independent classifications of each individual scene, using comparable classification strategies. The two classifications are then compared, pixel by pixel, to generate an image that shows pixels placed in different classes on the two scenes. Successful application of this method requires accurate classifications of both scenes so that differences between the two scenes portray true differences in land use rather than differences in classification accuracy. In urban and sub-urban landscapes, the high percentages of mixed pixels (at Landsat MSS resolution) have tended to decrease classification accuracy and therefore to generate inflated estimates of the numbers of pixels that have experienced change. Because post-classification comparison permits compilation of the matrix of from-to changes, it provides more useful results than some other methods (e.g., image algebra that simply identifies pixels that have changed, without specifying the classes involved).
3. Multidate composites are formed by assembling all image bands from two or more dates together into a single data set. The composite data set can then be examined using methods described in earlier chapters, including principal components analysis and image classification. Thus, for two dates of Landsat MSS data, the data would consist of eight bands of spectral values. A classification of the composite identifies not only the usual land-use categories, but also classes composed of

pixels that have experienced change from one date to the next. Due to the large size of the data set and its unwieldy character, this approach is usually inefficient and has been reported to be less accurate.

4. Spectral change vector analysis examines each pixel's position in mutispectral data space. If the corresponding pixel in an image from another data set occupies a nearby position, then the ground area represented by the pixel has not changed much during the interval between the two dates. If the two pixels occupy different positions, then the ground area has experienced changes. Usually the procedure is applied by preparing a pair of images representing the magnitude of the mutispectral changes and the detection of the change; these images can then be inspected by the analyst to set thresholds separating substantive changes from incidental changes caused by atmospheric effects, shadowing or other ephemeral cause.
5. Use of a binary change mask requires classification of the image from the first date. Image algebra is then applied to the original image data for both dates to generate an image of changes, as described in (1) above. The image is used to prepare a binary mask, representing only changed and unchanged pixels. The binary change mask is then superimposed over the image data for the second date and the classification of this image examines only those pixels that have been identified as changed. This method is often effective, provided that the binary change mask is accurate.
6. On-screen digitisation requires specialised image analysis software that permits the analysts to view both images side by side on the same screen and the outline changed areas manually using on-screen digitisation, based upon visual interpretation. This methods has been used primarily, if not exclusively, the large-scale digital images.
7. Change detection by image display is essentially a digital version of the photographic change detection methods mentioned above. Corresponding bands from different dates are used as separate overlays in a red-green-blue colour display. Pixels that have experienced change appear in distinctive colours (depending upon the assignment of images to colours), thereby flagging those pixels that have changes during the interval between the two dates. This technique does not reveal the form-to change information provided by some other techniques.

BROAD-SCALE LAND-COVER STUDIES

The availability of multispectral AVHRR data (and data from similar meteorological satellites) on a regular basis has provided the capability to directly compile broad-scale land-cover maps and data. In this context, broad scale refers to images that represent entire continents or even entire hemispheres, based on data collected over a short period of time, perhaps about 10 days to 2 weeks. Previously, data for such large regions could be acquired only by generalising more detailed information—a task that was difficult and inaccurate because of the incompleteness of the coverage and the inconsistencies of the many detailed maps required to prepare small-scale maps. The finer resolution data from the Landsat and SPOT systems provide information of local and regional interest, but are not really suitable for compilation of data at continental scales because 7of the effects of cloud cover, differences in sun angle and other factors that prevent convenient comparisons and mosaicking of many scenes into a single data set representing a large region.

AVHRR data, provide coverage of entire continents over relatively short time periods. Accumulation of data over a period of a week to 10 days usually permits each pixel to be observed at least once under cloud-free conditions. Although the scan angle varies greatly, data are acquired at such frequent intervals that it is often possible to select coverage of the region of interest from the central section of each scene to reduce the effects of the extreme perspective at the edges of each scene.

Tucker and others examined AVHRR data for Africa, using images acquired over a 19 month time interval. They examined changes in the vegetation index at intervals of 21 days; their results clearly illustrate the climatic and ecological differences between the major biomes, as observed using the vegetation index and seasonal variations in the vegetation index. They conducted a second analysis using eight of the 21 day segments selected from the 19 month interval mentioned above. They calculated principal components as a means of condensing the many variables into a concise yet potent data set that describes both seasonal and place-to-place variations in the vegetation index. Their land-cover map (based upon the first three principal components) is an extraordinary representation of key environmental conditions over an entire continent. It shows what are clearly major climate the ecological zones, as defined by conventional criteria, although they have been derived from data that are completely independent of the usual climatic data. The map has a uniformity, a level of detail and (apparently) an accuracy not obtainable using conventional vegetation and climatic analysis. Although the Tucker has not fully evaluated his map by systematic comparison with field observations, it seems clear that products of this sort will provide an opportunity to examine broad ecological zones at continental scales and furthermore, to examine seasonal and year-to-year changes in such zones.

More recently, AVHRR data have been used to compile other kinds of broad-scale land-cover maps.

SOURCES OF COMPILED LAND-USE DATA

During the past decades, remote sensing has contributed greatly to the ability for organisations to prepare comprehensive land-cover surveys of large regions. Satellite imagery in particular has provided near-simultaneous acquisition, broad areal coverage, uniform detail and other qualities not available from alternative sources.

In the United States, several governmental initiatives have exploited this capability to prepare broad-scale land-cover surveys.

Land Use and Land Cover

In 1990s the USGS developed a national land-cover mapping programme based on manual interpretation of high-altitude aerial photography at scales of 1:60000 and smaller. The resulting USGS Land Use and Land Cover (LULC) data files describe the vegetation, water, natural surfaces and cultural features for large regions of the United States. The USGS National Mapping Programme provides these data sets and associated maps using map bases at 1:2,50,000. (In some cases, such as Hawaii, 1:1,00,000 scale maps are also used as the base.)

Multiresolution Land Characteristics Consortium

To economise in the acquisition of image data, in 1992 several agencies of the US government formed a consortium designed to acquire satellite-based remote sensor data for their separate environmental monitoring programmes. The MultiResolution Land Characteristics (MRLC) Consortium was sponsored originally by the USGS, the US Environmental Protection Agency (EPA), the National Oceanographic and Atmospheric Administration (NOAA) and the US Forest Service (USFS). MRLC was designed as an effort to pool financial resources to acquire satellite remote sensing imagery data in a cost-effective manner. Mapping efforts are based upon TM data and future plans are directed at acquisition of Landsat 7 ETM data for all 50 states, to be used as the basis for land cover mapping.

During the 1990s, MRLC supported land-cover mapping programmes such as the GAP analysis project and the National Land Cover Data (NLCD) project, both mentioned below.

Gap Analysis

In the United States, a national programme to assess biodiversity and threats to biodiversity has been based on assessment of land cover derived from multispectral Landsat TM data. The objective of gap analysis is to identify 'gaps' in biodiversity by surveying land-cover patterns to assess cover types. For example, regions with high species diversity are often associated with high ranges of elevations, contrasts in soil characteristics and the presence of varied vegetation classes. Gap analysis permits identification of high priorities for conservation and for development and land-use policies.

Each state conducts its own survey, using its own classification, mapping and accuracy assessment strategy, developed in collaboration with neighbouring states. The national project is coordinated by the National Gap Analysis Programme within the USGS, Biological Resources Division (USGS-BRD).

National Land-Cover Data

One of the projects sponsored by the MRLC Consortium was production of land-cover data for the conterminous United States. Land cover was mapped using general land-cover classes. For example, forest is classified as either deciduous, evergreen or mixed. Land-cover classification was based on the Landsat 5 TM data archive and a host of ancillary sources. Once completed, NLCD will be the first national land-cover data set produced since the early 1990s, effectively replacing the land-cover data known to many as LUDA or GIRAS. Available data have been used for many environmental applications, including land-use planning, hydrological analyses, habitat assessments and many others. Assessments of the accuracy of the data are undertaken after completion of large regions.

22

Global Remote Sensing

INTRODUCTION

The history of remote sensing can be visualised as one of increasing scope of vision, with respect both to space and time (Fig. 22.1). Before the availability of aerial photography, human observation of the landscape was limited in scope to the area visible from a high hill or building. As aerial photography became available, it became possible to view larger areas over longer intervals. Later, as the routine availability of infrared emulsions permitted high-altitude aerial photography, larger areas could be represented within a single frame. Still later, the larger areas viewed by satellite images permitted analysts to consider even broader perspectives. Finally, by merging images from several dates to remove effects of cloud cover, it became possible to compile images representing continents, hemispheres and the entire globe. Such images have made it possible to directly examine broad-scale environmental patterns and their changes over years, decades and even longer intervals. This capability has had profound impact on perspectives that scientists and the general public apply to their consideration of broad-scale environmental issues. Issues that once could be only matters of speculation now can be considered in the light of data and information that are based on systematic observation.

The instruments and programmes outlined in this chapter are designated to gather data that will provide the geographic coverage and consistency required to compile global data sets and to examine fundamental questions concerning place-to-place variations in climate, vegetation patterns and biophysical processes and their changes over time.

BIOGEOCHEMICAL CYCLES

Such capabilities open new opportunities for understanding basic processes that underlie the earth's climatic and biologic patterns. The elements and nutrients that make life on earth possible reside differentially in biologic, geologic and atmospheric components of the earth. Over years, decades and centuries, atmospheric and geologic processes cycle these nutrients and chemicals varied through the components of the biosphere. The earth's atmosphere and oceans move at rates measured in minutes, hours or days. At the other extreme, minerals of the earth's crust can be considered mobile only when viewed over intervals of many millions of years.

Understanding the earth's environment requires examination of movements and interchanges between its varied components.

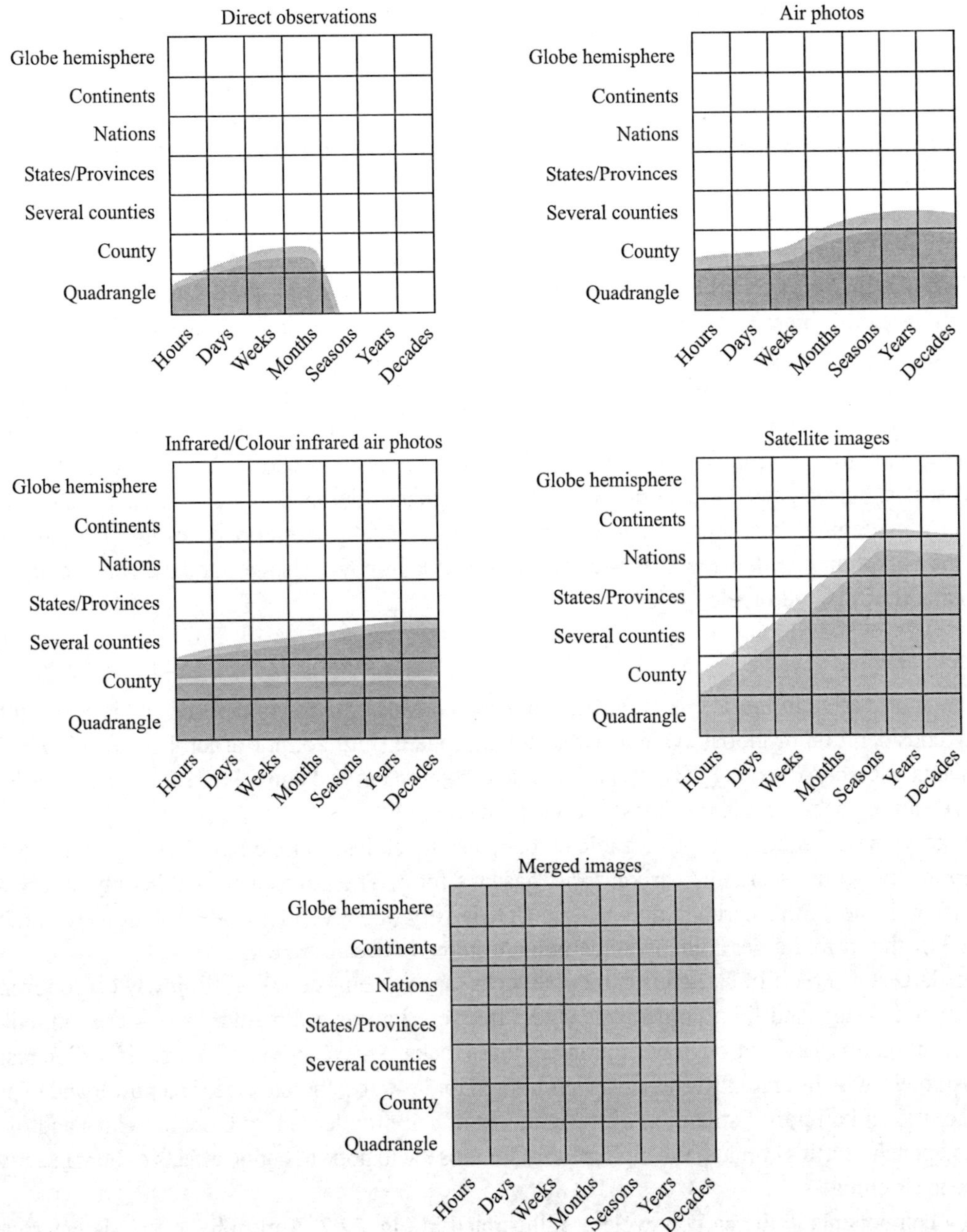

Fig. 22.1. Increasing scope of human vision of the earth. The horizontal axis in each graph represents time (in an arbitrary scale of increasing intervals from hours and days at one extreme to years and decades at the other). The vertical axis represents space (in arbitrary units, from quadrangle-sized areas at one extreme to continents and hemispheres at the other).

For example, minerals weather from geologic material, enter the soil, are absorbed by plant roots, then are incorporated into plant tissues as plants grow. As these plants die and decompose, nutrients are released into groundwater or surface run-off, then again assume geologic form as sedimentological and lithological processes concentrate and mineralise materials. Such are the biogeochemical processes that govern the movement of carbon, sulphur, nitrogen, oxygen and other elements.

The following sections outline major components of the most important biogeochemical cycles; these are not intended to provide complete descriptions, but to illustrate the kinds of issues that require global perspectives.

Hydrologic Cycle

The hydrologic cycle is the best known and most central of the many processes that cycle materials through the earth's biosphere. Because of the central role of moisture in biologic, climatic and geologic processes, the hydrologic cycle has obvious significance for all other processes that cycle materials through the earth's environment. Hydrologic processes at all scales are intimately connected with land-cover, so the broad-scale land-cover data provided by Advanced Very-High-Resolution Radiometer (AVHRR) data form a central component of efforts to examine the hydrologic cycle at continental and global scales. Further, aerial photography and the satellite data outlined in previous chapters provide, at least in some regions, a record of land-cover changes extending several decades into the past, which offer the opportunity to develop broad-scale analyses of land-cover changes and their impact upon key components of the hydrologic cycle.

Carbon Cycle

Carbon, in its varied forms, is one of the essential components of living organisms and is of key interest in any consideration of global cycling within the biosphere (Fig. 22.2). Carbon is available for living organisms as carbon dioxide (CO_2) and as organic carbon (plant and animal tissues), sometimes known as fixed carbon, because it is much less mobile than CO_2.

Photosynthesis reduces CO_2 to organic carbon, also much less mobile than CO_2; Within organisms respiration can convert organic carbon to its gaseous form. The atmosphere holds only a very small proportion of the earth's carbon, atmospheric CO_2 is very effective in absorbing long-wave radiation emitted by the earth. Larger amounts of carbon are stored in oceans.

The largest reservoir of carbon is carbonate rocks (such as limestone). Very slowly carbon from the atmosphere, oceans and living organisms enters this reservoir as sedimentary rocks are formed. And slowly carbon is released through weathering of these rocks. An exception, of course, is carbon residing as fossil fuels, which is rapidly released as it is burned for heat, to generate electrical power and to propel automobiles and aircraft. Estimation of the amounts of carbon released by these activities and of their effects upon the earth's climate, is a high priority for those who hope to gauge effects of human activities upon earth's climates.

Key components in the carbon cycle are illustrated in Fig. 22.2. Atmospheric CO_2 is incorporated into the structure of living organisms by photosynthesis. The decay of organic matter releases CO_2 into the atmosphere. CO_2 is also released by the burning of fossil fuels.

Remote sensing instruments assist scientists in understanding the carbon cycle by providing estimates of the areas covered by plants, identifying the kinds of plants and estimating the time period for which they are photosynthectically active.

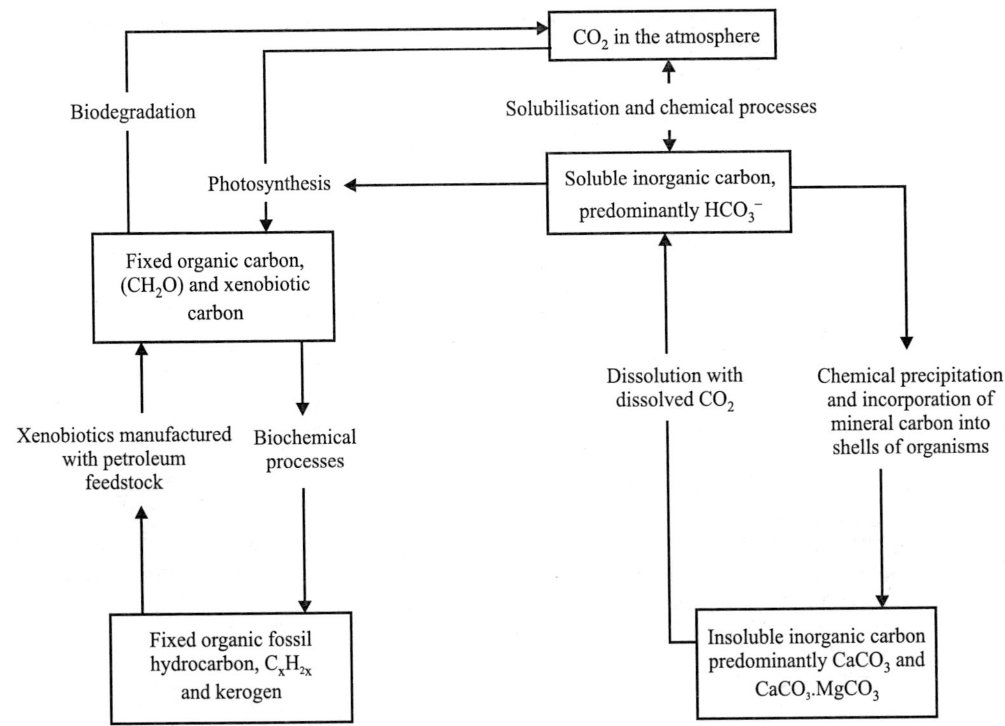

Fig. 22.2. Carbon cycle.

Nitrogen Cycle

Nitrogen occurs in large amounts on earth and is of great significance in the food chain, because it occurs as a principal element in the atmosphere and in tissues of plants and animals (Fig. 22.3). It occurs in several forms, both organic and inorganic and participates in important biological processes. Very large amounts of the earth's nitrogen is considered inactive; it is held in sedimentary and crustal rocks and does not participate in the short-term cycling of nitrogen. Within the active pool, the largest amount of nitrogen resides in the atmosphere, where it is one of the major constituents of the atmosphere. Atmospheric nitrogen, however, is not available for biological use.

Nitrogen becomes available for biological use through fixation, the chemical reaction in which nitrogen combines with hydrogen (H) to create ammonia (NH_3). Although nitrogen fixation can occur within the atmosphere (through lightening strikes), in the burning of fossil fuels and industrially (in the manufacture of artificial fertilisers), the most significant source by far is biologically based. Biological fixation occurs by the action of living plants that change atmospheric nitrogen (N_2) to a fixed form (NH_3) that can be used by plants and animals. Micro-organisms, both free-living and those symbiotic with specific plants (legumes), are the only animals that can accomplish this process. Amino acids from plant or animal tissue can be broken down by the process of ammonification, which releases energy, H_2O and CO_2. Ammonification is accomplished by decomposing micro-organisms.

By this process, nitrogen enters the food chain and the tissues of plants and animals. Denitrification, the process by which nitrites (NO_2^-) or nitrates (NO_3^-) are converted to molecular nitrogen or nitrous oxide, is accomplished by soil bacteria under anaerobic conditions. This process occurs in a two-step process during which ammonia is oxidised to nitrate in two steps. The first, completed by the bacteria *Nitrosommonas*, yields nitrate ions and water. The second step, accomplished by the bacteria *Nitrobacter*, consumes nitrite ions to yield nitrate. Industrial fixation accomplishes the same process using energy to transform atmospheric nitrogen to ammonia, which can be used in other industrial processes to manufacture fertilisers and explosives.

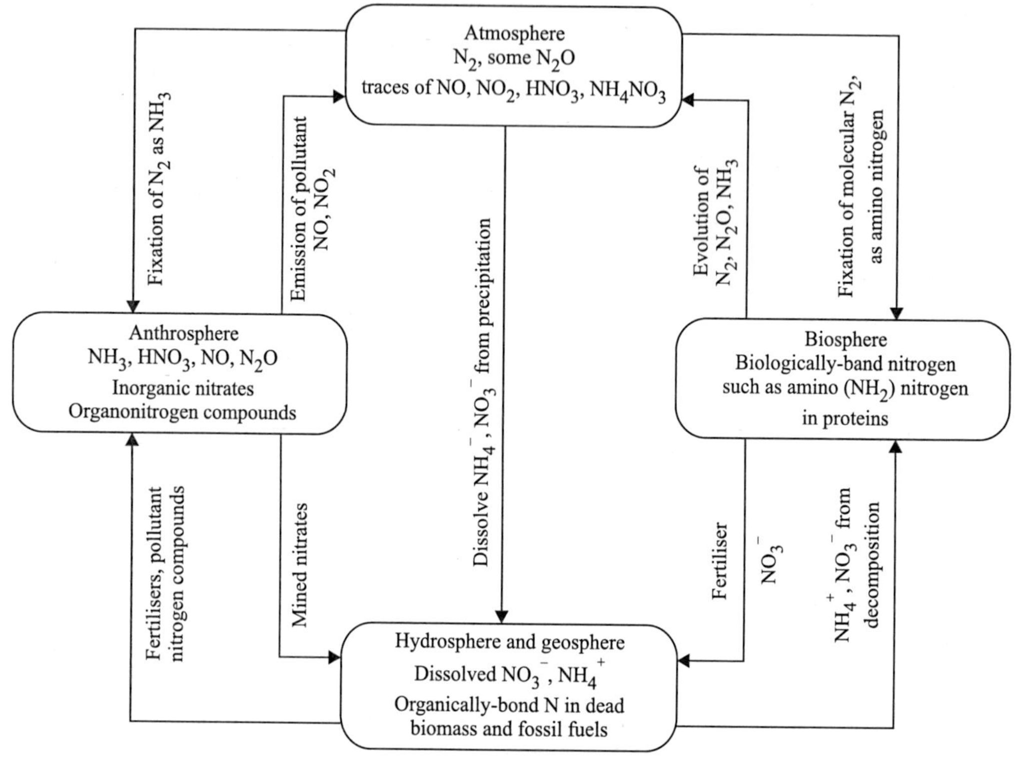

Fig. 22.3. Nitrogen cycle.

One of the largest reservoirs of nitrogen is decaying organic matter. Remote sensing assists in understanding the nitrogen cycle by providing accurate estimates of areas where organic matter accumulates for decay, such as swamps and marshes.

Sulphur Cycle

In comparison with other biogeochemical cycles discussed here, the sulphur cycle (Fig. 22.4) is somewhat less significant with respect to total amounts in active circulation and with respect to its role in the food chain. But it has great significance if we examine ways in which humans influence the sulphur cycle. Sulphur resembles nitrogen in the sense that it occurs in several forms within the environment and participates in several organic and inorganic reactions that alter its forms and behaviour. By far the largest amount of sulphur is in geologic form, in sedimentary deposits that are removed from short-term participation in the sulphur cycle. Weathering releases small amounts of geologic sulphur to the atmosphere. Of greater interest, however, is the release of sulphur into the atmosphere by the removal and burning of fossil fuels.

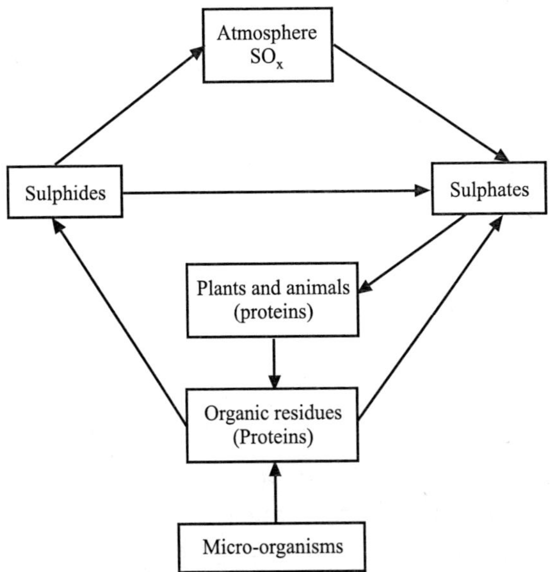

Fig. 22.4. Sulphur cycle.

Oceans form the main reservoir for sulphur in active circulation. Only small amounts reside in the atmosphere. On land, some is incorporated in the tissues of plants and animals and some is retained as decaying organic matter (e.g., in swamps and marshes). Sulphur enters the atmosphere from four sources: emissions from bacteria as organic matter decays, combustion of fossil fuels, airborne dust from evaporating sea spray and volcanic sources.

Accelerated release of geologic sulphur by burning of fossil fuels has contributed to reactions within the atmosphere that have increased the acidity of rainfall near industrialised regions of northern latitudes, which in turn is believed to have decreased the pH of lakes, rivers and even soils in some regions. Such changes in water and soil acidity, if sustained, would have profound impact on wildlife, vegetation patterns and soil fertility. Because such impacts have already been observed, governments have instituted efforts to reduce sulphur emissions and to encourage industries to switch to low-sulphur fuels.

Significance of Remote Sensing

Remote sensing is the primary means by which we can observe the dynamic character of the earth's biosphere. Although basic outlines of biogeochemical cycles are well known, specific quantities, rates of movement and regional variations are not well understood, nor is the true impact of human activities upon their functioning. Such detail is necessary for scientists to assess the significance of human influences on biogeochemical processes and their significance in relation to natural variations. Therefore, scientists seek not only to understand the general structure of such cycles but also to develop a more precise knowledge of quantities and rates of movement within these cycles.

Preparation of such estimates is very difficult because the figures commonly given are necessarily very rough estimates and conventional data are not adequate to provide the required data. For example, the existing network of climate stations consists of a series of point observations at locations not representative of specific environments. This network can provide only the very crudest estimates of temperature patterns and is clearly inadequate for answering the critical questions concerning the possible warming of the earth's atmosphere during recent history.

Mather and Sdasyuk review existing sources of environmental data suitable for assessing broad-scale environmental trends, identifying the many defects in the present sources of data. They, like many others, conclude that broad-scale remote sensing provides the only practical means to acquire data of sufficient scope for addressing these issues.

ADVANCED VERY-HIGH-RESOLUTION RADIOMETER

The advanced very-high-resolution radiometer (AVHRR) is a multispectral radiometer carried by a series of meteorological satellites operated by NOAA in near-polar, sun-synchronous orbits. They can acquire imagery over a swath width of approximately 2400 km. AVHRR acquires global coverage on a daily basis; the frequent global coverage is possible because of the wide angular field of view, but areas recorded near the edges of images suffer from severe geometric and angular effects. As a result, AVHRR data selected from the regions near the nadir provide the most accurate information. Although designed initially for much narrower purposes, AVHRR is the first sensor to provide the basis for collection of worldwide data sets that permit assessment of environmental issues.

AVHRR pixels are about 1.1 km on each side at nadir, with fine radiometric resolution at 10 bits. Details of spectral coverage vary with specific mission, but in general AVHRR sensors have recorded radiation in the visible and infrared regions of the spectrum. AVHRR spectral regions have been selected to attain meteorological objectives, including spectral data to distinguish clouds, snow, ice and open water. Nonetheless, AVHRR has been employed on an adhoc basis for land resource studies. The AVHRR sensor includes one channel in the visible spectrum, one in the near infrared and three in the thermal infrared. It is possible to use the data to calculate vegetation indices.

From these AVHRR data, the global vegetation index (GVI) data set has been prepared for the period 1998–2001. GVI data are presented using an arbitrary grid system, with cells that vary in size with latitude, from about 13 km at the equator to 26 km at the poles. Data collected within a 7 day period are examined for the brightest ('greenest') NDVI value in each cell for the reporting interval. GVI images remove effects of clouds, except for instances in which clouds are present in all seven images.

Such data provided one of the first tools that permitted study of the earth's major biomes. Previously, the areas and extents of major regions of forest, savanna, tundra, deserts and the like could only estimated roughly from climate and vegetation patterns as observed at ground level. Although satellite data show that these earlier approximations were quite accurate, the use of satellite data permits closer studies of detail of the patterns and examination of seasonal variations and long-term trends with accuracy and detail that were not previously possible. Specifically, AVHRR permits closer examination of effects of droughts and other broad-scale climatic changes, as well as changes related to human activities.

Pathfinder Data

In 1990 NASA and NOAA began a programme to compile Pathfinder data sets, designed to provide data for analysis of long-term environmental processes at continental and global scales. Pathfinder data are compiled for systems placed in service prior to the Earth Observing Systems (EOS), to provide experience with global-scale data systems and to extend to period of analysis to as early a date as possible. These objectives require use of systems with accurate calibration and consistent qualities to permit analysis over time and from one sensor system to another. The first Pathfinder data sets have been prepared from AVHRR data, other meteorological satellite data and selected Landsat data. Pathfinder data are sampled over time (in part to select cloud-free data and to reduce other atmospheric effects) and over space (to create consistent levels of detail and data sets of manageable sizes) and then processed to permit convenient use by a wide variety of users. Separate Pathfinder initiatives are underway to compile data describing ocean surface temperature, atmospheric conditions and land surfaces.

Pathfinder AVHRR land data are global in scope, but sampled over time and space. The daily data set consists of AVHRR terrestrial data, mapped to an equal area projection on an 8 km grid. Pixels near the edges of the AVHRR swath are excluded. The daily data can be used directly for analysis or as source data for composite data sets. The composite data set is derived from the daily data set; the compositing process filters out effects of clouds and selects data for each date from the scene with the highest NDVI. The climate data set is compiled to a 1° × 1° resolution, for 8 to 11 day composite periods. The result forms a set of cloud-free, averaged, NDVI data. Thirty-six such images are produced each year, to provide data for examination by scientists studying broad-scale climatic and biosphere changes. Browse images are prepared from the daily data set and the composite data set to provide a reduced data set to assist in data selection and evaluation.

EARTH OBSERVING SYSTEM

Although existing satellite data such as AVHRR and those described in previous chapters might seem at first consideration to provide a means to study global environmental problems, in fact these images provide piecemeal rather than systematic long-term coverage. Likewise, much of the existing archive of imagery records arbitrary regions of the spectrum (rather than regions targeted on those required for specific tasks) and are not coordinated with related data-collection efforts. Attacking these broad-scale, long-term data-collection requirements requires instruments tailored for specific tasks at hand. This is the context in which NASA, in the late 1980s and early 1990s, developed a programme to acquire the environmental data required to address questions posed by concerns over global environmental change.

Earth Science Enterprise (formerly Mission to Planet Earth [MTPE]) is one of NASA's four strategic enterprises designed to establish a long-term, coordinated research effort to study the total earth system and the effects of natural and human-induced changes on the global environment. Earth Science Enterprise is a long-term effort to observe the earth's environments and how they change over time, as an essential component to developing an understanding of the nature, rates and consequences of broad-scale environmental change. The early activities of Earth Science Enterprise (in the 1990s, when it was still named MTPE) focused on the design of numerous satellites that requires specialised orbits and instruments.

The second, long-term, component of the Earth Science Enterprise is a system of satellites that form an integrated system of earth-orbiting satellites designed to provide a continuous stream of data for a period of 15 years or more. The Earth Observing System (EOS) is to consist of several satellites carrying numerous sensors designed to monitor environmental variables on a worldwide basis.

EOS efforts have been coordinated nationally through various agencies of the US government and internationally through agreements with other nations. The design of EOS has changed in response to scientific, operational and budgetary considerations and will no doubt continue to change. Thus, the following sections outline some of the instruments likely to be of interest to readers of this text, but do not attempt an exhaustive description of the complete system.

EARTH OBSERVING SYSTEM INSTRUMENTS

EOS is designed to collect data to provide a comprehensive overview of the dynamic components of the earth's atmosphere and land and water surfaces (Fig. 22.5). To accomplish this objective, the EOS plan has included 30 or more instruments designed to monitor physical and biological components of the biosphere. However, the budget priorities have changed, so has the programme design evolved. No doubt, it will continue to evolve. Therefore, individual sensors have been re-designed or dropped from the plan. Here we briefly describe only a few of the many instruments proposed for EOS that are most closely related to those already discussed in this volume. The reader may find that further programme changes will alter even the brief list of instruments presented here.

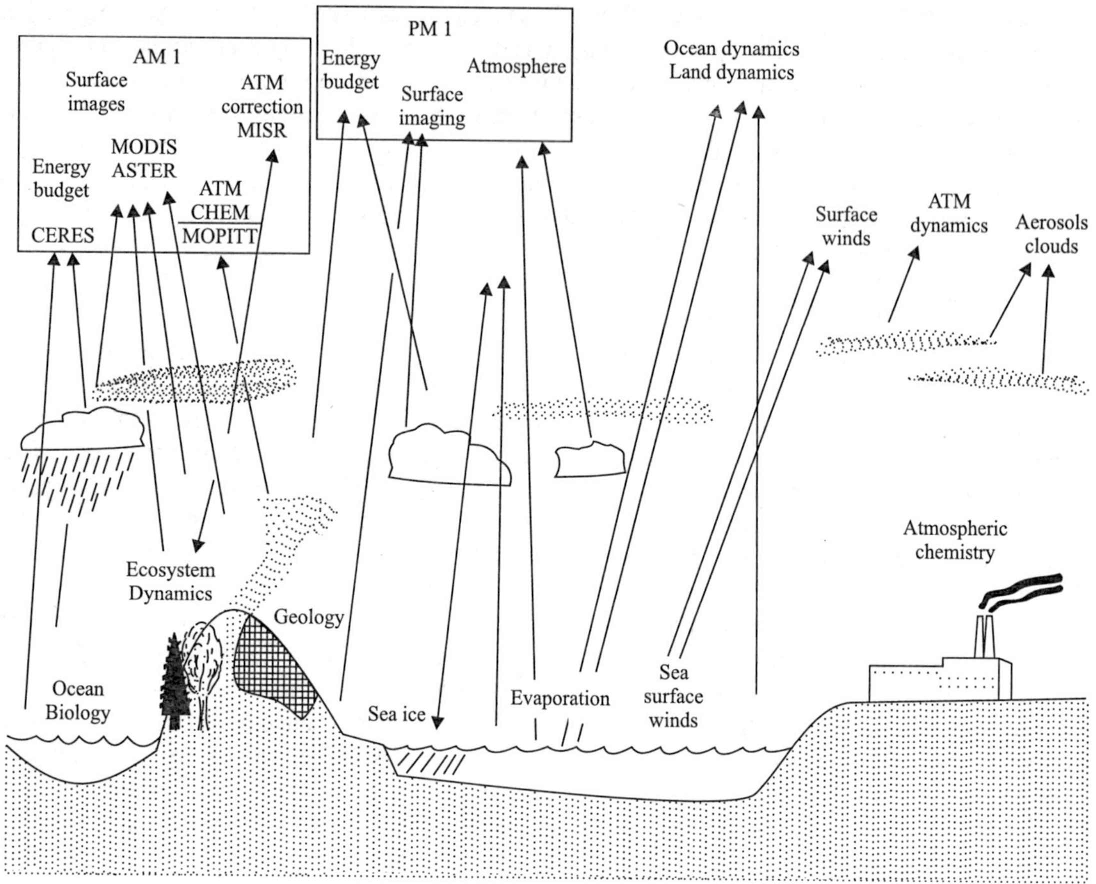

Fig. 22.5. EOS overview. This diagram represents the planned configuration for EOS missions.

Moderate-Resolution Imaging Spectroradiometer

The moderate-resolution imaging spectroradiometer (MODIS) (Fig. 22.6) was launched on the Terra satellite in December 1999. MODIS is designed to acquire imagery that will permit compilation of global data sets at frequent intervals. It uses a cross-track scanning mirror and CCD detectors in 36 spectral bands, covering spectral regions from the visible to the thermal infrared. Spatial resolutions will vary from 500 m to 1 km; the satellite provides coverage every 2 days. MODIS instruments are designed to extend the kinds of data collected by AVHRR, TM and some of the meteorological satellites.

MODIS is designed for monitoring the earth's land areas; in essence, it is an instrument similar to AVHRR, but tailored to monitoring land resources (rather than the meteorological mission of AVHRR). Moderate resolution refers to its 500 m pixels, which may seem course relative to SPOT or Landsat, but are fine relative to the 1 km pixels of AVHRR and achieve global coverage to meet EOS objectives.

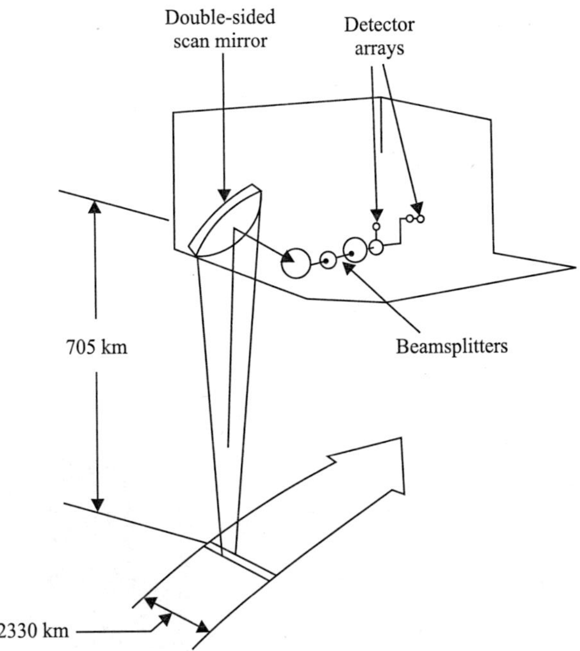

Fig. 22.6. Schematic sketch of MODIS.

MODIS data permit analysts to monitor biological and physical processes at the earth's land surfaces and water bodies and to collect data describing cloud cover and atmospheric qualities. MODIS collects data describing range and forest fires, snow cover, chlorophyll concentrations, surface temperature and other variables.

Earth Observing System Ocean Colour Experiment

The EOS Ocean Colour Experiment (EOS-Colour) is a optical-mechanical imaging radiometer provided for EOS service by Japan's Ministry of International Trade and Industry. It is designed to operate from a sun-synchronous orbit, with a noon equatorial crossing. It collects data in 8 spectral channels over a swath width of 2800 km. Spatial resolution at nadir is 1.1 km and as much as 4.5 km off-nadir.

The instrument is designed to acquire data to study marine phytoplankton, the oceanic role is the carbon cycle, mixing of oceanic and coastal water and the nature of heat exchange within the upper layers of the ocean.

Advanced Spaceborne Thermal Emission and Reflection Radiometer

The advanced spaceborne thermal emission and reflection radiometer (ASTER) is an imaging radiometer designed to collect data in 14 spectral channels (Fig. 22.7). Three channels in the visible and near infrared provide 15 m resolution in the region 0.5 μm to 0.9 μm; six channels in the short-wave infrared provide 30 m resolution in the interval 1.6 μm to 2.5 μm; and five channels in the thermal infrared provide 90 m resolution in the interval 8 μm to 12 μm. Imagery can be acquired in a 60 km swath centered on a pointable field of view ±8.5° in the mid-infrared and thermal infrared and ±2.4° in the visible and near infrared. The instrument acquires a stereo capability through use of an aft-pointing telescope that acquires imagery in channel 3. The ASTER can provide 16 day repeat coverage in all 14 bands and 5 day coverage in the visible and near infrared channels.

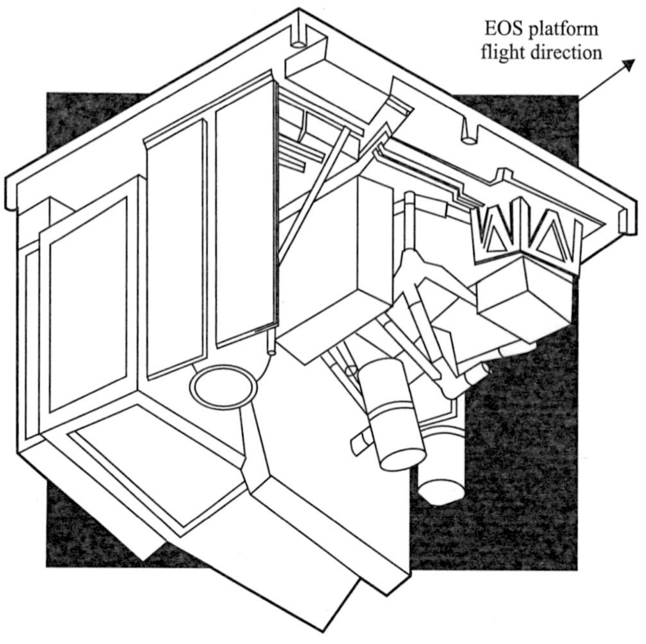

Fig. 22.7. Schematic sketch of ASTER.

The instrument is designed to provide data to describe land use, cloud coverage and kind and heights of clouds, land and ocean temperature, topographic data and information on glacial activity and snow cover.

Multi-Angle Imaging Spectroradiometer

The multi-angle imaging spectroradiometer (MISR) employs 9 CCDs to observe the earth's surface from nine angles (Fig. 22.9). One looks to the nadir and four each look to the fore and aft along the ground track of the satellite in each of four spectral regions, centered on 0.443 μm, 0.555 μm, 0.670 μm and 0.865 μm. These channels have resolutions of 240 m , 480 m, 960 m and 1.92 km, respectively.

The instrument is designed to observe the atmosphere at different angles and to observe features through differing path lengths and angles of observation. Data from MISR will permit the study of atmospheric properties, including effects of pollutants and the derivation of information to correct data from other sensors for atmospheric effects. The instrument will also contribute to the development of models for the optical behaviour of surfaces (e.g., forest canopies) by developing accurate BRDFs. The configuration of the sensors provides the ability to acquire stereo imagery of both ground surfaces and clouds.

Multifrequency Imaging Microwave Radiometer

The multifrequency imaging microwave radiometer (MIMR) is a passive microwave radiometer designed to acquire data at six frequencies (6.8, 10.65, 18.7, 23.8, 36.5 and 90 GHz) at dual polarisation. It observes a 1400 km swath at resolutions varying from 60 km to 5 km. It is designed to observe surface temperature, sea ice, sea surface, atmospheric water vapour and soil moisture patterns.

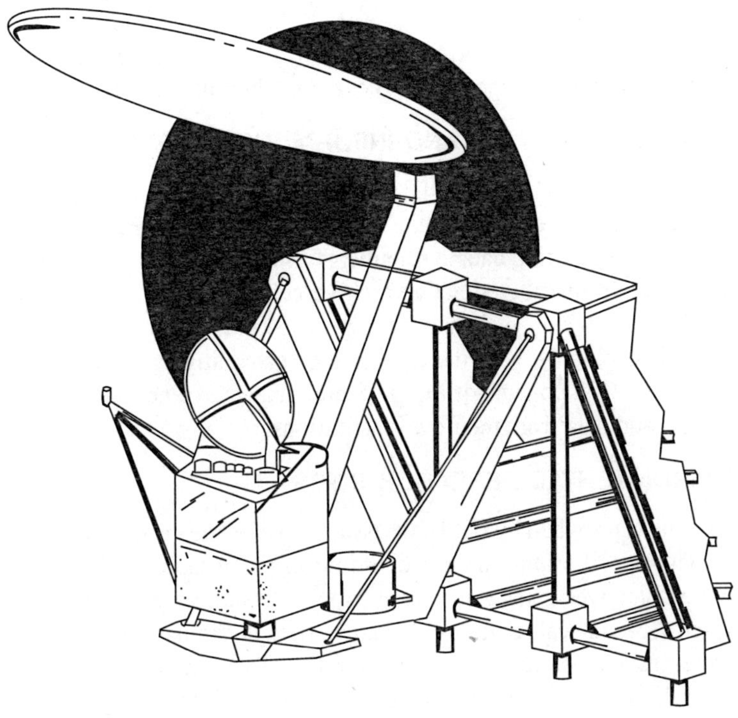

Fig. 22.8. Schematic sketch of MIMR.

Earth Orbiting System Synthetic Aperture Radar

The EOS programme includes a synthetic aperture radar (EOS-SAR), designed to monitor sea ice, glaciers, snow, soil moisture, patterns of deforestation and moisture in forest canopies. The EOS-SAR is planned to acquire imagery in L, C and X-bands, using multipolarisation. The SAR will use look angles from 15° to 40°, to either side of the ground track. The instrument is designed to operate in any of three modes, which provide different trade-offs between coverage and spatial resolution. At one extreme (local-high-resolution mode), the SAR uses a swath width of 30 km to 50 km to collect data with resolution of 20 m to 30 m. In the regional mapping mode, the SAR acquires data for a 100 km to 200 km swath width at 50 m to 100 m resolution. In global mapping mode, images can show a swath width of as much as 500 km, at resolutions of 250 m to 500 m.

EARTH OBSERVING SYSTEM BUS

EOS sensors are to be placed on series of satellites designed to provide standard support functions, including communications, thermal control, power supply and related functions. The standardised components are known as the EOS bus.

The first of the EOS buses, EOS-AM, known as Terra, was launched in December 1999 and placed in service in February 2000, carrying CERES, MISR, MODIS, ASTER and MOPITT sensors. Terra was placed in an orbit designed for morning observation (local sun time), which optimises observation of terrestrial surfaces by minimising land areas obscured by cloud cover. A second satellite, EOS-PM, will be launched later to observe the earth at a later time of day, designed for optimum observation of ocean and atmospheric features, as well as selected terrestrial phenomena. EOS-PM will carry some of the same sensors (e.g., MODIS) carried on Terra, to permit features to be imaged by the same instrument at different times of day, providing an opportunity to examine diurnal changes.

EARTH OBSERVING SYSTEM DATA AND INFORMATION SYSTEM

The EOS Data and Information System (EOSDIS) was established to handle the unprecedented volume of data to be acquired by the system of satellite sensors. Operation of EOS will require a system for acquiring, processing and distributing data to scientists for interpretation and analysis. Key components within EOSDIS are the eight distributed active archive centers (DAACs), established to process and distribute data. Each DAAC specialises in handling specific kinds of data (e.g., 'land processes, 'sea ice and polar processes', 'hydrology'), with the objective of providing sustained access to the data for a broad community of users. Components of EOSDIS are connected electronically, so users can quickly access archives, indices and data from their own institutions.

LONG-TERM ENVIRONMENTAL RESEARCH SITES

In this context, information provided by field data assumes a new meaning. The usual field observations, collected to match with specific images on a one-time basis, at isolated times and places, have less significance when the objectives extend over very large areas and very long time intervals. To support the search for long-term, broad-scale patterns of change, field data must exhibit continuity over time and be positioned to represent ecosystems at continental scales. To address these needs, a network of long-term ecological research sites has been established within many of the earth's major ecological zones. At each site long-term studies are underway to document ecological behaviour and changes over time and to understand relationships between natural changes and those that might be caused or accelerated by human activities. Research conducted at some sites records local patterns of nutrient cycling as a component in understanding changes in the global cycles. These sites represent many of the principal ecological zones of our hemisphere. Although these sites are defined as a national (US) programme, they represent a broad sample of global environment. Similar efforts are underway throughout the world to establish a network of international sites representing a full range of biomes.

EARTH EXPLORER

Earth explorer, developed by the USGS EROS Data Center, is an interactive computer system designed to permit scientists to identify information pertaining to the earth's land surfaces. Earth explorer consists of metadata describing dates, coverages, cloud cover, quality ratings and other characteristics of broad-scale data sets of the earth's land areas. Included are summaries of land cover, soil, geologic, cultural, topographic and remotely sensed data. Users can connect to Earth Explorer computers remotely to review data for their specific regions of interest. Earth explorer permits examination of the suitability of data for specific projects and inspection of sample data project and provides a vehicle for placing orders to acquire data. Earth explorer descriptions are organised to permit users to search for coverages of specific regions by date to ascertain availability of data from specific years or by class of data (aerial photography, digital line graphs, maps, elevation data or satellite imagery).

23

Natural Hazards

INTRODUCTION

One of the most important tools available to the regional planner is the remote sensing of the environment. Not only is it very useful in the planning process in general, but it is also valuable in detecting and mapping many types of natural hazards when, as is often the case, detailed descriptions of their effects do not exist. If susceptibility to natural hazards can be identified in the early stages of an integrated development planning study, measures can be introduced to reduce the social and economic impacts of potential disasters.

All natural hazards are amenable in some degree to study by remote sensing because nearly all geologic, hydrologic and atmospheric phenomena that create hazardous situations are recurring events or processes that leave evidence of their previous occurrence. This evidence can be recorded, analysed and integrated into the planning process. Most remote sensing studies concerned with natural hazards have been about an area's vulnerability to a disaster, the monitoring of events which could precipitate a disaster and the magnitude, extent and duration of a disaster.

While both aerial and satellite remote sensing techniques are presented, emphasis is placed on satellite-derived sensing because the data provide the synoptic view required by the broad scale of integrated development planning studies. Aerial remote sensing data are useful to natural hazard management for focusing on priority areas, verifying small-scale data interpretations and providing information about features that are too small for detection by satellite imagery, but extensive aerial surveys commonly exceed the budget constraints of a planning study and may also provide more information than is necessary, particularly during the early stages of the study.

It will become evident that some of these hazards are interrelated, e.g., floods and hurricanes; earthquakes, volcanoes and landslides.

The ability to identify these natural hazards or their potential for occurring depends on the resolution of the image, the acquisition scale of the sensor data, the working scale, scenes free of clouds and heavy haze and adequate textural and tonal or colour contrast. The availability of stereo models of the scene being studied can greatly enhance the interpretation. After a hazard is identified, formulating appropriate mitigation measures and developing response plans may require different remote sensing data sets. This additional remote sensing data needed are most likely to include greater detail of the infrastructure, e.g., roads and facilities. This may have to be derived from aerial photography.

APPLICATIONS OF REMOTE SENSING TECHNOLOGY TO NATURAL HAZARD ASSESSMENTS

Remote Sensing

Remote sensing is the technology allowing to obtain information of an object, area or phenomenon by means of data coming from an apparatus, which is not in physical contact with this object, area or phenomenon. In practice, this means that the information of the Earth's surface is obtained by sensors mounted on an airplane or a satellite. Most remote sensing satellites are in polar orbit (about 900 km from the Earth), while communication and some weather satellites are in geostationary orbit (about 36000 km away from the Earth). Remote sensors record electromagnetic radiation emitted or reflected from the Earth's surface. Different types of vegetation, soils and other features emit and reflect energy differently. This characteristic makes it possible to identify different cover types on the surface. Using multi-temporal images it is possible to monitor the changes. Finally, since the images are digital they can then be re-formatted to constitute an accurate geometrical representation of the Earth, in other words the creation of accurate maps is possible using satellite images (Fig. 23.1).

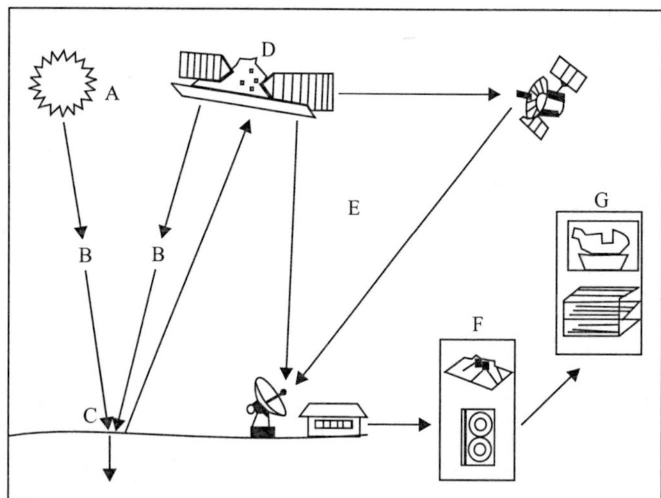

Fig. 23.1. Stages of remote sensing: (A) Energy source or illumination; (B) radiation and the atmosphere; (C) interaction with the target; (D) Recording of energy by the sensor; (E) transmission, reception and processing; (F) interpretation and analysis; and (G) application.

Planet Earth is actually surrounded by about 40 Earth observation satellites. A large amount of satellite remote sensing data is currently available from a number of agencies.

With remote sensors it is possible to update data more frequently than ground-based survey techniques and in theory, to monitor changes occurring in features in near-real or 'real enough' time. With frequently updated information, resource managers can monitor dynamic processes. In some places, they have to make decisions about isolated and sometimes inaccessible areas.

In such cases the analysis of remote sensing data is the way to acquire the most accurate, inexpensive and timely information needed to identify and assess different management options.

Different types of spatial and spectral resolutions are available. Very high ground resolution is the new generation of sensors with 4 m in multispectral mode and 1 m in panchromatic mode for Ikonos and

2.8 m in multispectral mode and 0.7 m in panchromatic mode for Quick Bird. These systems enable users to discriminate a greater number of features more quickly, they enhance decision making in fields such as natural resource exploration, city planning, vegetation monitoring, detection of pollution, disaster and crisis mitigation and economic analysis. Simultaneously, research continues into new ways in which remote sensing technologies can be used to facilitate strategic planning for environment and development issues. For purposes of assessing natural hazards in the context of integrated development planning studies, it is not necessary to have real-time or near real-time remote sensing imagery. What is required is the ability to define areas of potential exposure to natural hazards by identifying their occurrence or conditions under which they are likely to occur and to identify mechanisms to prevent or mitigate the effects of those hazards. This section considers the practical detectability by remote sensing technology of the potential for floods, hurricanes, earthquakes, volcanic eruptions and related hazards and landslides. It will become evident that some of these hazards are interrelated, e.g., floods and hurricanes; earthquakes, volcanoes and landslides.

Floods

Floods are the most common of natural hazards that can affect people, infrastructure and the natural environment. They can occur in many ways and in many environment. Riverine floods, the most prevalent, are due to heavy, prolonged rainfall, rapid snowmelt in upstream watersheds or the regular spring thaw. Other floods are caused by extremely heavy rainfall occurring over a short period in relatively flat terrain, the backup of estuaries due to high tides coinciding with storm surges, dam failures, dam overtopping due to landslides into a reservoir and seiche and wind tide effects in large lakes.

Occasionally an eruption on a glacier or snow-covered volcanic peak can cause a flood or a mudflow in which the terrain is radically changed and any agrarian development is totally destroyed, frequently with much loss of life.

It is impossible to define the entire flood potential in a given area (see images shown in Fig. 23.2). However, given the best remote sensing data for the situation and a competent interpreter, the evidence for potential flood situations can be found or inferred. The most obvious evidence of a major flood potential, outside of historical evidence, is identification of floodplain or flood-prone areas which are generally recognisable on remote sensing imagery. The most valuable application of remote sensing to flood hazard assessments, then, is in the mapping of areas susceptible to flooding.

Fig. 23.2. Flooded city of Mumbai (year 2005).

Synoptic satellite sensor coverage of a planning study area is the practical alternative to aerial photography because of cost and time factors. The application of Landsat MSS imagery to floodplain or flood-prone area delineation has already been demonstrated by comparing pre-flood scenes with scenes obtained at the height of the flood, using Landsat MSS band 7 (near IR) images in a colour additive viewer. This temporal comparison can now be done pixel by pixel in a computer. Landsat TM, with its greater spatial resolution than MSS data (30m versus 80m) and its additional spectral coverage (7 bands versus 4 bands), can be used for more detailed mapping of floodplains and flood-prone areas on larger scale maps of 1:50000 or greater. TM data have been used for discriminating land cover classification and to provide useful input to flood forecasting and flood damage models for urban and agricultural areas (Table 23.1).

Table 23.1. TM data—used for discriminating land cover classification. (Also provides useful inputs).

	Earthquake	*Volcanic eruption*	*Lansides*	*Tsunami*	*Desertification*	*Floods*	*Hurricans*
Information to be obtained	Land-use maps geoglogical maps	Maps of areas vulnerable to lava flows, ash fall, debris fall and fires	Slope slopes stability, elevation, geology, soil type, areas of standing water, land-use maps	Bathymetric/ topographic maps	Land-use maps, soil moisture content, crop condition and natural vetetation	Floodplain delineation maps, land-use classification, historical data, soil cover and soil moisture	Land-use maps
Spectral band	Visible and near IR	Visible, near IR and thermal IR	Visible	Visible including blue and near IR	Visible, near IR and microwave	Near IR, Thermal IR and microwave	Visible and near IR
Spatial resolution	20–80m	30–80m	10–30m	30m	80m–1 km	20m (for cultural features); 30–80m (for land use); 1 km (for snow cover and soil moisture)	20m (for cultural features); 30–80m (for land use)
Areal coverage	Large area	Large area	Large area	Large coastal area	Large regional area	Large regional area	Large area
All weather capability	No	No	No	No	No	No	No
Synoptic view	Yes	Yes	Yes	Yes	Yes	Yes	Yes
Stereo capability	Yes	Yes	Yes	Yes	No	Yes	No
Frequency of observations for planning study use	1 to 5 years	1 to 5 years	1 to 5 years	1 to 5 years	Monthly	Seasonal (except weekly for snow cover and soil moisture)	Yearly

This approach to floodplain delineation does have its limitations. The area of potential flooding delineated in this manner may represent a flood level that exceeds an acceptable degree of loss. Also, no floods may have occurred during the period of the sensor operation. In this case, indirect indicators of flood susceptibility are used.

There are large parts of tropical humid ecosystems where adequate Landsat or other similar imagery is not available due to cloud coverage or heavy haze. In some instances the heavy tropical vegetation masks many geomorphic features so obvious in drier climates. In this case the use of available radar imagery from space or previously acquired from an aircraft survey is desirable. The radar imagery, which has a resolution comparable to Landsat TM and SPOT from both space and sub-orbital altitudes, can satisfactorily penetrate the clouded sky and define many floodplain features. Moisture on the ground noticeably affects the radar return and together with the textural variations emphasised by the sensor, makes radar a potentially desirable tool for flood and floodplain mapping.

Hurricanes

To mitigate the impact of hurricanes, the planner needs to know the frequency of storms of given intensity in the study area, to what extent these storms could affect people and structures and what sub-areas would be most affected such as low-lying coastal, estuarine and reverie areas threatened by flooding and storm surge (Fig. 23.3). Also refer to Fig. 23.4 for the diagramatical representation of the formation of a hurricane.

Fig. 23.3. Sattelite images of the formation of hurricane.

The determination of past hurricane paths for the region can be derived from remote sensing data from the US National Oceanographic and Atmospheric Administration (NOAA) satellite sensors designed and operated for meteorological purposes. These data are already plotted by meteorological organisations in the U.S.A. and other countries where hurricanes are a threat. For plotting new data, the best sensor is the AVHRR which, with its 2700 km swath, makes coverage twice a day and has appropriate resolution. The red band is useful for defining daytime clouds and vegetation, while the thermal IR band (10.50 mm to 11.50 mm) is useful for both daytime and night time cloud observations.

The AVHRR is not useful in other aspects of hurricane contingency planning due to its limited spatial resolution. These planning needs require higher resolution available from other satellite sensors. If imagery of areas inundated by floods, hurricane storms or other storms is obtained with any sensor immediately after the event, it should be used, of course, regardless of its resolution. Any such information that is obtained in a timely fashion should be used to delineate the problem areas since their definition is more exact than can be interpreted from higher resolution data obtained during a non-flood period.

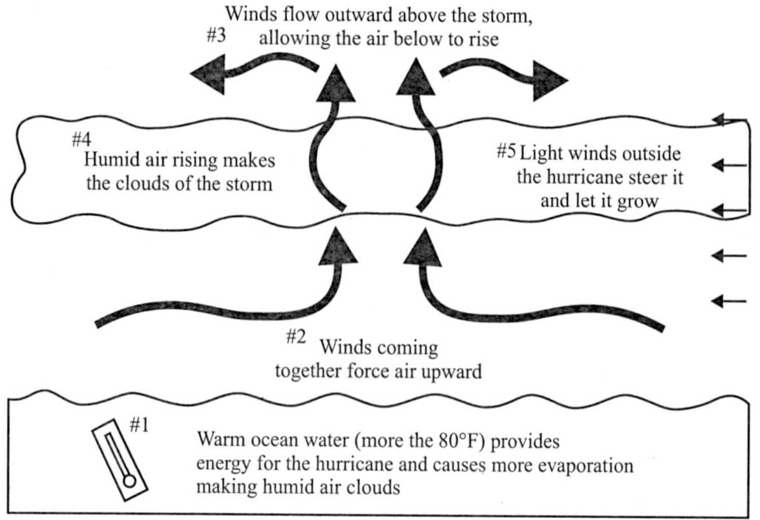

Fig. 23.4. Diagramatic representation of the formation of a hurricane.

Predicting areas of potential inundation along coasts and inland can be achieved using topographic maps with scales as large as 1:12500. When such maps are not available, remote sensing techniques can be used. In areas with a distinct wet and dry season, it is desirable to obtain information for the wet season from Landsat or comparable imagery in the near IR bands or use a colour IR composite made from Landsat MSS or TM imagery or from SPOT HRV imagery. These image products can be used to identify the moisture-saturated areas susceptible to flooding as well as the higher and drier ground for potential evacuation areas.

Likewise, consideration of development plans in view of this potential natural hazard can proceed in a way similar to that for areas prone to flood hazards. For flood hazard assessments, radar imagery from space or aircraft could be used (if available) in lieu of the Landsat MSS imagery. Since there is a general lack of relief in low-lying coastal areas and estuarine areas, stereoscopy would not normally play an important role in this situation. However, stereoscopic viewing even without significant relief enhancement can still reinforce the details of the scene, although at considerably greater cost.

The development planner also needs to consider the additional feature of a hurricane—its high winds. In identifying measures to mitigate wind effects, the planner may consider the type of crops grown, if an agricultural development is being planned and the design and construction materials used in buildings.

Earthquakes

The planning of development in earthquake-prone areas is laden with problems. There are large human settlements already located in earthquake/prone areas. Refer Fig. 23.5 for the damages done by earthquakes.

As with other geologic hazards, the frequency of occurrence can fall in cycles of decades or centuries. Earthquakes are particularly difficult to predict at this time. Thus, mitigation emphasis is on land use planning (non-intensive uses in most hazardous areas), on building strength and integrity on response planning and on incorporating mitigation measures into reconstruction efforts. The main problem is the identification of the earthquake damage-prone zones. While in most areas of great earthquake activity some seismic information is available, it may not be sufficient for planning purposes. Remote sensing techniques and resulting data interpretation can play a role in providing additional information.

Fig. 23.5. Consequences of earthquakes.

Tectonic activity is the main cause of destructive earthquakes, followed by earthquakes associated with volcanic activity. Where the history of earthquakes due to seismic activity is present in an area, the faults associated with the activity can frequently be identified on satellite imagery.

Where volcanic-related earthquakes occur, the source is generally not as obvious: it may be due to movement on a fault near the surface or deep within the Earth, to caldera's collapse or to magma movement within the volcanic conduit.

In order to identify earthquake hazards it is necessary to have the expertise to recognise them and then determine the correct remote sensing tools to best delimit them. Landsat imagery has been effectively and widely used for this purpose since it is less expensive and more readily available than other remote sensing data. Airborne radar mosaics have been successfully used for the delineation of fault zones. Generally, two mosaics can be made of an area: one with the far range portion of the SLAR and the other with the near range portion. The former is best used in areas of low relief where the relief needs to be enhanced and the latter in areas of high relief where the shadow effect is not needed or may be detrimental to the image.

Radar is applicable to delineate unconsolidated deposits sitting on fault zones-upon which most of the destruction occurs-to identify areas where an earthquake can trigger landslides. This is best accomplished on stereomodels using adjoining and overlapping radar flight lines. Conventional aerial photography, in black and white or colour, would also work well for this purpose.

An alternative, which is adequate but not as good as using radar and aerial photography, is to use multispectral imagery obtained from the Landsat TM and/or MSS or SPOT HRV sensors. Colour IR composites or straight near-IR imagery from these sensors at scales up to about 1:1,00,000 can be used to define active surface fault zones, but not as efficiently as with the radar images. The distinction between bedrock versus unconsolidated materials and the areas of potential landslide hazards can be defined but, again, only if stereocoverage is available. SPOT sensors can provide this capability.

While radar imagery is an ideal data source, available coverage is extremely limited and contracting airborne radar is usually prohibitively expensive. Landsat TM and MSS are the most practical data source, simply because of its availability and both provide sufficient resolution for regional planning studies.

Volcanic Eruptions and Related Hazards

Many hazards are associated with the conditions brought about by volcanic activity. Active volcanoes pose hazards which include the immediate release of expelled ash, lava, pyroclastic flows and/or poisonous hot gases; volcanic earthquakes; and the danger of mudflows and floods resulting from the rapid melting of snow and ice surrounding the vent during eruption (see Fig. 23.6 volcanic erruption). Some secondary hazards may threaten during volcanic activity or during periods of dormancy. These include landslides due to unstable accumulations of tephra, which may be triggered by heavy rains or by earthquakes.

Fig. 23.6. Volcanic eruption.

Each volcano has its own particular behaviour within a framework of given magmatic and tectonic settings. Prediction of a volcano's behaviour is extremely difficult and the best evidence for the frequency of activity and its severity is the recorded history of eruptions. Imminent eruptions are now best recognised by on-site seismic monitoring. Some classifications distinguish between active, inactive, dormant and extinct volcanoes. But since some of the most catastrophic eruptions have come from 'extinct' volcanoes, many volcanologists have abandoned such a classification, settling for a simple distinction between short-term and long-term periodicity.

Gawarecki first detected volcanic heat from satellite remote sensing using thermal IR imagery from the high resolution IR radiometer (HRIR). Remote sensing data interpretation can lead to the recognition of past catastrophic events associated with recently active volcanoes (recently in the geologic sense), as in the Andes and the Lesser Antilles. This information together with the available historical data can be used as the basis of assessing the risks of an area with potential volcano-related hazards.

The varied nature and sizes of volcanic hazards require the use of various types of sensors from both satellites and aircraft. The relatively small area involved with volcanoes should encourage the use of aerial photography in their analysis. Panchromatic black and white stereo aerial coverage at scales between 1:25000 to 1:60000 is usually adequate to recognise and map geomorphic evidence of recent activity and associated hazards. Colour and colour IR photography may be useful in determining the possible effects of volcanic activity on nearby vegetation, but the slower film speed, lower resolution and high cost diminish much of any advantage they provide.

The airborne thermal IR scanner is probably the most valuable tool in surveying the geothermal state of a volcano. The heat within a volcano and underlying it and its movement are amenable to detection. Because of the rapid decrease in resolution with increasing altitude (about 2m per 1000m) the surveys need to be made at low altitudes under 2000m.

An IR pattern of geothermal heat in the vicinity of a volcano is an indication of thermal activity which many inactive volcanoes display. Many volcanoes thought to be extinct may have to be reclassified if aerial IR surveys discover any abnormally high IR emissions from either the summit craters or the flanks. Changes in thermal patterns can be obtained for a volcano only through periodic aerial IR surveys taken under similar conditions of data acquisition. The temperature and gas emission changes, however, can be monitored on the ground at ideal locations identified on the thermal imagery, making periodic overflights unnecessary. Continuous electronic monitoring of these stations is possible by transmission through a geostationary data relay satellite, another phase of remote sensing.

The thermal IR bands of the satellite sensors now available have inadequate spatial and thermal resolution to be of any significant value to detect the dynamic change in volcanic geothermal activity. In addition to sensing geothermal heat, however, other remote sensing techniques are useful in preparing volcanic hazard zonation maps and in mitigating volcanic hazards. Mitigation techniques requiring photo interpretation and topographic maps include predicting the path of potential mudflows or lava flows and restricting development in those areas.

Example: Remote sensing-volcanic eruptions

In 1991 thousands of lives were protected when government geologists evacuated towns and villages on the slopes of Mt. Pinatubo in the Philippines. Soon after, the volcano exploded in a massive eruption that devastated vast tracts of countryside in the region. There are several different types of volcanoes and understanding how and why they differ is a key to understanding the threat posed to local populations. Every new eruption is an opportunity to gather information that someday might be used to save lives (Fig. 23.7).

Fig. 23.7. Volcanic eruptions are highly damaging and dangerous events. They also renew Earths surface and contribute important gases to the atmosphere.

Landslides

Landslides or mass movements of rock and unconsolidated materials such as soil, mud and volcanic debris, are much more common than is generally perceived by the public. Many are aware of the catastrophic landslides, but few are aware that small slides are of continuous concern to those involved in the design and construction business. These professionals can often exacerbate the problem of landsliding through poor planning, design or construction practices. Frequently, the engineer and builder are also forced into difficult construction or development situations as a result of ignoring the potential landslide hazard (Fig. 23.8). This can be avoided if there is early recognition of the hazard and there is effective consultation between planners and the construction team prior to detailed development planning.

The mass movement of bed rock and unconsolidated materials results in different types of slides, magnitudes and rates of movement. An area with a potential landslide hazard usually has some evidence of previous occurrences, if not some historical record. Unfortunately, some types of landslides, particularly those of small size, cannot be delineated on remote sensing imagery or through aerial photography. Usually the scars of the larger slides are evident and although the smaller slide features may not be individually discerned, the overall rough appearance of a particular slope can suggest that mass movement occurred. If a fairly accurate geologic map is available at a reasonable scale (1:50000 or larger) rock types and/or formations susceptible to landslides may be examined for evidence of movement. An example of this would be finding a shale in a steeper than usual slope environment, implying the strong possibility of a landslide history. An examination of stream traces frequently shows deflections of the bed course due to landslides. If one can separate out the tectonically controlled stream segments, those deflections due to slides or slumps often become evident.

Typical features that signify the occurrence of landslides include chaotic blocks of bedrock whose only source appears to be upslope; crescentic scarps or scars whose horns point downward on a normal-looking slope; abnormal bulges with disturbed vegetation at the base of the slope; large intact beds of competent sedimentary or other layered rock displaced down dip with no obvious tectonic relationship; and mudflow tongues stretching outward from the base of an obviously eroded scar of relatively unconsolidated material (Fig. 23.8). A good understanding of the structural geology of the study area frequently places these superficial anomalies into perspective. The susceptibility to landslides is relative to the area. Landslides can occur on gentle slopes as well as on steep slopes, depending on landscape characteristics.

Most landslide discussions do not address the problem of sinkholes, which are a form of circular collapse landslides. The karstic areas in which they occur are easy to identify even on some satellite imagery (MSS, TM, SPOT, etc.) due to their pitted appearance and evidence of the essentially internal drainage. Despite the obvious occurrence of many sinkholes, many individual small sinkholes are subtle and not easily recognised. These are frequently the sites of collapse and subsequent damage to any overlying structure when groundwater is removed to satisfy development needs, which results in lowering the water table and undermining the stability of the land.

The spatial resolution required for the recognition of most large landslide features is about 10 m. However, the recognition depends to a great extent on the ability and experience of the interpreter and is enhanced by the availability of stereoscopic coverage, which can be expensive to acquire. Stereoscopic coverage and the resolution requirements preclude use of most satellite-borne sensor imagery, although large block landslides can be detected on Landsat MSS and TM imagery.

Given the spatial resolution requirement, SPOT HRV-P (panchromatic mode) imagery can be useful with its 10 m resolution. Its broad band coverage, however, is not conducive to providing adequate contrast in scenes involving heavily vegetated tropics, where most of the potential hazards occur. Ameliorating this factor slightly is the availability of stereocoverage. It is important to understand that this is specifically programmed for the SPOT satellite and that stereocoverage is not normally acquired during sensor operation.

Fig. 23.8. Pictorial representation of a land slide, displaying the landslide in proccess of damage.

Detection of landslide features is more easily achieved using airborne sensors. Aerial photography with its normal stereoscopic coverage is the best sensor system with which to define landslides, both large and small. Aerial photographic scales as small as 1:60000 can be used. Black and white panchromatic or IR films are adequate in most cases, but colour IR may prove better in some instances. The IR-sensitive emulsions, as stated earlier, eliminate much of the haze found in the humid tropics. The open water or other moisture in back of recent slump features stands out as an anomaly in the aerial IR stereomodel, either in black and white or colour. The colour IR photography might, in some rare cases, show the stress on the vegetation caused by recent movement. If the scales are large enough, tree deformation caused by progressive tilting of the slope of the soil might also be detected.

A more sensitive detector of moisture associated with landslides is the thermal IR scanner. This sensor is particularly useful in locating seepage areas that lubricate slides. It is particularly effective during the night, when there is a maximum temperature difference between the terrain and the effluent groundwater. Despite its utility many factors rule out the widespread use of the thermal IR scanner. These factors include the low altitude required for reasonable spatial resolution, the large number of flight lines required for the large area involved and the geometrical distortions inherent in the system. If the terrain to be interpreted has some relief and is nondescript, these distortions become an even greater problem when the data are interpreted by making the location of features very difficult.

SLAR, especially the X-band synthetic aperture radar with its nominal 10 m resolution, can be marginally useful in a stereo mode because of its ability to define some larger textures related to landslides. In some cloud-prone environments radar may be the only sensor that can provide interpretable information.

Desertification

Desertification occurs when an ecosystem experiences a diminution or loss of productivity. This process can have a natural and an anthropic component, which may reinforce each other, creating a synergetic effect (Fig. 23.9). The degree of desertification risk is directly related to certain natural conditions such as climate, topography, natural vegetation, soil and hydrology, as well as to the intensity and type of anthropic activity in the area. Desertification is among the most serious problems of the region. This trend indicates the increasing need to consider desertification processes in integrated development planning studies. Remote sensing, both spaceborne and airborne, provides valuable tools for evaluating areas subject to desertification. Film transparencies, photographs and digital data can be used for the purpose of locating, assessing and monitoring deterioration of natural conditions in a given area. Information about these conditions can be obtained from direct measurements or inferred from indicators (keys to the recognition of a desertification process).

Fig. 23.9. Pictorial representation of the desertification of the mother nature.

In order to describe, evaluate and decide about the type of action to be taken, the following issues should be addressed:

1. Location: involves the identification of areas that are currently undergoing desertification and areas expected to be exposed to the forces that can lead to deterioration.
2. Assessment: involves the identification and quantification of vegetative cover types, soils, land forms and land-use change patterns. Vulnerability to change, rate of change and direction of change in desertification patterns can be studied through this assessment.

3. Monitoring: accomplished by detecting and measuring changes in landscape characteristics over a period of time. Comparisons are made between present conditions and previously observed conditions for the purpose of recording the reduction in biological productivity.

For a more detailed approach, four sets of data should be taken into consideration for a desertification study of a given area: a set taken at the end of the humid season, a set taken at the end of the last dry season and the same two seasons taken five or ten years earlier. Data selection for a given area will be directly related to the desired amount of detail, size of the area, required degree of precision and accuracy and available time frame.

Large-scale aerial photography provides a great amount of detail for this type of study. Systematic reconnaissance flights can be used for environmental monitoring and resource assessment. Radar sensors and infrared scanners may be used to monitor soil moisture and other desertification indicators. However, acquisition of this type of data is costly and time consuming.

The use of satellite imagery is recommended during the first stages of a detailed desertification study since it offers an overview of the entire region. Computer enhancements, false colour composites and classifications can offer useful information. Optical enhancements can be performed, but these lack the quantitative control available through an automated approach. Statistical data obtained from a quantitative analysis through the use of a geographic information system can be expressed as a histogram, a graph, a table or a new image.

AVHRR imagery is commercially available and has been used for vegetation change studies. Ground resolution of 1 to 4 km represents some limitation in making large continental area studies. Other studies have used Nimbus data to delineate moisture patterns and vegetation boundaries. Geostationary Operational Environmental Satellite (GOES) data have been used effectively to locate and measure dust plumes; and Seasat SAP imagery has been applied in the delineation of large dune morphology.

Landsat MSS and TM and SPOT data have proven to be useful and cost effective for regional assessments. Landsat transparencies of bands 5 and 7 have been used to monitor superficial changes in areas undergoing desertification and to map present water bodies and former drainage systems. Temporal tonal variations on Landsat MSS have been correlated with variations on the field. Movement of sand-dune belts has been detected using Landsat with a multi-temporal approach. Albedo changes in arid terrains have been calculated using Landsat digital data: phenomena that tend to lower productivity (increased erosion, loss of vegetation density, deposition of colic sedimentation) also tend to appear brighter on the image. On the contrary, phenomena that tend to increase productivity (increased vegetation, soil moisture), tend to darken the land. In this way, brightness variations can be detected in an area over a period of time. These data can also be calibrated with ground data collected from the areas where change has occurred.

Aerial and space remote sensing provide valuable tools for desertification studies, although, as for any other natural hazard related study, they must be combined with ground-collected data. The use of remote sensing methods should minimise the need for ground data, therefore saving time and resulting quite inexpensive per unit of data. The combination of remotely sensed and ground-collected data can then provide the basis for the assessment.

Tsunami

The phenomenon we call tsunami is a series of large waves of extremely long wavelength and period usually generated by a violent, impulsive undersea disturbance or activity near the coast or in the ocean. When a sudden displacement of a large volume of water occurs or if the sea floor is suddenly raised or dropped by an earthquake, big tsunami waves can be formed by forces of gravity. The waves travel out of the area of origin and can be extremely dangerous and damaging when they reach the shore. The word tsunami (pronounced tsoo-nah-mee) is composed of the Japanese words 'tsu' (which means harbour) and 'nami' (which means 'wave'). Often the term, 'seismic or tidal sea wave' is used to describe the same phenomenon; however the terms are misleading, because tsunami waves can be generated by other, non seismic disturbances such as volcanic eruptions or underwater landslides and have physical characteristics different of tidal waves.

By far, the most destructive tsunamis are generated from large, shallow earthquakes with an epicenter or fault line near or on the ocean floor. These usually occur in regions of the Earth characterised by tectonic subduction along tectonic plate boundaries. The high seismicity of such regions is caused by the collision of tectonic plates. When these plates move past each other, they cause large earthquakes, which tilt, offset or displace large areas of the ocean floor from a few kilometers to as much as a 1000 km or more. The sudden vertical displacements over such large areas disturb the ocean's surface, displace water and generate destructive tsunami waves. The waves can travel great distances from the source region, spreading destruction along their path. It should be noted that not all earthquakes generate tsunamis. Usually, it takes an earthquake with a Richter magnitude exceeding 7.5 to produce a destructive tsunami.

Tsunami 26th December 2004

An earthquake occurred off the west coast of northern Sumatra at 00:58:53 GMT (7:58:53 AM local time) on 26 December. The epicenter was located under the sea, at the confluence of the Australian and Burma plates at 3.32 N 95.85 E. The earthquake was rated at magnitude 9.0. This makes it the fourth largest since 1900. The earthquake generated three tsunamis, which swept across the Indian Ocean within hours. Most of the energy appears to have been transferred into a set of eastand west-tending waves. To the east, the north-western coast of Sumatra, especially the town of Banda Aceh and the Nicobar Islands, sat in the path of the waves (Fig. 23.10). Beyond them, the waves smashed into the Isthmus of Kra. Coastal towns in southern Burma, Thailand and northern Malaysia were inundated. To the west, the tsunamis crossed the Bay of Bengal in a matter of hours, crashing into the east coast of Sri Lanka and India. Sri Lanka, especially, suffered huge loss of life.

Fig. 23.10. The strong impact of high waves created by Tsunami.

Further south, the westbound waves reached the Maldives, where most of the capital, Male, was destroyed. Some 130 people were killed in Africa, some 4000 km away. On the positive side, Bangladesh, almost due north of the epicenter, was spared. More than a million people live in the low-lying mouths of the Ganges. They would be particularly vulnerable to this type of catastrophe.

Remote sensing activity

Most of the world's space-borne optical sensors have been looking at the Indian Ocean since Boxing Day. A spokesman for Spot Image in Toulouse said it acquired its first image of Banda Aceh about two hours after the earthquake, as part of an acquisition programme in the region.

DigitalGlobe was also able to capture an image on 26 December. QuickBird-1 actually captured tsunami water receding from Kalutara in Sri Lanka. NSPO in Taiwan claims Formosat-1 was the first satellite to retrieve imagery over Phuket.

Space Imaging also captured part of the region on 26 December. Imagery of the Andaman Islands in the Bay of Bengal was downloaded by CRISP. A UN agreement called the International Charter on Space and Major Disasters, which was activated by India, has co-ordinated much of the activity. France's national space agency, the CNES, was put in charge of co-ordinating observation programmes using Spot-5 and 4, India's IRS constellation, Canada's Radarsat-1 and the European Space Agency's Envisat. Eliane Cubero is managing this programme. In India, the Indian Space Research Organisation is using its IRS- 1C, 1D, Oceansat-1 and Resourcesat for analysis and damage assessment. Information is being provided to the Crisis Management Group of the Ministry of Home Affairs and state agencies. Satellite data has been acquired for Car Nicobar, Chennai and Kakinada, the Tamil Nadu coast (especially Nagapattinam), Andhra Pradesh and Kerala. Aerial photography has also been used by ISRO to assess the state of agriculture areas, coastal vegetation and breaches. Chennai-Nagapattinam, the Andhra Pradesh coast and Port Blair have already been covered. In the US, the military is providing imagery of affected areas to the US Agency for International Development's Office of Foreign Disaster Assistance on a daily basis. Primarily, the National Geospatial-Intelligence Agency appears to be relying on its commercial contracts with Orbimage, DigitalGlobe and Space Imaging to fulfill requests for information.

Downstations active

Receiving stations in the region able to download imagery from orbiting satellites have played a major role in speeding up the response to the disaster. Stations in Malayasia, Indonesia and Singapore have all been very active. The Centre for Remote Imaging, Sensing and Processing at the National University of Singapore was much in demand. Virtually all the regions affected by the tsunamis are within the footprint of the station, so satellites can downlink directly to the station, without the need to use tape recorders. CRISP is equipped with two reception antenna. One is six meters wide and was installed in October 2000. The other antenna is 13 meters across and dates from 1995. The station can receive imagery from the Spot constellation, both ERS 1 and 2, Radarsat-1, NOAA's SeaWiFS, the Chinese FengYun 1C and from Ikonos and the Israeli EROS-A1.

Warning was possible

Many of the deaths from the tsunami could have been avoided, if Indian Ocean nations had been equipped with an appropriate warning system. There are two warning systems in the Pacific, one run by the US, based in Hawaii and the other in Tokyo. Both these systems predicted a tsunami based on the size of the quake and its location under the sea. These systems can also directly detect a tsunami in the Pacific with a network of sensors all over the ocean. Tsunami are almost impossible to spot otherwise. Conventional ocean wave crests are separated by only a few meters at most, but 200 kilometers or more can separate tsunamis in the deep ocean. The time between their peaks can range from five minutes to an hour. However, the detection of a tsunami is of little use on its own.

There must also be a way of getting the message out to people in the path of the tsunami and the people must know what to do when they receive such a warning.

The Indian Ocean basin has no warning communications system comparable to the Pacific ones.

In India, the ministry of Science and Technology is planning meetings with the National Geophysical Research Institute, National Institute of Oceanography and the Department of Ocean Development for devising an appropriate system. Also, there are plans to strengthen the Indian station in Antarctica, Maitri, to monitor seismicity in and around Antarctica and the Indian Ocean.

Tracking the wave

Scientists at the US National Oceanic and Atmospheric Administration used radar data from the TOPEX/ Poseidon and Jason satellites operated by NASA and the French space agency, CNES; the European Space Agency's Envisat and the US Navy's Geosat Follow-On to measure the height of the tsunami as it travelled across the Indian ocean. The results confirm that while tsunami are small at sea, they swell as they approach shore. The scientists found that two hours after the Earthquake, the tsunami was about 600 mm high. An hour and 15 minutes later it was down to about 400 mm. After eight hours the main wave was down to about 70 mm high, though a portion in the Bay of Bengal was still at about 200 mm, the NOAA scientists said. Walter Smith, a geophysicist at NOAA, said that the office does not get satellite data until several hours after a tsunami has developed—too late to be used as a real-time forecast. 'Right now, this technique is not the first line of defence in tsunami hazard monitoring and warnings. It gives scientists a way of watching the tsunami even in the deep parts of the ocean basin, where it is too far away from coastal tide gauges and other instruments that can detect it,' he said.

Scientists explain origin of south Asia's deadly tsunami

A devastating earthquake of high magnitude has occurred on December, 26, 2004 off the west coast of Sumatra, Indonesia. The resulting Tsunami killed thousands of people in Southern India, Sri Lanka, Indonesia, etc. In India, Andaman and Nicobar islands, Tamil Nadu, Pondicherry, Andhra Pradesh, Kerala were worst hit.

This massive tsunamis resulted in killing more than 1,00,000 people and leaving millions more homeless, was centered deep under the Indian Ocean off the coast of Indonesia. As relief workers struggle to help survivors, scientists are working to better understand the forces that unleashed such devastation.

National Remote Sensing Agency, Dept. of Space, Govt. of India made all possible efforts to monitor this catastrophic event. Satellite data of different resolutions was acquired, analysed and the valueadded information is being disseminated to concerned.

The following pictures show some portions of the worst-hit Andaman and Nicobar islands and part of Andhra Pradesh and Chennai coast.

In the images, red depicts vegetation, white depicts clouds and shades of blue indicate types of water.

The most powerful earthquake in 40 years—measuring 9.0 on the Richter scale—occurred approximately four miles below the Indian Ocean near the Indonesian Island of Sumatra.

Scientists say this happened when two of the major plates that make up the Earth's crust, the India plate and the Burma plate, collided and created a tsunami or extremely powerful waves.

'The earthquake causes large-scale immediate uplifting of the terrain under the water that creates a massive wave. That wave travels very efficiently across the ocean. And so it shows up hundreds and even thousands of miles away with much of the same energy that it started with,' said Devine, a senior science adviser to the director of the US Geological Survey, the government agency in charge of monitoring earthquakes.

These large wave swells, some of which traveled 3000 miles to the African coast of Somalia, caused the majority of the death and destruction throughout Sri Lanka, India, Indonesia, Thailand and Malaysia.

The term tsunami, which is often incorrectly referred to as a tidal wave, was officially adopted for general use in 1963 during an international scientific conference. It is a Japanese word represented by two characters: 'tsu' which means harbor and 'nami' which means wave.

Most waves that hit the typical beach are wind generated. Smaller and less powerful than other waves, wind-generated waves have a period—the time between two successful waves—of five to twenty seconds. Their wavelength—the distance between two successful waves—is usually about 50 to 600 feet.

Tsunamis, on the other hand, can have periods between ten minutes and one hour and a wavelength in excess of 430 miles.

With an underwater disturbance like an earthquake, millions of gallons of seawater are suddenly and violently displaced. The waves they create radiate in all directions from the epicenter of the quake, moving at the speed of a commercial jet. As they get closer to a shoreline or coast the front of the tsunami wave slows due to friction. The waves behind stack up onto each other creating a pile of waves that can reach 30 feet, hitting land with enough force to flatten buildings and trees and carry boats and ships miles inland. Various satellite images related to Tsunami are shown in Figs. 23.11 and 23.12.

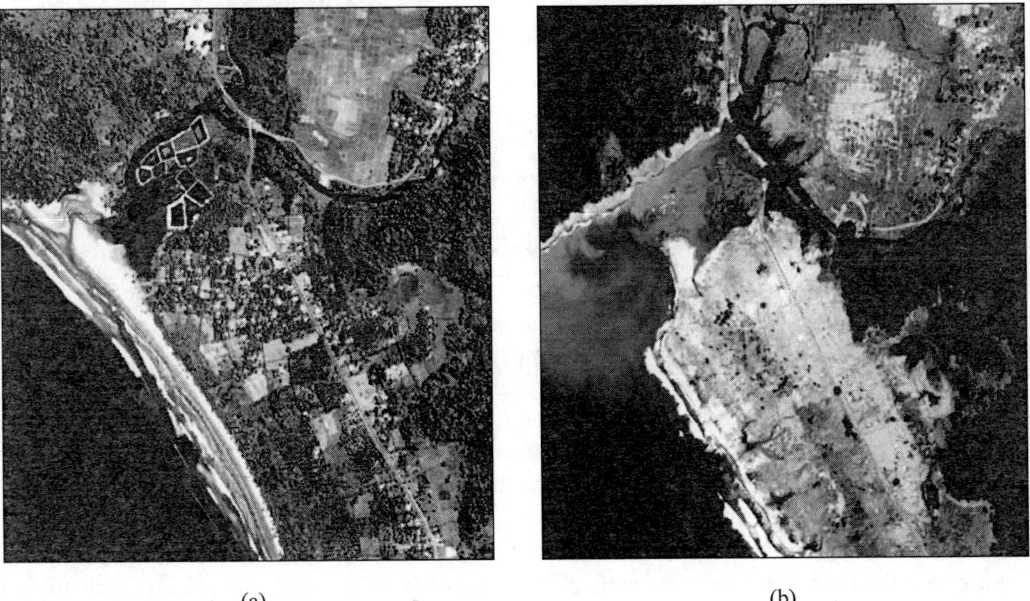

(a) (b)

Fig. 23.11. (a) Satellite image of Indonesia taken on 13 Jan 2003, i.e., before Tsunami. (b) Satellite image of Indonesia taken on 29 Dec., 2004, after disasterous Tsunami.

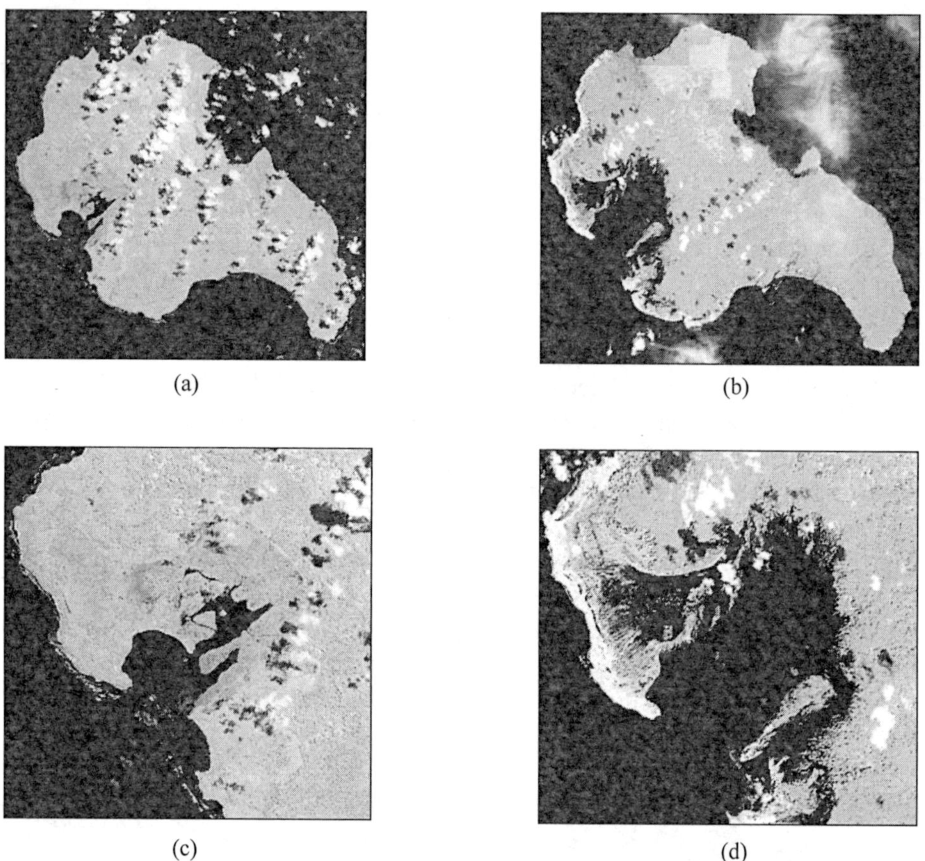

Fig. 23.12. (a) and (c) are the satellite images taken on 10 July 2004, of Katchall Island, India. These are the images of land before tsunami. (b) and (d) are the satellite images taken on 28 December 2004 of Katchal Island, India displaying the extend of Tsunami on land.

Remote Sensing–Melting Snows of Kilimanjaro

Sensors that measure environments are mounted on spacecraft, aircraft and ships that travel the skies and water above Earth's surface. This type of remote sensing reveals many aspects of Earth that improve our understanding of natural processes and human impacts.

Sensors collect data that record the topography, chemistry and biology of the air, water and crust. Some remote sensors capture wavelengths of energy that are not detectable to the human eye (such as infrared energy). Shipboard sensors use acoustic energy (sound waves) to map the seafloor. Because these instruments record their images digitally, geologists can mathematically enhance the data to bring out more detail. Remote sensing allows scientists to track environmental changes around the world. In this century scientists are most interested in how human are impacting Earth's climate.

One example of climate change is found in the loss of the world's mountain glaciers. Scientists using remote sensing have found that glaciers in most areas of the world are melting. Dr. Jeff Kargel of the US Geological Survey coordinates a project with over 100 researchers from 23 countries studying the problem. 'Glacier changes in the next 100 years could significantly affect agriculture, water supplies, hydroelectric power, transportation, mining, coastlines and ecological habitats. Melting ice may cause both serious problems and for the short term in some regions, helpful increases in water availability, but all these impacts will change with time', says Kargel.

Africa's highest peak, Mt. Kilimanjaro, has lost 82 per cent of its icecap in the last three decades (23.13). This ice supplies water for crops grown on the lower slopes of the mountain supporting the local lifestyle of hundreds of farmers. As the ice disappears the local population will have to move to new areas in search of water. The changes occurring on Mt. Kilimanjaro mirror similar changes occurring in mountainous regions around the planet.

Fig. 23.13. Mt. Kilimanjaro. Africa's highest mountain is losing its 11000 year old ice cap. Known as the 'Shining Mountain' for its white summit, the ice field shrank by 82 per cent over the past century and it could be gone by the year 2015. Almost half a meter of ice is lost each year due to rising surface temperatures. NASA's 'Landsat' satellites, first launched in 1972, captured this pair of images over Mount Kilimanjaro on February 17, 1993 (left) and February 21, 2000 (right).

Remote Sensing and Geographical Information System for natural disaster management

Natural Disasters are inevitable and Indian subcontinent is prone to all type of Natural Disaster either it is flood, drought, cyclone earthquakes or forest fires etc. Disasters can be classified in several ways. A possible sub-division of disaster is: (i) Natural Disasters; (ii) Human made disasters; (iii) Human induced disasters. Another sub-division is related to the main controlling factors leading to a disaster. These may be meteorologically, geomorphological/geological, ecological, technological, global environmental and extra terrestrial. Another useful distinction that can be made between disaster is regarding their duration of impact and the time of forewarning. Some disaster strikes within a short period with devastating outcomes; others have a slow onset period with equally or even more serious repercussions. According to the available statistics 60 per cent of the total area of Indian subcontinent is venerable to seismic activity of varying intensities, 16 per cent of the country's total area is drought prone. In India 68 per cent of total sown area of the country is drought prone. Coastal areas of India is exposed to tropical cyclones and among all the disaster occur in the country. River floods are the most frequent and often the most devastating.

Remote Sensing and GIS in Disaster Management Mitigation of natural disaster management can be successful only when detailed knowledge is obtained about the expected frequency, character and magnitude of hazard events in an area. Although, natural disaster have shown in the last decades a drastic increase in magnitude and frequency, it can as be observed that there is a dramatic increase in technical capabilities to mitigate them.

We now have access to information gathering and organising technologies like remote sensing and GIS, which have proven their usefulness in disaster management. Remote sensing and GIS provides a data base from which the evidence left behind by disaster that have occurred before can be interpreted and combine with the other information to arrive at hazard maps, indicating which area is potentially dangerous. Using remote sensing data, such as satellite imageries and ariel photos, allows us to map the variabilities of terrain properties, such as vegetation, water, geology, both in space and time. Satellite images give a synoptic overview and provide a very useful environmental information, for a wide range of scales, from entire continents to detail of a few meters. Many types of disasters, such as floods, droughts, cyclones, volcanic eruptions, etc. will have certain precursors that satellite can detect.

Remote sensing also allows monitoring the event during the time of occurrence while the forces are in full swing. The vantage position of satellite makes it ideal for us to think of, plan for and operationally monitor the event.

Finally, the impact and departure of the disaster event leaves behind an area of immense devastation. Remote Sensing can assists in damage assessment monitoring, providing a quantitative base for relief operation. After that it can be used to map the new situation and update the database used for the reconstruction of an area. It can help to prevent the occurrence of such disasters again in future.

Disaster Management

The use of remote sensing and GIS has become an integrated, well developed and successful tool in disaster management, as we are having our own Earth observation programmes and the requirement for hazard mitigation and monitoring rank high in the planning of new satellites. A very powerful tool in combination of these different types of data is GIS. It is defined as a 'powerful set of tools for collecting, storing, retrieving at will, transforming and displaying spatial data from a real world for a particular set of purpose'. GIS allows the combination of different kinds of data using models. GIS allows for the combination of the different kinds of spatial data, with non-spatial data, attribute data and use them as useful information in the various stages of disaster management.

A complete strategy for disaster management is required to effectively reduce the impact of natural disaster, which is as referred to as disaster management cycle. Disaster management consists of two phases that takes place before disaster occurs, disaster prevention and disaster preparedness, a three phases that happens after the occurrence of a disaster, i.e. disaster relief, rehabilitation and reconstruction. In disaster prevention phase, GIS is used to manage the large volume of data needed for the hazard and risk assessment. In disaster preparedness phase it is a tool for the planning of evacuation routes, for the design of centers for emergency operations and for integration of satellite data with other relevant data in the design of disaster warning systems. In the disaster relief phase, GIS is extremely useful in combination with Global Positioning System in search and rescue operations in areas that have been devastated and where it is difficult to orientate. In the disaster rehabilitation phase GIS is used to organise the damage information and the post-disaster census information and in the evaluation of sites for reconstruction. Hence, GIS is the useful tool in disaster management if it is used effectively and efficiently.

Remote Sensing and Geographical Information System for natural disaster management

Remote sensing and GIS for different application levels

Natural Hazard information should be included routinely in developmental planning and investment projects preparation. Development and investment projects should include a cost/benefit analysis of investing in hazard mitigation measures and weigh them against the losses that are likely to occur if these measures are not taken. Remote sensing and GIS can play a role at the following levels:

National level

At national level, GIS can provide useful information and create disaster awareness with politicians and the public, so that on a national level decisions are taken on the establishment of disaster management organisations. At such a general level, the objective is to give an inventory of disasters and the areas affected or threatened for an entire country. Mapping scales will be in order of 1:10,00,000 or smaller. The following types of information should be included:

1. Hazard free regions for development.
2. Regions with severe hazards where most development should be avoided.
3. Hazardous regions where development already has taken place and where measures are needed to reduce the venerability.
4. Regions where more hazards investigations are required.
5. National scale information is as required for these disaster that affect and entire country (drought, major hurricanes, floods etc.)

Regional level

At regional level the use of GIS for disaster management is intended for planner in the early phase of regional development projects or large engineering projects. It is used to investigate where hazards can be a constrain on the development of rural, urban or infrastructural projects. The areas to be investigated are large, generally several thousands or square kilometer and the required details of the input data is still rather low. Typical mapping scales for this level are between 1:10000 and 1:10,00,000. Synoptic Earth observation is the main source of information at this level, forming the basis for hazard assessment. Apart from the actual hazard information, as environmental and population and infrastructural information can be collected at a large detail than the national level. Therefore, the GIS can be utilised more for analysis at this scale, although the type of analysis will mostly be qualitative, due to the lack of detailed information.

Medium level

At this level GIS can be used for the prefeasibility study of developmental projects, at all inter-municipal or district level. The areas to be investigated will have an extend of a few hundred of square kilometer and a considerable higher details is required at this scale. Typical mapping scale is in the order of 1:25000–1:1,00,000. Slope information at this scale is sufficiently detailed to generate Digital Elevation Models and derivative products such as slope maps. GIS analysis capabilities for hazard zonation can be utilised extensively.

Local level

The level of application is typically that of a municipality. The use of GIS at this level is intended for planner to formulate projects at feasibility levels. But it is as used to generate hazard and risk map for existing settlements and cities and in the planning of disaster preparedness and disaster relief activities.

Typical mapping scales are 1:5000–1:25000. The details of information will be high, including for example cadastral information. The hazard data is more quantitative, derived from laboratory testing of materials and in field measurements. As the hazard assessment techniques will be more quantitative and based on deterministic/probabilistic models. The size of area under study is in the order of several tenths of square kilometer and the hazards classes on such maps should be absolute, indicating the probability of occurrence for mapping units, with areas down to one hectare or less.

Site investigation scale

At site investigation scale GIS is used in the planning and design of engineering structure and in detail engineering measures to mitigate natural hazards. Typical mapping scale are 1:2000 or larger. Nearly all of the data is of a quantitative nature. GIS is basically used for the data management and not for data analysis, since mostly external deterministic models are used for that. As 3-D GIS can be of great use at this level.

Thus, analysis of hazard is a complex task, as many factors can play important role in the occurrence of the disastrous event. Therefore, analysis requires a large number of input parameters and techniques of analysis may be very costly and time consuming. The increase availability of Remote Sensing data and GIS during the last decades has created opportunities for a more detailed and rapid analysis of natural hazard. The proper structure of information system for disaster management should be present to tackle the disaster and to manage it. The remote sensing and GIS database can be used to create elaborate and effective Disaster Management Information System (DMIS). An integrated approach using scientific and technological advances should be adopted to mitigate and to manage natural hazards. Moreover there should be a national policy for natural disaster management.

Glossary

Absorption band	:	Wavelength interval within which electromagnetic radiation is absorbed by the atmosphere or by other substances.
Absorptivity	:	Capacity of a material to absorb incident radiant energy.
Active remote sensing	:	Remote sensing methods that provide their own source of electromagnetic radiation to illuminate the terrain. Radar is one example.
Additive primary colours	:	Blue, green and red. Filters of these colours transmit the primary colour of the filter and absorb the other two colours.
Adiabatic cooling	:	Refers to decrease in temperature with increasing altitude.
Advanced very high resolution radio-meter (AVHRR)	:	Cross-track multispectral scanner on a NOAA polar-orbiting satellite that acquires five spectral bands of data (0.55 to 12.50 μm) with a ground resolution cell of 1.1 by 1.1 km.
Air base	:	Ground distance between optical centers of successive overlapping aerial photographs.
Aerial magnetic survey	:	Survey that records variations in the earth's magnetic field.
Airborne imaging spectrometer (AIS)	:	Along-track multispectral scanner with spectral bandwidth of 0.01 μm.
Airborne visible and infrared imaging spectrometer (AVIRIS)	:	Experimental airborne along-track multispectral scanner under development of JPL to acquire 224 images in the spectral region from 0.4 to 2.4 μm.
AIS	:	Airborne imaging spectrometer.
Albedo (A)	:	Ratio of the amount of electromagnetic energy reflected by a surface to the amount of energy incident upon it.
Along-track scanner	:	Scanner with a linear array of detectors oriented normal to flight path. The IFOV of each detector sweeps a path parallel with the flight direction.
Alteration	:	Changes in colour and mineralogy of rocks surrounding a mineral deposit that are caused by the solutions that formed the deposit. Suites of alteration minerals commonly occur in zones.
Amplitude	:	For waves, the vertical distance from crest to trough.
Analog display	:	A form of data display in which values are shown in graphic form, such as curves. Differs from digital displays, in which values are shown as arrays of numbers.
Angular beam width	:	In radar, the angle subtended in the horizontal plane by the radar beam.

Angular field of view : Angle subtended by lines from a remote sensing system to the outer margins of the strip of terrain that is viewed by the system.

Angular resolving power : Minimum separation between two resolvable targets, expressed as angular separation.

Anomaly : An area on an image that differs from the surrounding, normal area. For example, a concentration of vegetation within a desert scene constitutes an anomaly.

Antenna : Device that transmits and receives microwave and radio energy in radar systems.

Aperture : Opening in a remote sensing system that admits electromagnetic radiation to the film or detector.

Apollo : US lunar exploration programme of satellites with crews of three astronauts.

Apparent thermal inertia (ATI) : An approximation of thermal inertia calculated as one minus albedo divided by the difference between day time and night time radiant temperatures.

ASA index : Index of the American Standards Association designating film speed or sensitivity to light. Higher values indicate higher sensitivity. The ASA index has been replaced by the ISO index.

Atmosphere : Layer of gases that surrounds some planets.

Atmospheric correction : Image-processing procedure that compensates for effects of selectively scattered light in multispectral images.

Atmospheric window : Wavelength interval within which the atmosphere readily transmits electromagnetic radiation.

Attitude : Angular orientation of a remote sensing system with respect to a geographic reference system.

Azimuth : Geographic orientation of a line given as an angle measured in degrees clockwise from north.

Azimuth direction : In radar images, the direction in which the aircraft is heading. Also called flight direction.

Azimuth resolution : In radar images, the spatial resolution in the azimuth direction.

Background : Area on an image or the terrain that surrounds an area of interest or target.

Backscatter : In radar, the portion of the microwave energy scattered by the terrain surface directly back toward the antenna.

Backscatter coefficient : A quantitative measure of the intensity of energy returned to a radar antenna from the terrain.

Band : A wavelength interval in the electromagnetic spectrum. For example, in Landsat images the bands designate specific wavelength intervals at which images are acquired.

Base-height ratio : Air base divided by aircraft height. This ratio determines vertical exaggeration on stereo models.

Batch processing : Method of data processing in which data and programs are entered into a computer that carries out the entire processing operation with no further instructions.

Bathymetry : Configuration of the seafloor.

Beam : A focused pulse of energy.

Binary : Numerical system using the base 2.

Bit : Contraction of binary digit, which in digital computing represents an exponent of the base 2.

Blackbody : An ideal substance that absorbs all the radiant energy incident on it and emits radiant energy at the maximum possible rate per unit area at each wavelength for any given temperature. No actual substance is a true blackbody, although some substances, such as lampblack, approach its properties.

Brightness : Magnitude of the response produced in the eye by light.

Brute-force radar : See real-aperture radar.

Byte : A group of eight bits of digital data.

Calibration : Process of comparing an instrument's measurements with a standard.

Calorie : Amount of heat required to raise the temperature of 1 gram of water by 1°C.

Camouflage detection photographs : Another term for IR colour photograph.

Cardinal point effect : In radar, very bright signatures caused by optimally oriented corner reflectors, such as buildings.

Cathode ray tube (CRT) : A vacuum tube with a phosphorescent screen on which images are displayed by an electron beam.

Centerpoint : The optical center of a photograph.

Change-detection images : A difference image prepared by digitally comparing images acquired at different times. The gray tones or colours of each pixel record the amount of difference between the corresponding pixels of the original images.

Charge-coupled detector (CCD) : A device in which electrons are stored at the surface of a semi-conductor.

Chlorosis : Yellowing of plant leaves resulting from an imbalance in the iron metabolism caused by excess concentrations of copper, zinc, manganese or other elements in the plant.

Circular scanner : Scanner in which a faceted mirror rotates about a vertical axis to sweep the detector IFOV in a series of circular scan lines on the terrain.

Classification : Process of assigning individual pixels of an image to categories, generally on the basis of spectral reflectance characteristics.

Coastal zone colour scanner (CZCS) : A satellite-carried multispectral scanner designed to measure chlorophyll concentrations in the oceans.

Colour composite image : Colour image prepared by projecting individual black-and-white multispectral images, each through a different colour filter. When the projected images are superposed, a colour composite image results.

Colour ratio composite image : Colour composite image prepared by combining individual ratio images for a scene using a different colour for each ratio image.

Complementary colours : Two primary colour of light (one additive and the other subtractive) that produce white light when added together. Red and cyan are complementary colours.

Computer-compatible tape (CCT) : The magnetic tape on which the digital data for Landsat MSS and TM images are distributed.

Conduction : Transfer of electromagnetic energy through a solid material by molecular interaction.

Contact print : A reproduction from a photographic negative in direct contact with photosensitive paper.

Contrast enhancement : Image-processing procedure that improves the contrast ratio of images. The original narrow range of digital values is expanded to utilise the full range of available digital values.

Contrast ratio : On an image, the ratio of reflectances between the brightest and darkest parts of the image.

Convection : Transfer of heat through the physical movement of heated matter.

Corner reflector : Cavity formed by two or three smooth planar surfaces intersecting at right angles. Electromagnetic waves entering a corner reflector are reflected directly back toward the source.

COSMIC : Computer Software Management and Information Center, University of Georgia. This facility distributes computer programs developed by US government-funded projects.

Cross-polarised : Describes a radar pulse in which the polarisation direction of the return is normal to the polarisation direction of the transmission. Cross-polarised images may be HV (horizontal transmit, vertical return) or VH (vertical transmit, horizontal return).

Cross-track scanner : Scanner in which a faceted mirror rotates about a horizontal axis to sweep the detector IFOV in a series of parallel scan lines oriented normal to the flight direction.

CRT : Cathode ray tube.

Cycle : One complete oscillation of a wave.

Data collection system (DCS) : On Landsats 1 and 2, the system that acquired information from seismometers, flood gauges and other measuring devices. These data were relayed to ground receiving stations.

Densitometer : Optical device for measuring the density of photographic transparencies.

Density of images : Measure of the opacity or darkness, of a negative or positive transparency.

Density of materials (ρ) : Ratio of mass to volume of a material, typically expressed as grams per cubic centimeter.

Density slicing : Process of converting the continuous gray tones of an image into a series of density intervals or slices, each corresponding to a specific digital range. The density slices are then displayed either as uniform gray tones or as colours.

Depolarised : Refers to a change in polarisation of a transmitted radar pulse as a result of various interactions with the terrain surface.

Depression angle (γ) : In radar, the angle between the imaginary horizontal plane passing through the antenna and the line connecting the antenna and the target.

Detectability : Measure of the smallest object that can be discerned on an image.

Detector : Component of a remote sensing system that converts electromagnetic radiation into a recorded signal.

Developing : Chemical processing of an exposed photographic emulsion to produce an image.

Dielectric constant : Electrical property of matter that influences radar returns. Also referred to as complex dielectric constant.

Difference image : Image prepared by subtracting the digital values of pixels in one image from those in a second image to produce a third set of pixels. This third set is used to form the difference image.

Diffuse reflector : Surface that reflects incident radiation nearly equally in all directions.

Digital display : A form of data display in which values are shown as arrays of numbers.

Digital image processing : Computer manipulation of the digital-number values of an image.

Digital number (DN) : Value assigned to a pixel in a digital image.

Digitisation : Process of converting an analog display into a digital display.

Digitiser : Device for scanning an image and converting it into numerical format.

Directional filter : Mathematical filter designed to enhance on an image those linear features oriented in a particular direction.

Distortion : On an image, changes in shape and position of objects with respect to their true shape and position.

Diurnal : Daily.

Doppler principle : Describes the change in observed frequency that electromagnetic or other waves undergo as a result of the movement of the source of waves relative to the observer.

Dwell time : Time required for a detector IFOV to sweep across a ground resolution cell.

Earth-terrain camera (ETC) : A high-resolution camera carried on Skylab.

Edge enhancement : Image-processing technique that emphasises the appearance of edges and lines.

Ektachrome : A Kodak colour positive film.

Electromagnetic radiation : Energy propagated in the form of an advancing interaction between electric and magnetic fields. All electromagnetic radiation moves at the speed of light.

Electromagnetic spectrum : Continuous sequence of electromagnetic energy arranged according to wavelength or frequency.

Emission : Process by which a body radiates electromagnetic energy. Emission is determined by kinetic temperature and emissivity.

Emissivity ($\in$) : Ratio of radiant flux from a body to that from a blackbody at the same kinetic temperature.

Emulsion : Suspension of photosensitive silver halide grains in gelatine that constitutes the image-forming layer on photographic film.

Energy flux : Radiant flux.

Enhancement : Process of altering the appearance of an image so that the interpreter can extract more information.

EREP : Earth Resources Experiment Package, carried on Skylab and consisting of cameras and a multispectral scanner.

EROS : Earth Resource Observation System.

EROS data center (EDC) : Facility of the US Geological Survey at Sioux Falls, South Dakota, that archives, processes and distributes images.

ERTS : Earth Resource Technology Satellite, now called Landsat.

Evaporative cooling : Temperature drop caused by evaporation of water from a moist surface.

False colour photograph : Another term for IR colour photograph.

Far range : The portion of a radar image farthest from the aircraft or spacecraft flight path.

Film : Light-sensitive photographic emulsion and its base.

Film speed : Measure of the sensitivity of photographic film to light. Larger numbers indicate higher sensitivity.

Filter digital : Mathematical procedure for modifying values of numerical data.

Filter optical : A material that, by absorption or reflection, selectively modifies the radiation transmitted through an optical system.

Flight path : Line on the ground directly beneath a remote sensing aircraft or spacecraft. Also called flight line.

Fluorescence : Emission of light from a substance following exposure to radiation from an external source.

f-number : Representation of the speed of a lens determined by the focal length divided by diameter of the lens. Smaller numbers indicate faster lenses.

Focal length : In cameras, the distance from the optical center of the lens to the plane at which the image of a very distant object is brought into focus.

Format : Size of an image.

Forward overlap : The per cent of duplication by successive photographs along a flight line.

Frequency (ν) : Number of wave oscillations per unit time or the number of wavelengths that pass a point per unit time.

f-stop : Focal length of a lens divided by the diameter of the len's adjustable diaphragm. Smaller numbers indicate larger openings, which admit more light to the film.

Gemini : US programme of two-man earth-oribiting spacecraft in 1965 and 1966.

Geometric correction : Image-processing procedure that corrects spatial distortions in an image.

Geostationary : Refers to satellites travelling at the angular velocity at which the earth rotates; as a result, they remain above the same point on earth at all times.

Geostationary operational environmental satellite (GOES) : A NOAA satellite that acquires visible and thermal IR images for meteorologic purposes.

Geothermal : Refers to heat from sources within the earth.

Goddard space flight center (GSFC) : The NASA facility at Greenbelt, Maryland, that is also a Landsat ground receiving station.

GMT : Greenwich mean time. This international 24 hour system is used to designate the time at which Landsat images are acquired.

Gossan : Surface occurrence of iron oxide formed by the weathering of metallic sulphide ore minerals.

Granularity : Graininess of developed photographic film that is determined by the texture of the silver grains.

Gray scale	:	A sequence of gray tones ranging from black to white.
Ground-control point (GCP)	:	A geographic feature of known location that is recognisable on images and can be used to determine geometric corrections.
Ground range	:	On radar images, the distance from the ground track to an object.
Ground-range image	:	Radar image in which the scale in the range direction is constant.
Ground receiving station	:	Facility that records data transmitted by a satellite, such as Landsat.
Ground resolution cell	:	Area on the terrain that is covered by the IFOV of a detector.
Ground swath	:	Width of the strip of terrain that is imaged by a scanner system.
Harmonic	:	Refers to waves in which the component frequencies are whole-number multiples of the fundamental frequency.
Heat capacity (c)	:	Ratio of heat absorbed or released by a material to the corresponding temperature rise or fall. Expressed in calories per gram per degree centigrade. Also called thermal capacity.
Heat capacity mapping mission (HCMM)	:	NASA satellite orbited in 1978 to record day time and night time visible and thermal IR images of large areas.
Highlights	:	Areas of bright tone on an image.
Hue	:	In the IHS system, represents the dominant wavelength of a colour.
IHS	:	Intensity, hue and saturation system of colours.
Image	:	Pictorial representation of a scene recorded by a remote sensing system. Although image is a general term, it is commonly restricted to representations acquired by non-photographic methods.
Image swath	:	See *ground swath*.
Incidence angle	:	In radar, the angle formed between an imaginary line normal to the surface and another connecting the antenna and the target.
Incident energy	:	Electromagnetic radiation impinging on a surface.
Index of refraction (n)	:	Ratio of the wavelength or velocity of electromagnetic radiation in a vacuum to that in a substance.
Instantaneous field of view (IFOV)	:	Solid angle through which a detector is sensitive to radiation. In a scanning system, the solid angle subtended by the detector when the scanning motion is stopped.
Intensity	:	In the IHS system, brightness ranging from black to white.
Interactive processing	:	Method of image processing in which the operator views preliminary results and can alter the instructions to the computer to achieve desired results.
Interpretation	:	The process in which a person extracts information from an image.
Interpretation key	:	Characteristic or combination of characteristics that enable an interpreter to identify an object on an image.
IR	:	Infrared region of the electromagnetic spectrum that includes wavelengths from 0.7 μm to 1 mm.
IR colour photograph	:	Colour photograph in which the red-imaging layer is sensitive to photographic IR wavelengths, the green-imaging layer is sensitive to red light and the blue-imaging

layer is sensitive to green light. Also known as camouflage detection photographs and false-colour photographs.

ISO index	:	Index of the International Standards Organisation, designating film speed in photography. Higher values indicate higher sensitivity.
Isotherm	:	Contour line connecting points of equal temperature. Isotherm maps are used to portray surface-temperature patterns of water bodies.
Johnson space flight center	:	A NASA facility in Houston, Texas.
JPL	:	Jet Propulsion Laboratory, a NASA facility at Pasadena, California, operated under contract by the California Institute of Technology.
Ka band	:	Radar wavelength region from 0.8 to 1.1 cm.
Kernel	:	Two-dimensional array of digital numbers used in digital filtering.
Kinetic energy	:	The ability of a moving body to do work by virture of its motion. The molecular motion of matter is a form of kinetic energy.
Kinetic temperature	:	Internal temperature of an object determined by random molecular motion. Kinetic temperature is measured with a contact thermometer.
Kodachrome	:	A Kodak colour positive film.
LACIE	:	Large Area Crop Inventory Experiment.
Landsat	:	A series of unmanned earth-oribiting NASA satellites that acquire multispectral images in various visible and IR bands.
Laplacian filter	:	A form of non-directional digital filter.
Large-format camera (LFC)	:	An experiment first carried on the Space Shuttle in October 1984.
Latent image	:	Invisible image produced by the photochemical effect of light on silver halide grains in the emulsion of film. The latent image is not visible until after photographic development.
Layover	:	In radar images, the geometric displacement of the top of objects toward the near range relative to their base.
L band	:	Radar wavelength region from 15 to 30 cm.
Lens	:	One or more pieces of glass or other transparent material shaped to form an image by refraction of light.
Light	:	Electromagnetic radiation ranging from 0.4 to 0.7 μm in wavelength that is detectable by the human eye.
Light meter	:	Device for measuring the intensity of visible radiation and determining the appropriate exposure of photographic film in a camera.
Lineament	:	Linear topographic or tonal feature on the terrain and on images, maps and photographs that may represent a zone of structural weakness.
Linear	:	Adjective that describes the straight line-like nature of features on the terrain or on images and photographs.
Line-pair	:	Pair of light and dark bars of equal widths. The number of such line-pairs aligned side by side that can be distinguished per unit distance expresses the resolving power of an imaging system.

Lineation	:	The one-dimensional alignment of internal components of a rock that cannot be depicted as an individual feature on a map.
Look direction	:	Direction in which pulses of microwave energy are transmitted by a radar system. The look direction is normal to the azimuth direction. Also called range direction.
Low-sun-angle photograph	:	Aerial photograph acquired in the morning, evening or winter when the sun is at a low elevation above the horizon.
Luminance	:	Quantitative measure of the intensity of light from a source.
Mercury	:	US programme of one-man, earth-orbiting spacecraft in 1962 and 1963.
Microwave	:	Region of the electromagnetic spectrum in the wavelength range of 0.1 to 30 cm.
Minimum ground separation	:	Minimum distance on the ground between two targets at which they can be resolved on an image.
Minus-blue photographs	:	Black-and-white photographs acquired using filter that removes blue wavelengths to produce higher spatial resolution.
Modular optoelectric multispectral scanner (MOMS)	:	An along-track scanner carried on the Space Shuttle that recorded two bands of data.
Modulate	:	To vary the frequency, phase or amplitude of electromagnetic waves.
Modulation transfer function (MTF)	:	A method of describing spatial resolution.
Mosaic	:	Composite image or photograph made by piecing together individual images or photographs covering adjacent areas.
MSS	:	Multispectral scanner system of Landsat that acquires images at four wavelength bands in the visible and reflected IR regions.
Multiband camera	:	System that simultaneously acquires photographs of the same scene at different wavelengths.
Multispectral classification	:	Identification of terrain categories by digital processing of data acquired by multispectral scanners.
Multispectral scanner	:	Scanner system that simultaneously acquires images of the same scene at different wavelengths.
Nadir	:	Point on the ground directly in line with the remote sensing system and the center of the earth.
NASA	:	National Aeronautical and Space Administration.
Near range	:	Refers to the portion of a radar image closest to the aircraft or satellite flight path.
Negative photograph	:	Photograph on film or paper in which the relationship between bright and dark tones in the reverse of that of the features on the terrain.
NHAP	:	National High Altitude Photography programme of the US Geological Survey.
NOAA	:	National Oceanic and Atmospheric Administration.
Noise	:	Random or repetitive events that obscure or interfere with the desired information.
Non-directional filter	:	Mathematical filter that treats all orientations of linear features equally.
Non-systematic distortion	:	Geometric irregularities on images that are not constant and cannot be predicted from the characteristics of the imaging system.

Normal colour film : Film in which the colours are essentially true representations of the colours of the terrain.

NSSDC : National Space Science Data Center.

Oblique photograph : Photograph acquired with the camera intentionally directed at some angle between horizontal and vertical orientations.

OMS : Orbital maneuvering system.

Orbit : Path of a satellite around a body such as the earth, under the influence of gravity.

Overlap : Extent to which adjacent images or photographs cover the same terrain, expressed as a percentage.

Panchromatic film : Black and white film that is sensitive to all visible wavelengths.

Parallax : Displacement of the position of a target in an image caused by a shift in the observation position.

Parallel-polarised : Describes a radar pulse in which the polarisation of the return is the same as that of the transmission. Parallel-polarised images may be HH (horizontal transmit, horizontal return) or VV (vertical transmit, vertical return).

Pass : In digital filters, refers to the spatial frequency of data transmitted by the filter. High-pass filters transmit high-frequency data; low-pass filters transmit low-frequency data.

Passive remote sensing : Remote sensing of energy naturally reflected or radiated from the terrain.

Path-and-row index : System for locating Landsat MSS and TM images.

Pattern : Regular repetition of tonal variations on an image or photograph.

Periodic line dropout : Defect on Landsat MSS or TM images in which no data are recorded for every sixth or sixteenth scan line, causing a black line on the image.

Periodic line striping : Defect on Landsat MSS or TM images in which every sixth or sixteenth scan line is brighter or darker than the others. Caused by the sensitivity of one detector being higher or lower than the others.

Photodetector : Device for measuring energy in the visible-light band.

Photogeology : Mapping and interpretation of geologic features from aerial photographs.

Photograph : Representation of targets on film that results from the action of light on silver halide grains in film's emulsion.

Photographic IR : Short-wavelength portion (0.7 to 0.9 μm) of the IR band that is detectable by IR colour film or IR black-and-white film.

Photographic UV : Long-wavelength portion of the UV band (0.3 to 0.4 μm) that is transmitted through the atmosphere and is detectable by film.

Photomosaic : Mosaic composed of photographs.

Photon : Minimum discrete quantity of radiant energy.

Picture element : In a digitised image, the area on the ground represented by each digital number. Commonly contracted to pixel.

Pitch : Rotation of an aircraft about the horizontal axis normal to its longitudinal axis that causes a nose-up or nose-down attitude.

Pixel : Contraction of picture element.

Polarisation : The direction of orientation in which the electrical field vector of electromagnetic radiation vibrates.

Positive photograph : Photographic image in which the tones are directly proportional to the terrain brightness.

Previsual symptom : A vegetation anomaly that is recognisable on IR film before it is visible to the naked eye or on normal colour photographs. It results when stressed vegetation loses its ability to reflect photographic IR energy and is recognisable on IR colour film by a decrease in brightness of the red hues.

Primary colours : A set of three colours that in various combinations will produce the full range of colours in the visible spectrum. There are two sets of primary colours, additive and subtractive.

Principal-component (PC) image : Digitally processed image produced by a transformation that recognises maximum variance in multispectral images.

Principal point : Optical center of an aerial photograph.

Printout : Display of computer data in alphanumeric format.

Pulse : Short burst of electromagnetic radiation transmitted by a radar antenna.

Pulse length : Duration of a burst of energy transmitted by a radar antenna, measured in microseconds.

Pushbroom scanner : An alternate term for an along-track scanner.

Radar : Acronym for radio detection and ranging. Radar is an active form of remote sensing that operates in the microwave and radio wavelength regions.

Radar shadow : Dark signature on a radar image representing no signal return. A shadow extends in the far-range direction from an object that intercepts the radar beam.

Radian : Angle subtended by an arc of a circle equal in length to the radius of the circle 1 rad = 57.3°.

Radiant energy peak (λ_{max}) : Wavelength at which the maximum electromagnetic energy is radiated at a particular temperature.

Radiant flux : Rate of flow of electromagnetic radiation measured in watts per square centimeter.

Radiant temperature : Concentration of the radiant flux from a material. Radiant temperature is the kinetic temperature multiplied by the emissivity to the one-fourth power.

Radiation : Propagation of energy in the form of electromagnetic waves.

Radiometer : Device for quantitatively measuring radiant energy, especially thermal radiation.

Random line dropout : In scanner images, the loss of the data from individual scan lines in a non-systematic fashion.

Range direction : See look direction.

Range resolution : In radar images, the spatial resolution in the range direction, which is determined by the pulse length of the transmitted microwave energy.

Raster pattern : Pattern of horizontal lines swept by an electron beam across the face of a CRT that constitute the image display.

Ratio image : An image prepared by processing digital multispectral data as follows: for each pixel, the value for one band is divided by that of another. The resulting digital values are displayed as an image.

Rayleigh criterion : In radar, the relationship between surface roughness, depression angle and wavelength that determines whether a surface will respond in a rough or smooth fashion to the radar pulse.

Real-aperture radar : Radar system in which azimuth resolution is determined by the transmitted beam width, which is in turn determined by the physical length of the antenna and by the wavelength.

Real time : Refers to images or data made available for inspection simultaneously with their acquisition.

Recognisability : Ability to identify an object on an image.

Rectilinear : Refers to images with no geometric distortion in which the scales in the horizontal and vertical directions are identical.

Reflectance : Ratio of the radiant energy reflected by a body to the energy incident on it. Spectral reflectance is the reflectance measured within a specific wavelength interval.

Reflected energy peak : Wavelength (0.5 μm) at which maximum amount of energy is reflected from the earth's surface.

Reflected IR : Electromagnetic energy of wavelengths from 0.7 μm to about 3 μm that consists primarily of reflected solar radiation.

Reflectivity : Ability of a surface to reflect incident energy.

Refraction : Bending of electromagnetic rays as they pass from one medium into another when each medium has a different index of refraction.

Registration : Process of superposing two or more images or photographs so that equivalent geographic points coincide.

Relief : Vertical irregularities of a surface.

Relief displacement : Geometric distortion on vertical aerial photographs. The tops of objects appear in the photograph to be radially displaced from their bases outward from the photograph's centerpoint.

Remote sensing : Collection and interpretation of information about an object without being in physical contact with the object.

Reseau marks : Pattern of small crosses added to photographs.

Resolution : Ability to separate closely spaced objects on an image or photograph. Resolution is commonly expressed as the most closely spaced line-pairs per unit distance that can be distinguished. Also called spatial resolution.

Resolution target : Series of regularly spaced alternating light and dark bars used to evaluate the resolution of images or photographs.

Resolving power : A measure of the ability of individual components and of remote sensing systems, to separate closely spaced targets.

Reststrahlen band : In the thermal IR region, refers to absorption of energy as a function of silica content.

Return : In radar, a pulse of microwave energy reflected by the terrain and received at the radar antenna. The strength of a return is referred to as return intensity.

Return-beam vidicon (RBV)	:	A system in which images are formed on the photosensitive surface of a vacuum tube; the image is scanned with an electron beam and transmitted or recorded. Landsat 3 used a pair of RBVs to acquire images.
Roll	:	Rotation of an aircraft that causes a wing-up or wing-down attitude.
Roll compensation system	:	Component of an airborne scanner system that measures and records the roll of the aircraft. This information is used to correct the imagery for distortion due to roll.
Rough criterion	:	In radar, the relationship between surface roughness, depression angle and wavelength that determines whether a surface will scatter the incident radar pulse in a rough or intermediate fashion.
Roughness	:	In radar, the average vertical relief of small-scale irregularities of the terrain surface. Also called surface roughness.
Satellite	:	An object in orbit around a celestial body.
Saturation	:	In the IHS system, represents the purity of colour. Saturation is also the condition where energy flux exceeds the sensitivity range of a detector.
Scale	:	Ratio of distance on an image to the equivalent distance on the ground.
Scan line	:	Narrow strip on the ground that is swept by IFOV of a detector in a scanning system.
Scanner	:	An imaging system in which the IFOV of one or more detectors is swept across the terrain.
Scanner distortion	:	Geometric distortion that is characteristic of cross-track scanner images.
Scan skew	:	Distortion of scanner images caused by forward motion of the aircraft or satellite during the time required to complete a scan.
Scattering	:	Multiple reflections of electromagnetic waves by particles or surfaces.
Scattering coefficient curves	:	Display of scatterometer data in which relative backscatter is shown as a function of incidence angle.
Scatterometer	:	Non-imaging radar device that quantitatively records backscatter of terrain as a function of incidence angle.
Scene	:	Area on the ground that is covered by an image or photograph.
Seasat	:	NASA unmanned satellite that acquired L-band radar images in 1978.
Sensitivity	:	Degree to which a detector responds to electromagnetic energy incident on it.
Sensor	:	Device that receives electromagnetic radiation and converts it into a signal that can be recorded and displayed as either numerical data or an image.
Shuttle imaging radar (SIR)	:	L-band radar system deployed on the Space Shuttle.
Sidelap	:	Extent of lateral overlap between images acquired on adjacent flight lines.
Side-looking airborne radar (SLAR)	:	An airborne side scanning system for acquiring radar images.
Side-scanning sonar	:	Active system for acquiring images of the seafloor using pulsed sound waves.
Side scanning system	:	A system that acquires images of a strip of terrain parallel with the flight or orbit path but offset to one side.

Signal : Information recorded by a remote sensing system.

Signature : Set of characteristics by which a material or an object may be identified on an image or photograph.

Silver halide : Silver salts that are especially sensitive to visible light and convert to metallic silver when developed.

Skylab : US earth-orbiting workshop that housed three crews of three astronauts in 1973 and 1974.

Skylight : Component of light that is strongly scattered by the atmosphere and consists predominantly of shorter wavelengths.

Slant range : In radar, an imaginary line running between the antenna and the target.

Slant-range distance : Distance measured along the slat range.

Slant-range distortion : Geometric distortion of a slant-range image.

Slant-range image : In radar, an image in which objects are located at positions corresponding to their slant-range distances from the aircraft flight path. On slant-range images, the scale in the range direction is compressed in the near range region.

Smooth criterion : In radar, the relationship between surface roughness, depression angle and wavelength that determines whether a surface will scatter the incident radar pulse in a smooth or intermediate fashion.

Software : Programs that control computer operations.

Sonar : Acronym for sound navigation ranging. Sonar is an active form of remote sensing that employs sonic energy to image the seafloor.

Space Shuttle : US manned satellite programme in the 1980s, officially called the Space Transportation System (STS).

Spectral reflectance : Reflectance of electromagnetic energy at specified wavelength intervals.

Spectral sensitivity : Response or sensitivity, of a film or detector to radiation in different spectral regions.

Spectral vegetation index : An index of relative amount and vigour of vegetation. The index is calculated from two spectral bands of AVHRR imagery.

Spectrometer : Device for measuring intensity of radiation absorbed or reflected by a material as a function of wavelength.

Spectrum : Continuous sequence of electromagnetic energy arranged according to wavelength or frequency.

Specular : Refers to a surface that is smooth with respect to the wavelength of incident energy.

SPOT : Systeme Probatoire d'Observation de la Terre. Unmanned French remote sensing satellite orbiting in the late 1980s.

Stefan-Boltzmann constant : 5.68×10^{-12} W · cm^{-2} · °K^{-4}.

Stefan-Boltzmann law : States that radiant flux of a blackbody is equal to the temperature to the fourth power times the Stefan-Boltzmann constant.

Stereo base : Distance between a pair of correlative points on a stereo pair that are oriented for stereo viewing.

Stereo model : Three-dimensional visual impression produced by viewing a pair of overlapping images through a stereoscope.

Stereo pair : Two overlapping images or photographs that may be viewed stereoscopically.

Stereoscope : Binocular optical device for viewing overlapping images or diagrams. The left eye sees only the left image and the right eye sees only the right image.

Subscene : A portion of an image that is used for detailed analysis.

Subtractive primary colours : Yellow, magenta and cyan. When used as filters for white light, these colours remove blue, green and red light, respectively.

Sunglint : Bright reflectance of sunlight caused by ripples on water.

Sun-synchronous : Earth satellite orbit in which the orbit plane is nearly polar and the altitude is such that the satellite passes over all places on earth having the same latitude twice daily at the same local sun time.

Supervised classification : Digital-information extraction technique in which the operator provides training-site information that the computer uses to assign pixels to categories.

Surface phenomenon : Interaction between electromagnetic radiation and the surface of a material.

Surface roughness : See *roughness*.

Synthetic-aperture radar (SAR) : Radar system in which high azimuth resolution is achieved by storing and processing data on the Doppler shift of multiple return pulses in such a way as to give the effect of a much longer antenna.

Synthetic stereo images : Stereo images constructed through digital processing of a single image. Topographic data are used to calculate parallax.

System : Combination of components that constitute an imaging device.

Systematic distortion : Geometric irregularities on images that are caused by known and predictable characteristics.

Target : Object on the terrain of specific interest in a remote sensing investigation.

TDRS : Tracking and Data Relay Satellite.

Telemeter : To transmit data by radio or microwave links.

Terrain : Surface of the earth.

Texture : Frequency of change and arrangement of tones on an image.

Thematic mapper (TM) : A cross-track scanner deployed on Landsat that records seven bands of data from the visible through the thermal IR regions.

Thermal capacity (c) : See *heat capacity*.

Thermal conductivity (K) : Measure of the rate at which heat will pass through a material, expressed in calories per centimeter per second per degree Centigrade.

Thermal crossover : On a plot of radiant temperature versus time, the point at which temperature curves for two different materials intersect.

Thermal diffusivity (k) : Governs the rate at which temperature changes within a substance, expressed in centimeters squared per second.

Thermal inertia (P) : Measure of the response of a material to temperature changes, expressed in calories per square centimeter per square root of second.

Thermal IR : IR region from 3 to 14 μm that is employed in remote sensing. This spectral region spans the radiant power peak of the earth.

Thermal IR image : Image acquired by a scanner that records radiation within the thermal IR band.

Thermal IR multispectral scanner (TIMS) : Airborne scanner that acquires multispectral images within the 8-to-14 μm band of the thermal IR region.

Thermal model : Mathematical expression that relates thermal and other physical properties of a material to its temperature. Models may be used to predict temperature for given properties and conditions.

Thermography : Medical applications of thermal IR images. Images of the body, called thermograms, have been used to detect tumours and monitor blood circulation.

Tone : Each distinguishable shade of gray from white to black on an image.

Topographic inversion : An optical illusion that may occur on images with extensive shadows. Ridges appear to be valleys and valleys appear to be ridges. The illusion is corrected by orienting the image so that the shadows trend from the top margin of the image to the bottom.

Topographic reversal : A geomorphic phenomenon in which topographic lows coincide with structural highs and vice versa. Valleys are eroded on crests of anticlines to cause topographic lows and synclines form ridges or topographic highs.

Tracking and data relay satellite (TDRS) : Geostationary satellite used to communicate between ground receiving stations and satellites such as Landsat.

Trade-off : As a result of changing one factor in a remote sensing system, there are compensating changes elsewhere in the system; such as compensating change is known as a trade-off.

Training site : Area of terrain with known properties or characteristics that is used in supervised classification.

Transmissivity : Property of a material that determines the amount of energy that can pass through the material.

Transparency : Image on a transparent photographic material, normally a positive image.

Transpiration : Expulsion of water vapour and oxygen by vegetation.

Travel time : In radar, the time interval between the generation of a pulse of microwave energy and its return from the terrain.

Unsupervised classification : Digital information extraction technique in which the computer assigns pixels to categories with no instructions from the operator.

UV : Ultraviolet region of the electromagnetic spectrum ranging in wavelengths from 0.01 to 0.4 μm.

Vegetation anomaly : Deviation from the normal distribution or properties of vegetation. Vegetation anomalies may be caused by faults, trace elements in soil or other factors.

Vertical exaggeration : In a stereo model, the extent to which the vertical scale appears larger than the horizontal scale.

Visible radiation : Energy at wavelengths from 0.4 to 0.7 μm that is detectable by the human eye.

Volume scattering : In radar, interaction between electromagnetic radiation and the interior of a material.

Watt (W) : Unit of electrical power equal to rate of work done by one ampere under a potential of one volt.

Wavelength (λ) : Distance between successive wave crests or other equivalent points in a harmonic wave.

Wien's displacement law: Describes the shift of the radiant power peak to shorter wavelengths as temperature increases.

X band : Radar wavelength region from 2.4 to 3.8 cm.

Yaw : Rotation of an aircraft about its vertical axis so that the longitudinal axis deviates left or right from the flight line.

Appendices

APPENDIX I

ABBREVIATIONS AND SATELLITES

AATSR	:	Advanced along-track scanning radiometer
ACE	:	Atmosphere climate experiment
ACSYS	:	Arctic climate system studies
ADEOS	:	Satellite
AEM	:	Applications explorer mission
Aeolus	:	Atmospheric dynamics mission
AGCM	:	Atmospheric general circulation models
AIRS	:	Atmospheric infrared sounder
AMI	:	Active microwave instrument
AMSU	:	Advanced microwave sounding unit
Argos	:	Argos data collection and platform location system
ARTEMIS	:	Satellite
ASAR	:	Advanced synthetic aperture radar
ASCAT	:	Advanced scatterometer
ASTER	:	Advanced speceborne thermal emission and reflection radiometer
ATSR	:	Along-track scanning radiometer
AVNIR	:	Advanced visible and near infrared radiometer
BAHC	:	Biospheric aspects of hydrological cycle
BrO	:	Bromine species
BUV	:	Backscattered ultraviolet
CBD	:	Convention on biological diversity
CEOS	:	Committee on Earth observation satellites
Ceosat	:	Satellite
CERES	:	Clouds and Earth's radiant energy system
CHEM	:	Satellite
Clark	:	Satellite
CNES	:	Centre National d'Etudes Spatiales
COP	:	Conference of parties
CPU	:	Central processing unit

Cryosat : Satellite
CSD : Commission on sustainable development
CSIRO : Commonwealth scientific and industrial research organisation (Australia)
DAAC : Distributed active archive centres
DGVIII : Directorate general VIII (European commission)
DGXI : Directorate general XI (European commission)
DIS : Data and information system (IGBP)
DISCover : DIS land-cover dataset
DMS : Dimethylsulphide
DMSP : (US) Defence meteorological satellite programme
DORIS : Doppler orbitography and radio positioning integrated by satellite
DTM : Digital terrain model
Early Bird : Satellite
EARSeL : European Association of Remote Sensing Laboratories
Earth Explorer : Satellite
Earth Watch : Satellite
EC : European commission
ECMWF : European centre for medium-range weather forecasting
EEA : European environment agency
EIT : Economies in transition
Envisat : Satellite
EOPB : Earth observation programme board
EOS : Earth observing system; a US programme of planned satellites
EOS/ALT : Satellite
EOS/COLOUR : Satellite
EOSP : Earth observing scanning polarimeter
EPS : EUMETSAT Polar system
ER : Earth radiation
ERB : Earth radiation budget
ERBE : Satellite
ERS : Satellite (European remote sensing)
ESA : European space agency
ESAC : Earth science advisory committee
ESE : Earth science enterprise
ESF : European science foundation
ESM : Earth system models
ESSC : European space science committee
EU : European union
EUMETSAT : European organisation for meteorological satellites
FAO : Food and agriculture organisation (UN)
FCCC : Framework convention of climate change
FFT : Fast fourier transform
FIFE : First international satellite land surface climatology field experiment
FIRE : First international satellite cloud climatology regional experiment

FR	:	Full resolution
FTIR	:	Fourier transform infrared
FTP	:	File-transfer protocol
G3OS	:	Global climate, ocean and terrestrial observing systems (Combination of GCOS, GOOS and GTOS)
GAC	:	Global area coverage
GAIM	:	Global analysis, interpretation and modelling
GARP	:	Global atmospheric research programme
GCEC	:	Global change and ecological complexity
GCMs	:	General circulation models
GCOS	:	Global climate observing system
GCTE	:	Global change and terrestrial ecosystems
GERB	:	Geostationary Earth radiation budget experiment
GEWEX	:	Global energy and water cycle experiment
GFSSOC	:	Gravity field and steady state ocean circulation mission
GMS	:	Satellite
GOCE	:	Earth explorer gravity field and steady-state gravity circulation core mission
GOCM	:	Global ocean circulation models
GOEZS	:	Global ocean euphotic zone study
GOME	:	Global ozone monitoring experiment
GOMOS	:	Global ozone monitoring by occultation of stars
GOOS	:	Global ocean observing system
GOSMOS	:	Global ozone monitoring by occultation of stars
GOSSP	:	Global observing systems space panel
GPCP	:	Global precipitation climatology project
GRAS	:	Global navigation satellite system receiver for atmospheric sounding
GTOS	:	Global terrestrial observing system
HALOE	:	Halogen occultation experiment solar occultation
HFCs	:	Hydrofluorocarbons
HIRS	:	High resolution infrared radiation sounder
HRCs	:	High reflective clouds
HRDI	:	High resolution doppler imager
HRG	:	High resolution geometry
HRV	:	High (Haute) resolution visible sensor
IASI	:	Infrared atmospheric sounding interferometer
ICPD	:	International conference on population and development
ICSU	:	International council for science
ICT	:	Internal calibration target
IEA	:	Institute of economic affairs
IGAC	:	International global atmospheric chemistry project
IGBP	:	International geosphere–biosphere programme
IGBP-DIS	:	IGBP data and information system
IGFA	:	International group of funding agencies
IGOOS	:	Integrated global ocean observing system

IGOS	:	Integrated global observing strategy
IGY	:	International geophysical year
IHDP	:	International human dimensions programme
IKONOS	:	Satellite
Insat	:	Satellite
IOC	:	Intergovernmental oceanographic commission
IPCC	:	Intergovernmental panel on climate change
IQSY	:	International quiet Sun year
IRIS	:	Satellite
IRS	:	Satellite
ISAMS	:	Improved stratospheric and mesospheric sounder
ISCCP	:	International satellite cloud climatology project
ISRO	:	Indian space research organisation
ISS	:	International space station
Jason	:	NASA/NOAA/CMES satellites planned as successors to *Topex-Poseidon* as part of the EOS programme
JERS	:	Satellite
JGOFS	:	Joint global ocean flux study
LAI	:	Leaf area index
Landsat	:	Satellite
LCWG	:	Land cover working group
LISS	:	Linear imaging self-scanning sensor
LOICZ	:	Land–ocean interactions in the coastal zone
LRR	:	Laser retro-reflector
LSPI	:	Land surface processes and interaction mission
LUCC	:	Land use/cover change
LUCF	:	Land-use change and forestry
MCP	:	Mission communication package
MERIS	:	Medium resolution imaging spectrometer
Meteosat	:	Satellite
METOP	:	Satellite
MHS	:	Microwave humidity sounder
MIMR	:	Multifrequency imaging microwave radiometer
MIPAS	:	Michelson interferometer for passive atmospheric sounding
MISR	:	Multi-angle imaging spectro-radiometer
MLS	:	Microwave limb sounder
MLW	:	Mid-latitude winter
MODIS	:	Moderate resolution imaging spectroradiometer
MOPIT	:	Measurements of pollution in the troposphere
MSC	:	Meteorological satellite centre
MSG	:	Meteosat second generation
MSU	:	Microwave sounding unit
MSU-SK	:	A Soviet mechanical scanning imaging radiometer
MWR	:	Microwave radiometer

MWS : Microwave sounder
NASDA : National space development agency (Japan)
NCDC : National climate data center
NCEP : National center for environmental prediction
NDVI : Normalised difference vegetation index
NESDIS : National environmental satellite data and information service
NGDC : National geophysical data center
Nimbus : Satellite
NIMBY : Not in my backyard syndrome
NIST : National institute of standards and technology
NOAA : National oceanic and atmospheric administration; also satellite
NODC : National oceanographic data center
NRA : NASA radar altimeter
NWP : Numerical weather prediction
MWPM : Numerical weather prediction models
OCTS : Ocean colour and temperature sensor
OECD : Organisation for economic cooperation and development
OGCM : Ocean general circulation models
OLR : Outgoing long-wave radiation
OMI : Ozone monitoring instrument
OOPC : Ocean observing panel for climate
OPEC : Organisation of petroleum exporting countries
Orbview : Satellite
PAGES : Past global changes
PI : Principal investigators
PRARE : Precise range and range-rate equipment
PRT : Platinum resistance thermometer
Quickbird : Satellite
RA : Radar altimeter
Radarsat : Satellite
RDED : Rio declaration on environment and development
RESURS : Satellite
RFI : Radio-frequency interference
S & R : Search and rescue
SAGE : Stratospheric aerosol and gas experiment
SAM : Stratospheric aerosol measurement
SAMS : Stratosphere and mesosphere sounder
SBSTA : Subsidiary body for scientific and technological advice
SBUV : Solar backscatter ultraviolet
SCIAMACHY : Scanning imaging absorption spectrometer for atmospheric cartography
SDS : Strategic data sets
Seasat : Satellite
Sea WiFS : Sea-viewing wide-field-of-view sensor
SEM : Space environment monitor

SETI : Search for extraterrestrial intelligence
SEVIRI : Spinning enhanced visible and infrared imager
SGP97 : Southern great plains 1997 hydrology experiment
SI : Systeme international d'Unites
SMMR : Scanning multi-channel microwave radiometer
SMOS : Soil moisture of ocean circulation mission
SPARC : Stratospheric processes and their role in climate change
SPIN : Satellite
Sputnik : Satellite
SSM/I : Special sensor microwave/imager
SST : Sea surface temperature
SSU : Stratospheric sounding unit
START : Global change system for analysis, research and training
STIB : Stratosphere–troposphere interactions and the biosphere
SWARM : Name of and Earth explorer opportunity mission
SWIFT : Stratospheric wind interferometer for transport studies
TES : Tropospheric emission spectrometer
TFIS : Tropical forest information system
TIROS : Satellite
TOGA : Tropical oceans and global atmosphere
TOMS : Total ozone mapping spectrometer
TOPC : Terrestrial observing panel for climate
Topex-Poseidon : Satellite
TOVS : TIROS operational vertical sounder
TRMM : Tropical rainfall measuring mission
UARS : Upper atmosphere research satellite
UGCM : UGAMP global circulation model
UNCED-2 : Second united nations conference on environment and development
VISSR : Visible infrared spin scan radiometer
VWG : Validation working group
WCC-1 : First world climate conference
WCP : World climate programme
WCRP : World climate research programme
WCU : World conservation union
WGCV : Working group on calibration and validation
WGISS : Working group on information systems and services
WINDII : Wind imaging interferometer
WMO : World meteorological organisation
WOCE : World ocean circulation experiment
WRI : World resources institute
WWW : World weather watch; World wide web
WWWGOS : World weather watch global observing system

APPENDIX II

REMOTE SENSING JOURNALS AND SOCIETIES

Journal	*Publishing society*
Canadian Journal of Remote Sensing	Canadian Aeronautics and space institute Saxe Building 60–75 Sparks Street Ottawa, Canada K1P 5A5
IEEE Transaction on Geoscience and Remote Sensing	IEEE Remote Sensing and Geoscience Society Institute of Electrical and Electronics Engineers 445 Hoes Lane Piscataway, NJ 08854
International Journal of Remote Sensing	Remote Sensing Society c/o Taylor and Francis, Ltd. Rankine Road Basingstoke, Hants RG24 OPR United Kingdom
Photogrammetric Engineering and Remote Sensing	American Society for Photogrammetry and Remote Sensing 210 Little Falls Street Falls Church, VA 22046
Remote Sensing of the Environment	Elsevier Publishing Co. 52 Vanderbilt Avenue New York, NY 10017
Geo Abstracts—G. Remote Sensing, Photogrammetry and Cartography	Geo Abstracts Regency House 34 Duke Street Norwich NR3 3AP United Kingdom
Remote Sensing Reviews	Harwood Academic Publishers 50 West 23rd Street New York, NY 10010

APPENDIX III

REMOTE SENSING ORGANISATIONS AND CONFERENCES

Organisation	*Address*	*Conference*
Environmental Research Institute of Michigan	P.O. Box 618 Ann Arbor, MI 48107	'Remote Sensing of Environment'; 'Thematic Conferences on Remote Sensing'
EROS Data Center of U.S. Geological survey	Sioux Falls, SD 57198	'Pecora Symposium on Remote Sensing' (annual conference)
Geosat Committee	153 Kearny Street San Francisco, CA 94108	Annual workshop on exploration applications of Remote Sensing
Jet Propulsion Laboratory	4800 Oak Grove Drive Pasadena, CA 91103	Publishes reports; conducts conferences and workshops
Laboratory for Applications of Remote Sensing, Purdue University	1220 Potter Drive East Lafayette, IN 47906	'Machine Processing of Remote Sensed Data' (annual symposium)
IEEE Geoscience and Remote Sensing Society	345 East 47th Street New York, NY 10017	'IEEE International Geoscience and Remote Sensing Symposium' (annual symposium)

References

Amato, J.M., *Introduction to Remote Sensing and Environment*, Applied Science Publishers, London.

Atkinson, K.W. and Lloyd, R., *Introductory Digital Image Processing*, Butterworths, London.

Blom, R.G., *Geophysiology of Remote Sensing*, Pearson Education, Singapore.

Brown, R.L., *Geographic Information Systems for Geoscientists*, Spring field, New York.

Burton, G.W., *Basic Concepts of Remote Sensing*, Cambridge University Press, Cambridge.

Durbin, R. Eddy., *Photogrammetric Engineering and Remote Sensing*, Academic Press, London.

Fuller, R.L., *Introduction to Remote Sensing*, Harwood Academic Publishers, New York.

Gold burg, *Remote Sensing Image Classification*, Tata McGraw Hill, New York.

Hardin, C.M., *Implications for Remote Sensing and GIS Applications*, Castle Housing Publications Ltd., London.

Hay, A.M., *Remote Sensing in Alternatives to Deforestation*, Bio Scientic Publishers, Oxford.

Jones, J.B., *Forest Measurement*, Marcel Dekker Inc., New York.

Landis, J.G., *Linking Remote Sensing to Environment*, Cold Spring Horbor Press, UK.

Lowell, N. and Fletcher, W.W., *Remote Sensing Laboratory Manual*, Blackie, Glasgow and London.

Merser, *Thermal Radiation and Accuracy Assessment*, Reston Publishing Co., Reston, Virginia.

Meyer, M.J., *Manual of Remote Sensing*, Pergamon Press, Oxford, London.

Michael, P., *Uncertainity in Geographical Information*, Tata McGraw-Hill, New Delhi.

Munn, R.F., *Application of Space Images for Neotectonic Studies*, John Wiley & Sons, New York.

Nelson, L.N., *Introduction to Remote Sensing and GIS Analysis*, Applied Science Publishers, London.

Packwell, P.A., *Manual of Image Processing*, Chapman and Hall, New York.

Pugh, S.R., *Legacy of Change in Universe*, Academic Press, London.

Sabin, F.F., *Remote Sensing Change Detection*, Human Press Inc., New Jersey.

Schrowebel, J., *Geologic Application of Remote Sensing from Space*, Pergamon Press, New York.

Shelton, J.S., *Remote Sensing in Geologic Mapping*, Prentice Hall, London.

Solow, T.R., *Remote Sensed Data*, Chapman and Hall, London.

Steven E. Franklin., *Remote Sensing for Sustainable Forest Management*, Lewis Publishers, New York.

Tortora, R.A., *Digital Classification of Landsat Data for Vegetation*, Butterworth, London.

Trifonov, H.Y., *Land Cover Classification System*, Van Nostrand Reinhold, New York.

Wilbur, W.J., Lipman, D.J., *Integration of Remote Sensing with Image Processing*, Heinemann, London.

Index

E

F

G

H

I

N

O

P

Q

R

S